Matt

GREATER WORKS

Other Titles by Smith Wigglesworth

GREATER WORKS

Smith Wigglesworth

WHITAKER
HOUSE

Whitaker House gratefully acknowledges and thanks Glenn Gohr and the entire staff of the Assemblies of God Archives in Springfield, Missouri, for graciously assisting us in compiling Smith Wigglesworth's works for publication in this book.

Unless otherwise indicated, all Scripture quotations are taken from the *New King James Version* (NKJV), © 1979, 1980, 1982, 1984 by Thomas Nelson, Inc. Used by permission. All rights reserved. All Scripture quotations marked (KJV) are taken from the King James Version of the Holy Bible.

Publisher's note: This new edition from Whitaker House has been updated for the modern reader. Words, expressions, and sentence structure have been revised for clarity and readability. Although the more modern Bible translation quoted in this edition was not available to Smith Wigglesworth, it was carefully and prayerfully selected in order to make the language of the entire text readily understandable while maintaining his original premises and message.

GREATER WORKS: Experiencing God's Power

Titles included in this anthology:
Smith Wigglesworth on Healing
ISBN: 978-0-88368-426-9   © 1999 by Whitaker House
Smith Wigglesworth on the Holy Spirit
ISBN: 978-0-88368-544-0   © 1999 by Whitaker House
Smith Wigglesworth on Spiritual Gifts
ISBN: 978-0-88368-533-4   © 1998 by Whitaker House
Smith Wigglesworth on Faith
ISBN: 978-0-88368-531-0   © 1998 by Whitaker House

ISBN-13: 978- 0-88368-584-6
ISBN-10: 0-88368-584-1
Printed in the United States of America
© 2000 by Whitaker House

Whitaker House
1030 Hunt Valley Circle
New Kensington, PA 15068
www.whitakerhouse.com

Library of Congress Cataloging-in-Publication Data
Wigglesworth, Smith, 1859–1947.
Greater works : experiencing God's power / by Smith Wigglesworth.
   p.   cm.
ISBN 0-88368-584-1 (trade pbk. : alk. paper)
1. Spiritual life—Pentecostal churches. I. Title.
BV4501.2 .W5192 2000
234'.13—dc21   00-026803

5 6 7 8 9 10 11 12 13 14 15 16 ᴜᴜ 16 15 14 13 12 11 10 09 08 07

CONTENTS

The moment I reached the house, they brought in this blind woman. After we shook hands, she made her way to a room, and we went in. "Now," she said, "we are with God."

Have you ever been there? It is a lovely place.

After an hour and a half in His presence, the power of God fell upon us. Rushing to the window, she exclaimed, "I can see! Oh, I can see!"

****

There was a young man twenty-six years old who had been in bed eighteen years. His body was much bigger than an ordinary body because of inactivity, and his legs were like a child's.

I felt it was one of the opportunities of my life.

God said to me, "Command him in My name to walk." So I shouted, "Arise and walk in the name of Jesus." Did he do it? No, I declare he never walked. He was lifted up by the power of God in a moment, and he ran. The door was wide open; he ran out across the road into a field where he ran up and down and came back. Oh, it was a miracle!

****

Among the first people I met in Victoria Hall was a woman who had breast cancer. As soon as the cancer was cursed, it died and stopped bleeding. The next thing that happened was that her body cast it out, because the natural body has no room for dead matter. When it came out, it was like a big ball with thousands of fibers. All these fibers had spread out into the flesh, but the moment the evil power was destroyed, they had no power.

INTRODUCTION

An encounter with Smith Wigglesworth was an unforgettable experience. This seems to be the universal reaction of all who knew him or heard him speak. Smith Wigglesworth was a simple yet remarkable man who was used in an extraordinary way by our extraordinary God. He had a contagious and inspiring faith. Under his ministry, thousands of people came to salvation, committed themselves to a deeper faith in Christ, received the baptism in the Holy Spirit, and were miraculously healed. The power that brought these kinds of results was the presence of the Holy Spirit, who filled Smith Wigglesworth and used him in bringing the good news of the Gospel to people all over the world. Wigglesworth gave glory to God for everything that was accomplished through his ministry, and he wanted people to understand his work only in this context, because his sole desire was that people would see Jesus and not himself.

Smith Wigglesworth was born in England in 1859. Immediately after his conversion as a boy, he had a concern for the salvation of others and won people to Christ, including his mother. Even so, as a young man, he could not express himself well enough to give a testimony in church, much less preach a sermon. Wigglesworth said that his mother had the same difficulty in expressing herself that he did. This family trait, coupled with the fact that he had no formal education because he began working twelve hours a day at the age of seven to help support the family, contributed to Wigglesworth's awkward speaking style. He became a plumber by trade, yet he continued to devote himself to winning many people to Christ on an individual basis.

In 1882, he married Polly Featherstone, a vivacious young woman who loved God and had a gift of preaching and evangelism. It was she who taught him to read and who became his closest confidant and strongest supporter. They both had compassion for the

9

poor and needy in their community, and they opened a mission, at which Polly preached. Significantly, people were miraculously healed when Wigglesworth prayed for them.

In 1907, Wigglesworth's circumstances changed dramatically when, at the age of forty-eight, he was baptized in the Holy Spirit. Suddenly, he had a new power that enabled him to preach, and even his wife was amazed at the transformation. This was the beginning of what became a worldwide evangelistic and healing ministry that reached thousands. He eventually ministered in the United States, Australia, South Africa, and all over Europe. His ministry extended up to the time of his death in 1947.

Several emphases in Smith Wigglesworth's life and ministry characterize him: a genuine, deep compassion for the unsaved and sick; an unflinching belief in the Word of God; a desire that Christ should increase and he should decrease (John 3:30); a belief that he was called to exhort people to enlarge their faith and trust in God; an emphasis on the baptism in the Holy Spirit with the manifestation of the gifts of the Spirit as in the early church; and a belief in complete healing for everyone of all sickness.

Smith Wigglesworth was called "The Apostle of Faith" because absolute trust in God was a constant theme of both his life and his messages. In his meetings, he would quote passages from the Word of God and lead lively singing to help build people's faith and encourage them to act on it. He emphasized belief in the fact that God could do the impossible. He had great faith in what God could do, and God did great things through him.

Wigglesworth's unorthodox methods were often questioned. As a person, Wigglesworth was reportedly courteous, kind, and gentle. However, he became forceful when dealing with the Devil, whom he believed caused all sickness. Wigglesworth said the reason he spoke bluntly and acted forcefully with people was that he knew he needed to get their attention so they could focus on God. He also had such anger toward the Devil and sickness that he acted in a seemingly rough way. When he prayed for people to be healed, he would often hit or punch them at the place of their problem or illness. Yet, no one was hurt by this startling treatment. Instead, they were remarkably healed. When he was asked why he treated people in this manner, he said that he was not hitting the people but that he was hitting the Devil. He believed that Satan should never be treated gently or allowed to get away with anything.

About twenty people were reportedly raised from the dead after he prayed for them. Wigglesworth himself was healed of appendicitis and kidney stones, after which his personality softened and he was more gentle with those who came to him for prayer for healing. His abrupt manner in ministering may be attributed to the fact that he was very serious about his calling and got down to business quickly.

Although Wigglesworth believed in complete healing, he encountered illnesses and deaths that were difficult to understand. These included the deaths of his wife and son, his daughter's lifelong deafness, and his own battles with kidney stones and sciatica.

He often seemed paradoxical: compassionate but forceful, gentle but blunt, a well-dressed gentleman whose speech was often ungrammatical or confusing. However, he loved God with everything he had, he was steadfastly committed to God and to His Word, and he didn't rest until he saw God move in the lives of those who needed Him.

In 1936, Smith Wigglesworth prophesied about what we now know as the charismatic movement. He accurately predicted that the established mainline denominations would experience revival and the gifts of the Spirit in a way that would surpass even the Pentecostal movement. Wigglesworth did not live to see the renewal, but as an evangelist and prophet with a remarkable healing ministry, he had a tremendous influence on both the Pentecostal and charismatic movements, and his example and influence on believers is felt to this day.

Without the power of God that was so obviously present in his life and ministry, we might not be reading transcripts of his sermons, for his spoken messages were often disjointed and ungrammatical. However, true gems of spiritual insight shine through them because of the revelation he received through the Holy Spirit. It was his life of complete devotion and belief in God and his reliance on the Holy Spirit that brought the life-changing power of God into his messages.

As you read this book, it is important to remember that Wigglesworth's works span a period of several decades, from the early 1900s to the 1940s. They were originally presented as spoken rather than written messages, and necessarily retain some of the flavor of a church service or prayer meeting. Some of the messages were Bible studies that Wigglesworth led at various conferences. At his meetings, he would often speak in tongues and give the interpretation, and these messages have been included as well. Because of Wigglesworth's unique style, the sermons and Bible studies in this book have been edited for clarity, and archaic expressions that would be unfamiliar to modern readers have been updated.

In conclusion, we hope that as you read these words of Smith Wigglesworth, you will truly sense his complete trust and unwavering faith in God and take to heart one of his favorite sayings: "Only believe!"

Smith Wigglesworth on

HEALING

Contents

CHAPTER ONE

THE POWER OF THE NAME

All things are possible through the name of Jesus (Matt. 19:26). *"God also has highly exalted Him and given Him the name which is above every name, that at the name of Jesus every knee should bow"* (Phil. 2:9–10). There is power to overcome everything in the world through the name of Jesus. I am looking forward to a wonderful union through the name of Jesus. *"There is no other name under heaven given among men by which we must be saved"* (Acts 4:12).

SPEAKING THE NAME OF JESUS

I want to instill in you the power, the virtue, and the glory of that name. Six people went into the house of a sick man to pray for him. He was a leader in the Episcopal Church, and he lay in his bed utterly helpless. He had read a little tract about healing and had heard about people praying for the sick. So he sent for these friends, who, he thought, could pray *"the prayer of faith"* (James 5:15). He was anointed with oil according to James 5:14, but because he had no immediate manifestation of healing, he wept bitterly. The six people walked out of the room, somewhat crestfallen to see the man lying there in an unchanged condition.

When they were outside, one of the six said, "There is one thing we could have done. I wish you would all go back with me and try it." They all went back and got together in a group. This brother said, "Let us whisper the name of Jesus." At first, when they whispered this worthy name, nothing seemed to happen. But as they continued to whisper "Jesus! Jesus! Jesus!" the power began to fall. As they saw that God was beginning to work, their faith and joy increased, and they whispered the name louder and louder. As they did so, the man rose from his bed and dressed himself. The secret was just this: those six people had gotten their eyes off the sick man and were taken up with the Lord Jesus Himself. Their faith grasped the power in His name. Oh, if people would only appreciate the power in this name, there is no telling what would happen.

I know that through His name and through the power of His name we have access to God. The very face of Jesus fills the whole place with glory. All over the world there are people magnifying that name, and oh, what a joy it is for me to utter it.

RAISING LAZARUS

One day I went up onto a mountain to pray. I had a wonderful day. It was one of the mountains of Wales. I had heard of one man going up onto this mountain to pray and the Spirit of the Lord meeting him so wonderfully that his face shone like that of an angel when he returned. Everyone in the village was talking about it. As I went up onto this mountain and spent the day in the presence of the Lord, His wonderful power seemed to envelop and saturate and fill me.

Two years before this time, there had come to our house two lads from Wales. They were just ordinary lads, but they became very zealous for God. They came to our mission and saw some of the works of God. They said to me, "We would not be surprised if the Lord brings you down to Wales to raise our Lazarus." They explained that the leader of their church was a man who had spent his days working in a tin mine and his nights preaching, and the result was that he had collapsed and contracted tuberculosis. For four years he had been a helpless invalid, having to be fed with a spoon.

When I was up on that mountaintop, I was reminded of the Transfiguration (see Matthew 17:1–8), and I felt that the Lord's only purpose in taking us into the glory is to prepare us for greater usefulness in the valley.

> INTERPRETATION OF A MESSAGE IN TONGUES: "The living God has chosen us for His divine inheritance, and He it is who is preparing us for our ministry, that it may be of God and not of man."

As I was on the mountaintop that day, the Lord said to me, "I want you to go and raise Lazarus." I told the brother who had accompanied me about this, and when we got down to the valley, I wrote a postcard. It read, "When I was up on the mountain praying today, God told me that I was to go and raise Lazarus." I addressed the postcard to the man whose name had been given to me by the two lads. When we arrived at the place, we went to the man to whom I had addressed the postcard. He looked at me and asked, "Did you send this?" "Yes," I replied. He said, "Do you think we believe in this? Here, take it." And he threw it at me.

The man called a servant and said, "Take this man and show him Lazarus." Then he said to me, "The moment you see him, you will be ready to go home. Nothing will keep you here." Everything he said was true from the natural standpoint. The man was helpless. He was nothing but a mass of bones with skin stretched over them. There was no life to be seen. Everything in him spoke of decay.

I said to him, "Will you shout? You remember that at Jericho the people shouted while the walls were still up. God has a similar victory for you if you will only believe." But I could not get him to believe. There was not an atom of faith there. He had made up his mind not to have anything.

It is a blessed thing to learn that God's Word can never fail. Never listen to human plans. God can work mightily when you persist in believing Him in spite of discouragement from the human standpoint. When I got back to the man to whom I had sent the postcard, he asked, "Are you ready to go now?" I replied, "I am not moved by what I see. I am moved only by what I believe. I know this: no man looks at the circumstances if he believes. No man relies on his feelings if he believes. The man who believes God has his request. Every man who comes into the Pentecostal condition can laugh at all things and believe God."

There is something in the Pentecostal work that is different from anything else in the world. Somehow, in Pentecost you know that God is a reality. Wherever the Holy Spirit has the right-of-way, the gifts of the Spirit will be in manifestation. Where these gifts are never in manifestation, I question whether He is present. Pentecostal people are spoiled for anything other than Pentecostal meetings. We want none of the entertainments that other churches are offering. When God comes in, He entertains us Himself. We are entertained by the King of Kings and Lord of Lords! Oh, it is wonderful!

There were difficult conditions in that Welsh village, and it seemed impossible to get the people to believe. "Ready to go home?" I was asked. But a man and a woman there asked us to come and stay with them. I said to the people, "I want to know how many of you can pray." No one wanted to pray. I asked if I could get seven people to pray for the poor man's deliverance. I said to the two people we were to stay with, "I will count on you two, and there is my friend and myself. We need three others." I told the people that I trusted that some of them would awaken to their privilege and come in the morning and join us in prayer for the raising of Lazarus. It will never do to give way to human opinions. If God says a thing, you have to believe it.

I told the people that I would not eat anything that night. When I got to bed, it seemed as if the Devil tried to place on me everything that he had placed on that poor man on the sickbed. When I awoke in the middle of the night, I had a cough and all the weakness of a man with tuberculosis. I rolled out of bed onto the floor and cried out to God to deliver me from the power of the Devil. I shouted loud enough to wake everybody in the house, but nobody was disturbed. God gave the victory, and I got back into bed again as free as I had ever been in my life. At five o'clock the Lord awakened me and said to me, "Don't break bread until you break it around My table." At six o'clock He gave me these words: *"And I will raise him up"* (John 6:40). I elbowed the fellow who was sleeping in the same room. He said, "Ugh!" I elbowed him again and said, "Do you hear? The Lord says that He will raise him up."

At eight o'clock they said to me, "Have a little refreshment." But I have found prayer and fasting the greatest joy, and you will always find it so when you are led by God. When we went to the house where Lazarus lived, there were eight of us altogether. No one can prove to me that God does not always answer prayer. He always does more than that. He always gives *"exceedingly abundantly above all that we ask or think"* (Eph. 3:20).

I will never forget how the power of God fell on us as we went into that sick man's room. Oh, it was lovely! As we made a circle around the bed, I got one brother to hold the sick man's hand on one side, and I held the other, and we each held the hand of the person next to us. I said, "We are not going to pray; we are just going to use the name of Jesus." We all knelt down and whispered that one word, "Jesus! Jesus! Jesus!" The power of God fell, and then it lifted. Five times the power of God fell, and then it remained. But the man in the bed was unmoved. Two years previously, someone had come along and had tried to raise him up, and the Devil had used his lack of success as a means of discouraging Lazarus. I said, "I don't care what the Devil says. If God says He will raise you up, it must be so. Forget everything else except what God says about Jesus."

A sixth time the power fell, and the sick man's lips began moving, and the tears began to fall. I said to him, "The power of God is here; it is yours to accept it." He said, "I have been bitter in my heart, and I know I have grieved the Spirit of God. Here I am, helpless. I cannot lift my hands or even lift a spoon to my mouth." I said, "Repent, and God will hear you." He repented and cried out, "O God, let this be to Your glory." As he said this, the power of the Lord went right through him.

I have asked the Lord never to let me tell this story except the way it happened, for I realize that God can never bless exaggerations. As we again said "Jesus! Jesus! Jesus!" the bed shook, and the man shook. I said to the people who were with me, "You can all go downstairs now. This is all God. I'm not going to assist him." I sat and watched that man get up and dress himself. We sang the doxology as he walked down the steps. I said to him, "Now, tell what has happened."

It was soon told everywhere that Lazarus had been raised up. The people came from Llanelli and all the district around to see him and to hear his testimony. God brought salvation to many. Right out in the open air, this man told what God had done, and as a result, many were convicted and converted. All this occurred through the name of Jesus, *"through faith in His name"* (Acts 3:16). Yes, the faith that is by Him gave this sick man perfect soundness in the presence of them all (v. 16).

A LAME MAN HEALED

Let us read a passage from the book of Acts:

Now Peter and John went up together to the temple at the hour of prayer, the ninth hour. And a certain man lame from his mother's womb was carried, whom they laid daily at the

21

gate of the temple which is called Beautiful, to ask alms from those who entered the temple; who, seeing Peter and John about to go into the temple, asked for alms. And fixing his eyes on him, with John, Peter said, "Look at us," So he gave them his attention, expecting to receive something from them. Then Peter said, "Silver and gold I do not have, but what I do have I give you: In the name of Jesus Christ of Nazareth, rise up and walk," And he took him by the right hand and lifted him up, and immediately his feet and ankle bones received strength. So he, leaping up, stood and walked and entered the temple with them; walking, leaping, and praising God. And all the people saw him walking and praising God. Then they knew that it was he who sat begging alms at the Beautiful Gate of the temple; and they were filled with wonder and amazement at what had happened to him. Now as the lame man who was healed held on to Peter and John, all the people ran together to them in the porch which is called Solomon's, greatly amazed. So when Peter saw it, he responded to the people: "Men of Israel, why do you marvel at this? Or why look so intently at us, as though by our own power or godliness we had made this man walk? The God of Abraham, Isaac, and Jacob, the God of our fathers, glorified His Servant Jesus, whom you delivered up and denied in the presence of Pilate, when he was determined to let Him go. But you denied the Holy One and the Just, and asked for a murderer to be granted to you, and killed the Prince of life, whom God raised from the dead, of which we are witnesses. And His name, through faith in His name, has made this man strong, whom you see and know. Yes, the faith which comes through Him has given him this perfect soundness in the presence of you all."   (Acts 3:1–16)

Peter and John were helpless and uneducated. They had no college education; they had only some training in fishing. But they had been with Jesus. To them had come a wonderful revelation of the power of the name of Jesus. They had handed out the bread and fish after Jesus had multiplied them. They had sat at the table with Him, and John had often gazed into His face. Jesus often had had to rebuke Peter, but He had manifested His love to him through it all. Yes, He loved Peter, the wayward one. Oh, He's a loving Savior! I have been wayward and stubborn. I had an unmanageable temper at one time, but how patient He has been. I am here to tell you that there is power in Jesus and in His wondrous name to transform anyone, to heal anyone.

If only you will see Him as God's Lamb, as God's beloved Son, upon whom was laid *"the iniquity of us all"* (Isa. 53:6). If only you will see that Jesus paid the whole price for our redemption so that we might be free. Then you can enter into your purchased inheritance of salvation, of life, and of power.

Poor Peter and John! They had no money. I don't think there is a person in this building as poor as Peter and John were. But they had faith; they had the power of the Holy Spirit; they had God. You can have God even though you have nothing else. Even if you have lost your character, you can have God. I have seen the worst men saved by the power of God.

DEALING WITH A POTENTIAL MURDERER

I was preaching one day about the name of Jesus, and there was a man leaning against a lamppost, listening. He needed the lamppost to enable him to stay on his feet. We had finished our open-air meeting, and the man was still leaning against the lamppost. I asked him, "Are you sick?" He showed me his hand, and I saw that inside his coat he had a silver-handled dagger. He told me that he had been on his way to kill his unfaithful wife but that he had heard me speaking about the power of the name of Jesus and could not get away. He said that he felt just helpless. I said, "Kneel down." There on the square, with people passing back and forth, he got saved.

I took him to my home and clothed him with a new suit. I saw that there was something in that man that God could use. He said to me the next morning, "God has revealed Jesus to me. I see that all has been laid upon Jesus." I lent him some money, and he soon got together a wonderful little home. His faithless wife was living with another man, but he invited her back to the home that he had prepared for her. She came. Where enmity and hatred had been before, the whole situation was transformed by love. God made that man a minister wherever he went. Everywhere there is power in the name of Jesus. God can *"save to the uttermost"* (Heb. 7:25).

AN "INCURABLE" MAN HEALED

There comes to mind a meeting we had in Stockholm that I will always remember. There was a home for incurables there, and one of the patients was brought to the meeting. He had palsy and was shaking all over. He stood up in front of three thousand people and came to the platform, supported by two others. The power of God fell on him as I anointed him in the name of Jesus. The moment I touched him, he dropped his crutch and began to walk in the name of Jesus. He walked down the steps and around that great building in view of all the people. There is nothing that our God cannot do. He will do everything if you will dare to believe.

Grace = desire and power
to do God's will

CHAPTER TWO

HE HIMSELF TOOK
OUR INFIRMITIES

AND HE CAST OUT THE SPIRITS WITH A WORD, AND HEALED ALL
WHO WERE SICK, THAT IT MIGHT BE FULFILLED WHICH WAS SPOKEN
BY ISAIAH THE PROPHET, SAYING: "HE HIMSELF TOOK
OUR INFIRMITIES AND BORE OUR SICKNESSES."
—MATTHEW 8:16–17

Here we have a wonderful word. All of the Word is wonderful. This blessed Book brings such life, health, peace, and abundance that we should never be poor anymore. This Book is my heavenly bank. I find everything I want in it. I desire to show you how rich you may be, so that in everything you can be enriched in Christ Jesus (1 Cor. 1:5). For you He has *"abundance of grace and...the gift of righteousness"* (Rom. 5:17), and through His abundant grace *"all things are possible"* (Matt. 19:26). I want to show you that you can be a living branch of the living Vine, Christ Jesus, and that it is your privilege to be, right here in this world, what He is. John told us, *"As He is, so are we in this world"* (1 John 4:17). Not that we are anything in ourselves, but Christ within us is our All in All.

The Lord Jesus is always wanting to show forth His grace and love in order to draw us to Himself. God is willing to do things, to manifest His Word, and to let us know a measure of the mind of our God in this day and hour.

A LEPER IS MIRACULOUSLY CLEANSED

Today there are many needy ones, many afflicted ones, but I do not think anyone present is half as bad as this first case that we read of in Matthew 8:

25

When He had come down from the mountain, great multitudes followed Him. And behold, a leper came and worshiped Him, saying, "Lord, if You are willing, You can make me clean." Then Jesus put out His hand and touched him, saying, "I am willing; be cleansed." Immediately his leprosy was cleansed. And Jesus said to him, "See that you tell no one; but go your way, show yourself to the priest, and offer the gift that Moses commanded, as a testimony to them." (Matt. 8:1–4)

This man was a leper. You may be suffering from tuberculosis, cancer, or other things, but God will show forth His perfect cleansing, His perfect healing, if you have a living faith in Christ. He is a wonderful Jesus.

This leper must have been told about Jesus. How much is missed because people are not constantly telling what Jesus will do in our day. Probably someone had come to that leper and said, "Jesus can heal you." So he was filled with expectation as he saw the Lord coming down the mountainside. Lepers were not allowed to come within reach of people; they were shut out as unclean. Ordinarily, it would have been very difficult for him to get near because of the crowd that surrounded Jesus. But as Jesus came down from the mountain, He met the leper; He came to the leper.

Oh, leprosy is a terrible disease! There was no help for him, humanly speaking, but nothing is too hard for Jesus. The man cried, *"Lord, if You are willing, You can make me clean"* (v. 2). Was Jesus willing? You will never find Jesus missing an opportunity to do good. You will find that He is always more willing to work than we are to give Him an opportunity to work. The trouble is that we do not come to Him; we do not ask Him for what He is more than willing to give.

"Then Jesus put out His hand and touched him, saying, 'I am willing; be cleansed.' Immediately his leprosy was cleansed" (v. 3). I like that. If you are definite with Him, you will never go away disappointed. The divine life will flow into you, and instantaneously you will be delivered. This Jesus is just the same today, and He says to you, *"I am willing; be cleansed."* He has an overflowing cup for you, a fullness of life. He will meet you in your absolute helplessness. All things are possible if you will only believe (Mark 9:23). God has a real plan. It is very simple: just come to Jesus. You will find Him just the same as He was in days of old (Heb. 13:8).

JESUS HEALS BY SAYING A WORD

The next case we have in Matthew 8 is that of the centurion who came and pleaded with Jesus on behalf of his servant, who was paralyzed and was dreadfully tormented.

Now when Jesus had entered Capernaum, a centurion came to Him, pleading with Him, saying, "Lord, my servant is lying at home paralyzed, dreadfully tormented." And Jesus said to him, "I will come and heal him." The centurion answered and said, "Lord, I am not worthy that You should come under my roof. But only speak a word, and my servant will be healed. For I also am a man under authority, having soldiers under me. And I say to this one, 'Go,' and he goes; and to another, 'Come,' and he comes; and to my servant, 'Do this,' and he does it." When Jesus heard it, He marveled, and said to those who followed, "Assuredly, I say to you, I have not found such great faith, not even in Israel! And I say to you that many will come from east and west, and sit down with Abraham, Isaac, and Jacob in the kingdom of heaven. But the sons of the kingdom will be cast out into outer darkness. There will be weeping and gnashing of teeth." Then Jesus said to the centurion, "Go your way; and as you have believed, so let it be done for you." And his servant was healed that same hour.
(Matt. 8:5–13)

This man was so earnest that he came seeking Jesus. Notice that there is one thing that is certain: there is no such thing as seeking without finding. *"He who seeks finds."* (Matt. 7:8). Listen to the gracious words of Jesus: *"I will come and heal him"* (Matt. 8:7).

In most places where I go, there are many people whom I cannot pray for. In some places there are two or three hundred people who would like me to visit them, but I am not able to do so. Yet I am glad that the Lord Jesus is always willing to come and heal. He longs to help the sick ones. He loves to heal them of their afflictions. The Lord is healing many people today by means of handkerchiefs, even as He did in the days of Paul. (See Acts 19:11–12.)

A woman came to me in the city of Liverpool and said, "I would like you to help me by joining me in prayer. My husband is a drunkard and every night comes into the home under the influence of alcohol. Won't you join me in prayer for him?" I asked the woman, "Do you have a handkerchief?" She took out a handkerchief, and I prayed over it and told her to lay it on the pillow of the drunken man. He came home that night and laid his head on the pillow in which this handkerchief was tucked. He laid his head on more than the pillow that night, for he laid his head on the promise of God. In Mark 11:24, we read, *"Whatever things you ask when you pray, believe that you receive them, and you will have them."*

The next morning the man got up and, going into the first saloon that he had to pass on his way to work, ordered some beer. He tasted it and said to the bartender, "You put some poison in this beer." He could not drink it and went on to the next saloon and ordered some more beer. He tasted it and said to the man behind the counter, "You put some poison in this beer. I believe you folks have plotted to poison me." The bartender was indignant at being charged with this crime. The man said, "I will go somewhere else." He went to another saloon, and the same thing happened as in the two previous saloons. He made such a fuss that he was thrown out.

After he left work that evening, he went to another saloon to get some beer, and again he thought the bartender was trying to poison him. Again, he made such a disturbance that he was thrown out. He went to his home and told his wife what had happened and said, "It seems as though all the fellows have agreed to poison me." His wife said to him, "Can't you see the hand of the Lord in this, that He is making you dislike the stuff that has been your ruin?" This word brought conviction to the man's heart, and he came to the meeting and got saved. The Lord still has power to set the captives free.

Jesus was willing to go and heal the sick servant, but the centurion said, *"Lord, I am not worthy that You should come under my roof. But only speak a word, and my servant will be healed"* (Matt. 8:8). Jesus was delighted with this expression of faith and *"said to the centurion, 'Go your way; and as you have believed, so let it be done for you.' And his servant was healed that same hour"* (v. 13).

FACING A DEMON-POSSESSED WOMAN

I received a telegram once urging me to visit a case about two hundred miles from my home. As I went to this place, I met the father and mother and found them brokenhearted. They led me up a staircase to a room, and I saw a young woman on the floor. Five men were holding her down. She was a frail young woman, but the power in her was greater than the strength of all those young men. As I went into the room, the evil powers looked out of her eyes, and they used her lips, saying, "We are many; you can't cast us out." I said, "Jesus can."

Jesus is equal to every occasion. He is waiting for an opportunity to bless. He is ready for every opportunity to deliver souls. When we receive Jesus, the following verse is true of us: *"Greater is he that is in* [us], *than he that is in the world"* (1 John 4:4 KJV). He is greater than all the powers of darkness. No man can meet the Devil in his own strength, but any man filled with the knowledge of Jesus, filled with His presence, filled with His power, is more than a match for the powers of darkness. God has called us to be *"more than conquerors through Him who loved us"* (Rom. 8:37).

The living Word is able to destroy satanic forces. There is power in the name of Jesus. My desire is that every window on the street have the name of Jesus written on it.

Through faith in His name, deliverance was brought to this poor bound soul, and thirty-seven demons came out, giving their names as they came forth. The dear woman was completely delivered, and the family was able to give her back her child. That night there was heaven in that home, and the father, mother, son, and his wife were all united in glorifying Christ for His infinite grace. The next morning we had a gracious time in the breaking of bread.

All things are wonderful with our wonderful Jesus. If you would dare rest your all upon Him, things would take place, and He would change the whole situation. In a moment, through the name of Jesus, a new order of things can be brought in.

In the world, new diseases are always surfacing, and the doctors cannot identify them. A doctor said to me, "The science of medicine is in its infancy, and we doctors really have no confidence in our medicine. We are always experimenting." But the man of God does not experiment. He knows, or ought to know, redemption in its fullness. He knows, or ought to know, the mightiness of the Lord Jesus Christ. He is not, or should not be, moved by outward observation but should get a divine revelation of the mightiness of the name of Jesus and the power of His blood. If we exercise our faith in the Lord Jesus Christ, He will come forth and get glory over all the powers of darkness.

CHRIST BORE OUR SICKNESS AND SIN

When evening had come, they brought to Him many who were demon-possessed. And He cast out the spirits with a word, and healed all who were sick, that it might be fulfilled which was spoken by Isaiah the prophet, saying: "He Himself took our infirmities and bore our sicknesses." (Matt. 8:16–17)

The work is done if you will only believe it. It is done. "He Himself took our infirmities and bore our sicknesses." If only you can see the Lamb of God going to Calvary! He took on our flesh so that He could take upon Himself the full burden of all our sin and all the consequences of sin. There on the cross of Calvary, the results of sin were also dealt with.

Inasmuch then as the children have partaken of flesh and blood, He Himself likewise shared in the same, that through death He might destroy him who had the power of death, that is, the devil, and release those who through fear of death were all their lifetime subject to bondage. (Heb. 2:14–15)

Through His death there is deliverance for you today.

CHAPTER THREE

THE CONFIDENCE THAT WE HAVE IN HIM

NOW THIS IS THE CONFIDENCE THAT WE HAVE IN HIM,
THAT IF WE ASK ANYTHING ACCORDING TO HIS WILL, HE
HEARS US. AND IF WE KNOW THAT HE HEARS US,
WHATEVER WE ASK, WE KNOW THAT WE HAVE THE
PETITIONS THAT WE HAVE ASKED OF HIM.
—1 JOHN 5:14–15

 It is necessary to discover the meaning of these wonderful verses. There is nothing that will bring you such confidence as a life that is well pleasing to God. When Daniel's life pleased God, he could ask to be protected in the lions' den. But you cannot ask with confidence until there is a perfect union between you and God, as there was always a perfect union between God and Jesus. The foundation is confidence in and loyalty to God.

OBTAIN THE CONFIDENCE THAT CHRIST HAD

Some people think that when Jesus wept after Lazarus's death, his tears were due to the love that He had for Lazarus. But that was not the reason. Actually, He cried because He knew that the people who were around the grave, even Martha, had not come to the realization that whatever He would ask of the Father, the Father would give to Him. Their unbelief brought brokenness and sadness to the heart of Jesus, and He wept.

The moment you pray, you find that the heavens are opened. If you have to wait for the heavens to be opened, something is wrong. I tell you, what makes us lose confidence is disobedience to God and His laws.

31

At Lazarus's graveside, Jesus said that it was because of those who stood there that He prayed but that He knew that His Father always heard Him (John 11:42). And because He knew that His Father always heard Him, He knew that the dead could come forth.

There are times when there seems to be a stone wall in front of us. There are times when there are no feelings. There are times when everything seems as black as midnight, and there is nothing left but confidence in God. What you must do is have the devotion and confidence to believe that He will not fail, and cannot fail. You will never get anywhere if you depend on your feelings. There is something a thousand times better than feelings, and it is the powerful Word of God. There is a divine revelation within you that came when you were born from above, and this is real faith. To be born into the new kingdom is to be born into a new faith.

HOW TO BE USEFUL TO GOD

Paul spoke of two classes of Christians, one of which is obedient, and the other disobedient. The obedient always obey God when He first speaks. It is these people of God whom He will use to make the world know that there is a God. You cannot talk about things that you have never experienced. It seems to me that God has a process of training us. You cannot take people into the depths of God unless you have been broken yourself. I have been broken and broken and broken. Praise God, for *"the LORD is near to those who have a broken heart"* (Ps. 34:18). You must have a brokenness to get into the depths of God.

There is a rest of faith; there is a faith that rests in confidence on God. God's promises never fail. *"Faith comes by hearing, and hearing by the word of God"* (Rom. 10:17). The Word of God can create an irresistible faith, a faith that is never daunted, a faith that never gives up and never fails. We fail to realize the largeness of our Father's supply. We forget that He has a supply that cannot be exhausted. It pleases Him when we ask for much. *"If you then, being evil, know how to give good gifts to your children, how much more will your Father who is in heaven give good things to those who ask Him!"* (Matt. 7:11). It is the *"much more"* that God shows me.

I see that God has a plan of healing. It is along the lines of perfect confidence in Him. The confidence does not come from our much speaking; it comes from our fellowship with Him. There is a wonderful fellowship with Jesus. The chief thing is to be sure that we take time for communion with Him. There is a communion with Jesus that is life and that is better than preaching.

If God definitely tells you to do anything, do it, but be sure it is God who is telling you.

THE PRECIOUSNESS OF GOD'S WORD

I used to work with a man who had been a Baptist minister for twenty years. He was one of the sweetest souls I have ever met. He was getting to be an old man, and I used to walk by his side and listen to his instruction. God made the Word in his hand as a two-edged sword to me (see Hebrews 4:12), and I used to say, "Yes, Lord."

If the Sword ever comes to you, never harden yourself against it, but let it pierce you. You must be yielded to the Word of God. The Word will work out love in our hearts, and when practical love is in our hearts, there is no room to boast about ourselves. We see ourselves as nothing when we get lost in this divine love.

This man of God used to prune and prune me with the Sword of God, and God's Word is just as sweet to me today as it was then.

I praise God for the Sword that cuts us, and for a tender conscience. Oh, for that sweetness of fellowship with Jesus that when you hurt a fellow believer by word or act you can never let it rest until you make it right. First, we need to be converted, to become like little children (Matt. 18:3), and to have the hard heart taken away—to have a heart that is broken and melted with the love of God.

ONE WOMAN'S LAST DAY TO LIVE

The man of whom I have been speaking came to me and said, "The doctor says that this is the last day that my wife has to live." I said, "Oh, Brother Clark, why don't you believe God? God can raise her up if you will only believe Him." He replied, "I have looked at you when you have talked, and I have wept and said, 'Father, if You could give me this confidence, I would be so happy.'" I said, "Could you trust God?" I felt that the Lord would heal her.

I sent word to a certain man and asked if he would come with me to a dying woman, and I believed that if two of us would go and anoint her according to James 5:14–15, she would be raised up. This man said, "Oh, why do you come to me? I could not believe, although I believe the Lord would be sure to heal her if you would go."

Then I sent word to another man and asked him to go with me. This man could pray by the hour. When he was on his knees, he could go around the world three times and come out at the same place. I told him that whatever his impression was, to be sure to go on and pray right through. We entered the house. I asked this man to pray first. He cried in his desperation and prayed that this man might be comforted after he was left with these little motherless children, and that he might be strengthened to bear his sorrow! I could hardly wait until he was finished; my whole being was moved. I thought, "What an awful thing to bring this man all this way to pray that kind of a prayer." What was the matter with him? He was looking at the dying woman instead of looking at God. You can never pray *"the prayer of faith"* (James 5:15) if you look at the person who is needing it; there is only one place to look, and that is to Jesus. The Lord wants to help us right now to learn this truth and to keep our eyes on Him.

When this man had finished, I said to Brother Clark, "Now you pray." He took up the thread where the other man had left off and went on with the same kind of prayer. He got so down beneath the burden I thought he would never rise again, and I was glad when he was through. I could not have borne it much longer. These prayers seemed to be the most out-of-place prayers that I had ever heard; the whole atmosphere was being charged with unbelief. My soul was stirred. I was eager for God to get a chance to do something and to have His way. I did not wait to pray but rushed up to the bed and tipped the oil bottle, pouring nearly the whole contents on the woman. Then I saw Jesus just above the bed with the sweetest smile on His face, and I said to her, "Woman, Jesus Christ makes you whole." The woman stood up, perfectly healed, and she is a strong woman today.

Oh, beloved, may God help us to get our eyes off the conditions and symptoms, no matter how bad they may be, and get them fastened on Him. Then we will be able to pray *"the prayer of faith."*

CHAPTER FOUR

DELIVERANCE TO THE CAPTIVES

Our precious Lord Jesus has everything for everybody. Forgiveness of sin, healing of diseases, and the fullness of the Spirit all come from one source—the Lord Jesus Christ. Hear Him who is *"the same yesterday, today, and forever"* (Heb. 13:8) as He announces the purpose for which He came:

The Spirit of the LORD is upon Me, because He has anointed Me to preach the gospel to the poor; He has sent Me to heal the brokenhearted, to proclaim liberty to the captives and recovery of sight to the blind, to set at liberty those who are oppressed; to proclaim the acceptable year of the LORD. (Luke 4:18–19)

GOD'S POWER IS AVAILABLE TO YOU

Jesus was baptized by John in the Jordan, and the Holy Spirit descended in a bodily shape like a dove upon Him. Being full of the Holy Spirit, He was led by the Spirit into the wilderness, there to emerge more than a conqueror over the Archenemy. Then He returned *"in the power of the Spirit to Galilee"* (Luke 4:13) and preached in the synagogues. At last He came to His old hometown, Nazareth, where He announced His mission in the words I have just quoted from Luke 4:18–19. For a brief while, He ministered on the earth, and then He gave His life as a ransom for all (Matt. 20:28). But God raised Him from the dead.

Before Jesus returned to heaven, He told His disciples that they would receive the power of the Holy Spirit upon them, too (Acts 1:8). Thus, through them, His gracious ministry would continue. This power of the Holy Spirit was not only for a few apostles, but even for those who were *"afar off,"* even as many as our God would call (Acts 2:39), even for us way down in this century. Some ask, "But wasn't this power just for the privileged few in the first century?" No. Read the Master's Great Commission as recorded in Mark 16:15–18, and you will see it is for those who believe.

THE PURPOSE OF THE POWER

After I received the baptism in the Holy Spirit—and I know that I received it, for the Lord gave me the Spirit in just the same way that He gave Him to the disciples at Jerusalem—I sought the mind of the Lord as to why I had been baptized. One day I came home from work and went into the house, and my wife asked me, "Which way did you come in?" I told her that I had come in the back door. She said, "There is a woman upstairs, and she has brought an eighty-year-old man to be prayed for. He is raving up there, and a great crowd has gathered outside the front door, ringing the doorbell and wanting to know what is going on in the house." The Lord quietly whispered, "This is what I baptized you for."

I carefully opened the door of the room where the man was, desiring to be obedient to what my Lord would say to me. The man was crying and shouting in distress, "I am lost! I am lost! I have committed the unpardonable sin. I am lost! I am lost!" My wife asked, "Smith, what should we do?" The Spirit of the Lord moved me to cry out, "Come out, you lying spirit." In a moment the evil spirit went, and the man was free. God gives deliverance to the captives! And the Lord said again to me, "This is what I baptized you for."

There is a place where God, through the power of the Holy Spirit, reigns supreme in our lives. The Spirit reveals, unfolds, takes of the things of Christ and shows them to us (John 16:15), and prepares us to be more than a match for satanic forces.

MIRACLES ARE FOR TODAY

When Nicodemus came to Jesus, he said, *"Rabbi, we know that You are a teacher come from God; for no one can do these signs that You do unless God is with him"* (John 3:2). Jesus replied, *"Most assuredly, I say to you, unless one is born again, he cannot see the kingdom of God"* (v. 3).

Nicodemus was struck by Jesus' miracles, and Jesus pointed out the necessity of a miracle being done in every man who would see the kingdom. When a man is born of God—is brought *"from darkness to light"* (Acts 26:18)—a mighty miracle is performed. Jesus saw every touch of God as a miracle, and so we may expect to see miracles today. It is wonderful to have the Spirit of the Lord upon us. I would rather have the Spirit of God on me for five minutes than receive a million dollars.

THE ANTIDOTE FOR UNBELIEF

Do you see how Jesus mastered the Devil in the wilderness? (See Luke 4:1–14.) Jesus knew He was the Son of God, and Satan came along with an "if." How many times has Satan come along to you in this way? He says, "After all, you may be deceived. You know you really are not a child of God." If the Devil comes along and says that you are not saved, it is a pretty sure sign that you are. When he comes and tells you that you are not healed, it may be taken as good evidence that the Lord has sent His Word and healed you (Ps. 107:20). The Devil knows that if he can capture your thought life, he has won a mighty victory over you. His great business is injecting thoughts, but if you are pure and holy, you will instantly shrink from them. God wants us to let the mind that was in Christ Jesus, that pure, holy, humble mind of Christ, be in us (Phil. 2:5). *Richard*

I come across people everywhere I go who are held bound by deceptive conditions, and these conditions have come about simply because they have allowed the Devil to make their minds the place of his stronghold. How are we to guard against this? The Lord has provided us with weapons that are mighty through God for the pulling down of these strongholds of the Enemy (2 Cor. 10:4), by means of which every thought will be brought *"into captivity to the obedience of Christ"* (v. 5). Jesus' blood and His mighty name are an antidote to all the subtle seeds of unbelief that Satan would sow in your mind.

: Blood
° Name

CHRIST'S AMAZING WORKS TODAY

In the first chapter of Acts, we see that Jesus commanded the disciples to *"wait for the Promise of the Father"* (v. 4). He told them that not many days from then they would be baptized in the Holy Spirit (v. 5). Luke told us that he had written his former account concerning *"all that Jesus began both to do and teach"* (Acts 1:1). The ministry of Christ did not end at the Cross, but the book of Acts and the Epistles give us accounts of what He continued to do and teach through those whom He indwelt. And our blessed Lord Jesus is still alive and still continues His ministry through those who are filled with His Spirit. He is still healing the brokenhearted and delivering the captives through those on whom He places His Spirit.

I was traveling one day on a train in Sweden. At one station, an old lady boarded with her daughter. That old lady's expression was so troubled that I asked what was the matter with her. I heard that she was going to the hospital to have her leg amputated. She began to weep as she told me that the doctors had said that there was no hope for her except through having her leg amputated. She was seventy years old. I said to my interpreter, "Tell her that Jesus can heal her." The instant this was said to her, it was as though a veil had been taken off her face, it became so radiant. We stopped at another station, and the train filled up with people. A large group of men rushed to board the train, and the Devil said, "You're done." But I knew I had the best situation, for hard things are always opportunities to gain more glory for the Lord as He manifests His power.

Every trial is a blessing. There have been times when I have been hard-pressed through circumstances, and it seemed as if a dozen steamrollers were going over me, but I have found that the hardest things are just lifting places into the grace of God. We have such a lovely Jesus. He always proves Himself to be such a mighty Deliverer. He never fails to plan the best things for us.

The train began moving, and I crouched down and in the name of Jesus commanded the disease to leave. The old lady cried, "I'm healed! I know I'm healed!" She stamped her leg and said, "I'm going to prove it." So when we stopped at another station, she marched up and down and shouted, "I'm not going to the hospital!" Once again our wonderful Jesus had proven Himself a Healer of the brokenhearted, a Deliverer of one who was bound.

MY OWN REMARKABLE HEALING

At one time I was so bound that no human power could help me. My wife thought that I would pass away. There was no help. At that time I had just had a faint glimpse of Jesus as the Healer. For six months I had been suffering from appendicitis, occasionally getting temporary relief. I went to the mission of which I was the pastor, but I was brought to the floor in awful agony, and I was brought home to my bed. All night I was praying, pleading for deliverance, but none came. My wife was sure it was my call home to heaven and sent for a physician. He said that there was no possible chance for me—my body was too weak. Having had the appendicitis for six months, my whole system was drained, and, because of that, he thought that it was too late for an operation. He left my wife in a state of brokenheartedness.

After he left, a young man and an old lady came to our door. I knew that the old lady was a woman of real prayer. They came upstairs to my room. This young man jumped on the bed and commanded the evil spirit to come out of me. He shouted, "Come out, you devil! I command you to come out in the name of Jesus!" There was no chance for an argument or for me to tell him that I would never believe that there was a devil inside of me. The thing had to go in the name of Jesus, and it went. I was instantly healed.

I arose and dressed and went downstairs. I was still in the plumbing business, and I asked my wife, "Is there any work in? I'm all right now, and I am going to work." I found that there was a certain job to be done, and I picked up my tools and went off to do it. Just after I left, the doctor came in, put his hat down in the hall, and walked up to the bedroom. But the invalid was not there. "Where is Mr. Wigglesworth?" he asked. "Oh, doctor, he's gone out to work," said my wife. "You'll never see him alive again," said the doctor; "they'll bring him back a corpse."

Well, you see before you the corpse.

Since that time the Lord has given me the privilege of praying for people with appendicitis in many parts of the world, and I have seen a great many people up and dressed within a quarter of an hour from the time I prayed for them. We have a living Christ who is willing to meet people in every place.

A MAN WHOSE BRIDE WAS DYING

About eight years ago I met Brother Kerr, and he gave me a letter of introduction to a brother in Zion City named Cook. I took his letter to Brother Cook, and he said, "God has sent you here." He gave me the addresses of six people and asked me to go and pray for them and meet him again at twelve o'clock. I got back at about 12:30, and he told me about a young man who was to be married the following Monday. His sweetheart was dying of appendicitis. I went to the house and found that the physician had just been there and had pronounced that there was no hope. The mother was distraught and was pulling her hair and saying, "Is there no deliverance?" I said to her, "Woman, believe God, and your daughter will be healed and be up and dressed in fifteen minutes." But the mother went on screaming.

They took me into the bedroom, and I prayed for the girl and commanded the evil spirit to depart in the name of Jesus. She cried, "I am healed." I said to her, "Do you want me to believe that you are healed? If you are healed, get up." She said, "You get out of the room, and I'll get up." In less than ten minutes the doctor came in. He wanted to know what had happened. She said, "A man came in and prayed for me, and I am healed." The doctor pressed his finger right in the place that had been so sore, and the girl neither moaned nor cried. He said, "This is God." It made no difference whether he acknowledged it or not; I knew that God had worked.

Our God is real, and He has saving and healing power today. Our Jesus is just the same "yesterday, today, and forever" (Heb. 13:8). He saves and heals today just as of old, and He wants to be your Savior and your Healer.

Oh, if you would only believe God! What would happen? The greatest things. Some have never tasted the grace of God, have never had the peace of God. Unbelief robs them of these blessings. It is possible to hear and yet not perceive the truth. It is possible to read the Word and not share in the life it brings. It is necessary for us to have the Holy Spirit to unfold the Word and bring to us the life that is Christ. We can never fully understand the wonders of this redemption until we are full of the Holy Spirit.

DISEASE DUE TO IMMORALITY

One time I was at an afternoon meeting. The Lord had been graciously with us, and many had been healed by the power of God. Most of the people had gone home when I saw a young man who evidently was hanging back to have a word with me. I asked, "What do you want?" He said, "I wonder if I could ask you to pray for me." I said, "What's the trouble?" He said, "Can't you smell?" The young man had gone into sin and was suffering the consequences. He said, "I have been turned out of two hospitals. I am broken out all over. I have abscesses all over me." I could see that he was badly broken out on his nose. He said, "I heard you preach and could not understand about this healing business, and I was wondering if there was any hope for me."

I asked him, "Do you know Jesus?" He did not know the first thing about salvation, but I said to him, "Stand still." I placed my hands on him and cursed that terrible disease in the name of Jesus. He cried out, "I know I'm healed. I can feel a warmth and a glow all over me." I said, "Who did it?" He said, "Your prayers." I said, "No, it was Jesus!" He said, "Was it He? Oh, Jesus! Jesus! Jesus, save me." And that young man went away healed and saved. Oh, what a merciful God we have! What a wonderful Jesus is ours!

A PLACE OF DELIVERANCE

Are you oppressed? Cry out to God. It is always good for people to cry out. You may have to cry out. The Holy Spirit and the Word of God will bring to light every hidden, unclean thing that must be revealed. There is always a place of deliverance when you let God search out what is spoiling and marring your life. The evil spirit that was in the man in the synagogue cried out, *"Let us alone!"* (Mark 1:24). It is notable that the evil spirit never cried out like that until Jesus walked into the place where the man was. Jesus rebuked the thing, saying, *"Be quiet, and come out of him!"* (v. 25), and the man was delivered. He is just the same Jesus today, exposing the powers of evil, delivering the captives and letting the oppressed go free, purifying them and cleansing their hearts.

The evil spirits that inhabited the man who had the *"Legion"* did not want to be sent to the pit to be tormented before their time, and so they cried out to be sent into the swine. (See Luke 8:27–35.) Hell is such an awful place that even the demons hate the thought of going there. How much more should men seek to be saved from the pit?

God is compassionate and says, *"Seek the LORD while He may be found"* (Isa. 55:6). He has further stated, *"Whoever calls on the name of the LORD shall be saved"* (Acts 2:21). Seek Him now; call on His name right now. There is forgiveness, healing, redemption, deliverance—everything you need right here and now, and that which will satisfy you throughout eternity.

CHAPTER FIVE

DARE TO BELIEVE GOD!
THEN COMMAND!

MOST ASSUREDLY, I SAY TO YOU, HE WHO BELIEVES IN ME,
THE WORKS THAT I DO HE WILL DO ALSO; AND GREATER WORKS
THAN THESE HE WILL DO, BECAUSE I GO TO MY FATHER.
AND WHATEVER YOU ASK IN MY NAME, THAT I WILL DO, THAT
THE FATHER MAY BE GLORIFIED IN THE SON. IF YOU ASK
ANYTHING IN MY NAME, I WILL DO IT.
—JOHN 14:12–14

"*He who believes*." What a word! God's Word changes us, and we enter into fellowship and communion. We enter into assurance and Godlikeness, for we see the truth and believe. Faith is an effective power; God opens the understanding and reveals Himself. *"Therefore it is of faith that it might be according to grace"* (Rom. 4:16). Grace is God's blessing coming down to you. You open the door to God as an act of faith, and God does all you want.

Jesus drew the hearts of the people to Himself. They came to Him with all their needs, and He relieved them all. He talked to men, healed the sick, relieved the oppressed, and cast out demons. *"He who believes in Me, the works that I do he will do also"* (John 14:12).

"He who believes in Me"—the essence of divine life is in us by faith. To the one who believes, it will come to pass. We become supernatural by the power of God. If you believe, the power of the Enemy cannot stand, for God's Word is against him. Jesus gives us His Word to make faith effective. If you can believe in your heart, you begin to speak whatever you desire, and whatever you dare to

say is done. <u>You will have whatever you say after you believe in your heart</u>. (See Mark 11:23–24.) <u>Dare to believe</u>, and then <u>dare to speak</u>, for you will have whatever you say if you do not doubt.

Some time ago in England, the power of God was on a meeting that I was conducting, and I was telling the people they could be healed. I said that if they would rise up, I would pray for them, and the Lord would heal them. A man with broken ribs was healed. Then a fourteen-year-old girl said, "Will you pray for me?" After I prayed for her, she said, "Mother, I am being healed." She had straps on her feet, and when these were removed, God healed her right away. <u>Dare to believe God, and it will be as you believe</u>.

CHAPTER SIX

THE POWER TO BIND
AND TO LOOSE

THEN THE PHARISEES AND SADDUCEES CAME, AND TESTING
HIM ASKED THAT HE WOULD SHOW THEM A SIGN FROM HEAVEN. HE
ANSWERED AND SAID TO THEM, "WHEN IT IS EVENING YOU SAY, 'IT
WILL BE FAIR WEATHER, FOR THE SKY IS RED'; AND IN THE
MORNING, 'IT WILL BE FOUL WEATHER TODAY, FOR THE SKY IS
RED AND THREATENING.' HYPOCRITES! YOU KNOW HOW TO DISCERN
THE FACE OF THE SKY, BUT YOU CANNOT DISCERN THE SIGNS OF
THE TIMES. A WICKED AND ADULTEROUS GENERATION SEEKS AFTER
A SIGN, AND NO SIGN SHALL BE GIVEN TO IT EXCEPT
THE SIGN OF THE PROPHET JONAH."
—MATTHEW 16:1–4

The Pharisees and Sadducees had been tempting Jesus to show them a sign from heaven. He told them that they could discern the signs that appeared on the face of the sky and yet could not discern the signs of the times. He would give them no sign to satisfy their unbelieving curiosity, remarking that a wicked and adulterous generation sought a sign and that no sign would be given to them except the sign of the prophet Jonah. A wicked and adulterous generation stumbles over the story of Jonah, but faith can see in that story a wonderful picture of the death, burial, and resurrection of our Lord Jesus Christ.

REMEMBER GOD'S GOODNESS

After Jesus had departed from the Pharisees, He said to His disciples, *"Take heed and beware of the leaven of the Pharisees and the*

Sadducees" (Matt. 16:6). The disciples began to discuss this among themselves, and all they could think of was that they had brought no bread. What were they going to do? Then Jesus uttered these words: *"O you of little faith"* (v. 8). He had been with them for quite a while, yet they were still a great disappointment to Him because of their lack of comprehension and of faith. They could not grasp the profound spiritual truth He was bringing to them and could only think about having brought no bread. So Jesus said to them,

> *O you of little faith,....do you not yet understand, or remember the five loaves of the five thousand and how many baskets you took up? Nor the seven loaves of the four thousand and how many large baskets you took up?* (Matt. 16:8–10)

Do you keep in mind how God has been gracious in the past? God has done wonderful things for all of us. If we will keep these things in mind, we will become *"strong in faith"* (Rom. 4:20 KJV). We should be able to defy Satan in everything. Remember that the Lord has led all the way. When Joshua passed over the Jordan River on dry land, he told the people to pick up twelve stones and set them up in Gilgal. These were to be a constant reminder to the children of Israel that they came over the Jordan on dry land. (See Joshua 4:20–24.) How many times had Jesus shown to His disciples the mightiness of His power? Yet they failed in faith in the passage I just read.

THE POWER IN JESUS' WORDS

One time Jesus had the following conversation with Peter:

> *"What do you think, Simon? From whom do the kings of the earth take customs or taxes, from their sons or from strangers?" Peter said to Him, "From strangers." Jesus said to him, "Then the sons are free. Nevertheless, lest we offend them* [the collectors of the temple tax], *go to the sea, cast in a hook, and take the fish that comes up first. And when you have opened its mouth, you will find a piece of money; take that and give it to them for Me and you."* (Matt. 17:25–27)

Peter had been in the fishing business all his life, but he had never caught a fish with silver in its mouth. However, the Master does not want us to reason things out, for carnal reasoning will always land us in a bog of unbelief. He wants us simply to obey.

"This is a hard job," Peter must have said as he put the bait on his hook, "but since You told me to do it, I'll try." And he cast his line into the sea. There were millions of fish in the sea, but every fish had to stand aside and leave that bait alone and let the fish with the piece of money in its mouth come up and take it.

Do you not see that the words of the Master are the instruction of faith? It is impossible for anything that Jesus says to miss. All His words are spirit and life (John 6:63). If you will only have faith in Him, you will find that every word that God gives is life. You cannot be in close contact with Him and receive His Word in simple faith without feeling the effect of it in your body, as well as in your spirit and soul.

A woman came to me in Cardiff, Wales, who was filled with ulcers. She had fallen in the streets twice because of this trouble. When she came to the meeting, it seemed as if the evil power within her purposed to kill her right there. She fell, and the power of the Devil was attacking her severely. Not only was she helpless, but it seemed as if she had died. I cried, "O God, help this woman." Then I rebuked the evil power in the name of Jesus, and instantly the Lord healed her. She rose up and made a great to-do. She felt the power of God in her body and wanted to testify continually. After three days she went to another place and began to testify about the Lord's power to heal. She came to me and said, "I want to tell everyone about the Lord's healing power. Don't you have any tracts on this subject?" I handed her my Bible and said, "Matthew, Mark, Luke, and John—they are the best tracts on healing. They are full of incidents of the healing power of Jesus. They will never fail to accomplish the work of God if people will only read and believe them."

That is where men are lacking. All lack of faith is due to not feeding on God's Word. You need it every day. How can you enter into a life of faith? Feed on the living Christ of whom this Word is full. As you are taken up with the glorious fact and the wondrous presence of the living Christ, the faith of God will spring up within you. *"Faith comes by hearing, and hearing by the word of God"* (Rom. 10:17).

A PERSONAL REVELATION FROM GOD

Jesus asked His disciples who men were saying that He was. They told Him, *"Some say John the Baptist, some Elijah, and others*

Jeremiah or one of the prophets" (Matt. 16:14). Then He put the question to His disciples to see what they thought: *"But who do you say that I am?"* (v. 15). Peter answered, *"You are the Christ, the Son of the living God"* (v. 16). And Jesus said to him, *"Blessed are you, Simon Bar-Jonah, for flesh and blood has not revealed this to you, but My Father who is in heaven"* (v. 17).

It is so simple. Who do you say that He is? Who is He? Do you say with Peter, *"You are the Christ, the Son of the living God"*? How can you know this? He must be revealed to you. Flesh and blood do not reveal His identity; it is an inward revelation. God wants to reveal His Son within us and make us conscious of an inward presence. Then you can cry out, "I know He's mine. He's mine! He's mine!" *"Nor does anyone know the Father except the Son, and the one to whom the Son wills to **reveal Him**"* (Matt. 11:27, emphasis added). Seek God until you get from Him a mighty revelation of the Son, until that inward revelation moves you on to the place where you are always *"steadfast, immovable, always abounding in the work of the Lord"* (1 Cor. 15:58).

There is a wonderful power in this revelation. When Peter said to Jesus, *"You are the Christ"* (Matt. 16:16), He replied,

> *On this rock I will build My church, and the gates of Hades shall not prevail against it. And I will give you the keys of the kingdom of heaven, and whatever you bind on earth will be bound in heaven, and whatever you loose on earth will be loosed in heaven.* (Matt. 16:18–19)

Was Peter the *"rock"*? No. A few minutes later he was so full of the Devil that Christ had to say to him, *"Get behind Me, Satan! You are an offense to Me"* (v. 23). This *"rock"* was Christ. He is the Rock; there are many Scriptures to confirm this. And to everyone who knows that He is the Christ, He gives the key of faith, the power to bind and the power to loose. Establish your hearts with this fact. God wants you to have the inward revelation of this truth and of all the power contained in it.

WONDERFUL DEMONSTRATIONS OF GOD'S MIGHT

"On this rock I will build My church, and the gates of Hades shall not prevail against it" (v. 18). God is pleased when we stand

on the Rock and believe that He is unchangeable. If you will dare to believe God, you can defy all the powers of evil. There have been times in my experience when I have dared to believe Him and have had the most remarkable experiences.

One day I was traveling in a railway coach, and there were two people in the coach who were very sick, a mother and her daughter. I said to them, "Look, I've something in this bag that will cure every case in the world. It has never been known to fail." They became very much interested, and I went on to tell them more and more about this remedy that had never failed to remove disease and sickness. At last they summoned up the courage to ask for a dose. So I opened my bag, took out my Bible, and read them the verse that says, "*I am the LORD who heals you*" (Exod. 15:26).

God's Word never fails. He will always heal you if you dare to believe Him. Men are searching everywhere today for things with which they can heal themselves, and they ignore the fact that the Balm of Gilead (Jer. 8:22) is within easy reach. As I talked about this wonderful Physician, the faith of both mother and daughter went out toward Him, and He healed them both right in the train.

God has made His Word so precious that if I could not get another copy of it, I would not part with my Bible for all the world. There is life in the Word. There is power in it. I find Christ in it, and He is the One I need for spirit, soul, and body. It tells me of the power of His name and the power of His blood for cleansing. "*The young lions lack and suffer hunger; but those who seek the LORD shall not lack any good thing*" (Ps. 34:10).

A man came to me one time, brought by a little woman. I said, "What seems to be the problem?" She said, "He gets employment, but he fails every time. He is a slave to alcohol and nicotine poison. He is a bright, intelligent man in most areas, but he is in bondage to these two things." I was reminded of the words of the Master, giving us power to bind and to loose, and I told him to stick out his tongue. In the name of the Lord Jesus Christ, I cast out the evil powers that gave him the taste for these things. I said to him, "Man, you are free today." He was unsaved, but when he realized the power of the Lord in delivering him, he came to the services, publicly acknowledged that he was sinner, and was saved and baptized. A few days later I asked, "How are things with you?" He said, "I'm delivered." God has given us the power to bind and the power to loose.

Another person came and said, "What can you do for me? I have had sixteen operations and have had my eardrums taken out." I said, "God has not forgotten how to make eardrums." She was so deaf that I do not think she would have heard a cannon go off. I anointed her and prayed, asking the Lord to replace the eardrums. But she remained as deaf as it was possible to be afterward. However, she saw other people getting healed and rejoicing. Had "God forgotten to be gracious" (Ps. 77:9)? Wasn't His power just the same? She came the next night and said, "I have come to believe God tonight." Take care that you do not come in any other way. I prayed for her again and commanded her ears to be loosed in the name of Jesus. She believed, and the moment she believed, she heard. She ran and jumped on a chair and began to preach. Later I let a pin drop, and she heard it touch the floor. God can give drums to ears. "With God all things are possible" (Matt. 19:26). God can save the worst case.

Discouraged one, "cast your burden on the LORD, and He shall sustain you" (Ps. 55:22). Look to Him and be radiant (Ps. 34:5). Look to Him now.

49

CHAPTER SEVEN

YOU ARE THE CHRIST

I need not say how pleased I am to be among you again. We are coming in contact this afternoon with a living Christ. It is on the Rock that God is building His church, and the gates of hell will not prevail against it (Matt. 16:18).

We are more confident today than we were yesterday. God is building us up in this faith, so that we are living in great expectation. He is bringing us into a place with Himself where we can say, "I have seen God."

I have been asking God to send us something on fire from His Word—something that will live in our hearts, that will abide with us forever. It is important that every day we lay some new foundation that can never be uprooted. Oh, for a living touch from God, a new inspiration of power, and a deeper sense of His love!

THE KEY TO ALL REAL SUCCESS

I have been thinking about the sixteenth chapter of Matthew and Peter's answer to Jesus when He asked His disciples the question, *"Who do you say that I am?"* (Matt. 16:15). Peter answered, *"You are the Christ, the Son of the living God"* (v. 16). Beloved friend, do you know Him? Has this revelation come to your heart? Do you call Him Lord? Do you find comfort in the fact that He is yours?

"Who do you say that I am?" The Master knew what was in their thoughts before He asked them. This fact makes me long more and more to be really true; God is seeing right into my heart and reads my thoughts.

There is something in what Jesus said to Peter that is applicable to us: *"Blessed are you, Simon Bar-Jonah, for flesh and blood has not revealed this to you, but My Father who is in heaven"* (Matt. 16:17). If you can call Jesus Lord, it is by the Holy Spirit (1 Cor. 12:3). Therefore, there ought to be within us a deep response that says, *"You are the Christ"* (Matt. 16:16). When we can say this from our hearts, we know that we are not born of flesh and blood, but of the Spirit of the living God. (See John 3:5–6.)

If you will go back to the time when you first had the knowledge that you were born of God, you will see that there was within you a deep cry for your Father. You found you have a heavenly Father. If you want to know the reason for the real success of any life, it is this knowledge: *"You are the Christ."* This knowledge is the rock foundation, and the gates of hell will not prevail against it (Matt. 16:18). *"And I will give you the keys of the kingdom of heaven"* (v. 19).

It is about this rock, this blessed foundation truth, that I want to speak this afternoon—this knowledge of our personal acceptance by God, this life of faith that we have come into. It is because of this rock foundation that we have this living faith, and this foundation cannot be overthrown. Jesus has given us power to bind and to loose (v. 19). Everyone who has come to this rock foundation ought to be in the position where he can bind and loose. I want you to go away from this meeting knowing that you are on this rock foundation and are in this position, having that living faith so that you can pray and *know* you have the answer because of God's promises. It is on this rock that our faith must be based, and it will never fail; God has established it forever.

HOW TO OBTAIN SPIRITUAL POWER

From that time Jesus began to show to His disciples that He must go to Jerusalem, and suffer many things from the elders and chief priests and scribes, and be killed, and be raised the third day. Then Peter took Him aside and began to rebuke Him, saying, "Far be it from You, Lord; this shall not happen to You!" But He turned and said to Peter, "Get behind Me, Satan! You are an offense to Me, for you are not mindful of the things of God, but the things of men." Then Jesus said to His disciples, "If anyone desires to come after Me, let him deny himself, and take up his cross, and follow Me."

(Matt. 16:21–24)

We find that the fundamental truths of all the ages were planted right in the life of Peter. We see evidences of the spiritual power to which he had attained, and we see also the natural power working. Jesus saw that He must suffer if He would reach the spiritual life that God intended Him to reach. So Jesus said, "I must go forward. Your words, Peter, are an offense to Me." If you seek to save yourself, it is an offense to God. God has been impressing on me more and more that if at any time I were to seek man's favor or earthly power, I would lose favor with God and could not have faith. Jesus asked, *"How can you believe [if you] receive honor from one another?"* (John 5:44).

God is speaking to us, every one of us, and trying to get us to leave the shoreline. There is only one place where we can get the mind and will of God; it is alone with God. If we look to anybody else, we cannot get it. If we seek to save ourselves, we will never reach the place where we will be able to bind and loose. There is a close companionship between you and Jesus that nobody knows about, where every day you have to choose or refuse.

It is in the narrow way that you get the power to bind and the power to loose. I know that Jesus was separated from His own family and friends. He was deprived of the luxuries of life. It seems to me that God wants to get every one of us separated to Himself in this holy war, and we are not going to have faith if we do not give ourselves wholly to Him. Beloved, it is in these last days that I cannot have the power I want to have unless, as a sheep, I am willing to shear myself. The way is narrow. (See Matthew 7:13–14.)

Beloved, you will not be able to bind and loose if you have sin in you. There is not one person who is able to deal with the sins of others if he is not free himself. *"He breathed on them, and said to them, 'Receive the Holy Spirit'"* (John 20:22). He knew the Holy Spirit would give them both a revelation of themselves and a revelation of God. He must reveal to you your depravity. In Luke 22:29–30, we read,

> And I bestow upon you a kingdom, just as My Father be-stowed one upon Me, that you may eat and drink at My table in My kingdom, and sit on thrones judging the twelve tribes of Israel.

Do you believe that the Father in heaven would make you a judge over a kingdom if there were anything crooked in you? Do you believe you will be able to bind unless you are free yourself? But everyone who has this living Christ within him has the power that will put to death all sin.

With Jesus' last words on earth, He gave the disciples a commission. (See Mark 16:15–18.) The discipleship has never ceased. The churches are weak today because Christ the Rock is not abiding in them in the manifestations of the power of God. This is not because it is a special gift—this power to bind and loose—but it is contingent on whether you have the rock foundation in you. In the name of Jesus, you will loose, and in the name of Jesus, you will bind. If He is in you, you ought to bring forth evidences of that power.

One can see that Peter had great sympathy in the natural, and he did not want Jesus to be crucified. It was perfectly natural for Peter to say what he did, but Jesus said, *"Get behind Me"* (Matt. 16:23). He knew He must not be turned aside by any human sympathy. The only way we can retain our humility is to stay on this narrow line and say, "Get behind me, Satan." If you try to go the easy way, you cannot be Jesus' disciple (Luke 14:27).

Beloved, we are now living in the experience of the fact that Jesus is the Rock. I am glad, for we are within reach of wonderful possibilities because of the Rock. Take a stand on the fact that the Rock cannot be overthrown.

MANY EXAMPLES OF GOD'S HEALING TOUCH

At one meeting, there was a seventy-seven-year-old woman who was paralyzed. The power of God came into her, and she was so strengthened and blessed after prayer that she rushed up and down in a marvelous way.

Brothers and sisters, what I see in this woman's healing is an illustration of what God will do. I am trusting that we will all be so strengthened today with the power of God that we will not allow any doubt or fear to come into our hearts. On the contrary, we will know that we are created anew by a living faith and that there is in that faith within us power to accomplish wonderful things for God.

I want to say that the most wonderful and marvelous faith is the simple faith of a little child. It is the faith that dares. There is a boldness in childlike faith that causes us to say, "You will be healed."

A man brought his son to my meeting, and he was all drawn to one side from having fits for years. The father asked, "Can you do anything for my son?" I said in the name of Jesus, "Yes, he can be healed." I knew it was because of the Rock that it could be done. There is a Spirit who dwells within us, and He is nothing less than the life of Him who gave Himself for us, for He is the life of the Rock in us.

I wonder if you wait until some mighty power sweeps over you before you feel you have power to bind. That is not the power. The Rock is within you; you have power to bind and power to loose because you consist of the Rock. What you have to do is stand on that fact and use the power. Will you do it?

I said, "Father, in the name of Jesus, I bind the evil spirit in this young man." Oh, the name of Jesus! We make too little use of that name. Even the children cried, *"Hosanna"* (Matt. 21:15). If we would let ourselves go and praise Him more and more, God would give us the shout of victory.

The father brought the young man to the next meeting, and I did not need to ask if he was delivered. The brightness of his face and the shining of the father's face told the story. But I asked, "Is he all right now?" and he said, "Yes."

Oh, I see it is needed so much, this power to bind and power to loose. Brothers and sisters, wherever you are, you can set people free. God wants to change your name from Doubting Thomas to Prevailing Israel.

A young woman was brought to me who had cancer. Her spirits were very low. People need to be made glad. I said to her, "Cheer up," but I could not get her to cheer up. So I bound the evil power in the name of Jesus and then laid my hands on her and said, "Sister, you are free." She arose and asked if she could say something. She rubbed the place where the cancer had been and said, "It is all gone!"

Oh, brothers and sisters, I want you to see that that power is yours. God is delighted when we use the power He has given us. I believe every child of God has a measure of this power, but there is a fuller manifestation of the power when we get so filled that we speak in tongues. I want you to press on until you get the fullness. I must send you home with a loaf of bread and a cake of raisins, as David did with the people. (See 2 Samuel 6:19.)

When will we see all the people filled with the Holy Spirit and things done as they were in the Acts of the Apostles? It will be when all the people say, "Lord, You are God." I want you to come into a place of such relationship with God that you will know your prayers are answered because He has promised.

I dropped into a shoemaker's shop one morning, and there was a man who had his eyes covered with a green shade. They were so inflamed that he was suffering terribly. He said, "I cannot rest anywhere." I did not ask him what he believed but laid down my Bible and put my hands on those poor suffering eyes in the name of Jesus. He said, "This is strange; I have no pain. I am free."

Do you think the human mind can do that? I say, "No." We do these things with a consciousness that God will answer, and He is pleased with that kind of service.

A boy came into a meeting on crutches. He had a broken ankle. Several of us joined in prayer, and with joy I saw the boy so healed that he walked away carrying his crutches.

Beloved, Jesus is coming soon. There are so many things that seem to say, "He is at the door." Will you use the power of the Rock within you for His glory?

CHAPTER EIGHT

HOW MULTITUDES
WERE DELIVERED

Facts are stubborn things. We need all unbelief to be cut away so that the mind does not interfere with God's plan. The Devil has been at work. Men today try to put away what God has established. God has established truth in His Word, but men have tried to bring it to nothing. God has His Word in the earth; it is also *"settled in heaven"* (Ps. 119:89). If you are standing on the Word, you are eternally fixed. God has said it, and it is established; the Word of God *"abides forever"* (1 Pet. 1:23). Men pass away, things change, but God's Word *"abides forever."* Examine yourselves in the faith (2 Cor. 13:5).

SOMEONE GREATER THAN SATAN

"If You are willing, You can make me clean" (Matt. 8:2). Who said this? A leper. In Bible times, leprosy was incurable. It is a loathsome condition in which limbs rot and fall off. When a man had leprosy, he was doomed for life. Like cancer or tuberculosis, it was the Devil manifest in the flesh. And the Devil never lets go of the flesh until he is forced to. For deliverance you must have someone mightier than Satan. Here is a fact: in our midst is One greater than Satan. If you believe it, it will make all the difference to you. It will mean no more trouble, no more sickness. God's plan is wonderful. Allow God to do a deep work, cutting away unbelief. His ways are perfect.

Jesus always goes to the right place. Sometimes doctors say that they begin to operate at the wrong place and that when they get to the right place, they cannot do what is needed. When the patient dies, they say the operation was successful but that he died after it. No one dies after the operation of Jesus. This is rather hard on the doctors, some say. No, they need not worry; they will have plenty to do while the world is rolling on in sin. But the believer is in a place quite different from that of the world. Jesus asked the woman, "Can we take the children's bread and give it to the dogs?" (See Matthew 15:26.) Children of God have bread; it is the life of Jesus. Jesus has all the bread you want, for spirit, soul, and body.

I went into a hotel where there was a man whose arm had been poisoned. I looked at the arm; it was very swollen. His arm, neck, and face were blue. He opened his eyes and said, "Can you save me? I am dying." I took hold of the arm and turned it round twice. It was an act of faith. I said, "In the name of Jesus, you are free." He swung his arm round and round and said, "Look! Jesus is that mighty, wonderful name, which God has said is greater than all." This same Jesus is the Deliverer of all humanity.

YOU CAN BE FREE

Women often say to their children, "Run and fetch my purse; I cannot get along without my purse." Mother, have you ever run back for your Bible? It contains richer gold and greater power. If the Word of God is in your heart, you will be free. God is always making you free. The Gospel is full of liberty and has no bondage. It is full of liberty! How long does it take to get clean? Jesus said to the leper, "I am willing; be cleansed" (Matt. 8:3), and his leprosy was cleansed immediately.

Lots of people have a big barrier in their way. They say, "I wonder if it is God's will," and they hang their harps on the willows. (See Psalm 137:1–4.) Is it the will of God? The answer comes when we look at redemption. Is it the will of God to save? Some people say, "All men will be saved." That is not scriptural. Who will be saved, and who will be lost? The lost are those who do not believe. To all who believe, God's plan is clear. The plan is "I will when you will."

THE POWER OF TRUE FAITH

There was a woman sick and near death. She sent for me. I went with a mission leader to her house. There she was, lying in bed, dying. The Lord revealed to me that nothing could save her except His power. I bent near to her. She said, "I have faith; I have faith." She repeated this continually: "I have faith." I said, "You have no faith; you are dying, and you know it. You have only words." I asked her, "Do you want to live?" "Yes," she said, "but I have no power." The Spirit of the Lord came upon me, and I said, "In the name of Jesus." Then the Spirit of God raised her up.

Faith is actively refusing the power of the Devil. It is not saying mere words. You must have an activity of faith, refusing the conditions in the name of Jesus. We must have something more than words. Satan comes *"to kill, and to destroy"* (John 10:10). Jesus comes to give life abundantly (v. 10). He comes to give abounding life through the operation of the Holy Spirit. The leper said, *"If You are willing, You can make me clean"* (Matt. 8:2). Jesus said, *"I am willing"* (v. 3).

A TESTIMONY OF HEALING

In one place where I was, there came a woman to be healed. Crowds were present. Here was a case God wanted to make an exhibition of. Here she was, in pain, in weakness, with flesh gone, unable to eat solid food. I said to the crowds, "Look at her. Take in the details of her condition." Then in the name of Jesus, I cast out the evil spirit and laid my hands upon her. She told the people she was free. She came to the meeting that night and to the one the next day, magnifying God. I was surprised to see her; I thought she had gone to her home in the country. She said, "I cannot go until I have fully magnified the Lord." When she left, she said, "Goodbye. I am going to preach this life: *'He Himself took our infirmities and bore our sicknesses'* (Matt. 8:17)."

So many miss the way because they rely on their feelings. It is more important to have God's Word than anything else. Psalm 119:50 states, *"Your word has given me life."* Nothing but the Word can give life, and the Word is Jesus. *"Your word I have hidden in my heart"* (Ps. 119:11). All darkness, sin, and affliction must go. The Word of God is against them. You cannot have both them and the Word of God. To believe is to be saved, to be healed, to be free. Unbelief is neither salvation, healing, nor freedom. *"If you can believe, all things are possible to him who believes"* (Mark 9:23). This truth is established forever.

CHAPTER NINE

LIFE IN THE SPIRIT

L et us read the third chapter of 2 Corinthians, all eighteen verses. What a wonderful passage! It will form the basis of my comments during this service.

Do we begin again to commend ourselves? Or do we need, as some others, epistles of commendation to you or letters of commendation from you? You are our epistle written in our hearts, known and read by all men; clearly you are an epistle of Christ, ministered by us, written not with ink but by the Spirit of the living God, not on tablets of stone but on tablets of flesh, that is, of the heart. And we have such trust through Christ toward God. Not that we are sufficient of ourselves to think of anything as being from ourselves, but our sufficiency is from God, who also made us sufficient as ministers of the new covenant, not of the letter but of the Spirit; for the letter kills, but the Spirit gives life. But if the ministry of death, written and engraved on stones, was glorious, so that the children of Israel could not look steadily at the face of Moses because of the glory of his countenance, which glory was passing away ["done away" KJV], how will the ministry of the Spirit not be more glorious? For if the ministry of condemnation had glory, the ministry of righteousness exceeds much more in glory. For even what was made glorious had no glory in this respect, because of the glory that excels. For if what is passing away ["done away" KJV] was glorious, what remains is much more glorious. Therefore, since we have such hope, we use great boldness of speech; unlike Moses, who put a veil over his face so that the children of Israel could not look steadily at the end of what was passing away. But their minds were blinded. For until this day the same veil remains unlifted in the reading of the Old Testament, because the veil is taken away ["done away" KJV] in Christ. But even to this day, when ✳ *Moses is read, a veil lies on their heart. Nevertheless when one turns to the Lord, the veil is taken away. Now the Lord is the Spirit; and where the Spirit of the Lord is, there is liberty. But we all, with unveiled face, beholding as in a mirror the glory of the Lord, are being transformed into the same image from glory to glory, just as by the Spirit of the Lord.* (2 Cor. 3:1–18)

We are told in Hebrews 6:1–2 that we are to leave the discussion of the first principles of Christ and go on to perfection, not laying again the foundation of repentance from dead works and the doctrine of baptisms and the other first principles. What would you think of a builder who was continually pulling down his house and putting in fresh foundations✳Never look back if you want the power of God in your life. You will find out that in the measure you have allowed yourself to look back, you have missed what God had for you.

The Holy Spirit shows us that we must never look back to the law of sin and death from which we have been delivered. (See Romans 8:2.) God has brought us into a new order of things, a life of love and liberty in Christ Jesus that is beyond all human comprehension. Many are brought into this new life through the power of the Spirit of God, and then, like the Galatians, who ran well at the beginning, they try to perfect themselves through legalism. (See Galatians 3:1–3; 5:7.) They turn back from a life in the Spirit to a life along natural lines. God is not pleased with this, for He has no place for the person who has lost the vision. The only thing to do is to repent. Don't try to cover up anything. If you have been tripped up in any area, confess it; then look to God to bring you to a place of stability of faith where your whole walk will be in the Spirit.

THE JOY OF BEING GOD'S CHILD

We all ought to have a clear conviction that *"salvation is of the LORD"* (Jonah 2:9). Salvation is more than a human order of things. If the Enemy can move you from a place of faith, he can get you outside of the plan of God. The moment a man falls into sin, divine life ceases to flow, and his life becomes one of helplessness.
✳ But this is not God's plan for any of His children. Read the third

chapter of John's first epistle, and take your place as a child of God. Take the place of knowing that you are a child of God, and remember that as your hope is set in Christ, it should have a purifying effect on your life. The Holy Spirit says, *"Whoever has been born of God does not sin, for His seed remains in him; and he cannot sin, because he has been born of God"* (1 John 3:9). There is life and power in the seed of the Word that is implanted within. God is in that *"cannot,"* and there is more power in that Word of His than in any human objections. God's thought for every one of us is that we will *"reign in life"* by Jesus Christ (Rom. 5:17). You must come to see how wonderful you are in God and how helpless you are in yourself.

God declared Himself to be mightier than every opposing power when He cast out the powers of darkness from heaven. I want you to know that the same power that cast Satan out of heaven dwells in every person who is born of God. If you would only realize this, you would *"reign in life."* When you see people laid out under an evil power, when you see the powers of evil manifesting themselves, always ask them the question, "Did Jesus come in the flesh?" I have never heard an evil power answer in the affirmative. (See 1 John 4:2–3.) When you know you have an evil spirit to deal with, you have power to cast it out. Believe this fact, and act on it, for *"greater is he that is in you, than he that is in the world"* (1 John 4:4 KJV). God intends for you to overcome and has put a force within you whereby you may defeat the Devil.

TRIUMPHING IN TRIALS

Temptations will come to all. If you are not worth tempting, you are not worth much. Job said, *"When He has tested me, I shall come forth as gold"* (Job 23:10). In every temptation that comes, the Lord allows you to be tempted to the very hilt, but He will never allow you to be defeated if you walk in obedience. Right in the midst of the temptation, He will always *"make the way of escape"* (1 Cor. 10:13).

INTERPRETATION OF A MESSAGE IN TONGUES: "God comes forth and with His power 'sweeps away the refuge of lies' and all the powers of darkness and causes you 'always to triumph in Christ Jesus.' The Lord loves His saints and covers them with His almighty wings."

May God help us to see this truth. We cannot be *"to the praise of His glory"* (Eph. 1:12) until we are ready for trials and are able to triumph in them. We cannot get away from the fact that when we were born, we inherited a sinful nature, but God comes into our nature and puts sin into the place of death. Why? So that the Spirit of God may come into the temple in all His power and liberty (1 Cor. 3:16), and so that right here in this present, evil world Satan may be dethroned by the believer.

THE SPIRIT'S WORK IN OUR HEARTS

Satan is always endeavoring to bring the saints of God into disrepute by bringing against them slanderous accusations, but the Holy Spirit never comes with condemnation. He always reveals the blood of Christ. He always brings us help. The Lord Jesus referred to Him as the Comforter who would come (John 14:16 KJV). He is always on hand to help in the seasons of testing and trial. The Holy Spirit is the lifting power of the church of Christ.

Paul told us that we are *"clearly...an epistle of Christ...written not with ink but by the Spirit of the living God, not on tablets of stone but on tablets of flesh, that is, of the heart"* (2 Cor. 3:3). The Holy Spirit begins in the heart, right in the depths of human affections. He brings into the heart the riches of the revelation of Christ, implanting a purity and holiness there, so that out of the depths of the heart, praises well up continually.

The Holy Spirit will make us epistles of Christ, ever proclaiming that Jesus is our Lord and our Redeemer and that He is ever before God as a slain Lamb. God has never put away that revelation. Because of the perfect atonement of that slain Lamb, there is salvation, healing, and deliverance for all. Some people think that they have to be cleansed only once, but as we walk in the light, the blood of Jesus Christ is ever cleansing us (1 John 1:7).

The very life of Christ has been put within us and is moving within us—a perfect life. May the Lord help us to see the power of this life. The days of a man's life are seventy years (Ps. 90:10), and so in the natural order of things, my life will be finished in seven years. But I have begun a new life that will never end. *"From everlasting to everlasting, You are God"* (v. 2). This is the life I have come into, and there is no end to this life. In me is working a power that is stronger than every power. Christ, the power of God, is formed within me. I can see why we need to be clothed from above

(Luke 24:49), for the life within me is a thousand times bigger than I am outside. There must be a tremendous expansion. I see, and cannot help seeing, that this life cannot be understood in the natural. No natural reason can comprehend the divine plan.

OUR ALL-SUFFICIENT GOD

We are not *"sufficient of ourselves to think of anything as being from ourselves, but our sufficiency is from God"* (2 Cor. 3:5). We have left the old order of things. If we go back, we miss the plan. We can never have confidence in the flesh (Phil. 3:3); we cannot touch that. We are in a new order, a spiritual order. It is a new life of absolute faith in our God's sufficiency in everything that pertains to our salvation.

You could never come into this place and be a Seventh-day Adventist, for the law has no place in you. You are set free from it. At the same time, like Paul, you are bound in the Spirit (Acts 20:22) so that you would not do anything to grieve the Lord.

Paul further told us that God has *"made us sufficient as ministers of the new covenant, not of the letter but of the Spirit; for the letter kills, but the Spirit gives life"* (2 Cor. 3:6). It is one thing to read this and another thing to have the revelation of it and to see the spiritual force of it. Any man can live in the letter and become dry and wordy, limited in knowledge of spiritual truths and spending all his time splitting hairs. But as soon as he touches the realm of the Spirit, dryness goes; the spirit of criticism leaves. There can be no divisions in a life in the Spirit. The Spirit of God brings such pliability and such love! There is no love like the love in the Spirit. It is a pure, holy, divine love that is poured out in our hearts by the Spirit (Rom. 5:5). It loves to serve and to honor the Lord.

THE HOLY SPIRIT'S LIFE-CHANGING POWER

I can never estimate what the baptism in the Holy Spirit has meant to me these past fifteen years. It seems as if every year has had three years packed into it, so that I feel as if I have had forty-five years of happy service since 1907. Life is getting better all the time. It is a luxury to be filled with the Spirit, and at the same time it is a divine command for us: *"Do not be drunk with wine, in which is dissipation; but be filled with the Spirit"* (Eph. 5:18). No Pentecostal person ought to get out of bed without being lost in the Spirit and speaking in tongues as the Spirit gives utterance. No one should come through the door of the church without speaking in tongues or having a psalm or a note of praise (1 Cor. 14:26).

Regarding the incoming of the Spirit, I emphasize that He should so fill us that every member in the body is yielded to Him. I also emphasize that no one is baptized in the Spirit without speaking in tongues as the Spirit gives utterance. I maintain that with a constant filling, you will speak in tongues morning, noon, and night. As you live in the Spirit, when you walk down the steps of your house, the Devil will have to flee before you. You will be more than a conqueror over the Devil (Rom. 8:37).

I see everything as a failure except what is done in the Spirit. But as you live in the Spirit, you move, act, eat, drink, and do everything to the glory of God (1 Cor. 10:31). Our message is always this: *"Be filled with the Spirit."* This is God's place for you, and it is as far above the natural life as the heavens are above the earth. Yield yourself so that God will fill you.

THE WONDERFUL NEW COVENANT

The Israelites tried Moses tremendously. They were always in trouble. But as he went up onto the mountain and God unfolded to him the Ten Commandments, the glory fell. He rejoiced to bring those two tablets of stone down from the mountain, and his very face shone with the glory. He was bringing to Israel that which, if obeyed, would bring life.

I think of my Lord coming from heaven. I think all heaven was moved by the sight. The letter of the law was brought by Moses, and it was made glorious, but all its glory was dimmed before the excelling glory that Jesus brought to us in the Spirit of Life. The glory of Sinai paled before the glory of Pentecost. Those tablets of stone with their "Thou shalt not's" are done away with, for they never brought life to anyone. The Lord has brought in a new covenant, putting His law in our minds and writing it in our hearts (Jer. 31:33)—this new law of the Spirit of Life. As the Holy Spirit comes in, He fills us with love and liberty, and we shout for joy, "Done away! Done away!" (See 2 Corinthians 3:7–11 KJV.) Henceforth, there is a new cry in our hearts: *"I delight to do Your will, O my God"* (Ps. 40:8). *"He takes away the first that He may establish the second"* (Heb. 10:9). In other words, He takes away *"the ministry of death, written and engraved on stones"* (2 Cor. 3:7), so that He may establish *"the ministry of righteousness"* (v. 9), this life in the Spirit.

You ask, "Does a man who is filled with the Spirit cease to keep the commandments?" I simply repeat what the Spirit of God has told us here, that this *"ministry of death, written and engraved on stones"* (and you know that the Ten Commandments were written on stones) is *"done away* [with]" (v. 11 KJV). However, the man who becomes a living epistle of Christ, written by the Spirit of the living God, has ceased to be an adulterer or a murderer or a covetous man; the will of God is his delight. I love to do the will of God; there is no irksomeness to it. It is no trial to pray, no trouble to read the Word of God; it is not a hard thing to go to the place of worship. With the psalmist I say, *"I was glad when they said to me, 'Let us go into the house of the LORD'"* (Ps. 122:1).

How does this new life work out? It works out because God *"works in you both to will and to do for His good pleasure"* (Phil. 2:13). There is a big difference between a pump and a spring. The law is a pump; the baptism in the Holy Spirit is a spring. The old pump gets out of order; the parts wear out, and the well runs dry. *"The letter kills"* (2 Cor. 3:6). But the spring is ever bubbling up, and there is a ceaseless flow direct from the throne of God. There is life.

It is written of Christ, *"You love righteousness and hate wickedness"* (Ps. 45:7). In this new life in the Spirit, in this new covenant life, you love the things that are right and pure and holy, and you shudder at all things that are wrong. Jesus was able to say, *"The ruler of this world is coming, and he has nothing in Me"* (John 14:30), and the moment we are filled with the Spirit of God, we are brought into a wonderful condition like this. Furthermore, as we continue to be filled with the Spirit, the Enemy cannot have an inch of territory in us.

HOW TO BRING CONVICTION OF SIN

Do you not believe that you can be so filled with the Spirit that a person who is not living right can be judged and convicted by your presence? As we go on in the life of the Spirit, it will be said of us that a vile person is convicted in our presence. Jesus lived in this realm and moved in it, and His life was a constant reproof to the wickedness around Him. "But He was the Son of God," you say. God, through Him, has brought us into the place of sonship, and I believe that if the Holy Spirit has a chance at us, He can make something of us and bring us to the same place.

I don't want to boast. If I glory in anything, it is only in the Lord, who has been so gracious to me (1 Cor. 1:31). But I remember a wonderful time of conviction. I stepped out of a railway coach to wash my hands. I had a season of prayer, and the Lord just filled me to overflowing with His love. I was going to a convention in Ireland, and I could not get there fast enough. As I returned to my seat, I believe that the Spirit of the Lord was so heavy upon me that my face must have shone. (When the Spirit transforms a man's very countenance, he cannot tell this on his own.) There were two clerical men sitting together, and as I got into the coach again, one of them cried out, "You convict me of sin." Within three minutes everyone in the coach was crying to God for salvation. This has happened many times in my life. It is the ministry of the Spirit that Paul spoke of. This filling of the Spirit will make your life effective, so that even the people in the stores where you shop will want to leave your presence because they are brought under conviction.

We must move away from everything that pertains to the letter. All that we do must be done under the anointing of the Spirit. Our problem has been that we as Pentecostal people have been living in the letter. Believe what the Holy Spirit said through Paul—that this entire *"ministry of condemnation"* (2 Cor. 3:9) that has hindered your liberty in Christ is done away with. The law has been done away with! As far as you are concerned, that old order of things is forever done away with, and the Spirit of God has brought in a new life of purity and love. The Holy Spirit takes it for granted that you are finished with all the things of the old life when you become a new creation in Christ. In the life in the Spirit, the old allurements have lost their power. The Devil will meet you at every turn, but the Spirit of God will always *"lift up a standard against him"* (Isa. 59:19).

Oh, if God had His way, we would be like torches, purifying the very atmosphere wherever we go, moving back the forces of wickedness.

INTERPRETATION OF A MESSAGE IN TONGUES: "'The Lord is that Spirit.' He moves in your heart. He shows you that the power within you is mightier than all the powers of darkness."

What do I mean when I say that the law has been done away with? Do I mean that you will be disloyal? No, you will be more than loyal. Will you grumble when you are treated badly? No, you will turn the other cheek (Matt. 5:39). You will always do this when God lives in you. Leave yourself in God's hands. Enter into rest. *"For he who has entered His rest has himself also ceased from his works as God did from His"* (Heb. 4:10). Oh, this is a lovely rest! The whole life is a Sabbath. This is the only life that can glorify God. It is a life of joy, and every day is a day of heaven on earth.

DAILY TRANSFORMATION

There is a continual transformation in this life. Beholding the Lord and His glory, we are *"transformed into the same image from glory to glory, just as by the Spirit of the Lord"* (2 Cor. 3:18). There is a continual unveiling, a constant revelation, a repeated clothing from above. I want you to promise God never to look back, never to go back to what the Spirit has said is done away with. I promised the Lord that I would never allow myself to doubt His Word.

There is one thing about a baby: he takes all that comes to him. A so-called prudent man lets his reason cheat him out of God's best. But a baby takes all the milk his mother brings and even tries to swallow the bottle. The baby can't walk, but the mother carries him; the baby can't dress himself, but the mother dresses him. The baby can't even talk. Similarly, in the life of the Spirit, God undertakes to do what we cannot do. We are carried along by Him. He clothes us, and He gives us utterance. Oh, that we all had the simplicity of babes!

CHAPTER TEN

GREATER WORKS THAN THESE

I want all you people to have a good time, all to be at ease, all to be without pain. I want all to be free. There is a man here with great pain in his head. I am going to lay my hands on him in the name of Jesus, and he will tell you what God has done. I believe it is the right thing to do, before I begin preaching to you, to help this poor man so that he will enjoy the meeting like us, without any pain.

(The man referred to had his head wrapped up in a bandage and was in pain. After he was prayed for, he testified that he had no pain.)

GOD'S BLESSINGS AVAILABLE TO ALL

I want you all to be in a place where you receive much blessing from God. It will be impossible for any of you to leave with pain if you will only believe God. If you receive the Word of God tonight, it will give life to you; it gives deliverance to every captive. I want to preach the Word tonight so that all the people will know the truth. You will leave with a knowledge of the deliverance of God.

I want everyone to receive a blessing at the start of the meeting. Not one person needs to live outside of the plan of God. If you have pain in your knee, and if you believe when you stand up, you will definitely be free. I believe the Word of God. God has promised that if we will believe, we can have whatever we ask (Matt. 21:22).

I want you to be blessed now. I find I get blessed as I ask—on the street, everywhere! If you find me on the street or anywhere else, if I am alone, I will be talking to God. I make it my business to talk to God all the time. If I wake in the night, I make it my business to

68

pray, and I believe that's the reason that God keeps me right, always right, always ready. I believe that God the Holy Spirit keeps us living in communion with God. I want you to begin now; begin talking to God.

Jesus is the Way and the Truth (John 14:6); therefore, all that Jesus said was true. Jesus said, *"Most assuredly, I say to you, he who believes in Me, the works that I do he will do also; and greater works than these he will do, because I go to My Father"* (v. 12). Has He gone? Yes, He has gone to the Father.

SEND THE LIGHT

Do you see this electric light? This light is receiving power from the power plant; it has a receiver and transmitter. The power plant may be a mile or two away. The wires that are conveying the current to and from are covered. We are getting the light from the bare wire underneath; the power is passing through the bare wire and giving us light.

I want you to understand the life in Christ. Jesus sends the light—He sends His life through the light—and it illuminates the life and then returns. And just as you are holy inside, your life becomes full of illumination. My life is from Him, my life goes back to Him, and I am kept by the life of God.

I touch people, and instantly they are changed. The life of the Son of God goes through and passes on. I live by the faith of the Son of God (Gal. 2:20 KJV).

WHAT DOES IT MEAN TO BELIEVE?

"He who believes in Me" (John 14:12). *"He who believes."* The devils believe and tremble (James 2:19). In the same way, people follow Scripture as if it had nothing to do with their lives. The Scriptures may be life or letter. What is the Word? It is spirit and life-giving when we believe (John 6:63). What is believing? Believing is asking for the divine life that God gives. Who desires this? Everyone in this place can have divine life.

I do not believe in baptismal regeneration. Nor can you be saved by riches. Jesus says, *"You must be born again"* (John 3:7). The new birth comes through faith in the Lord Jesus Christ, and you can be saved in a field as well as in a church. The heart is the key. When the heart desires righteousness, God makes Himself known. I want you to be saved by the blood tonight. Someone is saying, "I want to be saved." Shall I bring you to the Word? *"Everyone who asks receives"* (Matt. 7:8). Who says this? Jesus says this. *"Everyone who asks receives."*

> If I ask Him to receive me
> Will He say me nay?
> Not till earth and not till heaven
> Pass away.

A NEW SONG

"Salvation is of the LORD" (Jonah 2:9). No man can save you; no man can heal you. If anyone has been healed in these meetings, it is the Lord who has healed him.

I would not claim under any circumstances that I can heal anybody, but I believe God's Word. *"He who believes in Me... greater works than these he will do, because I go to My Father"* (John 14:12). He is lovely. Lovely Jesus.

> He knows it all, He knows it all,
> My Father knows it all.
> The bitter tears how fast they fall,
> He knows, my Father knows it all.

Isn't He lovely? If you get saved tonight, you will have another song:

> He knows it all, He knows it all,
> My Father knows it all.
> The joy that comes that overflows
> He knows, my Father knows it all.

Before I was baptized in the Holy Spirit, there were many songs that I sang only as they were written. God began a change, and He changed many songs. I believe God wants to change the song in your heart. He changed the following song for me. This is how it is sung:

> Oh, then it will be glory for me,
> It will be glory for me.

But God changed it:

> Oh, it is now glory for me,
> It is now glory for me.
> As now by His grace I can look on His face,
> Now it is glory, glory for me.

I want you to have your tune changed. The present-tense songs are better than the future-tense songs. If you get a full salvation, you will have a present-tense song. Sometimes it is a good thing to be able to hope for something, but it is a better thing to have it.

I used to hope and trust that I would be baptized in the Holy Spirit. But when I spoke in tongues—no, when He spoke!—then I knew I was baptized. When you get baptized in the Holy Spirit, the Spirit speaks through you. Then you know that the Comforter has come.

Has He come to you? Has the Comforter come to you? You must have Him. You must be filled with the Spirit; you must have an overflowing. Jesus says, *"You shall receive power when the Holy Spirit has come upon you"* (Acts 1:8). I want you to have power.

THE WONDERFUL WORDS OF JESUS

Let's look at the following Scripture: *"Whatever you ask in My name, that I will do, that the Father may be glorified in the Son"* (John 14:13). If we ask anything in His name, He will do it! Who says this? Jesus—that blessed Jesus, that lovely Jesus, that Incarnation from heaven, that blessed Son of God. How He wants to bless! How He saves *"to the uttermost"* (Heb. 7:25)! No one has ever spoken as He spoke (John 7:46). What did He say? *"Come to Me, all you who labor and are heavy laden, and I will give you rest"* (Matt. 11:28). Hear what else Jesus says about Himself: *"For God did not send His Son into the world to condemn the world, but that the world through Him might be saved"* (John 3:17). How beautiful! Jesus wants us all to be saved.

Have you ever looked at Jesus in His sadness? Just take a look at Him on the Mount of Olives, looking over Jerusalem, weeping and saying, *"O Jerusalem, Jerusalem...How often I wanted to gather your children together, as a hen gathers her chicks under her wings, but you were not willing!"* (Matt. 23:37). Shall it be said of

71

you, *"How often I wanted to gather* [you], *as a hen gathers her chicks under her wings, but you were not willing"*? Will you come to Him?

Hear what He said: *"**Whatever you ask in My name, that I will do**"* (John 14:13, emphasis added). What do you want? How much do you want? Do you want anything? Are you thirsty? Jesus says, "Come to Me, all who thirst, and I will give you the water of life." (See Revelation 22:17.) Are you hungry? He who eats the flesh and drinks the blood of the Son of Man will live forever (John 6:54).

Do you want to live forever? Jesus saves *"to the uttermost"* (Heb. 7:25). He heals. He helps all who come to Him. How many are coming for healing? How many are coming for salvation? Listen. *"Whatever you ask in My name, that I will do."* This is the Word of the living God, the Son of God. How beautifully God speaks of Jesus! *"This is my beloved Son"* (Matt. 3:17). Yet Jesus gave Himself for us. He gave Himself as a ransom for us.

How many are going to receive Him? Take the water of life freely (Rev. 22:17). You may ask, "How can I receive Him?" *"Believe on the Lord Jesus Christ, and you will be saved"* (Acts 16:31). Jesus said, *"He who hears My word and believes in Him who sent Me has everlasting life"* (John 5:24).

Who were the people who followed Jesus? Those who loved Him in their hearts. Do you love Him in your heart? From this day, if you do love Him, you will begin to hate all kinds of sin, and you will love all kinds of righteousness. That is the secret. The man who says he loves God but truly loves the world is a liar. God says that *"the truth is not in him"* (1 John 2:4). *"If anyone loves the world, the love of the Father is not in him"* (v. 15). You can tell tonight whether you love God or not. Do you love the world? Then the love of the Father is not in you. If you hate the world, the love of the Lord Jesus is in you. Hallelujah!

I want to make you love Him. Is He worth loving? What has He done? He bought salvation. He died to deliver. *"The wages of sin is death, but the gift of God is eternal life"* (Rom. 6:23).

I leave the decision with you. Will you love Him? Will you serve Him? Will you? He knows it. He understands.

> There's no one that loves me like Jesus;
> There's no one that knows me like Him.

> He knows all your trials, He knows all your sickness;
> There's no one that knows me like Him.

"Come to Me" (Matt. 11:28). That's what Jesus says. He knows you are needy.

CHAPTER ELEVEN

THE FAITH THAT DELIVERS

BY FAITH ENOCH WAS TAKEN AWAY SO THAT HE
DID NOT SEE DEATH, "AND WAS NOT FOUND, BECAUSE
GOD HAD TAKEN HIM"; FOR BEFORE HE WAS TAKEN HE HAD THIS
TESTIMONY, THAT HE PLEASED GOD. BUT <u>WITHOUT FAITH IT IS
IMPOSSIBLE TO PLEASE HIM</u>, FOR HE WHO COMES TO
GOD MUST BELIEVE THAT HE IS.
—HEBREWS 11:5–6

Believe that God is able to work out His plan in your life. He will work mightily through you if you believe. Great possibilities are within your reach if you dare to believe.

Evil spirits can have no more control if I believe that God is, that He is living and active. I do believe! I know I am free from all the powers of darkness, free from all the powers of evil, and it is a wonderful thing to be free. Christ said, *"You shall know the truth, and the truth shall make you free"* (John 8:32). Because you are free, you step into the freedom of liberated men and claim the possessions of God.

DARE TO BELIEVE

This is the dispensation of the Holy Spirit. It has been thirty-three years since God filled me with the Holy Spirit. The fire burned in my bones then, and it is still burning, producing more activity for God than thirty-three years ago. The Holy Spirit's supply has not been exhausted.

 God is waiting for people who dare to believe, and when you believe, *"all things are possible"* (Mark 9:23).

74

Only believe, only believe;
   All things are possible, only believe.
Only believe, only believe;
   All things are possible, only believe.

God wants to sweep away all unbelief from your heart. He wants you to dare to believe His Word. It is the Word of the Spirit. If you allow anything to come between you and the Word, it will poison your whole system, and you will have no hope. One bit of unbelief against the Word is poison. It is like the Devil putting a spear into you. The Word of Life is the breath of heaven, the life-giving power by which your very self is changed. By it, you begin to bear the image of the Heavenly One.

MIRACLES IN SOUTH AFRICA

A young man in South Africa, who was dying of tuberculosis, read one of my books. He got saved, and then God healed him. This young man grew so much in the knowledge of God that he was made a pastor. When I arrived in South Africa five years ago, he came up to me like a son to a father and said, "If you like, I will go with you all over South Africa." He bought the best car for the job. If you go to South Africa, you must have a car that can go through the plowed fields, one that will handle rough terrain and wet conditions. That young man drove me many miles through all the territories, right among the Zulus, and God took us through everything. Talk about life! Why, this is overcoming life!

When I arrived in Cape Town, a man was there whose deathly face was filled with the very Devil's manifestation of cancer. I said to the people, "There is a man in this place suffering tremendously. He does not even know I am talking about him. I give you the choice. If you want me to deliver that man so that he can enjoy the meeting, I will go down in the name of the Lord and deliver him, or I will preach." They said, "Come down." I went down, and the people saw what God can do. They saw that man shouting and raving, for he was like an intoxicated man. He was shouting, "I was bound, but I am free!" It was a wonderful thing to see that man changed.

One man, after spending forty-five hundred dollars on his wife for operation after operation, year after year, brought her helpless to the meeting. I went to her and said, "Look here, this is the greatest opportunity of your life. I will give an altar call tonight.

Fifty people will come up, and when you see them loosed, believe, and you will be loosed like them. Then we will have a testimony from you." They came, and I laid my hands upon them in the name of the Lord. I said, "Testify," and they testified. This woman saw their faces, and when all these people were through, I asked her, "Do you believe?" She said, "I cannot help but believe." There is something in the manifestation of faith.

I laid my hands upon her in the name of Jesus, and the power of God went right through her. I said, "In the name of Jesus, arise and walk." An impossibility? If you do not venture out in faith, you remain ordinary as long as you live. If you dare the impossible, God will abundantly do far above all you ask or think (Eph. 3:20).

As if a cannon had blown her into the air, she rose. I thought her husband would go mad with joy and excitement because he saw his wife mightily moved and made free by the power of God. She was in the first meeting afterward to glorify God.

WONDERFUL JESUS!

The divine plan is so much greater than all human thought. When we are willing to yield to His sovereign will, when we have no reserve, how wonderful God is. He is always willing to open the door until our whole lives are filled with the fragrance of heaven.

Jesus is the substance and fullness of the divine nature (Col. 2:9), and He dwells in our hearts. Oh, this wonderful, fascinating Jesus! What a wonderful Jesus we have! Something about Him kindles fire in the darkest place. Something about our Lord makes all darkness light. When we have Him, we have more than we can speak or think about. God's Son can set the world ablaze and bring heaven right into the place where we live. Dare to believe God, and *"nothing will be impossible for you"* (Matt. 17:20).

CHAPTER TWELVE

THE MINISTRY OF THE FLAMING SWORD

This glorious inworking of Holy Spirit power is preparing us for rapture. Our greatest theme is the glory of the splendor of our Lord—His face, His tenderness, His sweetness! He makes our hearts long to be forever with Him. Amen! Let it be so!

> *What then shall we say to these things? If God is for us, who can be against us?...Who shall separate us from the love of Christ? Shall tribulation, or distress, or persecution, or famine, or nakedness, or peril, or sword?...Yet in all these things we are more than conquerors through Him who loved us. For I am persuaded that neither death nor life, nor angels nor principalities nor powers, nor things present nor things to come, nor height nor depth, nor any other created thing, shall be able to separate us from the love of God which is in Christ Jesus our Lord.* (Rom. 8:31, 35, 37–39)

Oh, the joy of the thought of this! *"Who shall separate us from the love of Christ?"* (v. 35). This is a place of confidence, assurance, and rest, where God has perfect control over all human weakness. You stand as if on the Mount of Transfiguration, manifested and glorified in the presence of God. You are able to say, "I know all things are working together for good within me" (see Romans 8:28); all that can be destroyed is silently being destroyed so that He can have preeminence in your body. *"If God is for us, who can be against us?"* (v. 31).

God is bringing forth a new creation. The sons of God are to be manifested, and you must see your inheritance in the Holy Spirit.

Nothing can separate you from Christ's love (Rom. 8:38–39)! What is it God wants you to know? Right in your earthly temple, God has brought forth a son with power, with manifestation, with grace, crowned already in the earth, crowned with glory. *"The glory which You gave Me I have given them, that they may be one just as We are one"* (John 17:22).

The Spirit of the Lord is showing me that God must get a people who can see that from before the foundation of the world, He has had them in mind. (See Ephesians 1:4.) God has been delivering us through all difficulty. Where sin abounded, He has brought in His grace (Rom. 5:20). Where disease came in to steal our lives, God raised up a standard. (See Isaiah 59:19.) We have come through tribulation. God has been purifying us, strengthening us, equipping us with divine boldness by His almighty power, until we can say, *"What then shall we say to these things? If God is for us, who can be against us?"* (Rom. 8:31).

Should we dethrone what we know has equipped us and brought us through to the present? Should we allow our hearts to fail us in the day of adversity? No! God has already strengthened and perfected! Weakness has been made strong! Corruption has been changed to purity! In tribulation the fire of God has purified us. *"What then shall we say to these things?"* *"Our light affliction...is working for us a far more exceeding and eternal weight of glory"* (2 Cor. 4:17).

THE POWER OF THE NEW CREATION

People have been in meetings where the glory of God has fallen, where the fingerprints of God have been upon everything, and where fortifications have been made in the body. The next morning the power of Satan has attacked them. Why does this happen? The spiritual life, the Son manifested, the glory of the new creation, is already in our mortal bodies, but the flesh, being a battleground for the Enemy, is tested. But what God is forming is greater than the mortal body, for the spirit that is awakening to the glorious liberty of a child of God is greater. *"What then shall we say?"* How can we compare this with what is to come?

"It is the Spirit who gives life; the flesh profits nothing" (John 6:63). Though *"worms destroy this body"* (Job 19:26 KJV), I have a life greater than this life that will look upon God (v. 26), that will

see Him in His perfection, that will behold Him in His glory, that will be changed to be like Him. By the presence of God, a new creation will so clothe us that we will be like Him. Knowing this, should I give place to the Devil? Should I fear? Should I let my feelings change the experience of the Word of God? Should I trust in my fears? No! A million times, no! There has never been any good thing in the flesh (Rom. 7:18), but God has given life to the spirit, and we live a new life divine and are eternally shaped for God.

"What then shall we say?" (Rom. 8:31). Are you going to let the past, in which God Himself has worked for you, bring you to a place of distress? Or are you standing during your testing, quoting God's Word—*"Now we are children of God"* (1 John 3:2)—and remembering how God has answered your prayers, brought light into your home, delivered you from carnality, and touched you when no power in the world could help? *"What then shall we say?"* *"Who shall lay any thing to the charge of God's elect?"* (Rom. 8:33 KJV). *"I know whom I have believed"* (2 Tim. 1:12), and I am persuaded that He who purposed us for God will surely bring us to the place where we will receive the *"crown of life"* (James 1:12) through the faith that God has given us. God is in you and is mightily forming within you a new creation by the Spirit in order to make you ready for the glory that will be revealed in Him.

Someone said to me the other day, "I am in terrible trouble; a man is cursing me all the time." *"If God is for us, who can be against us?"* (Rom. 8:31). God is never tightfisted with any of His blessings. He takes you into all He has. *"He who did not spare His own Son...how shall He not with Him also freely give us all things?"* (v. 32). God has given us Jesus, the heart of His love, *"the express image of His person"* (Heb. 1:3), perfect in brilliance, purity, righteousness, and glory. I have seen Him many times, and seeing Him always changes me. Victory over your struggle is one of the *"all things"* (Rom. 8:32). Many needs have broken my heart, but I could say to the troubled ones, "God is greater than your heart, greater than your circumstances, greater than the thing that holds you. God will deliver you if you dare to believe Him." But I have to emphasize it again and again and again before I can get the people to believe God.

A dear woman was marvelously delivered and saved, but she said, "I am addicted to smoking. What shall I do?" "Oh," I said, "smoke night and day." She said, "In our circumstances, we take a glass of wine, and it has a hold on me." "Oh," I said, "drink all you can." It brought some solace to her, but she was still in misery. She said, "We play cards." I said, "Play on!" But after being saved, she called her maid and said, "Wire to London and stop the shipment of those cigarettes." The new life does not want these things. It has no desire for them. The old is dethroned.

A clergyman came to me. He said, "I have a terrible craving for tobacco." I said, "Is it the old man or the new?" He broke down. "I know it's the old," he said. *"Put off the old man with his deeds"* (Col. 3:9).

Someone told me, "I have an unlawful affection for another." I said, "You need revelation. Since God has given you Jesus, He will give you all things. He will give you power over the thing, and it will be broken." And God broke it.

Allow God to touch your flesh. He has given life to your spirit. Allow Him to reign, for He will reign until all is subdued. He is King in your life and is preeminent over your affections, your will, your desires, your plans. He rules as Lord of Hosts over you, in you, and through you, to chasten you and bring you to the perfection of your desired haven. *"Christ in you* [is] *the hope of glory"* (Col. 1:27). *"Who shall separate us from the love of Christ?"* (Rom. 8:35). Once things could separate us, but no more. We have a vision. What is the vision? Those days when we have eaten of *"the hidden manna"* (Rev. 2:17).

THE BENEFIT OF THE FLAMING SWORD

When I was baptized in the Holy Spirit, God showed me a wonderful truth. After Adam and Eve transgressed and were driven out of the Garden, the Tree of Life was guarded by a flaming sword—a sword of death if they entered the Garden. But the baptism in the Holy Spirit put the Tree of Life right inside of me and a flaming sword right outside of me to keep the Devil from me, so that I can eat the eternal bread all the time. I am eating this wonderful bread of life. Nothing can separate us from this life. It is increasing tremendously, perpetually. Rapture has something to do with it.

"[What] *shall separate us?"* (Rom. 8:35). Tribulations come, but they only press us closer to persecution—the finest thing that can come. Among the persecuted you find those who are the ripest, the holiest, the purest, the most intent, those who are the most filled with divine order. All these things work together for our good (Rom. 8:28). Nothing comes except what is helpful. Trials lift you. Distresses give you a sigh, but God causes you to triumph. *"Greater is he that is in you"* (1 John 4:4 KJV) than all the powers of darkness.

Whatever befalls you as you abide in Him is the good hand of God upon you so that you won't lose your inheritance. Every trial is a boost, every burden a place of exchanging strength. God will work. *"Who shall lay any thing to the charge of God's elect?"* (Rom. 8:33 KJV). People do it, but it makes no difference; *"God is for us"* (v. 31). *"'Eye has not seen, nor ear heard, nor have entered into the heart of man the things which God has prepared for those who love Him.' But God has revealed them to us through His Spirit"* (1 Cor. 2:9–10). *"No weapon formed against you shall prosper"* (Isa. 54:17).

Know the wisdom and purpose of God's great hand upon you. Glorify God in distresses and persecution, for the Spirit of God is made manifest in these situations. Be chastened! Be perfected! Press on to heights, depths, breadths. Faith is the victory (1 John 5:4). The hope is within you (1 Pet. 3:15). The joy is set before you (Heb. 12:2). God gives the peace that passes all understanding (Phil. 4:7). We know that the flesh has withered in the presence of the purifying of the Word. He who has brought you to this point will take you to the end (Phil. 1:6). I have mourned and wept bitterly when I needed revelation from God, but I did not need to do so.

The Lord lifts up and changes and operates. He remakes body and soul until He can say, *"There is no spot in you"* (Song 4:7). Yes, it was persecution, tribulation, and distress that drew us near to Him. These places of trial were places of uplifting, places of change, where God operated by the Spirit. Do not bypass this way, but let God have His way.

God stretched out His hand, covered us with the mantle of His love, and brought us nearer and nearer to the channel of His grace. Then our hearts moved and yielded and so turned to the Lord that every moment has seen a divine place where God has met us and stretched out His arms and said, *"Seek My face"* (Ps. 27:8); *"look to Me"* (Isa. 45:22). Behold what great love the Master has for you, to lead you to the fountain of living water. Yield! Be led! Let God be glorified! Amen.

CHAPTER THIRTEEN

LAUNCH OUT

SO IT WAS, AS THE MULTITUDE PRESSED ABOUT HIM TO HEAR THE WORD OF GOD, THAT HE STOOD BY THE LAKE OF GENNESARET, AND SAW TWO BOATS STANDING BY THE LAKE; BUT THE FISHERMEN HAD GONE FROM THEM AND WERE WASHING THEIR NETS. THEN HE GOT INTO ONE OF THE BOATS, WHICH WAS SIMON'S, AND ASKED HIM TO PUT OUT A LITTLE FROM THE LAND. AND HE SAT DOWN AND TAUGHT THE MULTITUDES FROM THE BOAT. WHEN HE HAD STOPPED SPEAKING, HE SAID TO SIMON, "LAUNCH OUT INTO THE DEEP AND LET DOWN YOUR NETS FOR A CATCH." BUT SIMON ANSWERED AND SAID TO HIM, "MASTER, WE HAVE TOILED ALL NIGHT AND CAUGHT NOTHING; NEVERTHELESS AT YOUR WORD I WILL LET DOWN THE NET." AND WHEN THEY HAD DONE THIS, THEY CAUGHT A GREAT NUMBER OF FISH, AND THEIR NET WAS BREAKING. SO THEY SIGNALED TO THEIR PARTNERS IN THE OTHER BOAT TO COME AND HELP THEM. AND THEY CAME AND FILLED BOTH THE BOATS, SO THAT THEY BEGAN TO SINK. WHEN SIMON PETER SAW IT, HE FELL DOWN AT JESUS' KNEES, SAYING, "DEPART FROM ME, FOR I AM A SINFUL MAN, O LORD!" FOR HE AND ALL WHO WERE WITH HIM WERE ASTONISHED AT THE CATCH OF FISH WHICH THEY HAD TAKEN; AND SO ALSO WERE JAMES AND JOHN, THE SONS OF ZEBEDEE, WHO WERE PARTNERS WITH SIMON. AND JESUS SAID TO SIMON, "DO NOT BE AFRAID. FROM NOW ON YOU WILL CATCH MEN."
—LUKE 5:1-10

Every time I preach I am impressed with the fact that the Word of God is full of life and vitality, and it changes us. God's Word must come to pass in us.

How can we get more faith? God's Word tells us, *"Faith comes by hearing, and hearing by the word of God"* (Rom. 10:17). Faith is a gift. We receive our inheritance by faith. We are spiritual children—*"children of God without fault"* (Phil. 2:15). May God manifest this in us by the power of His might.

The people said to Jesus, *"Blessed is the womb that bore You"* (Luke 11:27). But Jesus said, *"Blessed are those who hear the word of God and keep it!"* (v. 28). This blessed Christ of God! They said, *"'No man ever spoke like this Man!'* (John 7:46). He does not speak as the scribes speak; He teaches us as one having authority." (See Matthew 7:29.)

The living Son of God—*"the Son of His love"* (Col. 1:13)—came to us with understanding, ministering the breath of His Father. The moment we believed, we had a new nature, a new life. We knew a life-giving Spirit. Jesus had a wonderful word, a sweet influence. Men saw love in His beautiful eyes and were convicted of sin in His presence.

A REMARKABLE CATCH

The people crowded around Jesus, and He sat in a boat and taught them. Then Jesus said to Peter, *"Launch out into the deep and let down your nets for a catch"* (Luke 5:4). Peter answered, *"We have toiled all night and caught nothing"* (v. 5). Perhaps he was thinking, "Lord, You know nothing about fishing. Daytime is the wrong time to fish." But he said, *"Nevertheless at Your word I will let down the net"* (v. 5). I believe every fish in the lake tried to get into that net. They wanted to see Jesus. I must see Jesus.

Peter filled one ship, then another. Oh, what would happen if you lowered all the nets? Believe God! He says, *"Look to **Me**, and be saved"* (Isa. 45:22, emphasis added). He says, *"Come to Me, all you who labor and are heavy laden, and I will give you rest"* (Matt. 11:28). He says, *"He who believes in Me has everlasting life"* (John 6:47). Believe! Oh, believe! It is the Word of God. *"There is a river whose streams shall make glad the city of God"* (Ps. 46:4).

Peter saw the ship sinking. He looked around and saw Jesus. He fell down at Jesus' feet, saying, *"Depart from me, for I am a sinful man, O Lord!"* (Luke 5:8). He and all who were with him were astonished at the number of fish that they had caught. That spotless Lamb was before them. *"They looked to Him and were radiant, and their faces were not ashamed"* (Ps. 34:5).

To see Jesus is to see a new way, to see all things differently. It means a new life and new plans. As we gaze at Him, we are satisfied; there is none like Him. Sin moves away.

83

Jesus was the express image of the Father (Heb. 1:3). The Father could not be in the midst, so He clothed Jesus with a body, with eternal resources. Let us gather together unto Him. Let us move toward Him. He has all we need. He will fulfill the desires of our hearts, granting all our petitions.

A CRIPPLE AND A CANCER PATIENT

There was a banquet for cripples, and in the middle of it a father brought a boy on his shoulder and lifted the boy up. I said, "In the name of Jesus." The boy said, "Papa! Papa! It is going all over me." Jesus healed him.

There was a man who had cancer in the rectum. Night and day he had morphine every ten minutes. I went to see him. He said, "I do not know how to believe God! Oh, if only I could believe. Oh, if only God would work a miracle." I placed my hand upon him in Jesus' name. I said to the nurse, "You go to the other room. God will work a miracle." The Spirit of God came upon me. In the name of Jesus I laid hold of the evil power, with hatred in my heart against the power of Satan. While I was praying, he was healed. I said to the nurse, "Come in." She did not understand, but the man knew that God had done it. Previously, this man had had a hobby; it was yachting. He had been very fond of his yacht; it had been all he had wanted to talk about. Did he want to talk about yachting now? No! He said, "Tell me about Jesus—the Sin-Bearer—the Lamb of God."

He who made things happen—will you let Him in?

THE IMPORTANCE OF COMMUNION, GOD'S WORD, AND PRAYER

In Christ, we are one body. The bread and the wine represent Christ. (See 1 Corinthians 11:23–26.) His body was *"broken for you"* (v. 24), broken to meet every human need.

"The word of God is living and powerful" (Heb. 4:12). How it works in spirit, soul, and body, separating the desires, heart, thought, word, deed, and intent! The Word enters into the *"joints and marrow"* (v. 12). It is the Word of the living God.

The Lord says, "Begin to pray if you want the furniture of God's place put in order." You kneel down; you begin to pray. You begin in the Spirit; the Spirit leads you to pray by the Spirit. As you begin, God will come in. God will lift you as you begin.

I am here to help you to a place of beginnings. You must begin. Come to a Person who has no end—Jesus. Feed upon Him; believe Him. The day is a day of communion. One body means unbroken fellowship. Look at Him. Reign with Him. Live in His presence.

> Peace, peace, sweet peace;
> Sweet peace—the gift of God's love.

God could give us many gifts, but God is satisfied with the lovely gift of Him who suffered and died for us. Keep the vision of one bread and one body.

Bring your ships to land. Forsake all, and follow Him. Peter was astonished, and all who were with him, at the catch of fish that they had taken. Jesus said to Peter, *"Do not be afraid. From now on you will catch men"* (Luke 5:10).

CHAPTER FOURTEEN

THE MOVING BREATH
OF THE SPIRIT

The Word is God Himself. *"In the beginning was the Word, and the Word was with God, and the Word was God"* (John 1:1). Herein lies our attitude of rest. All our hope is in the Word of the living God. The Word of God *"abides forever"* (1 Pet. 1:23). Oh, the glorious truths found in His Word. One man said, "Never compare this Book with other books. The Bible is from heaven. It does not contain the Word of God; it is the Word of God. It is supernatural in origin, eternal in duration, infinite in scope, and divine in authorship. Read it through; pray it in; write it down." *"The fear of the LORD is the beginning of wisdom"* (Ps. 111:10).

The knowledge of our weakness brought the greatness of redemption; knowledge is coupled with joy! You cannot have the knowledge of the Lord without joy. Rejoice in the knowledge of Him. Faith is peace. Not long petitions but faith is peace. Where faith is undisturbed, there is peace. I am speaking of eternal faith, daring to believe what God has said. If I dare to trust Him, I find that what He has said always comes to pass. We must not doubt. *"He who doubts is like a wave of the sea driven and tossed by the wind. For let not that man suppose that he will receive anything from the Lord"* (James 1:6–7). Have faith in God. *"Only believe"* (Mark 5:36).

THE BLESSEDNESS OF BEING FILLED

"Jesus, being filled with the Holy Spirit, returned from the Jordan" (Luke 4:1). Bringing out of the shadow the reality of the

substance, the One who had been promised had come. He, our glo-rious Lord, who could speak like no other (John 7:46), had come to help the oppressed. Jesus, I'll go through with You.

What does the Bible mean when it says, *"Be filled with the Spirit"* (Eph. 5:18)? Oh, what a difference when we understand Acts 2 and know the flow of the life of the Spirit! How the Word is illuminated! We leap for joy.

> INTERPRETATION OF A MESSAGE IN TONGUES: "The King unfolds His will, covering His child, flooding the soul with open vision, untiring zeal. Fire! Fire! Fire!—burning in-tensely in the human soul, until he becomes an expression of the King."

I know the Lord laid His hand on me. He filled me with the Holy Spirit.

This Jesus, this wonder-working Jesus, came to be King. Is He King? He must reign. Oh, to yield so that He always has the first place. Glory be to God! The Holy Spirit has come to abide forever, flooding our souls, for Jesus said, *"If I depart, I will send Him to you"* (John 16:7).

> Has He come to you?
> Has He come to you?
> Has the Comforter come to you?

"When He [the Comforter] *has come, He will convict the world of sin"* (v. 8). In Him God has enriched us and given us a perfection of revelation. The Holy Spirit came to fill the body and to bring forth what all the prophets had spoken of. Jesus said concerning the Holy Spirit, *"He will glorify Me, for He will take of what is Mine and declare it to you"* (v. 14).

The woman had a well. (See John 4:5–14.) But the Holy Spirit's coming was like a river, *"rivers of living water"* (John 7:38), giving life, giving truth, giving prophetic utterance. There was a divine in-coming, a *"fill*[ing] *with all the fullness of God"* (Eph. 3:19).

The baptism in the Holy Spirit is like a flash of lightning; it opens up divine revelation so that we can dance and sing in the Spirit, enjoying sweeter music and stronger character. *"Christ in you* [is] *the hope of glory"* (Col. 1:27). The baptism in the Holy

Spirit brings us a vision of *"the glory of God in the face of Jesus Christ"* (2 Cor. 4:6). *"Jesus* [was] *filled with the Holy Spirit"* (Luke 4:1).

> **INTERPRETATION OF A MESSAGE IN TONGUES:** "He is the Spirit of Truth, unveiling, making manifest, breathing through in such a way, burning, quickening, until men cry out, 'What must we do to be saved?' The breath of life burns with intensity until the world feels the warmth and cries, 'What must we do?'"

Oh, the joy of being filled with the Holy Spirit, with divine purpose! Oh, the satisfaction of being active *"in season and out of season"* (2 Tim. 4:2) with the sense of divine approval. As the apostles were in their day, so we are to be in our day: *"filled with all the fullness of God"* (Eph. 3:19). We are to have this same Holy Spirit, this same warmth, this same life, this same heaven in the soul. The Holy Spirit brings heaven to us as He reveals Jesus, who is the King of heaven. Oh, the perfection of belonging to Him! It prepares us for every need. He holds us in the divine moments. There is no need to groan, cry, agonize, or sigh.

"The Spirit of the Lord is upon [me]" (Luke 4:18)—the sense of the Holy Spirit, the knowledge of His power, the sweetness of His experience, the wonder of His presence, honoring the Word, making all new, meeting the present need. These are the last days. Very wonderful are they. They are blessed with mighty signs. The breath of the Spirit is unfolding, helping. I believe in the Holy Spirit. God gave us the Holy Spirit for true Sonlikeness.

THE MIGHTY MOVING OF THE SPIRIT IN SWEDEN

In a park in Sweden, a large platform was erected for meetings on the condition that I did not lay my hands on the people. I said, "Lord, You know all about this. You can work." And there the Lord revealed His presence and healed and saved the people. I said, "Who here is in need? Put your hands up." Hands went up all over. I saw a large woman. I said, "Tell your trouble!" She said pains were all over her body. She was in terrible distress. I said, "Lift up your hands in Jesus' name!" (Jesus came to heal the sick, to unbind, to set free. He said in John 14:12, *"He who believes in Me, the works that I do he will do also; and greater works than these he will do."*) I said, "In the name of Jesus, I set you free." Then I asked, "Are you free?" She replied, "Yes, perfectly free!"

Although I could not put my hands on the people, God put *His* hands on the people. God has wonderful ways of meeting the need. I believe I will see the glory of God setting people free from all weakness. Jesus said, *"The Spirit of the LORD is upon Me"* (Luke 4:18). He said to *"make disciples of all the nations"* (Matt. 28:19).

When I first preached this glorious truth in New Zealand, I saw hundreds baptized. But in Sweden some churches were not pleased. A woman in the king's household was healed; nevertheless, I had to leave the country.

BOUNTIFUL BLESSINGS

On one occasion, I stayed on a side street. I arrived at 9:30 in the morning. The meeting was at 4:30, so I went to the coast for a few hours' rest. When I came back, the street was full from one end to the other with wheelchairs and cars filled with the helpless and needy. The people in charge said, "What are we going to do?" I said, "The Holy Spirit came to abide, to reign in supreme royal dignity. Live in freedom, anointing, inspiration, like a river flowing. Settle for nothing less, so that God may be glorified." God loosed the people and brought deliverance to the captives. Was that all? No, it was only the beginning! The house was packed, too! Oh, the joy of being ready! God must set us all on fire. There is much land to be possessed. The fields are ripe for harvest (John 4:35).

Oh, the cry of the people! Talk about weeping! Oh, the joy of weeping. You are in an awful place when you cannot weep when the breath of God is upon you. I continued helping the people. Oh, the breath of the Spirit. Jesus said, *"The Spirit of the LORD is upon Me"* (Luke 4:18). God spoke to me as clearly as could be, saying, "Ask Me! I'll give you all in the place." I thought this was something too big, but He whispered again, "Ask; I will give you all in the house." I said, "O my God, say it again." "Ask of Me. I will give you all in the house." I said, "I ask! I ask in faith! I believe it!" The breath of heaven filled the place. The people continued to fall down, weeping, crying, repenting.

There is something wonderful in this breath of heaven. Jesus said, *"The Spirit of the LORD is upon Me."* I repeat, *"Upon Me"*! May God move our hearts to act in this anointing. Do you want God to have you in His splendid palace? Is it the longing of your heart to come to this place? God can choose only those filled to the utmost. How many long to step into line, filled to the utmost, hungering and thirsting after God's fullness? Stand in a living experience as Jesus did, saying, *"The Spirit of the Lord is upon* [me]" (Luke 4:18). May God grant it to every one of you. Amen.

CHAPTER FIFTEEN

HEALINGS AT MY MEETINGS IN MELBOURNE, AUSTRALIA

T he healings at the meetings were blessed. At every meeting I invited the sick to remain after the service, but in many of the meetings I prayed for all who would stand up and believe that the Lord would heal them. At other times I asked any who had pain to stand up, and I prayed for them from the platform.

At one meeting a lady stood saying she had pain in her head and was suffering from gallstones. When I prayed, the power of the Spirit came upon her.

A person in the hospital was healed of a tumor when a handkerchief was taken from me and laid on that person. (See Acts 19:11–12.)

Mrs. Ingram tells of visiting a hospital and taking a handkerchief with her. Her friend was to be operated on the following Monday. On the Wednesday after that, when she visited her again, her friend told her that she had been on the operating table and the ether had been administered. When she regained consciousness, she discovered they had not operated because there was no need now for the operation. She was able to get up, and the swelling was all gone.

Mrs. A. Lavery of Collingwood writes, "I thank God for His blessed healing power. Hands were laid on my head. I had had blood pressure pains in my head for one year and six months, night and day. I know I am healed."

Mrs. Green of East Brunswick testifies, "I had mastoid trouble in my ear and general weakness throughout my body. Both of my kidneys had dropped an inch. I suffered terribly but had relief when prayed for. My ear began discharging. Now I am free."

Mr. R. Eddison of West Richmond was injured in a car accident. He had his ribs broken, collar bone broken, and lungs pierced. He was in the hospital for three weeks and suffered much pain for three months until prayed for in the meeting.

A woman who had been ill in bed for sixteen weeks was raised up by the Lord, was later baptized in water, and the following day received the baptism in the Holy Spirit.

A dying baby was healed.

A woman who had suffered pain in her legs for eleven years was set free.

Mrs. Rose Jesule writes, "The Lord touched my body in the audience, and I am free."

Another writes, "I have received the second handkerchief that you prayed over, and the Lord is blessing. This cancer is slowly drying up. I have had no more hemorrhages, and the terrible odor is leaving. Praise the Lord."

CHAPTER SIXTEEN

ABIDING

BUT I TELL YOU TRULY, THERE ARE SOME STANDING
HERE WHO SHALL NOT TASTE DEATH TILL THEY SEE
THE KINGDOM OF GOD.
—LUKE 9:27

H ow God fascinates me with His Word. I read and read and read, and there is always something new, As I get deeper into the knowledge of the Bridegroom, I hear His voice saying, "The bride rejoices to hear the Bridegroom's voice." The Word is His voice, and the nearer we are to Jesus, the more we understand the principles of His mission. He came to take for Himself a people for His bride; He came to find those who would become the *"body of Christ"* (1 Cor. 12:27). God's message to us is that Jesus is going to take unto Himself a bride.

So, while we are here to talk about salvation, there are deeper truths God wants to show us. Not only is there salvation, but there is an eternal destiny awaiting us that is full of all the wonders God has in glory. God has given us this blessed revelation of how Jesus lived and loved and said these words: *"Some...shall not taste death till they see the kingdom of God* [come in power]" (Luke 9:27).

GOD'S GLORY MANIFESTED IN CHRIST

Jesus could pray until He was transfigured, until His face shone like the sun and His clothes became white and glistening (Matt. 17:2). Praise God, this same Jesus also said, *"I have power to lay* [My life] *down, and I have power to take it again"* (John 10:18). By wicked hands He was taken and crucified, but He was willing,

93

for He had all power and could have called on legions of angels to deliver Him (Matt. 26:53). But His purpose was to save us and bring us into fellowship and oneness with Himself, so that the same life principles might be ours.

Jesus never looked back; He never withheld Himself. He went through death so that His life might be our portion in time and in eternity. He is the Lord Jesus Christ—the atonement for the whole world, the Son of God, the sinner's Friend. *"He was wounded for our transgressions"* (Isa. 53:5). He lived to manifest, to bring forth, the glory of God on earth. He gives His disciples the glory He had with the Father before the world began. He said, *"The glory which You gave Me I have given them"* (John 17:22).

So today, God *"will give grace and glory; no good thing will He withhold from those who walk uprightly"* (Ps. 84:11). He gives health, peace, joy in the Holy Spirit, and a life in Christ Jesus. It is wonderful, lovely. Shall we ever go back to Egypt? Shall we look back? Never! (See Hebrews 11:13–16.)

> Oh, you need not look for me down in Egypt's sand,
> For I have pitched my tent far up in Beulah land.

There is redemption for all through the blood of Jesus. This redemption is heaven on earth; it is joy and peace in the Holy Spirit. It is a change from darkness to light, from the power of Satan to the power of God (Acts 26:18). It means to be made sons, heirs, and joint-heirs with Christ (Rom. 8:17).

Twice God rent the heavens with the words, *"This is My beloved Son, in whom I am well pleased"* (Matt. 3:17; 17:5). Yes, it is true that Jesus was born in Bethlehem, that He worked as a carpenter, that He took upon Himself flesh. It is also true that God indwelt that flesh and manifested His glory, so that Christ was a perfect overcomer. He kept the law and fulfilled His commission, so that He could redeem us by laying down His life. Glory to God! Jesus was manifested in the flesh to destroy the power of the Devil (1 John 3:8). What does that mean? It means this: He is God's example to show us that what God did for and in Jesus, He can do for and in us.

ALLOW CHRIST TO CHANGE YOU

He can make us overcomers by dwelling in us by His mighty power and destroying the power of sin. He can transform us until we *"love righteousness and hate wickedness"* (Ps. 45:7), so that we can be holy.

We receive sonship because of His obedience. *"He learned obedience by the things which He suffered"* (Heb. 5:8). His family said He was beside Himself (Mark 3:21). The scribes said, *"He has a demon"* (John 10:20) and *"'He has Beelzebub,' and, 'By the ruler of the demons He casts out demons'"* (Mark 3:22). They reviled Him and tried to kill Him by stoning Him, but He passed through the midst of the whole crowd. Then He saw a blind man and healed him as He was going through. (See John 8:59–9:7.)

Oh, He is lovely! Meditate on the beatitudes, the attributes, and the divine position Jesus manifested. This power of the new creation, this birth unto righteousness by faith in the Atonement, can transform and change you until you are controlled, dominated, and filled with the Spirit of Jesus. Though you are still in the body, you are governed by the Spirit, having *"fruit to holiness, and the end, everlasting life"* (Rom. 6:22). Christ was a firstfruits for us (1 Cor. 15:20–23).

O Lord, reveal Yourself to this people, and give them genuine love and faith. Then they will withstand persecution, ridicule, and slander.

Christ loved you when you were yet a sinner (Rom. 5:8), and He seeks your love in return. He imparts to you an in-wrought love by the Holy Spirit, changing you from faith to faith, *"from glory to glory"* (2 Cor. 3:18).

WHAT A SAVIOR!

I am not surprised at Christ's face shining or at the presence of God appearing on the Mount (Matt. 17:2, 5). I am not surprised at anything that glorifies the Christ of God, who would lay down His own life to save the lost. Oh, what a Christ! When we were His enemies, He died for us (Rom. 5:10)!

Notice that Jesus had chances that were offered to no other human soul in the world. It was not only the glory of God that was offered to Him, but also the manifestation of a human glory, for people in certain circles longed to make Him a king. Oh, if any of you heard that the whole country was longing to make you a king, you would lose your head and your senses and everything you have. But this blessed Christ of God retired and went to prayer. He was the greatest King that the world will ever know. He is the King of

Kings and the Lord of Lords. *"Of His kingdom there will be no end"* (Luke 1:33). *"He shall see His seed, He shall prolong His days, and the pleasure of the LORD shall prosper in His hand"* (Isa. 53:10).

I wonder if there is any seed of the Lord Jesus in this place. Oh, you who believe you are the seed of the Son of God through promise, and the seed of the Son of God through faith, and the seed of the Son of God because His seed (the Word of God) is in you—all the seed in this place, let me see your hands. *"He shall see His seed, He shall prolong His days, and the pleasure of the LORD shall prosper in His hand."* Oh, hallelujah!

> INTERPRETATION OF A MESSAGE IN TONGUES: "Glory to God, the living shall praise Him, for out of the dust of the earth He has brought forth a harvest of souls to praise Him for all eternity. He is 'seeing His seed,' and the 'pleasure of the Lord' is already 'prospering in His hand.'"

Yes, beloved, this is the day of the visitation of the Lord again in this place. Look at Him right now, you needy ones. As you gaze upon Him, you will be changed. A strength will come to you; you will exchange strength. He is the God of Jacob, the God of the helpless and the ruined.

The Devil had a big plan against Jacob, but there was one thing Jacob knew. He knew that God would fulfill His promise. At Bethel, God had let him see the ladder, where the angels began at the bottom and went to the top. Bethel was the place of prayer, the place of changing conditions, the place of the earthly entering the heavenly. God had promised him, and He brought him back to Bethel. But he was the same old Jacob, and as long as God allowed him to wrestle, he wrestled. That is a type of holding on to this world. Then God touched him. God has a way of touching us. Jacob cried, "Don't go until You have blessed me." (See Genesis 32:26.) God will bless you there. God will meet you at the place of helplessness and brokenness. Have you been there?

When Jesus was on the Mount in the glory, Moses and Elijah came to speak to Him about our salvation, about His death at Jerusalem. And when Jesus came down from the Mount of Transfiguration, He set His face forward to fulfill His commission for you and me. He went from the glory right to the cross. What a wonderful Jesus we have!

DON'T LOSE YOUR DELIVERANCE

When Jesus came down among the crowd, a man cried out and said, "Help me, Lord; help me. Here is my son. The Devil takes him and tears him until he foams at the mouth, and there he lies prostrate. I brought him to Your disciples, but they could not help me." Oh, brothers and sisters, may God strengthen our hands and take away unbelief. Jesus said, *"O faithless generation...how long shall I bear with you? Bring him to Me"* (Mark 9:19). They brought him to Jesus, and Jesus cast out the evil spirit.

Did you know that even in the presence of Jesus these evil spirits tore the boy and left him as one dead? Just think about satanic power. The Devil goes about to kill, *"seeking whom he may devour"* (1 Pet. 5:8). May God save us and keep us in the place where the Devil has no power and no victory.

He has come; our Lord has come. Bless His name; has He come to you? He wants to come to you. He wants to be a sharer in your whole life. No, truly, He wants to transform your life through His power right now.

I pray to God that the demon powers that come out of everyone tonight will never get back in again. Oh, if I could only show you what it means to be delivered by the power of Jesus, and what it means—now hear what I say—to lose your deliverance through your own folly.

There was a case like this. A man possessed with demon power came to Jesus. Jesus cast the evil spirit out, and the man was made whole. But then he did not seek the Holy Spirit and the light of God and walk as blind Bartimaeus walked with Jesus when he was healed. The evil spirit returned and found that, although it appeared that this man's life was swept clean and put in order, the man had no inhabitant in him. He did not have Christ and the power of the Spirit. So the evil spirits entered into that man, and his case was worse than before. (See Matthew 12:43–45.)

If you people want healing by the power of God, it means your lives have to be filled with God. Will it last? Get Jesus on board, and it will last forever. You cannot keep yourself. No man is capable of standing against the schemes of the Devil by himself. But when you get Jesus in you, you are equal to a million devils. Not only must our lives be swept clean and put in order, but we must see that the power of God comes to inhabit us. No one is safe without Christ, but the weak man is capable if he is in Christ Jesus. Are you willing to surrender yourself to God tonight so that Satan will have no dominion over you? In the name of Jesus, I ask you.

> The power of God is just the same today,
> It does not matter what the people say.
> Whatever God has promised He is able to perform,
> For the power of God is just the same today.

CHAPTER SEVENTEEN

COMMON SENSE

I have had people ask me, "Is it every Christian's privilege to have his eyes preserved so that he never needs to wear glasses?" That is the question I will answer here.

The aging process affects every person. There are many people who have been praying ever since they were ten years old, and if praying and the life within them could have altered the situation, it would have been altered. But I see that many are here today with gray hair and white hair; this shows that the natural man decays, and you cannot do what you like with it. But the supernatural man may so abound in the natural man that it never decays; it can be replaced by divine life.

There comes a time in life when at age fifty or so, all eyes, without exception, begin to grow dim. However, although the natural man has had a change, I believe and affirm that the supernatural power can be so ministered to us that even our eyesight can be preserved right through. But I say this: any person who professes to have faith and then gets a large-print Bible so that he will not need glasses is a fool. It presents a false impression before the people. He must see that if he wants to carry a Bible that is not huge, his eyesight may require some help, or he may not be able to read correctly.

I have been preaching faith to my people for thirty years. When my daughter came back from Africa and saw her mother and me with glasses, she was amazed. When our people saw us put glasses on the first time, they were very troubled. They were no more troubled than we were. But I found it was far better to be honest with the people and acknowledge my condition than get a Bible with large print and deceive the people and say that my eyesight was all right. I like to be honest.

My eyesight gave way at about age fifty-three, and somehow God is doing something. I am now sixty-eight, and I do not need a stronger prescription than I needed then, and I am satisfied that God is restoring me.

When I was seeking this way of divine healing, I was baffled because all the people who had mighty testimonies of divine healing were wearing glasses. I said, "I cannot go on with this thing. I am baffled every time I see the people preaching divine healing wearing glasses." And I got such a bitterness in my spirit that God had to settle me along that line—and I believe that I have not yet fully paid the price.

My eyes will be restored, but until then, I will not deceive anybody. I will wear glasses until I can see perfectly.

A woman came up to me one day, and I noticed that she had no teeth. "Why," I said, "your mouth is very uneven. Your gums have dropped in some places, and they are very uneven."

"Yes," she said, "I am trusting the Lord for a new set of teeth."

"That is very good," I said. "How long have you been trusting Him for them?"

"Three years."

"Look here," I said, "I would be like Gideon. I would put the fleece out, and I would tell the Lord that I would trust Him to send me teeth in ten days or money to buy a set in ten days. Whichever came first, I would believe it was from Him."

In eight days, fifty dollars came to her from a person whom she had never been acquainted with in any way, and it bought her a beautiful set of teeth—and she looked nice in them.

Often I pray for a person's eyesight, and as soon as he is prayed for, he believes, and God stimulates his faith, but his eyesight is about the same. "What should I do?" he asks. "Should I go away without my glasses?"

"Can you see perfectly?" I ask. "Do you need any help?"

"Yes. If I were to go without my glasses, I would stumble."

"Put your glasses on," I say, "for when your faith is perfected, you will no longer need your glasses. When God perfects your faith, your glasses will drop off. But as long as you need them, use them."

You can take that for what you like, but I believe in common sense.

CHAPTER EIGHTEEN

DIVINE LIFE BRINGS
DIVINE HEALTH

See from Mark 1 how Jesus was quickened by the power of the Spirit of God and how He was driven by the Spirit into the wilderness (vv. 9–12). See how John also was so filled with the Spirit of God that he had a "cry" within him, and the cry moved all Israel (vv. 2–5). When God gets hold of a man in the Spirit, he can have a new cry—something in God's order. A man may cry for fifty years without the Spirit of the Lord, and the more he cries, the less people notice him. But if he is filled with the Holy Spirit and cries once, people feel the effects.

ENERGIZED BY THE SPIRIT

So there is a necessity for every one of us to be filled with God. It is not sufficient to have just a touch or to be filled with just a desire. Only one thing will meet the needs of the people, and that is for you to be immersed in the life of God. This means that God takes you and fills you with His Spirit until you live right in God. He does this so that *"whether you eat or drink, or whatever you do,* [it may be] *all to the glory of God"* (1 Cor. 10:31). In that place you will find that all your strength and all your mind and all your soul are filled with a zeal, not only for worship, but also for proclamation. This proclamation is accompanied by all the power of God, which must move satanic power and disturb the world.

The reason the world is not seeing Jesus is that Christian people are not filled with Jesus. They are satisfied with attending meetings weekly, reading the Bible occasionally, and praying sometimes.

101

Beloved, if God lays hold of you by the Spirit, you will find that there is an end of everything and a beginning of God. Your whole body will become seasoned with a divine likeness. Not only will He have begun to use you, but He will have taken you in hand, so that you might be *"a vessel for honor"* (2 Tim. 2:21). Our lives are not to be for ourselves, for if we live for ourselves we will die (Rom. 8:13); but if *"by the Spirit* [we] *put to death the deeds of the body,* [we] *will live"* (v. 13). He who lives in the Spirit is subject to the powers of God, but he who lives for himself will die. The man who lives in the Spirit lives a life of freedom and joy and blessing and service—a life that brings blessing to others. God would have us see that we must live in the Spirit.

YOU CAN BE LIKE JESUS

In Mark 1, we have two important factors in the Spirit. One is Jesus filled with the Holy Spirit and driven by the Spirit's power. The other is John the Baptist, who was so filled with the Spirit of God that his one aim was to go out preaching. We find him in the wilderness. What a seemingly strange place to be! Beloved, it was quite natural for Jesus, after He had served a whole day among the multitudes, to want to go to His Father and pray all night. Why? He wanted a source of strength and power; He wanted an association with His Father that would bring everything else to a place of submission.

After Jesus had been on the mountain communing with His Father and after He had been clothed with God's holy presence and Spirit, when He met the demon power, it had to go. (See Matthew 17:1–9, 14–18.) When He met sickness, it had to leave. He came from the mountain with power to meet whatever needs the people had.

I do not know what your state of grace is—whether you are saved or not—but it is an awful thing for me to see people who profess to be Christians lifeless, powerless, and in a place where their lives are so parallel to unbelievers' lives that it is difficult to tell which place they are in, whether in the flesh or in the Spirit. Many people live in the place that is described to us by Paul in Romans 7:25: *"With the mind I myself serve the law of God, but with the flesh the law of sin."* That is the place where sin is in the ascendancy. But when the power of God comes to you, it is to separate you from yourself. It is destruction of yourself, annihilation. It is to move you from nature to grace, making you mighty over the powers of the Enemy and making you know that you have now begun to live a life of faith in the Son of God.

TURNING STRUGGLES INTO REST

I pray that God will give us a way out of difficulties and into rest. The writer to the Hebrews told us that *"there remains therefore a rest for the people of God"* (Heb. 4:9). Those who have entered into that rest have ceased from their own works (v. 10). Oh, what a blessed state of rest that is, to cease from your own works. There God is enthroned in your life, and you are working for Him by a new order. If you preach, you no longer struggle to preach in the old way of sermonettes. God wants to bring you forth as a flame of fire with a message from God, with a truth that will disturb the powers of Satan, and with an unlimited supply for every needy soul. Then, just as John moved all of Israel with a cry, you, by the power of the Holy Spirit, will move the people.

This is what Jesus meant when He said to Nicodemus,

Unless one is born again, he cannot see the kingdom of God....[For] *that which is born of the flesh is flesh, and that which is born of the Spirit is spirit. Do not marvel that I said to you, "You must be born again."* (John 3:3, 6–7)

Oh, if you only knew what those words mean! To be born of God! It means no less than a new order of God; a new plan; a new faith by God; a new child of God; a new life from God; a new creation living in the world but not of the world (John 17:11, 14–16), reigning in life over all the powers of the world (Rom. 5:17), over whom *"sin shall not have dominion"* (Rom. 6:14).

LIFE BY THE SPIRIT

How will we reach these beatitudes in the Spirit? How will we come into the presence of God? How will we attain to these divine principles? Beloved, it is not in the flesh and never was! How can it be, when the Scripture plainly says that if we live according to the flesh we will die (Rom. 8:13)? But if we live *"by the Spirit,"* we will *"put to death the deeds of the body"* (v. 13) and will find that

103

"mortality [will] *be swallowed up by life"* (2 Cor. 5:4) Life will prevail in the body and in the mind, over self, over disease, over everything in the world, so that we may walk around without being distracted by any bodily ailments. Are we in this place?

I daresay that many of you are in a bound condition, with lots of things to remind you that you have a body. Do you not know that Jesus Christ *"was manifested...*[to] *destroy the works of the devil"* (1 John 3:8), to loose you from the bondage of self, and to free you from the bondage of the present evil world? Do you not know that Jesus came for the express purpose of destroying the flesh?

Jesus proceeded from the Father and went to the Father (John 16:28). That blessed, blessed Jesus. Have you received Him? I have no doubt that if I were to ask you whether you believe in Jesus, many of you would say that you have believed in Jesus all your lives. But if I were to ask, "Are you saved?" many of you would unhesitatingly reply that you have never done anything wrong in your whole lives but have always done what is right and honorable. Oh, you hypocrites! You self-righteous vipers! There is no such person on the earth. *"All have sinned and fall short of the glory of God"* (Rom. 3:23, emphasis added). How will we get rid of our sins? *"The blood of Jesus Christ His Son cleanses us from all sin"* (1 John 1:7). How will we get rid of our diseases? *"The blood of Jesus Christ His Son cleanses us from all* [diseases]." You cannot think about that blessed One without becoming holy.

We have a Scripture that says, *"Whatever is born of God overcomes the world....Who is he who overcomes the world, but he who believes that Jesus is the Son of God?"* (1 John 5:4–5). The one who is born again overcomes the world, and if you find that the world overcomes you, you can be sure that you have never known this Jesus. Jesus *"was manifested...*[to] *destroy the works of the devil."*

I want to talk until you are shaken and disturbed, until you see where you are. If I can get you to search the Scriptures after I leave this place and to see if I have been preaching according to the Word of God, then I will be pleased. Wake up to see that the Scriptures have life and freedom for you. They have nothing less than power to make you sons of God, free in the Holy Spirit.

Now, Jesus came to bring back to us what was forfeited in the Garden. Adam and Eve were there—free from sin and disease—and first sin came, then disease, and then death. People want to say this is not so! But I tell you, "Get the Devil out of you, and you will have a different body. Get disease out, and you will get the Devil out."

Jesus rebuked sickness, and it went. So this morning, I want to bring you to a place where you will see that you are healed. You must give God your life. You must see that sickness has to go and that God has to come in. You must see that your life has to be clean and that God will keep you holy. You must see that you have to walk before God and that He will make you perfect, for God says, *"Pursue...holiness, without which no one will see the Lord"* (Heb. 12:14). Moreover, as *"we walk in the light as He is in the light, we have fellowship with one another, and the blood of Jesus Christ His Son cleanses us from all sin"* (1 John 1:7).

A PLACE OF VICTORY

I want to say to you believers that there is a very blessed place for you to attain to, and the place where God wants you is a place of victory. When the Spirit of the Lord comes into your life, there must be victory. The disciples, before they received the Holy Spirit, were always in bondage. Jesus said to them one day, just before the Crucifixion, *"One of you will betray Me"* (Matt. 26:21), and they were so conscious of their inability, helplessness, and human depravity that they said to Jesus, *"Is it I?"* (v. 22). Then Peter was ashamed that he had taken that stand, and he rose up and said, *"Even if all are made to stumble because of You, I will never be made to stumble"* (v. 33). Likewise, the others rose up and declared that neither would they (v. 35), but every one of them did leave Him.

However, beloved, after they received the power of the outpouring of the Holy Spirit, they were made as bold as lions to meet any difficulty. They were made to stand any test. When the power of God fell upon them in the Upper Room, these same men who had failed before the Crucifixion came out in front of all those people who were gathered together and accused them of crucifying the Lord of Glory. They were bold. What had made them like this? Purity. I tell you, purity is bold. Take, for instance, a little child. He will gaze straight into your eyes for as long as you like, without looking away once. The purer a person is, the bolder he is. I tell you, God wants to bring us into that divine purity of heart and life, that holy boldness. Not arrogance, not big-headedness, not self-righteousness, but a pure, holy, divine appointment by One who will come in and live with you. He will defy the powers of Satan and put you in a place of victory, a place of overcoming the world.

You never inherited that kind of victory from the flesh. That is a gift from God, by the Spirit, to all who obey. Therefore, no one can say he wishes he were an overcomer but that he has failed and failed until he has no hope. Beloved, God can make *you* an overcomer. When the Spirit of God comes into your body, He transforms you; He gives you life. Oh, there is a life in the Spirit that makes you *"free from the law of sin and death"* (Rom. 8:2) and gives you boldness and personality. It is the personality of the Deity. It is God in you.

I tell you that God is able to so transform you and bring you into order by the Spirit that you can become a new creation after God's order. There is no such thing as defeat for the believer. Without the Cross, without Christ's righteousness, without the new birth, without the indwelling Christ, without this divine incoming of God, I see myself as a failure. But God the Holy Spirit can come in and take our place until we are renewed in righteousness, until we are made the children of God.

Do you think that God made you in order to watch you fail? God never made men in order to see them fail. He made men in order that they might be sons who walk the earth in power. So when I look at you, I know that God can give you the capability to bring everything into subjection. Yes, you can have the power of Christ dwelling in you. His power can bring every evil thing under your feet and make you master over the flesh and the Devil. His power can work until nothing rises within you except what will magnify and glorify the Lord.

God wants me to show you Jesus' disciples, who were very frail like you and me, so that we, too, may now be filled with God and become ambassadors of this wonderful truth I am preaching. We see Peter, frail, helpless, and at every turn a failure. However, God filled that man with the Spirit of His righteousness until he went up and down as bold as a lion. Moreover, when he faced death—even crucifixion—he counted himself unworthy of being crucified like his Lord and asked that his murderers would put him upside down on the cross. He had a deep submissiveness and a power that was greater than all flesh. Peter had received the power of God.

GOD'S UNFAILING WORD

The Scriptures do not tell two different stories. They tell the truth. I want you to know the truth, *"and the truth shall make you free"* (John 8:32). What is truth? Jesus said, *"I am the way, the truth, and the life"* (John 14:6). He also said, *"He who believes in Me, as the Scripture has said, out of his heart will flow rivers of living water"* (John 7:38). He said this concerning the Spirit, who would be given after Jesus had been glorified (v. 39).

I find nothing in the Bible but holiness, and nothing in the world but worldliness. Therefore, if I live in the world, I will become worldly; on the other hand, if I live in the Bible, I will become holy. This is the truth, *"and the truth shall make you free"* (John 8:32).

GOD'S TRANSFORMING POWER

The power of God can remodel you. He can make you hate sin and love righteousness (Ps. 45:7). He can take away bitterness and hatred and covetousness and malice. He can so consecrate you by His power, through His blood, that you are made pure and every bit holy—pure in mind, heart, and actions, pure right through.

God has given me the way of life, and I want to faithfully give it to you, as though this were the last day I had to live. Jesus is the best blessing, and you can take Him away with you this morning. God gave His Son to be *"the propitiation for* [y]*our sins, and not for* [y]*ours only but also for the whole world"* (1 John 2:2).

Jesus came to make us free from sin, free from disease and pain. When I see a person diseased and in pain, I have great compassion on him. When I lay my hands upon him, I know God intends for men to be so filled with Him that the power of sin has no effect on them. He intends for them to go forth, as I am doing, to help the needy, sick, and afflicted. But what is the main thing? To preach *"the kingdom of God and His righteousness"* (Matt. 6:33). Jesus came to do this. John also came preaching repentance (Mark 1:4). The disciples began by preaching *"repentance toward God and faith toward our Lord Jesus Christ"* (Acts 20:21). I tell you, beloved, if you have really been changed by God, there is a repentance in your heart that you will never regret having there.

Through the revelation of the Word of God, we find that divine healing is solely for the glory of God. Moreover, salvation is to make you know that now you have to be inhabited by Another, even God, and that now you have to walk with God *"in newness of life"* (Rom. 6:4).

CHAPTER NINETEEN

THE GRACE OF LONG-SUFFERING AND THE GIFTS OF HEALING

TO ANOTHER [IS GIVEN] FAITH BY THE SAME SPIRIT; TO ANOTHER THE GIFTS OF HEALING BY THE SAME SPIRIT.
—1 CORINTHIANS 12:9 KJV

This morning we will move on to the gifts of healing. However, you cannot expect to understand the gifts and to understand the Epistles unless you have the Holy Spirit. All the Epistles are written to a baptized people, not to the unregenerate. They are written to those who have grown to maturity and now manifest the characteristics of the Christ of God. Do not jump into the Epistles before you have come in at the gate of the baptism in the Spirit.

I believe that this teaching that God is helping me bring to you will make you thoroughly restless and discontented until God is done dealing with you. If we want to know the mind of God through the Epistles, nothing will unveil the truth except the revelation of the Spirit Himself. He gives the utterance; He opens the door. Don't live in a state of poverty when we are surrounded by the rarest gems of the latest word from God. As Matthew states,

Ask, and it will be given to you; seek, and you will find; knock, and it will be opened to you. For everyone who asks receives, and he who seeks finds, and to him who knocks it will be opened. (Matthew 7:7–8)

These verses are backed by the authority of God's Word. Remember, the authority of God's Word is Jesus. These are the utterances by Jesus' Spirit to us this morning.

HIGHER HEIGHTS

I come to you with a great inward desire to wake you up to your great possibilities. Your responsibilities will be great, but not as great as your possibilities. You will always find that God's supply is more than abundant, and He wants you to agree with His way of thinking so that you are not restricted by yourself. Be enlarged in God!

> **INTERPRETATION OF A MESSAGE IN TONGUES:** "It is that which God has chosen for us, which is mightier than we. It is that which is bottomless, higher than the heights, more lovely than all beside. And God in a measure presses you out to believe all things so that you may 'endure all things' and 'lay hold on eternal life' through the power of the Spirit."

HOW TO MINISTER THE GIFTS OF HEALING

The gifts of healing are wonderful gifts. There is a difference between having a gift of healing and *"gifts of healing"* (1 Cor. 12:9 KJV). God wants us not to come short in anything (1 Cor. 1:7).

I like this term *"gifts of healing."* To have these gifts, I must bring myself into conformity with the mind and will of God. It would be impossible for you to have gifts of healing unless you possessed that blessed fruit of long-suffering (Gal. 5:22). You will find that these gifts run parallel to the fruit of the Spirit that will bring them into operation.

How is it possible to minister the gifts of healing considering the peculiarities there are in the churches and the many evil powers of Satan that confront us and possess bodies? The person who wants to go through with God and exercise the gifts of healing has to be a person of long-suffering, always having a word of comfort. If the one who is in distress and helpless doesn't see eye to eye with us about every matter and doesn't get all he wants, long-suffering will bear and forbear. Long-suffering is a grace Jesus lived in and moved in. He was filled with compassion, and God will never be able to move us to help the needy until we reach that place.

You might think by the way I went about praying for the sick that I was sometimes unloving and rough, but oh, friends, you have no idea what I see behind the sickness and the one who is afflicted. I am not dealing with the person; I am dealing with the satanic forces that are binding the afflicted. As far as people go, my heart is full of love and compassion for all, but I fail to see how you will ever reach a place where God will be able to use you until you get angry at the Devil.

One day a pet dog followed a lady out of her house and ran all around her feet. She said to the dog, "I cannot have you with me today." The dog wagged its tail and made a great fuss. "Go home, pet," she said, but it didn't go. At last she shouted roughly, "Go home!" and off it went.

Some people play with the Devil like that. "Poor thing!" they say. The Devil can stand all the comfort anybody in the world could give him. Cast him out! You are not dealing with the person; you are dealing with the Devil. If you say with authority, "Come out, you demons, in the name of the Lord!" they must come out. You will always be right when you dare to treat sickness as the Devil's work.

Gifts of healing are so varied that you will often find the gift of (discernment) operating in connection with them. Moreover, the manifestations of the Spirit are given to us *for the profit of all* (1 Cor. 12:7).

You must never treat a cancer case as anything else but a living evil spirit that is destroying the body. It is one of the worst kind of evil spirits I know. Not that the Devil has anything good—every disease of the Devil is bad, either to a greater or lesser degree—but this form of disease is one that you must cast out.

MIRACLES OF HEALING

Among the first people I met in Victoria Hall was a woman who had breast cancer. As soon as the cancer was cursed, it died and stopped bleeding. The next thing that happened was that her body cast it out, because the natural body has no room for dead matter. When it came out, it was like a big ball with thousands of fibers. All these fibers had spread out into the flesh, but the moment the evil power was destroyed, they had no power.

Jesus gave us power to bind and power to loose (Matt. 16:19); we must bind the evil powers and loose the afflicted and set them free. There are many cases where Satan has control of the mind, and not all those under satanic influence are in asylums.

I will tell you what freedom is. No one who enjoys the fullness of the Spirit and a clear knowledge of redemption should notice that he has a body. You ought to be able to sleep, eat, and digest your food and not be conscious of your body. You should be a living epistle of God's thought and mind, walking up and down in the world without pain. That is redemption. To be fully in the will of God, to fully possess the perfection of redemption, we should not have pain of any kind.

I have had some experience along these lines. When I was weak and helpless and friends were expecting me to die, it was in that distressing place that I saw the fullness of redemption. I read and reread the Ninety-first Psalm and claimed long life. *"With long life I will satisfy him"*—and what else?—*"and show him My salvation"* (Ps. 91:16). His salvation is greater than long life. The salvation of God is deliverance from everything, and here I am. At least twenty-five or thirty people were expecting me to die; now at sixty-three I feel young. So there is something more in this truth that I am preaching than mere words. God has not designed us for anything else than to be firstfruits (James 1:18), sons of God with power *"over all the power of the enemy"* (Luke 10:19), living in the world but not of it. (See John 17:11, 14–16.)

DEALING WITH DEMONS

In casting out demons, we have to be careful about who gives the command. Man may say, "Come out," but unless his command is by the Spirit of God, his words are useless.

In the past, during the middle of the night, the Devil would have a good time with me and would try to give me a bad time. I had a real conflict with evil powers, and the only deliverance I got was when I bound them in the name of the Lord.

I remember one day walking with a man who was demon-possessed. We were going through a thickly crowded place, and this man became loud and unruly. I boldly faced him, and the demons came out of him. However, I wasn't careful, and these demons fastened themselves on me right on the street so that I couldn't move.

Sometimes when I am ministering on the platform and the powers of the Devil attack me, the people think I am casting demons out of them, but I am casting them out of myself. The people couldn't understand the situation when I cast those evil spirits out of that man on the street, but I understood. The man who had that difficulty is now preaching and is one of the finest men we have. But the requirement for his deliverance was that someone *"bind the strong man"* (Matt. 12:29 KJV).

You must be sure of your ground; you must be sure that there is a power mightier than you that is destroying the Devil. Take your position from the first epistle of John and say, *"Greater is he that is in [me], than he that is in the world"* (1 John 4:4 KJV). If you think the power comes from you, you make a great mistake. It comes from your being filled with Him, from His acting in the place of you—your thoughts, your words, your all being used by the Spirit of God.

THE PRICE OF MIRACLES

Oh, we must wake up, stretch our faith, and believe God! Before God could bring me to this place of working miracles, He had to break me a thousand times. I have wept, I have groaned, I have travailed night after night until God broke me. Until God has mowed you down, you will never have this long-suffering for others.

When I was at Cardiff, Wales, the Lord healed a woman right in the meeting. She was afflicted with ulcers, and while we were singing, she fell full length and cried in such a way that I felt something must be done. I knelt down alongside of the woman and laid my hands on her body. Instantly the powers of the Devil were destroyed. She was delivered from ulcers, rose up, and joined in the singing.

We have been seeing wonderful miracles in these last days, and they are only a little of what we are going to see. When I say "going to see," I do not want to imply ten years from now, or even two years. I believe we are right on the threshold of wonderful things.

You must not think that these gifts fall on you like ripe cherries. You pay a price for everything you get from God. There is nothing worth having that you do not have to pay for, either temporally or spiritually.

MINISTERING TO A LAME MAN

I remember when I was at Antwerp and Brussels. The power of God was very mighty upon me there. Going on to London, I called on some friends. To show you the leading of the Lord, these friends said, "Oh, God sent you here. How much we need you!" They sent a wire to a place where there was a young man twenty-six years old who had been in bed eighteen years. His body was much bigger than an ordinary body because of inactivity, and his legs were like a child's. He had never been able to dress himself.

When his family got the wire, the father dressed him, and he was sitting in a chair. I felt it was one of the opportunities of my life. I said to this young man, "What is the greatest desire of your heart?" "Oh," he said, "to be filled with the Holy Spirit!" I put my hands upon him and said, "Receive; receive the Holy Spirit." Instantly he became drunk with the Spirit and fell off the chair like a big bag of potatoes. I saw what God could do with a helpless cripple. First, his head began shaking terrifically; then his back began moving very fast, and then his legs. Then he spoke clearly in tongues, and we wept and praised the Lord. Looking at his legs, I saw that they were still as they had been, by all appearances, and this is where I missed it.

These "missings" are sometimes God's opportunities of teaching us important lessons. He will teach us through our weaknesses what is not faith. It was not faith for me to look at that body, but human nature. The man who wants to work the works of God must never look at conditions but at Jesus, in whom everything is complete.

I looked at the boy, and there was absolutely no help. I turned to the Lord and said, "Lord, tell me what to do," and He did. He said, "Command him to walk in My name." This is where I missed it. I looked at his conditions, and I got the father to help lift him up to see if his legs had strength. We did our best, but he and I together could not move him. Then the Lord showed me my mistake, and I said, "God, forgive me." I got right down and repented and said to the Lord, "Please tell me again." God is so good. He never leaves us to ourselves. Again He said to me, "Command him in My name to walk." So I shouted, "Arise and walk in the name of Jesus." Did he do it? No, I declare he never walked. He was lifted up by the power of God in a moment, and he ran. The door was wide open; he ran out across the road into a field where he ran up and down and came back. Oh, it was a miracle!

CAN GOD USE YOU?

There are miracles to be performed, and these miracles will be accomplished by us when we understand the perfect plan of His spiritual graces that has come down to us. These things will come to us when we come to a place of brokenness, of surrender, of wholehearted yieldedness, where we decrease but God increases (John 3:30), and where we dwell and live in Him.

Will you allow Him to be the choice of your thoughts? Submit to Him, the God of all grace, so that you may be well furnished with faith for every good work, so that the mind of the Lord may have free course in you, so that it may run and be glorified (2 Thess. 3:1). Submit so that the heathen will know the truth, so that the uttermost parts of the earth will be filled with the glory of the Lord as the waters cover the deep (Isa. 11:9).

CHAPTER TWENTY

I AM THE LORD WHO HEALS YOU

IS ANYONE AMONG YOU SICK? LET HIM CALL FOR THE
ELDERS OF THE CHURCH, AND LET THEM PRAY OVER HIM,
ANOINTING HIM WITH OIL IN THE NAME OF THE LORD.
AND THE PRAYER OF FAITH WILL SAVE THE SICK, AND
THE LORD WILL RAISE HIM UP. AND IF HE HAS
COMMITTED SINS, HE WILL BE FORGIVEN.
—JAMES 5:14–15

We have in this precious Word a real basis for the truth of healing. In these verses God gives very definite instructions to the sick. If you are sick, your part is to call for the elders of the church; it is their part to anoint and pray for you in faith. Then the whole situation rests with the Lord. When you have been anointed and prayed for, you can rest assured that the Lord will raise you up. It is the Word of God.

I believe that we all can see that the church cannot play with this business. If believers turn away from these clear instructions, they are in a place of tremendous danger. Those who refuse to obey do so to their unspeakable loss.

In connection with this, James told us,

If anyone among you wanders from the truth, and someone turns him back, let him know that he who turns a sinner from the error of his way will save a soul from death and cover a multitude of sins. (James 5:19–20)

Many turn away from the Lord like King Asa, who *"in his disease...did not seek the LORD, but the physicians"* (2 Chron. 16:12).

Consequently, *"he died"* (v. 13). I take it that this passage in James means that if one induces another to turn back to the Lord, he will save that person from death, and God will forgive that person of a multitude of sins. This Scripture can also largely apply to salvation. If you turn away from any part of God's truth, the Enemy will certainly get an advantage over you.

Does the Lord meet those who look to Him for healing and who obey the instructions set forth in the book of James? Most assuredly. He will undertake for the most extreme case.

Only last night a woman came into the meeting suffering terribly. Her whole arm was filled with poison, and her blood was so poisoned that it was certain to bring her to her death. We rebuked the thing, and she was here this morning and told us that she was without pain and had slept all night, a thing she had not done for two months. To God be all the praise! You will find that He will do this kind of thing all along.

God provides the double cure, for even if sin has been the cause of the sickness, His Word declares in James 5:15, *"If he has committed sins, he will be forgiven."*

FAITH IN JESUS AND SUBMISSION TO OTHERS

You ask, "What is faith?" Faith is the principle of the Word of God. The Holy Spirit, who inspired the Word, is called the Spirit of Truth. As we *"receive with meekness the implanted word"* (James 1:21), faith springs up in our hearts—faith in the sacrifice of Calvary; faith in the shed blood of Jesus; faith in the fact that He took our weaknesses, bore our sicknesses, carried our pains, and is our life today.

God has chosen us to help one another. We dare not be independent. He brings us to a place where we submit ourselves to one another. If we refuse to do this, we get away from the Word of God and out of the place of faith. I have been in this place once, and I trust I will never be there again. It happened one time when I went to a meeting. I was very, very sick, and I got worse and worse. I knew the perfect will of God was for me to humble myself and ask the elders to pray for me. I put it off, and the meeting ended. I went home without being anointed and prayed for, and everyone in my household caught the thing I was suffering with.

My boys did not know anything else but to trust the Lord as the family Physician, and my youngest boy, George, cried down

117

from the attic, "Dadda, come." I cried, "I cannot come. The whole thing is from me. I will have to repent and ask the Lord to forgive me." I made up my mind to humble myself before the whole church. Then I rushed to the attic and laid my hands on my boy in the name of Jesus. I placed my hands on his head, and the pain left but went lower; he cried, "Put your hands lower." This continued until at last the pain went right down to his feet, and as I placed my hands on his feet, he was completely delivered. Some evil power had evidently gotten hold of him, and as I laid my hands on the different parts of the body, it left. (We have to see the difference between anointing the sick and casting out demons.) God will always be gracious when we humble ourselves before Him and come to a place of brokenness of spirit.

PRAYING FOR A PARALYTIC

I was in Le Havre, France, and the power of God was being mightily manifested. A Greek named Felix attended the meeting and became very zealous for God. He was very eager to get all the Catholics he could to the meeting in order that they could see that God was graciously visiting France. He found a certain bedridden woman who was fixed in a certain position and could not move, and he told her about the Lord's healing at the meetings and said that he would get me to come if she wished. She said, "My husband is a Catholic, and he would never allow anyone who is not a Catholic to see me."

She asked her husband to allow me to come and told him what Felix had told her about the power of God working in our midst. He said, "I will have no Protestant enter my house." She said, "You know that the doctors cannot help me, and the priests cannot help. Won't you let this man of God pray for me?" He finally consented, and I went to the house. The simplicity of this woman and her childlike faith were beautiful to see.

I showed her my oil bottle and said to her, "Here is oil. It is a symbol of the Holy Spirit. When that comes upon you, the Holy Spirit will begin to work, and the Lord will raise you up." God did something the moment the oil fell upon her. I looked toward the window, and I saw Jesus. (I have seen Him often. There is no painting that is a bit like Him; no artist can ever depict the beauty of my lovely Lord.) The woman felt the power of God in her body and cried, "I'm free! My hands are free, my shoulders are free, and oh, I see Jesus! I'm free! I'm free!"

The vision vanished, and the woman sat up in bed. Her legs were still bound, and I said to her, "I'll put my hands on your legs, and you will be free entirely." As I put my hands on those legs covered with bedclothes, I looked and saw the Lord again. She saw Him, too, and cried, "He's there again. I'm free! I'm free!" She rose from her bed and walked around the room praising God, and we were all in tears as we saw His wonderful works. As we are told in James 5:15, "the Lord will raise [them] up" when the conditions are met.

OUR WONDERFUL LORD

We have a big God. We have a wonderful Jesus. We have a glorious Comforter. God's canopy is over you and will cover you at all times, preserving you from evil. "Under His wings you shall take refuge" (Ps. 91:4). "The word of God is living and powerful" (Heb. 4:12), and in its treasures you will find eternal life. If you dare trust this wonderful Lord, this Lord of Life, you will find in Him everything you need.

So many are trying drugs, quacks, pills, and plasters. You will find that if you dare trust God, He will never fail. "The prayer of faith will save the sick, and the Lord will raise him up" (James 5:15). Do you trust Him? He is worthy to be trusted.

DELIVERING A MANIAC

One time I was asked to go to Weston-super-Mare, a seaside resort in the western part of England. I learned from a telegram that a man had lost his reason and had become a raving maniac, and some people there wanted me to come and pray for him. I arrived at the place, and the wife said to me, "Will you stay with my husband?" I agreed, and in the middle of the night, an evil power laid hold of him. It was awful. I put my hand on his head, and his hair was like toothpicks standing on end. God gave deliverance—a temporary deliverance. At six o'clock the next morning, I felt that it was necessary that I get out of that house for a short time.

The man saw me going and cried out, "If you leave me, there is no hope." But I felt that I had to go. As I left, I saw a woman with a

Salvation Army bonnet on, and I knew that she was going to their seven o'clock prayer meeting. I said to the captain who was in charge of the meeting, when I saw he was about to sing a hymn, "Captain, don't sing. Let's go to prayer." He agreed, and I prayed my heart out. Then I grabbed my hat and rushed out of the hall. They all thought they had had a madman in their prayer meeting that morning.

I went down the road, and there was the man I had spent the night with, rushing down toward the sea without a particle of clothing on, about to drown himself. I cried, "In the name of Jesus, come out of him." The man fell full length on the ground, and that evil power went out of him never to return. His wife came rushing after him, and the husband was restored to her in a perfect mental condition.

BEING KEPT BY GOD'S POWER

There are evil powers, but Jesus is greater than all evil powers. There are tremendous diseases, but Jesus is the Healer. There is no case too hard for Him. The Lion of Judah will break every chain. He came to relieve the oppressed and to set the captive free (Luke 4:18). He came to bring redemption, to make us as perfect as man was before the Fall.

People want to know how to be kept by the power of God. Every position of grace into which you are led—forgiveness, healing, any kind of deliverance—will be contested by Satan. He will contend for your body. When you are saved, Satan will come around and say, "See, you are not saved." The Devil is a liar.

I remember the story of the man whose life was swept and put in order. The evil power had been swept out of him. But the man remained in a stationary position. If the Lord heals you, you dare not remain in a stationary position. The evil spirit came back to that man, found his house swept, and took seven others worse than himself and dwelt there. The last stage of that man was worse than the first. (See Matthew 12:43–45.) Be sure to get filled with God. Get an Occupier. Be filled with the Spirit.

God has a million ways of undertaking for those who go to Him for help. He has deliverance for every captive. He loves you so much that He even says, *"Before they call, I will answer"* (Isa. 65:24). Don't turn Him away.

CHAPTER TWENTY-ONE

WHAT IT MEANS TO BE
FULL OF THE HOLY SPIRIT

I n the days when the number of disciples began to multiply, there arose a situation in which the Twelve had to make a definite decision not to occupy themselves with "serving tables," but to give themselves "continually to prayer and to the ministry of the word." We read about this instance in the sixth chapter of the book of Acts:

Now in those days, when the number of the disciples was multiplying, there arose a complaint against the Hebrews by the Hellenists, because their widows were neglected in the daily distribution. Then the twelve summoned the multitude of the disciples and said, "It is not desirable that we should leave the word of God and serve tables. Therefore, brethren, seek out from among you seven men of good reputation, full of the Holy Spirit and wisdom, whom we may appoint over this business; but we will give ourselves continually to prayer and to the ministry of the word." And the saying pleased the whole multitude. And they chose Stephen, a man full of faith and the Holy Spirit, and Philip, Prochorus, Nicanor, Timon, Parmenas, and Nicolas, a proselyte from Antioch, whom they set before the apostles; and when they had prayed, they laid hands on them. Then the word of God spread, and the number of the disciples multiplied greatly in Jerusalem, and a great many of the priests were obedient to the faith. And Stephen, full of faith and power, did great wonders and signs among the people. Then there arose some from what is called the Synagogue of the Freedmen (Cyrenians, Alexandrians,

my family
friends
fields of
Great
Falls,
Purcellville

121

and those from Cilicia and Asia), disputing with (Stephen). And they were not able to resist the wisdom and the Spirit by which he spoke. Then they secretly induced men to say, "We have heard him speak blasphemous words against Moses and God." And they stirred up the people, the elders, and the scribes; and they came upon him, seized him, and brought him to the council. They also set up false witnesses who said, "This man does not cease to speak blasphemous words against this holy place and the law; for we have heard him say that this Jesus of Nazareth will destroy this place and change the customs which Moses delivered to us." And all who sat in the council, looking steadfastly at him, saw his face as the face of an angel. Then the high priest said, "Are these things so?" And he said, "Brethren and fathers, listen....You stiffnecked and uncircumcised in heart and ears! You always resist the Holy Spirit; as your fathers did, so do you. Which of the prophets did your fathers not persecute? And they killed those who foretold the coming of the Just One, of whom you now have become the betrayers and murderers, who have received the law by the direction of angels and have not kept it." When they heard these things they were cut to the heart, and they gnashed at him with their teeth. But he, being full of the Holy Spirit, gazed into heaven and saw the glory of God, and Jesus standing at the right hand of God, and said, "Look! I see the heavens opened and the Son of Man standing at the right hand of God!" Then they cried out with a loud voice, stopped their ears, and ran at him with one accord; and they cast him out of the city and stoned him. And the witnesses laid down their clothes at the feet of a young man named Saul. And they stoned Stephen as he was calling on God and saying, "Lord Jesus, receive my spirit." Then he knelt down and cried out with a loud voice, "Lord, do not charge them with this sin." And when he had said this, he fell asleep. (Acts 6:1–7:2, 51–60)

How important it is for all God's ministers to be continually in prayer and constantly feeding on the Scriptures of Truth. I often offer a reward to anyone who can catch me anywhere without my Bible or my New Testament.

None of you can be strong in God unless you are diligently and constantly listening to what God has to say to you through His Word. You cannot know the power and the nature of God unless you partake of His inbreathed Word. Read it in the morning, in the evening, and at every opportunity you get. After every meal, instead of indulging in unprofitable conversation around the table, read a chapter from the Word, and then have a season of prayer. I endeavor to make a point of doing this no matter where or with whom I am staying.

The psalmist said that he had hidden God's Word in his heart so that he might not sin against Him (Ps. 119:11). You will find that the more of God's Word you hide in your heart, the easier it is to live a holy life. He also testified that God's Word had given him life (v. 50). As you receive God's Word, your whole physical being will be given life, and you will be made strong. As you receive with meekness the Word (James 1:21), you will find faith springing up within. You will have life through the Word.

A BETTER PLAN FOR YOU

The Twelve told the rest of the disciples to find seven men to look after the business side of things. They were to be men with a good reputation and filled with the Holy Spirit. Those who were chosen were just ordinary men, but they were filled with the Holy Spirit, and this infilling always lifts a man to a plane above the ordinary. It does not take a cultured or an educated man to fill a position in God's church. What God requires is a yielded, consecrated, holy life, and He can make it a flame of fire. He can baptize *"with the Holy Spirit and fire"* (Matt. 3:11)!

The multitude chose seven men to serve tables. Undoubtedly, they were faithful in their appointed tasks, but we see that God soon had a better plan for two of them—Philip and Stephen. Philip was so full of the Holy Spirit that he could have a revival wherever God put him down. (See Acts 8:5–8, 26–40.) Man chose him to serve tables, but God chose him to win souls.

Oh, if I could only stir you up to see that, as you are faithful in the humblest role, God can fill you with His Spirit, make you a chosen vessel for Himself, and promote you to a place of mighty ministry in the salvation of souls and in the healing of the sick. Nothing is impossible to a man filled with the Holy Spirit. The possibilities are beyond all human comprehension. When you are filled with the power of the Holy Spirit, God will wonderfully work wherever you go.

When you are filled with the Spirit, you will know the voice of God. I want to give you one illustration of this. When I was going to Australia recently, our boat stopped at Aden and Bombay. In Aden the people came around the ship selling their wares—beautiful carpets and all sorts of Oriental things. There was one man selling some ostrich feathers. As I was looking over the side of the ship watching the trading, a gentleman said to me, "Would you join me in buying that bunch of feathers?" What did I want with feathers? I had no use for such things and no room for them either. But the gentleman asked me again, "Will you join me in buying that bunch?" The Spirit of God said to me, "Do it."

The feathers were sold to us for three pounds, and the gentleman said, "I have no money on me, but if you will pay the man for them, I will send the cash down to you by the steward." I paid for the feathers and gave the gentleman his share. He was traveling first class, and I was traveling second class. I said to him, "No, please don't give that money to the steward. I want you to bring it to me personally in my cabin." I asked the Lord, "What about these feathers?" He showed me that He had a purpose in my purchasing them.

A little while later, the gentleman came to my cabin and said, "I've brought the money." I said to him, "It is not your money that I want; it is your soul that I am seeking for God." Right there he opened up the whole story of his life and began to seek God, and that morning he wept his way through to God's salvation.

You have no idea what God can do through you when you are filled with His Spirit. Every day and every hour you can have the divine leading of God. To be filled with the Holy Spirit is great in every respect. I have seen some who had been suffering for years, but when they have been filled with the Holy Spirit, every bit of their sickness has passed away. The Spirit of God has made real to them the life of Jesus, and they have been completely liberated from every sickness and infirmity.

Look at Stephen. He was just an ordinary man chosen to serve tables. But the Holy Spirit was in him, and he was *"full of faith and power"* (Acts 6:8); therefore, he *"did great wonders and miracles among the people"* (v. 8 KJV). There was no resisting *"the wisdom and the Spirit by which he spoke"* (v. 10). How important it is that every man be filled with the Holy Spirit.

INTERPRETATION OF A MESSAGE IN TONGUES: "The divine will is that you be filled with God, that the power of the

Spirit fill you with the mightiness of God. There is nothing God will withhold from a man filled with the Holy Spirit."

I want to impress the importance of this upon you. It is not healing that I am presenting to you in these meetings—it is the living Christ. It is a glorious fact that the Son of God came down to bring *"liberty to the captives"* (Luke 4:18). He is the One who baptizes *"with the Holy Spirit and fire"* (Matt. 3:11). He is the One who is pouring forth what we are now seeing and hearing (Acts 2:33).

The Blessing of Persecution

Why is it that the moment you are filled with the Holy Spirit persecution starts? It was so with the Lord Jesus Himself. We do not read of any persecution before the Holy Spirit came down upon Him like a dove. Shortly after this, we find that after He preached in His hometown, the people wanted to throw Him over the brow of a hill. (See Luke 4:16–30.) It was the same way with the twelve disciples. They had no persecution before the Day of Pentecost, but after they were filled with the Spirit, they were soon in prison. The Devil and the leaders of religion will always get stirred when a man is filled with the Spirit and does things in the power of the Spirit. Nevertheless, persecution is the greatest blessing to a church. When we have persecution, we have purity. If you desire to be filled with the Spirit, you can count on one thing, and that is persecution. The Lord came to bring division (Luke 12:51), and even in your own household you may find *"three against two"* (v. 52).

The Lord Jesus gives us peace, but soon after you get peace within, you get persecution without. If you remain stationary, the Devil and his agents will not disturb you much. But when you press on and go the whole length with God, the Enemy has you as a target. But God will vindicate you in the midst of the whole thing.

At a meeting I was holding, the Lord was working, and many were being healed. A man saw what was taking place and remarked, "I'd like to try this thing." He came up for prayer and told me that his body was broken in two places. I laid my hands on him in the name of the Lord and said to him, "Now believe God." The next night he was at the meeting, and he got up like a lion. He said, "I want to tell you people that this man here is deceiving you. He laid his hands on me last night for a rupture in two places, but I'm not a bit better." I stopped him and said, "You are healed; your trouble is that you won't believe it."

He was at the meeting the next night, and when there was opportunity for testimonies, this man arose. He said, "I'm a mason by trade. Today I was working with a laborer, and he had to put a big stone in place. I helped him and did not feel any pain. I said to myself, 'How did I do that?' I went to a private place where I could take off my clothes, and I found that I was healed." I told the people, "Last night this man was against the Word of God, but now he believes it. It is true that 'these signs will follow those who believe;...they will lay hands on the sick, and they will recover' (Mark 16:17–18). Healing is through the power that is in the name of Christ." It is the Spirit who has come to reveal the Word of God and to make it spirit and life to us (John 6:63).

Those of you who are seeking the baptism in the Holy Spirit are entering a place where you will have persecution. Your best friends will leave you—or those you may think are your best friends. No good friend will ever leave you. But be assured that your seeking is worthwhile. You will enter into a realm of illumination, a realm of revelation by the power of the Holy Spirit. He reveals the preciousness and the power of the blood of Christ. I find by the revelation of the Spirit that there is not one thing in me that the blood does not cleanse (1 John 1:9). I find that God sanctifies me by the blood and reveals the effectiveness of His work by the Spirit.

LIFE IN THE SPIRIT

Stephen was just an ordinary man, but he was clothed with the divine. He was "full of faith and power" (Acts 6:8), and "great wonders and miracles" (v. 8 KJV) were done by him. Oh, this life in the Holy Spirit! Oh, this life of deep inward revelation, of transformation from one state to another, of growing in grace, in all knowledge, and in the power of the Spirit. In this state, the life and the mind of Christ are renewed in you, and He gives constant revelations of the might of His power. It is only this kind of thing that will enable us to stand.

In this life, the Lord puts you in all sorts of places and then reveals His power. I had been preaching in New York, and one day

I sailed for England on the *Lusitania*. As soon as I got on board, I went down to my cabin. Two men were there, and one of them said, "Well, will I do for company?" He took out a bottle and poured a glass of whiskey and drank it, and then he filled it up for me. "I never touch that stuff," I said. "How can you live without it?" he asked. "How could I live with it?" I asked. He admitted, "I have been under the influence of this stuff for months, and they say my insides are all shriveled up. I know that I am dying. I wish I could be delivered, but I just have to keep on drinking. Oh, if I could only be delivered! My father died in England and has given me his fortune, but what good will it be to me except to hasten me to my grave?"

I said to this man, "Say the word, and you will be delivered." He asked, "What do you mean?" I said, "Say the word—show that you are willing to be delivered—and God will deliver you." But it was just as if I were talking to this platform for all the understanding he showed. I said to him, "Stand still," and I laid my hands on his head in the name of Jesus and cursed that alcohol demon that was taking his life. He cried out, "I'm free! I'm free! I know I'm free!" He took two bottles of whiskey and threw them overboard, and God saved, sobered, and healed him. I was preaching all the way across the ocean. He sat beside me at the table. Previous to this, he had not been able to eat, but now at every meal he went right through the menu.

You need only a touch from Jesus to have a good time. The power of God is just the same today. To me, He's lovely. To me, He's saving health. To me, He's the Lily of the Valley. Oh, this blessed Nazarene, this King of Kings! Hallelujah! Will you let Him have your will? Will you let Him have you? If so, all His power is at your disposal.

IT'S WORTH IT!

Those who disputed with Stephen *"were not able to resist the wisdom and the Spirit by which he spoke"* (Acts 6:10). Full of rage, they brought him to the council. However, God filled his face with a ray of heaven's light.

Being filled with the Spirit is worthwhile, no matter what it costs. Read in Acts 7 the mighty prophetic utterance by this holy man. Without fear he told them, *"You stiffnecked and uncircumcised in heart and ears! You always resist the Holy Spirit"* (Acts 7:51). When his enemies heard these things, *"they were cut to the heart"* (v. 54). There are two ways of being cut to the heart. Here they gnashed their teeth at him, cast him out of the city, and stoned him. On the Day of Pentecost, when the people were cut to the heart, they cried out, *"What shall we do?"* (Acts 2:37). They responded in the opposite way. The Devil, if he can have his way, will cause you to commit murder. If Jesus has His way, you will repent.

Stephen, full of the Holy Spirit, looked up steadfastly into heaven and saw the glory of God and the Son of Man standing on the right hand of God. Oh, this being full of the Holy Spirit! How much it means! I was riding for sixty miles one summer day, and as I looked up at the heavens, I had an open vision of Jesus all the way. It takes the Holy Spirit to give this.

Stephen cried out, *"Lord, do not charge them with this sin"* (Acts 7:60). Since he was full of the Spirit, he was full of love. He manifested the very same compassion for his enemies that Jesus did at Calvary. This being filled with the Holy Spirit is great in every respect. It means constant filling and a new life continually. Oh, it's lovely! We have a wonderful Gospel and a great Savior! If you will only be filled with the Holy Spirit, you will have a constant spring within. Yes, as your faith centers on the Lord Jesus, from within you *"will flow rivers of living water"* (John 7:38).

CHAPTER TWENTY-TWO

IS ANYONE SICK?

I s there anyone sick? Is there anyone sick in this place?" This is what I ask when I go into a sickroom. Why? I will tell you a story that will explain.

My daughter is a missionary to Africa. I am interested in helping to support missionaries in Africa and all over. I love missionary work.

We had a missionary out in China who by some means or other got rheumatism. I have no word for rheumatism, only "devil-possessed." Rheumatism, cancer, tumors, lumbago, neuralgia—all these things I give only one name: the power of the Devil working in humanity. When I see tuberculosis, I see demon power working there. All these things can be removed.

When Jesus went into Peter's house, where his wife's mother lay sick, what did He do? Did He cover her up with a blanket and put a hot water bottle on her feet? If He didn't do that, why didn't He? Because He knew that the demons had all the heat of hell in them. He did the right thing: He rebuked the fever, and it left. (See Luke 4:38–39.) We, too, ought to do the right thing with these diseases.

This missionary with rheumatism came home to Belfast from China, enraged against the work of God, enraged against God, enraged against everything. She was absolutely outside the plan of God.

While she was in Belfast, God allowed this missionary to fall down the steps and dislocate her backbone. Others had to lift her up and carry her to her bed. God allowed it.

Be careful about getting angry at God because of something wrong with your body. Get right with God.

On the day that I was to visit the sick, she asked me to come. When I went to her room, I looked at her and called out, "Is there

Repent

anyone sick in this room?" No response. "Is there anyone sick in this room?" No response. "Well," I said, "we will wait until somebody moves."

By and by, she said, "Yes, I am sick." I said, "All right, we have found you out then. You are in the room. Now, the Word of God says that when you are sick, you are to pray. When you pray, I will anoint you and pray for you, but not before."

It took her almost a quarter of an hour to yield, the Devil had such possession of her. But, thank God, she yielded. Then she cried and cried, and by the power of God her body was shaken loose, and she was set free. This happened when she repented, and not before. ✳

Oh, what would happen if everybody in this place would repent! Talk about blessings! The glory would fall so you couldn't get out of this place. We need to see that God wants us to be blessed, but first of all He wants us to be ready for the blessing.

BELIEVE AND BE HEALED

The God who told Moses to make a bronze serpent and put it on a pole so that whoever looked could be healed (see Numbers 21:5–9), now says, "The bronze serpent is not on the pole. Jesus is not on the cross. He has risen and has been given all power and authority. Believe. You will be healed if you believe."

You cannot literally look at the cross, you cannot literally look at the bronze serpent, but you can believe. If you believe, you can be healed. God means for you to believe today; God means for you to be helped today.

COMPLETE VERSUS PARTIAL HEALING

I want everybody to know that Wigglesworth does not believe in partial healings. Then what does Wigglesworth believe? I believe in complete healings. If the healing is not manifested, it is there all the same. It is inactive because of inactive faith, but it is there. God has given it. How do I know? *"They will lay hands on the sick, and **they will recover**"* (Mark 16:18, emphasis added). Whose word is that? That is God's Word. So I have faith today. Hallelujah! Even repeating the Word gives me more faith.

INTERPRETATION OF A MESSAGE IN TONGUES: "Why do you doubt when God, even the Lord, has come to cast the Devil out, so that you may know that you are free from all things by the blood of Jesus?"

We are in a great place. The Lord is in the midst of us. You are to go away free today.

A WOMAN SEES A VISION

I like the thought, *"He Himself took our infirmities and bore our sicknesses"* (Matt. 8:17).

I want to tell you a remarkable story. One day I was standing at the bottom of Shanklin Road, Belfast, Ireland, with a piece of paper in my hand, looking at the addresses of where I had to go, when a man came over and said to me, "Are you visiting the sick?" "Yes," I said. "Go there," he said, and pointed to a house nearby.

I knocked at the door. No reply. I knocked again, and then a voice inside said, "Come in!" So I opened the door and walked in. Then a young man pointed for me to go up the stairway.

When I got up onto the landing, there was a door wide open. So I walked right through the doorway and found a woman sitting up on the bed. As soon as I looked at her, I knew she couldn't speak to me, so I began to pray. She was rocking back and forth, gasping for breath. I knew she was beyond answering me.

When I prayed, the Lord said to me—the Holy Spirit said distinctly—"Read Isaiah 53." So I opened the Book and began to read,

Who has believed our report? And to whom has the arm of the LORD been revealed? For He shall grow up before Him as a tender plant, and as a root out of dry ground. (Isa. 53:1–2)

When I got to the fifth verse, *"But He was wounded for our transgressions, He was bruised for our iniquities; the chastisement for our peace was upon Him, and by His stripes we are healed,"* the woman shouted, "I am healed! I am healed!"

Amazed at this sudden exclamation, I said, "Tell me what happened."

"Two weeks ago I was cleaning the house," she said. "In moving some furniture, I strained my heart; it moved out of its place. The doctors examined me and said that I would die of suffocation. But last night, in the middle of the night, I saw you come into the room. When you saw me, you knew I could not speak, so you began to pray. Then you opened to Isaiah 53 and read until you came to the fifth verse, and when you read the fifth verse, I was completely healed. That was a vision; now it is a fact."

So I know the Word of God is still true.

> INTERPRETATION OF A MESSAGE IN TONGUES: "Stretch out your hand, for the Lord your God is so nigh unto you. He will take you and so place you in His pavilion of splendor that if you will not go out anymore but will remain stationary in the will of God, He will grant you the desire of your heart."

Now, that is a word from the Lord. You will never get anything more distinct than that from the Lord. People miss the greatest plan of healing because of moving from one thing to another. Become stationary. God wants you to take the Word, claim the Word, and believe the Word. That is the perfect way of healing. Do not turn to the right hand or to the left (Deut. 5:32), but believe God.

GOD'S PRESENCE HEALS

I believe we ought to have people in this meeting loosed from their infirmities even without having hands laid upon them. I see more and more that the day of the visitation of the Lord is upon us, (that the presence of the Lord is here to heal.) We should have people healed in these meetings while I am speaking, healed under the anointing of the Spirit.

I have been preaching faith so that you may definitely claim your healing. I believe that if you have listened to the Word and have been moved to believe, if you stand up while I pray, you will find that God's healing power will loose you from sickness.

> INTERPRETATION OF A MESSAGE IN TONGUES: "In the depths God has come and moves, and moves in the very inner working of the heart until the Spirit of the Lord has perfect choice, and brings forth that which will resound to His glory forever. The Lord is in the midst of it. Those who are bound are made free from captivity."

God wants you to have a living faith now; He wants you to get a vital touch, shaking the foundation of all weakness. When you were saved, you were saved the moment you believed, and you will be healed the moment you believe.

Father, I take these people and present them to You, giving them into Your gracious, glorious care, so that You may keep them from falling, keep them from the error of the ways of the wicked, and deliver them from all evil. Let Your mercy be with them in their homes, in their bodies, and in every way. Amen.

CHAPTER TWENTY-THREE

DO YOU WANT TO BE MADE WELL?

I believe the Word of God is so powerful that it can transform any and every life. There is power in God's Word to make that which does not exist to appear (Rom. 4:17). There is executive power in the words that proceed from His lips. The psalmist told us, *"He sent His Word and healed them"* (Ps. 107:20). Do you think the Word has diminished in its power? I tell you, it has not. God's Word can bring things to pass today as it did in the past.

The psalmist said, *"Before I was afflicted I went astray, but now I keep Your word"* (Ps. 119:67). And again, *"It is good for me that I have been afflicted, that I may learn Your statutes"* (v. 71). If our afflictions will bring us to the place where we see that we cannot *"live by bread alone, but by every word that proceeds from the mouth of God"* (Matt. 4:4), they will have served a blessed purpose. I want you to realize that there is a life of purity, a life made clean through the Word He has spoken (John 15:3), in which, through faith, you can glorify God with a body that is free from sickness, as well as with a spirit that has been set free from the bondage of Satan.

Around the pool of Bethesda lay a great multitude of sick folk—blind, lame, paralyzed—waiting for the moving of the water. (See John 5:2–4.) Did Jesus heal all of them? No, He left many around that pool unhealed. Undoubtedly, many had their eyes on the pool and had no eyes for Jesus. There are many today who always have their confidence in things they can see. If they would only get their eyes on God instead of on natural things, how quickly they would be helped.

The Bread of Healing

The following question arises: Is salvation and healing for all? It is for all who will press right in and claim their portion. Do you remember the case of that Syro-Phoenician woman who wanted the demon cast out of her daughter? Jesus said to her, *"Let the children be filled first, for it is not good to take the children's bread and throw it to the little dogs"* (Mark 7:27). Note that healing and deliverance are here spoken of by the Master as *"the children's bread"*; therefore, if you are a child of God, you can surely press in for your portion.

The Syro-Phoenician woman purposed to get from the Lord what she was after, and she said, *"Yes, Lord, yet even the little dogs under the table eat from the children's crumbs"* (v. 28). Jesus was stirred as He saw the faith of this woman, and He told her, *"For this saying go your way; the demon has gone out of your daughter"* (v. 29).

Today many children of God are refusing their blood-purchased portion of health in Christ and throwing it away. Meanwhile, sinners are pressing through and picking it up from under the table and are finding the cure, not only for their bodies, but also for their spirits and souls. The Syro-Phoenician woman went home and found that the demon had indeed gone out of her daughter. Today there is bread—there is life and health—for every child of God through His powerful Word.

The Word can drive every disease away from your body. Healing is your portion in Christ, who Himself is our bread, our life, our health, our All in All. Though you may be deep in sin, you can come to Him in repentance, and He will forgive and cleanse and heal you. His words are spirit and life to those who will receive them (John 6:63). There is a promise in the last verse of Joel that says, *"I will cleanse their blood that I have not cleansed"* (Joel 3:21 KJV). This as much as says that He will provide new life within. The life of Jesus Christ, God's Son, can so purify people's hearts and minds that they become entirely transformed—spirit, soul, and body.

The sick folk were around the pool of Bethesda, and one particular man had been there a long time. His infirmity was of thirty-eight years' standing. Now and again an opportunity to be healed would come as the angel stirred the waters, but he would be sick at heart as he saw another step in and be healed before him. Then one

135

day Jesus was passing that way, and seeing him lying there in that sad condition, He asked, *"Do you want to be made well?"* (John 5:6). Jesus said it, and His words are from everlasting to everlasting. These are His words today to you, tried and tested one. You may say, like this poor sick man, "I have missed every opportunity up until now." Never mind that. *"Do you want to be made well?"*

IS IT THE LORD'S WILL?

I visited a woman who had been suffering for many years. She was all twisted up with rheumatism and had been in bed two years. I asked her, "What makes you lie here?" She said, "I've come to the conclusion that I have a thorn in the flesh." I said, "To what wonderful degree of righteousness have you attained that you must have a thorn in the flesh? Have you had such an abundance of divine revelations that there is a danger of your being exalted above measure?" (See 2 Corinthians 12:7–9.) She said, "I believe it is the Lord who is causing me to suffer." I said, "You believe it is the Lord's will for you to suffer, but you are trying to get out of it as quickly as you can. You have medicine bottles all over the place. Get out of your hiding place, and confess that you are a sinner. If you'll get rid of your self-righteousness, God will do something for you. Drop the idea that you are so holy that God has to afflict you. Sin is the cause of your sickness, not righteousness. Disease is not caused by righteousness, but by sin."

There is healing through the blood of Christ and deliverance for every captive. God never intended His children to live in misery because of some affliction that comes directly from the Devil. A perfect atonement was made at Calvary. I believe that Jesus bore my sins, and I am free from them all. I am justified from all things if I dare to believe (Acts 13:39). *"He Himself took our infirmities and bore our sicknesses"* (Matt. 8:17), and if I dare to believe, I can be healed.

See this helpless man at the pool. Jesus asked him, *"Do you want to be made well?"* (John 5:6). But there was a difficulty in the way. The man had one eye on the pool and one eye on Jesus. If you will look only to Christ and put both of your eyes on Him, you can be made every bit whole—spirit, soul, and body. It is the promise of the living God that those who believe are justified, made free, from all things (Acts 13:39). And *"if the Son makes you free, you shall be free indeed"* (John 8:36).

You say, "Oh, if I could only believe!" Jesus understands. He knew that the helpless man had been in that condition for a long time. He is full of compassion. He knows about that kidney trouble; He knows about those corns; He knows about that neuralgia. There is nothing He does not know. He wants only a chance to show Himself merciful and gracious to you, but He wants to encourage you to believe Him. If you can only believe, you can be saved and healed. Dare to believe that Jesus was wounded for your transgressions, was bruised for your iniquities, was chastised that you might have peace, and that by His stripes there is healing for you here and now (Isa. 53:5). You have failed because you have not believed Him. Cry out to Him even now, *"Lord, I believe; help my unbelief!"* (Mark 9:24).

I was in Long Beach, California, one day. I was with a friend, and we were passing by a hotel. He told me of a doctor there who had a diseased leg. He had been suffering from it for six years and could not get around. We went up to his room and found four doctors there. I said, "Well, doctor, I see you have plenty going on. I'll come again another day." I was passing by another time, and the Spirit said, "Go see him." Poor doctor! He surely was in poor shape. He said, "I have been like this for six years, and nobody can help me." I said, "You need almighty God." People are trying to patch up their lives, but they cannot do anything without God. I talked to him for a while about the Lord and then prayed for him. I cried, "Come out of him in the name of Jesus." The doctor cried, "It's all gone!"

Oh, if we only knew Jesus! One touch of His might meets the need of everything that is not right. The trouble is getting people to believe Him. The simplicity of this salvation is so wonderful. One touch of living faith in Him is all that is required for wholeness to be your portion.

I was in Long Beach about six weeks later, and the sick were coming for prayer. Among those filling up the aisle was the doctor. I said, "What is the trouble?" He said, "Diabetes, but it will be all right tonight. I know it will be all right." There is no such thing as the Lord's not meeting your need. There are no *ifs* or *mays*; His promises are all *shall*s. *"All things are possible to him who believes"* (Mark 9:23). Oh, the name of Jesus! There is power in that name to meet every human need.

At that meeting there was an old man helping his son to the altar. He said, "He has fits—many every day." Then there was a woman with cancer. Oh, what sin has done! We read that when God brought forth His people from Egypt, *"there was not one feeble person among their tribes"* (Ps. 105:37 KJV). No disease! All healed by the power of God! I believe that God wants a people like that today.

I prayed for the woman who had the cancer, and she said, "I know I'm free and that God has delivered me." Then they brought the boy with the fits, and I commanded the evil spirits to leave in the name of Jesus. Then I prayed for the doctor. At the next night's meeting the house was full. I called out, "Now, doctor, what about the diabetes?" He said, "It is gone." Then I said to the old man, "What about your son?" He said, "He hasn't had any fits since." We have a God who answers prayer.

SIN AND SICKNESS

Jesus meant this man at the pool to be a testimony forever. When he had both eyes on Jesus, He said to him, "Do the impossible thing. *'Rise, take up your bed and walk'* (John 5:8)." Jesus once called on a man with a withered hand to do the impossible—to stretch forth his hand. The man did the impossible thing. He stretched out his hand, and it was made completely whole. (See Matthew 12:10–13.)

In the same way, this helpless man began to rise, and he found the power of God moving within him. He wrapped up his bed and began to walk off. It was the Sabbath day, and there were some folks who, because they thought much more of a day than they did of the Lord, began to make a fuss. When the power of God is being manifested, a protest will always come from some hypocrites. Jesus knew all about what the man was going through and met him again. This time He said to him, *"See, you have been made well. Sin no more, lest a worse thing come upon you"* (John 5:14).

There is a close relationship between sin and sickness. How many know that their sicknesses are a direct result of sin? I hope that no one will come to be prayed for who is living in sin. But if you will obey God and repent of your sin and stop it, God will meet you, and neither your sickness nor your sin will remain. *"The prayer of faith will save the sick, and the Lord will raise him up. And if he has committed sins, he will be forgiven"* (James 5:15).

Faith is just the open door through which the Lord comes. Do not say, "I was saved by faith" or "I was healed by faith." Faith does not save and heal. (God) saves and heals through that open door. You believe, and the power of Christ comes. Salvation and healing are for the glory of God. I am here because God healed me when I was dying, and I have been around the world preaching this full redemption, doing all I can to bring glory to the wonderful name of the One who healed me.

"*Sin no more, lest a worse thing come upon you*" (John 5:14). The Lord told us in one place about an evil spirit going out of a man. The house that the evil spirit left got all swept and put in order, but it received no new occupant. That evil spirit, with seven other spirits more wicked than himself, went back to that unoccupied house, and "*the last state of that man* [was] *worse than the first*" (Matt. 12:45).

The Lord does not heal you to go to a baseball game or to a racetrack. He heals you for His glory so that from that moment your life will glorify Him. But this man remained stationary. He did not magnify God. He did not seek to be filled with the Spirit. And his last state became "*worse than the first.*"

The Lord wants to so cleanse the motives and desires of our hearts that we will seek one thing only, and that is His glory. I went to a certain place one day and the Lord said, "This is for My glory." A young man had been sick for a long time. He had been confined to his bed in an utterly hopeless condition. He was fed with a spoon and was never dressed. The weather was damp, so I said to the people in the house, "I wish you would put the young man's clothes by the fire to air." At first they would not take any notice of my request, but because I was persistent, they at last got out his clothes. When they had been aired, I took them into his room.

The Lord said to me, "You will have nothing to do with this," and I just lay prostrate on the floor. The Lord showed me that He was going to shake the place with His glory. The very bed shook. I laid my hands on the young man in the name of Jesus, and the power fell in such a way that I fell with my face to the floor. In about a quarter of an hour, the young man got up and walked back and forth praising God. He dressed himself and then went out to the room where his father and mother were. He said, "God has healed me." Both the father and mother fell prostrate to the floor as the power of God surged through that room. There was a woman in that house who had been in an asylum for lunacy, and her condition was so bad that they were about to take her back. But the power of God healed her, too.

The power of God is just the same today as it was in the past. Men need to be taken back to the old paths, to the old-time faith, to believing God's Word and every "Thus says the Lord" in it. The Spirit of the Lord is moving in these days. God is coming forth. If you want to be in the rising tide, you must accept all God has said.

"Do you want to be made well?" (John 5:6). It is Jesus who asks this question. Give Him your answer. He will hear, and He will answer.

CHAPTER TWENTY-FOUR

THE WORDS OF THIS LIFE

The fifth chapter of Acts is full of glorious truths that I desire to share with you today. Let's read the first twenty verses of this wonderful chapter:

But a certain man named Ananias, with Sapphira his wife, sold a possession. And he kept back part of the proceeds, his wife also being aware of it, and brought a certain part and laid it at the apostles' feet. But Peter said, "Ananias, why has Satan filled your heart to lie to the Holy Spirit and keep back part of the price of the land for yourself? While it remained, was it not your own? And after it was sold, was it not in your own control? Why have you conceived this thing in your heart? You have not lied to men but to God." Then Ananias, hearing these words, fell down and breathed his last. So great fear came upon all those who heard these things. And the young men arose and wrapped him up, carried him out, and buried him. Now it was about three hours later when his wife came in, not knowing what had happened. And Peter answered her, "Tell me whether you sold the land for so much?" She said, "Yes, for so much." Then Peter said to her, "How is it that you have agreed together to test the Spirit of the Lord? Look, the feet of those who have buried your husband are at the door, and they will carry you out." Then immediately she fell down at his feet and breathed her last. And the young men came in and found her dead, and carrying her out, buried her by her husband. So great fear came upon all the church and upon all who heard these things. And through the hands of the apostles many signs and wonders were done among the people. And they were all with one accord in Solomon's Porch. Yet none of the rest dared join them, but the people esteemed them highly. And believers were increasingly added to the

Lord, multitudes of both men and women, so that they brought the sick out into the streets and laid them on beds and couches, that at least the shadow of Peter passing by might fall on some of them. Also a multitude gathered from the surrounding cities to Jerusalem, bringing sick people and those who were tormented by unclean spirits, and they were all healed. Then the high priest rose up, and all those who were with him (which is the sect of the Sadducees), and they were filled with indignation, and laid their hands on the apostles and put them in the common prison. But at night an angel of the Lord opened the prison doors and brought them out, and said, "Go, stand in the temple and speak to the people all the words of this life." (Acts 5:1–20)

Notice this expression that the Lord gives of the gospel message—*"the words of this life."* It is the most wonderful life possible—the life of faith in the Son of God. This is the life where God is present all the time. He is all around, and He is within. It is the life of many revelations and of many manifestations of God's Holy Spirit, a life in which the Lord is continually seen, known, felt, and heard. It is a life without spiritual death, for *"we have passed from death to life"* (1 John 3:14). The very life of God has come within us. Where that life is in its fullness, disease cannot exist. It would take me a month to tell what there is in this wonderful life. Everyone can enter in and possess and be possessed by this life.

It is possible for you to be within the vicinity of this life and yet miss it. It is possible for you to be in a place where God is pouring out His Spirit and yet miss the blessing that God is so willing to bestow. This is all due to a lack of revelation and a misunderstanding of the infinite grace of God and of *"the God of all grace"* (1 Pet. 5:10), who is willing to give to all who will reach out the hand of faith. This life that He freely bestows is a gift. Some think they have to earn it, and they miss the whole thing. Oh, for a simple faith to receive all that God so lavishly offers! You can never be ordinary from the day you receive this life from above. You become extraordinary, filled with the extraordinary power of our extraordinary God.

WHY DID ANANIAS AND SAPPHIRA DIE?

Ananias and Sapphira were in the wonderful revival that God gave to the early church, yet they missed it. They thought that possibly the thing might fail. They wanted to have a reserve for themselves in case it turned out to be a failure.

There are many people like them today. Many people make vows to God in times of great crisis in their lives but fail to keep their vows, and in the end they become spiritually bankrupt. Blessed is the man "*who swears to his own hurt and does not change*" (Ps. 15:4), who keeps the vow he has made to God, who is willing to lay his all at God's feet. The man who does this never becomes a lean soul. God has promised to "*strengthen* [his] *bones*" (Isa. 58:11). There is no dry place for such a man. He is always "*fresh and flourishing*" (Ps. 92:14), and he becomes stronger and stronger. It pays to trust God with all and to hold back nothing.

I wish I could make you see how great a God we have. Ananias and Sapphira were really doubting God and were questioning whether this work that He had begun would go on. They wanted to get some glory for selling their property, but because of their lack of faith, they kept part of the proceeds in reserve in case the work of God were to fail.

Many are doubting whether this Pentecostal revival will go on. Do you think this Pentecostal work will stop? Never. For fifteen years I have been in constant revival, and I am sure that it will never stop. When George Stephenson built his first locomotive engine, he took his sister Mary to see it. She looked at it and said to her brother, "George, it'll never go." He said to her, "Get in, Mary." She said again, "It'll never go." He said to her, "We'll see; you get in." Mary at last got in. The whistle blew, there was a puff and a rattle, and the engine started off. Then Mary cried out, "George, it'll never stop! It'll never stop!"

People are looking at this Pentecostal revival, and they are very critical. They are saying, "It'll never go." However, when they are induced to come into the work, they one and all say, "It'll never stop." This revival of God is sweeping on and on, and there is no stopping the current of life, of love, of inspiration, and of power.

INTERPRETATION OF A MESSAGE IN TONGUES: "It is the living Word who has brought this. It is the Lamb in the midst, 'the same yesterday, today, and forever.'"

God has brought unlimited resources for everyone. Do not doubt. Hear with the ear of faith. God is in the midst. See that it is God who has set forth what you see and hear today (Acts 2:33).

I want you to see that in the early church, which was controlled by the power of the Holy Spirit, it was not possible for a lie to exist. The moment it came into the church, there was instant death. And as the power of the Holy Spirit increases in these days of the latter rain, it will be impossible for any man to remain in our midst with a lying spirit. God will purify the church. The Word of God will be in such power in healing and other spiritual manifestations, that great fear will be upon all those who see these things.

To the natural mind, it seems a small thing for Ananias and Sapphira to want to have a little to fall back on, but I want to tell you that you can please God and get things from God only through a living faith. God never fails. God never can fail.

OUR MERCIFUL AND HEALING GOD

When I was in Bergen, Norway, there came to the meeting a young woman who was employed at the hospital as a nurse. A big cancerous tumor had developed on her nose. The nose was enlarged and had become black and very inflamed. She came for prayer, and I asked her, "What is your condition?" She said, "I dare not touch my nose; it gives me so much pain." I said to all the people, "I want you to look at this nurse and notice her terrible condition. I believe that our God is merciful, that He is faithful, and that He will bring to nothing this condition that the Devil has brought about. I am going to curse this disease in the all-powerful name of Jesus. The pain will go. I believe God will give us an exhibition of His grace, and I will ask this young woman to come to the meeting tomorrow night and declare what God has done for her."

Oh, the awfulness of sin! Oh, the awfulness of the power of sin! Oh, the awfulness of the consequences of the Fall! When I see a cancerous tumor, I ask, "Can this be the work of God?" May God help me to show you that this is the work of the Devil, and to show you the way out.

I do not condemn people who sin. I don't scold people. I know what is behind the sin. I know that Satan is always going about *"like a roaring lion, seeking whom he may devour"* (1 Pet. 5:8). I always remember the patience and love of the Lord Jesus Christ. When they brought to Him a woman whom they had taken in adultery, telling Him that they had caught her in the very act, He simply stooped down and wrote on the ground. Then He quietly said,

"He who is without sin among you, let him throw a stone at her first" (John 8:7). I have never seen a man without sin. *"All have sinned and fall short of the glory of God"* (Rom. 3:23). But I read in this blessed gospel message that God *"has laid on Him* [Jesus] *the iniquity of us all"* (Isa. 53:6).

When I see an evil condition, I feel that I must stand in my position and rebuke the condition. I laid my hands on the nose of that suffering nurse and cursed the evil power that was causing her so much distress. The next night the place was packed. The people were so jammed together that it seemed as if there was not room for one more to enter that house. How God's rain fell upon us! How good God is, so full of grace and so full of love. I saw the nurse in the audience and cried out, "Here's the woman whose nose I prayed for!" I asked her to come forward, and she came and showed everyone what God had done. He had perfectly healed her. Oh, I tell you, He is just the same Jesus. He is just the same today (Heb. 13:8). All things are possible if you dare to trust God (Mark 9:23).

CHURCH GROWTH AND NUMEROUS HEALINGS

When the power of God came so mightily upon the early church, even in the death of Ananias and Sapphira, great fear came upon all the people. And when we are in the presence of God, when God is working mightily in our midst, there comes a great fear, a reverence, a holiness of life, a purity that fears to displease God. We read that no man dared to join them, but God added to the church those who were being saved. I would rather have God add to our Pentecostal church than have all the town join it. God added daily to His own church.

The next thing that happened was that people became so assured that God was working that they knew that anything would be possible, and they brought their sick into the streets and laid them on beds and mats so that at least the shadow of Peter passing by might fall on them. Multitudes of sick people and those oppressed with evil spirits were brought to the apostles, and God healed every one of them. I do not believe that it was the shadow of Peter that healed them, but the power of God was mightily present, and the faith of the people was so aroused that they joined with one heart to believe God. God will always meet people on the basis of faith.

REVIVALS IN NORWAY AND IRELAND

God's tide is rising all over the earth. I had been preaching in Stavanger, Norway, and was very tired and wanted a few hours' rest. I went to my next speaking engagement, arriving at about 9:30 in the morning. My first meeting was to be at night. I said to my interpreter, "After we have had something to eat, let's go down to the sea." We spent three or four hours down by the sea and at about 4:30 returned. We found the end of the street, which had a narrow entrance, just filled with automobiles, wagons, and so on, containing invalids and sick people of every kind. I went up to the house and was told that the house was full of sick people, too. It reminded me of the scene that we read of in the fifth chapter of Acts. I began praying for the people in the street, and God began to heal the people. And how wonderfully He healed those people who were in the house! When we sat down to eat, the telephone rang, and someone at the other end was saying, "What are we going to do? The town hall is already full; the police cannot control things."

Beloved, the tide is rising; the fields are ripe for harvest (John 4:35). God gave us a wonderful revival. I want to be in a mighty revival. I was in one mighty revival in Wales, and I long to be in a great revival that will eclipse anything we have ever thought of. I have faith to believe it is coming.

In that little Norwegian town the people were jammed together, and oh, how the power of God fell upon us! A cry went up from everyone, "Isn't this the revival?" Revival is coming. The breath of the Almighty is coming. The breath of God shows every defect, and as it comes flowing in like a river, everybody will need a fresh anointing, a fresh cleansing of the blood. You can depend on it that that breath is upon us.

One time I was at a meeting in Ireland. Many sick people were carried to that meeting, and helpless ones were brought there. Many people in that place were seeking the baptism in the Holy Spirit. Some of them had been seeking for years. There were sinners there who were under mighty conviction. A moment came when the breath of God swept through the meeting. In about ten minutes every sinner in the place was saved. Everyone who had been seeking the Holy Spirit was baptized, and every sick one was healed. God is a reality, and His power can never fail. As our faith reaches out, God will meet us, and the same rain will fall. It is the

Blood

same blood that cleanses, the same power, the same Holy Spirit, and the same Jesus made real through the power of the Holy Spirit! What would happen if we would believe God?

The precious blood of the Lord Jesus Christ is effective; right now it will cleanse your heart and put this life, this wonderful life of God, within you. The blood will make you every bit whole if you dare to believe. The healing power of the blessed Son of God is right here for you, but so few will touch Him. The Bible is full of entreaty for you to come and partake and receive the grace, the power, the strength, the righteousness, and the full redemption of Jesus Christ. He never fails to hear when we believe. This same Jesus is in our midst to touch and to free you.

A LAME MAN AND HIS SON

In one place where I was, a lame man was brought to me who had been in bed for two years, with no hope of recovery. He was brought thirty miles to the meeting, and he came up on crutches to be prayed for. His boy was also afflicted in the knees, and they had four crutches between the two of them. The man's face was full of torture. But there is healing power in the Lord, and He never fails to heal when we believe. In the name of Jesus—that name so full of power—I put my hand down that leg that was so diseased. The man threw down his crutches, and all were astonished as they saw him walking up and down without aid. The little boy called out to his father, "Papa, me; papa, me, me, me!" The little boy who had two withered knees wanted the same touch. And the same Jesus was there to bring a real deliverance to the little captive. He was completely healed.

These were legs that were touched. If God will stretch out His mighty power to loose afflicted legs, what mercy will He extend to that soul of yours that must exist forever? Hear the Lord say,

> *The Spirit of the LORD is upon Me, because He has anointed Me to preach the gospel to the poor; He has sent Me to heal the brokenhearted, to proclaim liberty to the captives and recovery of sight to the blind, to set at liberty those who are oppressed.*
> (Luke 4:18)

He invites you, *"Come to Me, all you who labor and are heavy laden, and I will give you rest"* (Matt. 11:28). God is willing in His great mercy to touch your limbs with His mighty power, and if He is willing to do this, how much more eager He is to deliver you from the power of Satan and to make you a child of the King! How much more necessary it is for you to be healed of your soul sickness than of your bodily ailments! And God is willing to give the double cure.

A Young Man Who Had Fallen into Sin

I was passing through the city of London one time, and Mr. Mundell, the secretary of the Pentecostal Missionary Union, found out that I was there. He arranged for me to meet him at a certain place at 3:30 in the afternoon. I was to meet a certain boy whose father and mother lived in the city of Salisbury. They had sent this young man to London to take care of their business. He had been a leader in Sunday school work, but he had been betrayed and had fallen. Sin is awful, and *"the wages of sin is death"* (Rom. 6:23). But there is another side—*"the gift of God is eternal life"* (v. 23).

This young man was in great distress; he had contracted a horrible disease and was afraid to tell anyone. There was nothing but death ahead for him. When the father and mother found out about his condition, they suffered inexpressible grief.

When we got to the house, Brother Mundell suggested that we begin to pray. I said, "God does not say so. We are not going to pray yet. I want to quote a Scripture: *'Fools, because of their transgression, and because of their iniquities, were afflicted. Their soul abhorred all manner of food, and they drew near to the gates of death'* (Ps. 107:17)." The young man cried out, "I am that fool!" He broke down and told us the story of his fall. Oh, if men would only repent and confess their sins, how God would stretch out His hand to heal and to save! The moment that young man repented, a great abscess burst, and God sent power into that young man's life, giving him a mighty deliverance.

God is gracious and is *"not willing that any should perish"* (2 Pet. 3:9). How many are willing to make a clean break from their sins? I tell you that the moment you do this, God will open heaven. It is an easy thing for Him to save your soul and heal your disease if you will only come and take shelter today in *"the secret place of the Most High"* (Ps. 91:1). He will satisfy you with a long life and show you His salvation (Ps. 91:16). *"In* [His] *presence is fullness of joy; at* [His] *right hand are pleasures forevermore"* (Ps. 16:11). There is full redemption for all through the precious blood of the Son of God.

7 years

there was deceit in his spirit. soul
Fell into temptation — transgressed
    put me in a terrible place, dangerous
    • financially - poverty, unemployment
    • legally - property, debt
    • physical danger fires, speeding

Humble, loving   • self - deceived -
Prayer   and me
Loved Word   • pride
Worship   • lies
Hospitality   • greed - gambling
Giving   pride
Serving   gave over to Satan
Joyful   gambling
Affectionate   addictions

                                        pride
Photography   pursuit of riches
                 self

CHAPTER TWENTY-FIVE

THE ACTIVE LIFE OF THE SPIRIT-FILLED BELIEVER

These are the last days, the days of the falling away (2 Thess. 2:3). These are days when Satan is having a great deal of power. But we must keep in mind that Satan has no power except as he is allowed.

It is a great thing to know that God is loosing you from the world, loosing you from a thousand things. You must seek to have the mind of God in all things. If you don't, you will stop His working.

We will never know the mind of God until we learn to know the voice of God. The striking thing about Moses is that it took him forty years to learn human wisdom, forty years to know his helplessness, and forty years to live in the power of God. It took 120 years to teach that man, and sometimes it seems to me that it will take many years to bring us to the place where we can discern the voice of God, the leadings of God, and all His will concerning us.

I see that all revelation, all illumination, everything that God had in Christ was to be brought forth into perfect light so that we might be able to live the same way, produce the same things, and in every activity be children of God with power. It must be so. We must not limit the Holy One. And we must clearly see that God brought us forth to make us supernatural, so that we might be changed all the time along the lines of the supernatural; so that we might every day so live in the Spirit that all of the revelations of God are just like a canvas thrown before our eyes, on which we see clearly, step by step, all the divine will of God.

FREE IN THE SPIRIT

Any assembly that puts its hand on the working of the Spirit will surely dry up. The assembly must be as free in the Spirit as possible, and you must allow a certain amount of extravagance when people are getting through to God. Unless we are very wise, we can easily interfere with and quench the power of God that is upon us. It is an evident fact that one man in a meeting, filled with unbelief, can make a place for the Devil to have a seat. And it is very true that if we are not careful, we may quench the spirit of some person who is innocent but incapable of helping himself. *"We then that are strong ought to bear the infirmities of the weak"* (Rom. 15:1 KJV). If you want an assembly full of life, you must have one in which the Spirit of God is manifested. And in order to keep at the boiling point, you must be as simple as babes; you must be *"wise as serpents and harmless as doves"* (Matt. 10:16).

I always ask God for a leading of grace. It takes grace to be in a meeting because it is so easy, if you are not careful, to get on the natural side. If the preacher has lost the anointing, he will be well repaid if he will repent and get right with God and get the anointing back. It never pays to be less than spiritual. We must have a divine language, and the language must be of God. Beloved, if you come into perfect line with the grace of God, one thing will certainly take place in your life. You will change from that old position of the world where you are judging everybody and not trusting anybody, and you will come into a place where you will have a heart that will believe all things, a heart that under no circumstances retaliates when you are insulted.

THE SWEET TOUCH OF HEAVEN

I know that many of you think many times before you speak once. Here is a great word: *"For your obedience has become known to all. Therefore I am glad on your behalf; but I want you to be wise in what is good, and simple concerning evil"* (Rom. 16:19). Innocent. No inward corruption or defilement, that is, not full of distrust, but just a holy, divine likeness of Jesus that dares believe that almighty God will surely watch over all. Hallelujah! *"No evil shall befall you, nor shall any plague come near your dwelling. For He shall give His angels charge over you, to keep you in all your ways"* (Ps. 91:10–11). The child of God who is rocked in the bosom of the Father has the sweetest touch of heaven, and the honey of the Word is always in his life.

If the saints only knew how precious they are in the sight of God (Isa. 43:4), they would scarcely be able to sleep for thinking of His watchful, loving care. Oh, He is a precious Jesus! He is a lovely Savior! He is divine in all His attitudes toward us, and He makes our hearts burn. There is nothing like it. "Oh," said the two men who had traveled to Emmaus with Jesus, "didn't our hearts burn within us as He walked with us and talked with us?" (See Luke 24:32.) Oh, beloved, it must be so today.

Always keep in mind the fact that the Holy Spirit must bring manifestation. We must understand that the Holy Spirit is breath, the Holy Spirit is a person, and it is the most marvelous thing to me to know that this Holy Spirit power can be in every part of our bodies. You can feel it from the crown of your head to the soles of your feet. Oh, it is lovely to be burning all over with the Holy Spirit! And when that takes place, the tongue must give forth the glory and the praise.

You must be in the place of magnifying the Lord. The Holy Spirit is the great Magnifier of Jesus, the great Illuminator of Jesus. After the Holy Spirit comes in, it is impossible to keep your tongue still. Why, you would burst if you didn't give Him utterance! What about a silent baptized soul? Such a person is not to be found in the Scriptures. You will find that when you speak to God in the new tongue He gives you, you enter into a close communion with Him never experienced before. Talk about preaching! I would like to know how it will be possible for all the people filled with the Holy Spirit to stop preaching. Even the sons and daughters must prophesy (Joel 2:28). After the Holy Spirit comes in, a man is in a new order in God. You will find it so real that you will want to sing, talk, laugh, and shout. We are in a strange place when the Holy Spirit comes in.

If the incoming of the Spirit is lovely, what must be the outflow? The incoming is only to be an outflow.

I am very interested in scenery. When I was in Switzerland, I wasn't satisfied until I went to the top of the mountain, though I like the valleys also. On the summit of the mountain, the sun beats on the snow and sends the water trickling down the mountain right through to the meadows. Go there and see if you can stop the water. It is the same way in the spiritual realm. God begins with the divine flow of His eternal power, which is the Holy Spirit, and you cannot stop it.

SPIRITUAL GIANTS

We must always clearly see that the baptism in the Spirit must make us ministering spirits.

Peter and John had been baptized only a short time when they met the lame man at the temple. Did they know what they had? No. I challenge you to try to know what you have. No one knows what he has in the baptism in the Holy Spirit. You have no conception of it. You cannot measure it by any human standards. It is greater than any man can imagine; consequently, those two disciples had no idea what they had. After they had been baptized in the Holy Spirit, they came down to the Gate Beautiful. There they saw the man sitting who had been lame for over forty years. What was the first thing that happened after they saw him? Ministry. What was the second? Operation. What was the third? Manifestation, of course. (See Acts 3:1–10.) It could not be otherwise. You will always find that this order in the Scriptures will be carried out in everybody.

I clearly see that we ought to have spiritual giants in the earth, mighty in understanding, amazing in activity, always having a wonderful testimony because of their faith-filled activity. I find instead that there are many people who perhaps have better discernment than the average believer, better knowledge of the Word than the average believer, but they have failed to put their discernment and knowledge into practice, so the gifts lie dormant. I am here to help you to begin doing mighty acts in the power of God through the gifts of the Spirit. You will find that what I am speaking on is from personal knowledge derived from wonderful experiences in many lands. The man who is filled with the Holy Spirit is always acting. The first verse of the Acts of the Apostles says, *"Jesus began both to do and teach."* Jesus had to begin to do, and so must we.

HELP FOR THE SUFFERING

Beloved, we must see that the baptism in the Holy Spirit is an activity with an outward manifestation. When I was in Norway,

God was mightily moving there, though I had to talk through an interpreter. God always worked in a wonderful way. One day we met a man who stopped the three men I was with, one being the interpreter. I was walking on, but I saw he was in a dilemma, so I turned back and said to the interpreter, "What is the trouble?" "This man," he said, "is so full of neuralgia that he is almost blind, and he is in a terrible state." Just as soon as they finished the conversation, I said to the spirit that was afflicting him, "Come out of him in the name of Jesus." And the man said, "It is all gone! It is all gone! I am free." Ah, beloved, we have no conception of what God has for us!

I will tell you what happened in Sydney, Australia. A man with a cane passed by a friend and me. He had to get down and then twist over, and the torture on his face made a deep impression on my soul. I asked myself, "Is it right to pass by this man?" So I said to my friend, "There is a man in awful distress, and I cannot go farther. I must speak to him." I went over to this man and said to him, "You seem to be in great trouble." "Yes," he said, "I am no good and never will be." I said, "You see that hotel? Be in front of that door in five minutes, and I will pray for you, and you will be able to stand as straight as any man here." This is along the lines of activity in the faith of Jesus.

I came back after paying a bill, and he was there. I will never forget him wondering if he was going to be trapped, or why a man would stop him on the street and tell him he would be made to stand straight. However, I had said it, so it had to be. If you say anything, you must stand with God to make it so. Never say anything for bravado, or anything that you do not have the right to say. Always be sure of your ground, and be sure that you are honoring God. If there is anything about the situation that will make *you* anything, it will bring you sorrow. Your whole ministry has to be along the lines of grace and blessing.

We helped him up the two steps, took him to the elevator, and got him upstairs. It was difficult to get him from the elevator to my room, as though Satan was making the last attempt for his life, but we got him there. In five minutes' time this man walked out of that room with his body as straight as any man's in this place. He walked perfectly and declared he hadn't a pain in his body.

Oh, beloved, it is ministry; it is operation; it is manifestation! Those are three of the leading principles of the baptism in the Holy

Spirit. And we must see to it that God is producing these three through us.

The Bible is the Word of God. It has the truths, and whatever people may say of them, they stand stationary, unmovable. Not one word of all His good promises will fail (1 Kings 8:56). His Word will come forth. In heaven it is settled (Ps. 119:89). On earth the fact must be made manifest that He is the God of everlasting power.

BEGIN TO ACT

God wants manifestation, and He wants His glory to be seen. He wants us all to be filled with the thought that He can look upon us and delight in us subduing the world unto Him. You are going to miss a great deal if you don't begin to act. But once you begin to act in the order of God, you will find that God establishes your faith and from that day starts you along the line of the promises. When will you begin?

In a place in England, I was speaking about faith and what would take place if we believed God. Many things happened. When I left that place, it appeared that one man who worked in the coal mine had heard me. He had trouble with a stiff knee. He said to his wife, "I cannot help but think every day that that message of Wigglesworth's was to stir us to do something. I cannot get away from it. All the men in the pit know how I walk with a stiff knee, and you know how you have wrapped it with yards of flannel. Well, I am going to act. You have to be the congregation." He got his wife in front of him. "I am going to act and do just as Wigglesworth did." He got hold of his leg unmercifully, saying, "Come out, you devils; come out in the name of Jesus! Now, Jesus, help me. Come out, you devils; come out." Then he said, "Wife, they are gone! They are gone! This is too good. I am going to act now." So he went to his place of worship, and all the coal miners were there. It was a prayer meeting. As he told them this story, these men became delighted. They said, "Jack, come over here and help me." And Jack went. As soon as he was through in one home, he was invited to another; he loosed these people from the pains they had gotten in the coal mine.

Ah, brothers and sisters, we have no idea what God has for us if we will only begin! But, oh, the grace we need! We may make a mistake. If you do this work outside of Him, if you do it for yourself, and if you want to be someone, it will be a failure. We will be able to succeed only as we do the work in the name of Jesus. Oh, the love that God's Son can put into us if we are only humble enough, weak enough, and helpless enough to know that unless He does it, it will not be done! *"Whatever things you ask when you pray, believe that you receive them, and you will have them"* (Mark 11:24).

Live in the Spirit. Walk in the Spirit. Walk in communion with the Spirit. Talk with God. All leadings of the divine order are for you. I pray that if there are any who have turned to their own way and have made God second, they will come to repentance. Let go of what is earthly, and take hold of God's ideals. God will bring you to an end of yourself. Begin with God this moment.

Smith Wigglesworth on

THE HOLY
SPIRIT

CONTENTS

CHAPTER ONE

THE BAPTISM IN THE HOLY SPIRIT

How glad I am that God has baptized me in the Holy Spirit. What a wonderful difference it has made in my life. God has not promised that as Christians we will always feel very wonderful, but He has promised that if we stand on His Word, He will make His Word real in our lives. First we exercise faith; then it becomes fact. However, there are plenty of feelings in the fact, I assure you. God fills us with His own precious joy.

Samson is recorded in the eleventh chapter of Hebrews as being a man of faith. He was a man who was chosen by God from his mother's womb, but the power of God came upon him only on certain occasions. Yet we who have received the fullness of the Holy Spirit, the Comforter, may now have the anointing that abides forever.

The Lord has promised that we will have life and have it abundantly (John 10:10). Look at the fifth chapter of Romans and see how many times the expression *"much more"* is used. (See, for example, Romans 5:9.) Oh, that we might take this abundant grace of God, revel in the Word of God, and be so full of expectancy that we will have this *"much more"* manifested as fruit in our lives.

THE FULLNESS OF THE SPIRIT

Some people realize that they have had the power of the Lord upon them and yet have failed to receive the fullness of the Spirit. Friend, what about you? God, in His love and kindness, has listed

Samson in Hebrews 11 as an example for us. There came a time when, because of Samson's sin, his eyes were put out. His hair had been cut off, and he had lost his strength. He tried to break free of his bonds, but the Philistines got him. However, his hair grew again. The Philistines wanted him to entertain for them, but he prayed a prayer, and God answered. Oh, that we might turn to God and pray this prayer, as Samson did: *"O Lord GOD, remember me, I pray! Strengthen me, I pray, just this once, O God"* (Judg. 16:28). God is *"plenteous in mercy"* (Ps. 86:5 KJV), and if you will turn to Him with true repentance, He will forgive you. Repentance means getting back to God.

When Samson took hold of the pillars upon which the Philistine house stood, he pulled the walls down (Judg. 16:29–30). God can give you strength, and you can get hold of the posts, and He will work through you. No matter what kind of a backslider you have been, there is power in the blood. *"The blood of Jesus Christ His Son cleanses us from all sin"* (1 John 1:7). Oh, if I could only tell you how God so wonderfully restored me! I returned to my *"first love"* (Rev. 2:4), and He filled me with the Holy Spirit.

I want to draw your attention to a few verses from the second chapter of the Acts of the Apostles:

> *When the Day of Pentecost had fully come, they were all with one accord in one place. And suddenly there came a sound from heaven, as of a rushing mighty wind, and it filled the whole house where they were sitting. Then there appeared to them divided tongues, as of fire, and one sat upon each of them. And they were all filled with the Holy Spirit and began to speak with other tongues, as the Spirit gave them utterance.*
> (Acts 2:1–4)

What a wonderful, divine position God intends us all to have, to be filled with the Holy Spirit. It is something so remarkable, so divine; it is, as it were, a great open door into all the treasury of the Most High. As the Spirit comes like *"rain upon the mown grass"* (Ps. 72:6 KJV), He turns the barrenness into greenness and freshness and life. Oh, hallelujah! God wants you to know that there is a place you may come to, in which you are dispensed with and God comes to be your assurance and sustaining power spiritually—until your dryness is turned into springs, until your barrenness becomes floods, until your whole life becomes vitalized by heaven, until heaven sweeps through you and dwells within you and turns everything inside out, until you are so absolutely filled with divine possibilities that you begin to live as a new creation. The Spirit of the living God sweeps through all weaknesses.

Beloved, God the Holy Spirit wants to bring us to a great revelation of life. He wants us to be *"filled with all the fullness of God"* (Eph. 3:19). One of the most beautiful pictures we have in the Scriptures is of the Trinity. The Trinity was made manifest right on the banks of the Jordan River when Jesus was baptized. I want you to see how God unfolded heaven and how heaven and earth became the habitation of the Trinity. The voice of God came from the heavens as He looked at His well-beloved Son coming out of the waters, and there the Spirit was manifested in the shape of a dove. The dove is the only bird without gall; it is a creature so timid that at the least thing it moves and is afraid. No person can be baptized with the Holy Spirit and have bitterness, that is, gall.

A DOUBLE CURE

blood
water

My friend, you need a double cure. You first need saving and cleansing and then the baptism of the Holy Spirit, until the old man never rises anymore, until you are absolutely dead to sin and alive to God by His Spirit (Rom. 6:11) and know that *"old things have passed away"* (2 Cor. 5:17). When the Holy Spirit gets possession of a person, he is a new man entirely—his whole being becomes saturated with divine power. We become a habitation of Him who is all light, all revelation, all power, and all love. Yes, God the Holy Spirit is manifested within us in such a way that it is glorious.

There was a certain rich man in London whose business flourished. He used to count all his many assets, but he was still troubled inside; he didn't know what to do. Walking around his large building, he came upon a boy who was the doorkeeper and found the boy whistling. Looking at him, he sized up the whole situation completely and went back to his office again and puzzled over the matter. He went back to his business but he could find no peace. His bank could not help him; his money, his success, could not help him. He had an aching void. He was helpless within. My friend, having the world without having God is like being a whitewashed sepulcher. (See Matthew 23:27.)

When he could get no rest, he exclaimed, "I will go and see what the boy is doing." Again he went and found him whistling. "I want you to come into my office," he said. When they entered the office, the man said, "Tell me, what makes you so happy and cheerful?" "Oh," replied the boy, "I used to be so miserable until I went to a little mission and heard about Jesus. Then I was saved and filled with the Holy Spirit. I am always whistling inside; if I am not whistling, I am singing. I am just full!"

This rich man obtained the address of the mission from the boy, went to the services, and sat beside the door. But the power of God moved so strongly that when the altar call was given, he responded. God saved him and, a few days afterward, filled him with the Holy Spirit. The man found himself at his desk, shouting, "Oh, hallelujah!"

> I know the Lord, I know the Lord,
> I know the Lord's laid His hand on me.
> I know the Lord, I know the Lord,
> I know the Lord's laid His hand on me.

Oh, this blessed Son of God wants to fill us with such glory until our whole body is aflame with the power of the Holy Spirit. I see there is *"much more"* (Rom. 5:9). Glory to God! My daughter asked some African boys to tell us the difference between being saved and being filled with the Holy Spirit. "Ah," they said, "when we were saved, it was very good; but when we received the Holy Spirit, it was more so." Many of you have never received the "more so."

After the Holy Spirit comes upon you, you will have power. God will mightily move within your life; the power of the Holy Spirit will overshadow you, inwardly moving you until you know there is a divine plan different from anything that you have had in your life before.

Has He come? He is going to come to you. I am expecting that God will so manifest His presence and power that He will show you the necessity of receiving the Holy Spirit. Also, God will heal the people who need healing. Everything is to be had now: salvation, sanctification, the fullness of the Holy Spirit, and healing. God is working mightily by the power of His Spirit, bringing to us a fullness of His perfect redemption until every soul may know that God has all power.

CHAPTER TWO

FOUNDATIONAL TRUTHS
OF THE BAPTISM

What it means for people to have faith! What it will mean when we all have faith! We know that as soon as faith is in perfect operation, we will be in the perfect place where God is manifested right before our eyes. The pure in heart will see God (Matt. 5:8), and all the steps of purity are a divine appointment of more faith. The more purity, the more faith.

When Lazarus died and Jesus knew that Mary, Martha, and everyone around them had lost confidence and faith, He turned to the Father in prayer and said, *"Father,...I know that You always hear Me"* (John 11:41–42). Jesus commanded Lazarus to come out of the tomb; death had to give him up, and everything had to come to pass as He said.

Fellowship, purity, unity: these things reflect a living cooperation in which we are being changed from faith to faith. May the Lord grant to you this thought today: How may I more and more abandon myself from any earthly, human fellowship, until I am absolutely so bound to God that God has the right-of-way to the throne of my heart, until the seat of affection is blessedly purified, until there is no room for anything except the Son of God, who is the Author and Finisher of faith (Heb. 12:2)? Then Christ will be manifested in your flesh, destroying everything that is outside of Him.

When the Spirit of the Lord is upon us, we do not impart words but life. Words are only for the purpose of understanding what the Word is, but the Word itself is really life-giving. So when we are covered with the Spirit, we are imparting life. When we are filled with the Holy Spirit, every time we get up, we impart life. If you are ready to receive this life, it is amazing how it will quicken your mortal body every time you touch this life. (See Romans 8:11.) It is divine life. It is the life of the Son of God.

I want to lay down a foundation for understanding the baptism of the Holy Spirit by explaining why Jesus emphasized the baptism, how to receive the baptism, and the reason for the baptism. Jesus expressed all these things to His disciples. I want to dwell on this in order to provide you with a real foundation of the truth of the baptism. In this way, you will never wait before God without a clear understanding of what the baptism is for, what you are waiting for, and so on.

To begin with, we find a remarkable word from John the Baptist in Matthew:

> *I indeed baptize you with water unto repentance, but He who is coming after me is mightier than I, whose sandals I am not worthy to carry. He will baptize you with the Holy Spirit and fire.* (Matt. 3:11)

This is the statement of a man who was so filled with the Spirit of God that his very voice became the active process of a divine flame that moved the whole of creation that day. From east to west and north to south, he spoke by the power of the Holy Spirit until people gathered at the Jordan in multitudes, drawn by this voice of one crying in the Spirit. (See Matthew 3:3.) What a remarkable word he gave!

IMMERSED WITH THE SPIRIT

Most of us have seen water baptism in action so often that we know what it means. But I want you to see that God's very great desire is for you to be covered with the baptism of the Holy Spirit. He wants you to be so immersed and covered and flooded with the light and revelation of the Holy Spirit, the third person of the Trinity, that your whole body will be filled, and not only filled but also covered over until you walk in the presence of the power of God.

INTERPRETATION OF A MESSAGE IN TONGUES: "God's life for your life, His light for your darkness, His revelation for your

166

closed brain. He brings forth a new order in divine power until you will be changed into another man, until your very nature will be burning with a burning within you of divine purifying until you are like one who has come from the presence of the Glory to exhibit truths that God has revealed to you. In your lot, in your day, the power of another covering, girding you with the power of truth."

Oh, Jesus, let it come to pass that we never do anything in our own strength. Let all that we do be done to the glory of the Lord!

COME TO THE WATERS

We cannot stop there; that was the first breath of revelation of what would take place for individuals—yes, and for communities and for the world.

Let us turn now to John:

> *On the last day, that great day of the feast, Jesus stood and cried out, saying, "If anyone thirsts, let him come to Me and drink. He who believes in Me, as the Scripture has said, out of his heart will flow rivers of living water." But this He spoke concerning the Spirit, whom those believing in Him would receive; for the Holy Spirit was not yet given, because Jesus was not yet glorified.* (John 7:37–39)

Jesus saw all the people at the Feast of Tabernacles, and He not only had a great ability to scrutinize, to unfold the inward thoughts and intents of the heart, but He also saw things at a glance; He took in a situation in just a moment's time. He knew when the people were about to starve and die by the wayside, and He supplied all their needs.

We must not forget that He was filled with the Holy Spirit. He was lovely because He was full of the divine inflow of the life of God. Look at how He dealt with this situation. He saw the people who were at Jerusalem at the feast, and they were going home dissatisfied. My Lord could not have anybody dissatisfied. My Lord could never be satisfied when anybody was dissatisfied.

It is not in the canon of the history of the spiritual fellowship between heaven and earth that you should be famished, naked, full of discord, full of evil, full of disorder, full of sensuality, full of

167

carnality. That was what was taking place at the feast, and they came away hungrier than they were before. Jesus saw them like that, and He said, "*'Ho! Everyone who thirsts, come to the waters'* (Isa. 55:1). Come to Me, you who are thirsty, and I will give you drink."

Oh, the Master could give! The Master had it to give. Beloved, He is here to give, and I am sure He will give.

> **INTERPRETATION OF A MESSAGE IN TONGUES:** "God, First, Last, Alpha, Omega, Beginning and End. He is at the root of all things this morning. He will disturb what needs to be disturbed; He will unfold what needs to be unfolded; He will turn to death what needs to be broken and put to death. He will put a spring within you and lift you to life. God will deal with you in mercy but in severity, because all divine love is a sword and 'divides asunder soul and spirit, joint and marrow,' and deals with the inward desires of the heart."

Yes, the heavy hand of God is full of mercy. The *"two-edged sword"* is full of dividing (Heb. 4:12). His quickening Spirit puts to death everything that needs to die so that He might transform you by the resurrection of His life.

And this is the order of the Spirit. Can't you see how He says, "Come, thirsty one; come, needy one. I will give you a drink that will create a thirst in you that will prepare you for the coming of the Holy Spirit, that will make the spring that I give you a river of living water"?

Which do you have? Do you have the spring or the river? The spring is good because it has the same kind of water as the river. But the river means plentifulness, and the Holy Spirit is the river. Jesus was portraying, forecasting, sending out these wonderful words so that He might prepare the people for all the fullness that had to come forth.

BE EXTRAORDINARY

I want you to go away from these meetings just infused. Make up your mind that you won't be ordinary. You have an extraordinary God who gives revelation. Be determined that you won't go away as you came but that you will go away endued, infused with the living touch of the flame of the Master's torch.

These are not ordinary meetings; God would not want a meeting to be ordinary. I refuse to be an ordinary man. "Why?" you ask. Because I have an extraordinary God who makes extraordinary people, and because we either believe God's plan or we do not.

When we speak this way, we are at the root of the matter that can bring forth anything. Because Abram believed God, every person is blessed today through faithful Abraham. (See Galatians 3:8–9.) He was an extraordinary man of faith; he believed God in the face of everything.

You would like to be extraordinary, wouldn't you? If you are prayed for this morning, though you see no change at all, if you believe it is done, you may become extraordinary in that way. You who have been longing for the baptism of the Holy Spirit and have been waiting and tarrying every day, if you have come to a place of believing, you have come to a place where you have become extraordinary.

> INTERPRETATION OF A MESSAGE IN TONGUES: "The peace that comes from above is always full of purity and life-giving, and it never brings destruction to anyone. And the wisdom is on the same line; and all purification on every line never disturbs you. It is only what is earthly that disturbs you. You cannot be disturbed by a heavenly breath. God is with us on a heavenly breath, and in that action you cannot be disturbed. If you are disturbed from this day, know it is an earthly thing that is disturbing you."

GREATER WORKS

Now I want to explain the fourteenth chapter of John. It is the Master's word; it is the Master's desire. He said to His disciples in the twelfth verse, *"Greater works than these* [you] *will do."* Why was His perspective so full? Because He had admiration before Him. Jesus had great admiration before Him when He saw the disciples. He knew He had the material that would bring out what would prove to be a real satisfaction to the world—to heaven and to the world. The glorified, trained, wonderfully modified, and then again glorified positions of these fishermen were surely ideal places in which to be.

What were the disciples? For one thing, they were unlearned (not that I am going to build on an unlearned position). For another thing, they were ignorant men (not that I am going to build on ignorance, either). However, note this: they were unlearned, but God taught them. It is far better to have the learning of the Spirit than anything else. They were ignorant; He enlarged them. They were beside themselves because they had been touched with the divine life. If the Most High God touches you, you will be beside yourself. As long as you hold your own, the natural and the spiritual will be mixed; but if you ever jump over the lines by the power of the new creation, you will find He has gotten a hold of you.

Divine wisdom will never make you foolish. Divine wisdom will give you a sound mind; divine wisdom will give you a touch of divine nature. Divine life is full of divine appointment and equipping, and you cannot be filled with the power of God without a manifestation. It is my prayer today that we would understand that to be filled with the Holy Spirit is to be filled with manifestation, the glory of the Lord being in the midst of us, manifesting His divine power.

Jesus knew that these people He had before Him were going to do greater things than He had done (John 14:12). How could they do them? None of us is able; none of us is capable. But our incapability has to be clothed with His divine ability, and our helplessness has to be filled with His power of helpfulness. This is why He knew that they would do greater things.

He knew that He was going away and that, if He went away, it was expedient, it was necessary, it was important that Another come in His place and take up the same thing in them as He had been telling them (John 16:7, 14 KJV). *"You in Me, and I in you"* (John 14:20). There was a plan of divine order. So the Holy Spirit was to come.

I want you to see what has to take place when the Holy Spirit comes:

> *And I will pray the Father, and he shall give you another Comforter, that he may abide with you for ever; even the Spirit of truth; whom the world cannot receive, because it seeth him not, neither knoweth him: but ye know him; for he dwelleth with you, and shall be in you. I will not leave you comfortless: I will come to you.* (John 14:16–18 KJV)

I don't know a word that could be as fitting at this time as this word *"Comforter."* I want to take you with me into the coming of this Holy Spirit.

After Jesus ascended to heaven, He asked the Father to send the Comforter. It was a needy moment, a needy hour, a necessity. Why? Because the disciples would need comforting.

How could they be comforted? The Holy Spirit would take the word of Christ and reveal it to them (John 16:14). What could help them as much as a word by the Spirit? For the Spirit is breath, is life, is person, is power. He gives the breath of Himself to us, the nature of Him. How beautiful that, when the Spirit came, He should be called the *"Spirit of truth."* Oh, if we would only read that into our hearts!

Some people have wondered that if they were to ask for the baptism of the Holy Spirit, if an evil power could come instead or if an evil power could possess them while they were waiting for the Holy Spirit. Why, when you receive the Holy Spirit, you receive the Spirit of Truth, (the Spirit who gives revelation) the Spirit who takes the words of Jesus and makes them life to you. In your moment of need, He is the Comforter.

What will the Holy Spirit do? The Holy Spirit is prophetic. He says: *"Be of good cheer"* (v. 33). *"Take My yoke upon you and learn from Me"* (Matt. 11:29). *"Have peace with one another"* (Mark 9:50). You say, "But that is what Jesus said." It is what the Holy Spirit is taking and revealing to us and speaking to us. The Holy Spirit is the spokesman in these days. The Holy Spirit came to be the spokesman, and He spoke the Word. He is still taking the Word and speaking it. The Holy Spirit takes the words of Jesus, and He is so full of truth that He never adds anything to them. He gives you the unadulterated Word of Truth, the Word of Life.

"He will take of Mine and declare [reveal] it to you" (John 16:15). What is His? Truths like these: *"I am the light of the world"* (John 8:12), and *"For God did not send His Son into the world to condemn the world, but that the world through Him might be saved"* (John 3:17). The Holy Spirit takes these words and gives them to you. Here are some of the words of the Master: *"Come to Me, all you who labor and are heavy laden, and I will give you rest"* (Matt. 11:28).

Who is speaking? It is the Holy Spirit in the last days, the Spirit of Truth bringing forth the Word of Life. *"I will give you rest."* Rest? Oh, there is no rest like it! It can come in your moment of greatest trial.

When my dear wife was lying dead, the doctors could do nothing, and they said to me, "She is done; we cannot help you." My heart was so moved, and I said, "O God, I can't spare her!"

I went up to her and I said, "Oh, come back, come back and speak to me. Come back, come back!"

And the Spirit of the Lord moved, and she came back and smiled again.

Then the Holy Spirit said to me, "She is mine. Her work is done; she is mine."

Oh, the comforting word! No one else could have done it, but the Comforter came. At that moment, my dear wife passed away.

Ah, beloved, it is true to me that the Comforter has a word for us this day. He is the Comforter. There is only one Comforter, and He has been with the Father from the beginning. He comes only to give light. When the Holy Spirit comes into your body, He comes to unveil the King, to assure you of His presence.

BE SPECIFIC IN WHAT YOU ASK

The person who says "I am ready for anything" will never get it.

"What are you seeking, my brother?"

"Oh, I am ready for anything."

"You will never get 'anything.'"

"Oh! Well, tell me how to get it, then."

"One thing I have desired of the LORD, that will I seek" (Ps. 27:4). When the Lord reveals to you that you must be filled with the Holy Spirit, seek only that one thing, and God will give you that one thing. It is necessary for you to seek one thing first.

In a meeting one day, I went to two young men and said to them, "Young men, what about it? Would you like to receive the baptism?" They had just earned their degrees, and they were handsome young men.

"Oh!" they said. "We don't believe in it the same way you do. We don't believe in receiving the Holy Spirit as those people do."

There was a crowd of people waiting in the front.

"You are dressed up as if you would like to have it," I said. "You are dressed like preachers, and seeing that you are dressed like preachers, it is a pity for you to have the clothing without the Presence."

"Well, we don't believe it that way," they said.

"But look," I said, "the apostles believed it that way. Wouldn't you like to be an apostle? Wouldn't you like to go along the same lines as they did? They believed it that way."

Never forget, the baptism will always be as it was in the beginning. It has not changed. And if you want a real baptism, expect it to be just the same as they had it at the beginning.

"What did they have at the beginning?" you ask.

Well, the early believers knew when others had the same experience they had had at the beginning, for they heard them speak in tongues. That is the only way they did know, because they heard the others saying the same things in the Spirit that they had said at the beginning. It has never been changed; it has always been the same right down to today. As it was in the beginning, so it will be forever and ever.

When these two young men at the meeting realized that Peter and John and the rest of them had the baptism, they came up to receive it. They were beautifully dressed. In about half an hour's time, they looked strange. They had been rolling, somehow. I had not caused them to do it. But they had been so lost in and so controlled by the power of God that they were just rolling all around and their clothes were rumpled—but their faces were wonderful.

What had happened? They had received it just as the first Christians had received it at the beginning.

These young men had been ordained as pastors by men. I do not say anything against that; I think that is very good. However, there is an ordination that is better, and it is the ordination with the King. This is the only ordination that is going to equip you for the future. The King is already on His throne, but He needs crowning; when the Holy Spirit comes, He crowns the King inside of us.

The person who has passed through that ordination goes forth with fresh feet—the preparation of the Gospel (Eph. 6:15); he goes forth with a fresh voice, speaking as the Spirit gives utterance (Acts 2:4); he goes forth with a fresh mind, his mind being illuminated by the power of God (see Hebrews 8:10); he goes forth with a fresh vision and sees all things new (see 2 Corinthians 5:17).

When the Holy Spirit comes, He will reveal things to you. Has He revealed them yet? He is going to do it. Just expect Him to do so. The best thing for you is to expect Him to do it now.

OVERCOMING HINDRANCES TO RECEIVING

Put up with any disorder you like when you are coming through into the baptism. As far as I am concerned, you can have the biggest time on earth; you can scream as much as you like. Yet some people are frightened by this.

A woman in Switzerland came to me after I had helped her and asked to speak to me further.

"Now that I feel I am healed," she said, "and that terrible carnal passion that has bound and hindered me is gone, I feel that I have a new mind. I believe I would like to receive the Holy Spirit, but when I hear these people screaming, I feel like running away."

After that, we were at another meeting in Switzerland where a large hotel was joined to the building. At the close of one of the morning services, the power of God fell—that is the only way I can describe it, the power of God *fell*. This poor, timid creature who couldn't bear to hear anybody scream, screamed so loud that all the waiters in this big hotel came out with their aprons on and with their trays to see what was up. Nothing was especially up. Something had come down, and it had so altered the situation that this woman could stand anything after that.

When God begins dealing with you on the baptism, He begins on this line: He starts with the things that are the most difficult. He starts with your fear; He starts with your human nature. He puts the fear away; He gets the human nature out of the way. And just as you dissolve, just as the power of the Spirit brings a dissolving to your human nature, in the same act the Holy Spirit flows into the place where you are being dissolved, and you are quickened just where you come into death. As you die, naturally, humanly, carnally, selfishly, to every evil thing, the new life, the Holy Spirit, floods the whole condition until it becomes a transformed condition.

"No man can tame the tongue" (James 3:8); but when the Holy Spirit begins, He tames the whole body until the tongue, moved by the power of the Spirit, says things exactly as the Lord would be delighted for them to be said.

The Holy Spirit is the Comforter; the Holy Spirit takes the necessary word at the right time and gives it to you. After the Holy Spirit takes charge of you, He is the Comforter who brings thought and language to your life, and it is amazing.

If we get to the place where we take no thought for ourselves, then God takes thought for us; but as long as we are taking thought for ourselves, we are somewhat hindered in this divine order with God. Taking no thought for yourself, no desire for your human self, not seeking anything for your human condition but that God will be glorified in your body and spirit and that He will be the chief Worker on every line—this is divine appointment. This is holy order.

There is a holy order. There are sects today that call themselves "holy orders," but the only holy order is where God has gotten so through with your nature that the Trinity comes in with perfect blending. Where the human nature could not help itself, God turned the captivity of the wheels of nature and poured in His divine power until the nature itself became divine property.

YOU HAVE AN ANOINTING

Another of the roles of the Holy Spirit that is necessary for today we find in John:

> But the Comforter, which is the Holy [Spirit], whom the Father will send in my name, he shall teach you all things, and bring all things to your remembrance, whatsoever I have said unto you. (John 14:26 KJV)

Jesus said something very similar in a later chapter: "He will take of what is Mine and declare [reveal] it to you" (John 16:14). Everything that has been revealed to you was first taken. So, first, the Holy Spirit takes of what is Christ's and reveals it to you. Then you come to the place where you need another touch. What is it? In the necessity of your ministry, He will bring to your remembrance everything that you need in your ministry. That is an important thing for preachers. God will give us His Word, and if there is anything special we need, He will bring that to our memories, too. The Holy Spirit comes to bring the Word to us in remembrance.

I will throw this word out to you as a help for future reflection. In 1 John 2:20, we read, "You have an anointing from the Holy One." May God grant that we will not forget it! "You shall receive power" (Acts 1:8). Oh, may God grant that we will not forget it!

What do I mean by that? Many people, instead of standing on the rock-solid word of faith and believing that they have received the baptism with its anointing and power, say, "Oh, if I could only feel that I have received it!"

My friend, your feelings rob you of your greatest place of anointing. Your feelings are a place very often of discouragement. You have to get away from the sense of all human feeling or desire. Earthly desires are not God's desires. All thoughts of holiness, all thoughts of purity, all thoughts of power from the Holy Spirit are from above. Human thoughts are like clouds that belong to the earth. "[God's] *thoughts are not* [our] *thoughts*" (Isa. 55:8).

> INTERPRETATION OF A MESSAGE IN TONGUES: "It is the shadows that flee away. It is your feelings that have to be moved from you this day. It is the divine unction of a new creation moving in your human nature that has to change all, even your environment, and make you so that your heart, even your mind and your tongue and everything, will be in a place of magnifying the Lord. Remember, it is from above in your heart to change all your life until you will be as He has promised, sons of God with power."

"*You have an anointing*" (1 John 2:20).

Some things are of necessity. Suppose that all around me are people with needs: a woman is dying; a man has lost all the powers of his faculties; another person is apparently dying. Here they are. I see the great need, and I drop down on my knees and cry. Yet in doing so, I miss it all.

God does not want me to cry. God does not want me to labor. God does not want me to anguish and to be filled with anxiety and a sorrowful spirit. What does He want me to do?

"*Only believe*" (Mark 5:36). After you have received, only believe. Come to the authority of it; dare to believe. Say, "I will do it!"

So the baptism of the Holy Spirit says to me, "*You have an anointing.*" The anointing has come; the anointing remains; the anointing is with us (1 John 2:27). But what if you have not lived in the place in which the unction, the anointing, can be increased? Ah! Then the Spirit is grieved; then you are not moved. You are like one who is dead. You feel that all the joy is gone.

What is the matter? There is something between you and the Holy One; you are not clean, not pure, not desirous of Him alone. Something else has come in the way. Then the Spirit is grieved, and you have lost the unction.

Is the Unctioner still there? Yes. When He comes in, He comes to remain. He will either be grieved, full of groaning and travail, or He will be there to lift you above the powers of darkness, transform you by His power, and take you to a place where you may be fully equipped.

Many people lose all potential positions of attainment because they fail to understand this:

> *But the anointing which you have received from Him abides in you, and you do not need that anyone teach you; but as the same anointing teaches you concerning all things, and is true, and is not a lie, and just as it has taught you, you will abide in Him.* (1 John 2:27)

What *"anointing"* is referred to here? *"God anointed Jesus of Nazareth with the Holy Spirit and with power, who went about doing good"* (Acts 10:38). The same anointing is with you, *"and you do not need that anyone teach you."* The same anointing is with you and will teach you all things.

O lovely Jesus! Blessed Incarnation of holy display! Thank God for the Trinity displayed in our hearts today. Thank God for this glorious open way. Thank God for darkness that is turning into day. Thank God for life all along the way. Praise God for hope that we may all be changed today. Hallelujah!

> Peace, peace, sweet peace,
>> Coming down from the Father above;
> Peace, peace, wonderful peace,
>> Sweet peace, the gift of God's love.

This is the very position and presence that will bring everybody into a fullness.

CHAPTER THREE

THE FULLNESS
OF THE SPIRIT

AND NOW ABIDE FAITH, HOPE, LOVE, THESE THREE; BUT THE
GREATEST OF THESE IS LOVE. PURSUE LOVE, AND DESIRE
SPIRITUAL GIFTS, BUT ESPECIALLY THAT YOU MAY PROPHESY. FOR
HE WHO SPEAKS IN A TONGUE DOES NOT SPEAK TO MEN BUT TO
GOD, FOR NO ONE UNDERSTANDS HIM; HOWEVER, IN THE SPIRIT
HE SPEAKS MYSTERIES. BUT HE WHO PROPHESIES SPEAKS
EDIFICATION AND EXHORTATION AND COMFORT TO MEN.
—1 CORINTHIANS 13:13–14:3

It is quite easy to construct a building if the foundation is secure. On the other hand, a building will be unstable if it does
not have a solid understructure. Likewise, it is not very easy to
rise spiritually unless we have a real spiritual power working
within us. It will never do for us to be top-heavy—the base must
always be very firmly set. Many of us have not gone on in the Lord
because we have not had a secure foundation in Him, and we will
have to consider *"the pit from which* [we] *were dug"* (Isa. 51:1).
Unless we correctly understand the spiritual leadings, according to
the mind of God, we will never be able to stand when the winds
blow, when the trials come, and when Satan appears as *"an angel
of light"* (2 Cor. 11:14). We will never be able to stand unless we are
firmly fixed in the Word of God.

There must be three things in our lives if we wish to go all
the way with God in the fullness of Pentecost. First, we must be
grounded and settled in love; we must have a real knowledge of what
love is. Second, we must have a clear understanding of the Word, for
love must manifest the Word. Third, we must clearly understand our

own ground, because it is our own ground that needs to be looked after the most.

The Lord speaks at least twice of the good ground into which seed was sown, which also bore fruit and brought forth some one hundredfold, and some sixty, and some thirty (Matt. 13:8; Mark 4:8). Even in the good ground, the seed yielded different portions of fruit. I maintain truly that there is no limitation to the abundance of a harvest when the ground is perfectly in the hands of the Lord. So we must clearly understand that the Word of God can never come forth with all its primary purposes unless our ground is right. But God will help us, I believe, to see that He can make the ground in perfect order as it is put into His hands.

Let me speak about 1 Corinthians 13:13, and then I must continue on quickly. I want you to notice that the primary thought in the mind of the Spirit is that when love is in perfect progress, all other things will work in harmony, for prophetic utterances are all of no value unless they are perfectly covered with divine love. Our Lord Jesus would never have accomplished His great plan in this world except that He was so full of love for His Father, and love for us, that love never failed to accomplish its purpose. It worked in Him and through Him by the power of the Father's love in Him.

I believe that love will have to come into our lives. Christ must be the summit, the desire, the plan of all things. All our sayings, doings, and workings must be well pleasing in and to Him, and then our prophetic utterances will be a blessing through God; they will never be side issues. There is no imitation in a man filled with the Holy Spirit. Imitation is lost as the great plan of Christ becomes the ideal of his life.

God wants you to be so balanced in spiritual anointing that you will always be able to do what pleases Him, and not what will please other people or yourself. The ideal must be that it will all be to edification, and everything must go on to this end to please the Lord.

"Pursue love, and desire spiritual gifts, but especially that you may prophesy" (1 Cor. 14:1). When someone came to Moses and said that there were two others in the camp prophesying, Moses said, "Oh, that all the Lord's people were prophets" (Num. 11:29). That is a clear revelation along these lines that God wants us to be in such a spiritual, holy place that He could take our words and so fill them with divine power that we would speak only as the Spirit leads in prophetic utterances.

Beloved, there is spiritual language, and there is also human language, which always stays on the human plane. The divine comes into the same language so that it is changed by spiritual power and brings life to those who hear you speak. But this divine touch of prophecy will never come in any way except through the infilling of the Spirit.

If you wish to be anything for God, do not miss His plan. God has no room for you on ordinary lines. You must realize that within you there is the power of the Holy Spirit, who is forming within you everything you require.

I believe we have too much preaching and too little testifying. You will never have a living Pentecostal church with a preacher who is every night preaching, preaching, preaching. The people get tired of this constant preaching, but they never get tired when the whole place is on fire, when twenty or more jump up at once and will not sit down until they testify. So, remember, you must awake out of your lethargy.

> *And it shall come to pass afterward that I will pour out My Spirit on all flesh; your sons and your daughters shall prophesy, your old men shall dream dreams, your young men shall see visions. And also on My menservants and on My maidservants I will pour out My Spirit in those days.* (Joel 2:28–29)

This was spoken by the prophet Joel, and we know that this is what occurred on the Day of Pentecost. This was the first outpouring of the Spirit, but what would it be like now if we would only wake up to the words of our Master, *"Greater works than these [you] will do, because I go to My Father"* (John 14:12)?

Hear what the Scripture says to us: *"However, when He, the Spirit of truth, has come, He will guide you into all truth; for He will not speak on His own authority, but whatever He hears He will speak"* (John 16:13). The Holy Spirit is inspiration; the Holy Spirit is revelation; the Holy Spirit is manifestation; the Holy Spirit is operation. When a man comes into the fullness of the Holy Spirit, he is in perfect order, built up on scriptural foundations.

I have failed to see any man understand the twelfth, thirteenth, and fourteenth chapters of 1 Corinthians unless he had been baptized with the Holy Spirit. He may talk about the Holy Spirit and the gifts, but his understanding is only a superficial one.

However, when he gets baptized with the Holy Spirit, he speaks about a deep inward conviction by the power of the Spirit working in him a revelation of that Scripture. On the other hand, there is so much that a man receives when he is born again. He receives the *"first love"* (Rev. 2:4) and has a revelation of Jesus. *"But if we walk in the light as He is in the light, we have fellowship with one another, and the blood of Jesus Christ His Son cleanses us from all sin"* (1 John 1:7).

But God wants a man to be on fire so that he will always speak as an oracle of God. He wants to so build that man on the foundations of God that everyone who sees and hears him will say he is a new man after the order of the Spirit. *"Old things have passed away; behold, all things have become new"* (2 Cor. 5:17). New things have come, and he is now in the divine order. When a man is filled with the Holy Spirit, he has a vital power that makes people know he has seen God. He ought to be in such a place spiritually that when he goes into a neighbor's house, or out among people, they will feel that God has come into their midst.

"He who prophesies speaks edification and exhortation and comfort to men. He who speaks in a tongue edifies himself, but he who prophesies edifies the church" (1 Cor. 14:3–4). There are two edifications spoken of here. Which is the first? To edify yourself. After you have been edified by the Spirit, you are able to edify the church through the Spirit. What we need is more of the Holy Spirit. Oh, beloved, it is not merely a measure of the Spirit, it is a pressed-down measure. It is not merely a pressed-down measure, it is *"shaken together, and running over"* (Luke 6:38). Anybody can hold a full cup, but you cannot hold an overflowing cup, and the baptism of the Holy Spirit is an overflowing cup. Praise the Lord!

CHAPTER FOUR

BIBLICAL EVIDENCE
OF THE BAPTISM

There is much controversy today regarding the genuineness of this Pentecostal work. However, there is nothing so convincing as the fact that over twenty-five years ago, a revival on Holy Spirit lines began and has never ceased. You will find that in every region throughout the world, God has poured out His Spirit in a remarkable way, in a manner parallel to the glorious revival that inaugurated the church of the first century.

Our Lord Jesus said to His disciples, *"Behold, I send the Promise of My Father upon you; but tarry in the city of Jerusalem until you are endued with power from on high"* (Luke 24:49). God promised through the prophet Joel, *"I will pour out My Spirit on all flesh....On My menservants and on My maidservants I will pour out My Spirit in those days"* (Joel 2:28–29).

TONGUES AND THE BAPTISM

Let me tell you about my own experience of being baptized with the Holy Spirit. You know, beloved, that it had to be something that was based on solid facts in order to move me. I was as certain as possible that I had received the Holy Spirit, and I was absolutely rigid in this conviction. Many years ago, a man came to me and said, "Wigglesworth, do you know what is happening in Sunderland, England? People are being baptized in the Holy Spirit exactly the same way that the disciples were on the Day of Pentecost." I said, "I would like to go."

Immediately, I took a train and went to Sunderland and met with the people who had assembled for the purpose of receiving the Holy Spirit. I was continuously in those meetings causing disturbances, until the people wished I had never come. They said that I was disrupting the conditions for people to receive the baptism. But I was hungry and thirsty for God, and had gone to Sunderland because I had heard that God was pouring out His Spirit in a new way. I had heard that God had now visited His people and manifested His power, and that people were speaking in tongues as on the Day of Pentecost.

Therefore, when I first got to Sunderland, I said to the people, "I cannot understand this meeting. I have left a meeting in Bradford all on fire for God. The fire fell last night, and we were all laid out under the power of God. I have come here for tongues, and I don't hear them—I don't hear anything."

"Oh!" they said. "When you get baptized with the Holy Spirit, you will speak in tongues."

"Oh, is that it?" I said. "When the presence of God came upon me, my tongue was loosened, and when I went in the open air to preach, I really felt that I had a new tongue."

"Ah, no," they said, "that is not it."

"What is it, then?" I asked.

"When you get baptized in the Holy Spirit—"

"I am baptized," I interjected, "and there is no one here who can persuade me that I am not baptized."

So I was up against them, and they were up against me.

I remember a man getting up and saying, "You know, brothers and sisters, I was here three weeks and then the Lord baptized me with the Holy Spirit, and I began to speak with tongues."

I said, "Let us hear it. That's what I'm here for."

But he could not speak in tongues at will; he could only speak as the Spirit gave him the ability, and so my curiosity was not satisfied. I was doing what others are doing today, confusing the twelfth chapter of 1 Corinthians with the second chapter of Acts. These two chapters deal with different things; one deals with the gifts of the Spirit, and the other deals with the baptism of the Spirit with the accompanying sign of tongues.

I saw that these people were very earnest, and I became quite hungry for tongues. I was eager to see this new manifestation of the Spirit, and, as I said, I would be questioning all the time and spoiling a lot of the meetings. One man said to me, "I am a missionary, and I have come here to seek the baptism in the Holy Spirit. I am waiting on the Lord, but you have come in and are spoiling everything with your questions." I began to argue with him; the argument became so heated that when we walked home, he walked on one side of the road, and I walked on the other.

That night, there was to be another meeting, and I purposed to go. I changed my clothes and left my key in the clothes I had taken off. As we came from the meeting in the middle of the night, I found that I did not have my key with me, and this missionary brother said, "You will have to come and stay with me." But do you think we went to sleep that night? Oh, no, we spent the night in prayer. We received a precious shower from above. The breakfast bell rang, but that was nothing to me. For four days, I wanted nothing but God. If you only knew the unspeakably wonderful blessing of being filled with the third person of the Trinity, you would set aside everything else to wait for this infilling.

As the days passed, I became more and more hungry for God. I had opposed the meetings so much, but the Lord was gracious, and I will always remember that last day—the day I was to leave. God was with me so much. They were to have a meeting, and I went, but I could not rest. This revival was taking place at an Episcopal church. I went to the rectory to say goodbye, and I said to Sister Boddy, the rector's wife, "I cannot rest any longer; I must have these tongues."

She replied, "Brother Wigglesworth, it is not the tongues you need but the baptism. If you will allow God to baptize you, the other will be all right."

I answered, "My dear sister, I know I am baptized. You know that I have to leave here at four o'clock. Please lay hands on me so that I may receive the tongues."

She stood up and laid her hands on me, and the fire fell.

There came a persistent knock at the door, and she had to go out. That was the best thing that could have happened, for I was alone with God. Then He gave me a revelation. Oh, it was wonderful! He showed me an empty cross and Jesus glorified. I do thank God that the cross is empty, that Christ is no longer on the cross.

Then I saw that God had purified me. I was conscious of the cleansing of the precious blood of Jesus, and I cried out, "Clean!

Clean! Clean!" I was filled with the joy of the consciousness of the cleansing. As I was extolling, glorifying, and praising Him, I was speaking in tongues *"as the Spirit gave* [me] *utterance"* (Acts 2:4). I knew then that I had received the real baptism in the Holy Spirit.

It was all as beautiful and peaceful as when Jesus said, *"Peace, be still!"* (Mark 4:39). The tranquillity and the joy of that moment surpassed anything I had ever known up to that time. But hallelujah! These days have grown with greater, mightier, more wonderful divine manifestations and power. That was only the beginning. There is no end to this kind of beginning. You will never come to the end of the Holy Spirit until you have arrived in glory—until you are right in the presence of God forever. And even then we will always be conscious of His presence.

What had I received? I had received the biblical evidence. This biblical evidence is wonderful to me. I knew I had received the very evidence of the Spirit's incoming that the apostles had received on the Day of Pentecost. I knew that everything I had had up to that time was in the nature of an anointing, bringing me in line with God in preparation. However, now I knew I had the biblical baptism in the Spirit. It had the backing of the Scriptures. You are never right if you do not have a foundation for your testimony in the Word of God.

For many years, I have thrown out a challenge to any person who can prove to me that he has the baptism without the speaking in tongues as the Spirit gives utterance—to prove it by the Word that he has been baptized in the Holy Spirit without the biblical evidence—but so far, no one has accepted the challenge. I only say this because so many are like I was; they have a rigid idea that they have received the baptism, without having the biblical evidence. The Lord Jesus wants those who preach the Word to have the Word in evidence. Don't be misled by anything else. Have a biblical proof for everything you have, and then you will be in a place where no man can move you.

When I returned home from Sunderland, my wife said to me, "So you think you have received the baptism of the Holy Spirit? Why, I am as much baptized in the Holy Spirit as you are." We had sat on the platform together for twenty years, but that night she said, "Tonight you will go by yourself." I said, "All right." My wife went back to one of the furthermost seats in the hall, and she said to herself, "I will watch it."

As I went up to the platform that night, the Lord gave me the first few verses of the sixty-first chapter of Isaiah, starting with the first verse:

The Spirit of the Lord GOD is upon Me, because the LORD has anointed Me to preach good tidings to the poor; He has sent Me to heal the brokenhearted, to proclaim liberty to the captives, and the opening of the prison to those who are bound.
(Isa. 61:1)

I preached that night on the subject the Lord had given me, and I told what the Lord had done for me. I told the people that I was going to have God in my life and that I would gladly suffer a thousand deaths rather than forfeit this wonderful infilling that had come to me.

My wife was very restless, just as if she were sitting on a red-hot poker. She was moved in a new way and said, "That is not my Smith that is preaching. Lord, You have done something for him."

As soon as I finished, the secretary of the mission got up and said, "I want what the leader of our mission has gotten." He tried to sit down but missed his seat and fell on the floor. There were soon fourteen of them on the floor, my own wife included. We did not know what to do, but the Holy Spirit got hold of the situation, and the fire fell. A revival started and the crowds came. It was only the beginning of the flood tide of blessing. We had touched the reservoir of the Lord's life and power. Since that time, the Lord has taken me to many different lands, and I have witnessed many blessed outpourings of God's Holy Spirit.

THREE WITNESSES TO THE BAPTISM

I want to take you to the Scriptures to prove my position that tongues are the evidence of the baptism in the Holy Spirit. Businessmen know that in cases of law where there are two clear witnesses, they could win a case before any judge. On the clear evidence of two witnesses, any judge will give a verdict. What has God given us? He has given us three clear witnesses on the baptism in the Holy Spirit—more than is necessary in law courts.

The first is from the second chapter of Acts, which describes the Day of Pentecost:

They were all filled with the Holy Spirit and began to speak with other tongues, as the Spirit gave them utterance.

(Acts 2:4)

Here we have the original pattern. And God gave to Peter an eternal word that couples this experience with the promise that came before it: *"This is what was spoken by the prophet Joel"* (v. 16). God wants you to have this—nothing less than this. He wants you to receive the baptism in the Holy Spirit according to this original Pentecostal pattern.

In Acts 10, we have another witness. Cornelius had had a vision of a holy angel and had sent for Peter. When Peter arrived and proclaimed the gospel message, the Holy Spirit fell on all those who heard his words.

A person said to me one day, "You don't admit that I am filled and baptized with the Holy Spirit. Why, I was ten days and ten nights on my back before the Lord, and He was flooding my soul with joy." I said, "Praise the Lord, sister, that was only the beginning. The disciples were waiting for that length of time, and the mighty power of God fell upon them. The Bible tells us what happened when the power fell." And that is just what happened in the house of Cornelius. The Holy Spirit fell on all those who heard the Word.

And those of the circumcision who believed were astonished, as many as came with Peter, because the gift of the Holy Spirit had been poured out on the Gentiles also. (Acts 10:45)

What convinced these prejudiced Jews that the Holy Spirit had come? *"For they heard them speak with tongues and magnify God"* (v. 46). There was no other way for them to know. This evidence could not be contradicted. It is the biblical evidence. ✳

If some people were to have an angel come and talk to them as Cornelius did, they would say that they knew they were baptized. Do not be fooled by anything. Be sure that what you receive is according to the Word of God.

We have heard two witnesses. Now let us look at the third witness, the instance in which Paul ministered to certain disciples in Ephesus:

And when Paul had laid hands on them, the Holy Spirit came upon them, and they spoke with tongues and prophesied.

(Acts 19:6)

These Ephesians received the identical biblical evidence that the apostles had received at the beginning, and they prophesied in addition. Three times the Scriptures show us this evidence of the baptism in the Spirit. I do not glorify tongues. No, by God's grace, I glorify the Giver of tongues. And above all, I glorify Him whom the Holy Spirit has come to reveal to us, the Lord Jesus Christ. It is He who sends the Holy Spirit, and I glorify Him because He makes no distinction between us and those who believed at the beginning.

But what are tongues for? Look at the second verse of 1 Corinthians 14, and you will see a very blessed truth. Oh, hallelujah! Have you been there, beloved? I tell you, God wants to take you there. *"For he who speaks in a tongue does not speak to men but to God, for no one understands him; however, in the spirit he speaks mysteries."* The passage goes on to say, *"He who speaks in a tongue edifies himself"* (v. 4).

Enter into the promises of God. It is your inheritance. You will do more in one year if you are really filled with the Holy Spirit than you could do in fifty years apart from Him. I pray that you may be so filled with Him that it will not be possible for you to move without a revival of some kind resulting.

CHAPTER FIVE

PAUL'S CONVERSION
AND BAPTISM

S aul was probably the greatest persecutor that the early church had. Saul hated the Christians: *"He made havoc of the church, entering every house, and dragging off men and women, committing them to prison"* (Acts 8:3). In Acts 9, we read that he was breathing out threats and slaughter against the disciples of the Lord. He was on his way to Damascus for the purpose of destroying the church there (vv. 1–2).

How did God deal with such a person? We would have dealt with him in judgment. God dealt with him in mercy. Oh, the wondrous love of God! He loved the believers at Damascus, and the way He preserved them was through the salvation of the man who intended to scatter and destroy them. Our God delights to be merciful, and His grace is granted daily to both sinner and saint. He shows mercy to all. If we would just realize that we are alive today only through the grace of our God.

More and more, I see that it is through the grace of God that I am preserved every day. It is when we realize the goodness of God that we are brought to repentance (Rom. 2:4). Here was Saul, with letters from the high priest, hurrying to Damascus. He was struck down, and he saw a light, a light that was brighter than the sun. As he fell speechless to the ground, he heard a voice saying to him, *"Saul, Saul, why are you persecuting Me?"* He asked, *"Who are You, Lord?"* And the answer came back, *"I am Jesus, whom you are persecuting."* And Saul cried, *"Lord, what do You want me to do?"* (Acts 9:4–6).

I do not want to bring any word of condemnation to anyone, but I know that there are many who have felt very much the same way toward the children of God as Saul did, especially toward those who have received the Pentecostal baptism. I know that many people tell us, "You are mad," but the truth is that <u>the children of God are the only people who are really glad</u>. <u>We are glad inside, and we are glad outside</u>. Our gladness flows from the inside. God has filled us with *"joy inexpressible and full of glory"* (1 Pet. 1:8). We are so happy about what we have received that, if it were not for the desire to keep a little decorum, we might be doing strange things. This is probably how the apostle Paul felt when he referred to himself and his coworkers as being *"beside* [them]*selves"* (2 Cor. 5:13) in the Lord. This joy in the Holy Spirit is beyond anything else. And this joy of the Lord is our strength (Neh. 8:10).

When Saul went down to Damascus, he thought he would do wonderful things with that bunch of letters he had from the high priest. But I think he dropped them all on the road. If he ever wanted to pick them up, he was not able to, for he had lost his sight. The men who were with him had lost their speech—they were speechless—but they led him to Damascus.

There are some people who have an idea that it is only preachers who can know the will of God. However, this account of Saul shows us that the Lord had a disciple in Damascus, named Ananias, a man behind the scenes, who lived in a place where God could talk to him. His ears were open. He was one who listened in to the things from heaven. Oh, they are so much more marvelous than anything you can hear on earth. It was to this man that the Lord appeared in a vision. He told him to go down to the street called Straight and to inquire for Saul. And He told him that Saul had seen in a vision a man named Ananias coming in and putting his hand on him so that he might receive his sight. Ananias protested,

> *Lord, I have heard from many about this man, how much harm he has done to Your saints in Jerusalem. And here he has authority from the chief priests to bind all who call on Your name.* (Acts 9:13–14)

But the Lord reassured Ananias that Saul was a chosen vessel, and Ananias, doubting nothing, went on his errand of mercy.

The Lord had told Ananias concerning Saul, *"Behold, he is praying"* (Acts 9:11). Repentant prayer is always heard in heaven. The Lord never despises a broken and contrite heart (Ps. 51:17). Saul was given a vision that was soon to be a reality, the vision of Ananias coming to pray for him so that he would receive his sight.

I do thank God that visions have not ceased. The Holy Spirit can give visions, and we may expect them in these last days. God does not will the death of any sinner (Ezek. 33:11), and He will use all kinds of means for their salvation. I do praise God for this Gospel. It is always so entreating. *"Look to Me, and be saved, all you ends of the earth!"* (Isa. 45:22) is such an inviting message. Oh, what a Gospel! Whatever people say about it, it is surely a message of love.

Ananias went down to the house on Straight Street, and he laid his hands on the one who had before been a blasphemer and a persecutor, and he said to him, *"Brother Saul, the Lord Jesus, who appeared to you on the road as you came, has sent me that you may receive your sight and be filled with the Holy Spirit"* (Acts 9:17). He recognized him as a brother whose soul had already been saved and who had come into relationship with the Father and with all the family of God, but there was something necessary beyond this. Yes, the Lord had not forgotten his physical condition, and there was healing for him. But there was something beyond this. It was the filling with the Holy Spirit.

Oh, it always seems to me that the Gospel is robbed of its divine glory when we overlook this marvelous truth of the baptism of the Holy Spirit. To be saved is wonderful; to be a new creation (2 Cor. 5:17), to have *"passed from death to life"* (1 John 3:14), to have the witness of the Spirit that you are born of God (Rom. 8:16)—all this is unspeakably precious. But whereas we have the well of salvation bubbling up inside us, we need to go on to a place where from within us will flow *"rivers of living water"* (John 7:38). The Lord Jesus showed us very plainly that, if we believe in Him, from within us will flow these *"rivers of living water."* And this He spoke by the Spirit. The Lord wants us to be filled with the Spirit, to have the manifestation of the presence of His Spirit, the manifestation that is indeed given *"for the profit of all"* (1 Cor. 12:7). The Lord wants us to be His mouthpieces and to speak as the very *"oracles of God"* (1 Pet. 4:11).

God chose Saul. What was he? A blasphemer. A persecutor. That is grace. Our God is gracious, and He loves to show His mercy to the vilest and worst of men.

There was a notable character in the town in which I lived who was known as the worst man in town. He was so vile, and his language was so horrible, that even wicked men could not stand it. In England, they have what is known as the public hangman who has to perform all the executions. This man held that appointment, and he told me later that he believed that when he performed the execution of men who had committed murder, the demon power that was in them would come upon him, and that, in consequence, he had been possessed by a legion of demons.

His life was so miserable that he decided to kill himself. He went down to a certain train depot and purchased a ticket. English trains are much different from American trains. In every coach there are a number of small compartments, and it is easy for anyone who wants to commit suicide to open the door of his compartment and throw himself out of the train. This man purposed to throw himself out of the train in a certain tunnel just as the train coming from the opposite direction would be about to dash past; he thought this would make a quick end to his life.

There was a young man at the depot that night who had been saved the night before. He was all on fire to get others saved, and he purposed in his heart that every day of his life, he would get someone saved. He saw this dejected hangman and began to speak to him about his soul. He brought him down to our mission, and there he came under a mighty conviction of sin. For two-and-a-half hours he was literally sweating under conviction, and you could see a vapor rising up from him. At the end of two-and-a-half hours, he was graciously saved.

I said, "Lord, tell me what to do." The Lord said, "Don't leave him. Go home with him." I went to his house. When he saw his wife, he said, "God has saved me." The wife broke down, and she too was graciously saved. I tell you, there was a difference in that home. Even the cat knew the difference. Previous to this, the cat would always run away when that hangman came through the door. But the night that he was saved, the cat jumped onto his knee and went to sleep.

There were two sons in that house, and one of them said to his mother, "Mother, what is up in our house? It was never like this before. It is so peaceful. What is it?" She told him, "Father has gotten saved." The other son was also struck by the change.

I took this man to many special services, and the power of God was on him for many days. He would give his testimony, and as he grew in grace, he desired to preach the Gospel. He became an evangelist, and hundreds and hundreds were brought to a saving knowledge of the Lord Jesus Christ through his ministry. The grace of God is sufficient for the vilest, and He can take the most wicked men and make them monuments of His grace. He did this with Saul of Tarsus at the very time he was breathing out threats and slaughter against the disciples of the Lord. He did it with Berry the hangman. He will do it for hundreds more in response to our cries.

You will notice that when Ananias came into that house, he called the onetime enemy of the Gospel *"Brother Saul"* (Acts 9:17). He recognized that in those three days a blessed work had been accomplished and that Saul had been brought into relationship with the Father and with the Lord Jesus Christ. Was this not enough? No, there was something further, and for this purpose the Lord had sent Ananias to that house. The Lord Jesus had sent him to that house to put his hands upon this newly saved brother so that he might receive his sight and be filled with the Holy Spirit.

You say, "But it does not say that he spoke in tongues." We know that Paul did speak in tongues, that he spoke in tongues more than all the Corinthians (1 Cor. 14:18). In those early days, it was so soon after the time of that first Pentecostal outpouring that they would never have been satisfied with anyone receiving the baptism unless he received it according to the original pattern given on the Day of Pentecost.

When Peter was relating what had taken place in the house of Cornelius at Caesarea, he said, *"As I began to speak, the Holy Spirit fell upon them, as upon us at the beginning"* (Acts 11:15). Later, speaking of this incident, he said,

> *God, who knows the heart, acknowledged them by giving them the Holy Spirit, just as He did to us, and made no distinction between us and them, purifying their hearts by faith.*
> (Acts 15:8–9)

We know from the account of what took place at Cornelius's household that when the Holy Spirit fell, *"they heard them speak with tongues and magnify God"* (Acts 10:46).

Many people think that God makes a distinction between us and those who lived at the beginning of the church. But they have no Scripture for this. When anyone receives the gift of the Holy Spirit, there will assuredly be no difference between his experience today and what was given on the Day of Pentecost. And I cannot believe that, when Saul was filled with the Holy Spirit, the Lord made any difference in the experience that He gave him than the experience that He had given to Peter and the rest a short while before.

And so Saul was filled with the Holy Spirit, and in the later chapters of the Acts of the Apostles we see the result of this infilling. Oh, what a difference it makes.

The grace of God that was given to the persecuting Saul is available for you. The same infilling of the Holy Spirit that he received is likewise available. Do not rest satisfied with any lesser experience than the baptism that the disciples received on the Day of Pentecost. Then move on to a life of continuous receiving of more and more of the blessed Spirit of God.

CHAPTER SIX

RECEIVING THE BAPTISM

I believe God wants us to know more about the baptism of the Holy Spirit. And I believe that God wants us to know the truth in such a way that we may all have a clear understanding of what He means when He desires all His people to receive the Holy Spirit.

I want you to read this passage from the first chapter of the Acts of the Apostles:

The former account I made, O Theophilus, of all that Jesus began both to do and teach, until the day in which He was taken up, after He through the Holy Spirit had given commandments to the apostles whom He had chosen, to whom He also presented Himself alive after His suffering by many infallible proofs, being seen by them during forty days and speaking of the things pertaining to the kingdom of God. And being assembled together with them, He commanded them not to depart from Jerusalem, but to wait for the Promise of the Father, "which," He said, "you have heard from Me; for John truly baptized with water, but you shall be baptized with the Holy Spirit not many days from now." Therefore, when they had come together, they asked Him, saying, "Lord, will You at this time restore the kingdom to Israel?" And He said to them, "It is not for you to know times or seasons which the Father has put in His own authority. But you shall receive power when the Holy Spirit has come upon you; and you shall be witnesses to Me in Jerusalem, and in all Judea and Samaria, and to the end of the earth." Now when He had spoken these things, while they watched, He was taken up, and a cloud received

Him out of their sight. And while they looked steadfastly to-ward heaven as He went up, behold, two men stood by them in white apparel, who also said, "Men of Galilee, why do you stand gazing up into heaven? This same Jesus, who was taken up from you into heaven, will so come in like manner as you saw Him go into heaven." (Acts 1:1–11)

Jesus, our Mediator and Advocate, was filled with the Holy Spirit. He commanded His followers concerning these days we are in and gave instructions about the time through the Holy Spirit. I can see that if we are going to accomplish anything, we are going to accomplish it because we are under the power of the Holy Spirit.

During my lifetime, I have seen lots of satanic forces, Spiritualists, and all other "ists." I tell you that there is a power that is satanic, and there is a power that is the Holy Spirit. I remember that after we received the Holy Spirit and when people were speaking in tongues as the Spirit gave utterance—we don't know the Holy Spirit in any other way—the Spiritualists heard about it and came to the meeting in good time to fill two rows of seats.

When the power of God fell upon us, these imitators began their shaking and moving, with utterances from the satanic forces. The Spirit of the Lord was mighty upon me. I went to them and said, "Now you demons, clear out of here!" And out they went. I followed them right out into the street, and then they turned around and cursed me. It made no difference; they were out.

Beloved, the Lord wants us to know in these days that there is a fullness of God where all other powers must cease to be. And I implore you to hear that the baptism in the Holy Spirit is to possess us so that we are, and may be continually, so full of the Holy Spirit that utterances and revelations and eyesight and everything else may be so remarkably controlled by the Spirit of God that we live and move in this glorious sphere of usefulness for the glory of God.

And I believe that God wants to help us to see that every child of God ought to receive the Holy Spirit. Beloved, God wants us to understand that this is not difficult when we are in the right order. And I want you to see what it means to seek the Holy Spirit.

If we were to examine John's gospel, we would see that Jesus predicted all that we are getting today with the coming of the Holy Spirit. Our Lord said that the Holy Spirit would take of the things of His Word and reveal them to us. (See John 14:26; 16:14.) He would live out in us all of the life of Jesus.

If we could only think of what this really means! It is one of the ideals. Talk about graduation! My word! Come into the graduation of the Holy Spirit, and you will simply outstrip everything they have in any college there ever was. You would leave them all behind, just as I have seen the sun leave the mist behind in San Francisco. You would leave what is as cold as ice and go into the sunshine.

God the Holy Spirit wants us to know the reality of this fullness of the Spirit so that we will neither be ignorant nor have mystic conceptions but will have a clear, unmistakable revelation of the entire mind of God for these days.

> **INTERPRETATION OF A MESSAGE IN TONGUES:** "The Spirit of the living God comes with such divine revelation, such unveiling about Him, such a clearness of what He was to the people, and He brings within us the breath of that eternal power that makes us know we are right here, this very hour, to carry out His plan for now and what God will have for the future, for there is no limitation but rather an enforcement of character, of clearness of vision, of an openness of countenance until we behold Him in every divine light."

Glory! Oh, it is grand! Thank God for that interpretation.

I implore you, beloved, in the name of Jesus, that you should see that you come right into all the mind of God. Jesus truly said, *"But you shall receive power when the Holy Spirit has come upon you"* (Acts 1:8). And I want you to know that *"He also presented Himself alive after His suffering by many infallible proofs, being seen by them during forty days"* (v. 3). He is all the time unfolding to every one of us the power of resurrection.

THE BAPTISM IS RESURRECTION

Remember that the baptism of the Holy Spirit is resurrection. If you can touch this ideal of God with its resurrection power, you will see that nothing earthly can remain; you will see that all disease will clear out. If you get filled with the Holy Spirit, all satanic forces that cause fits, all lameness, all these foot afflictions, all these kidney troubles, and all these nervous, fearful things will go. _Resurrection_ is the word for it. Resurrection shakes away death and breathes life in you; it lets you know that you are quickened from the dead by the Spirit and that you are made like Jesus (Eph. 2:1, 5). Glory to God!

Oh, the word _resurrection!_ I wish I could say it on the same level as the word _Jesus._ They very harmoniously go together. Jesus is resurrection, and to know Jesus in this resurrection power is simply to see that you no longer have to be dead; you are alive unto God by the Spirit.

ENTERING INTO A NEW REALM

If you are a businessman, you need to be baptized in the Holy Spirit. For any kind of business, you need to know the power of the Holy Spirit, because if you are not baptized with the Holy Spirit, Satan has a tremendous power to interfere with the progress of your life. If you come into the baptism of the Holy Spirit, there is a new realm for your business.

I remember one day being in London at a meeting. About eleven o'clock, they said to me, "We will have to close the meeting. We are not allowed to have this place any later than eleven o'clock." There were several who were under the power of the Spirit. A man rose up and looked at me, saying, "Oh, don't leave me, please. I feel that I do not dare be left. I must receive the Holy Spirit. Will you go home with us?" "Yes," I said, "I will go." His wife was there as well. They were two hungry people just being awakened by the power of the Spirit to know that they were lacking in their lives and that they needed the power of God.

In about an hour's time, we arrived at their big, beautiful house in the country. It was wintertime. He began stirring the fire up and putting coal on, and he said, "We will soon have a tremendous fire, so we will get warmed. Then we will have a big supper." And I suppose the next thing would have been going to bed.

"No, thank you," I said. "I have not come here for your supper or for your bed. I thought you wanted me to come with you so that you might receive the Holy Spirit."

"Oh," he replied. "Will you pray with us?"

"I have come for nothing else." I knew I could keep myself warm in a prayer meeting without a fire.

About half past three in the morning, his wife was as full as could be, speaking in tongues. God was doing wonderful things that night. I went to the end of the table. There he was, groaning terribly. So I said, "Your wife has received the Holy Spirit." "Oh," he said, "this is going to be a big night for me." I tell you, you also will have big nights like this man had, whether you receive the baptism or not, if you will seek God with all your heart.

I often say there is more done in the seeking than in any other way. In the Scriptures, there is no such thing as seeking for the Holy Spirit. But we have to get to a place where we know that unless we meet face to face with God and get all the crooked places out of our lives, there will be no room for the Holy Spirit, for the indwelling presence of God. But when God gets a chance at us, and by the vision of the blood of Jesus we see ourselves as God sees us, then we have a revelation. Without this, we are undone and helpless.

At five o'clock in the morning, this man stood up and said, "I am through." He was not baptized. "I am settled," he continued. "God has settled me. Now I must have a few hours' rest before I go to my business at eight o'clock."

My word! That was quite a day at his business. In many years, he had never lived a day like that. He went about his business among all his men, and they said, "What is up with the man? What is up with the boss? What has taken place? Oh, what a change!"

The whole place was electrified. God had turned the lion into the lamb. Oh, formerly he had been like a great big lion prowling about, but God had touched him. The touch of Omnipotence had broken this man down until right there in his business the men were broken up in his presence. Oh, I tell you, there is something in pursuing; there is something in waiting. What is it? It is this: God slays a man so that he may begin on a new plane in his life. We will have to be utterly slain if we want to know that resurrection power of Jesus.

That night, at about ten o'clock, he was baptized in the Holy Spirit in a meeting. A short time afterward, when I was passing through the grounds toward this man's house, his two sons rushed out to where I was, threw their arms around me, and kissed me, saying, "You have sent us a new father."

Oh, the power of the Holy Spirit creates new men and new women. The Holy Spirit takes away your stony heart and gives you a heart of flesh (Ezek. 36:26–27). And when God gets His way like that, there is a tremendous shaking among the dry bones (see Ezekiel 37:4–10), for God gets His way with the people.

★ We must see that we are no good unless God takes charge of us. But when He gets real charge of us, what a plan for the future! What a wonderful open door for God!

Oh, beloved, we must see this ideal by the Spirit! What should we do? We do not dare to do anything but go through and receive the baptism. Submit to the power of God. If you yield, other people are saved. You will die unless you have a power of resurrection, a touch for others. But if you live only for God, then other people will be raised out of death and all kinds of evil into a blessed life through the Spirit.

Beloved, we must see that this baptism of the Spirit is greater than everything. You can talk as you like, say what you like, do as you like, but until you have the Holy Spirit, you won't know what the resurrection touch is. Resurrection is by the power of the Spirit. And remember, when I talk about resurrection, I am talking about one of the greatest things in the Scriptures. Resurrection is evidence that we have awakened with a new line of truth that cannot cease to be, but will always go on with a greater force and increasing power with God.

> INTERPRETATION OF A MESSAGE IN TONGUES: "Hallelujah! The Spirit breathes, the Spirit lifts, the Spirit renews, the Spirit quickens. He brings life where death was. He brings truth where no vision was. He brings revelation, for God is in that man. He is in the power of the Spirit, lost, hidden, clothed, filled, and resurrected."

Hallelujah! Thank God for that. See to it that today you press on with a new order of the Spirit so that you can never be where you were before. This is a new day for us all. You say, "What about the people who are already baptized in the Spirit?" Oh, this is a new day also for those who have been baptized, for the Spirit is an unlimited source of power. He is in no way stationary. Nothing in God is stationary. God has no place for a person who is stationary. The man who is going to catch the fire, hold forth the truth, and always be on the watchtower (Ezek. 33:7), is the one who is going to be a beacon for all saints, having a light greater than he would have naturally. He must see that God's grace, God's life, and God's Spirit are a million times mightier than he.

The man who is baptized in the Holy Spirit is baptized into a new order altogether. You cannot ever be ordinary after that. You are on an extraordinary plane; you are brought into line with the mind of God. You have come into touch with ideals in every way.

If you want oratory, it is in the baptism of the Spirit. If you want the touch of quickened sense that moves your body until you know that you are completely renewed, it is by the Holy Spirit. And while I say so much about the Holy Spirit, I withdraw everything that doesn't put Jesus in the place He belongs. For when I speak about the Holy Spirit, it is always with reference to revelations of Jesus. The Holy Spirit is only the Revealer of the mighty Christ who has everything for us so that we may never know any weakness. All limitations are gone. And you are now in a place where God has taken the ideal and moved you on with His own velocity, which has a speed beyond all human mind and thought. Glory to God!

INTERPRETATION OF A MESSAGE IN TONGUES: "Wake, you who sleep, and allow the Lord to wake you into righteousness. The liberty with which God has set you free—God has made you free to enlarge others who are bound."

So the Spirit of the Lord must have His way in everything. Oh, what would happen if we would all loosen ourselves up! Sometimes I think it is almost necessary to give an address to those who are already baptized in the Holy Spirit. I feel that, just like the Corinthian church, we may have, as it were, gifts and graces, and we may use them all, but we sit in them and do not go on beyond where we are. (See 1 Corinthians 14:12.)

I maintain that all gifts and graces are only for one thing: to make you desire gifts and graces. Don't miss what I say. Every touch of the divine life by the Spirit is only for one purpose: to make your life go on to a higher height than where you are. Beloved, if anybody has to rise up in the meeting to tell me how they were baptized with the Holy Spirit in order for me to know they are baptized, I say, "You have fallen from grace. You ought to have such a baptism that everybody can tell you are baptized without your telling how you were baptized." That would make a new day.

That would be a sermon in itself to everybody, not only in here but also outside. Then people would follow you to get to know where you have come from and where you are going. (See John 3:8.) You say, "I want that. I won't rest until I get that." God will surely give it to you.

The Holy Spirit never comes until there is a place ready for Him. The Holy Spirit can only come into us (His temples) when we are fully yielded to Him, for the Spirit *"does not dwell in temples made with hands"* (Acts 7:48) but in *"tablets of flesh, that is, of the heart"* (2 Cor. 3:3). So it doesn't matter what kind of a building you get; you cannot count on the building being a substitute for the Holy Spirit. You will all have to be temples of the Holy Spirit for the building to be anything like Holy Spirit order.

The Holy Spirit could not come until the apostles and the other disciples who were in the Upper Room on the Day of Pentecost were all of one mind and heart, all of one accord with each other and with God. Let me quote one verse to help you, because I am talking about the truth of what the fullness of *"the latter rain"* (Zech. 10:1) and the rapture of the church mean. James 5:7 is a beautiful verse regarding these things: *"Therefore be patient, brethren, until the coming of the Lord. See how the farmer waits for the precious fruit of the earth."*

What is the precious fruit of the earth? Is it cabbages? Is it grapes? The precious fruit of the earth is the church, the body of Christ. And God has no thought for other things. He causes the vegetation of the earth to grow and creates the glory of the flower. He gives attention to the beauty of flowers because He knows it will please us. But when speaking about the precious fruit of the earth, our Lord has His mind upon you today, and He says,

> *See how the farmer waits for the precious fruit of the earth, waiting patiently for it until it receives the early and latter rain. You also be patient. Establish your hearts, for the coming of the Lord is at hand.* (James 5:7–8)

So if you desire the coming of the Lord, you must certainly advocate having every believer filled with the Holy Spirit. The more a man is filled with the Holy Spirit, the more he will be ready to broadcast and send forth this glorious truth of the Lord's return.

The Holy Spirit cannot come until the church is ready. And you say, "When will the church be ready?" If believers were in an attitude of <u>yieldedness</u> and were in <u>unity with God</u> and <u>each other,</u> God could send the breath right now to make the church ready in ten minutes, even less than that.

So we can clearly say that the coming of the Lord is near to us, but it will be even closer to us as we are ready to receive a fuller and greater manifestation. What will be the manifestation of the coming of the Lord? If we were ready, and if the power of God were stressing that truth today, we would be rushing up to one another, saying, "He is coming; I know He is coming." "He is coming!" "Yes, I know He is." Every person around would be saying, "He is coming," and you would know He is coming.

That is the only hope of the future, and there is nothing except the Holy Spirit that can prepare the hearts of the people to rush up and down and say, "He is coming. He is coming soon." Praise God, He will come as surely as we are in this place. He is coming!

ALLOW GOD TO USE YOU

There are things I have had to learn about the baptism.

One day, in England, a lady wrote to ask if I would come and help her. She said she was blind, having two blood clots behind her eyes. I had been in London recently, and I didn't feel I wanted to go. However, I sent a letter, not knowing who she was, saying that if she was willing to go into a room with me and shut the door and never come out until she had perfect sight, I would come. She sent word, "Oh, come!"

The moment I reached the house, they brought in this blind woman. After we shook hands, she made her way to a room, opened the door, allowed me to go in, and then came in and shut the door. "Now," she said, "we are with God."

Have you ever been there? It is a lovely place.

In an hour and a half, the power of God fell upon us. Rushing to the window, she exclaimed, "I can see! Oh, I can see! The blood is gone; I can see!" Sitting down in a chair, she asked, "Could I receive the Holy Spirit?"

"Yes," I replied, "if all is right with God."

"You don't know me," she continued, "but for ten years I have been fighting your position. I couldn't bear these tongues, but God settled it today. I want the baptism of the Holy Spirit."

After she had prayed and repented of what she had said about tongues, she was filled with the Holy Spirit and began speaking in tongues.

When you put your hands upon people to pray, you can tell when the Holy Spirit is present. And if you will only yield to the Holy Spirit and allow Him to move, my word, what will happen!

RECEIVE THE SPIRIT AS A CHILD

I wonder how many people there are today who are prepared to be baptized? Oh, you say you couldn't be baptized? Then you have been an adult too long. You need to become childlike again. Do you know that there is a difference between being a baby and anything else in the world? Many people have been waiting for years for the baptism, and what has been the problem? We are told in the Scriptures,

> At that time Jesus answered and said, "I thank You, Father, Lord of heaven and earth, that You have hidden these things from the wise and prudent and have revealed them to babes."
> (Matt. 11:25)

What is the wise man's difficulty? A wise man is too careful. And while he is in the operation of the Spirit, he wants to know what he is saying. No man can know what he is saying when the Spirit is upon him. His own mind is inactive. If you get into that place in which you are near God, your mind is entirely obliterated, and the mind of Christ comes by the power of the Spirit. Under these conditions, Christ prays and speaks in the Spirit through you as the Spirit gives utterance.

It is the mind and plan of God for us to receive the Holy Spirit. What is the difference between the *"wise and prudent"* man and a baby? If you will get childlike enough this afternoon, at least fifty people will be baptized in the Holy Spirit. If you will only yield to God and let the Spirit have His way, God will fill you with the Holy Spirit.

In Sweden, the power of God was upon us, and I believe that more than a hundred people received the Holy Spirit in a quarter of an hour. May God grant it this afternoon. Beloved, it will be so, for God is with us.

The natural man cannot receive the Spirit of God (1 Cor. 2:14). But when you get into a supernatural place, then you receive the mind of God. Again, what is the difference between a *"wise and prudent"* man and a baby? The man drinks cautiously, but the baby swallows it all, and the mother has to hold the bottle, or some of that will go down, too. This is how God wants it to be in the Spirit: The spiritually minded baby cannot walk; however, God walks in him. The spiritually minded baby cannot talk, but God talks through him. The spiritually minded baby cannot dress himself, but God dresses him and clothes him with His righteousness.

Oh, beloved, if we can only be infants in this way today, great things will take place along the lines and thought of the Spirit of God. The Lord wants us all to be so like-minded with Him that He can put His seal upon us.

There are some in this meeting who no doubt have never been saved. Where the saints are seeking, and leaving themselves to the operation of the Spirit, there will be newborn children in the midst. God will save in our midst. God will use this means of blessing if we will only let ourselves go. You say, "What can I do?" The fiddler will drop his fiddle, the drummer his drum. If there is anybody here who has anything hanging around him, weighing him down, it will fall off. If you will become childlike enough today, everything else will fall off, and you will be free. You will be able to run and skip in the street, and you will be happy.

Does the baby ever lose his intelligence? Does he ever lose his common sense? Does the baby who comes into the will of God lose his reason or his credentials in any way? No, God will increase your abilities and help you in everything. I am not talking here about just being a baby. I am talking about being a baby in the Spirit. Paul said in 1 Corinthians 14:20, *"In malice be babes, but in under-standing be mature."* And I believe the Spirit would breathe through all the attributes of the Spirit so that we may understand what the mind of the Lord is concerning us in the Holy Spirit.

Oh, this blessed thought. I want to help all who are being baptized to help others. If you have ever spoken in tongues in your life, let yourself go today, and God will speak through you. You must have a day you have never had before. This must be an ideal day in the Spirit, a day with the anointing of the Spirit, a day with the mind of God in the Spirit.

CHAPTER SEVEN

OUR HEAVENLY DWELLING

I believe the Lord would be pleased for us to turn to the fourth chapter of 2 Corinthians and read from the sixteenth verse, concluding with the seventh verse of the fifth chapter:

> *For which cause we faint not; but though our outward man perish, yet the inward man is renewed day by day. For our light affliction, which is but for a moment, worketh for us a far more exceeding and eternal weight of glory; while we look not at the things which are seen, but at the things which are not seen: for the things which are seen are temporal; but the things which are not seen are eternal. For we know that if our earthly house of this tabernacle were dissolved, we have a building of God, an house not made with hands, eternal in the heavens. For in this we groan, earnestly desiring to be clothed upon with our house which is from heaven: if so be that being clothed we shall not be found naked. For we that are in this tabernacle do groan, being burdened: not for that we would be unclothed, but clothed upon, that mortality might be swallowed up of life. Now he that hath wrought us for the selfsame thing is God, who also hath given unto us the earnest of the Spirit. Therefore we are always confident, knowing that, whilst we are at home in the body, we are absent from the Lord: (for we walk by faith, not by sight).* (2 Cor. 4:16–5:7 KJV)

I believe the Lord has in His mind the further freedom of life. Nothing will please the Lord so much as for us to come into our fullness of redemption, because I believe that *"the Lord is the Spirit; and where the Spirit of the Lord is, there is liberty"* (2 Cor. 3:17).

WHAT ABOUT MANIFESTATIONS?

Liberty is beautiful when we never use it to satisfy ourselves but use it in the Lord. We must never transgress because of liberty. What I mean is this: it would be wrong for me to take opportunities just because the Spirit of the Lord is upon me. But it would be perfectly justifiable if I clearly allow the Spirit of the Lord to have His liberty with me. However, we are not to behave inappropriately in our liberty, for the flesh is more extravagant than the Spirit.

The Spirit's extravagances are always for edification, strengthening character, and bringing us all more into conformity with the life of Christ. But fleshly extravagances always mar and bring the saints into a place of trial for a moment. As the Spirit of the Lord takes further hold of a person, we may get liberty in it, but we are tried through the manifestations of it.

I believe we have come to a liberty of the Spirit that is so pure it will never bring a frown of distraction over another person's mind. I have seen many people who were in the power of the Spirit and yet exhibited a manifestation that was not foundational or even helpful. I have seen people under the mighty power of the Holy Spirit who have waved their hands wildly and moved on the floor and gone on in such a state that no one could say the body was not under the power. However, there was more natural power than spiritual power there, and the natural condition of the person, along with the spiritual condition, caused the manifestation. Though we know the Spirit of the Lord was there, the manifestation was not something that would elevate or please the people or grant them a desire for more of that. It wasn't an edification of the Spirit.

If there are any here who have those manifestations, I want to help you. I don't want to hurt you. It is good that you should have the Spirit upon you; people need to be filled with the Spirit. But you never have a right to say you couldn't help doing this, that, or the other manifestation.

No manifestation of the body ever glorifies the Lord except the tongue. If you seek to be free in the operation of the Spirit through the mouth, then the tongue which may be under a kind of subconscious control by the Spirit, brings out the glory of the Lord, and that will always bring edification, consolation, and comfort.

No other manifestation will do this. Still, I believe that it is necessary to have all these other manifestations when someone is filled with the Spirit for the first time. It seems to be almost necessary for some people to kick. I have seen some people leaping in the air so that you could hardly see across the room.

When the Spirit is there, the flesh must find some way out, and so, through past experience, we allow all these things at the beginning. But I believe the Holy Spirit brings a sound condition of mind, and the first thing must pass away so that the divine position may remain. And so there are various manifestations, including kicking and waving, that take place at the incoming of the Holy Spirit, when the flesh and the Spirit are in conflict. One must decrease and die, and the other must increase and multiply.

Consequently, when you come to understand this, you are in a place of sound judgment and know that now the Holy Spirit has come to take you on with God.

Suppose I were to read this Scripture verse in a meeting:

We do not look at the things which are seen, but at the things which are not seen. For the things which are seen are temporary, but the things which are not seen are eternal.
(2 Cor. 4:18)

What would you think if, at this point, I had to stop because of a great kicking sensation, and I had to lie down on the floor for three hours before I could go on with what the Spirit of the Lord was saying because my body and spirit were in disagreement? The glory of the Lord is upon me, and the Lord is speaking through me, but now I must stop to have a half hour of kicking. All the people in the audience are waiting to see Wigglesworth kick through a half hour before he goes on. I wonder if you would think that was in the will of God?

★ I don't believe it is in the will of God, and I never believe you have a license to do it. I will never believe that God would baptize you with the Holy Spirit and then make you like a machine so that you couldn't begin at any time and stop at any time.

All these things that I am speaking about are necessary for you for further advancement in the Spirit. To me it is a very marvelous thing that the Spirit can have such mightiness over a body to kick out the flesh.

I have known some people, when they have gone through to receiving the baptism in the Holy Spirit, whom God has begun in a new way. When the Lord baptized me with the Holy Spirit, at first there was so much flesh that needed to be done away with that I went all around the dining room on my knees, clapping my hands. I went through it, and at the end of it was tongues. Then I stopped because there was no more kick left. It couldn't go out through my feet when tongues were coming out through my mouth.

When the Holy Spirit is allowed full reign over the operation of human life, He always works out divine wisdom. And when He gets perfect control of a life, the divine source flows through so that all the people may receive edification in the Spirit. If you act foolishly after you have had wisdom taught you, nobody will give you much leeway.

"We then that are strong ought to bear the infirmities of the weak" (Rom. 15:1 KJV). Some who come to these meetings know nothing about the power of the Holy Spirit. They get saved and are quickened, and after the Spirit comes upon them, you will see all these manifestations. In love and grace, you should bear with them as newborn babes in the Spirit and rejoice with them because that is only a beginning to an end. The Lord wouldn't want us to be anything but *"strong in the Lord and in the power of His might"* (Eph. 6:10) to help everyone around us.

LIVING THE ASCENSION LIFE

I want you to keep these four verses primary in your mind throughout the rest of this message:

> *For we know that if our earthly house of this tabernacle were dissolved, we have a building of God, an house not made with hands, eternal in the heavens. For in this we groan, earnestly desiring to be clothed upon with our house which is from heaven: if so be that being clothed we shall not be found naked. For we that are in this tabernacle do groan, being burdened: not for that we would be unclothed, but clothed upon, that mortality might be swallowed up of life.* (2 Cor. 5:1–4 KJV)

I feel I may speak to you with perfect freedom because I believe the Lord is helping us to comprehend a very deep spiritual condition.

In the first place, I believe that we will all grasp the truth that we are not our own (1 Cor. 6:19). In the second place, we belong to a spiritual order; we don't belong to the earth. And not only that, but our minds and our bodies—our whole position through the eternal Spirit—always have to be on the ascending position. To descend is to be conformed. To ascend is to be transformed.

In this transforming condition, we may, by the power of the Spirit, as God gives us revelation, be lifted up into a very blessed state of fellowship with God, of power with God. And in that place of power with God, we will have power over everything else, for to have all power over the earth, we must first have power with God.

We know we are heavenly citizens (Phil. 3:20). We know we have to exit this earth and have been preparing for our exit. Yet while we are on earth, we must live in the place where we groan over everything that binds us from being loosed from the world.

What will hold me? Association will hold me in this present world. I must have no earthly associations that have a greater influence over me than God does—and you know it is as natural to have an earthly association as it is to live. I must hold every earthly association at a distance. It must never tie me or bind me. It must never have any persuasion over me. Hear what the Scripture says: *"Being conformed to His death"* (Phil. 3:10).

What does it mean to conform to the death of Jesus? It leads me to that death of separation to God, of yieldedness, of exchange, where God takes me to Himself and leaves the old nature behind. *"While we do not look at the things which are seen, but at the things which are not seen"* (2 Cor. 4:18).

Then we may grasp some idea of what it will mean if we die to ourselves. I want us to see, by the grace of God, that the dissolving (see 2 Corinthians 5:1 KJV) is a great thought. There is a position in God that we must clearly understand: *"Not because we want to be unclothed, but further clothed, that mortality may be swallowed up by life"* (2 Cor. 5:4).

"Mortality" is a great word. While it is necessary, it is a hindrance. While mortality has done a great deal to produce everything we see, it is a hindrance if we live in it. It is a helpful position if we live over it.

Then we must understand how mortality can be *"swallowed up."* We must know how the old body, the old tendencies to the fallen nature, may be swallowed up. There is a verse we must come to. It would serve us to look at it now: *"Always carrying about in the body the dying of the Lord Jesus, that the life of Jesus also may be manifested in our body"* (2 Cor. 4:10).

What is this *"dying of the Lord"*? It is dying to desire. In the measure that we look to one another for our help, we lose faith in God. If you rely upon any man or woman, upon any human assistance, to help you, you fall out of the greater purpose God has for you.

You must learn that no earthly source can ever assist you in this. You are going to this realm of life only by mortality being swallowed up by life: *"And the life which I now live in the flesh I live by faith in the Son of God"* (Gal. 2:20). It is a process of dying and living.

God will help us today. I know He will. I believe that the Lord will not let the preacher be anything anymore. All these messages that God is giving me show me that I have nothing in myself. But thank God, I am in Christ. Truly so.

I do not dare give way to my own self because I would only look like a fool. But I tell you, this life I am speaking about absolutely ravishes you. It absolutely severs you from earthly connections. It absolutely disjoins you from all earthly help. And I can understand this word now more than ever: *"You have not yet resisted to bloodshed, striving against sin"* (Heb. 12:4).

The great striving to the point of bloodshed—blood being the very essence of life—we have not yet resisted to that degree, but we will. I know the Scripture says we have not, but I know it means that we have not arrived there yet. But thank God, we are in it in a measure.

The apostle Paul could see that if he had any communion with flesh and blood, he couldn't go forward in the Lord. (See Galatians 1:15–17.) It was even necessary for Jesus' flesh and blood ties to be put in this context. Jesus said,

> *"Who is My mother and who are My brothers?" And He stretched out His hand toward His disciples and said, "Here are My mother and My brothers! For whoever does the will of My Father in heaven is My brother and sister and mother."*
>
> (Matt. 12:48–50)

Flesh and blood were nothing to Jesus. The body that brought Him forth was nothing to Him. God brought Him into the world as a seed of life. To Him, that obedient believer was His mother, that servant of God was His brother, that follower of Christ was His sister. But this is a higher ideal; this takes spiritual knowledge.

Let us look at another example of dying to self taken from Jesus' life. In the Garden of Gethsemane, Jesus faced His suffering from two different standpoints. His human nature instantly cried out, *"If it is possible, let this cup pass from Me"* (Matt. 26:39). The next moment, he was saying, with His divine nature, *"Nevertheless, not as I will, but as You will"* (v. 39). He also said, *"But for this purpose I came to this hour"* (John 12:27). His human nature had no more choices left. He was off to face the cross.

When God the Holy Spirit brings us to see these truths, we will deny ourselves for the sake of the Cross. We will deny ourselves of anything that would cause our brother to stumble. We will die to all fleshly indulgences, lest we should miss the great swallowing up by life (2 Cor. 5:4). We will not even mention or ever pay attention to anything along natural lines.

If we will allow God to govern us, He will lift us up into a higher state of grace than we have ever been in before. If believers could take hold of this spiritual power, they could stand anything along the lines of ridicule by a husband or wife. When are we distracted and disturbed? When we don't reach the ideals in the Spirit. When we reach the ideals in the Spirit, what does it matter? I find that the power of God sanctifies husband and wife.

One half of the trouble in the assemblies is the people's murmuring over the conditions they are in. The Bible teaches us not to murmur. If you reach that standard, you will never murmur anymore. You will be above murmuring. You will be in the place where God is absolutely the exchanger of thought, the exchanger of actions, and the exchanger of your inward purity. He will be purifying you all the time and lifting you higher, and you will know you are not of this world (John 15:19).

★ You are not of this world. If you want to stay in the world, you cannot go on with God. If you are not of this world, your position in the world in your banking affairs and everything else will have the least effect on you. Yet you will know that everything will work for your good if you climb the ladder of faith with God (Rom. 8:28). God will keep the world in perfect order and give you success in the end.

But you will not allow God to work for you; you are so involved in the world that He cannot get your attention. How can someone get into this divine order when he is torn between these two things: God and the world? He cannot let himself go and let God take him.

Let us read the passage from 2 Corinthians again, starting from the seventeenth verse:

*For our light affliction, which is but for a moment, worketh
for us a far more exceeding and eternal weight of glory; while
we look not at the things which are seen, but at the things
which are not seen: for the things which are seen are temporal; but the things which are not seen are eternal. For we
know that if our earthly house of this tabernacle were dissolved, we have a building of God, an house not made with
hands, eternal in the heavens.* (2 Cor. 4:17–5:1 KJV)

I maintain that, by the grace of God, we are so rich, we are so
abounding, we have such a treasure-house, we have such a storehouse of God, we have such an unlimited faith to share in all that
God has, for it is ours. We are the cream of the earth; we are the
precious fruit of the earth.

God has told us that all things will work together for our good
(Rom. 8:28). God has said that we will be the *"children of the Highest"* (Luke 6:35 KJV) and that we will be the *"salt of the earth"*
(Matt. 5:13). God has declared all that in His Word, and you will
never reach those beatitudes if you are holding on to the lower
things of this world; they will keep you down.

How am I to have all the treasures of heaven and all the treasures of God? Not by getting my eyes on the things that are seen, for
they will fade away. I must get my eyes on the things that are not
seen, for they will remain as long as God reigns.

Where are we? Are our eyes on the earth? You once had your
eyes on the earth. All your members were in the earth, working out
the plan of the earth. But now a change is taking place. I read in
the Scriptures: *"That you may be married to another; to Him who
was raised from the dead, that we should bear fruit to God"* (Rom.
7:4).

✶ You are joined to Another; you belong to Another. You have a
new life; you have a new place. God has changed you. Is it a living
fact? If it is only a word, it will end there. But if it is a spiritual fact,
and you reign in it, you will go away from this meeting and say,
"Thank God, I never knew I was so rich!" How to loose and how to
bind in the Spirit—these are great ideals.

DISSOLVED AND MADE LIKE CHRIST

I want you to see that there are two aspects to this: there is a
swallowing up (2 Cor. 5:4) and a dissolving (v. 1 KJV). I like the

213

thought of dissolving. Will that dissolving take place while we are still living on earth? We will not want it to be any other way. When will the clothing upon take place so that we may not be naked (2 Cor. 5:3)? It will take place while we live on earth. People believe that these conditions are not attainable while we live, but all these are spiritual blessings that *are* attainable while we live. These beatitudes dovetail so perfectly with those in the fifth chapter of Matthew's gospel. We will have to wake up and see that there are so many things in that fifth chapter of Matthew's gospel that are as practical as can be. Then God will be able to trust us with them along these lines.

I want us to grasp this idea of dissolving: *"For we know that if our earthly house of this tabernacle were dissolved, we have a building of God, an house not made with hands, eternal in the heavens"* (v. 1 KJV).

That is a perfect condition of a heavenly atmosphere and dwelling place. Let me take you there today. If I live on the earth, I fail everything. If I continue on the earth, everything I do will be mortal and will die. If I live in the heavenly realms, in the heavenly places, everything I touch will become spiritual, vital, purified, and eternal.

We must comprehend today by the faith of God how everything can be dissolved. I will explain it to you first in its heavenly connotation because you will understand it better that way. I will talk about it in regard to the Rapture, for that is what everyone focuses on in this passage. They say, "Some day we will leave the earth, and everything will be dissolved, and we will be clothed with new bodies for heavenly conditions."

But let me now explain a different way of looking at it. What is the good of having a white raiment to cover your nakedness so that it may not be seen in heaven? You know very well that isn't a heavenly condition. There will be no flesh in heaven. No nakedness will be seen in heaven. Then what does it really mean? It means that the power of God can so dwell in us that it can burn up everything that is not spiritual and dissolve it to the perfection of beauty and holiness that Jesus has. He walked on this earth, and when Satan came, he could find nothing in Him. (See John 14:30.) Jesus was perfectly dissolved in regard to everything in His human nature, and He lived in the Spirit over everything else. As He is, so we have to be. (See 1 John 4:17.)

We shouldn't be troubled in the flesh. Was Jesus troubled in the flesh? Didn't He go forth with perfect victory? It is impossible for any avenue of flesh, or anything that you touch in your natural body, to be helpful. Even your eyes have to be sanctified by the power of God so that they strike fire every time you look at a sinner, and the sinner will be changed.

We will be clothed with a robe of righteousness in God so that wherever we walk, there will be a whiteness of effectiveness that will bring people to a place of conviction of sin. You say, "There are so many things in my house that would have to be thrown out the window if Jesus came to my home." I pray that we could understand that He is already in the house all the time. Everything ought to go out the window that couldn't stand His eyes on it. Every impression of our hearts that would bring trouble if He looked at us ought to go forever.

You ask, "What are we to do?" It is in the message I am preaching; we are to be *"swallowed up by life"* (2 Cor. 5:4). The great I AM in perfect holiness—is He only an example? By the grace of God, He isn't just the example, but He clothes us with His own nature.

It is impossible for us to subdue kingdoms (see Hebrews 11:33), impossible for the greater works to be accomplished (see John 14:12), impossible for the Son of God to be making sons on earth except as we stand exactly in His place. It is lovely, and I must win Him. There isn't a place in Scripture that God spoke about that He doesn't have for us and that He won't take us into, beloved.

INTERPRETATION OF A MESSAGE IN TONGUES: "It is a whole burnt offering. It is a perfect sacrifice. It is a place where we are perfectly justified, where we have been 'partakers of His divine nature,' and become personated with His holiness, where we still are there, and He is still in the place of working out His great purpose in us, which is the work of God. 'For it is God who works in you to will and to do' these things when we are still and dissolved and put to death, where only the life of Christ is being manifested."

And that is the interpretation of the Spirit. It is both a lofty look and a lowly place.

Understand what "a whole burnt offering" means: a place of ashes, a place of helplessness, a place of wholehearted surrender where you do not refer to yourself. You have no justification of your own in regard to anything. You are prepared to be slandered, to be despised by everybody. You are of no importance to anybody but God. But because of His personality in you, He reserves you for Himself because you are godly (Ps. 4:3), and He sets you on high because you have known His name (Ps. 91:14). He causes you to be the fruit of His loins and to bring forth His glory so that you will not in any way rest in yourself or have any confidence in yourself. Your confidence will be in God. Ah, it is lovely.

"The Lord is the Spirit; and where the Spirit of the Lord is, there is liberty (2 Cor. 3:17).

> INTERPRETATION OF A MESSAGE IN TONGUES: "And in the depths of the heart there comes forth to us this morning this truth: 'Set your house in order.' See to it that you do not allow anything that could be there that He could see that He could be displeased with. Your house is your body; 'your body is the temple of the Spirit.'"

See to it that you obey that message.

I wonder how much we know about groaning to be delivered? (See Acts 7:34.) I think I can get an illustration of it by turning to the book of Nehemiah. But before we read a passage from there, please understand that to the Jews, Jerusalem was everything. Jerusalem to the Jews is a great deal now, but it is nothing more to us than any other city. Why? Theirs is an earthly type, but ours is a heavenly one. Our Jerusalem is the glory.

Now, Nehemiah said that one day a report was brought to him:

> *Hanani one of my brethren came with men from Judah; and I asked them concerning the Jews who had escaped, who had survived the captivity, and concerning Jerusalem. And they said to me, "The survivors who are left from the captivity in the province are there in great distress and reproach. The wall of Jerusalem is also broken down, and its gates are burned with fire." So it was, when I heard these words, that I sat down and wept, and mourned for many days; I was fasting and praying before the God of heaven.* (Neh. 1:2–4)

Nehemiah mourned, fasted, and prayed until his humility and yieldedness before God brought the same thing that God's Word brings to us: it dissolved him. It brought everything of his old nature into a dissolved place where he went right through into the presence of God.

Now, Nehemiah was the cupbearer for the Persian king Artaxerxes. The moment the king saw Nehemiah's sad expression, he asked, "What is the matter with you, Nehemiah? I have never seen your countenance changed like this." (See Nehemiah 2:1–2.) Nehemiah was so near almightiness before the king that he could pray and move the heavens and move the king and move the world until Jerusalem was restored.

He mourned. When we reach a place where the Spirit takes us to see our weaknesses, our depravity, our failings—when we mourn before God—we will be dissolved, and in the dissolving, we will be clothed with our house from heaven. We will walk in white; we will be robed with a new robe, and this *"mortality* [will] *be swallowed up by life"* (2 Cor. 5:4).

Beloved, Christ can bring every one of us, if we will, into a wholehearted dependency where God will never fail us but we will *"reign in life"* (Rom. 5:17). We will travail and bring forth fruit; for Zion, when she travails, will make the house of hell shake. (See Isaiah 66:8.)

Will we reach this place? Our blessed Lord reached it. Every night He went alone and reached ideals and walked the world in white. He was clothed with the Holy Spirit from heaven.

Daniel entered into the same negotiations with heaven through the same inward aspiration. He groaned and travailed until for three weeks he shook the heavens and moved Gabriel to come. Gabriel passed through all the regions of the damned to bring the message to him.

There was something so beautiful about the whole thing that even Daniel, in his most holy, beautiful state, became as corruption before the presence of Gabriel. And Gabriel strengthened Daniel by his right hand and lifted him up and gave him the visions of the world's history that are to be fulfilled. (See Daniel 9–12.)

INTERPRETATION OF A MESSAGE IN TONGUES: "The lamentable condition where God travails through the soul, touches by the Almighty the man of God like Gabriel, touches the human flesh and changes it and makes it bring forth and 'blossom even like the rose'; out of death into life, the powers of God will be."

You cannot get into life except through death, and you cannot get into death except by life. The only way to go into fullness with God is for the life of Christ to swallow up the natural life. For the natural life to be swallowed up, there must be nothing there but helplessness until the life of Christ strengthens the natural life. Yet instead of the natural life being strengthened, the spiritual life comes forth with abounding conditions.

KNOW NO MAN ACCORDING TO THE FLESH

Much has been given this morning in the Spirit that has never been given by me before, and I know that God has brought this message through a travail; it has come this morning for us. It will mean a lot more to us if we don't let these things slip. Let us grasp something from the sixteenth verse: *"Therefore, from now on, we regard no one according to the flesh. Even though we have known Christ according to the flesh, yet now we know Him thus no longer"* (2 Cor. 5:16).

To no longer know any man according to the flesh is a great thing. Beloved, we will no longer know any man along natural lines. From this moment, we will know everything only on a spiritual basis. Conversation must be spiritual. We can get distracted after we have had a really good meal; instead of no longer knowing any man according to the flesh, so that everything is in spiritual fellowship and union, we lower the standard by talking about natural things.

If you ride with me in a train compartment, you will have to pray or testify. If you don't, you will hear a whole lot of talk that will lower the anointing, bring you into a kind of bondage, and make you feel you wish you were out of the compartment. But if you break in and have a prayer meeting, you will turn the whole thing around. Go in and pray until you know everybody has been touched by it.

If you go out to dinner with anybody today, don't get sidetracked by listening to a long story about the state of their businesses. You must know only one Man now, and that is Christ, and He hasn't any businesses. Yet He is Lord over all businesses. Live

in the Spirit, and all things will work together for good to you
(Rom. 8:28). If you live for your businesses, you will not know the
mind of the Spirit. However, if you live in the *"heavenly places"*
(Eph. 2:6), you will cause your businesses and all things to come
out of their difficulties, for God will fight for you.

"We regard no one according to the flesh" (2 Cor. 5:16). I won't
enter into anything that is lower than spiritual fidelity. When I am
preaching spiritually anointing thoughts, I must see that I lift my
people into a place where I know the Spirit is leading me to know
Jesus.

Suppose you know Jesus. What do you say? That He lost out?
No, He didn't. But a great deal was put upon Him by the people
who said,

> *Is this not the carpenter's son? Is not His mother called Mary?*
> *And His brothers James, Joses, Simon, and Judas? And His*
> *sisters, are they not all with us? Where then did this Man get*
> *all these things?* (Matt. 13:55–56)

They said, "He is only an ordinary man. He was born the same
way we all were. You see Him. So what is He?"

You will never get anything that way. He wasn't an ordinary
man if He was born out of the "loins of Abraham." Two sons were
born to Abraham: Isaac and Ishmael. One was the son of promise,
the other wasn't. But Isaac, the son of promise, got the blessings.
Isaac was a type of Christ. You can never enter into God's conditions in any way but the spiritual way.

For a time, a cloud overshadowed Jesus because of His ances-
try. With the Jews, it overshadows Him today because the veil is
over their eyes; but the veil will be lifted. (See 2 Corinthians 3:14–
16.) With the Gentiles, the veil is already lifted.

We see Him as the Incarnation, as the Holy One of God, as the
Son of God, as the *"only begotten of the Father, full of grace and
truth"* (John 1:14). We see Him as the Burden-Bearer, as our Sanc-
tifier, as our Cleanser, as our Baptizer. Know no man according to
the flesh, but see Him! As we behold Him in all His glory, we will
rise; we cannot help but rise in the power of God.

Know no man according to the flesh. You will draw people if
you refuse to be contaminated by the world. People want holiness.

People want righteousness. People want purity. People have an inward longing to be clothed with the Spirit.

May the Lord lead you to the supply of every need, far more than you can *"ask or think"* (Eph. 3:20). May the Lord bless you as you are led to dedicate yourself afresh to God this very day. Amen.

CHAPTER EIGHT

CLOTHED WITH THE SPIRIT

G od has a plan for us in this life of the Spirit, this abundant life. Jesus came so that we might have life (John 10:10). Satan comes to steal and kill and destroy (v. 10), but God has abundance for us—full measure, pressed down, shaken together, overflowing, abundant measure (Luke 6:38). This abundance is God filling us with His own personality and presence, making us salt and light and giving us a revelation of Himself. It is God with us in all circumstances, afflictions, persecutions, and trials, girding us with truth. Christ the Initiative, the Triune God, is in control, and our every thought, word, and action must be in line with Him, with no weakness or failure. Our God is a God of might, light, and revelation, preparing us for heaven. Our lives are *"hidden with Christ in God"* (Col. 3:3). When He *"who is our life"* is manifested, we will also *"appear with Him in glory"* (v. 4).

THE GUARANTEE OF THE SPIRIT

For we know that if our earthly house, this tent, is destroyed, we have a building from God, a house not made with hands, eternal in the heavens....For we who are in this tent groan, being burdened, not because we want to be unclothed, but further clothed, that mortality may be swallowed up by life. Now He who has prepared us for this very thing is God, who also has given us the Spirit as a guarantee. (2 Cor. 5:1, 4–5)

God's Word is a tremendous word, a productive word. It produces what it is—power. It produces Godlikeness. We get to heaven through Christ, the Word of God; we have peace through the blood of His cross. Redemption is ours through the knowledge of the Word. I am saved because God's Word says so: *"If you confess with your mouth the Lord Jesus and believe in your heart that God has raised Him from the dead, you will be saved"* (Rom. 10:9).

If I am baptized with the Holy Spirit, it is because Jesus said, *"You shall receive power when the Holy Spirit has come upon you"* (Acts 1:8). We must all have one thought—to be filled with the Holy Spirit, to be filled with God.

> INTERPRETATION OF A MESSAGE IN TONGUES: "God has 'sent His Word' to free us from the 'law of sin and death.' Except we die, we cannot live; except we cease to be, God cannot be."

The Holy Spirit has a royal plan, a heavenly plan. He came to unveil the King, to show the character of God, to unveil the precious blood of Jesus. Because I have the Holy Spirit within me, I see Jesus clothed for humanity. He was moved by the Spirit, led by the Spirit. We read of some who heard the Word of God but did not benefit from it because faith was lacking in them (Heb. 4:2). We must have a living faith in God's Word, a faith that is quickened by the Spirit.

A man may be saved and still be carnally minded. When many people hear about the baptism of the Holy Spirit, their carnal minds at once arise against the Holy Spirit. *"The carnal mind...is not subject to the law of God, nor indeed can be"* (Rom. 8:7). One time, Jesus' disciples wanted to call down fire from heaven as a punishment against a Samaritan village for not welcoming Him. But Jesus said to them, *"You do not know what manner of spirit you are of"* (Luke 9:55).

> *For we who are in this tent groan, being burdened, not because we want to be unclothed, but further clothed, that mortality may be swallowed up by life. Now He who has prepared us for this very thing is God, who also has given us the Spirit as a guarantee.* (2 Cor. 5:4–5)

When we are clothed with the Spirit, our human depravity is covered and everything that is contrary to the mind of God is destroyed. God must have people for Himself who are being clothed with a heavenly habitation, perfectly prepared by the Holy Spirit for the Day of the Lord. *"For in this we groan, earnestly desiring to be clothed with our habitation which is from heaven"* (2 Cor. 5:2).

Was Paul speaking here only about the coming of the Lord? No. Yet this condition of preparedness on earth is related to our heavenly state. The Holy Spirit is coming to take out of the world a church that is a perfect bride. He must find in us perfect yieldedness, with every desire subjected to Him. He has come to reveal Christ in us so that the glorious flow of the life of God may flow out of us, bringing *"rivers of living water"* (John 7:38) to the thirsty land.

"If Christ is in you, the body is dead because of sin, but the Spirit is life because of righteousness" (Rom. 8:10).

THE PLAN OF THE SPIRIT

INTERPRETATION OF A MESSAGE IN TONGUES: "This is what God has declared: freedom from the law. 'If we love the world, the love of the Father is not in us.'"

"For all that is in the world; the lust of the flesh, the lust of the eyes, and the pride of life; is not of the Father but is of the world" (1 John 2:16).

The Spirit has to breathe into us a new occupancy, a new order. He came to give the vision of a new life.

[God] *has saved us and called us with a holy calling, not according to our works, but according to His own purpose and grace which was given to us in Christ Jesus before time began, but has now been revealed by the appearing of our Savior Jesus Christ, who has abolished death and brought life and immortality to light through the gospel.* (2 Tim. 1:9–10)

We are *"saved,"* called with *"a holy calling"*—*"called to be saints"* (Rom. 1:7), holy, pure, Godlike, sons with power (John 1:12 KJV). It has been a long time now since the debt of sin was settled, our redemption was secured, and death was abolished. Mortality is a hindrance, but death no longer has power. Sin no longer has dominion. You reign in Christ; you appropriate His finished work. Don't groan and travail for a week if you are in need; *"only believe"* (Mark 5:36). Don't fight to get some special thing; *"only believe."* It is according to your faith that you will receive (Matt. 9:29). God blesses you with faith. *"Have faith in God"* (Mark 11:22). If you are free in God, believe, and it will come to pass.

"If then you were raised with Christ, seek those things which are above, where Christ is, sitting at the right hand of God" (Col. 3:1). Stir yourselves up, beloved! Where are you? I have been planted with Christ in the likeness of His death, and I am risen with Christ (Rom. 6:5 KJV). It was a beautiful planting. I am seated with Him in heavenly places (Eph. 2:6). God credits me with righteousness through faith in Christ (Rom. 4:5), and I believe Him. Why should I doubt?

INTERPRETATION OF A MESSAGE IN TONGUES: "Why do you doubt? Faith reigns. God makes it possible. How many receive the Holy Spirit, and Satan gets a doubt in? Don't doubt; believe. There is power and strength in Him; who will dare to believe God?"

Leave Doubting Street; live on Faith-Victory Street. Jesus sent the seventy out, and they came back in victory. (See Luke 10:1–18.) It takes God to make it real. Dare to believe until there is not a sick person, until there is no sickness, until everything that is not of God is withered, and the life of Jesus is implanted within.

CHAPTER NINE

FILLED WITH GOD

L et us begin by reading the second chapter of Hebrews. This passage, like every other Scripture, is very important for us. At first read, we could scarcely pick any special Scripture out of this passage, for it is all so full of truth. It means so much to us.

Therefore we must give the more earnest heed to the things we have heard, lest we drift away. For if the word spoken through angels proved steadfast, and every transgression and disobedience received a just reward, how shall we escape if we neglect so great a salvation, which at the first began to be spoken by the Lord, and was confirmed to us by those who heard Him, God also bearing witness both with signs and wonders, with various miracles, and gifts of the Holy Spirit, according to His own will? For He has not put the world to come, of which we speak, in subjection to angels. But one testified in a certain place, saying: "What is man that You are mindful of him, or the son of man that You take care of him? You have made him a little lower than the angels; You have crowned him with glory and honor, and set him over the works of Your hands. You have put all things in subjection under his feet." For in that He put all in subjection under him, He left nothing that is not put under him. But now we do not yet see all things put under him. But we see Jesus, who was made a little lower than the angels, for the suffering of death crowned with glory and honor, that He, by the grace of God, might taste death for everyone. For it was fitting for Him, for whom are all things and by whom are all things, in bringing many sons to glory, to make the captain of their salvation perfect through sufferings. For both He who sanctifies and those who are being sanctified are all of one, for which reason He is not ashamed to call them brethren, saying: "I will declare Your name to My brethren; in the midst of the assembly I will sing praise to You." And again: "I will put My trust in Him." And again: "Here am I and the children whom God has given Me." Inasmuch then as the children have partaken of flesh and blood, He Himself likewise shared in the same, that through death He might destroy him who had the power of death, that is, the devil, and release those who through fear of death were all their lifetime subject to bondage. For indeed He does not give aid to angels, but He does give aid to the seed of Abraham. Therefore, in all things He had to be made like His brethren, that He might be a merciful and faithful High Priest in things pertaining to God, to make propitiation for the sins of the people. For in that He Himself has suffered, being tempted, He is able to aid those who are tempted. (Heb. 2:1–18)

We must understand that God, in these times, wants to bring us into perfect life so that we never, under any circumstances, need to go outside of His Word for anything.

Some people come to God with only a very small idea of His fullness, and a lot of people are satisfied with just a thimbleful. You can just imagine God saying, "Oh, if they only knew how much they could receive!" Other people come with a larger vessel, and they go away satisfied. But you can feel how much God is longing for us to have such a desire for more, such a desire as only He Himself can satisfy.

ONLY GOD CAN SATISFY

I suppose the women here would have a good idea of what I mean from the illustration of a screaming child being taken around from one person to another but never being satisfied until he gets to the arms of his mother. You will find that there is no peace, no help, no source of strength, no power, no life, nothing that can satisfy the cry of the child of God but the Word of God. God has a special way of satisfying the cry of His children. He is waiting to open to us the windows of heaven until He has so moved in the depths of our hearts that everything unlike Himself has been destroyed. No one in this place needs to go away dry. God wants you to be filled. My brother, my sister, God wants you today to be like a watered garden, filled with the fragrance of His own heavenly joy, until you know at last that you have touched immensity. The Son of God came for no other purpose than to lift and lift and mold and fashion and remold us until we become conformed to His own mind.

I know that the dry ground can have floods, and may God save me from ever wanting anything less than a flood. I will not stoop for small things when I have such a big God. Through the blood of Christ's atonement, we may have riches and riches. We need the warming atmosphere of the Spirit's power to bring us closer and closer until nothing but God can satisfy, and then we may have some idea of what God has left over after we have taken all that we can. It is just like a sparrow taking a drink of the ocean and then looking around and saying, "What a vast ocean! What a lot more I could have taken if I had only had room."

You may sometimes have things you can use, and not know it. Don't you know that you can be dying of thirst right in the middle of a river of plenty? There was once a vessel in the mouth of the Amazon river. Those on board thought they were still in the ocean, and they were dying of thirst; some of them had nearly been driven mad. They saw a ship and asked if they could have some water, for some of them were dying of thirst. Those on the other ship replied, "Dip your bucket right over; you are in the mouth of the river." There are many people today who are in the midst of a great river of life but are dying of thirst because they do not dip down and take it. Dear friend, you may have the Word, but you need an awakened spirit. The Word is not alive until it is moved upon by the Spirit of God, and in the right sense it becomes Spirit and life (John 6:63) when it is touched by His hand alone.

Beloved, there is a stream that makes glad the city of God (Ps. 46:4). There is a stream of life that makes everything move. There is a touch of divine life and likeness through the Word of God that comes from nowhere else. There is a death that has no life in it, and there is a death-likeness with Christ that is full of life.

Beloved, there is no such thing as an end to God's beginnings. But we must be in Him; we must know Him. The Holy Spirit is not a touch or a breath. He is the almighty God. He is a person. He is the Holy One dwelling in the temple "not made with hands" (2 Cor. 5:1). Beloved, He touches, and it is done. He is the same God over

227

all who is rich unto all who call upon Him (Rom. 10:12). Pentecost is the last thing that God has to touch the earth with. The baptism is the last thing; if you do not get this, you are living in a weak and impoverished condition that is no good to yourself or anybody else. May God move us on to a place where there is no measure to this fullness that He wants to give us. God exalted Jesus and gave Him a name above every name (Phil. 2:9). Notice that everything has been put under Him (Eph. 1:22).

In the last eight years or so, I have seen thousands and thousands of people healed by the power of God. Last year in Sweden, the last five months of the year, we saw over seven thousand people saved by the power of God. The tide is rolling in; let us see to it today that we get right out into the tide, for it will bear us. The heart of God's love is the center of all things. Get your eyes off yourself; lift them up high and see the Lord, *"for in the LORD...is everlasting strength"* (Isa. 26:4 KJV).

DOCTOR JESUS

If you went to see a doctor, the more you told him, the more he would know. But when you come to Doctor Jesus, He knows everything from the beginning, and He never gives you the wrong medicine. I went to see a doctor today, and someone in the doctor's office said, "Here is a person who has been poisoned through and through by another doctor giving him the wrong medicine." But Jesus sends His healing power and brings His restoring grace, and so there is nothing to fear. The only thing that is wrong is your wrong conception of the mightiness of His redemption.

He was wounded so that He might be touched with a feeling of your infirmities. He took your flesh and laid it upon the cross so that *"he might destroy him that had the power of death, that is, the devil; and deliver them who through fear of death were all their lifetime subject to bondage"* (Heb. 2:14–15 KJV).

You will find that almost all the ailments that you are heir to are satanically caused, and they must be dealt with as satanic; they must be cast out. Do not listen to what Satan says to you, for the Devil has been a liar from the beginning (John 8:44). If people would only listen to the truth of God, they would find out that they are over the Devil, over all satanic forces; they would realize that every evil spirit is subject to them. They would find out that they are always in the place of triumph, and they would *"reign in life"* (Rom. 5:17) by King Jesus.

Never live in a place that is less than where God has called you to, and He has called you up on high to live with Him. God has designed that everything will be subject to man. Through Christ, He has given you *"power...over all the power of the enemy"* (Luke 10:19 KJV). He has worked out your eternal redemption.

RECEIVE EVERYTHING YOU CAME FOR

When I had finished a meeting one day in Switzerland, and when I and those with me had ministered to all the sick, we went out to see some people. Two boys came to us and said that there was a blind man present at the meeting that afternoon who had heard all the words of the preacher. He said he was surprised that he had not been prayed for. They went on to say that this blind man had heard so much that he would not leave that place until he could see. I said, "This is positively unique. God will do something today for that man."

We went back to the place. This blind man said he had never seen before; he had been born blind, but because of the word he had heard preached in the afternoon, he was not going home until he could see. If I ever have joy, it is when I have a lot of people who will not be satisfied until they get all that they have come for. With great joy, I anointed him that day and laid my hands on his eyes, and then immediately God opened his eyes. The man acted very strangely. There were some electric lights in the building; first he counted them and then he counted us. Oh, the ecstatic pleasure that man experienced every moment because he had gained his sight! It made us all feel like weeping and dancing and shouting. Then he pulled out his watch and said that for years he had been feeling the raised figures on the watch in order to tell the time, but now he could look at it and tell us the time. Then, looking as if he had been awakened from some deep sleep or some long, strange dream, he realized that he had never seen the faces of his father and mother, and he went to the door and rushed out. That night, he was the first one in the meeting. All the people knew him as the blind man, and I had to give him a long time to talk about his new sight.

Beloved, I wonder how much you want to take away today. You could not carry it if it were an actual substance. But there is something about the grace and the power and the blessings of God that can be carried, no matter how big they are. Oh, what a Savior! What a place we are in, by grace, that He may come in to commune with us!

 He is willing to say to every heart, *"Peace, be still!"* (Mark 4:39), and to every weak body, "Be strong."

Are you going halfway, or are you going right to the end? Do not be deceived today by Satan, but believe God.

CHAPTER TEN

THE PENTECOSTAL POWER

Our Scripture text is from the nineteenth chapter of Acts. This passage has many things in it that indicate to us that there was something more marvelous than human power that was manifested in Ephesus:

And it happened, while Apollos was at Corinth, that Paul, having passed through the upper regions, came to Ephesus. And finding some disciples he said to them, "Did you receive the Holy Spirit when you believed?" So they said to him, "We have not so much as heard whether there is a Holy Spirit." And he said to them, "Into what then were you baptized?" So they said, "Into John's baptism." Then Paul said, "John indeed baptized with a baptism of repentance, saying to the people that they should believe on Him who would come after him, that is, on Christ Jesus." When they heard this, they were baptized in the name of the Lord Jesus. And when Paul had laid hands on them, the Holy Spirit came upon them, and they spoke with tongues and prophesied. Now the men were about twelve in all. And he went into the synagogue and spoke boldly for three months, reasoning and persuading concerning the things of the kingdom of God. But when some were hardened and did not believe, but spoke evil of the Way before the multitude, he departed from them and withdrew the disciples, reasoning daily in the school of Tyrannus. And this continued for two years, so that all who dwelt in Asia heard the word of the Lord Jesus, both Jews and Greeks. Now God worked unusual miracles by the hands of Paul, so that even *handkerchiefs or aprons were brought from his body to the sick, and the diseases left them and the evil spirits went out of* *them. Then some of the itinerant Jewish exorcists took it upon themselves to call the name of the Lord Jesus over those who had evil spirits, saying, "We exorcise you by the Jesus whom Paul preaches." Also there were seven sons of Sceva, a Jewish chief priest, who did so. And the evil spirit answered and said, "Jesus I know, and Paul I know; but who are you?" Then the man in whom the evil spirit was leaped on them, overpowered them, and prevailed against them, so that they fled out of that house naked and wounded. This became known both to all Jews and Greeks dwelling in Ephesus; and fear fell on them all, and <u>the name of the Lord Jesus was magnified</u>. And many who had believed came confessing and telling their deeds. Also, many of those who had practiced magic brought their books together and burned them in the sight of all. And they counted up the value of them, and it totaled fifty thousand pieces of silver. So the word of the Lord grew mightily and prevailed.* (Acts 19:1–20)

This is a wonderful Scripture passage. When I think about Pentecost, I am astonished from day to day because of its mightiness, its wonderfulness, and how the glory overshadows it. I think sometimes about these things, and they make me feel that we have only just touched the surface of it. Truly it is so, but we must thank God that we have touched it. We must not give in because we have only touched the surface. Whatever God has done in the past, <u>His name is still the same.</u> When hearts are burdened and they come face to face with the need of the day, they look into God's Word, and it brings in a propeller of power or an anointing that makes them know that He has truly visited.

<u>It was a wonderful day when Jesus left the glory to come to earth</u>. I can imagine God the Father and all the angels and all heaven so wonderfully stirred that day when the angels were sent to tell the wonderful story of "peace on earth and good will to men." (See Luke 2:14.) It was a glorious day when they beheld the Babe for the first time and God was looking on. I suppose it would take a big book to contain all that happened after that day up until Jesus was thirty years old. <u>Everything in His life was working up to a great climax</u>. The mother of Jesus hid many of these things in her heart. (See Luke 2:19.)

I know that Pentecost in my life is working up to a climax; it is not all accomplished in a day. There are many waters and all kinds of experiences that we go through before we get to the real summit of everything. The power of God is here to prevail. God is with us.

Now, when Jesus was thirty years old, the time came when it was made manifest at the Jordan River that He was the Son of God. Oh, how beautifully it was made known! It had to be made known first to one who was full of the vision of God. The vision comes to those who are full. Did it ever strike you that we cannot be too full for a vision, that we cannot have too much of God? When a person is full of God, then the visions begin. When God has you in His own plan, what a change; how things operate! You wonder; you see things in a new light. God is being greatly glorified as you yield from day to day. The Spirit seems to lay hold of you and bring you further along. Yes, it is a pressing on, and then He gives us touches of His wonderful power, manifestations of the glory of these things and indications of greater things to follow. These days that we are living in now speak of even better days. How wonderful!

Where would we be today if we had stopped short, if we had not fulfilled the vision that God gave us? I am thinking about the time when Christ sent the Spirit. Saul, who later became the apostle Paul, did not know much about the Spirit. His heart was stirred against the followers of Jesus, his eyes were blinded to the truth, and he was going to put the newborn church to an end in a short time; but Jesus was looking on. We can scarcely understand the whole process—only as God seems to show us—when He gets us into His plan and works with us little by little.

We are all amazed that we are among the "tongues people." It is altogether out of order according to the natural. Some of us would never have been in this Pentecostal movement if we had not been drawn, but God has a wonderful way of drawing us. Paul never intended to be among the disciples; he never intended to have anything to do with this Man called Jesus. But God was working. In the same way, God has been working with us and has brought us to this place. It is marvelous! Oh, the vision of God, the wonderful manifestation that God has for Israel!

I have one purpose in my heart, and it is surely God's plan for me: I want you to see that Jesus Christ is the greatest manifestation in all the world and that His power is unequaled, but that there is only one way to minister it. I want you to notice that in the Scripture passage from Acts 19 that we just looked at, some of the people in Ephesus, after they had seen Paul working wonders by the power of Christ, began to act along natural lines. If I want to do anything for God, I see that it is necessary for me to get the knowledge of God. I cannot work on my own; I must get the vision of God. It must be a divine revelation of the Son of God. It must be that.

I can see as clearly as anything that Saul, in his mad pursuit, had to be stopped along the way. After he was stopped and had the vision from heaven and the light from heaven, he instantly realized that he had been working in the wrong way. As soon as the power of the Holy Spirit fell upon him, he began in the way in which God wanted him to go. And it was wonderful how he had to suffer to come into the way. (See Acts 9:1–20.) A broken spirit, a tried life, and being driven into a corner as if some strange thing had happened (1 Pet. 4:12)—these are surely the ways in which we get to know the way of God.

POWER IN THE NAME OF JESUS

Paul did not have any power of his own that enabled him to use the name of Jesus as he did. But when he had to go through the privations and the difficulties, and even when all things seemed as if they were shipwrecked, God stood by him and caused him to know that there was Someone with him, supporting him all the time, who was able to carry him through and bring out what his heart was longing for all the time. He seemed to be so unconsciously filled with the Holy Spirit that all that was needed was to bring the aprons and the handkerchiefs to him and then send them forth to heal and deliver. I can imagine these itinerant Jewish exorcists and these seven sons of Sceva in Ephesus looking on and seeing him and saying, "The power seems to be all in the name. Don't you notice that when he sends out the handkerchiefs and the aprons, he says, 'In the name of the Lord Jesus, I command the evil spirit to come out'?"

These people had been looking around and watching, and they thought, "It is only the name; that is all that is needed," and so they said, "We will do the same." They were determined to make this thing work, and they came to a man who was possessed with an evil power. As they entered into the house where he was, they said, "We charge you in the name of Jesus, whom Paul preaches, to come out." The demon said, *"Jesus I know, and Paul I know; but who are you?"* (Acts 19:15). Then the evil power leaped upon them and tore their clothes off their backs, and they went out naked and wounded.

It is indeed the name of Jesus that brings power over evil spirits, only they did not understand it. Oh, that God would help us to understand the name of Jesus! There is something in that name that attracts the whole world. It is the name, oh, it is still the name, but you must understand that there is the ministry of the name. It is the Holy Spirit who is behind the ministry. The power is in the knowledge of Him; it is in the ministry of the knowledge of Him, and I can understand that it is only that.

I want to speak about the ministry of the knowledge of Him. This is important. May God help us to understand it. I am satisfied with two things. First, I am satisfied that the power is in the knowledge of His blood and of His perfect holiness. I am perfectly cleansed from all sin and made holy in the knowledge of His holiness. Second, I am satisfied that as I know Him, as I know His power—the same power that works in me as I minister only through the knowledge of Him—and as I know the Christ who is manifested by it, such knowledge will be effective to accomplish the very thing that the Word of God says it will: it will have power over all evil. I minister today in the power of the knowledge of Him. Beyond that, there is a certain sense in which I overcome the world according to my faith in Him. I am more than a conqueror (Rom. 8:37) over everything through the knowledge that I have that He is over everything (Eph. 1:22). He has been crowned by the Father to bring everything into subjection (v. 22).

Shouting won't cast out an evil spirit, but there is an anointing that is gloriously felt within and brings the act of casting out the demon into perfect harmony with the will of God. We cannot help shouting, though shouting won't do it. The power over evil spirits is in the ministry of the knowledge that He is Lord over all demons, over all powers of wickedness.

> **INTERPRETATION OF A MESSAGE IN TONGUES:** "The Holy One who anointed Jesus is so abiding by the Spirit in the one who is clothed upon to use the name until the glory is manifested and the demons flee; they cannot stand the glory of the manifestation of the Spirit that is manifest."

So I am realizing that Paul went about clothed in the Spirit. This was wonderful. Was his body full of power? No! He sent forth handkerchiefs and aprons that had touched him, and when they touched the needy, they were healed and demons were cast out. Was there power in his body? No! There was power in Jesus. Paul ministered through the power of the anointing of the Holy Spirit and through faith in the name of Jesus.

INTERPRETATION OF A MESSAGE IN TONGUES: "The liberty of the Spirit brings the office."

It is an office; it is a position; it is a place of rest, of faith. Sometimes the demon powers are dealt with in very different ways; they are not all dealt with in the same way. But the ministry of the Spirit is administered by the power of the word *Jesus,* and it never fails to accomplish the purpose that the one in charge has wisdom or discernment to see. This is because along with the Spirit of ministry, there comes the revelation of the need of the one who is bound.

The Spirit ministers the name of Jesus in many ways. I see it continually happening. I see it working, and all the time the Lord is building up a structure of His own power by a living faith in the sovereignty of Jesus' name. If I turn to John's gospel, I get the whole thing practically in a nutshell: *"This is eternal life, that they may know You, the only true God, and Jesus Christ whom You have sent"* (John 17:3). We must have the knowledge and power of God and the knowledge of Jesus Christ, the embodiment of God, in order to be clothed with God.

I see that there are those who have come into line: they have the blessed Christ within and the power of the baptism, which is (the revelation of the Christ of God within) This is so evidenced in the person who is baptized in the Spirit, and the Christ is so plainly abiding, that the moment the person is confronted with evil, he is instantly sensitive to the nature of this confrontation, and he is able to deal with it accordingly.

The difference between the sons of Sceva and Paul was this: They said, "It is only the use of the name that is important." How many people only use the name; how many times are people defeated because they think it is just the name; how many people have been brokenhearted because it did not work when they used the name? If I read this into my text, "He who believes will speak in tongues; he who believes will cast out devils; he who believes will

236

lay hands on the sick and they will recover" (see Mark 16:17–18), it seems perfectly easy on the surface of it. But you must understand this: there are volumes to be applied to the word *believe.* To believe is to believe in the need of the majesty of the glory of God's power. This is all power, and it brings all other powers into subjection.

WHAT DOES IT MEAN TO BELIEVE?

And what is belief? Let me sum it up in a few sentences. To believe is to have the knowledge of Him in whom you believe. It is not to believe in the word *Jesus,* but to believe in the nature of Christ, to believe in the vision of Christ, for all power has been given unto Him, and greater is He who is within you in the revelation of faith than he who is in the world. (See 1 John 4:4.) And so I say to you, do not be discouraged if every demon has not gone out; do not think that is the end of it. What we have to do is to see that if all it takes is using the name of Jesus, those evil powers would have gone out in that name by the sons of Sceva. It is not that. It is the power of the Holy Spirit with the revelation of the deity of our Christ of glory; it is knowing that *"all power is given unto* [Him]*"* (Matt. 28:18 KJV). Through the knowledge of Christ, and through faith in who He is, demons must surrender, demons must go out. I say this reverently: these bodies of ours are so constructed by God that we may be filled with the divine revelation of the Son of God until it is manifest to the devils we confront, and they will have to go. The Master is in; they see the Master. *"Jesus I know, and Paul I know"* (Acts 19:15). The ministry of the Master! How we need to get to know Him until within us we are full of the manifestation of the King over all demons.

Brothers and sisters, my heart is full. The depths of my yearnings are for the Pentecostal people. My cry is that we will not miss the opportunity of the baptism of the Holy Spirit, that Christ may be manifested in our human frames (2 Cor. 4:10) until every power of evil will be subject to the Christ who is manifested in us. The devils know Jesus.

Two important things are before me. First, to master the situation of myself. You are not going to oppose devils if you cannot master yourself, because you will soon find the devils to be bigger than yourself. It is only when you are conquered by Christ that He is enthroned. Then the embodiment of the Spirit gloriously covers your life so that Jesus is glorified to the full. So first it is the losing of ourselves, and then it is the incoming of Another; it is the glorifying of Him that will fulfill all things, and when He gets hold of lives, He can do it. When God gets hold of your life because you have yielded yourself to Him in this way, He will be delighted to allow the Christ to be so manifested in you that it will be no difficulty for the Devil to know who you are.

I am satisfied that the purpose of Pentecost is to allow God to work through human flesh. Do I need to say it again? The power of the Holy Spirit has to come to be enthroned in the human life so that it does not matter where we find ourselves. Christ is manifested in the place where devils are, the place where religious devils are, the place where false religion and unbelief are, the place where formal religion has taken the place of holiness and righteousness. You need to have holiness—the righteousness and Spirit of the Master—so that in every walk of life, everything that is not like our Lord Jesus will have to depart. That is what is needed today.

I ask you in the Holy Spirit to seek the place where He is in power. *"Jesus I know, and Paul I know; but who are you?"* (Acts 19:15). May God stamp this sobering question upon us, for the Devil is not afraid of us. May the Holy Spirit make us terrors of evildoers today, for the Holy Spirit came into us to judge the world of sin, of unbelief, and of righteousness; that is the purpose of the Holy Spirit. (See John 16:7–11.) Then Jesus will know us, and the devils will know us.

CHAPTER ELEVEN

CHRIST IN US

I believe that God wants to bring to our eyes and our ears a living realization of what the Word of God is, what the Lord God means by what He says, and what we may expect if we believe it. I am certain that the Lord wishes to put before us a living fact that will, by our faith, bring into action a principle that is within our own hearts so that Christ can dethrone every power of Satan.

Only this truth revealed to our hearts can make us so much greater than we ever had any idea we could be. I believe there are volumes of truth right in the midst of our own hearts. There is only the need of revelation and of stirring ourselves up to understand the mightiness that God has within us. We may prove what He has accomplished in us if we will only be willing to carry through what He has already accomplished in us.

For God has not accomplished something in us that should lie dormant, but He has brought within us a power, a revelation, a life that is so great that I believe God wants to reveal the greatness of it. Oh, the possibilities of man in the hands of God! There isn't anything you can imagine that is greater than what man may accomplish through Him.

But everything on a natural basis is very limited compared with what God has for us on a spiritual basis. If man can accomplish much in a short time, what may we accomplish if we will believe the revealed Word and take it as truth that God has given us and that He wants to bring out in revelation and force?

Let us read a passage from the eleventh chapter of the Gospel According to Matthew:

Now it came to pass, when Jesus finished commanding His twelve disciples, that He departed from there to teach and to

239

preach in their cities. And when John had heard in prison about the works of Christ, he sent two of his disciples and said to Him, "Are You the Coming One, or do we look for another?" Jesus answered and said to them, "Go and tell John the things which you hear and see: the blind see and the lame walk; the lepers are cleansed and the deaf hear; the dead are raised up and the poor have the gospel preached to them. And blessed is he who is not offended because of Me." As they departed, Jesus began to say to the multitudes concerning John: "What did you go out into the wilderness to see? A reed shaken by the wind? But what did you go out to see? A man clothed in soft garments? Indeed, those who wear soft clothing are in kings' houses. But what did you go out to see? A prophet? Yes, I say to you, and more than a prophet. For this is he of whom it is written: 'Behold, I send My messenger before Your face, who will prepare Your way before You.' Assuredly, I say to you, among those born of women there has not risen one greater than John the Baptist; but he who is least in the kingdom of heaven is greater than he. And from the days of John the Baptist until now the kingdom of heaven suffers violence, and the violent take it by force." (Matt. 11:1–12)

In the first place, notice the fact that John the Baptist was the forerunner of Jesus. Within his own short history, John the Baptist had the power of God revealed to him as probably no other man in the old dispensation had. He had a wonderful revelation. He had a mighty anointing.

I want you to see how he moved Israel. I want you to see how the power of God rested upon him. I want you to see how he had the vision of Jesus and went forth with power and turned the hearts of Israel to Him. And yet Jesus said about John,

Among those born of women there has not risen one greater than John the Baptist; but he who is least in the kingdom of heaven is greater than he. (Matt. 11:11)

Then I want you to see how satanic power can work in the mind. I find that Satan came to John when he was in prison. I find that Satan can come to any of us. Unless we are filled, or divinely insulated, with the power of God, we may be defeated by the power of Satan.

But I want to prove that we have a greater power than Satan's—in imagination, in thought, in everything. Satan came to John the Baptist in prison and said to him, "Don't you think you have made a mistake? Here you are in prison. Isn't there something wrong with the whole business? After all, you may be greatly deceived about being a forerunner of the Christ."

I find men who might be giants of faith, who might be leaders of society, who might rise to subdue kingdoms (Heb. 11:33), who might be noble among princes, but they are defeated because they allow the suggestions of Satan to dethrone their better knowledge of the power of God. May God help us.

See what John the Baptist did:

> *And when John had heard in prison about the works of Christ, he sent two of his disciples and said to Him, "Are You the Coming One, or do we look for another?"*   (Matt. 11:2–3)

How could Jesus send those men back with a stimulating truth, with a personal, effective power that would stir their hearts to know that they had met Him about whom all the prophets had spoken? What would declare it? How would they know? How could they tell it?

> *Jesus answered and said to them, "Go and tell John the things which you hear and see: the blind see, and the lame walk; the lepers are cleansed and the deaf hear; the dead are raised up and the poor have the gospel preached to them."*
> (Matt. 11:4–5)

And when they saw the miracles and wonders and heard the gracious words He spoke as the power of God rested upon Him, they were ready to believe.

Have miracles and wonders ceased? If they have not ceased, then I must put before you a living fact. I must cause you to understand why they will not cease. Instead of ceasing, they have to continue to occur. It is only by the grace of God that I dare to put these truths before you because of facts that will be proved.

SONS OF GOD WITH POWER

I have a message for those of you who are saved and a message for those of you who are unsaved, but I want you both to hear.

241

There are none so deaf as those who won't hear, and none so blind as those who won't see. But God has given you ears, and He wants you to hear. What should you hear? *"And you shall know the truth, and the truth shall make you free"* (John 8:32).

Hear what Jesus said:

> As they departed, Jesus began to say to the multitudes concerning John: "What did you go out into the wilderness to see? A reed shaken by the wind?" (Matt. 11:7)

Did you ever see a man of God who was like a reed? If you ever did, I would say that he was only an imitator. Has God ever made a man to be a reed or to be like smoking flax? (See Isaiah 42:3.) No. God wants to make men as flames of fire (Ps. 104:4). God wants to make men *"strong in the Lord and in the power of His might"* (Eph. 6:10).

Therefore, beloved, if you will hear the truth of the Gospel, you will see that God has made provision for you to be strong, to be on fire, to be as though you were quickened from the dead, as those who have seen the King, as those who have a resurrection touch. We know we are the sons of God with power as we believe His Word and stand in the truth of His Word (John 1:12).

> **INTERPRETATION OF A MESSAGE IN TONGUES:** "The Spirit of the Lord 'breathes upon the slain,' and upon the 'dry bones,' and upon the 'things which are not' and changes them in the flesh in a moment of time, and makes what is weak strong. And, behold, He is among us tonight to quicken what is dead and make the dead alive."

He is here!

"The dead will hear the voice of the Son of God; and those who hear will live" (John 5:25). Praise the Lord!

JESUS IS OUR LIFE

Let us move on to another very important thought in another verse: *"And from the days of John the Baptist until now the kingdom of heaven suffers violence, and the violent take it by force"* (Matt. 11:12).

This is a message to every believer. Every believer belongs to the kingdom of heaven. Every believer has the life of the Lord in him. And if Jesus, *"who is our life"* (Col. 3:4), were to come, instantly our life would go out to meet His life because we exist and consist of the life of the Son of God. (See verse 4.) *"Your life is hidden with Christ in God"* (v. 3).

If all believers understood this wonderful passage that is in the twenty-second chapter of Luke's gospel, there would be great joy in their hearts:

> *Then He said to them, "With fervent desire I have desired to eat this Passover with you before I suffer; for I say to you, I will no longer eat of it until it is fulfilled in the kingdom of God."* (Luke 22:15–16)

Everyone who is in Christ Jesus will be there when He sits down the first time to break bread in the kingdom of heaven. It is not possible for any child of God to remain on earth when Jesus comes. May the Lord help us to believe it.

I know there is a great deal of speculation on the Rapture and on the coming of the Lord. But let me tell you to hope for edification and comfort, for the Scripture by the Holy Spirit won't let me speak on anything except the edification, consolation, and comfort of the Spirit. (See 1 Corinthians 14:3.) Why? Because we are here for the purpose of giving everybody in the meeting comfort.

I don't mean that we are to cover sin up. God won't let us do that. But we must unveil truth. And what is truth? The Word of God is the truth. *"I am the way, the truth, and the life"* (John 14:6). *"You search the Scriptures, for in them you think you have eternal life; and these are they which testify of Me"* (John 5:39).

What does the truth say? It says that when Christ appears, all who are His at His coming will be changed *"in a moment, in the twinkling of an eye"* (1 Cor. 15:52). We will be presented at the same moment as all those who have fallen sleep in Him, and we will all go together.

> *We who are alive and remain until the coming of the Lord will by no means precede those who are asleep....And the dead in Christ will rise first. Then we who are alive and remain shall be caught up together with them in the clouds to meet the Lord*

in the air. And thus we shall always be with the Lord. There-fore comfort one another with these words. (1 Thess. 4:15–18)

Jesus said, *"For I say to you, I will not drink of the fruit of the vine until the kingdom of God comes"* (Luke 22:18). Two thousand years will soon have passed since the Lord broke bread around the table with His disciples. I am longing, the saints are longing, for the grand union when millions, billions, trillions will unite with Him in that great fellowship Supper. Praise the Lord! But now, what stimulation, what power, must be working every day until that Day appears!

THE KINGDOM OF HEAVEN

Listen to this carefully; this is my point. (No, it is not my point; it is God's revelation to us. I have nothing to do with it. If I ever say "I" or "my," you must look upon it and forgive me. I don't want to be here to speak my own words, my own thoughts. I want the Lord to be glorified in bringing every thought so that we will all be comforted and edified. But this is a strong message for us and a very helpful one, especially for the sick and needy believer.) This is the point: the kingdom of heaven is within us, within every believer (Luke 17:21). The kingdom of heaven is the Christ; it is the Word of God.

The kingdom of heaven must outstrip everything else, even your own lives. It has to be manifested so that you have to realize that even the death of Christ brings forth the life of Christ.

"The kingdom of heaven suffers violence" (Matt. 11:12). How does the kingdom of heaven suffer violence? If you are suffering, if you are needy—if you have paralysis, or an infirmity of the head, abdomen, or any other part of the body—if you feel distress in any way, it means that the kingdom of heaven is suffering violence at the hands of the Adversary.

Could the kingdom of heaven bring weaknesses or diseases? Could it bring imperfection on the body? Could it bring tuberculosis? Could it bring extreme fevers, cancers, or tumors?

"The kingdom of God is within you" (Luke 17:21). The kingdom of heaven is the life of Jesus; it is the power of the Highest. The kingdom of heaven is pure; it is holy. It has no disease, no imperfection. It is as holy as God is. And Satan with his evil power

244

"does not come except to steal, and to kill, and to destroy" (John 10:10) the body.

Every ailment that anyone has is from a satanic source. It is foolish and ridiculous to think that sickness purifies you. There is no purification in disease. I want you to see the wiles of Satan (Eph. 6:11), the power of the Devil. And I want to show you, in the name of Jesus, your power to dethrone the Enemy.

Oh, this blessed Lord! Oh, this lovely Jesus! Oh, this incarnation of the Lamb who was slain!

Beloved, I wouldn't stand on this platform if I didn't know that the whole Bible is true. Jesus said, *"The [Devil] does not come except to steal, and to kill, and to destroy. I have come that they may have life, and that they may have it more abundantly"* (John 10:10).

I want us to see the difference between the abundant life of Jesus and the power of Satan. Then—by the grace of God—to help us in our position, I want to keep before you this thought: *"The kingdom of heaven suffers"* (Matt. 11:12).

It is only fair and reasonable that I put before you the almightiness of God versus the might of Satan. If Satan were almighty, we would all have to quake with fear. But when we know that Satan is subject to the powers of God in everything, we can get this truth right into our hearts and be conquerors over every situation. I want to make everyone in this meeting *"strong in the Lord and in the power of His might"* (Eph. 6:10).

A POWER GREATER THAN THE ENEMY

I want you to have an inward knowledge that there is a power in you that is greater than any other power. And I trust that, by the help of the Spirit, I may bring you into a place of deliverance, a place of holy sanctification where you dare to stand against the *"wiles of the devil"* (v. 11), drive them back, and cast them out. May the Lord help us!

I want to wake you up! You ask, "Are we not awake?" You may be cognizant of what I am saying. You may be able to tell when I lift my hand and put it down. Still, you may be asleep concerning the deep things of God. I want God to give you an inward awakening, a revelation of truth within you, an audacity, a flaming indignation against the powers of Satan.

Lot had a righteous indignation—temporarily—but it came too late. He ought to have had it when he went into Sodom, not when he was coming out. But I don't want any one of you to go away dejected because you didn't take a step in the right direction sooner. Always be thankful that you are alive to hear and to change the situation.

It would be a serious thing for us to pay so much to rent this building, only to have you come in and sit for an hour and a half to two hours and then go out just the same as when you came in. I couldn't stand it. It would all be the biggest foolishness possible, and we would all need to be admitted to the insane asylum.

You must gain an inward knowledge that God is Lord over all the power of Satan. When I speak about you waking up, the thought in my heart is this: I don't doubt your sincerity about being saved, about having been justified in Christ. It is not for me to question a man's sincerity regarding his righteousness. And yet, as I preach to you, I feel I have a right to say that there is a deeper sincerity to reach to, there is a greater audacity of faith and fact to attain. There is something that you have to wake up to where you will never allow disease to have you or sin to have you or a weak heart or a pain in your back to have you; where you will never allow anything that isn't perfect life to have anything to do with you.

Let me continue now by showing you the weakness of believers. Does God know all about you? Is He acquainted with you altogether? Why not trust Him who knows all about you, instead of telling somebody else who knows only what you have told him.

Again, why should you, under any circumstances, believe that you will be better off by being diseased? When disease is impurity, why should you ever believe that you will be sanctified by having a great deal of sickness?

Some people talk about God being pleased to put disease on His children. "Here is a person I love," says God. "I will break his arm. Then, so that he will love Me more, I will break his leg. And so that he will love Me still more, I will give him a weak heart. And in order to increase that love, I will make him so that he cannot eat anything without having indigestion."

The whole thing won't stand daylight. And yet people are always talking in this way, and they never think to read the Word of God, which says, *"Before I was afflicted I went astray"* (Ps. 119:67). They have never read the following words into their lives:

Fools, (because of their transgression,) and (because of their iniquities) were afflicted. Their soul abhorred all manner of

*food, and they drew near to the gates of death. Then they cried
out to the LORD in their trouble, and He saved them out of
their distresses.* (Ps. 107:17–19)

Yes, we have that to praise the Lord for. Is it right now to say,
"You know, my brother, I have suffered so much in this affliction
that it has made me know God better"? Well, now, before you
agree, ask God for a lot more affliction so that you will get to know
Him still better. If you won't ask for more affliction to make you
still purer, I won't believe that the first affliction made you purer,
because if it had, you would have more faith in it. It appears that
you do not have faith in your afflictions. It is only talk, but talk
doesn't count unless it is backed up by fact. However, if people can
see that your words are backed up by fact, then they have some
grounds for believing in them.

THE KINGDOM SUFFERS VIOLENCE

I have looked through my Bible, and I cannot find where God
brings disease and sickness. I know there is glory, and I know it is
the power of God that brings the glory. Yet it is the Devil and not
God at all who brings sickness and disease. Why does he? I know
this: Satan is God's whip, and if you don't obey God, God will stand
to one side and Satan will devour you. But God will only allow him
to devour so much, as was the case with Job. The Lord told Satan,
"You may go only so far, and no further. Don't touch his life." (See
Job 2:6.)

"Let God be true but every man a liar" (Rom. 3:4). I am going
to take things on their real basis, on the truth as it is revealed to
me in the Scriptures: *"The kingdom of heaven suffers violence"*
(Matt. 11:12).

Why is Satan allowed to bring sickness? It is because we know
better than we act. And if people would do as well as they know, they
would have no sickness. If we would be true to our convictions and
walk according to the light we have been given, God would verify His
presence in the midst of us, and we would know that sickness cannot
"come near [our] *dwelling; for He shall give His angels charge over*
[us], *to keep* [us] *in all* [our] *ways"* (Ps. 91:10–11).

If there are weak persons here tonight, and they are suffering
terribly, I know they are sorry for their sicknesses. But if they

247

would be as sorry for their sins as they are for their sicknesses, they could be healed. If we ever get desperate about having our sins destroyed, they will go. May God help us!

Well, if you are whole from top to bottom and are not distracted by any pain in your body, it is easy to shout "Glory!" But if some people shouted "Glory," one side of them would ache. And so it is with those of you who are not free tonight. I want to put you in a place where you will shout "Glory!"

It is true that God keeps me, as it were, unaware that I have a body. I believe that is part of redemption. But I am not going to condemn people who are not there yet. I am here to help them. But I cannot help you out unless I give you Scripture. If I can lay down a basis in the Word of God for what I am saying, I can send you home and know that you will deliver yourselves.

If I could only get you to catch hold of faith, then, by the grace of God, every person here would be delivered. But I find that Satan has tremendous power over certain functions of the body, and I want to deal with that for a moment in order to help you.

When Satan can get to your body, he will, if possible, make the pain or the weakness so distracting that it will affect your mind and always bring your mind down to where the pain is. When that takes place, you do not have the same freedom in your spirit to lift up your heart and shout and praise the Lord, because the distraction of the pain brings the foundational power, which ought to be full of praise to God, down into the body. And through that—concerning everybody who is afflicted—*"the kingdom of heaven suffers violence"* (Matt. 11:12).

Beloved, I mean precisely this: anything that takes me from a position where I am in an attitude of worship, peace, and joy, where I have a consciousness of the presence of God, where there is an inward moving of the powers of God that makes me able to lift myself up and live in the world as though I were not of it (because I am not of it)—anything that dethrones me from that attitude is evil, is Satan.

I want to prove how the kingdom of heaven suffers violence. If it is only a finger or a tooth that aches, if it is only a corn on your foot that pinches you, or anything in the body that detracts from the highest spiritual attainment, the kingdom of heaven is dethroned to a degree; *"the kingdom of heaven suffers violence."*

By the Word of God, I am proving to you that the kingdom of heaven is within you. *"Greater is he that is in you"* (1 John 4:4 KJV)—the Son of God, the kingdom of heaven within you—*"than he that is in the world"* (v. 4 KJV)—the power of Satan outside you.

Disease or weakness, or any distraction in you, is a power of violence that can take the kingdom of heaven in you by force. The same spiritual power that will reveal this to you, will relieve you here in this meeting. For instance, I would like to show you a manifestation of a distraction. Is there a person here who is saved by the power of God but who is suffering in his back, in his legs, in his head, or in his shoulders? (A man raises his hand.)

Stand up, young man. Where are you suffering?

"In my leg."

Stand out in the aisle; this is an example for all the people. Are you saved?

"I am."

Do you believe the kingdom of God is within you?

"I do."

I can prove the Scriptures are true. Here the kingdom of heaven in this man is suffering violence because he has a pain in his leg that takes his mind, a hundred times a day, off the highest enthroned position—where he is seated in heavenly places with Christ Jesus (Eph. 2:6)—and onto his leg. I am going to tell this young man that tonight he has to treat this as an enemy, as the power of Satan down in his legs, and that he has to say that he is free in the name of Jesus. He has to say it by the power that is within him, in fact, by the personality and the presence of God, the power against Satan, the name of Jesus. I want you to say, "In the name of Jesus, come out!" Shout! Put your hand upon your leg and say, "In the name of Jesus, I command you to come out!" Go right to the bottom of your leg. Amen! Praise the Lord! Now walk around. Has he come out? Are you free?

"Yes."

Praise God! On the authority of the Word of God, I maintain that *"greater is he that is in you"* than any power of Satan that is around you. Suppose five or six people were standing up tonight, and I prayed with the fact in my heart that in me—by the power of Jesus—is a greater power than the power that is binding them. I pray, I believe, and the evil power goes out while I am praying. How much more would be done if you would inwardly claim your rights and deliver yourselves!

I believe the Bible from front to back. But the Bible won't have an atom of power in you if you don't put it into practice in yourself. If, by the power of God, I put in you an audacity, a determination, so that you won't let Satan rest there, you will be free. Praise the Lord!

Why do I take this attitude? Because for every step of my life since my baptism, I have had to pay the price of everything for others. God has to take me through to the place so that I may be able to show the people how to do it. Some people come up to me and say, "I have been waiting for the baptism, and I am having such a struggle. I am having to fight for every inch of it. Isn't it strange?" No. A thousand to one, God is preparing you to help somebody else who is desiring to receive it.

The reason I am so firm about the necessity of getting the baptism in the Holy Spirit, and about the significance of the Spirit's making a manifestation when He comes in, is this: I fought it. I went to a meeting because I had heard people were speaking in tongues there. I forced myself on the attention of those in the meeting almost like a man who was mad. I told the people there, "This meeting of yours is nothing. I have left better conditions at home. I am hungry and thirsty for something."

"What do you want?" they asked.

"I want tongues."

"You want the baptism?" they asked.

"Not I," I said. "I have the baptism. I want tongues."

I could have had a fight with anybody. The whole situation was this: God was training me for something else. The power of God fell upon my body with such ecstasy of joy that I could not satisfy the joy within with my natural tongue; then I found the Spirit speaking through me in other tongues.

What did it mean? I knew that I had had anointings of joy before this, and expressions of the blessed attitude of the Spirit of Life, and joy in the Holy Spirit; I had felt it all the way through my life. But when the fullness came with a high tide, with an overflowing life, I knew that was different from anything else. And I knew that was the baptism, but God had to show me.

People ask, "Do all speak with tongues?" Certainly not. But all people may speak as the Spirit gives utterance—as in the Upper Room (Acts 2:4) and at the house of Cornelius (Acts 10:44–45) and at Ephesus when Jesus' followers were filled with the Holy Spirit (Acts 19:1–6).

There is quite a difference between having a gift and speaking as the Spirit gives utterance. If I had been given the *gift* of tongues when I was filled with the Holy Spirit, then I could have spoken in tongues at any time, because gifts and calling remain (Rom. 11:29). But I couldn't speak in tongues at any time and any place after I was baptized. Why? It was because I had received the Holy Spirit with the evidence of speaking in tongues, but I hadn't received the gift of tongues.

However, I received the Holy Spirit, who is the Giver of all gifts. And nine months afterward, God gave me the gift of tongues so that I could speak in tongues at any time. But do I? God forbid! Why? Because no man ought to use a gift; the Holy Spirit uses the gift.

I will not be able to bring you into the miraculous regarding what I have been telling you, unless I can provoke you. "Why?" you ask. If I could cause every person who has a bad leg to be so provoked at the Devil that they would kick their bad leg off along with the Devil, then I could get somewhere. You say that I exaggerate. Well, I only exaggerate in order to wake you up.

I have a reason for talking like this. People come up to me all the time and say, "I have been prayed for, and I am just the same." It is enough to make you kick them. I don't mean that literally. I would be the last man to kick anybody in this place. God forbid. *"For the weapons of our warfare are not carnal but mighty in God for pulling down strongholds"* (2 Cor. 10:4). But if I can get you enraged against the powers of darkness and the powers of disease, if I can wake you up, you won't go to bed unless you prove that there is a Master in you who is greater than the power that is hanging around you.

Many times I have gone to a house in which an insane person lived and have been shut in with him in order to deliver him. I have gone in determined that he would be delivered. In the middle of the night, chiefly, sometimes in the middle of the day, the demon powers would come and bite me and handle me terribly roughly. But I never gave in. It would dethrone a higher principle if I had to give in.

There is a great cloud of witnesses of the satanic powers from hell. We are here on probation to slay the Enemy and destroy the kingdoms of darkness, to move among satanic forces and subdue them in the name of Jesus.

May the God of grace and mercy strengthen us. If the five or six hundred people in this place tonight were—in the will of God— to rise as one man to slay the Enemy, the evil host around us would feel the power. And in the measure that we destroy these evil powers, we make it easier for weak believers. For every time Satan overcomes a saint, it gives him ferocity for another attack; but when he is subdued, he will come to the place where defeat is written against him.

If you know God is within you, and you are suffering in any part of your body, please stand. I would like to take another case to prove my position in order to help all the people here. (A woman stands.) You know you are saved?

"Yes, sir."

Praise God! Do you know this truth from the fourth chapter of the first epistle of John: *"Greater is he that is in you, than he that is in the world"* (v. 4 KJV)? What is the trouble with you?

"I am suffering from neuralgic pains."

Then by the authority of Jesus, where the neuralgia is, you go like this: "I rebuke you in the name of Jesus! I am against you! In the name of Jesus, come out and leave me!" Now, go on.

"I rebuke you in the name of Jesus! I refuse this pain the right to remain in the name of Jesus."

I believe it is gone. Is it gone?

"It is gone!"

Let me read to you what I have been preaching, because I want to prove that it is the Word of God. It is in the eleventh chapter of Matthew: *"And from the days of John the Baptist until now* [right up to this moment] *the kingdom of heaven suffers violence"* (v. 12). That is, the inward presence of God suffers violence by the power of Satan, *"And the violent take it by force"* (v. 12).

How many people in this meeting are going to try that before going to bed? Glory to God! That is faith.

> I know the Lord, I know the Lord,
> I know the Lord's laid His hand on me.

If anyone were to say to me, "Wigglesworth, I will give you ten thousand dollars," in my estimation it would be as dust compared to the rising faith I have just seen. What I have seen by your uplifted hands along the lines of faith is of more value to me than anything you could count.

In your home, with your wife and children, you will have (audacity of determination,) along with (a righteous indignation) against the power of disease to cast it out. That is worth more to you than anything you could buy.

I have a clear conviction that through the preached Word, there are people who are going to take a new step. By the grace of God, we have seen tonight that we have to keep authority over the body, making the body subject to the higher powers. What about you who are in sickness or who are bound in other ways: don't you long to come into a fullness of God? Aren't you longing to know a Savior who can preserve you in the world over the powers of the Enemy? I pray tonight, in the name of Jesus, that you will yield.

Everyone who has an inward knowledge of an indwelling Christ, lift your right hand. Thank God! Put them down. No one can have a knowledge of an inward Christ without having a longing that there will be an increase of souls saved. The very first principle is that you have a *"first love"* (Rev. 2:4). And if you don't lose that love, it will keep you focused on winning souls all the time.

Those of you who did not put up your hands before, do you dare to put up your hands now and let all these four hundred believers pray for you? While we all appreciate the penitent bench being filled, I know that if you cannot be saved in your seats, you cannot be saved up here. You are not saved by coming forward, although it is a help for you to come forward. But if these four hundred saved people pray for you who have no knowledge of salvation, you can be saved right where you are.

So I am going to give you a real live opportunity to get near God by standing on your feet with these four hundred and sweeping into the kingdom of heaven by faith.

> Jesus paid it all,
> All to Him I owe;
> Sin had left a crimson stain;
> He washed it white as snow.

CHAPTER TWELVE

AFLAME FOR GOD

The word that I have for you is Hebrews 1:7: *"And of the angels He says: 'Who makes His angels spirits and His ministers a flame of fire.'"* His ministers are to be flames of fire! It seems to me that no man with a vision, especially a vision by the Spirit's power, can read that wonderful verse without being kindled to such a flame of fire for his Lord that it seems as if it would burn up everything that would interfere with his progress.

A flame of fire! It is a perpetual fire, a constant fire, a continual burning, a holy flame, which is exactly what God's Son was in the world. I can see that God has nothing less for us than to be flames! It seems to me that if Pentecost is to rise and be effective, we must have a living faith so that Christ's great might and power can flow through us until our lives become energized, moved, and aflame for God.

The important point of this message is that the Holy Spirit has come to make Jesus King. It seems to me that the seed, the life that was given to us when we believed—which is an eternal seed (1 Pet. 1:23)—has such resurrection power that I see a new creation rising from it with kingly qualities. I see that when we are baptized in the Holy Spirit, it is to crown Jesus King in our lives. Not only is the King to be within us, but also all the glories of His kingly manifestations are to be brought forth in us. Oh, for Him to work in us in this way, melting us, until a new order rises within us so that we are moved with His compassion. I see that we can come into the order of God where the vision becomes so much brighter and where the Lord is manifesting His glory with all His virtues and gifts; all His glory seems to fill the soul who is absolutely dead to himself and alive to God. There is much talk about death, but there is a

254

death that is so deep in God that, out of that death, God brings the splendor of His life and all His glory.

An opportunity to be a flame of fire for God came when I was traveling from Egypt to Italy. What I now tell you truly happened. On the ship and everywhere, God had been with me. A man on the ship suddenly collapsed; his wife was in a terrible state, and everybody else seemed to be, too. Some said that he would die, but oh, to be a flame, to have the living Christ dwelling within you!

We are backslidden if we have to pray for power, if we have to wait until we feel a sense of His presence. The baptism of the Holy Spirit has come upon you: *"You shall receive power when the Holy Spirit has come upon you"* (Acts 1:8). Within you is a greater power than there is in the world (1 John 4:4). Oh, to be awakened out of our unbelief into a place of daring for God on the authority of the blessed Book!

So in the name of Jesus, I rebuked the devil, and to the astonishment of the man's wife and the man himself, he was able to stand. He said, "What is this? It is going all over me. I have never felt anything like this before." From the top of his head to the soles of his feet, the power of God shook him. God has given us authority over the power of the Devil (Luke 10:19). Oh, that we may live in the place where the glory excels! It would make anyone a flame of fire.

Christ, who is the express image of God (Heb. 1:3), has come to our human weaknesses in order to change them and us into a divine likeness so that, by the power of His might, we may not only overcome but also rejoice in the fact that we are more than overcomers. God wants you to be *"more than conquerors"* (Rom. 8:37)! The baptism of the Spirit has come for nothing less than to possess the whole of our lives. It sets up Jesus as King, and nothing can stand in His holy presence when He is made King. Everything will wither before Him. I feel that the reason I come to a meeting like this is to stir you up and help you know that the inheritance of the Spirit is given to every man *"for the profit of all"* (1 Cor. 12:7). Praise the Lord! In the order of the Holy Spirit, we have to *"come short in no gift"* (1 Cor. 1:7).

This same Jesus has come for one purpose: that He might be made so manifest in us that the world will see Him. We must be burning and shining lights to reflect such a holy Jesus. We cannot do it with cold, indifferent experiences, and we never will. My dear wife used to say to our daughter, "Alice, what kind of a meeting have you had?" Alice would say, "Ask Father. He always has a good time!" His servants are to be flames. Jesus is life, and the Holy Spirit is the breath. He breathes through us the life of the Son of God, and we give it to others, and it gives life everywhere.

You should have been with me in Ceylon! I was having meetings in a Wesleyan chapel. The people there said, "You know, four days are not much to give us." "No," I said, "but it is a good share." They asked, "What are we going to do? We are not touching the people here at all." I said, "Can you have a meeting early in the morning, at eight o'clock?" They said they would, so I said, "We will tell all the mothers who want their babies to be healed and all the old people over seventy to come. Then after that, I will hope to give an address to the people to make them ready for the Holy Spirit."

Oh, it would have done you all good to see four hundred mothers there with their babies! It was fine! And then to see one hundred and fifty old black people, with their white hair, coming to be healed. I believe that you need to have something more than smoke to touch people; you need to be a burning light for that. His ministers must be flames of fire. There were thousands gathered outside the chapel to hear the Word of God. There were about three thousand people crying for mercy at the same time. I tell you, it was a sight.

After that, attendance at the meetings rose to such an extent that every night, five to six thousand people gathered there after I had preached in a temperature of 110 degrees. Then I had to minister to these people. But I tell you, a flame of fire can do anything. Things change in the fire. This is Pentecost. But what moved me more than anything else was this (and I say this carefully and with a broken spirit because I would not like to mislead anybody): there were hundreds who tried to touch me because they were so impressed with the power of God that was present. And they testified everywhere that with a touch, they were healed. It was *not* the power of Wigglesworth. It was because they had the same faith that was with those at Jerusalem who believed that Peter's shadow falling on them would heal them. (See Acts 5:14–15.)

You can receive something in three minutes that you can carry with you into glory. What do you want? Is anything too hard for God? God can meet you now. God sees inwardly. He knows all about you. Nothing is hidden from Him, and He can satisfy the soul and give you a spring of eternal blessing that will carry you right through.

CHAPTER THIRTEEN

"GLORY AND VIRTUE"

I want you to see two words that are closely connected: *glory* and *virtue.* They are beautiful words and are full of blessing for us this moment. Let me read the verse in which they are found: *"Through the knowledge of Him who called us by glory and virtue"* (2 Pet. 1:3).

People have a great misunderstanding about glory, though they often use the word. There are three things that ought to take place at the baptism of the Holy Spirit. First, it was necessary that the movement of the mighty rushing wind was made manifest in the Upper Room. Second, it was also necessary that the disciples were clothed with tongues as of fire. (See Acts 2:1–4.) Third, it was a necessity that they received not only the fire but also the rushing wind, the personality of the Spirit in the wind. The manifestation of the glory is in the wind, or breath, of God.

The inward man receives the Holy Spirit instantly with great joy and blessedness. He cannot express it. Then the power of the Spirit, this breath of God, takes of the things of Jesus (see John 16:14–15) and sends forth as a river the utterances of the Spirit. Again, when the body is filled with joy, sometimes so inexpressible, and the joy is thrown on the canvas of the mind, the canvas of the mind has great power to move the operation of the tongue to bring out the very depths of the inward heart's power, love, and joy to us. By the same process, the Spirit, which is the breath of God, brings forth the manifestation of the glory.

Peter said in 2 Peter 1:16–17,

For we did not follow cunningly devised fables when we made known to you the power and coming of our Lord Jesus Christ, but were eyewitnesses of His majesty. For He received from God the Father honor and glory when such a voice came to Him from the Excellent Glory: "This is My beloved Son, in whom I am well pleased." (2 Pet. 1:16–17)

Sometimes people wonder why it is that the Holy Spirit is always expressing Himself in words. It cannot be otherwise. You could not understand it otherwise. You cannot understand God by shakings, and yet shakings may be in perfect order sometimes. But you can always tell when the Spirit moves and brings forth the utterances. They are always the utterances that magnify God. The Holy Spirit has a perfect plan. He comes right through every man who is so filled and brings divine utterances so that we may understand what the mind of the Lord is.

I will show you some passages in the Bible that pertain to the glory. The first is Psalm 16:9: *"Therefore my heart is glad, and my glory rejoices."* Something has made the rejoicing bring forth the glory. It was because his heart was glad.

The second one is Psalm 108:1: *"O God, my heart is steadfast; I will sing and give praise, even with my glory."* You see, when the body is filled with the power of God, then the only thing that can express the glory is the tongue. Glory is presence, and the presence always comes by the tongue, which brings forth the revelations of God.

In Acts, we discover another aspect of this:

For David says concerning Him: "I foresaw the LORD always before my face, for He is at my right hand, that I may not be shaken. Therefore my heart rejoiced, and my tongue was glad." (Acts 2:25–26)

God first brings His power into us. Then He gives us verbal expressions by the same Spirit, the outward manifestation of what is within us. *"Out of the abundance of the heart the mouth speaks"* (Matt. 12:34).

Virtue has to be transmitted, and glory has to be expressed. Therefore, by filling us with the Holy Spirit, God has brought into us this glory so that out of us may come forth the glory. The Holy Spirit understands everything Christ has in the glory and brings through the heart of man God's latest thought. The world's needs, our manifestations, revivals, and all conditions are first settled in heaven, then worked out on the earth. We must be in touch with God Almighty in order to bring out on the face of the earth all the things that God has in the heavens. This is an ideal for us, and may God help us not to forsake the reality of holy communion with Him, of entering into private prayer so that publicly He may manifest His glory.

We must see the face of the Lord and understand His workings. There are things that God says to me that I know must take place. It does not matter what people say. I have been face to face with some of the most trying moments of men's lives, times when it made all the difference if I kept the vision and held fast to what God had said. A man must have immovable faith, and the voice of God must mean more to him than what he sees and feels, or what people say. He must have an originality born in heaven, transmitted or expressed in some way. We must bring heaven to earth.

Let us look again at 2 Peter 1:3: *"His divine power has given to us all things that pertain to life and godliness, through the knowledge of Him who called us by glory and virtue."* Oh, this is a lovely verse. There is so much depth in it for us. It is all real; it is all from heaven. It is as divinely appointed for this meeting as when the Holy Spirit was upon Peter. It is life to me. It is like the breath; it moves me. I must live in this grace. *"His divine power,"* there it is again, *"has given to us all things that pertain to life and godliness."* Oh, what wonderful things He has given us, *"through the knowledge of Him who called us by glory and virtue."* You cannot get away from Him. He is the center of all things. He moves the earth and transforms beings. He can live in every mind, plan every thought. Oh, He is there all the time.

You will find that Paul was full of the might of the Spirit breathing through him, and yet he came to a place where he felt he must stop. For there are greater things than he could utter even by prayer, when the Almighty breathes through the human soul.

At the end of Ephesians 3 are words that no human could ever think or write on his own. This passage is so mighty, so of God when it speaks about His being able to do all things, *"exceedingly abundantly above all that we ask or think"* (v. 20). The mighty God of revelation! The Holy Spirit gave these words of grandeur to stir our hearts, to move our affections, to transform us altogether. This is ideal! This is God. Shall we teach them? Shall we have them? Oh, they are ours. God has never put anything up on a pole where you could not reach it. He has brought His plan down to man, and if we are prepared, oh, what there is for us! I feel sometimes that we have just as much as we can digest. Yet such divine nuggets of precious truth are held before our hearts that it makes us understand that there are yet heights and depths and lengths and breadths of the knowledge of God stored up for us. (See Ephesians 3:17–19.) We might truly say,

> My heavenly bank, my heavenly bank,
> The house of God's treasure and store.
> I have plenty in here; I'm a real millionaire.

Glory! It is wonderful never to be poverty-stricken anymore, to have an inward knowledge of a bank that is greater than the Rothschilds, or any other wealthy person, has ever known about. It is stored up, nugget upon nugget—weights of glory, expressions of the invisible Christ to be seen by men.

God is shaking the earth to its foundations and causing us to understand that there is a principle in the Scriptures that can bring to man freedom from the natural order, and bring him into a place of holiness, righteousness, and the peace of God that passes all human understanding (Phil. 4:7). We must reach it. Praise God! God has brought us here on purpose so that we may enter that place. He has brought us here this morning, and you say, "How will I be able to get all that is stored up for me?" Brother, sister, I know no other way: "A broken and a contrite heart; these, O God, You will not despise" (Ps. 51:17).

What do you want? Be definite in your seeking. God knows what you need, and that one thing is for you this morning. Set it in your minds that you will know the "powers of the world to come" (Heb. 6:5 KJV).

Ask, and it will be given to you; seek, and you will find; knock, and it will be opened to you. For everyone who asks receives, and he who seeks finds, and to him who knocks it will be opened. (Matt. 7:7–8)

CHAPTER FOURTEEN

THE MIGHT OF THE SPIRIT

Our theme is power for service and power in service. This is a very wonderful subject, and we may not be able to cover it all today. But there is so much in it, which we are now comprehending, that was once obscure to us. There is much that we now know about, much that we are no longer groping around for, thinking about, or speaking as much about as something that is not yet quite clear. We are speaking of the things we do know and testifying to the things we have seen. Now we are on the Rock. We are coming to understand what Peter received on that memorable day when our Lord said to him, *"You are Peter, and on this rock I will build My church, and the gates of Hades shall not prevail against it"* (Matt. 16:18).

We are standing on the foundation: the Rock, Christ, the Word, the Living Word. The power is contained in substance there. Christ is the substance of our faith. He is the hope of our inheritance. He is the substance and sum of this whole conference we are attending. If we go outside of that, we will be altogether outside the plan of the great ideal of this conference, whose overall theme is "Christ the Center."

Let us look at a passage from the first chapter of Acts:

The former account I made, O Theophilus, of all that Jesus began both to do and teach, until the day in which He was taken up, after He through the Holy Spirit had given commandments to the apostles whom He had chosen, to whom He also presented Himself alive after His suffering by many infallible proofs, being seen by them during forty days and speaking of the things pertaining to the kingdom of God. And being assembled together with them, He commanded them not to depart from Jerusalem, but to wait for the Promise of the Father, "which," He said, "you have heard from Me; for John truly baptized with water, but you shall be baptized with the Holy Spirit not many days from now." Therefore, when they had come together, they asked Him, saying, "Lord, will You at this time restore the kingdom to Israel?" And He said to them, "It is not for you to know times or seasons which the Father has put in His own authority. But you shall receive power when the Holy Spirit has come upon you; and you shall be witnesses to Me in Jerusalem, and in all Judea and Samaria, and to the end of the earth." (Acts 1:1–8)

"You shall receive power when the Holy Spirit has come upon you." Jesus lived in the knowledge of that power. The Spirit of the Lord was upon Him.

Some of the important truths that I want to deal with today, as God breathes through me, are the fact of the power being there within us, the fact of a knowledge of that power, the fact of the substance being there, and the fact of what is being created or breathed or formed in us by God Himself.

We have come into a new order. We are dwelling in a place where Christ is the whole substance, and where man is but the body or the clay. (See Isaiah 64:8.) The body is the temple of the Holy Spirit (1 Cor. 6:19); within the temple, a living principle is laid down of rock, the Word of the living God. It is formed in us, and it is a thousand times mightier than the "self" in thought, in language, in activity, and in movement. There is an anointing, a force, a power mightier than dynamite that is stronger than the mightiest gun that has ever been made. It is able to resist the greatest pressure that the Devil can bring against it. Mighty power has no might against this almighty power. When we speak about evil power, we speak about mighty power. But when we speak about almighty power, we speak about a substance of rock dynamite that diffuses through a person and displays its might and brings everything else into insignificance.

I want you to think through what I am saying. I want us to be able to lay everything down on the Word. *"The people who know their God shall be strong, and carry out great exploits"* (Dan. 11:32). The Holy Spirit has come with one definite purpose, and that is to reveal to us the Father and the Son in all their different branches of helpfulness to humanity. The Spirit has come to display almighty power so that the weak may be made strong, and to bring to sickness such a manifestation of the blood of Christ, of the Atonement on Calvary, that the evil power of disease is conquered and forced to leave.

HOLY BOLDNESS

In this baptism of the Holy Spirit, there is a holy boldness—not superstition, but a boldness that stands unflinchingly and truly on what the Word of God says. To have holy boldness is to live in the Holy Spirit, to get to know the principles that are worked out by Him. I must understand that Jesus lived in a blessed, sweet fellowship with His Father, and He worked and operated because His Father worked (John 14:10). I must live in the same way. I must learn that the blessed principles of divine order are in me and that, as long as self doesn't take over, I am living only for Him.

Jesus is, and always ought to be, preeminent. Then there is no fear. Perfect love, perfect knowledge of God, of Jesus, brings me into a state where I have no fear. (See 1 John 4:18.) I have entered a new order in which Christ is working in me and bringing every thought into subjection. (See 2 Corinthians 10:5.) He is transforming my desires into what God desires, into a divine plan. Now I am working within a new plan in which self ceases, Christ does the work, and the work is accomplished.

"How does this happen?" you might be asking. I am going to mention a few things that will be helpful to you regarding this. You cannot have holy boldness unless you know God; do not attempt to exercise it unless you know Him. Daniel would never have survived the lions' den if he had not known God. What did the king say? He said, *"Daniel, servant of the living God, has your God, whom you serve continually, been able to deliver you from the lions?"* (Dan. 6:20). Daniel answered, *"O king, live forever! My God sent His angel and shut the lions' mouths, so that they have not hurt me"* (vv. 21–22).

In one sense, the mouths of the lions were shut when Daniel was in the den, and yet, in another sense, they were shut even before that. The lions' mouths were shut when the decree forbidding prayer to anyone except the king was signed and when Daniel trusted in God to deliver him. (See Daniel 6:1–23.) You will always

find that <u>victory occurs at the moment you open the door of your</u> ✳
<u>heart to believing.</u>

I arrived one day in a place where there was a great deal of strife and friction. I had a letter of introduction to a man there who was a stranger to me; I did not know a single person in town. I brought the letter to this man, and when he had read it, he said, "This letter is from Brother —— of Cleveland. I know him. The letter mentions much about you. There will be an open door for you here." Immediately, he added, "Go out and visit these people"—he gave me their names—"and then come back to dinner." I got back a little bit late, and as soon as I arrived, he said, "I am sorry you are late for dinner. We have already had dinner, for this reason: A heartbroken young man has been here. He was going to marry a beautiful young woman. But she is dying, and the doctor is by her side and cannot help her. That young man has promised to be here and will be here in a minute. You had better get ready." I replied, "I am ready now."

Just as I started to eat my dinner, in came this brokenhearted man. I did not question him. I went with him, and we arrived at the house where the young woman was. Her mother met me at the door, brokenhearted. I said to her, "<u>Cheer up.</u> Show me the girl; take me to her. It will be all right in a minute or two." Right away, I was taken into the house and upstairs. The young woman lay there in bed. She was suffering greatly from acute appendicitis. I said to her, "It will be all right in a minute or two." Then I said, "Come out!" and instantly she was healed. That was holy boldness!

<u>What do I mean by holy boldness?</u> We may say that <u>there is a divine position where a person may dwell and where he has such a knowledge of God that he knows God will not fail him.</u> It is not a miracle, although at times it almost seems as if it has a measure of the miraculous. At times it does not act exactly as the human mind would like it to act. God does not act in that way. He very often acts in quite an opposite way.

What I want you to know is that God has a plan for His children. What happened in that case I just mentioned? Here is the secret. The doctor came a short time after that girl had been healed, and he could not understand it. He saw this young woman; she was dressed and downstairs ten minutes after having been made well. Meanwhile, during the time it took her to dress, another four people were definitely healed. What was God's purpose? That young doctor had been investigating the power of healing, and he had not been able to find a single person who was able to heal in this way. He called to the young woman, "Are you downstairs?" "Yes," she replied. "Come here," he said. The young woman said, "A young man"—she called me a young man—"from England has been brought, and I was instantly healed." "Come here," he repeated. Then he pressed his long finger into the soft part of that tumor. It would have made her scream if she had still had appendicitis. But he could not find any symptoms, and he said, "This is God. This is God."

Did anything else happen in that town? Yes. They had built a new meetinghouse there, but it had never been filled to capacity. The leader said, "I am going to prophesy that there will be so many people, our place won't be able to hold them." And that's exactly the way it was. Did anything else happen? Yes, God healed over two hundred people in that place. Brothers and sisters, it is not we who do this. I am very aware of the fact that it is just as Jesus said in John 14:10, *"The words that I speak to you I do not speak on My own authority; but the Father who dwells in Me does the works."* Is that not beautiful? Just think of it, some of you who have been so busy in arranging plans for preaching. Think of how wonderful it is when the Holy Spirit comes and takes possession of you and speaks through you just the things that are needed.

Some people say, "Do these things last?" Praise God, His truth never fails to last; it goes on lasting. I received a letter the other day from Albany, Oregon, which is about seventy miles south of Portland. This person had not written to me since I visited there. The letter ran like this: "Do you remember my taking you to my wife's brother, who had lost all power of reason and everything? [Alcohol and the power of the Devil had taken hold of him.] My brother-in-law has been perfectly whole ever since, and has not tasted alcohol."

"You shall receive power" (Acts 1:8). Glory to God. I have come to understand that if I will be still, God can work; if I will be sure that I pay the price and do not come out of the divine order, God will certainly work.

Let me say a word to your hearts. Most of us here today are diligently seeking God's best. We feel that we would pay any price for His best. God knows my heart. I do not have an atom of desire outside the perfect will of God, and God knows this. But Wigglesworth, like everybody else, occasionally has to ask, "What is wrong with me? I do not feel the anointing," and if there is anything to repent of, I get right down before God and get it out. You cannot cover over sins; you cannot cover over faults. You must get to the bottom of them. I cannot have the anointing, the power of the Holy Spirit, the life of Christ, and the manifest glory except through self-abasement and complete renunciation of self—with God alone enthroned and Wigglesworth dead to himself. It must be of God, and if a person will only examine the conditions and act upon them, I tell you, things will come off wonderfully.

INTERPRETATION OF A MESSAGE IN TONGUES: "The deliverances of the Lord are as high as the righteousness of heaven, the purity of His saints is as white as linen, and the divine principles of His gracious will can only flow out when He is enthroned within. Christ first, last; always Christ. Through Christ and by the name of Jesus, 'whatever you shall ask in My name I will do.'"

I repeat: people sometimes say, "Do these things last; is this thing permanent?" The baptism of the Holy Spirit in my life is like a river flowing on. It has been eight years since I was baptized in the Holy Spirit, and the tide rises higher and higher. Holiness, purity of heart, divine thoughts, and revelations of God are far in advance of what they were even a short time ago.

We are living in a divine place where the Lord is blessedly having His way. I want you to hear what I have to say about one or two more things. Some people can have things rubbed out of their lives, but I want God Almighty to do something now that cannot be rubbed out. We are definitely told in the Word of God that if we ask God for the Holy Spirit, He will give Him (Luke 11:13). We hear people say this quite easily, but I find that many people who dwell on this promise do not receive the baptism. I know when a person is baptized in the Holy Spirit. There is a kindred spirit with a person who is baptized in the Holy Spirit that is not there with any other person.

The Holy Spirit is given *"to those who obey"* (Acts 5:32). To those who obey what? What Jesus said. What did Jesus say? *"Tarry...until you are endued with power from on high"* (Luke 24:49). Is that not clear? That is Scripture. You do not need to have anything more scriptural than that.

Now, the reason that God the Holy Spirit brings me into this place today is that I love the church of God. When I hear men and women who are as saved as I am speaking in a way that I know is not according to the Spirit of God, I know exactly of what spirit they are. May God save us from building on our own imaginations. Let us build on what the Word of God says. We will never be strong unless we believe what God says. If God tells me in His Word that Paul was the chief of sinners (1 Tim. 1:15), I say I will believe it; I will believe it forever. Whatever the Holy Spirit says through His Word, I believe it and keep to it. I will not move from it. And in Acts 1:8, the Holy Spirit says I will have power after He comes upon me through Jesus.

INTERPRETATION OF A MESSAGE IN TONGUES: "They who fear the Lord and they who keep His commandments will have the goodness of the land; and they who will do His will will know the doctrine, and God will declare unto their hearts the perfectness of His way. For 'there is a way that seems right to a man, but the way of that is death'; but the way of righteousness brings to pass that God's Word is true."

FIND YOUR PLACE IN THE HOLY SPIRIT

I am so pleased because there is a thought coming into my heart that all of you ought to know. I believe there is a great need today for us to find our place in the Holy Spirit. It would save us from so many burdens and many other things. I am going to give you a little illustration of this. There is a dear woman who lives at our house and who looks after my affairs. She perpetually makes herself a real slave-servant. I often think she does so much that is not needed. She is a slave-servant; that is her disposition. There are many people like this. Now, we have many people in our meetings whom God has been blessing and who have gone out to speak for Him in different places. This woman thought she ought to do the same. We had received many invitations for people to speak, and she accepted one of these invitations. She looked timid but said she had to lead this service. I got up with the needed boldness and set to work to strip away what was causing this timidity. With her heart full, she went out and found someone else to lead the meeting, and instantly she found relief. She came back with her face beaming. "What's up?" I asked. She said, "I've found relief." The burden was gone.

Some people, just because they have been baptized with the Holy Spirit and with fire (Matt. 3:11), think they have to go and be preachers. It is a pity—it is a thousand pities—that it is so. It is good that such a desire is in your heart, but it may not be God's purpose for you. If you would get to know your place in the Holy Spirit, it would save you from struggles and burdens and would relieve the whole situation. Get to know your place in the Holy Spirit, and God will bless you. There are people here whose hearts are crushed because they are not able to sing as well as our Welsh brother can. But it would not do for every one of us to be like him. We would be breaking all the glass in the place if we were all like him. We all have to get to know our positions in the Holy Spirit. God can work it so beautifully and harmonize it so that nothing will be out of order.

God will put you in the place you are to occupy if you will ask and trust Him for it. Then you will live in the Holy Spirit so that His glory will always be upon you. If you miss it, say, like David, "Lord, *restore to me the joy of Your salvation*' (Ps. 51:12)." If you feel out of touch with God, get back to Calvary; keep near the Cross. Let the God of Glory glorify Himself in you.

It is marvelous how all the gifts of the Spirit may be manifested in some people. Everybody acquainted with me knows that I used to be short of speech, slow at everything, and all out of order. My wife used to preach, and I carried the babies and the boots and everything. Then there came a time when my wife could not be there and I was forced to roll in somehow. Well, I rolled in, and I was very glad to roll out many times. But it is marvelous now. As a calling, God has allowed every one of the nine gifts of the Spirit to be ministered through me. (See 1 Corinthians 12:8–10.) There is not a single gift that has not been ministered through me. What I mean is this. You won't hear me say that I *have* these gifts. But, living in the Holy Spirit, I am in a place where God can manifest any gift at any moment that it is needed. You also may live in this glorious place. Then it is heaven to live, it is heaven to eat, it is heaven to sleep—it is heaven all the time. And when heaven comes, it will only be more fullness, for the kingdom of heaven is already within.

I am speaking from my heart this morning. It is no good for me to speak unless I speak from my heart. I have put my hands to this work, and I feel that God the Holy Spirit has done something, and I just want to speak about it in closing. I know you will believe it; I know it is true. God has helped me to go into different places and bring about revivals. Over and over again, revivals begin with people who are baptized in the Holy Spirit, and God does great things. Last night, there was a preacher here. There he was. He knelt down. He was as stiff as a board. You need to have discernment to see whether there is a real desire in people who are seeking the baptism. This preacher was frightened to let go. I said, "Come, brother, receive the Holy Spirit," and he replied, "I cannot." I told him, "You are not in earnest; you are not real. There is no resoluteness about you. You must begin to move. Receive the Holy Spirit." Then, when I knew that he was really being stirred up, according to God's divine order, I put my hands on him and said, "Receive the Holy Spirit." God the Holy Spirit shook him from top to bottom and inside out. What a wonderful baptism he had!

Brothers and sisters, do you want the Holy Spirit? We sing some hymns that speak of the breath of the Holy Spirit. In the Bible, we read that Jesus breathed upon His disciples, and they received the anointing in His breath (John 20:22). As people breathe in the Holy Spirit, they become so possessed with the power of God that they have no possessions in themselves. They simply fall into God, and God takes possession of everything—hands, feet, body, and tongue—for His glory. My heart yearns for you to be so filled with the divine power of the Holy Spirit that you will return to your own meetings and assemblies in the order of God. You are not to take any special notice of your fullness, but the fact will remain in you that you have the power of the Holy Spirit. Let the Word of God act upon this power in such a way that God will let it flow through you to others. In what way? In His way. You cannot baptize people, but He can do it. How? *"Receive the Holy Spirit"* (John 20:22). Let Him have His way.

CHAPTER FIFTEEN

THE PLACE OF VICTORY

Today I have been led to deal with an important truth that will be helpful for us in our Christian lives. The thought that has been pressing on my mind for some time is the thought of abiding in God. There is joy in being at the place where we can always count on being in the presence of Power—where we know that God's presence is with us, leading us to the place where victory is assured. This is the important truth that I have been led to think of. We are here to get hold of the thought that if we keep in the right place with God, God can do anything with us.

Let us look at a few passages of Scripture. The first is Luke 4:1–2: *"Then Jesus, being filled with the Holy Spirit, returned from the Jordan and was led by the Spirit into the wilderness, being tempted for forty days by the devil."* In Mark's account of Jesus' temptation, he spoke about Jesus being "driven" by the Spirit into the wilderness. (See Mark 1:12.)

Whatever Luke and Mark meant by Jesus being *"led"* or "driven" by the Holy Spirit, one thing is certain: a power, a majesty, had fallen on Jesus, and He was no longer the same man. He had received this mighty anointing power of God, and He realized that the only thing for Him to do was to submit. As He submitted, He was more and more covered with the power and led by the Spirit. The Holy Spirit took Him away into the wilderness, with its darkness and great privations. For forty days He was without food, but because of the presence and the power within and on Him, He was certain of victory. With this power, He faced the wild beasts of the wilderness (Mark 1:13) and the lack of every human sustenance. Then, at the end of the forty days, in that holy attainment,

270

He was brought into a state of persecution and trial such as a man likely has never been attacked by before or since.

In that place of persecution and trial, God sustained Him mightily. With what did God sustain Him? With this holy, blessed anointing. I want you to really think about this. God sustained Jesus with the holy, blessed anointing that was upon Him and that so brought the Word of God to bear upon Satan that Jesus was like the *"pen of a ready writer"* (Ps. 45:1) and slew Satan every time with God's Word.

Let us look at another passage of Scripture. In Luke 4:14–15, you will see that *"Jesus returned in the power of the Spirit to Galilee, and news of Him went out through all the surrounding region. And He taught in their synagogues, being glorified by all."* I want you to understand that after the trials, after all the temptations, and everything else, He came out more full of God, more clothed with the Spirit, and more ready for the fight. The endowment with power had such an effect on Him that other people saw it and flocked to hear Him, and great blessings came to the land. He was among His kinsfolk and relatives, and in the spirit of this kind of holy attainment, He went into the synagogue. He was given a scroll of the Scriptures, and He read, *"The Spirit of the LORD is upon Me, because He has anointed Me to preach the gospel to the poor"* (Luke 4:18).

I want you to keep in mind where the anointing came from. How was Jesus anointed? How did it come to Him? You remember how that came about: *"Jesus also was baptized; and while He prayed, the heaven was opened. And the Holy Spirit descended in bodily form like a dove upon Him"* (Luke 3:21–22). In just the same manner, I see that the Holy Spirit also fell upon the disciples at Pentecost. (See Acts 2:1–4.) I see that they were anointed with the same power; I see that they went forth, and success attended their ministry until the power of God swept through the whole earth. I want you to see that it was because of this anointing, this power, that when Peter and John spoke to the lame man at the gate of the temple, the man was able to rise and leap for joy. (See Acts 3:1–8.)

The Holy Spirit's coming upon an individual is capable of changing him, fertilizing his spiritual life, and filling him with such power and grace that he wouldn't be able to say that anything was impossible but that all things are possible with God (Matt. 19:26). What could happen, what is possible, if we reach this place and stay in it—if we abide in it? Some people have an idea that they have to be doing something. I implore you, by the power of the Holy Spirit, that you see that there is only one thing that is going to accomplish the purposes of God, and that is being in the Spirit. I don't care how dry the land is. I don't care how thirsty the land is. I don't care how many or how few vessels are available. I implore you, in the name of Jesus, to keep in the Spirit. That's the secret.

Now, let us go to the book of Ezekiel. The Lord asked the prophet Ezekiel, *"Son of man, can these bones live?"* (Ezek. 37:3). He answered, *"O Lord GOD, You know"* (v. 3). When you are in the Spirit and the dry bones surround you and barren conditions are all around you; when you think everything is exactly the opposite of your desires and you can see no deliverance by human power; then, knowing that your condition is known to God and that God wants men and women who are willing to submit and submit and yield and yield to the Holy Spirit until their bodies are saturated and soaked with God, you realize that God your Father has you in such a condition that, at any moment, He can reveal His will to you.

I want you to understand that there is something more in this. I want you to see that God is everything to us. I believe that we have come to a place where we have to submit ourselves to the mighty anointing power of God and where we will see that we are in the will of God. I pray to God the Holy Spirit that if He does one thing among us today, it will be to show us our leanness and our distance from this place. It is not that we are not contending for it, but what we need is a great hunger and thirst for God.

Ezekiel said, *"O dry bones, hear the word of the LORD!"* (v. 4). I would like you to understand that God spoke first. He spoke so loudly and clearly and so distinctly that this man, Ezekiel, who was filled with the Spirit, heard every word. I want you to understand that there was not any movement in that valley of dry bones; until the word of the Lord was spoken by the prophet, the bones were as dry as at the beginning. God had spoken, and the message had gone forth. But nothing had yet happened. What was the matter? Ah! It was only that the word of God needed to go forth through His servant the prophet. The world has to be brought to a knowledge of the truth, but this will only be brought about through human instrumentality. This will occur when the human instrument is at a place where he will say all that the Holy Spirit directs him to say.

Ezekiel rose up and, clothed with divine power, began to speak; he began to prophesy. Then there was a rattling among the bones; bone came together with bone at the voice of the man filled with the Spirit of the living God. God had given him the victory. God wants to give us the victory in a similar way.

What does the Word say? *"Be still, and know that I am God"* (Ps. 46:10). This is the place of tranquillity, where we know that He is controlling and moving us by the mighty power of His Spirit. Beloved, this is the place that we need to reach. This prophecy is for us. Truly, God wants to begin this in us. There are many dry places. What does that have to do with you? You are to be the Lord's instrument. *"The Lord's hand is not shortened, that it cannot save"* (Isa. 59:1). Man's extremity is God's opportunity; His Word will awaken to meet the need. *"All things are possible to him who believes"* (Mark 9:23). But if we are to do the will of God at the right time and place, we must get into the Spirit and, in so doing, give God a fair chance.

Ezekiel said, *"So I prophesied as I was commanded"* (Ezek. 37:7). He did just what he was told to do. It takes more to live in that place than any other that I know of—to live in the place where you hear God's voice. It is only by the power of the Holy Spirit that you can quickly do as you are told. Ezekiel continued, *"And as I prophesied, there was a noise, and suddenly a rattling; and the bones came together, bone to bone"* (v. 7). There is something worth your notice in this. It is only the Spirit who can make what is crooked straight. (See Isaiah 42:16.) Only yield so that He may have full control of all that you are. We must get to the place where we will see God and know His voice when He sends us with a message that brings life, power, and victory.

What happened when the prophet spoke the word of the Lord? *"And breath came into them, and they lived, and stood upon their feet, an exceedingly great army"* (Ezek. 37:10).

CHAPTER SIXTEEN

"THE BEST WITH IMPROVEMENT"

L et the Spirit cover you today so that you may be intensely earnest about the deep things of God. You should be so in the order of the Spirit that you may know this: that your will, your mind, and your heart may be so centered in God that He may lift you into the pavilion of splendor where you hear His voice—lift you to the place where the breath of the Almighty can send you to pray and send you to preach, the Spirit of the Lord being upon you.

You are at God's banquet, a banquet at which you are never separated from Him and He multiplies spiritual blessings and fruit in your life. It is a banquet where you have to increase with all increasing, where God has for you riches beyond all things—not fleshly things, not carnal things, but spiritual manifestations, gifts, fruits of the Spirit, and beautiful beatitudes, the blessing of God always being upon you. (See 2 Corinthians 9:10–11.)

Are you ready to enter into this glorious place where you no longer live for yourself? God will take over your life and send you out to win thousands of people to Christ, so that they also may enter into eternal grace.

> INTERPRETATION OF A MESSAGE IN TONGUES: "The Spirit moves and changes His operation, bringing the soul into the place of hunger and desire until the whole of the being 'cries out for the living God.' Truly the creature must be delivered from this present evil thing. So God is operating through us by these meetings and letting us know that 'all flesh is grass.'

But He is bringing the Spirit of revelation, that we may know that this inheritance we are having is to endure forever and ever, for we belong to the new creation of God, clothed upon with the Spirit, made like unto Him, because our whole hearts now are bringing forth what God has established. It is out of the fullness of the truth of the hidden heart that God flows forth His glory, His power—His might and His revelation and His power in association—and makes us one and says, 'You are Mine.'"

For our study, the Lord has led me to select the first chapter of James. This is a marvelous subject in itself. This is the Master's subject, and He will be able to manage it. I would have to give up if it were my subject, but seeing it is the Master's subject, I will begin.

James, a bondservant of God and of the Lord Jesus Christ, to the twelve tribes which are scattered abroad: Greetings. My brethren, count it all joy when you fall into various trials.

(James 1:1–2)

Victorious in Battle

No person is ever able to talk about victory over temptation unless he goes through it. All the victories are won in battles.

There are tens of thousands of people in Europe, America, and in other parts of the world, who wear badges to show they have been in battle, and they rejoice in it. They would be ashamed to wear such badges if they had not been in battle. The battle is what gives them the right to wear the badge.

It is those who have been in the fight who can tell about the victories. It is those who have been tried to the utmost who can come out and tell you a story about it. It was only James and Peter and Paul, those who were in the front lines of the battle, who told us how we have to rejoice in our trials because wonderful blessings will come out of them. It is in the trials that we are made.

Tribulation, Patience, Experience

You want a spiritual experience, do you? Read this Scripture passage; it will give you an experience. I know nothing like it:

Therefore being justified by faith, we have peace with God through our Lord Jesus Christ: by whom also we have access by faith into this grace wherein we stand, and rejoice in hope of the glory of God. And not only so, but we glory in tribulations also: knowing that tribulation worketh patience; and patience, experience. (Rom. 5:1–4 KJV)

And out of the experience, we tell what is being done in our lives. Do you want to have a big story to tell? Well, it is here: *"Count it all joy"* (James 1:2) in the midst of temptations. When the trial is severe; when you think that no one is being tried as much as you; when you feel as if some strange thing has happened (1 Pet. 4:12) so that you are altogether in a new order; when the trial is so hard you cannot sleep and you do not know what to do, *"count it all joy."* God has something in it, something of a divine nature. You are in a good place when you do not know what to do.

After Abraham was tried, he could offer Isaac, but not before he was tried. God put him through all kinds of tests. For twenty-five years, he was tested, and he was called "the father of the faithful" (see Romans 4:9–16) because he would not give in. We have blessing today because one man dared to believe God for twenty-five years without budging.

Living in Faith for Twelve Months

A woman came up to me in a meeting one day and said, "I have come for you to heal me. Can you see this big goiter?"

"I can hardly see anything else," I answered.

She had told her father and mother and the rest of her family before she came that she believed she was going to be healed because Wigglesworth was going to pray for her. As soon as she was prayed for, we had a testimony meeting. Her testimony was wonderful. "Oh!" she said. "I thank God because He has perfectly healed me!" She went home, and they were all glad to hear what she said. "When I was prayed for, I was perfectly healed!" she exultantly exclaimed.

For twelve months, she went everywhere among the assemblies, telling how God had healed her. After those twelve months, I returned to the same place to hold meetings, and she came again, filled with joy. When she came in, the people said, "Look who's here. Oh, look how big that goiter is!" They were all staring at her.

After a while, we had a testimony meeting. "Twelve months ago," she said, "I was prayed for here, and I was marvelously healed. I have had twelve months of the most wonderful time on earth because God so wonderfully healed me twelve months ago."

After the meeting, she went home. When she got there, she said to her mother, "Oh, if you had been there and seen the people, how they were moved when they heard me tell how God healed me."

"Look," the mother said, "you don't know—you don't seem to know—but the people are believing there is something wrong with your mind, and they believe the entire family is affected by it, as well! You are bringing disgrace upon the whole family. It is shameful. We are disgusted with you. The whole thing is being rolled onto us because you are not right in the head. Why don't you go look in the mirror, and you will see that the thing has not moved at all."

She went to her room and prayed, "Lord, I do not want to look in the mirror. I believe You have done it, but let all the people know that You have done it. Let them all know that You have done it, just the same as You have let me know it." The next morning, she came downstairs as perfect as anybody could be, and the family knew that the Lord had done it.

"MORE PRECIOUS THAN GOLD"

Some of you wonder what is up when you are not healed in a moment. God never breaks His promise. The trial of your faith is *"much more precious than gold"* (1 Pet. 1:7).

God has you on this earth for the purpose of bringing out His character in you. He wants to destroy the power of the Devil. He wants to move you so that in the face of difficulties and hardships, you will praise the Lord. *"Count it all joy"* (James 1:2). You have to take a leap today; you have to leap into the promises. You have to believe that God never fails you; you have to believe it is impossible for God to break His word. He is *"from everlasting to everlasting"* (Ps. 90:2).

> Forever and ever, not for a day,
> He keepeth His promise forever;
> To all who believe,
> To all who obey,
> He keepeth His promise forever.

There is no variableness with God; there is no *"shadow of turning"* (James 1:17). He is the same. He manifests His divine glory.

Jesus said to Mary and Martha, *"If you would believe you would see the glory of God"* (John 11:40). We must understand that there will be times of testing, but they are only to make us more like the Master. He was *"in all points tempted as we are, yet without sin"* (Heb. 4:15). He endured all things. He is our example.

Oh, that God would place us in an earnest, intent position in which flesh and blood have to yield to the Spirit of God! We will go forward; we will not be moved by our feelings.

Suppose that a man who is prayed for today gets a blessing, but tomorrow he begins murmuring because he does not feel exactly as he ought to feel. What is he doing? He is replacing the Word of God with his feelings. What an awful disgrace it is for you to replace the Word of God with your feelings. Let God have His perfect work.

"My brethren, count it all joy" (James 1:2). This does not mean "Count a bit of it as joy" but *"count it all joy."* It doesn't matter from what source the trial comes, whether it is your business or your home or what. *"Count it all joy."* Why? Because *"we know that all things work together for good to those who love God, to those who are the called according to His purpose"* (Rom. 8:28).

That is a great Scripture. It means that you have a special position. God is electrifying the very position that you hold so that the Devil will see that you have a godly character, and he will have to say about you what he said about Job.

Recall the scene. God asked, "Satan, what is your opinion about Job?" Then the Lord went on and said, "Don't you think he is wonderful? Don't you think he is the most excellent man in all the earth?"

Satan replied, "Yes, but You know, You are keeping him."

Praise the Lord! I am glad the Devil has to tell the truth. And don't you know that God can keep you, also?

"If You touch everything he has," the Devil said, "he will curse You to Your face."

God answered, "You can touch all he has, but you cannot touch him." (See Job 1:8–12.)

The Scripture says that Jesus was dead but is alive again and has power over death and hell. To this, the Scripture adds a big

"Amen" (Rev. 1:18). The Devil cannot take your life unless the Lord allows it. "You cannot touch Job's life," God told Satan. (See Job 2:6.)

Satan thought he could destroy Job, and you know the calamity that befell this righteous man. But Job said, *"Naked I came from my mother's womb, and naked shall I return there....Blessed be the name of the LORD"* (Job 1:21). Oh, it is lovely! The Lord can give us that kind of language. It is not the language of the head. This is divine language; this is heart acquaintance.

I want you to know that we can have heart acquaintance. It is far more for me to speak out of the abundance of my heart than out of the abundance of my head. I learned a long time ago that libraries often create swelled heads, but nothing except the Library, the Bible, can make swelled hearts. You are to have swelled hearts because out of the heart full of the fragrance of the love of God, the living life of the Lord flows.

INTERPRETATION OF A MESSAGE IN TONGUES: "It is the Spirit who gives liberty. The prophet is nothing, but the Spirit brings us into attainment where we sit at His feet and seek with Him and have communications of things divine. For now we are not belonging to the earth; we are 'transformed by the renewing of our minds' and set 'in heavenly places with Christ Jesus.'"

You must cease to be. That is a difficult thing—for both you and me—but it is no trouble at all when you are in the hands of the Potter (Isa. 64:8). You are only wrong when you are kicking. You are all right when you are still and He is forming you afresh. So let Him form you afresh today into a new vessel so that you will stand the stress.

"THAT YOU MAY BE PERFECT"

"But let patience have its perfect work, that you may be perfect" (James 1:4).

Is this possible? Certainly, it is possible. Who was speaking in this verse? It was the breath of the Spirit; it was also the hidden man of the heart who had a heart like his Brother. This was James, the Lord's brother, who was speaking. He spoke very much like his Brother. When we read these wonderful words, we might very likely be encountering a true kindred spirit with Christ.

James had to learn patience. It was not an easy thing for him to understand how his Brother could be the Son of God and be in the same family as he, Judas, and the other brothers. (See Matthew 13:55.) It was not an easy thing for him, and he had to learn to be patient to see how it worked out.

There are many things in your life that you cannot understand. But be patient, for when the hand of God is upon something, it may grind very slowly, but it will form the finest thing possible if you dare to wait until it is completed. Do not kick until you have gone through the process—and when you are dead enough to yourself, you will never kick at all. It is a death we die so that we might be alive unto God. It is only by the deaths we die that we are able to be still before God.

Jesus said, "The cross? I can endure the cross. The shame? I can despise it." (See Hebrews 12:2.) He withstood the bitter language spoken to Him at the cross: "If You are the Christ, come down, and we will believe." (See Matthew 27:40, 42.) They struck Him, but He *did not revile in return*" (1 Pet. 2:23).

He is the picture for us. Why did He do it? He was patient. Why? He knew that when He came to the uttermost end of the Cross, He would forever save all those who would believe.

You cannot tell what God has in mind for you. As you are still before God—pliable in His hands—He will be working out a greater vessel than you could ever imagine in all your life.

"COMPLETE, LACKING NOTHING"

"Let patience have its perfect work, that you may be perfect and complete, lacking nothing" (James 1:4). To be *"complete"* means that you are not moved by anything, that you are living only in the divine position of God. It means that you are not moved, that you are not changed by what people say. There is something about divine acquaintance that is instilled; it is worked within a person by the mighty God. It becomes like intuition.

The new life of God is not just on the surface. It builds the character of a person in purity until his inward heart is filled with divine love and has nothing but thoughts of God alone. *"That you may be perfect and complete, lacking nothing."*

When I was in New Zealand, some people came to me and said, "We would like to give you a Christmas present, if you can tell us what you would like." "I haven't a desire in the world," I said. "I cannot tell you anything I would like. I have no desire for anything except God."

One day, I was walking down the street with a millionaire. I was feeling wonderfully happy over the way the Lord was blessing in our meetings. As we walked together, I said, "Brother, I haven't a care in the world. I am as happy as a bird!"

"Oh!" he said. "Stop! Say it again! Say it again!" And he stood still, waiting for me to repeat it. "Brother, I haven't a care in the world. I am as happy as a bird!" He exclaimed, "I would give all my money, I would give everything I have, to have that!"

To be lacking nothing—hallelujah!

The Spirit of the Lord is moving us mightily to see that this is resurrection power. We were planted with Him, and we have been raised with Him (Rom. 6:5 KJV). We are from above (see Colossians 3:1–3); we do not belong to what is below. We *"reign in life"* (Rom. 5:17) by Another. It is the life of God's Son manifested in this human body.

ASK GOD FOR WISDOM

"If any of you lacks wisdom, let him ask of God, who gives to all liberally and without reproach, and it will be given to him" (James 1:5). This is a very remarkable Scripture. Many people come to me and ask if I will pray for them to have faith. I want to encourage them, but I cannot depart from God's Word. I cannot grant people faith. But by the power of the Spirit, I can stimulate you until you dare to believe and rest on the authority of God's Word. The Spirit of the living God quickens you, and I see that *"faith comes by hearing, and hearing by the word of God"* (Rom. 10:17).

This is a living word of faith: *"If any of you lacks wisdom, let him ask of God, who gives to all liberally."* You will never find that God ever judges you for the wisdom He gives you or for the blessing He gives you. He makes it so that when you come to Him again, He gives again, never asking what you did with what He gave you before. That is the way God gives. God *"gives to all liberally and without reproach."* So you have a chance today to come for much more. Do you want wisdom? Ask of God.

INTERPRETATION OF A MESSAGE IN TONGUES: "It is not the wisdom that you get from the earth: it is divine wisdom. It brings a peaceful position; it rules with diligence, and it causes you to live in quietness. You know the difference between the 'wisdom that is from above' and the wisdom that is from below, and so the Spirit breathes through our brother to show you that you have to be so in the perfect will of God in asking for these things until one thing must be fulfilled in your heart: if you ask, you must believe, for God is only pleased when you believe."

You have to be in the right condition for asking. This is the condition: *"But let him ask in faith, with no doubting"* (James 1:6).

I am satisfied that God, who is the builder of divine order, never brings confusion into His order. It is only when things are out of order that God brings confusion. God brought confusion upon the men who were building the Tower of Babel because they were out of order. (See Genesis 11:1–9.) What were they doing? They were trying to get into heaven by a way that was not God's way, and they were thieves and robbers. (See John 10:1.) So He turned their language to confusion. There is a way into the kingdom of heaven, and it is through the blood of the Lord Jesus Christ.

If you want this divine order in your life, if you want wisdom, you have to come to God believing. I want to impress upon you the fact—and I am learning it more every day—that if you ask six times for anything, just for the sake of asking, it shows you are an unbelieving person. If you really believe, you will ask God and know that He has abundance for your every need. But if you go right in the face of belief and ask six times, He knows very well that you do not mean what you ask, so you do not get it. God does not honor unbelief; He honors faith.

If you would really get down to business about the baptism of the Holy Spirit and ask God once and definitely to fill you, believing it, what would you do? You would begin to praise Him for it because you would know He had given it.

If you ask God once for healing, you will get it. But if you ask a thousand times a day until you do not even know you are asking, you will get nothing. If you would ask God for your healing now and begin praising Him because He never breaks His word, you would go out of here perfect. *"Only believe"* (Mark 5:36).

God wants to promote us. He wants us to get away from our own thoughts and our own foolishness, and get to a definite place, believing that He exists and that *"He is a rewarder of those who diligently seek Him"* (Heb. 11:6).

Have you gotten to the place where you dare to do this? Have you gotten to the place where you are no longer going to murmur when you are undergoing a trial? Are you going to go around weeping, telling people about it, or are you going to say, "Thank you, Lord, for putting me on the top"?

A great number of ministers and evangelists do not get checks sent to them any longer because they didn't thank the donor for the last one. Many people receive no blessing because they did not thank God for the last blessing. A thankful heart is a receiving heart. God wants to keep you in the place of constant believing.

> Keep on believing, Jesus is near;
>   Keep on believing, there's nothing to fear;
>   Keep on believing, this is the way;
>   Faith in the night, the same as the day.

ENDURED TEMPTATION BRINGS THE CROWN

"Blessed is the man who endures temptation; for when he has been approved, he will receive the crown of life" (James 1:12). People do not know what they are getting when they are in a great place of temptation. Temptation endured brings the *"crown of life."*

> *He will receive the crown of life which the Lord has promised to those who love Him. Let no one say when he is tempted, "I am tempted by God"; for God cannot be tempted by evil, nor does He Himself tempt anyone. But each one is tempted when he is drawn away by his own desires and enticed. Then, when desire has conceived, it gives birth to sin; and sin, when it is full-grown, brings forth death. Do not be deceived, my beloved brethren.* (James 1:12–16)

There is nothing outside of purity except what is sin. All unbelief is sin. God wants you to have a pure, active faith so that you will be living in an advanced place of believing God all the time, and so that you will be on the mountaintop and singing when other people are crying.

I want to speak now about lust. I am not speaking about the base things, the carnal desires. I am not speaking so much about adultery, fornication, and such things, but I am speaking about what has turned you aside to some other thing instead of God. God has been offering you better things all the time, and you have missed them.

There are three things in life, and I notice that many people are satisfied with just one of them. There is blessing in justification, there is blessing in sanctification, and there is blessing in the baptism of the Holy Spirit. Salvation is a wonderful thing, and we know it. Sanctification is a process that takes us on to a higher level with God. Salvation, sanctification, and the fullness of the Spirit are processes.

Many people are satisfied with "good"—that is, with salvation. Other people are satisfied with "better"—a sanctified life, purified by God. Still other people are satisfied with the "best"— the fullness of God with revelation from on high. I am not satisfied with any of the three. I am only satisfied with the "best with improvement."

So I come to you not with good, but better; not with better, but best; not with best, but best with improvement—going on with God. Why? Because *"when desire has conceived, it gives birth to sin; and sin, when it is full-grown, brings forth death"* (James 1:15). When anything has taken me from God, it means death in some way.

When Jesus said to the disciples, "The Son of Man will be put into the hands of sinners and crucified," Peter rebuked Him (see Matthew 16:21–22), but Jesus said, *"Get behind Me, Satan! You are an offense to Me, for you are not mindful of the things of God, but the things of men"* (v. 23).

✶ Anything that hinders me from denying myself and taking up my cross (v. 24) is of the Devil; anything that hinders me from being separated unto God is of the Devil; and anything that hinders me from being purified every day is carnal, and it is death. So I implore you today to make certain that there is no lustful thing in you that would rob you of the glory. Then God will take you to the very summit of the blessing where you can be increased day by day into all His fullness.

Here is another Scripture I want you to receive. I understand clearly by this that God has worked out the whole plan of our inheritance. He is showing us that the whole thing is so beautiful and that we are brought into existence in the spiritual order through the Word:

So then, my beloved brethren, let every man be swift to hear, slow to speak, slow to wrath; for the wrath of man does not produce the righteousness of God. Therefore lay aside all filthiness and overflow of wickedness, and receive with meekness the implanted word, which is able to save your souls.

(James 1:19–21)

Do not neglect the Word of God. Take time to think about the Word of God; it is the only place of safety.

CHAPTER SEVENTEEN

UNCONDITIONAL
SURRENDER

I t is Pentecost that has made me rejoice in Jesus. God has been confirming His power by His Holy Spirit. I have an intense yearning to see Pentecost, and I am not seeing it. I may feel a little of the glow, but what we need is a deeper work of the Holy Spirit in order for God's message to come full of life and power and sharper than a *"two-edged sword"* (Heb. 4:12). At Pentecost, Peter stood up in the power of the Holy Spirit, and three thousand people were saved. Not long after this, he preached again, and five thousand people were saved.

I am positive about the fact that we are on the wrong side of the cross. We talk about love, love, love, but it ought to be repent, repent, repent. John the Baptist came, and his message was *"Repent"* (Matt. 3:2). Jesus came with the same message: *"Repent"* (Matt. 4:17). The Holy Spirit came, and the message was the same: Repent, repent, repent and believe. (See Acts 2:38.) What has all this to do with Pentecost? Everything! It is the secret of our failure.

Daniel carried on his heart the burden of the people. He mourned for the captivity of Zion, he confessed his sin and the people's sin, and he identified himself with Israel until God made him a flame of fire. (See Daniel 9.) The result: a remnant returned to Zion to walk in the despised way of obedience to God.

Nehemiah was brokenhearted when he learned of the desolations of Jerusalem. He pleaded for months before God, confessing his sin and the sin of his people (see Nehemiah 1), and God opened the way, and the walls and gates were built up.

It is the spirit of deep repentance that is needed. You had an offering for foreign missionary work here yesterday. Fifty pounds was pledged, and you all seemed satisfied. May the Lord bless you for your gifts. They mean something, but they do not signify Pentecost. We have a lack of compassion. God says, *"You will seek Me and find Me, when you search for Me with all your heart"* (Jer. 29:13). Then the dry bones will move (see Ezekiel 37:5–10), and the Spirit will be poured out upon us without measure (John 3:34).

"Bring all the tithes into the storehouse, that there may be food in My house, and try Me now in this," says the LORD of hosts, "if I will not open for you the windows of heaven and pour out for you such blessing that there will not be room enough to receive it." (Mal. 3:10)

With the baptism of the Holy Spirit comes a demolishing of the whole man and a compassion for the world.

Much that I see in the children of God these days is strange to me. Where does the fault lie for the state of things we see today? It is in the lack of a deep spirit of repentance. Weeping is not repentance; sorrow is not repentance. Repentance is turning away from sin and doing the work of righteousness and holiness. The baptism of the Holy Spirit brings a deep repentance and a demolished and impoverished spirit.

What can we do to receive it? Don't ask anymore! Instead, repent, repent, repent. God will hear and God will baptize. Will you repent? Is it possible, after we have been baptized with the Holy Spirit, to be satisfied with what we see? What made Jesus weep over Jerusalem? He had a heart of compassion. There are sin-sick souls everywhere. We need a baptism of love that goes to the bottom of the disease. We need to cry to God until He brings us up to the *"measure of the stature of the fullness of Christ"* (Eph. 4:13).

Jesus told a parable about *"a certain man [who] went down from Jerusalem to Jericho, and fell among thieves"* (Luke 10:30). Who among those who passed by and saw his predicament was his neighbor? The one who had mercy on him and helped him (vv. 36–37). Are you awake to the great fact that God has given you eternal life? With the power God has put at your disposal, how can you rest as you look out upon your neighbors? How we have sinned against God! How we lack this spirit of compassion! Do we weep as we look out upon the unsaved? If not, we are not Pentecost-full. Jesus was moved with compassion. Are you?

We have not yet grasped the plight of the heathen. Since my only daughter went to Africa, I have a little less dim idea of what it meant that God so loved the world that He gave Jesus (John 3:16). God gave Jesus. What does that mean? Compassion. *"You shall receive power when the Holy Spirit has come upon you"* (Acts 1:8). If you have no power, you have not repented. You say, "That's hard language." It is truth.

Who is your brother's keeper? (See Genesis 4:9.) Who is the son and heir? (See Galatians 4:7.) Are you salted? (See Matthew 5:13.) Do you have a pure life? Don't be fooled; don't live in a false position. The world wants to know how to be saved, and power is at our disposal. Will we meet the conditions? God says, "If you will, I will." God will do it.

Daniel knew the time in which he was living; he responded to God, and a nation was saved. Nehemiah met God's conditions for his time, and the city was rebuilt. God has made the conditions. He will pour out His Spirit.

If we do not go on, we will have it to face. It may be up to us to bring the Gospel to the nations. We can win the world for Jesus. We can turn the tap on. What is the condition? It is unconditional surrender. *"'Not by might nor by power, but by My Spirit,' says the LORD of hosts"* (Zech. 4:6). Depart from sin; holiness opens the windows of heaven. The Spirit of God will be poured out without measure, until the people say, *"What must* [we] *do to be saved?"* (Acts 16:30).

CHAPTER EIGHTEEN

NEW WINE

I t is a settled thing in the glory that <u>in the fullness of time the latter rain has to be greater than the former</u>. (See Zechariah 10:1; James 5:7.) Some of our hearts have been greatly moved by the former rain, but it is the latter rain we are crying out for. What will it be like when the fullness comes and the heart of God is satisfied?

On the Day of Pentecost, *"they were all filled with the Holy Spirit and began to speak with other tongues, as the Spirit gave them utterance"* (Acts 2:4). What a lovely thought, that the Holy Spirit had such sway that the words were all His! We are having to learn, whether we like it or not, that <u>our end is God's beginning</u>. Then it is all God; the Lord Jesus stands forth in the midst with such divine glory, and men are impelled, filled, led so perfectly. Nothing else will meet the need of the world.

We see that there was something beautiful about Peter and John when we read that people *<u>"realized that they had been with Jesus"</u>* (Acts 4:13). There was something so real, so after the order of the Master, about them.

> *Now when they saw the boldness of Peter and John, and perceived that they were uneducated and untrained men, they marveled. And they realized that they had been with Jesus.* (Acts 4:13)

<u>May all in the temple glorify Jesus;</u> it can be so.

The one thing that was more marked than anything else in the life of Jesus was the fact that the people glorified God in Him. And when God is glorified and gets the right-of-way and the wholehearted attention of His people, everyone is as He is, filled with God. Whatever it costs, it must be. Let it be so. Filled with God! The only thing that will help people is to speak the latest thing God has given us from the glory.

There is nothing outside salvation. We are filled, immersed, clothed upon with the Spirit. There must be nothing felt, seen, or spoken about except the mighty power of the Holy Spirit. We are new creatures in Christ Jesus, baptized into a new nature. *"He who believes in Me, as the Scripture has said, out of his heart will flow rivers of living water"* (John 7:38). The very life of the risen Christ is to be in everything we are and do, moving us to do His will.

There is something we have not yet touched in the spiritual realm, but praise God for the thirst to be in this meeting! Praise God, the thirst is of God, the desire is of God, the plan is of God, the purpose is of God. It is God's plan, God's thought, God's vessel, and God's servant. We are in the world to meet the need, but we are not of the world or of its spirit. (See John 17:14–16.) We are *"partakers of the divine nature"* (2 Pet. 1:4) to manifest the life of Jesus to the world.

On the Day of Pentecost, *"others mocking said, 'They are full of new wine'"* (Acts 2:13). That is what we want, you say? *"New wine"*—a new order, a new inspiration, a new manifestation. New, new, new, new wine. A power all new in itself, as if you were born, as you are, into a new day, a new creation. *"No man ever spoke like this Man!"* (John 7:46).

This new wine has a freshness about it! It has a beauty about it! It has a quality about it! It creates in others the desire for the same taste. At Pentecost, some saw, but three thousand felt, tasted, and enjoyed. Some looked on; others drank with a new faith never before seen—a new manifestation, a new realization all divine, a new thing. It came straight from heaven, from the throne of the glorified Lord. It is God's purpose to fill us with that wine, to make us ready to burst forth with new rivers, with fresh energy, with no tired feeling.

God manifested in the flesh. That is what we want, and it is what God wants, and it satisfies everybody. All the people said, "We have never seen anything like it." (See Acts 2:7–12.) The disciples rejoiced in its being new; others were *"cut to the heart, [crying out] to Peter and the rest of the apostles, 'Men and brethren, what shall we do?'"* (v. 37).

> *Then Peter said to them, "Repent, and let every one of you be baptized in the name of Jesus Christ for the remission of sins; and you shall receive the gift of the Holy Spirit. For the promise is to you and to your children, and to all who are afar off, as many as the Lord our God will call." And with many other words he testified and exhorted them, saying, "Be saved from this perverse generation."* (Acts 2:38–40)

"What shall we do?" "Men and brethren, what shall we do?" Believe! Stretch out! Press on! Let there be a new entering in, a new passion to have it. We must be *"beside ourselves"* (2 Cor. 5:13); we must drink deeply of the new wine so that multitudes may be satisfied and find satisfaction, too.

The new wine must have a new wineskin—that is the necessity of a new vessel. (See Matthew 9:17.) If anything of the old is left, not put to death, destroyed, there will be a tearing and a breaking. The new wine and the old vessel will not work in harmony. It must be new wine and a new wineskin. Then there will be nothing to discard when Jesus comes.

> *For the Lord Himself will descend from heaven with a shout, with the voice of an archangel, and with the trumpet of God. And the dead in Christ will rise first. Then we who are alive and remain shall be caught up together with them in the clouds to meet the Lord in the air. And thus we shall always be with the Lord.* (1 Thess. 4:16–17)

The Spirit is continually working within us to change us until the day when we will be like Him:

> [The Lord Jesus Christ] *will transform our lowly body that it may be conformed to His glorious body, according to the working by which He is able even to subdue all things to Himself.* (Phil. 3:21)

I desire that all of you be so filled with the Spirit, so hungry, so thirsty, that nothing will satisfy you but seeing Jesus. We are to get more thirsty every day, more dry every day, until the floods come and the Master passes by, ministering to us and through us the same life, the same inspiration, so that *"as He is, so are we in this world"* (1 John 4:17).

When Jesus became the sacrifice for man, He was in great distress, but it was accomplished. It meant strong crying and tears (see Hebrews 5:7); it meant the cross manward but the glory heavenward. Glory descending on a cross! Truly, *"great is the mystery of godliness"* (1 Tim. 3:16). He cried, *"It is finished!"* (John 19:30). Let the cry never be stopped until the heart of Jesus is satisfied, until His plan for humanity is reached in the sons of God being manifested (Rom. 8:19) and in the earth being *"filled with the knowledge of the glory of the LORD, as the waters cover the sea"* (Hab. 2:14). Amen. Amen. Amen.

CHAPTER NINETEEN

QUESTIONS AND ANSWERS
ABOUT THE BAPTISM

Q: Is the Holy Spirit a personality?

A: Yes, He is. He is not an "it," not an influence, but He is a presence, a power, a person, the third person of the Trinity. That is the reason that the Lord said, *"When He, the Spirit of truth, has come, He will guide you into all truth"* (John 16:13).

Q: If you do not receive the baptism of the Holy Spirit, will you be lost?

A: Certainly not. You are not saved by the Holy Spirit. You are saved by the Word of God and the blood of Jesus.

Q: Is it as necessary to urge people to seek the baptism of the Holy Spirit as it is to urge them to be saved?

A: No, because the baptism of the Holy Spirit cannot come to anybody until he is saved. And a person could go to heaven without the baptism of the Holy Spirit—the thief on the cross did. You must understand that the most important thing to-day is getting people saved. But do not forget that after you are saved, you must seek so that you receive *"the Promise of the Father"* (Acts 1:4).

Q: The Holy Spirit said through John the Baptist, *"[Jesus] will baptize you with the Holy Spirit and fire"* (Matt. 3:11). Is it necessary that I receive the baptism of fire, and can I receive the Holy Spirit before I receive the baptism of fire?

A: It is one and the same thing. There is only one Holy Spirit, only one baptism, only one reception of the Spirit. When He comes in, He comes to abide.

We can't always give all the figurative descriptions of the Holy Spirit, but the fire of the Holy Spirit is more than figurative. When He comes in, you will feel fire going through your body. You will feel a burning of all inward corruption.

The baptism of the Holy Spirit is essential for bringing into you a divine, holy fire that burns up all dross and quickens all purity, making you ablaze so that perfect love may continue.

The baptism of the Holy Spirit and the baptism of fire are one and the same. The baptism is the infilling of the divine third person of the Trinity.

Q: But on the Day of Pentecost, the fire fell upon them as tongues of fire, and afterward the Holy Spirit came. Will you explain that?

A: Before there were tongues of fire, there first was the *"rushing mighty wind"* (Acts 2:2). Let me explain the importance of this by looking at the life of our Lord. Jesus was a person, but He was a person of ideal perfection; the Father manifested all fullness in Him (Col. 2:9). And yet when all fullness came, it was necessary for Jesus to receive the flow of the Spirit's breath to formulate the Word; the Spirit breathed and Jesus said the words. Christ said, *"The words that I speak unto you I speak not of myself: but the Father that dwelleth in me, he doeth the works"* (John 14:10 KJV). The Spirit was the breath, the power, that was making the language.

Now, why did the Holy Spirit have to come at Pentecost? Simply because when Jesus was here, He was local. But the Holy Spirit can fill people in England, in America, in China, in Africa, in the islands of the sea, everywhere, all over the world. When He came, the breath, the power, could fill the whole universe because it was the breath of the mighty power of God Himself.

Also, the Holy Spirit was a flame. Tongues of fire—what could be more inspiring? Flames of fire, tongues of fire, burning up what was inflammable within. The disciples saw this on the Day of Pentecost, and it has been seen many times since then. But they were not baptized in the wind; they were not baptized in the fire. When were they baptized? When the wind and the fire got inside and caused eruption.

Q: Can a person receive the baptism of the Holy Spirit before being sanctified?

A: Yes. Do you know what it is to be saved? As you go on with God, you are being saved, and the more you go on with God, the more confident you are that you are saved. It was an accomplished fact that you were saved when you believed, but you are being saved as you walk in the light to a greater depth of knowledge of salvation. You were sanctified, but you are also being sanctified according to light, and you are not what you were yesterday.

Light, light, light! When you received the Holy Spirit, it is certain that the Lord was pleased with the place at which you had arrived, but it is not where you are going to. Every believer is sanctified, but no believer has received sanctification who does not also have an increased sanctification. There is no man being saved today who does not need to have an increased salvation, truth upon truth, *"line upon line"* (Isa. 28:10), knowing that he is ripe for heaven but that he is also going on to perfection (Heb. 6:1). He is being changed *"from glory to glory"* (2 Cor. 3:18). The process is wonderful: being saved, being sanctified, being made ready every day!

Q: Is sanctification a definite work of grace?

A: Yes, and salvation also. And the next day, you will find out that as light comes, you will be like Isaiah in the presence of God; you will find you need another cleansing. (See Isaiah 6:5–7.) Light makes cleansing necessary.

Q: After being baptized in water, if one goes back in sin and then repents, is it necessary to be baptized again?

A: There has to come into your life a real knowledge that after you have had hands laid upon you, you do not have to expect that hands will need to be laid upon you again. After you have received the baptism, you are not to expect to be baptized again, in water or anywhere else. The Word of God is very clear; as you *"go on to perfection,"* you are leaving the first principles (Heb. 6:1). You are leaving them behind because God says, "Come on!" Don't repeat anything that has passed by. Believe it is finished.

Q: Are the results mentioned in Mark 16:17–18 meant only for those who are baptized with the Holy Spirit?

A: Thousands of people who have never received the baptism of the Holy Spirit are very specially led and blessed in healing the sick. Some of the finest people that I have ever known have never come into the same experience as I am in today regarding the baptism of the Holy Spirit, yet they are mightily and wonderfully used in healing all kinds of sicknesses. But they do not have what is in the sixteenth chapter of Mark.

Only baptized believers speak in tongues. The Scripture says, "If you believe, you will lay hands on the sick" and "If you believe, you will speak in new tongues." (See Mark 16:17–18.) This means that after the Holy Spirit comes, you are in the place of command. You can command. How do I know this? Because Paul, in 2 Timothy 1, was very clear when he said, "Stir up the gift" (v. 6). What was the trouble with Timothy? He was downcast. He was a young man who had been called out by Paul, but he had been among other clergymen. Because of his youth, he had been somewhat put off to the side, and he was grieved. Paul found him in a distressed place, so Paul stirred him up.

Every one of you, if you have faith, can "stir up the gift" within you. The Holy Spirit can be so manifested in you that you can speak in utterances with tongues as He gives you the ability, even though you may not have actually received the gift of tongues. And I believe that everybody baptized in the Holy Spirit has a right to allow the Spirit to have perfect control and to speak every day, morning, noon, and night, in this way.

Therefore, do not put out your hand to stop anybody who is doing good, but encourage him to do good; then bring him into the baptism of much good.

Q: When the Lord gives an interpretation of a message in tongues, does He give it to the interpreter while the tongues are being given or when the interpretation is given?

A: The interpretation is not known to the interpreter at the time the tongues are given. The interpreter speaks as the Spirit gives him unction; he does not know what he is going to say or what he is saying. He speaks as the Spirit gives him liberty. Interpretation is like tongues. You do not know what you are saying when you speak in tongues. Likewise, you don't know what you are saying when you give interpretation. But you know what you have said.

Q: I have been waiting for the baptism of the Holy Spirit for a long time. I have been told that if I will say "Glory!" or "Hallelujah!" until I have lost myself, I will receive, but so far I have not received.

A: You have had a great deal of things in your mind as to what ought to bring the baptism, and you are forgetting what will bring it, and that is Jesus. Jesus is the Baptizer. As soon as you are ready, He will fill you.

Q: Can anyone receive the baptism of the Holy Spirit in his own room?

A: Yes. I believe that after hands have been laid upon you to receive the Holy Spirit, you can go away believing that you will certainly receive, whether it is in your bed or anywhere else. I laid my hands on a very remarkable man in London; we considered him one of the finest men we had. He went home and received the baptism of the Holy Spirit in his bed.

Remember that no person is a baptizer. Jesus is the only Baptizer, and you never get away from His presence. He is with you in your bedroom; He is with you at your workplace; He is with you everywhere. *"Lo, I am with you always"* (Matt. 28:20).

Smith Wigglesworth on

SPIRITUAL
GIFTS

CONTENTS

CHAPTER ONE

CONCERNING SPIRITUAL GIFTS

God wants us to enter into the rest of faith. He desires us to have all confidence in Him. He purposes that His Word will be established in our hearts; and, as we believe His Word, we will see that *"all things are possible"* (Matt. 19:26).

In 1 Corinthians 12:1 we read, *"Now concerning spiritual gifts, brethren, I do not want you to be ignorant."* There is a great weakness in the church of Christ because of an awful ignorance concerning the Spirit of God and the gifts He has come to bring. God wants us to be powerful in every way because of the revelation of the knowledge of His will concerning the power and manifestation of His Spirit. He desires us to be continually hungry to receive more and more of His Spirit.

In the past, I have organized many conferences, and I have found that it is better to have a man on my platform who has not received the baptism but who is hungry for all that God has for him, than a man who has received the baptism and is satisfied and has settled down and become stationary and stagnant. But of course I would prefer a man who is baptized with the Holy Spirit and is still hungry for more of God. A man who is not hungry to receive more of God is out of order in any Christian conference.

THE IMPORTANCE OF BEING FILLED

Richard

It is impossible to overestimate the importance of being filled with the Spirit. It is impossible for us to meet the conditions of the day, to *"walk in the light as He is in the light"* (1 John 1:7), to subdue kingdoms and work righteousness and bind the power of Satan, unless we are filled with the Holy Spirit.

We read that, in the early church, *"they continued steadfastly in the apostles' doctrine and fellowship, in the breaking of bread, and in prayers"* (Acts 2:42). It is important for us also to continue steadfastly in these same things.

For some years I was associated with the Plymouth Brethren. They are very strong on the Word and are sound on water baptism. They do not neglect the communion service; rather, they have it on the morning of every Lord's Day, as the early church did. These people seem to have the wood and the kindling, but not the match. If they had the fire, then they would be all ablaze.

Because they lack the fire of the Holy Spirit, there is no life in their meetings. One young man who attended their meetings received the baptism with the speaking in other tongues as the Spirit gave utterance (Acts 2:4). The brethren were very upset about this, and they came to the young man's father and said to him, "You must take your son aside and tell him to cease." They did not want any disturbance. The father told the son, "My boy, I have been attending this church for twenty years and have never seen anything of this kind. We are established in the truth and do not want anything new. We won't have it." The son replied, "If that is God's plan, I will obey, but somehow or other I don't think it is." As they were going home, the horse stood still; the wheels of their carriage were in deep ruts. The father pulled at the reins, but the horse did not move. He asked, "What do you think is up?" The son answered, "It has gotten established." God save us from becoming stationary.

God wants us to understand spiritual gifts and to *"earnestly desire the best gifts"* (1 Cor. 12:31). He also wants us to enter into the *"more excellent way"* (v. 31) of the fruit of the Spirit. We must implore God for these gifts. It is a serious thing to have the baptism and yet be stationary. To live two days in succession on the same spiritual plane is a tragedy. We must be willing to deny ourselves everything to receive the revelation of God's truth, and to receive the fullness of the Spirit. Only that will satisfy God, and nothing less must satisfy us.

A young Russian received the Holy Spirit and was mightily clothed with power from on high. The secret of his power was a continuous waiting upon God. As the Holy Spirit filled him, it seemed as though every breath became a prayer, and so his entire ministry was continually increasing.

I knew a man who was full of the Holy Spirit and would only preach when he knew that he was mightily anointed by the power of God. He was once asked to preach at a Methodist church. He was staying at the minister's house, and he said, "You go on to church and I will follow." The place was packed with people, but this man did not show up. The Methodist minister, becoming anxious, sent his little girl to inquire why he did not come. As she came to the bedroom door, she heard him crying out three times, "I will not go." She went back and reported that she had heard the man say three times that he would not go. The minister was troubled about it, but almost immediately afterward the man came in. As he preached that night, the power of God was tremendously manifested. The preacher later asked him, "Why did you tell my daughter that you were not coming?" He answered, "I know when I am filled. I am an ordinary man, and I told the Lord that I did not dare to go and would not go until He gave me a fresh filling of the Spirit. The moment the glory filled me and overflowed, I came to the meeting."

✗ Yes, there is a power, a blessing, an assurance, a rest in the presence of the Holy Spirit. You can feel His presence and know that He is with you. You do not need to spend an hour without this inner knowledge of His holy presence. With His power upon you, there can be no failure. You are above par all the time.

"*You know that you were Gentiles, carried away to these dumb idols, however you were led*" (1 Cor. 12:2). This is the age of the Gentiles. When the Jews refused the blessings of God, He scattered them, and He has grafted the Gentiles into the olive tree where many of the Jews were broken off. (See Romans 11:17–25.) There has never been a time when God has been so favorable to a people who were not a people. (See 1 Peter 2:9–10.) He has brought in the Gentiles to carry out His purpose of preaching the Gospel to all nations and receiving the power of the Holy Spirit to accomplish this task. It is because of the mercy of God that He has turned to the Gentiles and made us partakers of all the blessings that belong to the Jews. Here, under this canopy of glory, because we believe, we get all the blessings of faithful Abraham. (See Galatians 3:8–9.)

GUARD AGAINST ERROR

Therefore I make known to you that no one speaking by the Spirit of God calls Jesus accursed, and no one can say that Jesus is Lord except by the Holy Spirit. (1 Cor. 12:3)

Many evil, deceiving spirits have been sent forth in these last days who endeavor to rob Jesus of His lordship and of His rightful place. Many people are opening the doors to these latest devils, such as New Theology and New Thought and Christian Science. These evil cults deny the fundamental truths of God's Word. They all deny eternal punishment and the deity of Jesus Christ. You will never see the baptism of the Holy Spirit come upon a man who accepts these errors. Nor will you see anyone receive the baptism who puts Mary in the place of the Holy Spirit. No one can know he is saved by works. If you ever speak to someone who believes this, you will know that he is not definite on the matter of the new birth. He cannot be. And there is another thing: you will never find a Jehovah's Witness baptized in the Holy Spirit. The same is true for a member of any other cult who does not believe that the Lord Jesus Christ is preeminent.

The all-important thing is to make Jesus Lord of your life. Men can become lopsided by emphasizing the truth of divine healing. Men can get into error by preaching on water baptism all the time. But we never go wrong in exalting the Lord Jesus Christ, in giving Him the preeminent place and glorifying Him as both Lord and Christ, yes, as "very God of very God." As we are filled with the Holy Spirit, our one desire is to glorify Him. We need to be filled with the Spirit to get the full revelation of the Lord Jesus Christ.

God's command is for us to "be filled with the Spirit" (Eph. 5:18). We are no good if we only have a full cup. We need to have an overflowing cup all the time. It is a tragedy not to live in the fullness of overflowing. See that you never live below the overflowing tide.

USE THE GIFTS PROPERLY

"There are diversities of gifts, but the same Spirit" (1 Cor. 12:4). Every manifestation of the Spirit is given "for the profit of all" (v. 7). When the Holy Spirit is moving in an assembly of believers and His gifts are in operation, everyone will profit.

I have seen some people who have been terribly off track. They believe in gifts—prophecy, in particular—and they use these gifts apart from the power of the Holy Spirit. We must look to the Holy Spirit to show us how to use the gifts, what they are for, and when to use them, so that we may never use them without the power of the Holy Spirit. I do not know of anything that is so awful today as people using a gift without the power. Never do it. May God save us from doing it.

While a man who is filled with the Holy Spirit may not be conscious of having any gift of the Spirit, the gifts can be made manifest through him. I have gone to many places to minister, and I have found that, under the unction, or anointing, of the Holy Spirit, many wonderful things have happened in the midst of the assembly when the glory of the Lord was upon the people. Any man who is filled with God and filled with His Spirit might at any moment have any of the nine gifts listed in 1 Corinthians 12 made manifest through him, without knowing that he has a gift.

Sometimes I have wondered whether it is better to be always full of the Holy Spirit and to see signs and wonders and miracles without any consciousness of possessing a gift or whether it is better to know one has a gift. If you have received the gifts of the Spirit and they have been blessed, you should never under any circumstances use them without the power of God upon you pressing the gift through. Some have used the prophetic gift without the holy touch, and they have come into the realm of the natural. It has brought ruin, caused dissatisfaction, broken hearts, and upset assemblies. Do not seek the gifts unless you have purposed to abide in the Holy Spirit. They should be manifested only in the power of the Holy Spirit.

USE THE GIFTS WITH WISDOM

The Lord will allow you to be very drunk in the Spirit in His presence, but sober among people. I like to see people so filled with the Spirit that they are drunk in the Spirit like the 120 disciples were on the Day of Pentecost, but I don't like to see people drunk in the Spirit in the wrong place. That is what troubles us: somebody being drunk in the Spirit in a place of worship where a lot of people come in who know nothing about the Word. If you allow yourself to be drunk there, you send people away; they look at you instead of seeing God. They condemn the whole thing because you have not been sober at the right time.

Paul wrote, *"For if we are beside ourselves, it is for God; or if we are of sound mind, it is for you"* (2 Cor. 5:13). You can be beside yourself. You can go a bit further than being drunk; you can dance, if you will do it at the right time. So many things are commendable when all the people are in the Spirit. Many things are very foolish if the people around you are not in the Spirit. We must be careful not to have a good time in the Lord at the expense of somebody else. When you have a good time, you must see that the spiritual conditions in the place lend themselves to it and that the people are falling in line with you. Then you will always find it a blessing.

While it is right to earnestly desire the best gifts, you must recognize that the all-important thing is to be filled with the power of the Holy Spirit Himself. You will never have trouble with people who are filled with the power of the Holy Spirit, but you will have a lot of trouble with people who have the gifts but no power. The Lord does not want us to *"come short"* in any gift (1 Cor. 1:7). But at the same time, He wants us to be so filled with the Holy Spirit that it will be the Holy Spirit manifesting Himself through the gifts. Where the glory of God alone is desired, you can expect that every gift that is needed will be made manifest. To glorify God is better than to idolize gifts. We prefer the Spirit of God to any gift; but we can see the manifestation of the Trinity in the gifts: different gifts but the same Spirit, different administrations but the same Lord, diversities of operation but the same God working all in all (1 Cor. 12:4–6). Can you conceive of what it will mean for our triune God to be manifesting Himself in His fullness in our assemblies?

Imagine a large locomotive boiler that is being filled with steam. You can see the engine letting off some of the steam as it remains stationary. It looks as though the whole thing might burst. You can see believers who are like that. They start to scream, but that does not edify anyone. However, when the locomotive moves on, it serves the purpose for which it was built and pulls along many cars with goods in them. It is the same way with believers when they are operating in the gifts of the Spirit properly.

INWARD POWER MANIFESTED OUTWARDLY

It is wonderful to be filled with the power of the Holy Spirit and for Him to serve His own purposes through us. Through our lips, divine utterances flow; our hearts rejoice, and our tongues are glad. It is an inward power that is manifested in outward expression. Jesus Christ is glorified. As your faith in Him is quickened, from within you there *"will flow rivers of living water"* (John 7:38). The Holy Spirit will pour through you like a great river of life, and thousands will be blessed because you are a yielded channel through whom the Spirit may flow.

CHAPTER TWO

UNDERSTANDING THE GIFTS

L et us review the twelfth chapter of 1 Corinthians. The first verse reads, *"Now concerning spiritual gifts, brethren, I do not want you to be ignorant."* When the Holy Spirit says that, He expects us to understand what the gifts are, and He wants us to understand that the church may be able to profit by them.

First, let us examine the nature of those who are led by the Spirit. *"No one can say that Jesus is Lord except by the Holy Spirit"* (1 Cor. 12:3). Whenever I have come in contact with people who have acknowledged the Lord Jesus, I have known whether they knew anything about the Spirit of God. For every spirit that is of God testifies of Jesus, and you will always be able to tell people's spiritual condition by that. If they do not confess that Jesus was manifested in the flesh, you may know that they do not have the Spirit of God (v. 3). Beloved, on the contrary, we find that every spirit that confesses that Jesus is Lord does so by the Holy Spirit.

GREAT POSSIBILITIES

Everyone who has received the Holy Spirit has within him great possibilities and unlimited power. He also has great possessions, not only of things that are present but also of things that are to come (1 Cor. 3:22). The Holy Spirit has power to equip you for every emergency. The reason people are not thus equipped is that they do not receive Him and do not yield to Him. They are timid and they doubt, and in the measure that they doubt, they are defeated. But if you will yield to His leading and not doubt, it will lead you to success and victory. You will grow in grace, and you will have not only a controlling power, but also a power that reveals the mind of God and the purposes He has for you. I see that all things are in the power of the Holy Spirit, and I must not fail to give you the same truth.

MANIFESTING THE GLORY OF GOD

We must remember that we have entered into the manifestation of the glory of God, and there is great power and strength in that. Many believers might be far ahead of where they are now spiritually, but they have doubted. If by any means the Enemy can come in and make you believe a lie, he will do so. We have had to struggle to maintain our standing in our salvation, for the Enemy would beat us out of it, if possible. It is in the closeness of the association and oneness with Christ that there is no fear, but perfect confidence all the time. The child of God does not need to go back a day for his experience, for the presence of the Lord is with him and the Holy Spirit is in him, in mighty power, if he will believe. I see that we should stir one another up and provoke one another to good works (Heb. 10:24).

The Pentecostal people have a "know" in their experience. We know that we have the Spirit abiding within, and if we are not moved upon by the Spirit, we move the Spirit; that is what we mean by "stirring up the Spirit." And yet it is not we but the living faith within us—it is the Spirit who stirs Himself up.

FAITH

We should ask ourselves, "Where are we living?" I do not mean in the natural. We are a spiritual people, *"a royal priesthood,"* a holy people (1 Pet. 2:9). If we find that there is unbelief in us, we must search our hearts to see why it is there. Where there is a living faith, there is no unbelief, and we go on from faith to faith until it becomes as natural to live there as can be. But if you try to live by faith before you have been justified in Christ, you will fail, for *"the just shall live by faith"* (Rom. 1:17). When you are justified, it is a natural consequence for you to live by faith. It is easy; it is joyful. It is more than that: it is our life and spiritual inheritance.

If the Spirit can stir you up, you will not *"come short"* in any gift (1 Cor. 1:7). God wants us to see that we do not need to come short in any gift, and He wants to bring us to a place where we will be on fire because of what He has called us to. We should always move the tent every night; we cannot stay in one place. The land is before us; there are wonderful possessions to be had. God says, "They are yours; go in and claim them."

Paul prayed that we might *"be able to comprehend with all the saints"* (Eph. 3:18). I see the place where Paul was in the Holy Spirit, and I believe that God is calling us today to comprehend as much as Paul comprehended. It is in the perfect will of God that we should possess the needed gifts, but there must be unity between God and you. When the gifts are in evidence, the whole church is built up, Christ being the Head (Eph. 5:23).

> *There are diversities of activities, but it is the same God who works all in all. But the manifestation of the Spirit is given to each one for the profit of all.* (1 Cor. 12:6–7)

THE POWER OF YIELDING TO GOD

Jesus said, *"Behold, I have come to do Your will, O God!"* (Heb. 10:9), and as we surrender in that way, God will be delighted to hand to us the gift that is necessary. The more we realize that God has furnished us with a gift, the more completely we will be united with Jesus, so that people will be conscious of Him rather than of His gift.

Oh, beloved, if everything is not of the Holy Spirit, and if we are not so lost and controlled in the ministry of the gift that it is only to be Jesus, it will all be a failure and come to nothing. There were none so self-conscious as those who said, *"In Your name, [we have] cast out demons"* (Matt. 7:22). They were so controlled by the natural and the thought that they had done it all, that God was not in it. But when He comes forth and does it, it is all right.

There is a place in the Holy Spirit where we will not allow unbelief to affect us, for God has all power in heaven and earth. And now that I am in the secret knowledge of this power, I stand in a place where my faith is not to be limited because I have the knowledge that He is in me and I in Him.

Some of you have come from your homes with broken hearts; you have a longing for something to strengthen you in the midst of the conditions that exist there, and a power to make these conditions different. You say you are *"unequally yoked together with unbelievers"* (2 Cor. 6:14). You have a mighty power that is greater than all natural power. You can take victory over your homes and your spouses and children, and you must do it in the Lord's way. Suppose you do see many things that ought to be different; if it is your cross, you must take it and win the victory for God. It can be done, for He who is in you is greater than all the power of hell (1 John 4:4). I believe that anyone filled with the Holy Spirit is equal to a legion of demons any day.

In a meeting in Glasgow, a man got up and said, "I have power to cast out demons." A man full of demons got up and came to him, and this man did everything he could, but he could not cast out the demons. Do you want to cast out demons? You be sure it is the Holy Spirit who does it. Recall that a slave girl who had a spirit of divination followed Paul around for many days before he cast the demon out (Acts 16:16–18).

The Holy Spirit has His dwelling place within me and is stirring up my heart and life to adore Jesus. Other things must be left behind; I must adore Him.

WHAT IS YOUR MOTIVE?

God says, *"Everyone who asks receives"* (Matt. 7:8). What are you asking for? What is your motive? In the Scriptures we read, *"You ask and do not receive, because you ask amiss, that you may spend it on your pleasures"* (James 4:3). There is a need for the gifts, and God will reveal to you what you ought to have, and you should never be satisfied until you receive it.

It is important that we know we can do nothing in ourselves. However, we may know that we are clothed with the power of God so that, in a sense, we are not in the natural man. As we go forth in this power, things will take place as they took place in the days of the disciples.

When I received the new birth at eight years of age, it was so precious and lovely. Since that time, I have never lost the knowledge of my acceptance with God. Then, brothers and sisters, God did a wonderful work in me when I waited for the baptism.

I was in a strange position. For sixteen years I had testified to having received the baptism of the Holy Spirit, but I had really only received the anointing of the Spirit. In fact, I could not preach unless I had the anointing. My wife would come to me and say, "They

313

are waiting for you to come out and speak to the people." I would say, "I cannot and will not come without the anointing of the Spirit."

I can see now that I was calling the anointing the baptism. But when the Holy Spirit came into my body until I could not give satisfaction to the glory that was in me, God took this tongue, and I spoke as the Spirit gave utterance (Acts 2:4), which brought perfect satisfaction to me. When He comes in, He abides. I then began to reach out as the Holy Spirit showed me.

ASK AND YOU WILL RECEIVE

In the call of the prophet Elisha, God saw the young man's willingness to obey. The twelve yoke of oxen, the plow, and all soon came to nothing; all bridges had to be burned behind him (1 Kings 19:19–21). Friend, the Lord has called you, too. Are you separated from the old things? You cannot go on unless you are.

As Elisha went on with the prophet Elijah, the young man heard wonderful things about Elijah's ministry, and he longed for the time when he would take his master's place. Now the time was getting close. His master said to him, "I am going to Gilgal today. I want you to remain here." "Master," he replied, "I must go with you." I see that other people also knew something about it, for they said to Elisha, "Do you know that your master is going to be taken away from you today?" He said, "Hold your peace; I know it." Later on, Elijah said, "I want to go on to Bethel. You stay here." But Elisha said, "No, I will not leave you." Something had been revealed to Elisha. Perhaps, in a similar way, God is drawing you to do something; you feel it.

Then Elijah said, "The Lord has sent me to Jordan. You stay here." It was the spirit of the old man that was stirring up the young man. If you see zeal in somebody else, reach out for it; it is for you. I am coming to realize that God wants all the members of His body joined together. In these days He is making us feel that when a person is failing to go on with God, we must restore that member.

When they came to the Jordan River, Elijah struck his cloak on it and they crossed. No doubt Elisha said, "I must follow his steps." And when they had gone over, the old man said, "You have done well; you would not stay back. What is the real desire of your heart?

I feel I am going to leave you. Ask what you like now, before I leave you." "Master," he said, "I have seen all that you have done. Master, I want twice as much as you have."

I believe it is the fainthearted who do not get much. As they went on up the hill, down came the chariot of fire, nearer and nearer, and as the old man departed, the young man said, "Father, Father, Father," and down came the cloak.

What have you asked for? Are you satisfied to continue on in the old way now that the Holy Spirit has come to give you an unlimited supply of power and says, "What will you have?" Why, we see that Peter was so filled with the Holy Spirit that his shadow falling on sick people healed them (Acts 5:15).

What do you want? Elisha asked, and he got it. He came down and said, "I don't feel any differently." However, he had the knowledge that feelings are not to be counted as anything; some of you are looking at your feelings all the time. He came to the waters of the Jordan as an ordinary man. Then, in the knowledge in which he possessed the cloak (not in any feelings about it), he said, "Where is the God of Elijah?" and he struck the water with the cloak. The waters parted and Elisha put his feet down in the riverbed and crossed to the other side. When you put your feet down and say you are going to have a double portion, you will get it. After he had crossed, there were the people again (they always come where there is power), and they said, "The spirit of Elijah rests on Elisha." (See 2 Kings 2:1–15.)

You are to have the gifts and to claim them. The Lord will certainly change your lives, and you will be new men and women. Are you asking for a double portion? I trust that no one will "come short" in any gift (1 Cor. 1:7). You say, "I have asked. Do you think God will be pleased if I ask again?" Yes, do so before Him. Ask again, and we may go forth in the Spirit of the cloak. Then we will no longer be working in our own strength but in the Holy Spirit's strength, and we will see and know His power because we believe.

CHAPTER THREE

GOD'S TREASURE-HOUSE

How inexhaustible is the treasure-house of the Most High! How near God is to us when we are willing to draw near to Him (James 4:8)! And how He comes and refreshes us when our hearts are attuned to Him and desire Him alone, for *"the desire of the righteous will be granted"* (Prov. 10:24).

God has for us today a divine experience that quickens, a divine life flowing through our beings that will be sufficient for us in all times of need. When God is for you, who can be against you (Rom. 8:31)? What a blessed assurance this is to the hungry heart. How it thrills one to the very depths of one's soul!

My heart's desire is to bring you again to a banquet, that wonderful spiritual reserve, that great blessed day of appointment for us with the King, so that you may believe that all the precious promises are *"Yes"* and *"Amen"* (2 Cor. 1:20) to us as we dare to believe.

Oh, to believe God! Oh, to rest upon what He says, for there is not one *"jot"* or *"tittle"* of the Word that will fail until all is fulfilled (Matt. 5:18)! Has He not promised, and will He not also perform (Rom. 4:21)? Our blessed Lord of life and glory impressed upon us before He left that He would send the Holy Spirit, the Comforter, and that, when the Spirit came, He would take of the words of Jesus and declare them to us (John 16:14–15). The Holy Spirit would pray through us, and whatever we would ask, the Lord would hear us (1 John 5:14–15).

So I want you to get in a definite place, daring to ask God for something that will be the means of stimulating your life forever.

Are you ready? You say, "What for?" To have some of the promises fulfilled.

Are you ready? What for? For God to so clothe you with the Spirit this day that there will be nothing within you that will war against the Spirit. Are you ready? Search your heart diligently.

Are you ready? What for? For you to know the Word of God. For you to know that they who dwell and live in the Spirit of God are kept in a perfect state in which there is no condemnation. (See Romans 8:1.)

I want very much for you to get stirred up with the prospect of this state and then to come into the experience of this state, because that is what God wants you to have. He wants you to get so moved by the power of God that you believe that the things you are hearing about will be yours.

So many people miss a great many things because they are always thinking that they are for someone else. I want you to know that God's Word is for you and that you are to make a personal application of all there is in the Scriptures.

I do not believe that the Scriptures are only for pastors, teachers, evangelists, prophets, or apostles. They are for the whole body of Christ, for it is the body that has to be the epistle of Christ. (See 2 Corinthians 3:3.) So the Word of God has to abound in you until you are absolutely built and fixed upon the living Word.

ALL GIFTS ARE FOR EDIFICATION

I am going to remind you of 1 Corinthians 14:12, because I want to make it the keynote of everything I am presenting to you here on the topic of spiritual gifts: *"Even so you, since you are zealous for spiritual gifts, let it be for the edification of the church that you seek to excel."* Keep that definitely in mind because, whatever gifts are manifested in a service, they mean nothing to me unless they edify or comfort or console.

God wants to make you worthy of His wonderful name. You must always understand that all the gifts and graces of the Spirit are most helpful to you when you are a blessing to others. The Holy Spirit did not come to exalt you; He came so that you could exalt the Lord.

Before these services are over, I will be able to tell you definitely how to receive a gift and then how to use a gift or how to be in a place where the gift can be used. We should cover much ground because the Spirit is going to speak. If I were to use my own reasoning, you wouldn't be edified. There is only one edification that is going to last, and it is the spiritual, inward revelation of Christ. What is in the mind is no good unless it is spiritually quickened through the heart affections. So let us remember that it is more important that we are filled with the Holy Spirit, that the Spirit has His perfect control and way, than that we be filled with knowledge to no profit. *"Knowledge puffs up"* (1 Cor. 8:1). As the saying goes, "A little knowledge is dangerous." In fact, all knowledge is very dangerous unless it is balanced in a perfect place where God has the controlling position.

In the first few verses of 1 Corinthians 12, we find that the Holy Spirit is speaking through the apostle Paul. Paul's initial comment is that he does not want you to be ignorant concerning spiritual gifts. You are not to be ignorant of the best gift God has arranged for you. You are to come into possession. It is a will that has been left by God's Son. He rose to carry it out, and He is on the throne to carry out His own will. His will is that you should be filled with all the fullness of God. What a wonderful will!

The next thought is that, because we are Gentiles, God has entrusted to us the proclamation of the Gospel in the power and demonstration of the Spirit, so that we may not speak with man's wisdom but by the revelation of the operation of God.

So the Holy Spirit is to make us ready for every perfect work, ready in such a way that opportunities are taken advantage of. Just as much as if the Lord Jesus were in the world, we must be in the world, ready for the glorious, blessed anointing and equipping for service. In this way, the powers of hell will not prevail (Matt. 16:18); we will bind the powers of Satan. We will be in a great position to engage in spiritual battle.

INTERPRETATION OF A MESSAGE IN TONGUES: "The Spirit Himself brings forth light and truth to edify and build up the church in the most holy faith, that we might be ready for all activity in God. For the Spirit of the Lord is upon us to bring forth what God has declared and ordained, that we should go forth bearing 'precious fruit' and come forth rejoicing, singing, and harvesting together."

Oh, to keep in the covenant place where you are hidden in Christ, where He alone is superseding, controlling, leading, directing, and causing you to live only for the glory of God!

THE UNCHANGEABLE WORD OF GOD

Let us move on to 1 Corinthians 12:3: *"No one speaking by the Spirit of God calls Jesus accursed."* Don't forget that you are entrusted with the Word of Life, which speaks to you as the truth. Jesus is the Way, the Truth, and the Life (John 14:6), and He declared eternal life by the operation of the Gospel. For we receive immortality and life by the Gospel. (See 2 Timothy 1:10.) Seeing these things are so, you can understand that those who receive the life of Christ move out of condemnation into eternal life.

But what about those who do not? They are still under condemnation, *"having no hope and without God in the world"* (Eph. 2:12) and in danger of eternal destruction. God save them!

Hellfire will never be changed by what men say about it. Hellfire will be the same forever. You will never change the Word of God by men's opinions. The Word of God is fixed forever (Isa. 40:8).

The Lord wants you to be in a significant place in which the Holy Spirit has such control of your inner eyes that He may reveal the fullness of the Lord of Life until Jesus is glorified tremendously by the revelation of the Holy Spirit, until He becomes Lord over all things: your affections, your will, your purposes, your plans, and your wishes forever. Let Him be Lord.

> **INTERPRETATION OF A MESSAGE IN TONGUES:** "For when the Lord changes the situation, then you come out of the hiding of captivity into the fullness of the revelation of the blaze of His glory, for when He has molded you, then He can build you and change you until He is having His way."

BUILDING YOUR CROWN OF GLORY

> God has a great purpose for us in that we can be changed, and you are in a great place when you are willing to have this change take place. You are in a greater place when you are willing to drop everything that has brought you to where you thought you could not be changed; and when you have dropped all things that have hindered you, you have leaped forth and been tremendously changed.

If you have held anything from a human standpoint, no matter how it has come, that is not according to the biblical standard of the Word of God, let it be weeded out. If you do not get it weeded out, be warned: there is a time coming in which wood, hay, and stubble will be burned, but the gold, the silver, and the precious stones will stand the fire (1 Cor. 3:12–13).

Lots of people would like to know what kind of crown they will have when they get to glory. Well, the Lord will take everything that could not be burned by the fire and make your personal crown. So everybody is forming his own crown. Be careful not to be all wood, hay, and stubble. Have something left for the crown. There is a *"crown of glory that does not fade away"* (1 Pet. 5:4), which I am trying to help you build today.

A GIFT SPECIFICALLY FOR YOU

God has a special way of meeting the needs of individual people today. We all vary so much in our appearances, in how we are made. Yet God has a way of particularizing a gift so that it fits you perfectly, so that you will not be lopsided. I am trusting the Lord to help me to build you up so that you are not lopsided.

Lots of people have good things—but. Lots of people might be very remarkably used—but. Lots of people might soar into wonderful places of divine positions with God—but. And it is the "but" that spoils it.

Some people have very good gifts—all the gifts of God are good—but because the gifts have been made a blessing, these people transgress with the same gift and speak in tongues longer than they ought to. So it is the "but" that is in the way and that is spoiling the best.

Some people have prophecy, very wonderful prophecy, but there is a "but." They have prophesied, and the Lord has been with them in the prophecy, but because the people have applauded them, they have gone beyond divine prophecy and used their own human minds. The "but" has spoiled them until they do not want the hidden prophecy.

Mrs. So-and-So has a wonderful testimony, and we all like to hear her for three minutes, but we are all sick of it if she goes on for five minutes. Why is this so? There is a "but" about it.

Brother So-and-So ignites fire in every prayer meeting when he begins to speak, but after about five minutes, all the people say, "I wish he would stop." There is a "but" there.

It is because of the lopsidedness of people that I want to advise you so that you do not transgress. Do not use divine liberty to spoil God's position; rather, be wise, and the Lord will cause you to understand what it means. Be wise.

When you say that you have been baptized with the Holy Spirit, people look and say, "Well, if that is so, there ought to be something very beautiful about you."

Yes, it is true, and if there is something that is shady, something that is uncanny, something that does not express the glory or grace, the meekness or love, of Christ, there is a "but" about it. The "but" is that you have not really gotten your own human spirit under control by the divine Spirit; the human is mingled with it, and it is spoiling the divine.

Now, a word to the wise is sufficient, and if you are not wise after you have heard it, it shows that you are foolish. Do not be foolish; be wise!

"Do not let your good be spoken of as evil" (Rom. 14:16). God wants people in these days who are so fortified, so built in Christ, that they do not need to be ashamed.

INTERPRETATION OF A MESSAGE IN TONGUES: "For it is God who has called you for His own purpose. It is Christ who ordained you, and being ordained by Christ we go forth to bring forth much fruit. God is being glorified when our anointing or our covenant with Christ is being reserved for God only, and we live and move for the glory of the exhibition of Christ. Then that is the place where Jesus is highly honored, and when you pray, God is glorified in the Son, and when you preach, the unction abides, and the Lord brings forth blessing upon the hearers."

DIVERSITIES OF GIFTS

In 1 Corinthians 12:4–7, you notice very remarkable words. In these verses we are dealing with the Spirit, with the Lord, and with God—each One of them in cooperation with this position:

There are diversities of gifts, but the same Spirit. There are differences of ministries, but the same Lord. And there are diversities of activities, but it is the same God who works all in all. But the manifestation of the Spirit is given to each one for the profit of all.

There are diversities, varieties, of gifts that truly are to be in the believer. There are nine gifts listed in 1 Corinthians 12, and I would like you to notice that they never interfere with the gifts that Jesus gave. If you will turn to Ephesians 4, you will find that Jesus gave gifts:

> *But to each one of us grace was given according to the measure of Christ's gift. Therefore He says: "When He ascended on high, He led captivity captive, and gave gifts to men."*
> (Eph.4:7–8)

A little later in the chapter, these gifts are listed:

> *And He Himself gave some to be apostles, some prophets, some evangelists, and some pastors and teachers, for the equipping of the saints for the work of ministry, for the edifying of the body of Christ.* (Eph. 4:11–12)

Let us look at the gifts Jesus has. How beautifully He arranges things. *"When He ascended on high, He led captivity captive, and gave gifts to men"* (v. 8).

Now, the apostle Paul was in captivity. How do we know? He described his position as the chief of sinners (1 Tim. 1:15). By the way, as long as we know that the chief of sinners has been saved, every man that ever lives can be saved. Paul was the chief of sinners, and he was led captive when he was enraged with indignation against the disciples; he was rushing everywhere to apprehend them and put them in prison and make them blaspheme (Acts 8:3; 9:1–2; 26:9–11).

So Paul was in captivity. Yet Jesus took him out of captivity; then He took him into His captivity and gave him gifts.

Jesus has already made disciples; He has gone up on high leading captivity captive; now He is giving gifts. This is the divine position of our Lord, giving gifts to those He has in captivity.

Now, who do you think is most likely to be in captivity? It is the people who are lost in God, who are hidden in Him.

Baptizing in water is an emblem of death, and the moment a person is immersed in the water, he is lifted out. But this is not the case with the baptism in the Holy Spirit. To be baptized in the Holy Spirit is to be in deeper every day, never lifted out, never coming out; it is to be in captivity, ready for gifts.

Now, is a person made a prophet or an apostle or a teacher before the baptism of the Spirit or after? I want to speak to you very definitely, and I want you to keep in mind what the Spirit will say to us at this time.

When I went to New Zealand, the power of God was very present, and God wonderfully worked miracles and wonders there. The gifts that laid hold of the whole place were the gifts of tongues and interpretation. That entire city was moved until the place that held thirty-five hundred was often overcrowded, and we had two thousand and three thousand people who could not get in.

Now, when the Plymouth Brethren, who knew the Word of God, saw the grace of God upon me, they wanted to have some conversation with me. So I gave them an audience, and eighteen of them came.

As soon as they began they said, "Well, we know God is with you; it is evident."

(In ten days we had two thousand people saved, and we had fifteen hundred of those young converts sit down to communion; and it was the Plymouth Brethren who served us the wine and the bread.)

"Now," they said, "we want to examine the truth with you to see where things stand."

I said, "All right, brethren."

In a moment or two, they were quoting Ephesians to me.

"But, beloved," I said, "you know better than anybody that the man who climbs up some other way is a thief and a robber, don't you? How many times have you preached that? Jesus is the Door, and everyone entering that way will be saved. What does it mean? Jesus is Truth."

They continued quoting Ephesians to me.

"But, brethren," I said, "you have no right to Ephesians; you have no right to the epistles. The epistles are not for you. You are climbing up some other way."

Without fear of contradiction, on the authority of God, I say today that there is no person who has a right to the epistles until he has gone through the Acts of the Apostles and received the Holy Spirit.

They said I could not prove it. I said, "I can prove it very easily." And I read, *"For he who speaks in a tongue does not speak to men but to God, for no one understands him; however, in the spirit he speaks mysteries"* (1 Cor. 14:2).

"Now, brethren," I said, "tell me if you understand that."
They said, "No."

"That is simply because you have never received the Holy Spirit. Every person who receives the Holy Spirit receives that—speaking unto God by the Spirit. The Gospels are the Gospel of the kingdom of God. It is in the Acts of the Apostles that people see water baptism, sanctification, and also the receiving of the Holy Spirit fulfilled. So the moment you pass through the Acts of the Apostles, you are ready for the epistles, for the epistles were written to baptized believers.

"I will prove it another way," I continued, and I read Romans 8:26–27:

Likewise the Spirit also helps in our weaknesses. For we do not know what we should pray for as we ought, but the Spirit Himself makes intercession for us with groanings which cannot be uttered. Now He who searches the hearts knows what the mind of the Spirit is, because He makes intercession for the saints according to the will of God.

Here is another distinct condition of a man filled with the Holy Spirit.

INTERPRETATION OF A MESSAGE IN TONGUES: "For the Lord Himself is the chief director of all truth, for He is the Way and the Truth; therefore, the Spirit takes the Word, which is Christ, and reveals it unto us, for He is the life by the Word. 'He that heareth my word, and believeth on him that sent me, hath everlasting life.' Jesus is the Way; Jesus is the Truth; Jesus is the Life."

The Holy Spirit is jealous over you. The Holy Spirit has a godly jealousy over you. Why? Lest you turn to yourself. He wants you to exhibit the Lord entirely. Therefore, He girds you. He sees to you in every way so that you will not be drawn aside by human desires but that, instead, Jesus will become the Alpha and Omega in all your desires.

Now, to this end the Spirit knows the great hunger of the heart. Hunger for what? For gifts, graces, beatitudes.

Oh, it is lovely when we are at a point at which we can only pray in the Holy Spirit!

PRAYING IN THE SPIRIT

I am going to give you a very important word about the usefulness of praying in the Spirit. Lots of people are still without an understanding of <u>what it is to pray in the Spirit.</u> In 1 Corinthians 14:15 we read, *"I will pray with the spirit, and I will also pray with the understanding. I will sing with the spirit, and I will also sing with the understanding."*

I am going to tell you a story that will help you to see how necessary it is that you be so lost in the order of the Holy Spirit that you will pray in the Holy Spirit.

Our missionary work in the center of Africa was opened by Brothers Burton and Salter, the latter being my daughter's husband. He is now there in the Congo. When they went there, there were four of them: Brothers Burton and Salter, an old man who wanted to go to help them build, and a young man who believed he was called to go. The old man died on the road and the young man turned back, so there were only two left.

They worked and labored. God was with them in a wonderful way. But Burton took sick, and all hopes were gone. Fevers are dreadful there; mosquitoes swarm; great evils are there. There he was, laid out; there was no hope. They covered him over and went outside very sorrowfully, because he truly was a pioneer missionary. They were in great distress and uttered words like this: "He has preached his last sermon."

When they were in that state, without any prompting whatever, Brother Burton stood right in the midst of them. He had arisen from his bed and had walked outside, and he now stood in the midst of them. They were astonished and asked how and what had happened.

All he could say was that he had been awakened out of a deep sleep with a warm thrill that went over his head, right down his body, and out through his toes.

"I feel so well," he said. "I don't know anything about my sickness."

It remained a mystery. Later, when he was over in England visiting, a lady said to him, "Brother Burton, do you keep a diary?"

"Yes," he said.

"Don't open the diary," she said, "until I talk with you."

"All right."

This is the story she told.

"At a certain time on a certain day, the Spirit of the Lord moved upon me. I was so moved by the power of the Spirit that I went alone into a place to pray. As I went there, believing that, just as usual, I was going to open my mouth and pray, the Spirit laid hold of me and I was praying in the Spirit—not with understanding, but praying in the Spirit.

"As I prayed, I saw right into Africa; I saw you laid out helpless and, to all appearances, apparently dead. I prayed on until the Spirit lifted me, I knew I was in victory, and I saw you had risen up from that bed.

"Look at your diary, will you?"

He looked in the diary and found that it was exactly the same day.

So there are revivals to come; there are wonderful things to be done, when we can be lost in the Spirit until the Spirit prays through to victory.

> INTERPRETATION OF A MESSAGE IN TONGUES: "It is only He; it is He who rolls away the cloud. He alone is the One who lifts the fallen, cheers the faint, brings fresh oil, and changes the countenance. It is the Lord your God. He has seen your misery, He has known your brokenheartedness, and He has known how near you seem to be to despair."

Oh, beloved, God is in the midst of us to help us into these wonderful divine places of appointment!

Are you ready? You say, "What for?" To let all differences cease and to have the same evidence the disciples had in the Upper Room.

Are you ready? What for? To be so in the place in which God's Son will be pleased that He gives you all the desires of your heart.

Are you ready? What for? So that God can fill you with new life, stimulate you with new fire. He can inflame you with great desire. We are in the midst of blessing; I want you to be blessed.

Faith has the greatest ability to position us. Faith is what will lift you into every place, if you do not interfere with it.

Don't forget you are in the presence of God. This day has to be covered with a greater day. It is not what you are; it is what you are intending to be.

If you have ever spoken in tongues, believe it is your right and your privilege to have anything in the Bible. Don't let your human mind interfere with the great plan of God. Submit yourself to God.

May the divine likeness of Him who is the express image of the Father (Heb. 1:3) dwell in you richly, abounding through all, supplying every need, bringing you into a place where you know the hand of God is leading you from treasure to treasure, from grace to grace, from victory to victory, from *"glory to glory"* (2 Cor. 3:18), by the Spirit of the Lord.

CHAPTER FOUR

THE FRUIT AND THE GIFTS

As a preparation for the study of the gifts of the Spirit, we should read the twelfth chapter of Romans. All that is done and said in these meetings is upon the authority of the Word of God. I am sure it would not please God if we were to turn aside to any human thing when we have such a valuable, wonderful display of wisdom and authority in this living Word.

PARTAKERS OF THE DIVINE NATURE

We thank You, Lord, that You have made sufficient atonement for sin, sickness, deficiencies, all our weakness, and everything.

As we take our minds off human things and are clothed with the Spirit, we will be natural but also supernatural. This is a lovely condition. We are still natural, with just the same physique, just the same expression. We are the same people, only we are supernatural, inwardly displaying the revelation of the power of God through the same body. What a divine state!

Don't be afraid to understand that God intends for you to be *"partakers of the divine nature"* (2 Pet. 1:4), of divine life in the human frame, of divine thoughts over the human mind. You are to have your human minds transformed. The divine mind is to take its place so that you will always be the children of the Lord and act like people who are *"from above"* (John 3:31). You are *"from above"*; you are born of a *"new creation"* (2 Cor. 5:17). You were planted with Him (Rom. 6:5 KJV); you were risen, and you are to be seated with Him in the place of victory over the power of the Enemy.

Don't forget that God is in all, over all, through all. He is in you so that He might bring about in your daily ministries a divine plan as active and as perfect as the apostles had at the beginning, as Jesus had in His ministry. Jesus portrayed, showed forth, emphasized to His disciples this word: *"Be ye therefore perfect, even as your Father which is in heaven is perfect"* (Matt. 5:48 KJV).

We do not need to regard people according to the flesh anymore (2 Cor. 5:16). From this day, let us learn that we only need to know the character of the people according to the Spirit. Remember that the disciples came to a perfect place when they said, "We won't know Jesus anymore according to the flesh." (See verse 16.)

They wouldn't remember Him in terms of His fleshly ministry. I don't mean a fleshly power, but His fleshly body. There were any number of things to remember about Jesus in terms of His natural human need, such as when He needed food from the tree and when He sat by the well and asked for water. We won't know Him that way anymore; we will know Jesus according to the Spirit.

What is the difference? He no longer has any human weakness but has perfect power over all weaknesses. May the Lord grant to us in these days a divine familiarity with the Master so that we begin from this day to be more and more spiritual until we live in the Spirit, not fulfilling the lusts of the flesh (Gal. 5:16), but living in Christ.

> **INTERPRETATION OF A MESSAGE IN TONGUES:** "The Lord Himself feeds us with the finest of the wheat. He seeks only to bring us into favor with the Father. He says, '"Until now you have asked nothing"; ask large things, for "my Father and I are one."' And as you ask, it will be given you, a measure full, 'pressed down, shaken together, and running over,' that there will be no leanness in you, but you will be full, overflowing, expressive, God manifest in you, the glory of the Lord upon you, and He bringing forth songs in the earth."

FRUITS AND GIFTS UNITED

I want to speak a little about the dovetailing, the uniting together of the fruits and the gifts of the Spirit. I am just going to enumerate them so that you will know their relationship. This will be very profitable to you because you must be careful that whatever gift is manifested in you, it has to coincide, have a joint fellowship, with its corresponding fruit, so that you will never miss the plan of God in this holy order. Any gift that God may give you will never go to waste; it will always profit others.

The fruit of the Spirit is listed in Galatians 5:22–23: *"But the fruit of the Spirit is love, joy, peace, longsuffering, kindness, goodness, faithfulness, gentleness, self-control."* Now, let us see how the fruit corresponds to the gifts of the Spirit.

The first gift of the Spirit Paul mentioned in 1 Corinthians 12 is *"wisdom"* (v. 8), which must always be connected with love. Love is the first fruit; wisdom is the first gift.

The next gift is *"knowledge"* (v. 8). You will find, if you work this out, that knowledge will always bring joy and will be accompanied by joy. Knowledge produces joy, and they coincide.

The third is *"faith"* (v. 9). You never find that faith is to any profit unless there is peace, so the gift of faith coincides with the fruit of peace.

The next is *"healings"* (v. 9). You always find that the person who is used in healing is long-suffering. If he loses that, if the person who ministers to the needy does not enter into their need, well, remember the words in Philippians: *"The fellowship of His sufferings"* (Phil. 3:10). It doesn't mean that you have to go to the cross, but you have to be so in spirit with the needy sufferer that you enter right into his need.

In this regard, remember that you must be brought into a place of justification, because it may be that many of you are judging me and saying, "Isn't he rough when he ministers to people in healing!" Now, we must understand every man in his own way. You can't fill my boat, and I couldn't fill yours; but we can fill the boat God has made for us. We cannot turn aside to please humanity, because we have one Master, who is Christ.

A woman came before me in Australia where thousands were looking on, and I ministered to her for healing. She was a very large woman. As she came to me, the Spirit of the Lord revealed to me that inwardly there was an adversary destroying her life. Instantly, God helped me to rise up against the adversary, not against the woman.

In the name of Jesus, I dealt with this evil thing that had distressed the woman. With the whole crowd looking on, she cried, "You're killing me! You're killing me! Oh, you're killing me!"

She fell down on the floor. "Bring her back again," I said. I knew I had not finished the work.

Then I went at it again, destroying the evil that was there, and I knew I had to do it. The people did not understand as again she cried, "Oh, you're killing me!"

"Bring her back again," I said.

I laid my hands on her again in the name of Jesus, and the work was done. She walked five yards in the aisle, and the big cancer dropped off her.

You who are judging me, please leave your judgment outside, for I obey God. If you are afraid to be touched, don't come to me to pray for you. If you are not prepared to be dealt with as God leads me to deal, keep away. But if you can believe that God has me for a purpose, come, and I will help you.

How we need to have the mind of Christ and to live for Christ. What a serious thing it would be for me at sixty-eight years of age to try to please people when I have my Father in heaven to please!

INTERPRETATION OF A MESSAGE IN TONGUES: "It is the way into the treasure-house the Lord brings you. It is not your way of thinking; it is the way in which He brings you through. Don't forget that Jesus said, 'Straight is the gate, narrow the way' that brought you in to the plan and place of redemption with fullness. Therefore, do not resist the Spirit, do not judge the things, even prophecy, but lay hold of it that God is in the midst of you to bring you to the place of your desired health."

1 CORINTHIANS 13: A BALANCER

I now want to discuss the thirteenth chapter of 1 Corinthians. This chapter on love falls appropriately between the twelfth and the fourteenth chapters; it dovetails or unites the three chapters, bringing us into a place where we can understand them. The twelfth chapter deals with the gifts of the Spirit, the fourteenth chapter deals with the ministry of the gifts, and the thirteenth chapter deals with balance.

If you know anything about an engine, you know that right over the main throttle valve that lets the steam into the cylinder, with the piston driving it backward and forward, there are two little governor balls running around. Sometimes they go fast; sometimes they go slowly. They control the condition of the pistons so that the engine doesn't run away and so that it maintains an even motion.

That is exactly the purpose of the thirteenth chapter of 1 Corinthians; it shows believers how to keep the gifts in perfect harmony until we learn not to run away with them, not to get out of order. It shows that *"the wisdom that is from above"* (James 3:17) lies in a human vessel; it never loses its luster or glory or expression or force of character of divine origin.

So God has a plan for us. He wants to show us that even though our lives may be wonderful—for example, we may have the gift of divine prophecy, which is beautiful, or we may have all faith to move mountains (1 Cor. 13:2)—if we do not understand the Scriptures, if we lose the main factor, which will produce the governing principles, we become nothing. But if we are balanced by the power of the Spirit, every act will be an act of such divine quality that people will recognize that fact in a moment; their judgment will be accurate, as it was that day when the people saw Peter and John. (See Acts 3:1–4:4.) Although these disciples were humble men and had not gone through college courses, they had something that expressed a fact to the people: they had been in a place that had changed their character and their language; they had been with the Master (Acts 4:13).

While I know that many good things come out of colleges, you must not forget that you must occasionally go to night school, as Nicodemus did, and see the Master. (See John 3:1–21.)

A personal acquaintance with the Lord Jesus, by the revelation of the Spirit, can so move you that, in an instant, you may have revelation that causes you to see that you are now encased by an enthronement of wisdom from on high.

> **INTERPRETATION OF A MESSAGE IN TONGUES:** "'The wisdom which is from above is first peaceable, easily entreated, without partiality, full of goodness and truth,' and the Lord of Hosts has us in His great pavilion of opening the avenue of our human nature, flowing forth through the natural life, divine life, quickened from on high, because we are the children of the King."

Thank you, Lord. We are the children of the King. We belong to the Lord; therefore, no other power has a right to us. We belong to Him.

INTERPRETATION OF A MESSAGE IN TONGUES: "From your mother's womb I called you. Though I have chastened you and put you through the fire, yet it was necessary to bring out of you and to bring you out into a land of promise. It is true that you have passed through deep waters and that the fire has many times seared you, but this was all to chasten you and to prove you, to see if you loved the Lord with all your heart. And now the Lord has brought you to the banquet. Eat, my beloved; 'eat, and be satisfied.'"

CHAPTER FIVE

How to Receive a Spiritual Gift

The gift of the Holy Spirit, which He breathes into you, will make you wonderfully alive. It will almost seem as though you had never been born before. The jealousy God has over us, the interest He has in us, the purpose He has for us, the grandeur of His glory are so marvelous. God has called us into this place to receive gifts.

Now I want to tell you how to receive a gift. I will illustrate this by explaining the nature of a gift and telling you what happened to me when I received the gift of tongues.

The difference between speaking in tongues as a gift and speaking in tongues by receiving the Spirit is this: everybody who is baptized speaks as the Spirit gives utterance. The tongues that are manifested when someone receives the baptism are an evidence of the baptism. However, this is not the gift of tongues. The gift is a special manifestation in a person's life that he knows, and he can speak in tongues as long as he wants to. Nevertheless, a person should never speak longer than the Spirit gives the anointing; he should never go beyond the Spirit's leading. Like someone giving a prophecy, he should never go beyond the spiritual anointing.

The trouble is this: after we have been blessed with tongues, our human nature often steps in. Everything that is not the rising tide of the Spirit is either law or letter. (See Romans 7:6–7.) What does this mean? When you are following the law, it means that you have fallen into your human nature. When you are following the letter, it means that you are depending on the Word without the power. These two things will work against you instead of working for you.

The letter and the law bring harshness; the Spirit brings joy and happiness. One is perfect harmony; the other produces strife. One is the higher tide of the Spirit; the other is earthly. One gets into the bliss of the presence of heaven; the other never rises from earthly associations.

Claim your right; claim your position. The person who asks for a gift twice will never get it under any circumstances. I am not moved by what you think about it. I believe this is sovereign from God's altar. You never get a gift if you ask for it twice. But God will have mercy upon you if you stop asking and believe.

There is not a higher order that God puts in motion with a person who believes than this: *"Ask, and you will receive"* (John 16:24). If you dare to ask for any gift, if you really believe that it is a necessary gift, if you dare to ask and will not move from it but begin to act in it, you will find that the gift is there.

If you want to be in the will of God, you will have to be stubborn. What do I mean by this? I mean that you will have to be unchangeable. Do you think that if you get a gift, you will feel it? It is nothing like that. If you ask for a gift, do not expect that there will be a feeling with it. There is something better; there is a fact with it, and the fact will bring the feeling after the manifestation. People want feelings for gifts. There is no such thing. You will make the biggest mistake if you dare to continue praying about anything until you feel like doing something. As sure as can be, you have lost your faith. You have to believe that after you receive, you have the power, and that you begin to act in the power.

The morning after I received the gift of tongues, I went out of the house with a box of tools on my back; I was going down the street to do some work. The power of God lit me up and I broke out in tongues—loudly. My, they were loud! The street was filled with people, and there were some gardeners trimming some hedges and cutting the grass. When they heard me, they stuck their heads over the hedges, looking as if they had swan necks.

"Whatever is up? Why, it is the plumber."

I said, "Lord, I am not responsible for this, and I won't go from this place until I have the interpretation."

God knows that I wouldn't have moved from that place. And out came the interpretation:

Over the hills and far away before the brink of day, the Lord your God will send you forth and prosper all your way.

This is the point: the gift was there. I did not pray for it. I did not say, "Lord, give me the interpretation." I said, "If you don't give it to me, I won't move." By this I meant that I was determined to have the gift.

It has been surprising, but at every place where I am, the Spirit of the Lord moves upon me.

I want to say something about the gift of interpretation because it is so sublime, it is so divine, it is such a union with the Christ. It is a pleasing place with the Christ. It is not the Holy Spirit who is using it so much, but it is the Christ who is to be glorified in that act, for the Trinity moves absolutely collectively in the body.

As soon as that incident had taken place, wherever I went, when anybody spoke in tongues, I did not say, "Lord, give me the interpretation." That would have been wrong. I lived in a fact. Now, what is a fact? A fact is what produces. Fact produces; fact has it. Faith is a fact. Faith moves fear and faction. Faith is audacity. Faith is a personality. Faith is the living Christ manifested in the believer.

Now, what is interpretation? Interpretation moves and brings forth the words of God without the person thinking about it. If you get words before you have received from God, that is not interpretation. The person who interprets does not have the words. The gift breathes forth, and the person speaks, never stopping until he is through. He does not know what he is going to say until the words are out. He does not form them; he does not plan them. Interpretation is a divine flood, just as tongues are a flood. So it requires continual faith to produce this thing.

A divine gift has divine comprehension. It is also full of prophetic utterances. There is no such thing as an end to the divine vocabulary.

What is faith? Is it a pledge? It is more than that. Is it a present? It is more than that. It is relationship. Now, is there something better than relationship? Yes. What is it? Sonship is relationship, but heirship is closer still; and faith is *"God... manifested in the flesh"* (1 Tim. 3:16).

"What was Jesus?" you ask.

Jesus was the glory manifested in human incarnation.

"Was He anything else?"

Yes. Jesus was the fullness of the *"express image"* of the Father (Heb. 1:3). Is that fullness ours? Yes. Who are the chosen ones? They are those who ask and believe and see it done. God will make you chosen if you believe it.

Let us repent of everything that is hindering us; let us give place to God. Let us lose ourselves in Him. Let us have no self-righteousness, but let us have brokenness, humbleness, submission. Oh, may there be such brokenheartedness in us today! May we be dead indeed and alive indeed with refreshing from the presence of the Most High God!

Some of you have been saying, "Oh, I wish I could know how to get a gift." Some of you have felt the striving of the Holy Spirit within you. Oh, beloved, rise to the occasion this day. Believe God. Ask God for gifts, and it may come to pass in your life. But do not ask unless you know it is the desire of your heart. May God grant to us gifts and graces!

CHAPTER SIX

THE WORD OF WISDOM

FOR TO ONE IS GIVEN THE WORD OF WISDOM
THROUGH THE SPIRIT.
—1 CORINTHIANS 12:8

G od bless you! When He blesses, no one can curse. <u>When God is with you, it is impossible for anyone to be against you</u> (Rom. 8:31). When God has put His hand upon you, every way will open with blessing to others. The greatest thing that God has allowed us to come into is <u>the plan of distributing His blessing to others.</u>

"I will bless you and...you shall be a blessing" (Gen. 12:2). When we know the power of almighty God, we never need to be afraid of any weapon that is formed against us (Isa. 54:17), believing that the Lord of Hosts will rise up and stand against the enemy. *"The LORD will cause your enemies who rise against you to be defeated before your face; they shall come out against you one way and flee before you seven ways"* (Deut. 28:7).

God's power upon us, His wonderful blessing of us, His providential promise written down for us are to make us ready, every day and under all circumstances, to know that He who promised will surely fulfill.

What a wonderful Christ! God has chosen a blessing for us in the midst of anything we encounter. The power of the Highest overshadows us; the glory of the Lord is behind us and before us. (See Isaiah 58:8.) Who is able to withstand that almightiness!

God, breathe upon us so that we may be *"endued with power from on high"* (Luke 24:49), enriched with all the enrichment of heaven, crowned with blessing.

The Lord will lead us forth from victory to victory as His people. Oh, what a blessing to know that we are the fruit of the Lord! His people are the precious fruit of the earth.

I am not afraid to say these things to you because I know God wants to bless you. Why should you go away without blessing when God has promised that you will have a portion that cannot be measured (John 3:34)? Why should you fear when God wants to remove fear?

Are you ready? You say, "What for?" Oh, for His blessing that will fill your life, overflow you, change you.

Are you ready? Ready for what? To get a childlike simplicity and to look into the face of the Father and believe that all His promises are "Yes" and "Amen" (2 Cor. 1:20) to you.

Are you ready? Ready for what? To be awakened into that "Spirit of adoption" (Rom. 8:15) that believes all things and dares to ask the Father.

SPIRITUAL GIFTS

We have carefully gone through a few verses in the twelfth chapter of 1 Corinthians, so I hope you are well established in the thought that you are not to be ignorant about the gifts of the Holy Spirit. God does not intend for you to be ignorant concerning spiritual gifts: gifts that have revelation, that have divine knowledge, that have within them the power to deliver others and the power to pray through.

The gift of intercession, the gift of laying hands on the sick, the gift of prophecy, the gift of the word of wisdom, the gift of the word of knowledge, the gift of discerning spirits, the gift of tongues, and the gift of interpretation—all these are included in this one verse: "Now concerning spiritual gifts, brethren, I do not want you to be ignorant" (1 Cor. 12:1).

So I implore you to think seriously in your heart—because you have to be in the world but not of it (John 17:14–16)—that you need to be a personal manifestation of the living Christ. Just as Christ walked about the earth, you have to walk about as a child of God, with power and manifestation. People do not take time to read the Bible, so you have to be a walking epistle, "known and read by all men" (2 Cor. 3:2).

Seeing that this is so and that you have to correctly comprehend that Jesus is the Word and that you have to believe the Word of God and not change it because of people who have other opinions, take the Word of God. Yes, take the Word of God; it will furnish you as you stand strong in the Lord. It is there that you will find out that you do not need anything better; there is nothing better. It is there that you will find all you need: food for hunger, light for darkness, largeness of heart, conceptions of thought, and inspiration.

I like the words of Paul. They are beautiful, and they come forth so often by the power of the Spirit, such as this word: *"Strengthened with might through His Spirit in the inner man"* (Eph. 3:16). This might of the Spirit can fill everybody, and it brings forth the revelation of the Word.

THE GIVER, THEN GIFTS

We have clearly seen, I believe, why gifts were particularized, why there are varieties of gifts and varieties of positions in which to hold gifts. We must not forget that the Giver is to be received before the gifts.

Salvation always precedes sanctification, and sanctification will always precede the baptism of the Holy Spirit. Sanctification prepares the body for the Holy Spirit, and when the body is rightly prepared for the Spirit, then it is the work of Jesus to baptize with the Holy Spirit.

The Holy Spirit then makes Jesus King in your life; you regard Him as Lord and Master over all things, and you become submissive to Him in all things. You are not afraid to say, "You are mine! I love You!"

I love Him. He is so beautiful; He is so sweet; He is so loving; He is so kind! He never turns a deaf ear; He never leaves you in distress. He heals brokenheartedness; He liberates the captive (Luke 4:18); and for those who are down-and-out, He comes right into that place and lifts the burden.

It is truly said of Him, "He came to His own and His own had no room for Him; but to as many as had room for Him, He gave them power to become the sons of God." (See John 1:11–12.)

Thus I bring you again to the nature of sonship: it is grace bestowed, poured out, pressed through, or covering you, preserving you from all evil. It is boundless grace, grace that brings capability for your lack of ability, until God has you in His own mind and purpose.

THE GIFT OF THE WORD OF WISDOM

In 1 Corinthians 12:8, the Word of God tells us about the word of wisdom: *"For to one is given the word of wisdom through the Spirit."* It does not say—and you must clearly understand it—it does not say "the gift of wisdom," but the gift of *"the word of wisdom."* You have to *"rightly* [handle] *the word of truth"* (2 Tim. 2:15) because it will mean so much to us.

The gift of the word of wisdom is necessary in many instances. For example, when you want to build another church building, maybe larger than the one you are in, so that everybody can speak and be heard without any trouble, a word of wisdom is needed regarding how to build the place for God's service.

A word of wisdom is necessary when you are faced with a choice and it is difficult for you to know in what direction to go. That word can come to you in a moment and prepare you for the right way.

The gift of the word of wisdom is meant for a needy hour when you are under great stress concerning some business transaction; provided it is a godly transaction, you can ask God what to do, and you will receive wisdom along two lines.

It may come through the gift of the word of wisdom, or it may come forth just because the power of the Holy Spirit is upon you. I have been trying to show you that if you are filled with the Holy Spirit, the Holy Spirit can manifest any gift. At the same time, you are not to forget that the Word of God urges you to desire earnestly the best gifts (1 Cor. 12:31); so while the best gift might be to you the word of wisdom, or some other gift, you should not be lacking in any gift.

That is a remarkable statement for me to make, but I declare to you that Scripture lends itself to me to be extravagant. When God speaks to me, He says, "Anything you ask." (See John 15:7.) When God is speaking of the world's salvation, He says, "Whosoever believes." (See John 3:16.) So I have an extravagant God with extravagant language to make me an extravagant person—in wisdom.

If you have extravagance without wisdom, you will know very well that it is going to be of no profit. You have to learn not to be extravagant in this way so that you will not waste anything, and you have to learn above all things that you have to be out and God has to be in. The trouble with so many people is that they have never gotten out so He could get in. But if God ever gets in, you will first have gotten out, never to come in anymore.

To this end, we pray that God will show us now why we really need the word of wisdom and how we may be in a place in which we will surely know it is of God. I am going to give you an example of the word of wisdom through an experience I had, and it will help you more than anything else.

A QUESTIONABLE WORD AND A WORD OF WISDOM

One day I went out of my house and saw a friend of mine named John who lived opposite me. He crossed the road, came up to me, and said, "Now, Smith, how are you?"

"Very well, John," I said.

"Well," he said, "my wife and I have been thinking and praying and talking together about selling our house, and every time we think about it in any way, your name is the only one we think about."

That was a strange thing to me.

"Will you buy it?" he asked.

Now, if you remember, when David went wrong he only went wrong because he violated the holy communion and knowledge of what kept him. What was it? What was the word that would have saved him? *"You shall not covet your neighbor's wife"* (Exod. 20:17). He had to break that law to commit sin.

I was not dealing with a sin; however, looking back, I see that there were many questionable things about the situation, so that if I had thought about it for a moment, I would have been saved from many weeks of brokenheartedness and sorrow.

What was the first thing that I should have asked myself? "Can I live in two houses? No. Well, then, one is sufficient."

The next thing was, "Do I have the money to buy the house? No."

That is sufficient in itself, for God does not want any person to be in debt, and when you learn that secret, it will save you from thousands of sleepless nights. But I was like many people; we are all learning, and none of us is perfect. However, I do thank God that we are called to perfection, whether we come into it at once or not. If you miss the mark of holiness ten times a day, fortify yourself to believe that God intends for you to be holy, and then stand again. Do not give in when you miss the mark.

There is a saying that goes something like this: "No man fails to succeed in life because he makes a blunder; it is when he makes the blunder twice." No person who fails once loses his *"high calling"* (Phil. 3:14 KJV). Therefore, when you repent with godly repentance, you will never do the same thing again. (See 2 Corinthians 7:9–11 KJV.)

It is not for you to give in; you have to fortify yourself. The day is young; the opportunities are tremendously large. May God help you not to give in. Believe that God can make you new and turn you into another person.

Now, what was the trouble with me? It was that I didn't discuss this transaction with God. Many of you are in the same place. What do we do afterward? We begin working our way out. So I began working this thing out.

"How much will you take for it?" I asked.

He named the price. I thought to myself—this was a human thought—"Now, the banking society will give me all I want. They are well acquainted with me; that will be no trouble."

So the loan officer came to look over the house.

"It is a beautiful house," he said. "It is very reasonable. You will lose nothing on this if you ever sell it. It is well worth the money. But I cannot give you within five hundred dollars of what you need."

I did not have five hundred dollars; I couldn't get it out of the business I had at that time, so I still tried a human way. I did not go to God. If I had, I could have gotten out of it. But I tried to work my way out by myself. Why? Because I knew I was wrong from the beginning.

The first thing I did was to try my relatives. Have you ever done that? What was wrong? They were all so pleased to see me, but I was either a bit too soon or a little bit too late; I absolutely just missed it. They all wanted to lend me the money, but I was there at the wrong time. I tell you, every time I saw a relative, I had a Turkish bath without paying for it.

I had another human plan then: I tried my friends. The same thing happened.

Then I went to my lovely wife. Oh, she was a darling! She was holy! I went to her, and I said, "Oh, Mother, I am in a hard place."

"I know," she said. "I will tell you what you have never done, my dear."

"What?"

"You have never gone to God once about this thing."

That is the secret. When you get out of the will of God, then you try your own way.

So then I knew she knew, and I knew what I would get if I went to prayer.

"All right, my dear, I will go pray."

It is lovely to have a place to go in which to pray—those places where you open your eyes to see if you can see Him in reality because He is so near. Ah, to walk with God!

"Father," I said, "You know all about it. If you will forgive me this time, I will never trouble you again as long as I live with anything like this."

And then came the word of wisdom. He has it. And yet it was the most ridiculous word I ever heard in all my life. The Lord said, "Go see Brother Webster."

I came downstairs. I said, "He has spoken."

"I knew He would."

"Yes, but you see He said such a ridiculous thing."

"Believe it," she said. "It will be all right. When God speaks, you know it means it is all right."

"But Mother, you could hardly think it could be right. He has told me to go see Brother Webster."

"Go," she said.

Brother Webster was a man who kilned lime. The most he ever got per week, to my knowledge, was $3.50. He wore corduroy trousers and a pair of big work boots. But he was a godly man.

Early in the morning, I jumped onto my bicycle and went to his house. I got there at eight o'clock.

"Why, Brother Wigglesworth, what brings you so early?" he asked.

"I was speaking to the Lord last night about a little trouble," I said, "and He told me to come and see you."

"If that is the case," he said, "we will go down to my house and talk to the Lord."

We went to the house, and he locked the door.

"Now, tell me," he said.

"Well, three weeks ago I arranged to buy a house. I found out I was short five hundred dollars. I have tried everything I know and have failed. My wife told me last night to go to God, and while I was there, God said, 'Go see Brother Webster,' so here I am."

"How long have you needed it?"

"Three weeks."

"And you have never come to see me before?"

"No, God never told me."

I could have been able to know the next day if I had gone to God, but I tried my way and went to every man possible without going straight to God. I hope you won't do that now that you are to have the word of wisdom God is going to give you.

Brother Webster said to me, "For twenty years I have been putting aside a little more than half a dollar a week into a cooperative society. Three weeks ago they told me that I had five hundred dollars and that I must take it out because I was not doing business with them. I brought it home. I put it under the mattresses, under the floor boards, in the ceiling, everywhere. Oh, I have been so troubled by it! If it will do you any good, you can have it."

> He knows it all, He knows it all;
>   My Father knows it all.
> Your bitter tears, how oft they flow,
>   He knows, my Father knows it all.

I would like to change that verse somewhat. I will sing it the way God changed it for me:

> He knows it all, He knows it all;
>   My Father knows it all.
> The joy that comes and overflows,
>   He knows, my Father sends it all.

Yes, He knows. Glory to God!

"I had so much trouble," Brother Webster said, "that I took it to the bank yesterday to get rid of it. If I can get it out today, you can have it."

He went to the bank and asked, "How much can I have?"

"Why, it is your own," they said. "You can have it all."

He came out, gave it to me, and said, "There it is! If it is as much blessing to you as it has been trouble to me, you will have a lot of blessing."

Yes, beloved, He knows just what you need. Don't you know that if I had gone to the right place right away, I would never have

345

been in trouble? What I ought to have known was this: there was no need for the house at all.

I could not rest. I got rid of the house and took the money back to Brother Webster and said, "Take it back; take the money back. It will be trouble to me if I keep that money; take it."

Oh, to be in the will of God!

Don't you see, beloved, there is the word, the word of wisdom. One word is sufficient; you don't need a lot. One little word from God is all you require. You can count on it; it will never fail. It will bring forth what God has desired.

May the Lord give wisdom to you so that you may *"rightly* [handle] *the word of truth"* (2 Tim. 2:15), walk in the *"fear of the LORD"* (2 Chron. 19:7), and be an example to other believers (1 Tim. 4:12). Never take advantage of the Holy Spirit, but allow the Holy Spirit to take advantage of you.

I have come to a conclusion that is very beautiful, in my estimation. I once thought I possessed the Holy Spirit, but I have come to the conclusion that He has to be entirely the Possessor of me.

God can tame your tongue. God can so reserve you for Himself that your entire body will be operating in the Spirit.

INTERPRETATION OF A MESSAGE IN TONGUES: "The Lord of Hosts is in the place, waiting to change the human race and fit it for a heavenly place."

CHAPTER SEVEN

THE WORD OF KNOWLEDGE AND GIFT OF FAITH

TO ANOTHER [IS GIVEN] THE WORD OF KNOWLEDGE THROUGH THE
SAME SPIRIT, TO ANOTHER FAITH BY THE SAME SPIRIT.
—1 CORINTHIANS 12:8–9

We have not passed this way before. I believe that Satan has many devices and that they are worse today than ever before. But I also believe that there is to be a full manifestation on the earth of the power and glory of God to defeat every device of Satan.

In Ephesians 4 we are told to endeavor *"to keep the unity of the Spirit in the bond of peace,"* for *"there is one body and one Spirit,... one Lord, one faith, one baptism; one God and Father of all"* (vv. 3–6). The baptism of the Spirit is to make us all one. Paul told us that *"by one Spirit we were all baptized into one body...and have all been made to drink into one Spirit"* (1 Cor. 12:13). It is God's intention that we speak the same thing. If we all have the full revelation of the Spirit of God, we will all see the same thing. Paul asked the Corinthians, *"Is Christ divided?"* (1 Cor. 1:13). When the Holy Spirit has full control, Christ is never divided. His body is not divided; there is no division. Schism and division are products of the carnal mind.

THE WORD OF KNOWLEDGE

How important it is that we have the manifestation of *"the word of knowledge"* in our midst. The same Spirit who brings forth the word of wisdom brings forth the word of knowledge. The revelation of the mysteries of God comes by the Spirit, and we must have a supernatural word of knowledge in order to convey to others the things that the Spirit of God has revealed. The Spirit of God reveals Christ in all His wonderful fullness, and He shows Him to us from the beginning to the end of the Scriptures. It is the Scriptures that make us *"wise for salvation"* (2 Tim. 3:15) and that open to us the depths of the kingdom of heaven, revealing all of the divine mind to us.

There are thousands of people who read and study the Word of God, but it is not quickened to them. The Bible is a dead letter except by the Spirit. The words that Christ spoke were not just dead words, but they were spirit and life (John 6:63). And so it is the intention of God that a living word, a word of truth, the word of God, a supernatural word of knowledge will come forth from us through the power of the Spirit of God. It is the Holy Spirit who will bring forth utterances from our lips and a divine revelation of all the mind of God.

The child of God ought to thirst for the Word. He should know nothing else but the Word, and he should know nothing among men except Jesus (1 Cor. 2:2). *"Man shall not live by bread alone, but by every word that proceeds from the mouth of God"* (Matt. 4:4). It is as we feed on the Word and meditate on the message it contains that the Spirit of God can vitalize what we have received and bring forth through us the word of knowledge. This word will be as full of power and life as when He, the Spirit of God, moved upon holy men in ancient times and gave them the inspired Scriptures (2 Pet. 1:21). All the Scriptures were inspired by God (2 Tim. 3:16) as they came forth at the beginning, and through the same Spirit they should come forth from us vitalized, *"living and powerful, and sharper than any two-edged sword"* (Heb. 4:12).

With the gifts of the Spirit should come the fruit of the Spirit. With wisdom we should have love, with knowledge we should have joy, and with faith we should have the fruit of peace. Faith is always accompanied by peace. Faith always rests. Faith laughs at impossibilities. Salvation is by faith, through grace, and *"it is the gift of God"* (Eph. 2:8).

THE POWER OF FAITH

We are *"kept by the power of God through faith"* (1 Pet. 1:5). God gives faith, and nothing can take it away. By faith we have power to enter into the wonderful things of God. There are three kinds of faith: saving faith, which is the gift of God; the faith of the Lord Jesus; and the gift of faith. You will remember the word that the Lord Jesus Christ gave to Paul, to which he referred in Acts 26, where the Lord commissioned him to go to the Gentiles:

> To open their eyes, in order to turn them from darkness to light, and from the power of Satan to God, that they may receive forgiveness of sins and an inheritance among those who are sanctified by faith in Me.　　　　　(Acts 26:18)

Oh, this wonderful faith of the Lord Jesus. Our faith comes to an end. Many times I have been to the place where I have had to tell the Lord, "I have used all the faith I have," and then He has placed His own faith within me.

One of my fellow workers in ministry said to me at Christmastime, "Wigglesworth, I was never so near the end of my finances in my life." I replied, "Thank God, you are just at the opening of God's treasures." It is when we are at the end of our own resources that we can enter into the riches of God's resources. It is when we possess nothing that we can possess all things. (See 2 Corinthians 6:10.) The Lord will always meet you when you are on the edge of living.

I was in Ireland one time, and I went to a house and said to the lady who came to the door, "Is Brother Wallace here?" She replied, "Oh, he has gone to Bangor, but God has sent you here for me. I need you. Come in." She told me her husband was a deacon of the Presbyterian church. She herself had received the baptism of the Spirit while she was a member of the Presbyterian church, but they did not accept it as from God. The people of the church said to her husband, "This thing cannot go on. We don't want you to be a deacon any longer, and your wife is not wanted in the church."

The man was very enraged, and he became incensed against his wife. It seemed as though an evil spirit had possessed him, and the home that had once been peaceful became very terrible. Finally, he left home without leaving behind any money for his wife. The woman asked me what she should do.

We went to prayer, and before we had prayed five minutes, the woman was mightily filled with the Holy Spirit. I said to her, "Sit down and let me talk to you. Are you often in the Spirit like this?" She said, "Yes, and what could I do without the Holy Spirit now?" I said to her, "The situation is yours. The Word of God says that you have power to sanctify your husband. (See 1 Corinthians 7:14.) Dare to believe the Word of God. Now, the first thing we must do is to pray that your husband comes back tonight." She said, "I know he won't." I replied, "If we agree together, it is done." She said, "I will agree." Then I said to her, "When he comes home, show him all possible love; lavish everything upon him. If he won't hear what you have to say, let him go to bed. The situation is yours. Get down before God and claim him for the Lord. Get into the glory just as you have gotten into it today, and as the Spirit of God prays through you, you will find that God will grant all the desires of your heart."

A month later I saw this sister at a conference. She told how her husband came home that night. He went to bed, but she prayed right through to victory and then put her hands on him and prayed. He cried out for mercy. The Lord saved him and baptized him in the Holy Spirit. The power of God is beyond all our conception. The trouble is that we do not have the power of God in a full manifestation because of our finite thoughts, but as we go on and let God have His way, there is no limit to what our limitless God will do in response to a limitless faith. But you will never get anywhere unless you are in constant pursuit of all the power of God.

One day when I came home from our open-air meeting at eleven o'clock, I found that my wife was out. I asked, "Where is she?" I was told that she was down at Mitchell's. I had seen Mitchell that day and knew that he was at the point of death. I knew that it would be impossible for him to survive the day unless the Lord undertook to heal him.

There are many who let up in sickness and do not take hold of the life of the Lord Jesus Christ that is provided for them. For example, I was taken to see a woman who was dying, and I said to her, "How are things with you?" She answered, "I have faith; I believe." I said, "You know that you do not have faith. You know that you are dying. It is not faith that you have; it is language." There is a difference between language and faith. I saw that she was in the hands of the Devil. There was no possibility of life until he was removed from the premises. I hate the Devil, and I laid hold of the woman and shouted, "Come out, you demon of death. I command you to come out in the name of Jesus." In one minute she stood on her feet in victory.

But to return to the case of Brother Mitchell, I hurried down to the house, and as I got near I heard terrible screams. I knew that something had happened. I saw Mrs. Mitchell on the staircase and asked, "What is up?" She replied, "He is gone! He is gone!" I just passed by her and went into the room. Immediately I saw that Mitchell had gone. I could not understand it, but I began to pray. My wife was always afraid that I would go too far, and she laid hold of me and said, "Don't, Dad! Don't you see that he is dead?" I continued to pray and my wife continued to cry out to me, "Don't, Dad. Don't you see that he is dead?" But I continued praying. I got as far as I could with my own faith, and then God laid hold of me. Oh, it was such a laying hold that I could believe for anything. The faith of the Lord Jesus laid hold of me, and a solid peace came into my heart. I shouted, "He lives! He lives! He lives!" And he is living today.

There is a difference between our faith and the faith of the Lord Jesus. The faith of the Lord Jesus is needed. We must change faith from time to time. Your faith may get to a place where it wavers. The faith of Christ never wavers. When you have His faith, the thing is finished. When you have that faith, you will never look at things as they are. You will see the things of nature give way to the things of the Spirit; you will see the temporal swallowed up in the eternal.

The Gift of Faith

People say to me, "Do you not have the gift of faith?" I say that it is an important gift, but that what is still more important is for us to be making an advancement in God every moment. Looking at the Word of God, I find that its realities are greater to me today than they were yesterday. It is the most sublime, joyful truth that God brings an enlargement, always an enlargement. There is nothing dead, dry, or barren in this life of the Spirit; God is always moving us on to something higher, and as we move on in the Spirit, our faith will always rise to the occasion as different circumstances arise.

This is how the gift of faith is manifested. You see something, and you know that your own faith is nothing in the situation. The other day I was in San Francisco. I was sitting on a streetcar, and I saw a boy in great agony on the street. I said, "Let me get out." I rushed to where the boy was. He was in agony because of stomach cramps. I put my hand on his stomach in the name of Jesus. The boy jumped and stared at me with astonishment. He found himself instantly free of pain. The gift of faith dared in the face of everything. It is as we are in the Spirit that the Spirit of God will operate this gift anywhere and at any time.

When the Spirit of God is operating this gift within a person, He causes him to know what God is going to do. When the man with the withered hand was in the synagogue, Jesus got all the people to look to see what would happen. The gift of faith always knows the results. Jesus said to the man, *"Stretch out your hand"* (Matt. 12:13). His word had creative force. He was not living on the edge of speculation. He spoke and something happened. He spoke at the beginning, and the world came into being. (See John 1:1–3.) He speaks today, and things such as I have just described have to come to pass. He is the Son of God, and He came to bring us into sonship. He was the *"firstfruits"* of the Resurrection (1 Cor. 15:20), and He calls us to be *"firstfruits"* (James 1:18), to be the same kind of fruit as Himself.

There is an important point here. You cannot have the gifts by mere human desire. The Spirit of God distributes them *"to each one individually as He wills"* (1 Cor. 12:11). God cannot trust some people with a gift, but those who have a humble, broken, contrite heart He can trust (Isa. 66:2).

One day I was in a meeting where there were a lot of doctors and eminent men and many ministers. It was at a conference, and the power of God fell on the meeting. One humble little girl who served as a waitress opened her being to the Lord and was immediately filled with the Holy Spirit and began to speak in tongues. All these big men stretched their necks and looked up to see what was happening. They were saying, "Who is it?" Then they learned it was "the servant." Nobody received except the servant! These things are hidden and kept back from the *"wise and prudent,"* but the little children, the humble ones, are the ones who receive (Matt. 11:25). We cannot have faith if we show undue deference to one another. A man who is going on with God won't accept honor from his fellow beings. God honors the man who has a broken, contrite spirit. How can I get to that place?

So many people want to do great things and to be seen doing them, but the one whom God will use is the one who is willing to be told what to do. My Lord Jesus never said He could do things, but He did them. When that funeral procession was coming up from Nain with the widow's son being carried in an open coffin, Jesus made them lay the coffin down. (See Luke 7:11–14.) He spoke the word, *"Arise"* (v. 14), and gave the son back to the widow. He had compassion for her. And you and I will never do anything except along the lines of compassion. We will never be able to remove the cancer until we are immersed so deeply in the power of the Holy Spirit that the compassion of Christ is moving through us.

I find that in everything my Lord did, He said that He did not do it but that Another who was in Him did the work (John 14:10). What a holy submission! He was just an instrument for the glory of God. Have we reached a place where we dare to be trusted with the gift? I see in 1 Corinthians 13 that if I have faith to move mountains and do not have love, all is a failure. When my love is so deepened in God that I only move for the glory of God, then the gifts can be made manifest. God wants to be manifested and to manifest His glory to those who are humble.

A faint heart can never have a gift. Two things are essential: first, love; and second, determination—a boldness of faith that will cause God to fulfill His Word.

When I was baptized in the Holy Spirit, I had a wonderful time and had utterances in the Spirit, but for some time afterward, I did not again speak in tongues. One day, as I was ministering to another, the Lord again gave me utterances in the Spirit. After this, I was going down the road one day and speaking in tongues a long while. There were some gardeners doing their work, and they stuck their heads out over the hedges to see what was going on. I said, "Lord, You have something new for me. You said that when a man speaks in tongues, he should ask for the interpretation. I ask for the interpretation, and I'll stay right here until I get it." And from that hour, the Lord has given me interpretation.

One time I was in Lincolnshire in England and came in touch with the old rector of the church there. He became very interested in what I had to say, and he asked me into his library. I never heard anything sweeter than the prayer the old man uttered as he got down to pray. He began to pray, "Lord, make me holy. Lord, sanctify me." I called out, "Wake up! Wake up now! Get up and sit in your chair." He sat up and looked at me. I said to him, "I thought you were holy." He answered, "Yes." "Then what makes you ask God to do what He has already done for you?" He began to laugh and then to speak in tongues. Let us move into the realm of faith and live in the realm of faith and let God have His way.

CHAPTER EIGHT

GIFTS OF HEALING AND THE WORKING OF MIRACLES

TO ANOTHER [ARE GIVEN] THE GIFTS OF HEALING BY THE SAME
SPIRIT; TO ANOTHER THE WORKING OF MIRACLES.
—1 CORINTHIANS 12:9–10 (KJV)

G od has given us much in these last days, and where much is given, much will be required (Luke 12:48). The Lord has said to us,

You are the salt of the earth; but if the salt loses its flavor, how shall it be seasoned? It is then good for nothing but to be thrown out and trampled underfoot by men. (Matt. 5:13)

Our Lord Jesus expressed a similar thought when He said, *"If anyone does not abide in Me, he is cast out as a branch and is withered; and they gather them and throw them into the fire, and they are burned"* (John 15:6). On the other hand, He told us, *"If you abide in Me, and My words abide in you, you will ask what you desire, and it shall be done for you"* (John 15:7).

If we do not move on with the Lord in these days, if we do not walk in the light of revealed truth, we will become as flavorless salt or a withered branch. This one thing we must do: *"Forgetting those things which are behind"*—both the past failures and the past blessings—we must reach forth for those things that are before us and *"press toward the mark for the prize of the high calling of God in Christ Jesus"* (Phil. 3:13–14 KJV).

For many years, the Lord has been moving me on and keeping me from spiritual stagnation. When I was in the Wesleyan Methodist

Church, I was sure I was saved, and I was sure I was all right. The Lord said to me, "Come out," and I came out. When I was with the people known as the Brethren, I was sure I was all right then. But the Lord said, "Come out." Then I went into the Salvation Army. At that time, it was full of life, and there were revivals everywhere. But the Salvation Army went into natural things, and the great revivals that they had in those early days ceased. The Lord said to me, "Come out," and I came out. I have had to come out three times since. I believe that this Pentecostal revival that we are now in is the best thing that the Lord has on the earth today; and yet I believe that God will bring something out of this revival that is going to be still better. God has no use for anyone who is not hungering and thirsting for even more of Himself and His righteousness.

The Lord has told us to *"earnestly desire the best gifts"* (1 Cor. 12:31), and we need to earnestly desire those gifts that will bring Him the most glory. We need to see the gifts of healing and the working of miracles in operation today. Some say that it is necessary for us to have the gift of discernment in operation with the gifts of healing, but even apart from this gift, I believe that the Holy Spirit will have a divine revelation for us as we deal with the sick.

Most people think they have discernment; but if they would turn their discernment on themselves for twelve months, they would never want to "discern" again. The gift of discernment is not criticism. I am satisfied that in Pentecostal circles today, our paramount need is more perfect love.

Perfect love will never want the preeminence in everything; it will never want to take the place of another; it will always be willing to take the back seat. If you go to a Bible conference, there is always someone who wants to give a message, who wants to be heard. If you have a desire to go to a conference, you should have three things settled in your mind: Do I want to be heard? Do I want to be seen? Do I want anything on the line of finances? If I have these things in my heart, I have no right to be there.

The one thing that must move us is the constraining love of God to minister for Him (2 Cor. 5:14 KJV). A preacher always loses out when he gets his mind on finances. It is advisable for Pentecostal preachers to avoid making much of finances except to stir people up to help support our missionaries financially. A preacher who gets big collections for the missionaries never needs to fear; the Lord will take care of his finances.

A preacher should not arrive at a place and say that God has sent him. I am always fearful when I hear a man advertising this. If he is sent by God, the believers will know it. God has His plans for His servants, and we must live in His plans so completely that He will place us where He wants us. If you seek nothing but the will of God, He will always put you in the right place at the right time.

I want you to see that the gifts of healing and the working of miracles are part of the Spirit's plan and will come forth in operation as we are working along that plan. I must know the movement of the Spirit and the voice of God. I must understand the will of God if I am to see the gifts of the Spirit in operation.

HEALING POWER

The people of the Holy Spirit have a ministry. Everyone who has received the Holy Spirit is so filled with the Spirit that, without having the specific gift of healing, the Holy Spirit within him may bring forth healing power.

That is the reason I say to you, "Never be afraid of coming near me when I am praying for the sick." I love to have people help me. Why? Because I know that there are people who have a very dim conception of what they have. I believe that the power of the Holy Spirit you have received has power to bring you into focus in such a way that you will dare to believe God for healing, apart from knowing you have a gift.

THE GIFTS OF HEALING

Now I will deal with the gift itself. It is actually "gifts" of healing, not the "gift" of healing. There is a difference, and we must give it the proper name. Gifts of healing can deal with every case of sickness, every disease that there is. These gifts are so full that they are beyond human expression, but you come into the fullness of them as the light brings revelation to you.

There is something about a divine healing meeting that may be different in some respects than other meetings. I have people continually coming to me and saying, "When you are preaching, I see a halo around you," or "When you are preaching, I have seen angels standing around you."

I hear these things from time to time, and I am thankful that people have such spiritual vision. I do not have that kind of vision; however, I have the express glory, the glory of the Lord, covering me, the intense inner working of His power, until every time I have stood before you, I have known that I have not had to choose the words I have spoken. The language has been chosen, the thoughts have been chosen, and I have been speaking in prophecy more than in any other way. So I know we have been in the school of the Holy Spirit in a great way.

The only vision I have had in a divine healing meeting is this: so often, when I have laid hands upon the people, I have seen two hands go before my hands. This has happened many, many times.

The person who has the gifts of healing does not look to see what is happening. You will notice that after I have finished ministering, many things are manifested, but they don't move me. I am not moved by anything I see.

The divine gifts of healing are so profound in the person who has them that there is no such thing as doubt, and there could not be; whatever happens could not change the person's opinion or thought or act. He expects the very thing that God intends him to have as he lays hands upon the seeker.

Wherever I go, the manifestation of divine healing is considerably greater in every way after I leave than when I am there. Why? It is God's plan for me. God has great grace over me. Wonderful things have been accomplished, and people have told me what happened when I was there, but these things were hidden from me. God has a reason that He hides things from me.

When I lay hands upon people for a specific thing, I tell you, that thing will take place. I believe it will be so, and I never turn my ears or my eyes from the fact. It has to be so.

The gift of divine healing is more than audacity; it is more than an unction. Those are two big things; however, the gift of healing is the solid fact of a divine nature within the person pressing forward the very nature and act of the Lord, as if He were there. We are in this place to glorify the Father, and the Father will be glorified in the Son since we are not afraid of taking action in this day.

The gift of healing is a fact. It is a production; it is a faith; it is an unwavering trust; it is a confidence; it is a reliability; it knows it will be.

People sometimes come to me very troubled. They say, "I had the gift of healing once, but something has happened and I do not have it now."

They never had it. *"The gifts and the calling of God are irrevocable"* (Rom. 11:29), and they remain under every circumstance except this: if you fall from grace and use a gift, it will work against you. If you use tongues out of the will of God, interpretation will condemn you. If you have been used and the gift has been exercised and then you have fallen from your high place, it will work against you.

MINISTERING HEALING

The gifts of healing are so varied. You may go to see ten people, and every case will be different. I am never happier in the Lord than when I am in a bedroom with a sick person. I have had more revelations of the Lord's presence when I have ministered to the sick at their bedsides than at any other time. It is as your heart goes out to the needy ones in deep compassion that the Lord manifests His presence. You are able to discern their conditions. It is then that you know you must be filled with the Spirit to deal with the conditions before you.

When people are sick, you frequently find that they are ignorant about Scripture. They usually know three Scriptures, though. They know about Paul's *"thorn in the flesh"* (2 Cor. 12:7); they know that Paul told Timothy to take *"a little wine"* for his *"stomach's sake"* (1 Tim. 5:23); and they know that Paul left someone sick somewhere, but they don't remember his name or the place, and they don't know in what chapter of the Bible it is found. (See 2 Timothy 4:20.) Most people think they have a thorn in the flesh. The chief thing in dealing with a person who is sick is to discern his exact condition. As you are ministering under the Spirit's power, the Lord will let you see just what will be the most helpful and the most faith-inspiring to him.

When I was in the plumbing business, I enjoyed praying for the sick. Urgent calls would come, and I would have no time to wash. With my hands all black, I would preach to these sick ones, my heart all aglow with love. Ah, your heart must be in it when you pray for the sick. You have to get right to the bottom of the cancer with a divine compassion, and then you will see the gifts of the Spirit in operation.

I was called at ten o'clock one night to pray for a young person who was dying of consumption and whom the doctor had given up on. As I looked, I saw that unless God intervened, it would be impossible for her to live. I turned to the mother and said, "Well, Mother, you will have to go to bed." She said, "Oh, I have not had my clothes off for three weeks." I said to the daughters, "You will have to go to bed," but they did not want to go. It was the same with the son. I put on my overcoat and said, "Goodbye, I'm leaving." They said, "Oh, don't leave us." I said, "I can do nothing here." They said, "Oh, if you will stay, we will all go to bed."

I knew that God would not move in an atmosphere of mere natural sympathy and unbelief. They all went to bed, and I stayed, and that was surely a time as I knelt by that bed face to face with death and the Devil. But God can change the hardest situation and make you know that He is almighty.

Then the fight came. It seemed as though the heavens were brass. I prayed from 11:00 P.M. to 3:30 A.M. I saw the glimmering light on the face of the sufferer and saw her pass away. The Devil said, "Now you are done for. You have come from Bradford, and the girl has died on your hands." I said, "It can't be. God did not send me here for nothing. This is a time to change strength." I remembered the passage that said, *"Men always ought to pray and not lose heart"* (Luke 18:1). Death had taken place, but I knew that my God was all-powerful and that He who had split the Red Sea is just the same today. It was a time when I would not accept "No," and God said "Yes."

I looked at the window, and at that moment, the face of Jesus appeared. It seemed as though a million rays of light were coming from His face. As He looked at the one who had just passed away, the color came back to her face. She rolled over and fell asleep. Then I had a glorious time. In the morning she woke early, put on a dressing gown, and walked to the piano. She started to play and to sing a wonderful song. The mother and the sister and the brother all came down to listen. The Lord had intervened. A miracle had been worked.

The Lord is calling us along this way. I thank God for difficult cases. The Lord has called us into heart union with Himself; He wants His bride to have one heart and one Spirit with Him and to do what He Himself loved to do. That case had to be a miracle. The lungs were gone; they were just in shreds. Yet the Lord restored her lungs, making them perfectly sound.

A fruit of the Spirit that must accompany the gift of healing is long-suffering. The man who is persevering with God to be used in healing must be a man of long-suffering. He must always be ready with a word of comfort. If the sick one is in distress and helpless and does not see everything eye to eye with you, you must bear with him. Our Lord Jesus Christ was filled with compassion and lived and moved in a place of long-suffering, and we will have to get into this place if we are to help needy ones.

There are some times when you pray for the sick, and you seem to be rough with them. But you are not dealing with a person; you are dealing with satanic forces that are binding the person. Your heart is full of love and compassion toward all; however, you are moved to a holy anger as you see the place the Devil has taken in the body of the sick one, and you deal with his position with a real forcefulness.

One day a pet dog followed a lady out of her house and ran all around her feet. She said to the dog, "My dear, I cannot have you with me today." The dog wagged its tail and made a big fuss. She said, "Go home, my dear." But the dog did not go. At last she shouted roughly, "Go home," and off it went. Some people deal with the Devil like that. The Devil can stand all the comfort you like to give him. Cast him out! You are not dealing with the person; you are dealing with the Devil. Demon power must be dislodged in the name of the Lord.

You are always right when you dare to deal with sickness as with the Devil. Much sickness is caused by some misconduct; there is something wrong, there is some neglect somewhere, and Satan has had a chance to get in. It is necessary to repent and confess where you have given place to the Devil (Eph. 4:27), and then he can be dealt with.

When you deal with a cancer case, recognize that a living evil spirit is destroying the body. I had to pray for a woman in Los Angeles one time who was suffering with cancer, and as soon as it was cursed, it stopped bleeding. It was dead. The next thing that happened was that the natural body pushed it out, because the natural body had no room for dead matter. It came out like a great big ball with tens of thousands of fibers. All these fibers had been pressing into the flesh. These evil powers move to get further hold of the body's system, but the moment they are destroyed, their hold is gone. Jesus told His disciples that He gave them power to loose and power to bind (Matt. 16:19). It is our privilege in the power of the Holy Spirit to loose the prisoners of Satan and to let the oppressed go free.

Take your position from the first epistle of John and declare, *"He who is in* [me] *is greater than he who is in the world"* (1 John 4:4). Then recognize that it is not you who has to deal with the power of the Devil, but the Greater One who is in you. Oh, what it means to be filled with Him! You can do nothing in yourself, but He who is in you will win the victory. Your being has become the temple of the Spirit (1 Cor. 3:16). Your mouth, your mind, your whole being may be used and worked upon by the Spirit of God.

I was called to a certain town in Norway. The hall seated about fifteen hundred people. When I got to the place, it was packed, and hundreds were trying to get in. There were some policemen there. The first thing I did was to preach to the people outside the building. Then I said to the policemen, "It hurts me very much that there are more people outside than inside, and I feel I must preach to the people. I would like you to get me the marketplace to preach in." They secured a large park for me, and a big stand was erected, and I was able to preach to thousands.

After the preaching, we had some marvelous cases of healing. One man came a hundred miles, bringing his food with him. He had not been passing anything through his stomach for over a month because there was a great cancerous growth there. He was healed at that meeting, and opening his package, he began eating for all the people to see.

There was a young woman there with a stiff hand. When she was a child, her mother, instead of making her use her arm, had allowed her to keep it dormant until it was stiff. This young woman was like the woman in the Bible who was bent over with the spirit of infirmity (Luke 13:11). As she stood before me, I cursed the spirit of infirmity in the name of Jesus. It was instantly cast out and the arm was free. Then she waved her hand all around.

At the close of the meeting, the Devil threw two people to the ground with fits. When the Devil is manifesting himself, then is the time to deal with him. Both of these people were delivered, and when they stood up and thanked and praised the Lord, what a wonderful time we had.

We need to wake up and strive to believe God. Before God could bring me to this place, He broke me a thousand times. I have wept; I have groaned. I have travailed many a night until God broke me. It seems to me that until God has mowed you down, you can never have this long-suffering for others. We will never have the gifts of healing and the working of miracles in operation unless we stand in the divine power that God gives us, unless we stand believing God and, *"having done all"* (Eph. 6:13), we still stand believing.

We have been seeing wonderful miracles during these last days, and they are only a little of what we are going to see. I believe that we are right on the threshold of wonderful things, but I want to emphasize that all these things will be only through the power of the Holy Spirit. You must not think that these gifts will fall upon you like ripe cherries. There is a sense in which you have to pay the price for everything you get. We must earnestly desire God's best gifts and say "Amen" to any preparation the Lord takes us through. In this way, we will be humble, useable vessels through whom He Himself can operate by means of the Spirit's power.

CHAPTER NINE

THE GIFT OF PROPHECY

TO ANOTHER [IS GIVEN] PROPHECY.
—1 CORINTHIANS 12:10

I want you to understand clearly that there are three kinds of prophecy. Get this in your heart, because Paul said, *"I wish you all spoke with tongues, but even more that you prophesied"* (1 Cor. 14:5).

TESTIMONIAL PROPHECY

First, there is the prophecy that is the testimony of the saved person regarding what Jesus has done for him. Everyone, every newborn soul, has this kind of prophecy. Through the new birth that results in righteousness, God has given an anointing of the Spirit, a real unction of the Spirit of Christ. We felt when we were saved that we wanted everybody to be saved. That mindset has to be continuous; the whole world can be regenerated by the spirit of prophecy as we testify of our salvation in Christ. This kind of prophecy was described by an inhabitant of heaven to the apostle John in Revelation 19:10:

And I fell at his feet to worship him. But he said to me, "See that you do not do that! I am your fellow servant, and of your brethren who have the testimony of Jesus. Worship God! For the testimony of Jesus is the spirit of prophecy."

This is the same prophecy that Paul spoke about in 1 Corinthians 14:1: *"Pursue love, and desire spiritual gifts, but especially that you may prophesy."* This verse identifies prophecy as being more important than other gifts. Think about that: prophecy is to be chosen and desired above all the other gifts; the greatest among all the gifts is prophecy.

Why prophecy? Because prophecy by the power of the Spirit is the only power that saves humanity. We are told in the Word of God that the Gospel that is presented through prophecy has power to bring immortality and light. (See 2 Timothy 1:10.) Immortality is what abides forever. Light is what opens the understanding of your heart. Light and immortality come by the Gospel.

Prophecy is to be desired above all things, and every Christian has to have it. Every believer may have gifts, though there are very few who do; however, every believer has testimonial prophecy.

Now, from that same reference in Revelation 19:10, let us see what testimonial prophecy is and how it comes forth.

"I fell at his feet." Who is this inhabitant of heaven? The one speaking to John is a man who has been on the earth. Lots of people are foolishly led by the Devil to believe that after they die, their spirits will be asleep in the grave; this is absolutely contrary to the Word of God. Don't you know that even if you live until the Lord comes, the body that you have must be put off and another must be put on, because you cannot go into heaven with your present body? Nothing makes you so foolish as to turn aside from the Word of God. If you ever want to be a fool, turn aside from the Word of God, and you will find yourself in a fool's paradise.

This man has been on the earth in the body and is now in heaven in the spirit, and he wants you to hear what he has to say: *"I am your fellow servant, and of your brethren who have the testimony of Jesus....For the testimony of Jesus is the spirit of prophecy"* (Rev. 19:10).

What is the testimony of Jesus? The testimony is: "Jesus has saved me." What the world wants to know today is how they can be saved.

Testify that you are saved. Your knees may knock together; you may be trembling as you do it; but when you get it out, you enter into the spirit of prophecy. Before you know where you are, you are saying things that the Spirit is saying.

There are thousands of Christians who have never received the baptism of the Holy Spirit but who have this wonderful spirit of prophecy. People are being saved everywhere by the testimony of such believers.

John Wesley was moved by the power of God, and he created revivals all over the world. After the people were saved, they testified.

If you cease from testifying, you will be sorry when you give an account of your life before God (Rom. 14:12). As you testify, you will be a vessel through which the power of God can bring salvation to people (Rom. 1:16). Testify wherever you are.

> **INTERPRETATION OF A MESSAGE IN TONGUES:** "'You have not chosen me, but I have chosen you, and ordained you,' that you should go forth, 'your feet shod with the preparation of the gospel of peace.' What lovely feet! What lovely desire! A desire in your heart, because you are saved, to get everybody saved. The spirit of prophecy!"

You must all preach from now on. Every one of you must be a preacher. You have a prophecy that has come from heaven to change you from vile inward corruption, to do away with your human, evil nature, and to put within you a spirit of testimony. You know that where once you were dead, behold, you are alive! (See Luke 15:24.)

> **INTERPRETATION OF A MESSAGE IN TONGUES:** "Live in the place where the Lord your God moves you, not to go from house to house nor speak from person to person, but where the Lord directs you, for He has the person who is in need of truth waiting for watering with your watering can."

Oh, how the Lord wants to cheer you today! Do not forget that you are ambassadors for Christ (2 Cor. 5:20). Do not forget that you are now in the place where the prophets have a chance.

The Lord can bring you into a great place of splendor. He has His hand upon you. Whatever you do, desire to be holy, seek to be clean, so that you might always bear about in your body not only the dying of the Lord, but also the life of the resurrection of the Lord (2 Cor. 4:10).

> **INTERPRETATION OF A MESSAGE IN TONGUES:** "Lift up your hands and never be feeble, for the Lord has said, 'Lift up holy hands.' Don't be afraid of coming into the treasury, of making your hands clean, for they who 'bear the vessels of the Lord'

have to be only unto the Lord. So the Lord is bringing you to this great place of His pavilion so that He may clothe you upon with the Spirit, that your water will not fail. He will give you water and seed for your ministry, for remember, it is the same water and it is the same Sower. So don't forget, beloved, you are coworkers together with Him, and your ministry in the Lord is not to be in vain. See to it that you live so that your seed is well watered."

Now, that is one kind of prophecy. General Booth, the founder of the Salvation Army, knew it. He got the vision as clear as anything from Wesley. The greatest revival that has ever swept the earth that we remember is the revival the Salvation Army brought.

God revealed Himself to Booth. Those who were saved testified. God moved the people who were saved—former drunkards and prostitutes—into the streets to prophesy in the Spirit of Jesus. This is the prophecy that you all have when you are saved. The spirit of prophecy is the testimony that you are saved by the blood of the Lamb.

ANOINTED PROPHECY

The next type of prophecy is given by the preacher who lives in anointing, in prophetic utterances. You will find that I mostly speak in prophecy. Why? Well, it has pleased the Lord to bring me into this way of ministering so that I do not come to the platform with thought—that is, not with any thoughts of what I am going to say.

I want you to know another thing: I never say what I think. It is very much below a prophet of the Lord to begin to speak what he thinks to the people. The prophet must always say what he knows, because the people he is speaking to are the ones who have to think it out; but he is in the place of knowledge. The Holy Spirit takes the thoughts of Jesus and fills the prophet with divine life until he speaks divine utterances, until he knows.

Sometimes I speak quite a bit; I never take any thought at all concerning what I am speaking, but it flows out like rivers, prophecy of divine power. My natural makeup is not full, but my supernatural makeup is an overflowing full. I depend on an overflowing full so that you may get something out of it, so that you also may be full to overflowing.

It is very important and very essential that the person who preaches should live in prophetic utterances. Then a preacher will never be lamentable in his divine position. He is standing before people as a chosen one of God. He is not in any way to preach anything unless he knows it is the Word of God, and there he is to be clothed with holiness like a garment of salvation.

Oh, this is true! The Spirit of the Lord is upon me now. I know it; I feel it. It is moving me; it chastens me; it is bringing me to a place where I know that if you listen, you will be blessed. The blessing of the Lord is upon you. Hear, for the Spirit speaks to you.

This is prophecy as the Spirit gives forth. It is the illumination of truth by the Word of Life. The Holy Spirit has the chief position in the place, taking words, actions, and everything else until the prophet stands there complete, the oracle of God, speaking words absolutely as if the Lord were here saying them (1 Pet. 4:11).

These first two kinds of prophecy are divine inspiration, Holy Spirit utterances. In a very remarkable way by the Spirit of Jesus, every person can feel burnings and movings, chastenings and thrillings. It is wonderful. All you have to do is begin and you cannot stop.

There was something done on the cross that is truly wonderful. Don't you know you were made every bit whole? You were made holy; you were made a saint; you were absolutely cleansed from all unrighteousness. The new birth is a revelation of God in the soul. You are made His forever when you are saved by His power. No one can estimate the new birth; it is beyond all human power to estimate. The new birth is larger than our human capacities. And, thank God, we have touches from Him that make us on fire.

The Gift of Prophecy

We will now look at divine prophecy as a gift. I trust that many of you will have this gift.

This is the most wonderful of all prophecy and yet the most dangerous. There is a great deal of trouble in relation to the gift of prophecy; there always has been. So I want you to guard this gift. With the gift of prophecy, what you need to watch is this (it is the same with the gift of tongues and the gifts of healing): even though the gift has been received and the people have been blessed through the gift, you are never to use the gift unless the power of the Spirit brings into you a great thirst and longing to do it. It would be a serious thing for me to speak in tongues at any moment just because I had the gift; without the unction of the Spirit, it would fall to nothing.

All gifts are of no account at all unless they are brought forth by the Giver of the gifts, and the Holy Spirit is the One who gives the nine gifts listed in 1 Corinthians 12. He brings anointing, fire, confirmation, and utterance, until those who hear are moved. When the Lord speaks, it changes and moves the natural, because it is supernatural. Supernatural always changes natural.

Prophecy is lovely because it makes the body very full of expressions of joy. It is lovely, for people all like to hear it. It is lovely when it is the Spirit moving.

Be careful when people are very pleased to hear you prophesy. Prophecy is like tongues; no man who speaks and speaks and speaks and speaks in tongues is to have control in a meeting. That is not what it means to have the advantage in a meeting. Having the advantage means that when the Spirit is upon you, you will speak in tongues, and you will close down the moment you know you are at the end. What spoils it is when people go on and on, and the hearers get tired of it because they want something that God can bring in and move quickly.

Don't think you will be heard by your *"many words"* (Matt. 6:7), either by tongues, prayer, or anything else. You are not heard because of your many words; you are heard because you are definite. All your spiritual abilities are going to be acceptable with others as you learn how to obey the Spirit and never to take advantage just because you are present in a meeting.

Here is another thing you have to learn: people rush up and down sometimes, and then they say to you, "Oh, I had to do that! I had to jump up and do that. I had to do that—and that—and that."

Don't believe them; it isn't true. There never was a person in the world, as long as he was in the body, who didn't have power over his spirit. And so, when people rush to you and say they have to do this, that, and the other, don't believe it. What are you to believe? You are to believe that when the Spirit is manifested in the order it should be, it will have three things with it: comfort, exhortation, and edification (1 Cor. 14:3).

369

If any of you find that I do not speak by the Spirit of God and teach the Scriptures only, which is what God desires, you meet me at the door and tell me. I have declared that this will be my constant purpose. I have declared that as long as I live, I will never exaggerate. Exaggeration is lying. What God wants is a people who are full of truth. I want God to so have you that your word will be your bond. Whenever you say anything, the people will be able to believe it; you have said it, and you will do it.

When the unction is upon you, when the power of God is manifested through you, one thing that will be accomplished by prophecy is comfort. The Holy Spirit can so have you in prophecy that all the people will be comforted.

But if you get away from that prophecy because you begin and the people are delighted, and if you go on until you come out with your own human words, you will lead people astray. People have been led to buy houses, to do all sorts of silly things, because of people who did not obey the Lord but brought in some human prophecy.

If anybody ever comes to you with human prophecy, say, "I know God, and unless God tells me, I won't move."

Don't be deluded by anybody. You can tell what is of the Lord. The Word of God distinctly says, *"Do not despise prophecies"* (1 Thess. 5:20). So whatever you do, do not despise them. However, in the next verse you are told to *"test all things"* (v. 21). Therefore, you may say, "Well now, if that is of the Lord, I will see if it corresponds to the Word of God." And you will have clear revelation as to whether it is the word of the Lord.

This is the day in which we need comforting, and the power of the Spirit can comfort you and send you away from these meetings knowing that you have been in the presence of God and have heard the Word of God.

There are people who, like Isaiah, have the gift of prophecy. Isaiah was so filled with this prophecy. He said, *"Unto us a Son is given"* (Isa. 9:6). This was definite, personal, truth, and knowledge. It took over five hundred years to bring it to pass, but there it was, definitely declared beforehand:

> *And the government will be upon His shoulder. And His name will be called Wonderful, Counselor, Mighty God, Everlasting Father, Prince of Peace.* (Isa. 9:6)

Oh, hallelujah! All the way down through the Scriptures you will find such distinct prophecy. You will see the book of Isaiah filled with prophetic utterances. Begin with Genesis and go right through, and you will find the golden or the scarlet thread right through all the prophecies, declaring, "He is coming, He is coming! He is on the way; He will surely come!"

At the birth of Christ, the angels sang; the Babe was born. Prophecy was fulfilled!

And you shall call His name JESUS, for He will save His people from their sins. (Matt. 1:21)

And this will be the sign to you: You will find a Babe wrapped in swaddling cloths, lying in a manger. (Luke 2:12)

Prophecy was also fulfilled in Jesus' crucifixion and resurrection:

You know that after two days is the Passover, and the Son of Man will be delivered up to be crucified. (Matt. 26:2)

As Moses lifted up the serpent in the wilderness, even so must the Son of Man be lifted up. (John 3:14)

Ah, beloved, God can give you prophecy that will fulfill the past to a perfect degree, chapter and verse.

He is coming. Glory to God! The saints will be awakened; prophecy will appear. People will say, "Yes, He is coming; we know He is coming!"

And He will come!

CHAPTER TEN

THE DISCERNING OF SPIRITS

TO ANOTHER [IS GIVEN] DISCERNING OF SPIRITS.
—1 CORINTHIANS 12:10

Discernment is a very necessary gift to understand, and I want you to keep your mind clearly balanced about this. I want you to rightly divide this truth (2 Tim. 2:15), to keep clear in your mind what it is.

DISCERNMENT VERSUS JUDGING

In 1 Corinthians 12:10, it clearly says that there is a gift of *"discerning of spirits,"* but most people seem to think it is a discerning of human persons. It is amazing to find that all the people I come across—or most of them—seem to have a tremendous bent toward "discerning" others. If you carefully put this discerning of one another into real practice upon yourself for twelve months, you will never presume to try it upon another. You will see so many faults, so many crooked things about yourself, that you will say, "O God, make me right!"

There is a vast difference between natural discernment and spiritual discernment. This statement of Jesus is remarkable:

How can you say to your brother, "Let me remove the speck from your eye"; and look, a plank is in your own eye? Hypocrite! First remove the plank from your own eye, and then you will see clearly to remove the speck from your brother's eye.

(Matt. 7:4–5)

Remember that if you begin judging, it will lead you to judgment (Matt. 7:1–2). If you begin using your discernment to weigh people by your standards, it will lead you to judgment. Ever since God showed me a certain passage in Romans 2, I have been very careful to examine myself before I begin judging:

> *Therefore you are inexcusable, O man, whoever you are who judge, for in whatever you judge another you condemn yourself; for you who judge practice the same things. But we know that the judgment of God is according to truth against those who practice such things. And do you think this, O man, you who judge those practicing such things, and doing the same, that you will escape the judgment of God?* (Rom. 2:1–3)

Balance that in your heart. It will save you from judging.

I have found that there are many notable people in the world, whom I have known personally, who have gotten to running another person down and finding fault. They are always faultfinding and judging people outright. I find that those people always fall in the mire. If I were to mention these people by name, you would know that what I am saying is true.

God save us from criticism! When we are pure in heart, we only think about pure things. When we are impure in heart, we speak and act and think as we are in our hearts. The pure in heart see purity. May God give us that inward desire for purity so that He can take away judging.

In the sixth chapter of Isaiah, we read of the prophet being in the presence of God. He found that even his lips were unclean, that everything was unclean (Isa. 6:5). But praise God, there is the same live coal for us today (vv. 6–7), the baptism of fire, the perfecting of the heart, the purifying of the mind, the regeneration of the spirit. How important it is that the fire of God touches our tongues!

DISCERNING SPIRITS

But it is the discerning of spirits that I want to talk about, as well as what to do when you have no discernment.

In 1 John 4:1 we are told, *"Beloved, do not believe every spirit, but test the spirits, whether they are of God."* We are further told:

And every spirit that does not confess that Jesus Christ has come in the flesh is not of God. And this is the spirit of the Antichrist, which you have heard was coming, and is now already in the world. (1 John 4:3)

From time to time, as I have seen a person under a power of evil or having a fit, I have said to the power of evil or satanic force that is within the possessed person, "Did Jesus Christ come in the flesh?" and right away they have answered no. They either say no or hold their tongues, refusing altogether to acknowledge that the Lord Jesus Christ came in the flesh. It is at a time like this when, remembering that further statement of John's, *"He who is in you is greater than he who is in the world"* (v. 4), you can, in the name of the Lord Jesus Christ, deal with the evil powers and command them to come out. We, as Pentecostal people, must know the tactics of the Evil One, and we must be able to displace and dislodge him from his position.

To discern spirits, we must dwell with Him who is holy, and He will give the revelation and unveil the mask of satanic power, whatever it is. In Australia, I went to one place where there were disrupted and broken homes. The people were so deluded by the evil power of Satan that men had left their wives and wives had left their husbands and they had gotten into spiritual affinity with one another. That is the Devil! May God deliver us from such evils in these days. There is no one better than the companion God has given you. I have seen so many broken hearts and so many homes that have been wrecked. We need a real revelation of these evil seducing spirits who come in and fascinate through the eyes, and who destroy lives, bringing the work of God into disrepute. But there is always flesh behind it. It is never clean; it is unholy, impure, satanic, devilish; and hell is behind it. If the Enemy comes in to tempt you in any way like this, I implore you to look instantly to the Lord Jesus. He can deliver you from any such satanic power. You must be separated in every way if you are going to have faith.

★ The Holy Spirit will give us this gift of the discerning of spirits if we desire it so that we may perceive by revelation this evil power that comes in to destroy. We can reach out and get this unction of the Spirit that will reveal these things to us.

People will come to your meetings who are Spiritualists. You must be able to deal with spiritualistic conditions. You can deal with them in such a way that they will not have any power in the meetings. If you ever have mystics or Christian Scientists in your meetings, you must be able to discern them and deal with them. Never play with them; always clear them out. They are always better with their own company, unless they are willing to be delivered from the delusion they are in. Remember the warning of the Lord Jesus: *"The thief does not come except to steal, and to kill, and to destroy"* (John 10:10).

Seek the Lord, and He will sanctify every thought, every action, until your whole being is ablaze with holy purity and your one desire is for Him who has created you in holiness. Oh, this holiness! Can we be made pure? We can. Every inbred sin must go. God can cleanse away every evil thought. Can we have a hatred for sin and a love for righteousness? Yes, God will create within you a pure heart. He will take away your stony heart and give you a heart of flesh. He will sprinkle you with clean water, and you will be cleansed from all your filthiness (Ezek. 36:25–26). When will He do it? When you seek Him for such inward purity.

DELIVERANCE

Let me tell you what may seem to be a horrible story for you to hear; nevertheless, it is a situation in which discernment is necessary. This is happening all the time, and I do thank God for it because it is teaching me how to minister to people in the Lord.

Messages came to me again and again by telegraph, letters, and other things, asking that I come to London. I wired back and wrote, but so many calls came and no hint was given in any way as to the reason I was to go there. The only thing they said was that they were in great distress.

When I got there, the dear father and mother of the needy one both took me by the hand and broke down and wept.

"Surely this is deep sorrow of heart," I said.

They led me up onto the balcony. Then they pointed to a door that was open a little, and both of them left me. I went in that door, and I have never seen a sight like it in all my life. I saw a young woman who was beautiful to look at, but she had four big men holding her down to the floor, and her clothing was torn from the struggle.

When I got into the room and looked into her eyes, her eyes rolled but she could not speak. She was exactly like the man in the

Bible who came out of the tombs and ran to Jesus when he saw Him. As soon as he got to Jesus, he couldn't speak, but the demon powers spoke. (See Mark 5:1–13.) And the demon powers in this young girl spoke and said, "I know you. You can't cast us out; we are many."

"Yes," I said, "I know you are many, but my Lord Jesus will cast you all out."

It was a wonderful moment; it was a moment when it was only He alone who could do it.

The power of Satan was so great upon this beautiful girl that she whirled and broke away from these four strong men.

The Spirit of the Lord was wonderful in me, and I went right up to her and looked into her face. I saw the evil powers there; her very eyes flashed with demon power.

"In the name of Jesus," I said, "I command you to leave. Though you are many, I command you to leave this moment, in the name of Jesus."

She instantly became sick and began vomiting. She vomited out thirty-seven evil spirits and gave their names as they came out. That day she was made as perfect as anybody.

The next morning at ten o'clock, we all shared a meal together. Praise the Lord!

With the gift of discernment, you are in pursuit of divine thought; you are in pursuit of divine character; you are in pursuit of the deep, holy, inward intuition so that you might know what to do. The Lord of Hosts is in you, and the Lord of Hosts is with you; His desire is that you should know how you will be able to do it.

I arrived one night at Gottenberg in Sweden and was asked to hold a meeting there. In the midst of the meeting, a man fell full length in the doorway. The evil spirit threw him down, manifesting itself and disturbing the whole meeting. I rushed to the door and laid hold of this man and cried out to the evil spirit within him, "Come out, you devil! In the name of Jesus, we cast you out as an evil spirit." I lifted him up and said, "Stand on your feet and walk in the name of Jesus." I don't know whether anybody in the meeting understood me except the interpreter, but the devils knew what I said. I spoke in English, but these demons in Sweden cleared out. A similar thing happened in Oslo, Norway.

The Devil will endeavor to fascinate people through the eyes and through the mind. One time a beautiful young woman was brought to me who had been fascinated with some preacher; just because he had not given her satisfaction on the lines of courtship and marriage, the Devil had taken advantage of the situation and had made her delirious and insane. They had brought her 250 miles in that condition. She had previously received the baptism in the Spirit.

You ask, "Is there any place for the Enemy in one who has been baptized in the Holy Spirit?" Our only safety is in going on with God and in constantly being filled with the Holy Spirit. You must not forget Demas. He must have been baptized with the Holy Spirit, for he appears to have been one of Paul's right-hand workers, but the Enemy got him to the place where he loved this present world, and he fell away (2 Tim. 4:10).

When they brought this young woman to me, I discerned the evil power right away and immediately cast the thing out in the name of Jesus. It was a great joy to present her before all the people in her right mind again.

There is a life of perfect deliverance, and this is where God wants you to be. If I find that my peace is disturbed in any way, I know it is the Enemy who is trying to work. How do I know this? Because the Lord has promised to keep your mind in perfect peace when it is focused on Him (Isa. 26:3). Paul told us to present our bodies as *"a living sacrifice, holy, acceptable to God, which is* [our] *reasonable service"* (Rom. 12:1). The Holy Spirit also spoke this word through Paul: *"And do not be conformed to this world, but be transformed by the renewing of your mind, that you may prove what is that good and acceptable and perfect will of God"* (v. 2).

Paul further told us in Philippians 4:8,

Finally, brethren, whatever things are true, whatever things are noble, whatever things are just, whatever things are pure, whatever things are lovely, whatever things are of good report, if there is any virtue and if there is anything praiseworthy; meditate on these things.

As we think about what is pure, we become pure. As we think about what is holy, we become holy. And as we think about our Lord Jesus Christ, we become like Him. We are changed into the likeness of the object on which our gaze is fixed.

HOW TO KNOW THE MIND OF GOD

Now we come to the place of how to know the nature of the spirit we are dealing with. That is a very important thing. You are always in a dangerous place if you trust in your own knowledge. Let me say to you that whatever the Holy Spirit does in these days, He does in order to give you a new mind. Our new mind is to have the thoughts of Christ, the mind of Christ.

To have the thoughts and mind of Christ means that you will never seek to assert yourself for your own glory; now Another who is greater than you has to take your place and lead you to where you are in the place of Jesus. And in that way, the Lord will give you power to discern evil spirits.

We have struck one of the most holy chords that could be struck. I have clear confidence that we are in the will of God in this meeting, and I know the Lord is helping me to speak to you.

HINDRANCES TO DISCERNMENT

I want you to see clearly that you will never be able to discern or deal with evil powers as long as there is anything in you that the Devil can touch. You are only able to do what God desires for you to do as you have come into the depths of death to self, so that the supernatural life of Christ is abounding in you to destroy the powers of evil.

Before Satan can bring his evil spirits, there has to be an open door. Hear what the Scriptures say: *"The wicked one does not touch him"* (1 John 5:18), and *"The LORD shall preserve you from all evil; He shall preserve your soul"* (Ps. 121:7). How does Satan get an opening? When the believer ceases to seek holiness, purity, righteousness, truth; when he ceases to pray, stops reading the Word, and gives way to carnal appetites. Then it is that Satan comes. So often sickness comes as a result of disobedience. David said, *"Before I was afflicted I went astray"* (Ps. 119:67).

You will never be able to reach out your hand to destroy the power of Satan as long as there is the vestige of human desire or attainment in you. It is in the death of the death that you are in the life of the life. Don't fool yourself; don't mislead yourself. Never think that God overlooks sins. Sins have to be dealt with, and the only way God ever deals with sin is to absolutely destroy its power.

You can be made so clean that the Devil comes and finds nothing in you. (See John 14:30.) And then you have power by the power of God over the powers of Satan.

Discernment is not mind or eye. Discernment is an intuition. Your heart knows exactly what you are dealing with, and you are dealing with it because of your heart purity against evil and uncleanness.

God is purifying me in every meeting. I can safely say that unless the power of the Spirit purges me through and through, I cannot help you. First of all, before I can give any life to you, the life must be in me. And remember that the Scriptures are very clear: death works in us so that life may work in you. (See 2 Corinthians 4:12.)

Now, what we are being purified from is all carnal, evil, sensual. Don't forget the remarkable thing in the Scriptures that leads us to this; there are sixty-six evil things listed in the Bible, such as murder, covetousness, evil propensities. But I am here to say by the power of God that one fruit will destroy every evil thing. *"Seek first the kingdom of God and His righteousness, and all these things shall be added to you"* (Matt. 6:33).

CHAPTER ELEVEN

HOW TO DISCERN VOICES

There are many voices in the world. I want you to be able to understand voices, to understand spiritual voices, to understand exactly what the Scripture means about these things.

Now, I know there are a good many people who are big on the author Sir Arthur Conan Doyle, who, you will find, is trying to delve into mysteries. There is nothing mystical about what we are doing, and I want to tell everybody who comes to this place that you will have no share with us if you have anything to do with spiritualism. We denounce it as being of the Devil, and we don't want fellowship with you. If you want to join up with two things—the Lord and the Devil—the Devil will get you in the end.

Now, what is the difference between the spirit of *"disobedience"* (Eph. 2:2) and the spirit of *"lawlessness"* (2 Thess. 2:7–8)? They are one and the same. They are the spirit of antichrist, and they are right in the midst of things. Spiritualism, Jehovah's Witnesses, Christian Science—they are all related. They have no room for the blood of Jesus, and you cannot get near God except by the blood; it is impossible. The blood is the only power that can make a clear road into the kingdom for you—the blood of Jesus.

TESTING THE SPIRITS

Beloved, do not believe every spirit, but test the spirits, whether they are of God; because many false prophets have gone out into the world. By this you know the Spirit of God: Every spirit that confesses that Jesus Christ has come in the flesh is of God, and every spirit that does not confess that Jesus Christ has come in the flesh is not of God. And this is the spirit of the Antichrist, which you have heard was coming, and is now already in the world. You are of God, little children, and have overcome them, because He who is in you is greater than he who is in the world. They are of the world. Therefore they speak as of the world, and the world hears them. We are of God. He who knows God hears us; he who is not of God does not hear us. By this we know the spirit of truth and the spirit of error. (1 John 4:1–6)

Beloved, you have to be in a position to try the spirits to see whether they are of God. Why should believers try the spirits? You can always try the spirits to see whether they are of God for this reason: you will be able to tell the true revelation, and the true revelation that will come to you will always sanctify the heart; it will never have an "if" in it. When the Devil came to Jesus, he had an "if." He said, *"If You are the Son of God"* (Matt. 4:3), and *"If You will fall down and worship me"* (v. 9). The Holy Spirit never comes with an "if." The Holy Spirit is the divine Orator of this wonderful Word, but the position of the mystic Conan Doyle, and others like him, is satanic.

I have often dealt with people under evil powers, people in fits and other things, and sometimes I have come across people so much controlled by evil powers that every time they want to speak, the evil powers speak. It is a very dangerous condition; but, it is true: people get possessed by the Devil.

Do you remember the biblical account of the man in the tomb who was terribly afflicted with evil powers (Mark 5:2–15)? Strong cords and chains could not hold him. Night and day, there he was in the tombs, *"crying out and cutting himself with stones"* (v. 5). Jesus came on the scene, and these evil powers caused the man to run. Now, it was all in the power of the Devil, and as soon as the man got in front of Jesus, the evil spirit said, *"Have You come here to torment us before the time?"* (Matt. 8:29). This man had no power to get free, but these evil spirits were so troubled in the presence of Jesus that they cried out, *"Have You come here to torment us before the time?"*

Oh, thank God for Jesus. I want you to notice that Jesus wants you to be so under His power, so controlled by and filled with the Holy Spirit, that the power of authority in you will resent all evil.

This is an important lesson for believers, because there are so many believers who are not on their guard. I want to impress you with the fact that every believer should reach a place in the Holy Spirit where he has no desire except the desire of God. The Holy Spirit has to possess us until we are filled, led, yes, divinely led, by the Holy Spirit. It is a mighty thing to be filled with the Holy Spirit.

> **Interpretation of a Message in Tongues:** "The Lord, He is the mighty power of government, for the Scripture says, 'The government shall be upon His shoulders,' and now He has taken us on His shoulders; therefore, let Him lead you where He will."

Do not desire to lead Jesus; if He leads you, He will lead you into truth. He will lead you into nothingness, but when you are in nothingness, you will be in power. He will lead you into weakness, but when you are in weakness, God will be with you in might; everything that seems weak from a human perspective will be under the control of divine power.

RECEIVING IMPRESSIONS

Now I want to deal with a very important thing. I have people by the hundreds who are continually pressing on me with their difficulties, with their strange and yet holy and noble desires, where two ways meet and they do not know which one to take. Some have received impressions in their minds and hearts, but I want to show you what comes of impressions.

A person came to me one day and said, "Oh, you know the Spirit of the Lord was mighty upon me this morning."

I said, "Good!"

"Oh, I want to tell you about it. I want you to tell me if there is such a place as Ingerow anywhere near here."

I answered, "Yes, there is."

"Well, that place has been on my mind; I have to go and preach there."

There was nothing wrong with her desire to go preach, was there?

But I asked, "What is the message?"

"I don't exactly know."

"Now come, what is the message?" I asked.

"Oh, I have to speak to someone about his soul."

"And you don't know that there is such a place? The place is toward Skipton," I replied.

"But I have to go."

"Now come," I said, "I want you to think. You are working, are you not? Do you think anybody in the mill will approve of your going to a place you don't know, to speak to someone you don't know?"

Was it of God? That is the first thing. It was an impression, coming from a desire to be something special. That's the danger. My daughter tried to stop her, but she went the first chance she got. She got to the station, and there was nobody there. The result was that she was soon in an asylum.

What was it? An impression. How will we know when this is the case?

A lady came to me yesterday and said, "Don't you know, the Spirit of the Lord is upon me; I have to preach the Gospel."

I said, "There is nothing wrong in that."

"I want to know where I have to go to preach, so I have come to you to see if the Lord has told you where I am to go."

"Yes, you have to begin at home. Begin at Jerusalem, and if you are successful, go to Judea; then if you are successful, God will send you to the uttermost parts of the world." (See Acts 1:8.)

God is not going to send you to the uttermost parts of the world until you have been successful around Jerusalem. We have a tremendously big job; it is well worth doing, and I want to do it well. I want to tell you the difference between the right and the wrong way to discern voices and thoughts that may come into your minds.

You have the Scriptures, and you have the Holy Spirit. The Holy Spirit has wisdom, and He does not expect you to be foolish. The Holy Spirit has perfect insight into knowledge and wisdom, and truth always gives you balance.

You always need to have one thing removed from you: being terribly afraid. However, fear leaves, and power and confidence come in its place. You also need to have another thing that must remain, and that is love: love in order to obey God rather than your inclinations to be something; but if God wants to make you someone, that is different.

My wife tried her best to make me someone, but she could not do it. Her heart was right; her love was right; she did her best to make me a preacher. She used to say, "Now, Father, you could do it if you wanted to, and I want you to preach next Sunday."

I did everything to get ready; I tried everything. I don't know what I did not try—it would be best not to tell you what I did try. I had as many notes as would suit a clergyman for a week.

My wife's heart, her love, her desires were all right, but when I got up to preach, I would give out my text and then say, "If anybody can preach, now is your chance, for I have finished." That did not take place once, but many times. She was determined, and I was willing. When I ministered to those who had come forward to repent and receive Jesus, I could bring them right into the kingdom. I could nurse the children while my wife preached, and I was pleased to do it. But, don't you know, when the Holy Spirit came, then I was ready. Then the preaching abilities were not mine but the Lord's. To be filled with the Holy Spirit is to be filled with divine equipping. It must all be for Jesus.

Oh, I tell you, whatever you may think about it, the whole thing is that there is nothing good without Jesus. Anyone could jump on this platform and say, "I am right." But when you have no confidence, then Jesus is all the confidence you require. God must have men and women on fire for Him. God will mightily send you forth in the anointing of the Spirit, and sinners will feel convicted, but it will never be accomplished if you have it in your mind that you are going to be something. The baptism is a baptism of death, and you live only unto God.

THE HOLY SPIRIT VERSUS DECEPTIVE VOICES

A lot of people are very much troubled by voices. Some people are so troubled that they get very distressed. Some people take it as a great thing; they think it is very remarkable, and they go astray. Lots of people go astray by foolish prophecy, and lots of people are foolish enough to believe that they have tongues and interpretation and that they can be told what they should do. This is altogether outside the plan of God and bordering on blasphemy.

I do not preach my own ideas. That is, I never come on this platform and tell you what I think, because everybody can think. I come on this platform to tell you what I know. Therefore, what you need to do is to listen to what I know so that you may learn it. Then you can tell others what you have learned so that they will learn also.

How can I dislodge the power of Satan? How can I deal with satanic power? How may I know whether a voice is of God or not? Are there not voices that come from God? Yes. I am here believing that I am in the right place to build you on the authority of the Word of God. I believe I am in the right place to build you so that you will be able to deal with the things that I am talking about. I have come with a knowledge of how to deal with these things, because I myself have been dealing with them.

By this you know the Spirit of God: Every spirit that confesses that Jesus Christ has come in the flesh is of God, and every spirit that does not confess that Jesus Christ has come in the flesh is not of God. (1 John 4:2–3)

The grace of the Lord Jesus Christ, and the love of God, and the communion of the Holy Spirit be with you all. (2 Cor. 13:14)

The first Scripture tells us how to deal with power that is not of God but is satanic. The second Scripture reveals that we have within us a secure position in God so that we may have the communion of the Holy Spirit, who has all the latest plans, thoughts, and language from heaven. You know that a business executive is one who has a right to declare everything for the board of directors. And the Chief Executive of the world is the Holy Spirit. He is here today as a communication to our hearts, to our minds, to our thoughts, of what God wants us to know. So this Holy Executive, who is in us, can speak wonderful words. In fact, you will find that the Holy Executive will speak most of the words in this sermon.

I am dealing now with what you may know when you are fully in the Holy Spirit. The Spirit will teach you; He will *"bring to your remembrance all things"* (John 14:26). Now you do not need any man to teach you. But the anointing remains (1 John 2:27). You do not need teachers, but you need the Teacher, who is the Holy Spirit, to bring all things to your remembrance. This is the office of the Holy Spirit. This is the power of His communication. This is what John meant when he said, *"God is love"* (1 John 4:8). Jesus, who is grace, is with you. But the Holy Spirit is the speaker, and He speaks everything concerning Jesus.

There may be people here who have been hearing voices, and it has put them in a situation in which they have been moving from place to place. I am referring to voices that have caused tremendous issues in your lives, brought a great amount of distress and brokenheartedness, and led you into confusion and trouble. Why? You did not know how to judge the voices.

If a voice comes and tells you what to do, if a person comes and says he has a special prophecy that God has given him for you, you have as much right to ask God for that prophecy as they had to give it to you, and you have as much right to judge that prophecy according to the Word of God. You need to do this, for there are people going about pretending to be tremendous people, and they are sending people nearly off their wits' end because they believe their damnable prophecies, which never are of God but are of the Devil. I am very severe on this thing. God won't let me rest; I have to deal with these things because I find people everywhere in a terrible state because of these voices. How will we get to know the difference between the voice of God and the voice of Satan? The Scripture tells us.

> **INTERPRETATION OF A MESSAGE IN TONGUES:** "God brings liberty and fruit, 'precious fruit,' holy fruit, inward piety, holiness, entirety, separateness from the world, chastened by the Lord, filled with light, admiration of Jesus, and you see Him above all, full of light and truth, bringing forth into your hearts perfect peace and joy. This is tranquillity; this is God's desire for you, every one of you, to be filled with the joy of the Lord."

THE SPIRIT GIVES JOY AND GLADNESS

The difference between those who are being led by the Holy Spirit and those who are being deceived by Satan is joy, gladness, and a good countenance instead of sadness, sorrow, and depression. When Jesus comes with joy into the soul and lifts you higher and higher, it is the Spirit who gives light. When satanic power begins to rule, then there is weariness; then people's faces are like a tragedy; then their eyes glare as though they had passed through a terrible trial.

You are always right to *"test the spirits, whether they are of God"* (1 John 4:1). If you do not do it, then you will be sure to be caught napping.

MISLED BY A "VOICE"

I want to describe some specific cases to further explain this. Two sisters were saved in our meetings and were filled with the Holy Spirit. They were very lovely women, full of purity, truth, and righteousness. Their expressions were good; no one could look at them without admiring them.

Both of them worked in a telegraph office, and they both desired to be missionaries. They were so zealous to be missionaries that they were laying aside money and everything they could in order to be prepared to go to the mission field. They were zealous for God. Their very lives would reveal this in a meeting or anywhere else. They were so zealous for God that they would do anything.

One of them was operating a telegraph machine when she heard a voice in her head, a voice that said something along these lines: "Will you obey me? If you will obey me, I will make you the most wonderful missionary that ever lived." Oh, beloved, try the voices, try the spirits. Only the Devil promises such a thing, but she did not know this; she did not understand. This was exactly what she wanted; it was her heart's desire, do you see? And she was so moved by this. The voice added, "And I will find you all the money you need."

I never knew this kind of "leading" to come true, and you never will as long as you live.

For example, a man came to me and said, "I have in my hands a certain food for invalids that can raise millions of dollars for the missionaries."

I said to him, "I will not have anything to do with it." These things are not a success. God does not work in that way. If God wanted you to have gold, He could make it rain on your houses while you were away. He has all the gold, and the cattle on a thousand hills are His (Ps. 50:10).

Beloved, I want you to see that Jesus was the meekest man in the world. He had power to make bread or gold, and yet He never made it except for somebody else.

When anybody preaches for the kingdom's sake, God will provide. Seek to be filled with the Holy Spirit for the people's sake. Seek only God, and the rain will fall. The enduement of power will be made manifest in your mortal bodies if you are really in the Spirit.

387

Now, this young woman was so excited that her sister noticed it and went to her.

"What is it?" she asked.

"Oh! God is speaking to me," she said, "saying wonderful things to me."

She became so excited that her sister asked their supervisor if they could be excused for a while, because she saw that she would have to protect her. So the overseer allowed them both to be excused for a time, and they went into a room. The first sister became so excited with these messages, so believing that it was of God, that her white blouse became spotted with blood as she pricked her flesh with the nails of her hand.

That is never of God. What do I read about the wisdom of God? I read that it is full of peace and gentleness; it is willing to submit; it is without partiality; it is full of goodness and truth. (See James 3:17.) And, remember, if you ever know anything about God, it will be peace. If you ever know anything about the world, it will be disorder. The peace of God, which passes all understanding (Phil. 4:7), comes to the heart after you are saved. We are *"justified by faith,"* and *"we have peace with God through our Lord Jesus Christ"* (Rom. 5:1). The peace continues until it makes us full of the *"hope of the glory of God"* (v. 2).

God showed me a long time ago, and it has not been taken out of my mind, that if I was disturbed in my spirit and was not at rest, I had missed the plan. How can you miss it? In three ways.

First of all, you can miss it because you have taken on someone else's burden. All the time you are told to cast your burden on the Lord (1 Pet. 5:7). Any number of people are overflowing with sorrow because they are taking on someone else's burden. That is wrong. You must teach them and teach yourself that you have to cast your burdens on the Lord.

Second, if you do not have peace, you have gotten out of the will of God in some way. You may not have sinned. You can be out of the will of God without sinning. You can be out of the will of God if you are not making progress. If you have not made progress since yesterday morning, you are a backslider. Everybody is a backslider who is not going on with God. You are a backslider if you do not increase in the divine character and likeness of Christ. You have to move from state to state, *"from glory to glory,"* by the Spirit of the Lord (2 Cor. 3:18).

INTERPRETATION OF A MESSAGE IN TONGUES: "The Spirit quickens, moves, chastens, builds, builds, builds, and makes you free."

> This is like heaven to me,
> This is like heaven to me;
> I've crossed over Jordan to Canaan's fair land,
> And this is like heaven to me.

You won't be down in the dumps then. Do you know what Jordan represents? Jordan represents death, and you have crossed over death. Do not drop into it again.

You can lose your peace by missing some divine plan of God, and you can lose your peace because you have gotten your mind on something natural. A natural thing is a carnal thing. The Word of God says that the carnal things have to be destroyed because they are not subject to the law of God and cannot be subject to them (Rom. 8:7). Every carnal thing must be destroyed.

So you can miss the plan. Now, what is the plan? *"You will keep him in perfect peace, whose mind is stayed on You, because he trusts in You"* (Isa. 26:3). Examine yourself to see where you are. If you are not in perfect peace, you are out of the will of God.

Therefore, if these voices take away your peace, you will know they are not the will of God. But if the Spirit speaks, He will bring harmony and joy. The Spirit always brings three things: comfort, exhortation, and edification. He will make you sing *"songs in the night"* (Job 35:10). You will rise in high places, and you will not be afraid of declaring the works of the Lord. When the Spirit of the Lord is upon you and greatly active, you may *"go from strength to strength"* (Ps. 84:7), praising the Lord.

My wife and I were visiting at the home of these two sisters when they came in from work that day. We saw the distress. We saw the wild condition. If you are wild, that is the Devil. If you go breathlessly to the Bible, looking for confirmation of the voice, that is the Devil. The Word of God brings light. I must use it as the Word of Light. I must see it as the Light of Light. I must have it as the Light. I must not run up and down as if I had been hit with a stick.

I must be wise, because if I say I am baptized with the Holy Spirit, if I say I am a child of God, I must act so that people will know that I have been with God. (See Acts 4:13.) If there is anything I would resound through this meeting like a trumpet, it is this: *"Do not let your good be spoken of as evil"* (Rom. 14:16)!

Who is speaking now? It is the Spirit speaking to us, saying that He wants us in the world in such a way that we would not have anything—neither tongues, interpretations, prophecy, discernment, nor any kind of actions—except what would affirm that we have been with Jesus and that now the light has come, the truth has fallen upon us, and we have come into the wisdom of the Most High God. If you ever find a person who has given a prophecy but who will not allow that prophecy to be judged, as sure as anything, that prophecy never was right. Everybody who has a true prophecy is willing to come to the light so that everything will be made true according to the Word of God. So don't receive these things unless you know they are of God.

Well, what happened to the young woman? The voice came with such tremendous force that she could not let it go. Try the spirits. God will never do anything like that. He will never send you an unreasonable, unmanageable message.

The moment the girl became obsessed with what the voice said, what did the Devil say next? "You keep this a secret. Don't tell anybody. If you confide in anybody, let it be your sister, because she seems to understand you." So they confided in each other.

Now, that is surely as satanic as anything you ever heard in your life, because every true thing, every holy thing, does not need to be kept a secret under any circumstances. Anything that is holy can be told on the housetops; God wants you to be able to tell all.

My wife and I tried to help them. "Oh, God is speaking to me!" the young woman said. And we could not change her. That night she said that the evil power continued speaking, saying to her, "Tell no one but your sister. Go to the station tonight and wait for the train. The train will come in at thirty-two minutes past seven. Buy two tickets for Glasgow. After you have bought your tickets, you will have sixpence left."

This could be confirmed, and no one had to know but her sister. They went to the station. The train came in exactly at the right time. And there was just sixpence left after they had bought the tickets. Marvelous! Wonderful! This was sure to be right.

"See!" she said. "I have just the amount of money left after I have bought the tickets that the voice said I would." The train came in. The voice had said that a gentleman would be sitting in one of the coaches with all the money she would ever need. Directly opposite this gentleman, a woman with a nurse's cap would be sitting. The man would give her all the money, and they were to take it to a certain bank at a certain street corner in Glasgow.

Here was lack of presentation of thought. There are no banks open at half past seven, and, after investigation, it was discovered that there was no such bank in that place. Then what caused the young woman to obey the voice? It got her ear, and I will tell you what the danger is. If I had only five minutes I would say this to you: If you cannot be reasoned with, you are wrong. If you are right and everybody else is wrong, I don't care who you are, if you cannot bear examination, if what you hold cannot bear the light of the truth, you are wrong. It will save a lot of you if you will just think.

You may say, "Oh, but I know, I *know*." It is a very serious thing when nobody else knows but you. May God deliver us from such a condition. If you think you have some specialty, it is not unique; it can be repeated.

The train came in. They rushed from one end of the train to the other. There were no such people on the train. Then the voice came, "On the next platform, the next train." And they rushed over. Would you believe, those two young women were kept moving from platform to platform by those voices until half past nine at night?

Those voices went on. Ah, those evil voices. How will we know whether they are of God? When God speaks, He will speak with wisdom. When the Devil came to Jesus, he said, *"If You are the Son of God"* (Matt. 4:3). The Devil knew that He was the Son of God, and Jesus knew and answered, *"It is written, 'You shall worship the LORD your God, and Him only you shall serve'"* (v. 10).

Now, was there anything wrong with what was happening with these two young women? The wrong was that the first young woman ought to have judged the spirits. If she had asked, "Did Jesus come in the flesh?" the voice would have answered no. (See 1 John 4:3.) No satanic voice in the world and no Spiritualist medium will acknowledge that Jesus came in the flesh. The Devil never will, and he is the father of spiritualism mediums.

The same power said to the young woman, "Now that I know you will obey me in everything, I will make you the greatest missionary in the world."

We tried to console them, but nothing could be done; she was convinced it was the voice of the Lord.

There are two workings; the workings of the Spirit are always contrary to the workings of the flesh.

How could the two women have known at that moment that this was a false voice? Why, they could have known according to the Word of God. What does it say? *"Many false prophets have gone out into the world"* (1 John 4:1). Many, many voices, the Scripture says. Who are these false prophets after? Perhaps those with sincerity, earnestness, zeal, and purity. Who knows? These evil powers know. What is necessary to keep in our minds all the time? We must keep these things clearly in mind: What am I living for? What is the hope of my life? Do I have to be the greatest missionary in the world and a wonderful Christian worker, or does Jesus need to be glorified in my life to do as He wills with me for the world? The ripe grape is never as pure and perfect as it is just before it decays. The child of God is never as near to God—right at the summit—as he is when the Devil can come and say, "You are wonderful!"

It is satanic to feel that you are different from anybody else, that God has a special message for you, and that you are someone very particular. Every place that God brings you to in a rising tide of perfection is a place of humility, brokenness of heart, and fullness of surrender, where only God can rule in authority. It is not where you are somebody, but where God is everything and where you will be living for the exhibition of His glory.

It was three months before these two young women were delivered from this delusion. It took months and months of pleading, of crying bitterly. But God did deliver them, and they have been really wonderful missionaries in China. Thank God, there is a way out. The Devil's plan was defeated, but it was at tremendous cost, almost of their lives.

How could they have known that it was a false voice? How can you know? When a voice comes, no matter how it seems to you, you must test it. When a voice comes and it is strange, when it is persistently pressing you to do something and you are taken to a hard place and you know the difficulties are such that you can hardly conceive how this thing is possible, you have a position in the power of the Word of God to say to this evil power, "Did Jesus come in the flesh?" (See 1 John 4:3.) And the satanic power will say no. There never yet was a Spiritualist or anybody else who was under satanic power, anybody in a fit, anybody losing his mind, who has ever said that Jesus came in the flesh. Satanic forces will not admit it.

But the Spirit of the living God, the Holy Spirit, always says yes. And so you can get to know the difference. You have to listen. The Scriptures are clear on these things. We have to live in the place of knowing so that we are able to spiritually, divinely, discern whether these things are of God or not.

Did Jesus come in the flesh? Yes, and now the living Christ is within you. Christ came into you the moment you believed. There is a manifestation of it. You may live in such a way that Christ is greater than you. You may live in such a way that your language, your expressions, your actions, and everything speak of Christ. *"They realized that they had been with Jesus"* (Acts 4:13). You can live in such a way that the personality of Christ is exactly what Paul said: "Not I—I don't live anymore. Christ lives in me." (See Galatians 2:20.)

The Christ life, the Christ power, the personality of His presence may be in you in such a way that you could not doubt the Word of God. If you prayed, it would always be in faith, and as you preached, it would always be in faith. You *"live by the faith of the Son of God"* (Gal. 2:20 KJV) until your whole body is aflame with the faith of God. This is a divine position of a living attitude in which we live and reign in this beautiful place with Jesus.

This is an important word, and I am saying everything I can, by the grace of God and the revelation of the Spirit, to make you careful and yet careless: careful of satanic powers and careless when the power of God is upon you with anointing force, so that He Himself will be manifested, and not you.

A RUINED LIFE

Lots of people are brought down by the same thing that ruined the life of a young Christian I want to tell you about. For many years after I was baptized, the Lord graciously helped me. I laid hands upon people, and they received the Holy Spirit. I thank God that that power has not stopped. I believe in asking God, in *"lifting up holy hands"* (1 Tim. 2:8) and saying, "Father, grant that who-ever I place my hands upon will receive the Holy Spirit."

People have called me from various places to come and help them when they have had people they wanted to receive the Holy Spirit. Once a group from York, England, sent word saying that they had fourteen people whom they wanted to have baptized in the Holy Spirit, and would I come? They had all been saved since the last time I was there.

So I went. I have never in all my life met a group of people who were so intoxicated with a certain thing, which had happened since I had been there. In the open-air preaching, the power of God had been upon them, and many people had been gathered from the marketplace. Right there in the midst of them, they had drawn in a young man who had developed such a gift of teaching and such a gift of leading the people forward with God through the power of the Spirit that they said they did not believe there was another man like him in all of England. They were intoxicated beyond any-thing; they were drunk with it.

Did I rejoice with them? Certainly.

If there is anything that I love, it is the young men and young women. When Jesus began His ministry, He laid hands upon eleven who turned out to be the most marvelous men, and they were young men. When Paul was brought into the knowledge of the truth, he was a young man. Jesus began the great ministry of worldwide revival with young life.

World War I showed us that no man over forty years of age was good enough for that war. They had to have young blood, young life that could stand the stress of frost, heat, and all kinds of things.

God wants young people filled with the power of God to go into the harvest field, because they can stand the stress. Jesus knew this, and He got all young men around Him.

Weren't the disciples a lovely group? Yes, when He was in the midst of them. You are a lovely group of people because Jesus is in the midst of you, and you will be more lovely as you keep Him in your midst. You will be more lovely still if you refuse to live unless He is in your midst.

Moses said, *"If Your Presence does not go with us, do not bring us up from here"* (Exod. 33:15). And we have a right today to live in the presence of the power of the Holy Spirit.

As soon as I got to York, the people came around me and said, "Oh, we've gotten him! We've gotten him! The only thing that is needed now is that we want him to receive the Holy Spirit, and as soon as he receives, we will know we have gotten him."

Was anything wrong with that? No, I rejoiced with them.

Then the power of God fell. You know, we allow anything in a meeting before people receive the Spirit. Don't be afraid when people are on the floor. Lots of people roll around the floor and get their black clothes made white. Any number of things take place when the flesh is giving way to the Spirit. But after the Holy Spirit has come in, then we do not expect you to roll again on the floor. We only expect you to roll on the floor until the life of the personality of the Holy Spirit has gotten right in and turned you out; then you will be able to stand up and preach instead of rolling on the floor.

The new believers were all lying on the floor. It was a wonderful sight. The people came to me and said, "Oh! Oh! We've gotten him now!" Oh, it was so lovely! And when that young man spoke in tongues, they almost went wild. They shouted, they wept, they prayed. Oh, they were so excited!

The leaders came and said they were overjoyed at the fact. I said, "Be still; the Lord will do His own work."

In a short time, he was through in the Spirit, and everybody was rejoicing and applauding. They fell into great error there.

Oh, I do pray that God will save you from anything like this. I hope nobody would say to me, "Oh, you did preach well tonight." It's as surely of the Devil as anything that ever came to anybody. God has never yet allowed any human being to be applauded.

This young man was in the power of the Holy Spirit, and it was lovely. But they came around him, shaking his hand and saying, "Now we have the greatest teacher there is."

Was this wrong? It was perfectly right, and yet it was the worst thing they could have done; they should have been thankful in their hearts. I want to tell you that the Devil never knows your thoughts, and if you won't let your thoughts out in public, you will be safe. He can suggest a thought; he can suggest thoughts of evil. But that is not sin; all these things are from outside of you. The Devil can suggest evil things for you to receive, but if you are pure, it is like water off a duck's back.

One woman came up and said, "I wouldn't be surprised if you had another John the Baptist."

And they were all around him, shaking hands and saying, "Oh, now we've gotten him! Now we know you are the best teacher that has ever been in Pentecost yet."

Thank God, the young man was able to throw it all off, and he was in a beautiful place.

Again, before we left, this woman came up and said, "Will you believe? It is a prophecy I have received that you have to be John the Baptist."

Thank God, he put it off again. But how satanic, how devilish, how unrighteous, and how untrue it was!

That night, as he was walking home along a country road, another voice came, louder than the woman's, right in the open air: "You are John the Baptist!"

Again the young man was able to guard it off. In the middle of the night, he was awakened out of his sleep, and this voice came again: "Rise; get up. You are John the Baptist. Declare it!"

And the poor man this time was not able to deal with it. He did not know what I am now telling you. I tell you with a sorrowful heart that for hours that morning he was walking around York, shouting, "I am John the Baptist!" Nothing could be done. He had to be detained.

Who did it? Why, the people, of course.

You have no right to come around me or anybody else and say, "You are wonderful!" That is satanic. I tell you, we have plenty of the Devil to deal with without your causing a thousand demons to come and help. We need common sense.

How could that young man have been delivered? He could have said, "Did Jesus come in the flesh?" The demon power would have said no, and then the Comforter would have come.

Lord, bring us to a place of humility and brokenheartedness where we will see the danger of satanic powers.

Don't think that the Devil is a big ugly monster; he comes as an angel of light (2 Cor. 11:14). He comes at a time when you have done well, and he tells you about it. He comes to make you feel you are somebody. The Devil is an exalted demon.

Oh, look at the Master. If you could see Him as I see Him sometimes: He was rich, and yet He became poor (2 Cor. 8:9); He was in the glory, yet He took upon Himself the form of a servant (Phil. 2:6–7). Yes, a servant, that is the Lord. May God give us the mindset of the Beatitudes (Matt. 5:3–12) where we will be broken and humble and in the dust; then God will raise us and place us in a high place.

These are days when God wants you to build. God does not want to take away your glory; He wants you to have the glory, for Jesus came and said, *"And the glory which You gave Me I have given them"* (John 17:22). But what is the glory for? To place on the Master. Give Him all; let Him have all: your heart's joy, your very life. Let Him have it. He is worthy. He is King of Kings. He is Lord of Lords. He is my Savior. He died to deliver me. He should have the crown.

CHAPTER TWELVE

TESTING THE SPIRITS

God has never changed His mind concerning His promises. They are *"Yes"* and *"Amen"* (2 Cor. 1:20) to those who believe. God is the same yesterday and forever (Heb. 13:8). To doubt Him is sin. All unbelief is sin. So we have to believe He can heal, save, fill with the Holy Spirit, and transform us altogether.

Are you ready? What for? To be so chastened by the Lord, so corrected by Him that, as you pass through the fire, as you pass through all temptations, you may come out as Jesus came out of the wilderness, filled with the Spirit.

Are you ready? What for? To be so brought in touch with the Father's will that you may know that whatever you ask, believing, you will receive (Matt. 21:22). This is the promise; this is the reality God brings to us.

Are you ready? What for? To no longer know yourself according to the flesh (see 2 Corinthians 5:16), to no longer yield to the flesh, but to be quickened by the Spirit, living in the Spirit without condemnation, your testimony bright, cheerful, and full of life. This is the inheritance for you today.

DO NOT BELIEVE EVERY SPIRIT

The message the Lord wants me to speak to you about is in the fourth chapter of 1 John. I would like the day to come in which we would never come to a meeting without having the Word of God with us. The great need today is to have more of the Word. There is no foundation apart from the Word. The Word not only gives you a foundation, but it also puts you in a place where you can stand and, after the battle, keep on standing. Nothing else will do it. When the Word is in your heart, it will preserve you from desiring sin. The Word is the living presence of that divine power that overcomes the world. You need the Word of God in your hearts so that you might be able to overcome the world.

> *Beloved, do not believe every spirit, but test the spirits, whether they are of God; because many false prophets have gone out into the world. By this you know the Spirit of God: Every spirit that confesses that Jesus Christ has come in the flesh is of God, and every spirit that does not confess that Jesus Christ has come in the flesh is not of God. And this is the spirit of the Antichrist, which you have heard was coming, and is now already in the world.* (1 John 4:1–3)

If this passage were honeycombed right through our own circumstances, there would be no room for fear. We are dealing with a subject concerning satanic power so that we may be able to discern evil spirits.

We can so live in this divine communion with Christ that we can sense evil in any part of the world. In this present world, powers of evil are rampant. The man who lives in God is afraid of nothing. The plan of God is that we might be so in Him that we will be equal to any occasion.

"Beloved" (v. 1). That is a good word. It means that we are now in a place where God has set His love upon us. He wants us to listen to what He has to say to us because when His beloved are hearing His voice, then they understand what He has for them.

The passage continues:

> *You are of God, little children, and have overcome them, because He who is in you is greater than he who is in the world. They are of the world. Therefore they speak as of the world, and the world hears them. We are of God. He who knows God hears us; he who is not of God does not hear us. By this we know the spirit of truth and the spirit of error. Beloved, let us love one another, for love is of God; and everyone who loves is born of God and knows God. He who does not love does not know God, for God is love. In this the love of God was manifested toward us, that God has sent His only begotten Son into the world, that we might live through Him. In this is love, not*

399

that we loved God, but that He loved us and sent His Son to be the propitiation for our sins. Beloved, if God so loved us, we also ought to love one another. No one has seen God at any time. If we love one another, God abides in us, and His love has been perfected in us. By this we know that we abide in Him, and He in us, because He has given us of His Spirit. And we have seen and testify that the Father has sent the Son as Savior of the world. Whoever confesses that Jesus is the Son of God, God abides in him, and he in God. And we have known and believed the love that God has for us. God is love, and he who abides in love abides in God, and God in him. Love has been perfected among us in this: that we may have boldness in the day of judgment; because as He is, so are we in this world. There is no fear in love; but perfect love casts out fear, because fear involves torment. But he who fears has not been made perfect in love. We love Him because He first loved us. (1 John 4:4–19)

This is an inexhaustible subject. We should get a great deal out of this message that will serve us for an evil day and the day of temptation.

God is dealing with us as sons; He calls us *"beloved."* We are in the truth, but we want to know the truth in a way that will keep us free. (See John 8:32.) I want to help the people who have been so troubled with voices and with things that have happened that they have felt they had no control over them. And I want to help those people who are bound in many ways and have been trying in every way to get free. I believe the Lord wants me very definitely to deal with things that will be of an important nature to you as long as you live.

The fourth chapter of 1 John tells us specifically how to deal with evil powers, with evil voices. It tells us how we may be able to dethrone them and be in a place where we are over them. It shows us how we may live in the world not subject to fear, not subject to bondage, not subject to pain, but in a place where we are defeating evil powers, ruling over them, reigning in the world by this life of Christ. In this way, we will be from above, and we will know it. We will not be subject to the world, but we will reign over the world so that disease, sin, and death will not have dominion.

A keynote that runs through the entire Scriptures is that Jesus has vanquished and overcome all of the powers of the Devil and has destroyed his power, even the power of death. Whether we are going to believe it or not, this is for us. God sends out the challenge, and He says, "If you believe it, it will be so."

What will hinder us? Our human nature will. This has a lot to do with hindering God: when the human will is not wholly surrendered, when there is some mixture, part spirit and part flesh, when there is a division in your own heart.

In a house where there are two children, one may desire to obey his father and mother, and he is loved and is very well treated. The other is loved just the same, but the difficulty is this: the wayward boy who wants his own way does many things to grieve his parents, and he gets the whip. They are both children in the house; one is getting the whip, the other is getting the blessing without the whip.

There are any number of God's children who are getting the whip who know better than they are doing. So I want you to wake up to do what you know ought to be done, because there is a whipping for those who won't obey. Sin is never covered by your appearance, your presence, your prayers, or your tears. Sin can only be removed by repentance. When you repent deeply enough, you will find that the thing goes away forever. Never cover up sin. Sins must be judged. Sins must be brought to the blood of Christ. When you have a perfect confidence between you and God, it is amazing how your prayers rise. You catch fire, you are filled with zeal, your inspiration is tremendous, you find out that the Spirit prays through you, and you live in a place of blessing.

DEALING WITH EVIL POWERS

There are many people living today who are called Spiritualists. I call them "Devilists." I never give any quarter to them. If I see a spiritualism meeting advertised, I say, "There is a Devil-possessed meeting." I never encounter a Christian Scientist without knowing that he is also working the powers of darkness and that he is on the Devil's side. I never meet a Jehovah's Witness without knowing that he has changed the Word of God, and I know that God has removed him from the blessing.

INTERPRETATION OF A MESSAGE IN TONGUES: "On the housetop things will be declared. God will bring everything to light that has been in darkness. There is not one thing but what will have to be judged, and in the present time the believer in Christ is in the position of judging the Devil. 'The Prince of this World is judged,' and God is fulfilling His divine power when He is bringing us into perfect order through the Spirit, so that we voice the power of the Word of God, so that we deal with satanic influences, satanic power. In this world we are to overcome until we deal with every demon power, so that Christ comes at the top and reigns over us, because He has given us 'power and authority over all the power of the Devil.'"

So God, by the power of the Spirit, has given us a revelation of our position in Christ. Whatever happens in the world, we must see that every demon power must be dislodged, cast into the pit forever. We must recognize that God's Son is placed in power over the power of the Enemy; we must understand that anybody who deals falsely with the Word of God nullifies the position of authority that Christ has given him over Satan.

What did Christ say? In a very definite way, He said,

> If your hand causes you to sin, cut it off. It is better for you to enter into life maimed, rather than having two hands, to go to hell, into the fire that shall never be quenched; where "their worm does not die, and the fire is not quenched." And if your foot causes you to sin, cut it off. It is better for you to enter life lame, rather than having two feet, to be cast into hell, into the fire that shall never be quenched; where "their worm does not die, and the fire is not quenched." And if your eye causes you to sin, pluck it out. It is better for you to enter the kingdom of God with one eye, rather than having two eyes, to be cast into hell fire; where "their worm does not die, and the fire is not quenched." (Mark 9:43–48)

It is better to go into the presence of God with half your faculties than to go into hell with all your faculties. Jesus knew that hell is a reality, and He gave no quarter to it. And when He was dealing with demons, they were referred to as *"unclean spirit*[s]," (Mark 9:25 KJV), meaning that there is no clean demon power. All demon powers are unclean.

God wants a clean people. He is cleansing us from all the filthiness of the flesh so that when the Devil comes, he will find nothing in us. (See John 14:30.)

JUDGE YOURSELF BY GOD'S WORD

There are two ways of being in the place where God wants you to be. One is to see that you obey. The next is to examine yourself to see that *"you are in the faith"* (2 Cor. 13:5). If you do not judge yourself, you will be judged (1 Cor. 11:31). But if you judge yourself by the Word of God, you will not be condemned with the present evil world (v. 32).

SPIRITUALISTS REMOVED

One day we were having a meeting after the Holy Spirit came upon us, and the word got around that we had received the baptism of the Spirit, as we called it, and were speaking in tongues. Many people said we had received satanic power and were speaking in tongues through the power of the Devil. So the whole city was awakened. At this meeting there were two rows of Spiritualists— these demon-possessed people. The power of the Spirit was upon me, and I began speaking in tongues, and these demon powers began muttering, shaking, rolling, and all kinds of things.

I went off the platform, stood at the end of the two rows, and said, "Come out, you demons, in the name of Jesus!" The two rows of people filed out of their seats and went down the aisle and outside. When they got outside, they cursed and blasphemed and said all kinds of evil things. But thank God they were outside!

MEDIUMS HINDERED

One day I met a friend of mine in the street, and I said, "Fred, where are you going?"

"I am going—. Oh, I don't feel I ought to tell you," he said. "It is a secret between me and the Lord."

"Now, we have prayed together, we have had nights of communication, we have been living together in the Spirit," I said. "Surely there is no secret that could be hidden between you and me."

"I will tell you," he said. "I am going to a spiritualism meeting."

"Don't you think it is dangerous? I don't think it is wise for believers to go to these places," I said.

"I am led to go to test it according to Scripture," he replied. "They are having some special mediums from London."

He meant that they were having some people from London who were more filled with the Devil than the Spiritualists we had in our city of Bradford. They were special devils.

"I am going," he continued, "and I am going with the clear knowledge that I am under the blood of Jesus."

"Tell me the results, will you?"

"Yes, I will."

Now, beloved, I advise none of you to go to these places.

My friend went and sat down in the midst of the séance meeting, and the medium began to take control. The lights went low; everything was in a dismal state. My friend did not speak, but just kept himself under the blood, whispering the preciousness of the blood of Jesus. These more-possessed devils were on the platform. They tried every possible thing they could to get under control for more than an hour, and then the lights went up. The leader said, "We can do nothing tonight; there is somebody here who believes in the blood of Christ."

Hallelujah! Do you all believe in the blood, beloved?

INTERPRETATION OF A MESSAGE IN TONGUES: "See that you keep your heart in a place where the blood is covering you, where the Wicked One does not touch you, for has He not given 'charge over you to keep you in all your ways'? He will send His angels, and 'they will bear you up, lest you dash your foot against a stone.' It is the Lord your God who overshadows; it is the Lord your God who protects, for He 'will not slumber or sleep,' but He keeps you in the perfect place, like 'the apple of His eye,' in perfection."

GREATER IS HE WHO IS IN YOU

"Test the spirits, whether they are of God" (1 John 4:1). Be ready to challenge the Devil. Don't be afraid. You will be delivered from fear if you believe. You can have *"ears to hear"* (Matt. 11:15) or ears that do not hear. Ears that hear are the ears of faith, and

your ears will be so open to what is spiritual that they will lay hold of it.

When the Word of God becomes the life and nature of you, you will find that the minute you open it, it becomes life to you; you will find that you have to be joined up with the Word. You are to be the epistles of Christ (2 Cor. 3:3). This means that Christ is the Word, and He will be known in us by our fruits. (See Matthew 7:16–20.) He is the life and the nature of you. It is a new nature: a new life, a new breath, a new spiritual atmosphere. There is no limitation in this standard, but in everything else you are limited. *"He who is in you is greater than he who is in the world"* (1 John 4:4). When the Word of Life is lived out in you because it is your life, then it is enacted, and it brings forth what God has desired. When we quote something from the Scriptures, we must be careful that we are living according to it. The Word of God has to abide in you, for the Word is life and it brings forth life, and this is the life that makes you *"free from the law of sin and death"* (Rom. 8:2).

How to Test the Spirits

There are evil thoughts, and there are thoughts of evil. Evil thoughts are suggestive of the Evil One. We must be able to understand what the evil is and how to deal with it. The Word of God makes us strong. All evil powers are weak. There is nothing strong in the Devil; the weakest believer dethrones the Enemy when he mentions Jesus. "Young men, you are strong because you know the Word." (See 1 John 2:14.)

There are evil thoughts and thoughts of evil. Where do thoughts of evil come from? They come from the unclean believer, the man who is not entirely sanctified. Remember that the Devil does not know your thoughts; that is where the Devil is held. But God knows your thoughts; God knows all things. Satan can only suggest evil thoughts to try to arouse your carnal nature.

Yet if you are disturbed, if you are weak, if you are troubled or depressed, then you are in a wonderful place. If you never tell anybody about your evil thoughts, and you are not disturbed about them, the carnal powers have never been destroyed in you. But if you tell anybody, then it is proof that you are clean; it is because you are clean that you weep. If you are not disturbed, if you have no conviction, it is because of your uncleansed heart; you have let sin come in.

OVERCOMING EVIL POWERS

How can the believer believe so that he will not be tormented? The question is: How can we be master of the situation? We must know this Scripture: *"Every spirit that confesses that Jesus Christ has come in the flesh is of God"* (1 John 4:2). Did Jesus come in the flesh? Mary produced a Son in the likeness of God. In a similar way, the eternal seed that came into us when we believed produces a life, a person, which is *"Christ in [us]"* (Col. 1:27) and which rises up in us until the reflection of the Son of God is in everything we do. Mary produced a Son for redemption. God's seed in us produces a son of perfect redemption, until we live in Him and move by Him (Acts 17:28). In the name of Jesus, cast self out, and you will be instantly free.

The Holy Spirit has all power and all language. If you won't tell anybody when these suggestive evil powers come, it is proof that you are not sanctified. A Spiritualist will never say that Jesus came in the flesh. The Lord wants us to understand that spiritualistic evidences, and the like, are of the Devil.

A PLACE OF DISCERNMENT

We must be in a place where we can discern evil things and evil spirits. There is a place where we can bind these evil powers and, loosing the people, set them free. Read the ninth chapter of Mark. There is an exchange of life, of power, until it is absolutely as the Word says: *"He who is in you is greater than he who is in the world"* (1 John 4:4). God can change you until you will not be afraid of anything.

Life comes after you have been filled with the Holy Spirit. Get down and pray for power. You ask, "What is the problem when I come away from prayer and nothing changes?" There are two reasons for this. First, when you go into your place, lock the door. Should you pray silently? No—pray loudly. The Devil has never disturbed anybody who prayed aloud. There the Holy Spirit's power is a proof.

Next, if you will, you can rebuke, you can cast out, satanic powers. Rebuke Satan. Never cast a demon out twice, or he will run about and laugh at you. He will know you did not believe it the first time. *"Ask, and you will receive"* (John 16:24). The moment you ask, believe you will receive, and you will have it.

Now I am going to pray, "Father, in the name of Jesus, increase my compassion." Thank You, Lord, I have it. I know I have it.

CHAPTER THIRTEEN

QUESTIONS AND ANSWERS ON TESTING SPIRITS

Q: Do you claim that there is no shaking of the body after the baptism of the Holy Spirit?

A: I maintain that after anyone has received the Holy Spirit, there is no shaking and no falling on the ground. Shaking and falling on the ground is a very limited position, instead of an unlimited position. There may be a manifestation, but it is not edifying, and the manifestation you are to have is to be for edification. (See 1 Corinthians 14:12.)

If somebody were to stand up now and shake and shake until her hair came down, no one in the place would be edified, and no one would want it. If the person knew it was not edifying, she would seek a place that is better. What is that better place? To seek a gift.

I declare to you that no one can shake and do all these things and speak in tongues; the Spirit has a way out. And no one when giving an interpretation has these manifestations, because the Holy Spirit has a way out. You need to seek so that you may excel and not be doing things that bring discord and discredit to your position.

Q: Is it true that tongues and interpretation are not for personal guidance at any time?

A: Tongues and interpretation are never for guidance. There is no such thing in the Scriptures. Tongues and interpretation are similar to prophecy; they are to edify the church.

408

Q: Can satanic influences come to us in thought as well as audibly, in word?

A: Any number of people are troubled with thoughts. There are two kinds of thoughts: evil thoughts and thoughts of evil. Evil thoughts are suggestive powers that the Devil gives to see if he can arouse your carnal nature. If he can, it shows you have never been changed from your corruption and sin. If he cannot, it shows you are pure; the blood has cleansed you, and carnality is defeated. This is what Jesus meant when He said that when the Devil comes, he finds nothing in you. (See John 14:30.)

The Devil does not know your thoughts; he does not know the desire of your hearts; he does not know your language. Therefore, the Devil always suggests something in order to get something from you. If we would only realize that fact, we could come into meetings and bind this power so that Satan would have no chance at all. Jesus said, *"I give you the authority...over all the power of the enemy"* (Luke 10:19). We have a right to bind his power. If a person is troubled about evil thoughts, he is safe; if he is not troubled, he is in danger.

If you are troubled by evil thoughts, test them and say, "Did Jesus come in the flesh?" That demon will go. You have a right to know these things because they will keep you in a place of real victory. If you are not troubled about evil thoughts, you need to repent and ask God to purify your hearts.

Until you voice anything, the Devil does not know it. You have desired to have converts, you have desired to have a glorious time in your meetings, and you have voiced it, and then you have had to fight as if for life and death to get it. Why? Because all the Adversary's power came. Why? Because you declared it. He would not have known if you had not declared it.

Q: Should you ask God for inspirations in secret, so that the Devil cannot know?

A: No. Always pray aloud so the Devil will clear out. When Jesus said to pray in secret (Matt. 6:6), He did not mean that you are to pray silently. He meant that you are to go in your prayer closet and shout aloud. If you do not, you will find that the Devil will battle you in every way; you will fall asleep, for example. Pray aloud.

Q: If a person has made the mistake of declaring his position against the Devil so that the forces of hell are arrayed against him, what will be effective in destroying Satan's power?

A: It is no mistake to declare yourself against the Devil. We are talking about two different situations here. Suppose you declare something such as this: "We are going to have the greatest time on earth. We will have a revival. We will have a time of fasting," or something similar. You have guaranteed that those will be difficult times, because Satan will assail himself against you. He cannot dethrone you, he cannot hinder you, but he will do all he can to do it. He will hinder you from having the blessing sooner. If you are fighting demon powers, there is not the same liberty as if there were no demon powers fighting you. Nevertheless, it is a good thing to have them to fight. Don't be afraid of demon powers; don't be afraid of being in temptation, because the Scriptures are clear that if you are not worthy to be tempted, you are no good. (See 2 Thessalonians 1:4–5.)

Now, suppose I came into this meeting and I said, "Jesus, in Your name I bind the powers of darkness"? It is finished. Satan won't come here. But if I declare such and such a thing without guarding myself, I will have to fight to get it.

CHAPTER FOURTEEN

TONGUES AND THE INTERPRETATION OF TONGUES

TO ANOTHER [ARE GIVEN] DIFFERENT KINDS OF TONGUES, TO
ANOTHER THE INTERPRETATION OF TONGUES.
—1 CORINTHIANS 12:10

The manifestations of tongues and the interpretation of tongues are so closely related that it would be very difficult to deal with one without the other, and I believe that it will be very profitable for you if I explain the two together.

Why tongues? Why has God brought this gift into operation? There is a reason. If there were not a reason, it would not be there.

I love the concept of "God over all, through all, in all." I love the concept that God has all power over all the powers of the Enemy (see Luke 10:19)—in the heavenlies, on the earth, and under the earth. Where can you go where He is not present (Ps. 139:7–12)?

Why did God design it all? You must see with me that the gift of tongues was never in evidence before the Holy Spirit came.

INTERPRETATION OF A MESSAGE IN TONGUES: "The Spirit leads and will direct every thought, and so bring into your hearts the fruit, until the fruit in your own life will be a manifestation that God is truly in you."

May the Lord grant that to us. That is a very important word.

The old dispensation was very wonderful in prophetic utterances. Every person, whoever he is, who receives the Holy Spirit will have prophetic utterances in the Spirit unto God or in a human language supernaturally coming forth, so that all the people will know that it is the Spirit.

This is the reason we want all the people filled with the Holy Spirit: they are to be prophetic. When a prophecy is given, it means that God has a thought, a word in season, that has never been in season before—things both new and old. The Holy Spirit brings things to pass!

So when God fulfilled the promise, when the time was appointed (and it is a wonderful appointment), the Holy Spirit came and filled the apostles. The gift that had never been in operation before came into operation that wonderful day in the Upper Room, and for the first time in all of history, men were speaking in a new order; it was not an old language, but language that was to be interpreted.

This is very profound because we recognize that God is speaking. No man understands it. The Spirit is speaking, and the Spirit opens the revelation that we will have, without adulteration; God's word flows through the whole place.

Tongues are a wonderful display of this; they are to revive the people; they are to give new depths of thought.

If you ever want to know why the Holy Spirit was greatly needed, you will find it in the third chapter of Ephesians. You will be amazed. The language is wonderful. Paul said that he was *"the least of all the saints"* (Eph. 3:8), and yet God had called him to be a *"minister"* (v. 7). His language is wonderful, and yet he felt in his heart and life that there was something greater, that the Spirit had him, and he bowed his knees unto the Father (v. 14).

You cannot find in all the Scriptures words with such profound fruit as those that ring through the verses of Paul's remarkable prayer in the Holy Spirit. He prayed *"that you may be filled with all the fullness of God"* (v. 19), and *"that you...may be able to comprehend with all the saints"* (vv. 17–18). He prayed that you may be able to ask and think, and think and ask, and that it will not only be abundantly but that it will also be *"exceeding abundantly above all that"* you can *"ask or think"* (v. 20).

There is a man closing down and the Holy Spirit praying.

INTERPRETATION OF A MESSAGE IN TONGUES: "To this end He brings you together that He might pour into you the hidden treasure, for it is in you. God has refined you, first cleansed you, made you just like a vessel, that He might dwell in you and make all His acquaintance with you, that the Father, the Son, and the Holy Spirit should be primary over you, and you should just be exalted in Him, not in yourself, but He should have the glory."

THE REASON FOR TONGUES

You may have heard that three years ago I was in Los Angeles. God's blessing was upon those meetings. Some of you remember blessings received. But since the time I left, you have not known what I have done, because you have not been with me; you do not live with me. I might have lost anointing or favor with God. I might be like many people today who have lived holy lives and have received holy language, but now are living in a backslidden condition a life that is not worthy of the language. There are people today who have lived holy lives, preached sanctification, and their language has been helpful, but something has come in the way. They have kept their language. They have lost their zeal and fire, but they still hold onto the language. This can take place in anyone's life. So I ask you, you who think you stand, *"take heed lest* [you] *fall"* (1 Cor. 10:12). You cannot play with this.

I would like you to know that the speaker is no good unless he judges himself every day. If I do not judge myself, I will be judged (1 Cor. 11:31). It is not sufficient for me to have your good word; I must have the Master's good word. It is no good to me if I look good to you. If there were one thing between me and God, I would not dare to come onto this platform unless I knew that God had made me holy, for they who carry the vessels of the Lord must be holy unto the Lord (Isa. 52:11). And I praise God because I know:

> His blood can make the vilest clean,
>   His blood can make the vilest clean,
> His blood avails for me,
>   His blood avails for me.

Holiness! Whiteness! Purity! Zeal!

INTERPRETATION OF A MESSAGE IN TONGUES: "'Grieve not the Holy Spirit whereby you are saved,' but 'let everything be done decently and in order' so that God will have preeminence in all things and Christ will reign over the house, even

His house, of which He says, 'Whose house you are if you hold fast the profession of your faith without doubting.' So God is bringing us this morning to this holy place to bring us to see that we must only obey the Spirit."

WHEN A PROPHET IS OUT OF GOD'S WILL

As I said, you do not know what has taken place in my life since I was here. When the good people of the Angelus Temple wired to see if I could give them June or July, they did not know that I was still living in the center of God's holy will. Because I am only a man, it is possible that I might have grieved the Spirit. When I got up to speak here, what I said might have been only formal language without unction, nothing that would move the people. In this type of situation, someone in the place—and this is what tongues are for—someone in the place who is hungry for God and cannot rest because he is not getting the cream of the truth would begin travailing and groaning in the Spirit and speaking in tongues. Another person would travail in the same way, receiving the interpretation of these tongues, and would arise and give that interpretation, thus lifting the people where the prophet could not because he was out of the will of God.

TO KNOW THE MIND OF GOD

Then, you ask, what about situations in which you are preaching and prophesying and we are all getting blessed, and then we have tongues?

From time to time as I speak, I am so full of the glory and of the joy that my body is more full than my language can express. Then, instantly, the Spirit pours forth His word in tongues, and the power of God just lifts the whole place into revelation and words of life far beyond where we were.

Therefore, the church is to come together so that in the Spirit, the power of God can fall on Mary or John or William or Henry and move them, until, with the power of God moving through them, the people get the mind of God.

HOW TO USE TONGUES CORRECTLY

In the fourteenth chapter of 1 Corinthians, we have very definite instructions about tongues:

If anyone speaks in a tongue, let there be two or at the most three, each in turn, and let one interpret. But if there is no interpreter, let him keep silent in church, and let him speak to himself and to God. (1 Cor. 14:27–28)

There are three types of tongues, and the spiritual law concerning them is laid down in the Scriptures. But before we come to that, we must understand verse thirty-two of 1 Corinthians 14, or else there will be no success in this place: *"And the spirits of the prophets are subject to the prophets."*

YIELD TO THE HOLY SPIRIT

Unless you adhere to this word, every assembly where you are will be broken up, and you will cause trouble. Until you come to a right understanding of the Scriptures, you will never be pleasing to God. You are not to consider, under any circumstances, that, because you have a spiritual gift, it is right for you to use that gift, unless the unction of the Spirit is upon you.

You have to be very careful that you never use tongues and interpretation in confusion with prophecy. When prophecy is going forth and the truth is being heard and all the people are receiving it with joy and are being built up, then there is no room for tongues or interpretation. But just at the time when the language in my heart seems too big to express, then tongues come forth and God looses the whole thing, and we get a new purpose in that.

So you who have this wonderful gift of tongues must see to it that you never break in where the Spirit is having perfect right-of-way. But when the Spirit is working with you and you know there is a line of truth that the Lord desires to express, then let the name of God be glorified.

You see, God wants everything to be in perfect order by the Spirit. That is why Paul said, *"If anyone speaks in a tongue, let there be two or at the most three"* (v. 27). You will never find me speaking if three have spoken before me. And you will never find me interpreting any word in tongues if three have spoken already. This is in order to keep the bonds of peace in the body so that the people will not be weary, because there are some people who have known nothing about what is right.

Unless you come to God's Word, you will be in confusion and you will be in judgment. God does not want you to be in confusion or in judgment, but He wants you to be built up by the Scriptures, for the Scriptures are clear.

If the Lord reveals truth to me, and if I have said anything previously in relation to this that has not been absolutely scriptural, I will no longer say it. I allow God's Word to be my judge. If I find that anything I have said is not scriptural, I repent before God. As God is my Judge, I never say anything unless I believe it is the sincere truth. But if I find out later that it is not exactly in the most perfect keeping with the Word of God, I never say it again.

I believe there is a place to come to in which, after we have repented of a thing, we never have to repent of that thing anymore. I pray that God will give us that kind of superabundant revelation of common sense. It is because there is not a superabundant revelation of common sense that everybody is using nonsense. May the Lord help us to be true to God first; then, if we are true to God, we will be true to ourselves. Let God be first in the choice of our desires and our plans. Jesus must be glorified.

In 1 Corinthians 14:30 we read: *"If anything is revealed to another who sits by, let the first keep silent."* I hope that someday the church will so completely come into its beauty that if I am preaching and you have a revelation on that very thing, a deep revelation from God, and if you stand, I will stop preaching at that moment. Why? Because the Scripture says that if, when a prophet is speaking, anything is revealed to someone in the audience, let the first hold his peace and then let that other one speak.

Then the Scripture says, *"For you can all prophesy one by one, that all may learn and all may be encouraged"* (v. 31). This refers to the one who is preaching. He may be led to hold his peace while one in the midst of the congregation speaks his line of thought that is divinely appointed; then, after he finishes, another may have a prophecy, and he may get up, and so on, until you may have several who have prophesied and you have such revelations in this manner that the whole church is ablaze. I believe that God is going to help us so that we might be sound in mind, right in thought, holy in judgment, separated unto God, and one in the Spirit. Imagine all the people in this place being comforted and edified and going away from the church feeling that they have been in the presence of God, just because they have been obedient to the will of God.

Allow me to say this, and then you judge it afterward. You are not in the right place if you do not judge what I say. You are not to swallow everything I say; you are to judge everything I say by the Scriptures. But you must always use righteous judgment. Righteous judgment is not judging through condemnation, but it is judging something according to the Word of God. Righteous judgment is not focused on criticism, but righteous judgment judges the truth of something. In this way, the church may receive edification so that all the people may be built up according to the Word of God. That is the right judgment.

Perhaps not everyone will affirm and believe what I have to say about this. However, I truly affirm and believe, because God has thus revealed it to me, that the words *"Let there be two or at the most three, each in turn"* (1 Cor. 14:27) mean that very often the speaker will not have finished his message after giving the first insight. So often I have seen in an assembly of believers that the first person has spoken and the Spirit of the Lord has been mightily upon him, but the anointing is such that he did not finish his message with his first insight of truth, and he realizes that he is not through with that message. He speaks in the Spirit again, and we feel that the tide is higher. Then he speaks a third time, and the tide is higher still, and then he stops.

This has led me to believe that *"each in turn"* means that one person may be permitted to speak in tongues three times in one meeting. In our conferences in England, we very often have nine utterances in tongues, but there will only be three people speaking. You can have nine, but it is not necessary unless the Lord is prompting it. Sometimes I find that the Spirit will take us through in prophecy in such a way that there will not be more than one, sometimes two, people speaking. If I am correct, and I believe I am correct when I say this, when we are full of prophecy, the Spirit has taken our hearts and has moved them by His power. When this happens to me, I speak as fast as I can, but I am not expressing my own thoughts. The Holy Spirit is the thought, the language, and everything; the power of the Spirit is speaking. And when the power of the Holy Spirit is speaking like this, there is no need for tongues or interpretation because you are getting right from the throne the very language of the heart and the man. Then when the person's language gives out, the Spirit will speak and the Lord will give tongues and interpretation, and that will lift the whole place.

"At the most three." Don't say four or five, but three at the most. The Holy Spirit says it.

Now, three things are important before we go further.

THREE TYPES OF TONGUES

There are three types of tongues, and this is where the confusion comes in; this is where the people judge you, and this is where people have gone wrong.

I know, and every person who interprets tongues knows, that there is an intuition of divine appointment at this time. Every person who has been given the interpretation of tongues when they have had nothing before them except the glory of God will agree with this.

Now, the first type of tongues is when people are receiving the Holy Spirit, and they speak in tongues as an evidence of their baptism.

There is another approach to tongues when you are in a prayer meeting. You need to know exactly one thing: if you are in a prayer meeting when people are praying in the Spirit, never seek the interpretation. The Scripture declares it clearly: *"For he who speaks in a tongue does not speak to men but to God, for no one understands him; however, in the spirit he speaks mysteries"* (1 Cor. 14:2).

You will find that in a prayer meeting people will pray and speak in the Spirit, but it will be unto God and not for interpretation. Do not try to seek interpretation, for if you do you will find it is wrong. Never under any circumstances expect tongues to be interpreted where it is continually routine—the same and the same and the same. It is a spiritual language, but it is not the gift of tongues. What is it? You will find that it is adoration. It happens when the soul has been in a real definite position with God. Do not seek interpretation.

The third type of tongues is for interpretation. What type of tongues is this? *"Different kinds of tongues"* (1 Cor. 12:10). What are these *"different kinds of tongues"*? They are languages with perfect syllables. When a person gets up with a perfect language by the Spirit, you will find it is decisive, it is instructive, it is lovely to hear, it is divine in its appointment. It has to have interpretation because God is speaking to us in words that are not in our native language.

Tongues are to bring forth revelation and power in the church, to save it from lack and from being bound. Tongues and interpretation are for liberty among the people, to lift the saints and fill the place with the glory. God will open this to you; you will see what it means to have people among you full of the Spirit, and you will long to get the Spirit's mind.

The Interpretation of Tongues

Now, what is the interpretation of tongues? Interpretation is given by the same Spirit who moved the person with tongues. They are so moved by the power of the Spirit that they are in a place where they know that what God is burning within has to come out.

It is a common occurrence for me, after I give an interpretation, to meet people at the door as I go out who say, "Oh, that interpretation was lovely! I had it, too."

Another will come and say, "Oh, that interpretation was beautiful! I had it, you know."

I have had three in one meeting say that to me. "Oh, the interpretation was lovely! I had it."

Is it true? No. There is no truth in it at all. Why?

No interpreter has the interpretation, not one. I haven't gotten it myself. Then what do they have? They have the spirit of it. They knew it was the spirit of it, and they knew it was according to the mind of God. They got the sense of the knowledge that God was speaking and that it was the Spirit, and they knew it was right. The interpreter never has it. Why? Because he is in the channel where the Spirit is breathing every word. He does not get the word, the sentences and everything, ready-made. The Spirit breathes the whole thing, and the interpreter speaks as the Spirit gives utterance (Acts 2:4). So it is as divine and as original as the throne of God.

I want to show you the difference between genuine and false tongues. There are some people who get up and speak in tongues who give a little bit of tongues, and then a little more, and a little more, and they repeat themselves. Never give interpretation to such foolishness.

There are other people who get up and profess to interpret it, and they stutter and stammer, giving a word now and then. Is that interpretation? No. Do you think that the Holy Spirit is short of language? If you are stammering and stuttering and giving a word of interpretation now and then, don't believe it. It is not of God. What is it, then? People are waiting while some word in their minds comes forth, and they are giving you their minds. It is not interpretation.

I say all these things to save you from foolishness, to save you from people who want to be somebody. The Holy Spirit has shown me that all the time He is helping me, I have to be nothing. There is not a place where any man can ever be anything. It is in the death, union, and likeness of Christ that He becomes all in all. If we have not gone to death in the baptism of the Spirit, it shows me that we are altogether out of order.

The Spirit of the Lord has been speaking to you. I have felt the unction, I have realized the power, I have been speaking as fast as I could get it out, and the Spirit has given everything. For once in our lifetimes, we have been in the presence of the Holy Spirit. We have been where there has been the manifestation of the glory, where God is speaking to our hearts, where He is bringing us to a place of inhabitation in the Spirit.

We need to cherish this meeting as a holy meeting with God. See that you are built squarely on the authority of God. See that your testimony on salvation, sanctification, the gifts, the baptism, is biblical. Then you cannot be troubled by the Enemy. You will be above the Enemy; you will be able to say to the Enemy, *"Get thee behind me"* (Matt. 16:23 KJV), and he will get!

What are you ready for now? Are you ready for anything? Don't forget you have to go over the top. The top of what? The top of yourself, the top of your opinions and fancies and whims and foolish acts. You have to dethrone them; you have to have a biblical building; you have to be in the Scriptures. *"For God has not given us a spirit of fear, but of power and of love and of a sound mind"* (2 Tim. 1:7).

When people say to me, "Oh, I have nervous symptoms; I have a nervous weakness," I know immediately that only one thing is wrong. What is it? It is a lack of knowing the Word. *"Perfect love casts out fear."* And there is no torment, no fear, in love (1 John 4:18).

I want you to get the Word of God into your heart until the demon powers have no power over you. You are over the powers of fear. Then I want you to understand that the baptism of the Holy Spirit is a love beyond any you have ever had; you are to have power after the Holy Spirit comes (Acts 1:8), and it is power over the Enemy, over yourself, and over your human mind. Self has to be dethroned, Christ has to be enthroned, and the Holy Spirit has to enlarge His position.

Go over the top and never slide down again the back way. If you go, you go forward, and you go into victory from victory, triumphing over the Enemy, having liberty in your captivity (see Ephesians 4:8), rightly rejoicing in the triumph of God.

Faith is the victory (1 John 5:4). Faith is the operation in your heart. Faith is the stimulation of the life of the Master. When you stand in faith, you are in a position in which God can take you to the place where you are *"over all"* (Luke 10:19) by the power of God.

Believe that no power of the Enemy will have power over you. Rebuke him. Stand on the authority of the Word and go forth into victory. I want you to be saved, healed, and blessed through what God's Word says.

CHAPTER FIFTEEN

THE PURPOSE OF TONGUES

I THANK MY GOD I SPEAK WITH TONGUES MORE THAN YOU ALL;
YET IN THE CHURCH I WOULD RATHER SPEAK FIVE WORDS WITH MY
UNDERSTANDING, THAT I MAY TEACH OTHERS ALSO, THAN TEN
THOUSAND WORDS IN A TONGUE.
—1 CORINTHIANS 14:18–19

This Scripture has been greatly misunderstood. Here the apostle Paul was saying that he spoke in tongues more than any others. Now, you can understand that he felt he spoke in tongues more than all of them, meaning that he lived in the utterances of the Spirit. Very likely, this would be lovely!

I remember one time in London when I asked for a meeting to commence at 7:30 P.M. I was not well acquainted with London, and I knew I had two hours to spare before the meeting. I was walking in one of the busiest places in London; all the theaters were just getting ready for their big Saturday night.

"Now, Lord," I said, "let me just be enveloped in Your glory for these two hours in the midst of the world."

And I went up and down Fleet Street and the Strand, lost in the Spirit, in tongues the whole time. It was lovely. Yes, the world was filled with *"the lust of the flesh, the lust of the eyes, and the pride of life"* (1 John 2:16), but God had His child in the midst of these blazing worldly affairs, lost in the Spirit.

I want you, I implore you, beloved, to desire earnestly to be in God's will so that at any time, wherever you are, you may pray in the Spirit, you may sing in the Spirit, you may have a good time thinking about the Lord. Remember that it is at these places and times and seasons when the Father and the Son come and make themselves known to you.

Now, a word in season regarding the next point. Paul knew that if the whole church turned to tongues, and tongues only, there would be confusion and much distress, and there would not be that lift of divine power and fellowship that Paul knew was needed.

So Paul's great heart as a builder of churches was moved; he saw that the Lord was breathing through him this glorious desire to form these churches, and he said to the Corinthians, in effect, "Think seriously, and let your speaking be with carefulness. The people who have been filled with the Spirit and speak in tongues should not go on constantly with that; they should not come to the meeting and continually have it taken up with speaking in tongues."

You know, the flow of the Spirit through you is very lovely; yes, it is very lovely, but we must always be mindful that our brother and sister sitting next to us have to be helped. There are weak people in the church who need your careful attention. Then there are people of different kinds of temperament and makeup. We must always remember that we have to guard the church, look after it, keep it with sober mind, until no person coming in may be taken up with the thought, "Why, these people are mad! There they are, all speaking in tongues." (See 1 Corinthians 14:23.)

Paul said, "I would rather speak five words with my understanding than ten thousand words that they couldn't understand." (See verse 19.)

Wasn't he right? Wouldn't I prefer the same thing? Is there anybody who is really in wisdom who would dare to continue speaking in tongues without interpretation and without opening the knowledge of God to the people? Who would dare to do that? It would be foolishness, it would be madness, and you would lose the opinion of the people.

You need to remember that whatever you do when you are in the church of God, you must seek to excel to the edifying of the body of Christ.

TONGUES, A SIGN TO THE UNBELIEVER

There is a word here that says that tongues are *"a sign"* for the unbeliever: *"Therefore tongues are for a sign, not to those who believe but to unbelievers"* (1 Cor. 14:22). We have a wonderful word there, and I know it will require some explanation. It is important, and I want to explain it so that it edifies you.

A friend of mine was attending a Wesleyan brotherhood meeting in England, a large, packed meeting. He saw a young man there who was full of desire for the salvation of his people. He looked it, and his body posture and his face looked it. My friend knew he was laboring there under great difficulty.

At the close of the service, he wrote him a check. He said, "Take this check and go to Bradford to Brother Wigglesworth, a friend of mine, and have a rest in his home. All you have to do is to say that I have sent you. They will take you in and make you comfortable."

When this young man got the check, he was in need of a rest, and he said to my friend, "Yes, I will go, and I thank you."

He arranged to go the next Friday. The first thing he did when he got to Bradford was to go to the Young Men's Christian Association to inquire if they knew anything about Wigglesworth.

"Oh, yes, we know everything about him. Why?"

"I have brought a letter of introduction to him and have been advised to go to his home for a rest."

"Now, you be very careful," they said. "This man is among those people who believe in tongues, and we believe it is of the Devil. So you be careful lest you be taken in."

"Oh!" he said. "Don't be afraid; they will not take me in. I am too wise for that."

So he came.

I want you to notice that the Scripture passage we are dealing with now is about tongues as an evidence to the unbeliever—not to the believer, but to the unbeliever.

This man came to my house full of unbelief. He is a great preacher and a wonderful man with great abilities, and I tell you— I know him well—that he is a godly man. But he was full of unbelief.

There are any number of people who are believers filled with unbelief. I have very little difficulty when I am dealing with a sinner about being healed. I scarcely ever see a sinner who knows nothing about Jesus fail to be healed when I pray for him. But if I pray for a believer, I very often find that he is not healed. Why? There is unbelief in the believer. It is a very astounding thing.

God speaks in the old prophetic language nine times as much to the backslider as He does to the sinner. So I want you to know there is no place for you except only to believe what God says.

When you come to that place, God will bless you; you will be amazed at how much He will bless you.

INTERPRETATION OF A MESSAGE IN TONGUES: "For God has not chosen you that He might make you as a waster, but He has chosen you to bring you on the hill of perfection, that you might know that there will not be weakness in you but strength and character, for God has chosen you."

This message is for someone in the meeting: "God has chosen you." Do not be afraid. God has chosen you.

To resume my story, when the young man got to my house, my wife was in the house alone. He went in and he talked, and talked, and talked, and talked. When I got home, my wife came out and said to me, "We have the strangest man we have ever had in our house. He has been in there for half an hour, and he has never stopped talking. You never heard such a talker."

"Let him alone," I said. "He will come to an end."

I was introduced to him, and he went on talking. He talked through the dinner hour and right through to nighttime.

That night we were having a meeting at our house. He didn't stop talking. He knew that if he stopped, he would allow something else into his mind, so he was going to talk and block everyone else who talked. He wasn't willing to be taken in with this.

The meeting began to fill up; the room was packed.

"Brother," I said, "you have talked ever since you came. We are now going to pray. It is our meeting night; you must cease to speak."

He got down before God. My, it was wonderful! The power of God fell upon us, and something happened that never happened before, as far as I can remember. We always began our meeting with a song—always—but this time we began it in an attitude of prayer.

At one side of the fireplace knelt one young woman and at the other side of the fireplace knelt another. I have never known it to happen before or since, but, deliberately, instead of praying, those two began speaking in tongues.

As soon as they began speaking in tongues, this man jumped up, startled. He ran to the one nearest him, his hands on his ears, and bent down over the girl; then frantically he ran to the other, then back to the first, then to the other one.

Finally he came and said to me, "Can I go to my room?"

"Yes, Brother."

He was shown to his room.

We had a wonderful meeting. At about 3:30 the next morning, he came to my door and knocked.

"May I come in?" he called.

"Yes," I said. "Come in."

As soon as he got in, he stammered, "Bl—bl—bl—" with his hand to his mouth. "It's come! It's come!"

"Go back to bed, Brother," I said.

The next morning he came down to breakfast.

"Oh, wasn't that a wonderful night!" he exclaimed.

"Which do you mean?" I asked.

We had had a wonderful time. I wanted to know what he had done.

"Oh!" he said. "When I came here, I heard in Bradford that you had received the power of the working of evils; I was warned to keep away, and I was filled with unbelief. I was determined that nothing of that would affect me. I made up my mind that I would talk every moment. But when you told the people to go to prayer, the moment those people began speaking in tongues, I went to them. I know Greek and I know Hebrew, and one was saying to me in Greek, 'Get right with God,' and the other was saying in Hebrew, 'Get right with God.'"

Oh, yes, God has a way to do it, and God can do it. When we get unbelief out of the way, the baptism of fire, revelation, the gifts of the Spirit, the harmony, the comfort, the blessed unction will abound until there will never be a dry meeting; every meeting will be filled with life and power and joy in the Holy Spirit.

Continuing his story, this man said, "When I heard that, I knew it was for me. I went upstairs and I repented. I knew I had been wrongly interpreting what God meant, and I repented. As I repented, I found myself overcome by the power of the Spirit. I tried to resist, but God was dealing with me in such a way that I fell down under the power of the Spirit over and over, until God sanctified me. At 3:30 the power of God fell upon me. I found myself speaking as the Spirit gave utterance, and I came to your door."

That man is a wonderful man today. God has blessed him everywhere.

CHAPTER SIXTEEN

A MORE EXCELLENT WAY

P raise the Lord! The Word of God is very clear regarding this: *"Let everything that has breath praise the LORD. Praise the LORD!"* (Ps. 150:6). If you ever get to the place where you cannot praise the Lord, it is a calamity in your life, and it is a calamity to the people who are around you. If you want to take blessing into homes and make all the people around you know that you have something more than an ordinary life, you must know that God has come to supplant you and put within you a perfect praise.

God has a great place for us, so that His will may be done and we may be subject to His perfect will. When that comes to pass, no one can tell what may happen, for Jesus reached the highest place when He said, *"For I have come down from heaven, not to do My own will, but the will of Him who sent Me"* (John 6:38). So there is something in a place of yielding where God can have us for His own.

God has a choice for us all so that we might lose ourselves in God in a way we have never done before. I want to provoke you to love so that you will come into a place of blessing, for God wants you to be blessed so that you will be a blessing.

Beloved, believe today that God has a way for you. Perhaps you have never come that way before. God has a way beyond all your ways of thought. He has a choice and a plan for you.

There is a great need today. People are hungry for truth. People are thirsting, wanting to know God better. There are thousands *"in the valley of decision"* (Joel 3:14), wanting someone to take them right into the depths of God.

Are you ready to pray? You say, "What should I ask for?"

You may not know what to ask for, but if you begin, the Spirit knows the desire of your heart, and He will pray according to the mind of God. You do not know, but God knows everything, and He is acquainted with you altogether and desires to promote you.

So I say, "Are you ready?" You say, "What for?" Are you ready to come promptly into the presence of God so that you may ask this day as you have never asked before? Ask in faith, nothing doubting, believing that God is on the throne waiting to anoint you afresh today.

Are you ready? What for? Are you ready to be brought into the banquet house of God, even as Esther came in before King Ahasuerus? God will put out the scepter, and all that your heart desires He will give to you. (See Esther 5–7.)

Father, in Jesus' name we come before You believing in Your almightiness, that the power of Your hand does move us and chasten us. Build us. Let the Word of God sink into our hearts this day. Make us, O God, worthy of the name we bear, that we may go about as real, holy saints of God. Just as if You were on the earth, fill us with Your anointing, Your power, and Your grace. Amen.

HUMILITY AND COMPASSION

It is very important to minister in the gifts of the Spirit in the proper way. What a serious thing it would be, after waiting for the enduement of power for months and months and months, to fail God because we turned to some human desire just because we liked it.

I want to say at the beginning that there is no anointing like the unction that comes out of death, when we are dead with Christ. It is that position that makes us live with Him. If we have been conformed to His death, then, in that same death, like Paul, we will be made like Him in His resurrection power (Phil. 3:10–11).

But do not forget that Jesus was coequal with the Father and that He made Himself of no reputation when He became man and came to earth (Phil. 2:6–7). He did not come out and say that He was this, that, or the other. No, that was not His position. Jesus had all the gifts. He could have stood up and said to Peter and John and James and the rest of them, when the dead son was being carried through the gate of the city of Nain (see Luke 7:11–15), "Stand to one side, Peter. Clear out of the way, John. Make room for Me,

Thomas. Don't you know who I am? I am coequal with the Father. I have all power; I have all gifts; I have all graces. Stand to one side; I will show you how to raise the dead!"

Is that how He did it? No! Never. Then what made it come to pass?

He was observant. The disciples were there, but they did not have the same observance. Observance comes from an inward holy flame kindled by God.

What did He see? He saw the widow and knew that she was carrying to burial that day all her help, all her life. Her love was bound up in that son. There she was, broken and bent over with sorrow, all her hopes blighted.

Jesus had compassion upon her, and the compassion of Jesus was greater than death. His compassion was so marvelous that it went beyond the powers of death and all the powers of demons.

"Bless the LORD, O my soul, and forget not all His benefits" (Ps. 103:2). Isn't He a lovely Jesus! Isn't He a precious Savior! Don't you see that if we bear in our body the marks of Jesus (Gal. 6:17) or the life of the manifestation of Jesus, if we live only as Jesus is manifested, if people realize that we have *"been with Jesus"* (Acts 4:13), as they realized it of Peter and John, then that would pay for everything? Oh, it would surely be beautiful!

PRESUMPTION

These meetings are not ordinary meetings. The Holy Spirit is among us; Jesus is being glorified. We are not seeking our own in these meetings, but we are seeking to provoke one another to holiness and character (Heb. 10:24) so that we may be of the same mind as Jesus. The same manifestation that was in Him has to be in us.

I must never, under any circumstances, as long as I live, take advantage of God or Jesus or the Holy Spirit. I have to be subservient to the power of God.

Let me give you a little illustration that will help you in thinking about this.

One day a young man got very elated because he had received the baptism in the Holy Spirit, and he got into a place that most people seemed to fail to see was the wrong place. This young man was on the platform during a meeting, and he said, "I am baptized with the Holy Spirit. I can cast out devils. Come, I can cast them out!"

There was a poor man there who had been bound by the Devil for many, many years, so bound that he was helpless. He could not help himself; he was bound in every way. He had never heard such words before, and when he heard them, he was so moved that he struggled out of his seat, took hold of the chairs, and went down among the people in the aisle. He was a poor helpless man who was seeking relief the first time he heard that he could be delivered.

He went up and stood before the preacher and cried out, "Cast them out! Please cast them out! Help me; please cast them out!"

The young man did all he could, but he could not do it. The church was broken; the whole place was brought into travail. Oh, they wept and they cried because it was not done.

A PERFECT WAY

It never will be done that way. That isn't the way to do it. But there is a way to minister in all the gifts of the Spirit, and it is the way that is in the Scriptures. Let us look into this perfect way that is found in 1 Corinthians 13, starting with the first verse: *"Though I speak with the tongues of men and of angels, but have not love, I have become sounding brass or a clanging cymbal."*

Did you ever read a verse like this? It is the state of being brought into a treasury. Do you know what a treasury is? A treasury holds or handles priceless things.

God puts you into the treasury to hold or handle the precious gifts of the Spirit. Therefore, so that you may not fail to handle them correctly, He gives you a picture of how you may handle them.

What a high position of authority, of grace, the Lord speaks about in this verse! *"Speak with the tongues of men and of angels."* Oh, isn't that wonderful!

There are men who have such wonderful qualifications for speaking. Their knowledge in the natural realm is so surpassing that many people go to hear their eloquent addresses because the language in them is so beautiful. Yet, through the baptism in the Holy Spirit, God puts you right in the midst of them and says that He has given you the capability to speak like men, with power of thought and language at your disposal, so that you can say anything.

People are failing God all the time all over the world because they are taken up with their own eloquence, and God is not in it. They are lost with the pretentiousness of their great authority over language, and they use it on purpose to tickle the ears and the sensations of the people, and it profits nothing. It is nothing. It will wither up, and the people who use it will wither up.

Yet God has said there is a way. Now, how would language *"of men and of angels"* (1 Cor. 13:1) come to prosper?

When you wept through to victory before, you were able to do anything. You were so undone that unless God helped you to do it, you couldn't do it. You were so broken in spirit that your whole body seemed to be at an end unless God reinstated you. Then the unction came, and every word was glorifying Jesus. Every sentence lifted the people, and they felt as they listened, "Surely God is in this place! He has sent His Word and healed us." (See Psalm 107:20.) They saw no man there except Jesus. Jesus was so manifested that they all said, "Oh, wasn't Jesus speaking to our hearts this morning!"

If you minister in this way, you will never become nothing. Tongues of men and angels alone will come to nothing. Yet if you speak with tongues of men and angels that are bathed in the love of God until it is to Him alone that you speak, then it will be written down forever in the history of the glory.

Never think for a moment that the Acts of the Apostles has been completed. It is an incomplete book. When you read Revelation, it is complete. You cannot add to or take from this wonderful truth of prophecy. It is complete. And so, when you are used only for and desire only the glory of God, your acts, life, ministry, and power will be an endless recording in the glory of heaven—for the acts of the apostles are being recorded in the glory.

So let the Lord help us to know how to act in the Holy Spirit.

INTERPRETATION OF A MESSAGE IN TONGUES: "Set your house in order, for unless you die, you cannot live. For God is coming today and taking us—others may be left, but we are taken—taken on with God, taken into God, moved by the power of God, until we live and move in God and God has us as His channel, breathing through, divinely fixing, bringing forth words 'new and old.' And God is moving in the midst, and His people are being fed with 'the finest of the wheat.'"

We have a great salvation, but some people limit it. I believe in eternal salvation. The question has been asked me, "Do you believe that after you are saved, you are forever saved?" The Scriptures are very clear on this, and they are the words of Jesus. What does He say? *"My sheep hear My voice, and I know them, and they follow Me"* (John 10:27).

I do not believe that you are a sheep if you do not follow. But if you follow, you are all right; if you do not follow, it shows you were never right. So if you are all right, you will remain right, and you will end up right.

Do not forget that it is only those who hear His voice who belong to the fold. And so, if you are acting indiscreetly, carelessly, frivolously, and sinfully, you have never been in it; you are a stranger to it. *"My sheep hear My voice...and they follow Me."* They will not listen to the voice of a stranger (v. 5), and they have not turned aside to everything else. They live—and, oh, it is a lovely life—they live in the will of God.

PROPHECY AND GOODNESS

Let us look at the second verse of 1 Corinthians 13:

And though I have the gift of prophecy, and understand all mysteries and all knowledge, and though I have all faith, so that I could remove mountains, but have not love, I am nothing. (1 Cor. 13:2)

This second verse is like the first, only the Word of God is very remarkable. It starts like this, brings you to a place where there is no condemnation, and then fills you up where there is no separation. That is God's plan.

Lots of people desire to have faith; lots of people desire to have prophecy; lots of people long to know mysteries. Who knows mysteries? *"The secret of the LORD is with those who fear Him"* (Ps. 25:14). Don't change the Scriptures. *"The just shall live by faith"* (Rom. 1:17). Do not alter the Scriptures. It takes a just man to live by faith.

Do not forget that prophecy is beautiful when you understand the principle of it. Prophecy is the sixth gift mentioned in 1 Corinthians 12. What fruit or grace do you think would coincide with prophecy? Why, goodness, of course.

Why goodness? Because if you are living in holiness, entire sanctification, perfection, you would never take advantage of the Holy Spirit and would speak only as the Spirit gave prophecy. You would never say human things just because you had the gift of prophecy. You would speak according to the Spirit, giving prophecy because you are holy.

When you speak in the natural after you have received the gift of prophecy, it is because you have come to be nothing; you are nothing; you are not counted in the great plan of the great purpose of God. But if you are hidden in Christ and your whole heart is perfected in God, and you will prophesy only when the Spirit of the Lord is upon you, then it will be something that lasts forever. People will be blessed forever, and God will be glorified forever.

FAITH WITHOUT LOVE

Suppose that I have all faith so that I could move mountains. Now, suppose that I also have a big farm, but that some of my farmland is not very profitable. It is stony; it has many rocks on it as well as some little mountains that are absolutely untillable and do no good. But because I have faith without love, I say, "I will use my faith, and I will move this land. I do not care where it goes as long as my land is clean."

So I use my faith to clear my land. The next day, my poor next-door neighbor comes and says, "I am in great trouble. All your wasteland and stony, rocky land has been tipped onto mine, and my good land is ruined."

And I, who have faith without love, say to him, "You get faith and move it back!"

That profits nothing. If God brings you into a place of faith, let it be for the glory of God. Then, when you pray, God will wonderfully answer you; nothing will hinder your being used for God, for God delights to use us.

Gifts are not only given; they are also increased to those who can be used, who can keep in a place of usableness. God keeps these yielded ones in a place of being continually supplanted—a new place that is deeper, higher, holier, richer, more heavenly.

In addition, gifts are not only useable, but God is also glorified in Jesus when you pray *"the prayer of faith"* (James 5:15). Jesus Himself said, "When you pray believing, the Father will be glorified in the Son." (See John 14:12–13.)

SACRIFICE NOTHING WITHOUT LOVE

We will move on now to the third verse:

And though I bestow all my goods to feed the poor, and though I give my body to be burned, but have not love, it profits me nothing. (1 Cor. 13:3)

Though I have such means that I can lay my hands on millions of dollars, though I can do all kinds of things with the money, and though, after I have given it all, I show the people more by giving my body to be burned, saying, "I will show the people what kind of material I am made of!" this is nothing, nothing! Your gifts will perish unless the gifts are used for the glory of Jesus. Five dollars given in the name of the Lord is of more value than thousands without acknowledging Him.

A man came to me, and we had long talks about the workings of the Lord. He told me, "I was in a very difficult place. I had been working very hard in the church and had given all my strength...."

Oh, I see such godly, holy people doing more than they ought to, thereby giving themselves away. Don't you know that your body belongs to God (1 Cor. 6:19–20), and that, if you overtax your body, God says He will judge you for it? We have to be careful because the body that is given to us is to exhibit His power and His glory, and we cannot do this if we give ourselves all the time to work, work, work, work, work and think that that is the only way. It is not the way.

The Scriptures teach us that Jesus had to go and renew His spiritual vision and power in solitude with His Father (Mark 1:35), and it was also necessary for the disciples to draw aside and rest awhile (Mark 6:30–31). Couldn't Jesus give them all they needed? My dear brother, whatever God gives you, He will never take away your common sense.

Suppose I unwisely overextended my body and knew that I had done so? How could I ask anyone to pray for me unless I repented? We must be careful. Our bodies are the temples of the Holy Spirit, and He has to dwell in them, and they have to be for His purpose in the world. We are not working for ourselves; God is to be glorified in our bodies. Lots of people today are absolutely withered up, years before their time, because they went beyond their knowledge. But dare to believe.

Let me tell you a personal story to illustrate this. In 1914 the Lord moved upon me in England to tell the people that I was going to America, coming in through Canada.

"Well, Lord," I said, "You know You will have to do a miracle, and You must do it sharp if You mean business, because I want to be in haste about this if it is Your plan. The first thing is that, as you know, I have a bad memory. You will have to work a miracle there. The next thing is that You will have to find me all the money because I cannot leave my children without money, and I have no money to go, so You will have to find a lot."

It was amazing how the Lord began to provide it. It was coming so fast that I said to the people, "Oh, the Lord has sent so much money that I am sure I am going!"

Then He stopped. There was no more money.

"Lord! Lord!" I said, "I know I have grieved You, and I repent. If You begin again to show me it is Your will, I won't tell anybody."

And it commenced again, falling as gently as rain.

My boy said to me, "Father, Mother has gone to heaven. If you go on this trip, it will be very lonely for me without you."

The front doorbell rang. I said to him, "George, go answer the front door, and let the Lord speak to you through this ring at the door whether I have to go or not."

There was a letter.

"Now, George," I said, "open that letter, and whatever is in the letter, read it, and let that suffice you whether I have to go or not."

George opened the letter. That letter had been traveling for six weeks; it began coming just about the time I repented. In it was a check for twenty-five pounds.

"What about it, George?" I asked.

"Oh!" he said. "Father, I won't say anything else."

I was rushing onto the ship one day not long afterward, when a poor woman who was dressed very shabbily, and whom I didn't know, came and gave me a big red sugar bag. I was packed with things, and I couldn't say a word to her because there were so many people to see me off and everything, so I just put the bag on one side. When the ship began moving, I thought, "Well, I will look in the sugar bag."

And there were twenty-five gold coins! Can't He provide it!

Just as I had been getting on the ship, a man had come and given me a book and said, "There is a page for every day in the

435

year." And the Lord had said to me, "Put down everything that takes place in the month." I did so, and I had a memory like an encyclopedia. You see, I never learned geography, and God sent me all over the world to see it.

Beloved, let the Lord do things. He knows how to do them.

Because I felt that my coming to America and Canada was all the Lord's doing, I said, "Lord, I will never let an opportunity slip." I traveled at night to preach during the day, took advantage of every opportunity, and went so far that I got to the point that I could not eat.

After one meeting, the people said, "You have lifted the meeting, lifted the meeting."

"Yes," I said, "God is with us."

They went to eat, but I could not. Then they said to me, "Wigglesworth, you do not understand your body. You are helping everybody in the Spirit, but your body has gotten so run down that if you do not go home, you may never be able to come back."

Ah! I had zeal without knowledge (Rom. 10:2); I had a love for God, but there was no wisdom in it. God showed me that if I would take care of my body, He could use me for years and years to come, and I find today that I am stronger and better and more ready for action than I was thirty years ago.

INTERPRETATION OF A MESSAGE IN TONGUES: "For it is the Lord your God 'who opens and no man shuts.' When He blesses, it will surely tend to blessing. And remember this, God has not called you in to keep your face down; He has called you in to laden you with the treasures and then pass you out to scatter the good things. God is at the right hand of those people who are seeking diligently only to follow Him, for God has set His heart upon you. David says, 'When I was poor and needy, then the Lord thought about me.' It is in the poverty of our weaknesses that God becomes the refreshing and strength of our human nature and spiritual quality and keeps us in the earth, fresh and ready."

Oh, Father, we do thank you for this!

Beloved, make sure that you see to these things. God will give you faith. God will give you prophecies. God will give gifts. And remember this, God will enrich you.

Did you ever know a time in your life when you were poorer after you began to serve the Lord? No. God blesses in basket and store, and He blesses in the body. It pays to serve the Lord in holiness, for God has a purpose in it. It is when you get out of the will of God that you have a hard time. Let God's will be done. There is money that *"leads to poverty"* (Prov. 11:24), and there are gifts of God that bring you into riches. So I implore you to serve God with all your heart.

I had hoped to go deeper into this thirteenth chapter of 1 Corinthians, but if we had gone deeper, we would not have come out again. There are many things to say about this chapter. For instance, how beautiful it would be to know what this really means: *"Love suffers long and is kind"* (1 Cor. 13:4).

I do not have time for any more, except this: the time is not past for much more. It is past for any more from me, but you are on the threshold of much more from God. May the Lord bless you in such a way that you will be in a place where God will be at your right hand (Ps. 16:8).

Faith is an act; faith is a leap; faith jumps in; faith claims. Faith has an author, and faith's author is Jesus. He is the Author and the Finisher of faith (Heb. 12:2).

Now, how much do you dare to ask for? How much do you dare to imagine? How much do you dare to expect will come? How much? May I move you to this banquet, this place of treasure, this "much more," this "abundant," this "abounding," this "exceeding"? (See Ephesians 3:20.) Jump up into God. Dare to believe. Faith is enough; ask and believe.

Give me grace, Lord—any how, any way—only have Your way.

CHAPTER SEVENTEEN

LOVE AND THE GIFTS

Thank God for the Word that comes to us afresh! Early this morning I was thinking and wondering if the Lord would speak through me, and I was strongly impressed that I should read to you 1 Corinthians 13.

I am so thankful to God that He has dovetailed this thirteenth chapter of 1 Corinthians between the twelfth and the fourteenth. The twelfth chapter deals expressly with the gifts of the Spirit, and the fourteenth chapter is on the lines of the manifestations and the gifts of the Spirit; the thirteenth chapter functions similarly to the governor balls that control a steam engine. If you ever see this type of engine working, you will find that right over the main valve that lets in the steam, there are two little balls that go around. Often they go as fast as they can, though sometimes they go slowly. They open and shut the valve that sends the steam to the pistons. These are constructed so that the engine does not get out of control.

I find that God, the Holy Spirit, in His remarkable wisdom, has placed the thirteenth chapter right between these wonderful chapters on the gifts that we love to dwell upon so much. How wonderful, how magnificent they are! God has given them to us so that we may be useful, not ornamental, and prove in every case and under every circumstance that we might be available at the right time with these gifts. They are enduement for power; they are expressive of His love; they are for the edification and comfort of so many weary souls.

We find that God brings these gifts in perfect order so that the church may receive blessings. Yet how many people, how many of us, have failed to come to the summit of perfection because the governor balls were not working well, because we were more taken

438

up with the gift than the power that moved the gift, because we were more frequently delighted in the gift than the Giver of the gift! Then the gift became fruitless and helpless, and we were sorry. Sometimes it brought on rebuke, and sometimes we suffered, suffered more or suffered less.

INTERPRETATION OF A MESSAGE IN TONGUES: "The love that constrains, the grace that adorns, the power that sustains, the gift that remains may be in excellence, when He is the Governor, the Controller, the Worker."

I do thank God for tongues and interpretation, because they introduce new vision; they open the larger avenue. Let it please You today, Lord, to show us how to work and how to walk and not stumble.

THE GIFTS

Now, beloved, the topic of love and the gifts is a very large one. However, I will do all I can, by the grace of God, so that I may say things that will live after I have gone away. For it is very necessary that we receive the Holy Spirit in the first place; after receiving the Holy Spirit, we must earnestly desire the gifts. Then, after receiving the gifts, we must never forget that the gift is entrusted to us for bringing the blessings of God to the people.

For instance, divine healing is a gift for ministering to the needs of the people. The gift of wisdom is a word in season at the moment of need, to show you just what to do. The gift of knowledge, or the word of knowledge, is to inspire you because of the consecutiveness of the Word of God, to bring you life and joy. This is what God intends.

Then there is the gift of discernment. We are not to discern one another, but to discern evil powers and deal with them and command them back to the pit from which they came. Regarding the gift of miracles, God intends for us to come to the place where we will see miracles worked. God also wants us to understand that tongues are profitable only when they exalt and glorify the Lord. And oh, that we might really know what it means when interpretation is given! It is not merely to have beautiful sensations and think that that is interpretation, but it is such that the man who has it does not know what is coming, for if he did, it would not be interpretation. Interpretation is not knowing what you are going to say, but it is being in the place where you say exactly what God says. So when I have to interpret a message, I purposely keep my mind from anything that would hinder, and I sometimes say "Praise the Lord" and "Hallelujah" so that everything will be a word through the Spirit, and not my word, but the word of the Lord!

Now, I understand that we can have these divine gifts so perfectly balanced by divine love that they will be a blessing all the time. However, there is sometimes such a desire in the flesh to do something attention-getting. How the people listen and long for divine prophecy, just as interpretation comes forth. How it thrills! There is nothing wrong with it; it is beautiful. We thank God for the office and the purpose that has caused it to come, but let us be careful to finish when we are through and not continue on our own. That is how prophecy is spoiled. If you continue on your own, at the end of the anointing, you are using false fire; at the end of the message, you will try to continue. Don't fail, beloved, because the people know the difference. They know what is full of life, what is the real thing.

Then again, it is the same with a person praying. We love people to pray in the Holy Spirit; how we love to hear them pray even the first sentences because the fire is there. However, what spoils the most holy person in prayer is when, after the spirit of prayer has gone forth, he continues on and people say, "I wish he would stop," and the church becomes silent. They say, "I wish that brother would stop. How beautifully he began; now he is dry!" But he doesn't stop.

A preacher was once having a wonderful time, and the people enjoyed it, but when he was through, he continued. A man came and said to someone at the door, "Has he finished?" "Yes," said the man, "long since, but he won't stop!" May God save us from that. People know when you are praying in the Spirit. Why should you take time and spoil everything because the natural side has come into it? God never intended that. God has a supernatural side; that is the true side, and how beautiful it is! People sometimes know better than we do, and we would also know if we were more careful.

May the Lord grant us revelation; we need discernment; we need intuition. It is the life inside. It is salvation inside, cleansing, filling; it is all inside. Revelation is inside. It is for exhibition outside, but always remember that it is inside. God's Son said as much when He said, "The pure in heart will see God." (See Matthew 5:8.) There is an inward sight of God, and it is the pure in heart who see God.

Lord, keep us pure so that we will never block the way.

LOVE

Love is always in the place of revelation.

Though I speak with the tongues of men and of angels, but have not love, I have become sounding brass or a clanging cymbal. And though I have the gift of prophecy, and understand all mysteries and all knowledge, and though I have all faith, so that I could remove mountains, but have not love, I am nothing. (1 Cor. 13:1–2)

Now, it is a remarkable fact that God intends us to be examples of the truth. These are divine truths, and God intends us to be examples of these truths. Beloved, it is lovely to be in the will of God. Now then, how may we be something? By just being nothing, by receiving the Holy Spirit, by being in the place where we can be operated by God and filled with the power to operate.

What it must be to have speaking ability, to have a beautiful language, as so many men have! There are men who are wonderful in language. I used to like to read Talmadge when he was alive; how his messages used to inspire me. But, oh, this divine power! It is wonderful to have the tongue of an angel so that all the people who hear you are moved by your use of language. Yet how I would weep, how my heart would be broken, if I came to speak before you in beautiful language without the power!

If I had an angel's language and the people were all taken with what I said, but Jesus was not glorified at all, it would all be hopeless, barren, and unfruitful. I myself should be nothing. But if I speak and say, "Lord, let them hear Your voice. Lord, let them be compelled to hear Your truth. Lord, any how, any way, hide me today," then He becomes glorious, and all the people say, "We have seen Jesus!"

When I was in California, I spent many days with our dear Brother Montgomery when I had a chance. During this time, a man

441

wrote to Brother Montgomery. This man had been saved but had lost his joy; he had lost all he had. He wrote, "I am through with everything. I am not going to touch this thing again; I am through." Brother Montgomery wrote back to him and said, "I will never try to persuade you again if you will hear once. There is a man from England, and if you will only hear him once, I will pay all your expenses." So he came. He listened, and at the end of the time he said to me, "This is the truth I am telling you. I have seen the Lord standing beside you, and I heard His voice. I never even saw you.

"I have a lot of money," he continued, "and I have a valley five hundred miles long. If you speak the word to me, I will go on your word, and I will open that valley for the Lord."

I have preached in several of his places, and God has used him wonderfully to speak throughout that valley. What I would have missed when he came the first day, if I had been trying to say something of my own instead of the Lord being there and speaking His words through me! Never let us do anything to lose this divine love, this close affection in our hearts that says, "Not I, but Christ; not I, but Christ!"

I want to say, "Forget yourself and get lost in Him." Lose all your identity in the Son of God. Let Him become all in all. Seek only the Lord, and let Him be glorified. You will have gifts; you will have grace and wisdom. God is waiting for the person who will lay all on the altar, fifty-two weeks in the year, three hundred and sixty-five days in the year, and then continue perpetually in the Holy Spirit.

I would have liked to have gone on with this topic. I have such joy in this. Beloved, go on for every blessing from the Lord, so that the Lord will be large in you, so that the wood and the hay and the stubble will be burned up (1 Cor. 3:12–13 KJV), and the Lord will bring you to a great harvesttime. Now, beloved, shall we not present ourselves to the Lord so that He may put His hand upon us and say, "My child, My child, be obedient to the message; hear what the Spirit says to you so that you may go on and possess the land"? The Lord will give you a great inheritance.

CHAPTER EIGHTEEN

A FINAL WORD ABOUT THE GIFTS

EVEN SO YOU, SINCE YOU ARE ZEALOUS FOR SPIRITUAL GIFTS, LET
IT BE FOR THE EDIFICATION OF THE CHURCH
THAT YOU SEEK TO EXCEL.
—1 CORINTHIANS 14:12

This Scripture is the Word of God, and it is most important that when we read the Word, we do so with hearts that have purposed to obey its every precept. We have no right to open the Word of God carelessly or indifferently. I have no right to come to you with any message unless it is absolutely in the perfect order of God. I believe we are in order to consider further the subject that we greatly need to be informed about in these days. So many people are receiving the baptism of the Holy Spirit, but then they do not know which way to go.

We have a great need today. It is that we may be supplied with revelation according to the mind of the Lord, that we may be instructed by the mind of the Spirit, that we may be able to rightly divide the Word of Truth (2 Tim. 2:15), and that we may not be novices, considering the fact that the Spirit of the Lord has come to us in revelation. We ought to be alert to every touch of divine, spiritual illumination.

We should carefully consider what the apostle Paul said to us: *"Do not grieve the Holy Spirit of God, by whom you were sealed for the day of redemption"* (Eph. 4:30). The sealing of the Spirit is very remarkable, and I pray to God that not one of you may lose the divine inheritance that God has chosen for you, which is greater than you could choose if your mind had ten times its normal faculties. God's mind is greater than yours. His thoughts are higher than the heavens over you (Isa. 55:9), so that you do not need to be afraid.

I have great love for my sons in England, great love for my daughter here; but it is nothing in comparison with God's love toward us. God's love wants us to walk up and down the earth as His Son did: clothed, filled, radiant, with fire beaming forth from our countenances, setting forth the power of the Spirit so that the people jump into liberty.

But there is deplorable ignorance among those who have gifts. It is not right for you to think that because you have a gift, you are to wave it before the people and try to get their minds upon that, because, if you do, you will be out of the will of God. Gifts and callings in the body of Christ may be irrevocable (Rom. 11:29), but remember that God calls you to account for properly administering the gift in a spiritual way after you have received it. It is not given to adorn you, but to sustain, build, edify, and bless the church. When God ministers through a member of the body of Christ and the church receives this edification, then all the members will rejoice together. God moves upon us as His offspring, as His choice, and as the fruit of the earth. He wants us to be elegantly clothed in wonderful raiment, even as our Master is.

His workings upon us may be painful, but the wise saint will remember that among those whom God chastens, it is the one who is trained by that chastening to whom *"it yields the peaceable fruit of righteousness"* (Heb. 12:11). Therefore, let Him do with you what seems good to Him, for He has His hand upon you; He will not willingly take it off until He has performed the thing He knows you need. So if He comes to sift you, be ready for the sifting. If He comes with chastisement, be ready for chastisement. If He comes with correction, be ready for correction. Whatever He wills, let Him do it, and He will bring you to the land of plenty. Oh, it is worth the world to be under the power of the Holy Spirit!

If He does not chasten you, if you sail placidly along without incident, without crosses, without persecutions, without trials, remember that *"if you are without chastening, of which all have become partakers, then you are illegitimate and not sons"* (Heb. 12:8). Therefore, *"examine yourselves as to whether you are in the faith"* (2 Cor. 13:5). Never forget that Jesus said this word: "They who hear My voice follow Me." (See John 10:27.) Jesus wants you all to follow; He wants you to have a clear ring to your testimony.

You are eternally saved by the power of God. Do not be led astray by anything; do not mistake your feelings for your salvation; do not take anybody's word for your salvation. Believe that God's Word is true. What does it say? *"He who believes in the Son has everlasting life; and he who does not believe the Son shall not see life, but the wrath of God abides on him"* (John 3:36).

When your will becomes entirely the will of God, then you are clearly in the place where the Holy Spirit can make Jesus Lord in your life, Lord over your purchases, Lord over your selling, Lord over your eating and your drinking, Lord over your clothing, and Lord over your choice of companions.

> *There are diversities of gifts, but the same Spirit. There are differences of ministries, but the same Lord. And there are diversities of activities, but it is the same God who works all in all. But the manifestation of the Spirit is given to each one for the profit of all.* (1 Cor. 12:4–7)

The variation of humanity is tremendous. Faces are different, so are physiques. Your whole body may be put together in such a way that one particular gift would not suit you at all, while it would suit another person.

So the Word of God deals here with varieties of gifts, meaning that these gifts perfectly meet the condition of each believer. That is God's plan. It may be that not one person would be led to claim all the gifts. Nevertheless, do not be afraid; the Scriptures are definite. Paul said that you do not need to come short in any gift (1 Cor. 1:7). God has wonderful things for you beyond what you have ever known. The Holy Spirit is so full of prophetic operations of divine power that it is marvelous what may happen after the Holy Spirit comes.

How He loosed me! I am no good without the Holy Spirit. The power of the Holy Spirit loosed my language. I was like my mother. She had no ability to speak. If she began to tell a story, she couldn't finish it. My father would say, "Mother, you will have to begin again." I was like that. I couldn't tell a story. I was bound. I had plenty of thoughts, but no language. But oh, after the Holy Spirit came!

When He came, I had a great desire for gifts. So the Lord caused me to see that it is possible for every believer to live in such

445

holy anointing, such divine communion, such pressed-down measure (Luke 6:38) by the power of the Spirit, that every gift can be his.

But is there not a vast and appalling unconcern about possessing the gifts? You may ask a score of believers, chosen at random from almost any church, "Do you have any of the gifts of the Spirit?" The answer from all will be, "No," and it will be given in a tone and with a manner that conveys the thought that the believer is not surprised that he does not have the gifts, that he doesn't expect to have any of them, and that he does not expect to seek them. Isn't this terrible, when the living Word specifically exhorts us to *"earnestly desire the best gifts"* (1 Cor. 12:31)?

So in order that the gifts might be everything and in evidence, we have to see that we cease to live without His glory. He works with us, and we work with Him—cooperating, working together. This is divine. Surely this is God's plan.

God has brought you to the banquet, and He wants to send you away full. We are in a place where God wants to give us visions. We are in a place where, in His great love, He is bending over us with kisses. Oh, how lovely is the kiss of Jesus, the expression of His love!

Oh, come, let us seek Him for the best gifts, and let us strive to be wise and to rightly divide the Word of Truth (2 Tim. 2:15), giving it forth in power so that the church may be edified and sinners may be saved.

Smith Wigglesworth on

FAITH

CONTENTS

CHAPTER ONE

THE AUTHOR AND FINISHER OF OUR FAITH

P raise the Lord that I have had the opportunity to spend over a month in Canaan. I have crossed the river of Jordan; been on the lake of Galilee; bathed in the Dead Sea; drunk at Jacob's well; had a drink at Elijah's fountain; preached on the top of the Mount of Olives; stood with tears running down my face just opposite Mount Calvary and, with hands lifted up, seen the place of sacrifice; and passed by the spot where the holy inn stood in Bethlehem. As I thought of all the holy associations connected with that land, my heart was melted. God has been very good to me.

GLORIOUS JESUS

One of my favorite texts is in the twelfth chapter of Hebrews. I want to look at a few verses there. What a wonderful revelation Hebrews is to us.

Therefore we also, since we are surrounded by so great a cloud of witnesses, let us lay aside every weight, and the sin which so easily ensnares us, and let us run with endurance the race that is set before us, looking unto Jesus, the author and finisher of our faith. (Heb. 12:1–2)

The thought here is Jesus as the Author and Finisher of our faith. Glory to God. What a sight to see our Lord Jesus Christ come forth robed in His own majesty and glory, as no man was ever robed. He is clothed in majesty. What compassion He had when He saw the struggling multitude! When He saw the crowds in need, His heart yearned with compassion. How He handled the bread! (See Matthew 14:15–21; 15:32–38.) No man ever handled bread like Jesus did. I can almost look into His face and see His eyes glisten as He sees the multitude. He said to Philip, "I would like to feed these people; how much would it take to feed them?" Philip said, "Eight months' wages is not sufficient, and besides, this is a desert place." (See John 6:5–7; Matthew 14:15.)

If you have been to Palestine and seen the sights I have seen, you understand what is meant by a desert place. I looked for many things in the Scriptures while I was over there, and God has spoken to me through the experience. They have the early and the latter rain there (see James 5:7), and the land is a beautiful land. Praise the Lord!

It was lovely to be there and see these things, but, beloved, it made me cherish the Bible as I have never cherished it before. Why? Because God has given us the assurance that makes our hearts know it is true. Even if you never see the Holy Land, you can live in the Holy Land and see all the wonderful things as you read of them in your Bible.

Beloved, I want to speak on the Author and the Finisher of our faith, and I want us to remember that Abraham, Daniel, and all the prophets were men of faith. We must not look at the things that have been done in the past; we must look at Jesus, the Author and the Finisher of our faith. We must *"run with endurance the race that is set before us, looking unto Jesus"* (Heb. 12:1–2). We must so look at the Author and the Finisher of our faith that the same glory and power will be resting upon us as was upon Him. We must have such grace, such holiness, that we will be landmarks, showing that His power is upon us.

Praise the Lord. Don't stumble at what I am going to say, but praise God that not only do we have the abiding presence of the Spirit's power in our midst, but we have the living Word, the living Christ. He is the Author and the Finisher of our faith. He has given eternal life to us, that is, if we have His Word and believe.

My dear wife has now entered glory, but during her lifetime she was a great revivalist. She was a preacher. I have seen the mighty power of God fall upon her and have seen her face light up with a heavenly light as she preached, and there are many ministers of the Gospel today because of her preaching and her faithfulness, and others are missionaries and are working for God. We will never know the extent of her work until the Last Day. You see, beloved, as we are faithful to God and come into line with Him and labor for Him, our work will be rewarded. A great crowd is looking on. God is doing a work in these days, and these are days of opportunity.

FAITH IS WORKING NOW

God has been blessing New Zealand, and you must hear all about that land. In Australia, four hundred people were baptized in the Holy Spirit. The Holy Spirit is being poured out everywhere, and the tide of blessing is rising. The power of the Holy Spirit is greater than we have ever conceived. The basis of the Pentecostal testimony should be holiness. What is the strength of our position today? Holiness. I say to you, if you fall a thousand times in a week, strive to be holy. It does not matter how many times you fall; do not give in because you fall.

I was staying in a house, and the lady of the house prepared a room and a bed for me to rest on, because I had just gotten off the train and was very tired. When I awoke she said, "I want you to lie in my son's bed. I would like him to know you have lain in the bed." I slept in that bed for three nights, and later two people slept in the same bed and both got baptized in the Spirit. Hallelujah! I desire that everyone who is seeking would get baptized.

That lady had such a sense of the presence of God that she said, "Lie in my son's bed." As soon as I opened my eyes, I looked across the room and saw these words: "A man does not fall because he makes a blunder, he falls because he makes a blunder the second time." God does not want us to fall but to be kept from falling by His grace, and He wants us to strive for holiness. I see the Word of God is the living Word, and Jesus is the Author of the Word. The Holy Spirit is the Enlightener of the Word. If you look at Acts 1, you will see these words: "[Jesus] *through the Holy Spirit had given commandments*" (v. 2).

We will find as we go on that the Lord Jesus Christ is the Author of our lives. He is the source of our life, our spiritual life, and He is producing holiness.

I want you to see what David said in the sixty-third Psalm: "*So I have looked for You in the sanctuary, to see Your power and Your glory*" (v. 2). Jesus said, "*Father, glorify Me together with Yourself, with the glory which I had with You before the world was"* (John 17:5). The greatest glory that was ever seen was manifested on the cross. The glory was manifested when Jesus offered Himself, *"through the eternal Spirit"* (Heb. 9:14), on the cross. He said to Judas, *"What you do, do quickly....Now the Son of Man is glorified"* (John 13:27, 31). So we see that God was glorified in Jesus; He was reconciling the world unto Himself (2 Cor. 5:19).

Everyone who has desires for God should believe the Word of God and take Jesus as the Author and the Finisher of his faith. All the desires and purposes of your heart will be accomplished, because God is faithful. God cannot fail; His Word is true. But what is real Pentecost? It is the manifestation of the power of God, and it is the manifestation of the power of the Holy Spirit. Real Pentecost is the manifestation of the signs and wonders. Real Pentecost is manifested in those who are *"determined not to know anything among* [men] *except Jesus Christ and Him crucified"* (1 Cor. 2:2). I say now, as I have said before, *"Whom have I in heaven but You? And there is none upon earth that I desire besides You"* (Ps. 73:25). He is my All in All. Amen.

CHAPTER TWO

DOMINANT FAITH

NOW FAITH IS THE SUBSTANCE OF THINGS HOPED FOR, THE
EVIDENCE OF THINGS NOT SEEN. FOR BY IT THE ELDERS OBTAINED
A GOOD TESTIMONY. BY FAITH WE UNDERSTAND THAT THE WORLDS
WERE FRAMED BY THE WORD OF GOD, SO THAT THE THINGS WHICH
ARE SEEN WERE NOT MADE OF THINGS WHICH ARE VISIBLE.
—HEBREWS 11:1–3

F aith is the substance, and it is a reality. God wants to bring us to the fact of it. He wants to know that we have something greater than we can see or handle, because everything we can see and handle is going to pass away. The heavens are going to be wrapped up (Heb. 1:10–12), the earth will *melt with fervent heat*" (2 Pet. 3:10), but the Word of the Lord will abide forever (1 Pet. 1:23). *"By faith we understand that the worlds were framed by the word of God, so that the things which are seen were not made of things which are visible."*

God spoke the Word and made the world, and I want to impress upon you this wonderful Word that made the world. I am saved by the incorruptible Word, the Word that made the world, and so my position by faith is to lay hold of the things that cannot be seen and believe the things that cannot be understood.

LIVE IN A PLACE OF COMMAND

The Lord has a way of making you equal to living in the power of the Holy Spirit as long as you have learned the needed lesson. God will make us know how to live.

I went to a Quakers' meeting, quiet and still, and there was such a silence that I was moved. It was of faith, and so I jumped up and had the time of my life. All these Quakers came round me, and they said, "You are the first man that we have ever seen in this place who was so quickly led by the Spirit." I said, "If the Spirit does not move me, I move the Spirit. John said that it is the anointing of the Holy One (1 John 2:20), and that you need no man to teach you (v. 27). It is the Holy Spirit who teaches. It is simplicity itself."

While on a ship, I said to the people, "I am going to preach on this ship on Sunday; will you come and hear me preach?"

They said no. Later they came around again and said, "We are going to have some entertainment, and we'd like you to be in it."

So I said, "Come in a quarter of an hour, and I will tell you."

They came round again and said, "Are you ready?"

"Yes," I told them, "I have gotten a clear witness that I have to be in the entertainment."

They said, "Well, what can you do?"

I replied, "I can sing."

They said, "Now, we want to know what position you would like to have on the program."

I answered, "Tell me what you are going to have on the program."

They said, "Recitations, instruments, and many things."

I asked, "What will you finish up with?"

"A dance."

"Well, put me down just before the dance."

I went to the entertainment, and when I saw the clergymen trying to please the people, it turned me to prayer. When they had all done their pieces, my turn came, and I went up to the piano with my "Redemption Songs." When the lady, who was rather less than half dressed, saw the music, she said, "I cannot play this kind of music."

I said, "Be at peace, young lady. I have music and words inside." So I sang,

> If I could only tell Him as I know Him,
>> My Redeemer who has brightened all my way;
> If I could tell how precious is His presence,
>> I am sure that you would make Him yours today.

> Could I tell it, could I tell it,
> How the sunshine of His presence lights my way,
> I would tell it, I would tell it,
> And I'm sure that you would make Him yours today.

God took it up, and from the least to the greatest they were weeping. They never had a dance, but they had a prayer meeting. Six young men were saved in my cabin by the power of God.

Live in the Acts of the Apostles, and every day you will see some miracle worked by the power of the living God. It comes right to the threshold, and God brings everything along to you.

CLAIM YOUR HOLY POSITION

Do not fail to claim your holy position, so that you will overcome the power of the Devil. The best time you have is when you are in the most difficult position.

You know, sometimes it seems as though the strangest things happen for the furtherance of the Gospel. I was at Southampton station, and there were four men to see me into the train. They knew everything, and I knew nothing, only I soon found that I was in the wrong carriage. There was a man in the carriage, and I said to him, "I have been to Bournemouth before, but I do not seem to be going the right way. Where are you going?"

He said, "I am going to South Wales."

I said, "What is the Lord Jesus Christ to you? He is my personal Friend and Savior."

The man replied, "I do not thank you to speak to me about these things."

The train stopped, and I said to the porter, "Am I on the way to Bournemouth? How many stops?" He said three.

I said to the man in the carriage with me, "It has to be settled before I leave the train; you are going to hell." That man wished he had never met me. The train stopped, and I had to get out. I said, "What are you going to do?"

He answered, "I will make Him my own."

We are of the incorruptible Word of God that lives and abides forever (1 Pet. 1:23), which made the world and brought into existence things that were not there (Heb. 11:3). There was nothing made except what He made (John 1:3), and so I realize I am made twice. I was made first by the creation of God. The next time I was born again in a moment of time, eternally begotten. If you believe in your heart, you can begin to speak, and whatever you say will come to pass if you believe in your heart. Ask God to give you the grace to use the faith you have.

CHAPTER THREE

FAITH BASED UPON KNOWLEDGE

THEN THEY SAID TO HIM, "WHAT SHALL WE DO, THAT WE MAY
WORK THE WORKS OF GOD?" JESUS ANSWERED AND SAID TO THEM,
"THIS IS THE WORK OF GOD, THAT YOU BELIEVE IN
HIM WHOM HE SENT."
—JOHN 6:28–29

Nothing in the world glorifies God as much as simple rest of faith in what God's Word says. *"This is the work of God, that you believe."* Jesus said, *"My Father has been working until now, and I have been working"* (John 5:17). He saw the way the Father did the works; it was on the groundwork of knowledge, faith based upon knowledge. When I know Him, there are so many promises I can lay hold of, and then there is no struggle, *"for* [he] *who asks receives, and he who seeks finds, and to him who knocks it will be opened"* (Matt. 7:8).

Jesus lived to manifest God's glory in the earth, to show forth what God is like, so that many sons might be brought to glory (Heb. 2:10). John the Baptist came as a forerunner, testifying beforehand to the coming revelation of the Son. The Son came, and in the power of the Holy Spirit revealed faith. The living God has chosen us in the midst of His people. The power is not of us, but of God. Yes, beloved, it is the power of Another within us.

JESUS, THE SON OF GOD

In the measure we are clothed and covered and hidden in Him, His inner working is manifested. Jesus said, *"My Father has been working until now, and I have been working"* (John 5:17). Oh, the joy of knowing Him! We know if we look back on how God has taken us on. We love to shout "Hallelujah," pressed out beyond measure by the Spirit as He brings us face to face with reality, while He is dwelling in us and manifesting the works. I must know the sovereignty of His grace and the manifestation of His power. The Holy Spirit, the great Revealer of the Son, is in us for revelation to manifest the Christ of God. Therefore, let it be known to you that *"the Father who dwells in* [Christ] *does the works"* (John 14:10). *"The law of the Spirit of life in Christ Jesus has made* [us] *free from the law of sin and death"* (Rom. 8:2).

ALL UNBELIEF IS DETHRONED

The Spirit working in righteousness has brought us to the place where Christ is made our Head; *"this was the Lord's doing, and it is marvelous in our eyes"* (Matt. 21:42). It is a glorious fact that we are in God's presence, possessed by Him. We are not our own; we are clothed with Another. And what for? For the deliverance of the people.

Many can testify to the day and hour when they were delivered from sickness by a supernatural power. Some would have passed away with influenza if God had not intervened, but God stepped in with a new revelation, showing us we are born from above, born by a new power, God dwelling in us and superseding the old. *"If you ask anything in My name, I will do it"* (John 14:14). If you dare to believe, *"ask, and you will receive, that your joy may be full"* (John 16:24). *"What shall we do, that we may work the works of God?...This is the work of God, that you believe in Him whom He sent"* (John 6:28–29). God is more eager to answer than we are to ask. I am speaking of faith based upon knowledge.

TESTIMONIES TO THIS FAITH

I was healed of appendicitis, because of faith based upon the knowledge of the experience of faith. When I have ministered to others, God has met and answered according to His will. The knowledge that God will not fail us if we will only believe is in our trust and our knowledge of the power of God. The centurion had this faith when he said to Jesus, *"Speak a word, and my servant will be healed"* (Matt. 8:8). Jesus answered him, *"'Go your way;*

and as you have believed, so let it be done for you.' And his servant was healed that same hour" (Matt. 8:13).

In one place where I was staying, a young man came in telling us his sweetheart was dying; there was no hope. I said, "Only believe." And this was faith based upon knowledge. I knew that what God had done for me He could do for her. We went to the house. Her sufferings were terrible to witness. I said, "In the name of Jesus, come out of her." She cried, "Mother, Mother, I am well." Then I said that the only way to make us believe it was for her to get up and dress. Presently she came down dressed. The doctor came in and examined her carefully. He said, "This is of God; this is the finger of God." It was faith based upon knowledge.

If I were to receive a check for a thousand pounds and knew only imperfectly the character of the man who sent it, I would be careful of him. I would be careful not to rely on the money until the check was honored. Jesus, on the other hand, did great works because of His knowledge of His Father. Faith begets knowledge, fellowship, and communion. If you see imperfect faith, full of doubt, a wavering condition, it always comes because of imperfect knowledge.

> *Jesus...said, "Father,...I know that You always hear Me, but because of the people who are standing by I said this, that they may believe that You sent Me."...He cried with a loud voice, "Lazarus, come forth!"*   (John 11:41–43)

> *Now God worked unusual miracles by the hands of Paul, so that even handkerchiefs or aprons were brought from his body to the sick, and the diseases left them and the evil spirits went out of them.*   (Acts 19:11–12)

> *For our citizenship is in heaven, from which we also eagerly wait for the Savior, the Lord Jesus Christ, who will transform our lowly body that it may be conformed to His glorious body, according to the working by which He is able even to subdue all things to Himself.*   (Phil. 3:20–21)

How God has cared for me and blessed me these twelve years, giving me such a sense of His presence! How bountiful God is when we depend on Him! He gives us enough to spare for others.

Lately God has enabled me to gain victory along new lines, an indwelling Holy-Spirit attitude in a new way. As we meet Him, the glory falls immediately. The Holy Spirit has the latest news from the Godhead and has designed for us the right place at the right time. Events happen in a remarkable way. You drop in where the need is.

I have come across several mental cases lately. How difficult they are naturally, but how easy for God to deal with. One lady came saying, "Just over the way there is a young man terribly afflicted, with no rest day or night." I went with a very imperfect knowledge as to what I had to do, but in the weak places God helps our infirmities. I rebuked the demon in the name of Jesus, and then I said, "I'll come again tomorrow." The next day when I went, he was quite well and with his father in the field.

Here is another case. Fifty miles away there was a fine young man, twenty-five years of age. He had lost his reason, could have no communication with his mother, and was always wandering up and down. I knew God was waiting to bless. I cast out the demon power and heard long after that he had become quite well. Thus the blessed Holy Spirit takes us on from one place to another. So many things happen; I live in heaven on earth. Just the other day, at Coventry, God relieved the people. Thus He takes us on and on and on. Do not wait for inspiration if you are in need; the Holy Spirit is here, and you can have perfect deliverance.

I was taken to three persons, one in care of an attendant. As I entered the room, there was a terrible din and quarreling. It was such a noise it seemed as if all the powers of hell were stirred. I had to wait for God's time. The Holy Spirit rose in me at the right time, and the three were delivered and at night were singing praises to God. There had to be activity and testimony.

Let it be known to you that this Man Christ is the same today. Which man? God's Man, who has to have the glory, power, and dominion. *"For He must reign till He has put all enemies under His feet"* (1 Cor. 15:25). When He reigns in you, you know how to obey and how to work in conjunction with His will, His power, His light, and His life. When we have faith based upon knowledge, we know He has come. *"You shall receive power when the Holy Spirit has come upon you"* (Acts 1:8). We are in the experience of it.

Sometimes a live word comes to me. In the presence of a need, a revelation of the Spirit comes to my mind, "You will be loosed."

Loosed now? It looks like presumption, but God is with the man who dares to stand upon His Word. I remember, for instance, a person who had not been able to smell anything for four years. I said, "You will smell now if you believe." This stirred another who had not smelled for twenty years. I said, "You will smell tonight." She went about smelling everything and was quite excited. The next day she gave her testimony.

Another came and asked, "Is it possible for God to heal my ears?" The eardrums had been removed. I said, "Only believe." She went down into the audience in great distress; others were healed, but she could not hear. The next night she came again. She said, "I am going to believe tonight." The glory fell. The first time she came feeling; the second time she came believing.

"'What shall we do, that we may work the works of God?' Jesus answered and said to them, 'This is the work of God, that you believe in Him whom He sent'" (John 6:28–29). Anything else? Yes. He *"took our infirmities"* and healed all our diseases (Matt. 8:17). I myself am a marvel of healing. If I failed to glorify God, the stones would cry out.

> Salvation is for all,
>> Healing is for all.
> The baptism of the Holy Spirit is for all.

Consider yourselves *"dead indeed unto sin, but alive unto God"* (Rom. 6:11 KJV). By His grace get the victory every time. It is possible to live a holy life.

> He breaks the power of canceled sin,
>> He sets the prisoner free;
> His blood can make the foulest clean,
>> His blood avails for me.

"What shall we do, that we may work the works of God?" Jesus answered and said to them, "This is the work of God, that you believe in Him whom He sent." (John 6:28–29)

CHAPTER FOUR

FAITH IS THE VICTORY

We may be in a very low ebb of the tide, but it is good to be in a place where the tide can rise. I pray that the Holy Spirit will so have His right-of-way that there will not be one person here who will not be moved upon by the Spirit of God. Everything depends upon our being filled with the Holy Spirit. And there is nothing you can come short of if the Holy Spirit is the prime mover in your thoughts and life, for He has a plan greater than ours. If He can only get us in readiness for His plan to be worked out, it will be wonderful.

FAITH TO BELIEVE GOD

Hebrews 11:1–10 is a very remarkable passage of Scripture for us when we are talking about faith. Everything depends upon our believing God. If we are saved, it is only because God's Word says so. We cannot rest on our feelings. We cannot do anything without a living faith. It is surely God Himself who comes to us in the person of His beloved Son and so strengthens us that we realize that our bodies are surrounded by His power and are being lifted into the almightiness of His power. All things are possible for us in God (Matt. 19:26).

The purpose of God for us is that we might be on the earth for a manifestation of His glory, that every time satanic power is confronted, God might be able to say of us as He did of Job, "What do you think about him?" (See Job 1:8.) God wants us so manifested in His divine plan in the earth that Satan will have to hear God. The joy of the Lord can be so manifested in us that we will be so filled with God that we will be able to rebuke the power of the Devil.

God has shown me in the night watches that everything that is not of faith is sin (Rom. 14:23). I have seen this in the Word so many times. God wants very much to bring us into harmony with His will so that we will see that if we do not come right up to the Word of God to believe it all, there is something in us that is not purely sanctified to accept the fullness of His Word. Many people are putting their human wisdom right in the place of God, and God is not able to give the best because the human is confronting God in such a way. God is not able to get the best through us until the human will is dissolved.

"Faith is the substance of things hoped for" (Heb. 11:1). I want to speak about *"substance"*; it is a remarkable word. Many people come to me and say, "I want things to be tangible. I want something to appeal to my human reasoning." My response to this is that everything that you cannot see is eternal. Everything you can see is natural and fades away. Everything you see now will fade away and will be consumed, but what you cannot see, what is more real than you, is the substance of all things: God in the human soul, mightier than you by a million times.

Beloved, we have to go out and be faced with all evil powers. Even your own heart, if it is not entirely immersed in the Spirit, will deceive you. So I am praying that there will not be a vestige of your human nature that will not be clothed upon with the power of the Spirit. I pray that the Spirit of the living God may be so imparted to your heart that nothing will in any way be able to move you. *"Faith is the substance of things hoped for, the evidence of things not seen"* (v. 1).

FAITH TO PLACE JESUS IN YOU

God has mightily blessed to me 1 Peter 1:23: *"Having been born again, not of corruptible seed but incorruptible, through the word of God which lives and abides forever."* We read, *"In the beginning was the Word, and the Word was with God, and the Word was God"* (John 1:1). Then we read that *"the Word became flesh and dwelt among us, and we beheld His glory, the glory as of the only begotten of the Father, full of grace and truth"* (v. 14). And He is manifested in the midst of us. His disciples went out and manifested that they had seen and touched Him, the Word of Life.

If you turn to 2 Peter 1:4, you will find that we have received His divine nature, which is infinite power, infinite knowledge, infinite pleasure, and infinite revelation. People are missing it because we have failed to apply it. But God is making up a people who will have to be *"firstfruits"* (James 1:18). By simple faith, you entered in and claimed your rights and became Christians, being born again because you believed. But there is something different in knowing God, in having fellowship with Him; there are heights and depths in this wonderful blessing in the knowledge of Him. Everybody can see Jacob, but do not forget, beloved, that God changed Jacob into Israel. The Holy Spirit wants everybody to see the unveiling of Jesus. The unveiling of Jesus is to take away yourself and to place Him in you, to take away all your human weakness and put within you that wonderful Word of eternal power and of eternal life that makes you believe that *"all things are possible"* (Matt. 19:26).

EXAMPLES OF FAITH

A man traveled with me from Montreal to Vancouver and then on ship to New Zealand. He was a dealer of race horses. It seemed he could not leave me. He was frivolous and talked about races, but he could not keep his end of the conversation up. I did not struggle to keep my end up because mine is a living power. No person who has Jesus as the inward power of his body needs to be trembling when Satan comes around. All he has to do is to *"stand still, and see the salvation of the LORD"* (Exod. 14:13).

This man entered into a good deal of frivolity and talk of this world. Coming upon a certain island of the Fiji group, we all went out, and God gave me wonderful liberty in preaching. The man came back afterward; he did not go to his racing and card-playing chums. He came stealing back to the ship, and with tears in his eyes, he said, "I am dying. I have been bitten by a snake." His skin had turned to a dark green, and his leg was swollen. "Can you help me?" he asked. If we only knew the power of God!

If we are in a place of substance, of reality, of ideal purpose, it is not human; we are dealing with almightiness. I have a present God, I have a living faith, and the living faith is the Word. The Word is life, and the Word is equipment, and the Lord is *"the same yesterday, today, and forever"* (Heb. 13:8). Placing my hand upon the serpent bite, I said, "In the name of Jesus, come out!" He looked at me, and the tears came. The swelling went down before his eyes, and he was perfect in a moment.

Yes, *"faith is the substance of things hoped for, the evidence of things not seen"* (Heb. 11:1). Faith is what came into me when I believed. I was born of the incorruptible Word (1 Pet. 1:23) by the living virtue, life, and personality of God. I was instantly changed from nature to grace. I became a servant of God, and I became an enemy of unrighteousness.

The Holy Spirit wants us to clearly understand that we are a million times bigger than we know. Every Christian has no conception of what he is. My heart is so big that I want to look in your faces and tell you if you only knew what you had, your body would scarcely be able to contain you. Oh, that God would so bring us into divine attractiveness by His almightiness that all our bodies would wake up to resurrection force, to the divine, inward flow of eternal power coursing through the human frame.

Let us read Ephesians 4:7–8, 11–13:

> *But to each one of us grace was given according to the measure of Christ's gift. Therefore He says: "When He ascended on high, He led captivity captive, and gave gifts to men."...And He Himself gave some to be apostles, some prophets, some evangelists, and some pastors and teachers, for the equipping of the saints for the work of ministry, for the edifying of the body of Christ, till we all come to the unity of the faith and of the knowledge of the Son of God, to a perfect man, to the measure of the stature of the fullness of Christ.*

God took you into His pavilion and began to clothe you and give you the gifts of the Spirit. He did this so that in that ministry by the power of God you would bring all the church into the perfect possession of the fullness of Christ. Oh, the wonder of it! Oh, the adaptability of His equipment!

INTERPRETATION OF A MESSAGE IN TONGUES: "God has designed it. In the pavilion of His splendor, with the majesty of His glory He comes and, touching human weakness, beautifies it in the Spirit of holiness until the effectiveness of this wonderful sonship is made manifest in us, until we all become the edification of the 'fullness of Christ.'"

I believe God wants something to be in you that could never be unless you cease to be for yourself. God wants you to be for Him, to be for everybody. But, oh, to have the touch of God! Beloved, the Holy Spirit is the Comforter. The Holy Spirit did not come to speak of Himself, but He came to unveil Him who said, *"Take My yoke upon you and learn from Me, for I am gentle and lowly in heart, and you will find rest for your souls"* (Matt. 11:29). The Holy Spirit came to thrill you with resurrection power, and He came so that you would be anointed with fresh oil that overflows in the splendor of His almightiness. Then right through you will come forth a river of divine anointing that will sustain you in the bitterest place. It will give life to the deadest formality and say to the weak, "Be strong," and to them who have no might, "The Lord of Hosts is here to comfort you." God wants us to be like the rising of the sun, filled with the rays of heaven, all the time beaming forth the gladness of the Spirit of the Almighty. Possibility is the greatest thing of your life.

I came to the tent yesterday afternoon. No one but myself could understand my feelings. Was it emotion? No, it was an inward inspiration to find hearts that God had touched and that had met me with such love that it was almost more than I could bear. I have to thank God for it and take courage that He has been with me in the past, and He will be with me in the future. I am satisfied that love is the essential. *"Love is of God"* (1 John 4:7); no, more than this, *"God is love"* (v. 8). Love is the Trinity working in the human to break it up so that it may be displaced with God's fullness.

When I was ministering to the sick, a man came among the crowd. If you had seen him, your heart would have ached for him. He was shriveled and weakened; his cheek bones were sticking out, his eyes sunken, and his neck all shriveled. He was just a form of a man. His coat hung on him as you would put it on some stick. He whispered, for he could only speak with a weak voice, "Can you help me?"

I asked, "What is it?" He said that he had had cancer of his stomach, and on the operation table they had taken away the cancer. But in the operation they made it so that the man could not swallow.

He said, "I have tried to take the juice of a cherry today, but it would not go down." Then he pulled out a tube about nine inches long, which had a cup at the top. He whispered, "I have a hole in my stomach. As I pour liquid in, my stomach receives that. I have been living this way for three months."

You could call it a shadow of life he was living. Could I help him? Look! This Book can help anybody. This Book is the essence of life. God moves as you believe. This Book is the Word of God. Could I help him? I said, "On the authority of this Word, this night you will have a big supper."

But he said he could not eat. "Do as I tell you," I answered.

"How can it be?"

"It is time," I said, "to go and eat a good supper." He went home and told his wife.

She could not understand it. She said, "You cannot eat. You cannot swallow."

But he whispered, "The man said I had to do it." He got hungry and hungrier and ventured, "I will try it." His wife got his supper ready. He got a mouth full, and it went down just as easy as possible. He went on eating food until he was filled up. Then he and his wife had one of the best times of their lives. The next morning he was so full of joy because he had eaten again. He looked down out of curiosity to see the hole and found that God had closed it up!

But you ask, Can He do it for me? Yes, if you believe it. Faith is the victory. Here I am, so thankful this morning. Thirty years ago this body you see was sick and helpless and dying. God, in an instant, healed me. I will be sixty-five years old in a day or two, and I am so free and healthy; oh, it is wonderful! There are people in this place who ought to be healed in a moment, people who ought to receive the Holy Spirit in a moment. The power of possibility is within the reach of every man. The Holy Spirit is full of the rising tide. Every one of us can be filled to overflowing. God is here with His divine purpose to change our weakness into mighty strength and faith. The Word of God, oh, brother, sister, have you gotten it? It is marrow to your bones. It is anointing. It is resurrection from every weakness; it is life from the dead.

If there is anything I want to shake you loose from, it is having a word of faith without the power of it. What are we here for? Surely we are not to hear only; we are to obey. Obedience is better than sacrifice (1 Sam. 15:22). God the Holy Spirit wants to give us such a revelation of Christ that we would go away as men who had seen the King. We would go away with our faces lit up with the brilliancy of heaven.

How many are willing to believe? The people who would like God to know they are in sincerity and they will do whatever His Spirit tells them, cry to God until you have all you want. Let God have His way. Touch God now. Faith is the victory.

CHAPTER FIVE

A FIRM FAITH

You know, beloved, there are many wonderful treasures in the storehouse of God that we have not yet gotten to. But praise God, we have the promise in 1 Corinthians: *"Eye has not seen, nor ear heard, nor have entered into the heart of man the things which God has prepared for those who love Him"* (1 Cor. 2:9).

> **INTERPRETATION OF A MESSAGE IN TONGUES:** "'Fear not, neither be dismayed,' for the God who has led will descend upon you, will surely carry you where you cannot go. But to this end He has called you out to take you on, to move upon you with a divine anointing of the Spirit, so that you should not be entertained by nature, but caught up with Him to hear His words, to speak His truth, to have His mind, to know His will, to commune and be still, to 'see Him who is invisible,' to be able to pour out to others the great stream of life, and to quicken everything wherever it moves. For the Spirit is not given 'by measure,' but He is given to us by faith, the measureless measure, that we may 'know Him and the power of His resurrection' in the coming day. And now is the day set for us that is the opening for the coming day."

THE FOUNDATION OF FAITH

I pray to God that there may be within us a deep hunger and thirst with the penetration that is centered entirely upon the axle of Him, for surely He is *"all and in all"* (Col. 3:11).

Now, you will clearly see that God wants to bring us to a foundation. If we are ever going to make any progress in the divine life, we will have to have a real foundation. And there is no foundation except the foundation of faith for us.

All our movements, and all that ever will come to us that is of any importance, will be because we have a Rock. If you are on the Rock, no powers can move you. And today we need to have our faith firmly built on the Rock. In any area or principle of your faith, you must have something established in you to bring it forth. And there is no establishment outside God's Word for you. Everything else is sand. Everything else will break apart. (See Matthew 7:26–27.)

If you build on anything else—on imaginations, sentimentality, any feelings, or any special joy—but the Word of God, it will mean nothing without the foundation, and the foundation will have to be in the Word of God.

I was once going on a tram to Blackpool. It is a fashionable resort, and many people go there because of the high tides and the wonderful sights they see as the ocean throws up its large, massive mountain of sea. When we were going on the tram, I looked over and said to a builder, "The men are building those houses upon the sands."

"Oh," he said, "you don't know. You are not a builder. Don't you know that we can pound that sand until it becomes like rock?"

I said, "Nonsense!" I saw the argument was not going to profit, so I dropped it. By and by we reached Blackpool, where the mountainous waves come over. I was looking and taking notice of so many things. I saw a row of houses that had fallen flat, and drawing the attention of this man, I said, "Oh, look at those houses. See how flat they are." He forgot our previous conversation and said, "You know here we have very large tides, and these houses, being on the sands when the floods came, fell."

We must have something better than sand, and everything is sand except the Word. There isn't anything that will remain. We are told that heaven and earth will be melted with fervent heat (2 Pet. 3:10). But we are told the Word of God will be forever (1 Pet. 1:23), and not *"one jot or...tittle"* of the Word of God will fail (Matt. 5:18). And if there is anything that is satisfying me today more than another, it is, *"Your word is settled in heaven"* (Ps. 119:89). And another passage in Psalm 138 says, *"You have magnified Your word above all Your name"* (v. 2). The very establishment for me is the Word of God. It is not on any other line.

Let us come to the principle of the matter. If you turn to John's gospel, you will find a wonderful passage there. It is worth our notice and great consideration:

In the beginning was the Word, and the Word was with God, and the Word was God. He was in the beginning with God. All things were made through Him, and without Him nothing was made that was made. (John 1:1–3)

There we have the foundation of all things, which is the Word. It is a substance; it is a power. It is more than relationship; it is personality. It is a divine injunction to every soul that enters into this privilege to be born of this Word. What it means to us will be very important for us. For remember, it is a *"substance"*; it is an *"evidence of things not seen"* (Heb. 11:1). It brings about what you cannot see. It brings forth what is not there, and it takes away what is there and substitutes for it.

God took the Word and made the world of the things that did not appear (v. 3). And we live in the world that was made by the Word of God, and it is inhabited by millions of people. And you say it is a substance. Jesus, the Word of God, made it with the things that did not appear. And nothing has been made that has not been made by the Word (John 1:3). And when we come to the truth of what that Word means, we will be able not only to build, but also to know, not only to know, but also to have. For if there is anything helping me today more than anything else, it is the fact that I am living in facts; I am moving in facts; I am in the knowledge of the principles of the Most High.

THE WISDOM OF DIVINE REVELATION

God is making manifest His power. God is a reality and is proving His mightiness in the midst of us. And as we open ourselves to divine revelation and get rid of all things that are not of the Spirit, then we will understand how mightily God can take us on in the Spirit, move the things that appear, and bring the things that do not appear into prominence.

Oh, the riches, the depths of the wisdom of the Most High God (Rom. 11:33)! Jabez knew that there were divine principles that we needed to know, and he said, *"Enlarge [me]"* (1 Chron. 4:10). David knew that there was a mightiness beyond and within, and he said, *"He has dealt bountifully with me"* (Ps. 13:6), knowing that all the springs that were in him and had made his face to shine had come from God (Ps. 87:7). And God is an inward witness of a power, of a truth, of a revelation, of an inward presence, of a divine knowledge. He is! He is!

Then I must understand. I must clearly understand. I must have a basis of knowledge for everything that I say. We must never say what we think; we must say what we know. Any man can think. You must be beyond the thinking. You must have the knowledge. And God wants to make us so loyal to Him that He unveils Himself. He rolls the clouds away; the mists disappear at His presence. He is almighty in His movements. God has nothing small. He is all large, an immensity of wisdom, unfolding the grandeur of His design or plan for humanity so that humanity may sink into insignificance, and the mightiness of the mighty power of God may move upon us until we are the sons of God with power, in revelation and might and strength in the knowledge of God. Oh, this wonderful salvation! Now let us think about it, it is so beautiful. Seeing then that God took the Word—what was the Word? The Word was Jesus. *"The Word became flesh and dwelt among us,"* and we beheld and saw the glory of God (John 1:14).

John has a wonderful passage on this that may lead us to edification at this moment. It is very powerful in its revelation to me as often as I gaze into the *"perfect law of liberty"* (James 1:25).

> *That which was from the beginning, which we have heard, which we have seen with our eyes, which we have looked upon, and our hands have handled, concerning the Word of life; the life was manifested, and we have seen, and bear witness, and declare to you that eternal life which was with the Father and was manifested to us; that which we have seen and heard we declare to you, that you also may have fellowship with us; and truly our fellowship is with the Father and with His Son Jesus Christ.* (1 John 1:1–3)

Oh, beloved, He is the Word! He is the principle of God. He is the revelation sent forth from God. All fullness dwelt in Him (Col. 2:9). We have all received a grand word of *"His fullness,"* and *"grace for grace"* (John 1:16).

In weakness, strength, poverty, and wealth is this Word! It is a flame of fire. It may burn in your bones. (See Jeremiah 20:9.) It may move in every tissue of your body. It may bring out of you so forcibly the plan and purpose and life of God until you cease to be, for God has taken you.

BORN AGAIN WITH POWER

It is a fact that we may be taken, hallelujah! into all the knowledge of the wisdom of God. Then I want to build, if I am created anew, for it is a great creation. It took nine months to bring us forth into the world after we were conceived, but it only takes one moment to beget us as God's sons. The first formation was a long period of nine months. The second formation is a moment, an act, a faith, for *"he who believes...has"* (John 3:36). And as you receive Him, you are begotten, not made.

Oh, the fact that I am *"begotten...again"* (1 Pet. 1:3) is wonderful! I am begotten of the same seed that begot Him. Remember, as He was conceived in the womb by the Holy Spirit, so we were conceived the moment we believed and became sons of God with promise.

And oh, how the whole creation groans for sonship! (See Romans 8:22.) There is a passage in Romans, and I think it would help us to read it. Some knowledge of sonship is needed; it is a beautiful word. I have so often looked at it with pleasure, for it is such a pleasure to me to read the Word of God. Oh, the hidden treasures there are! What a feast to have the Word of God! *"Man shall not live by bread alone, but by every word of God"* (Luke 4:4). How we need the Word! The Word is life.

> *Concerning His Son Jesus Christ our Lord, who was born of the seed of David according to the flesh, and declared to be the Son of God with power according to the Spirit of holiness, by the resurrection from the dead.*　　　(Rom. 1:3–4)

Oh, what a climax of beatitudes is here! How beautiful! God, breathe upon us this holy, inward way after His passion. Hear it: *"Declared to be the Son of God with power."*

Sons must have power. We must have power with God, power with man. We must be above all the world. We must have power over Satan and power over evil. I want you just for a moment to think with me because it will help you with this thought. You can never make evil pure. Anything that is evil never becomes pure in that sense. There is no such thing as ever transforming impurity into purity. The carnal mind is never subject to the will of God and cannot be (Rom. 8:7). There is only one thing for it; it must be destroyed. But I want you to go with me to when God cast out what was not pure. I want you to think about Satan in the glory with all the chances, and nothing spoiled him but his pride. And pride is an awful thing—pride in the heart, thinking we are something when we are nothing, building up a human constitution out of our own.

Oh yes, it is true the Devil is always trying to make you think about what you are. You never find God doing it. It is always Satan who comes around and says, "What a wonderful address you gave! How wonderful you did that, and how wonderful you prayed and sang that song." It is all of the Devil. There is not an atom of God in it, not from beginning to end. If we only knew how much better we could preach if we only would not miss the revelation! And Paul, in order that he might never miss the revelation, said, "Therefore I have never ceased; *I have kept the faith*' (2 Tim. 4:7)."

Oh, the vision is so needed today. It is more necessary than anything that man should have the visions of God. The people have always perished when there is no vision (Prov. 29:18 KJV). God wants us to have visions and revelations and manifestations. You cannot have the Holy Spirit without having revelations. You cannot have the Holy Spirit without being turned into another nature. It was the only credential by which Joshua and Caleb could enter the land, the fact that they were of *"another spirit."* (See Numbers 14:24, 30 KJV.) And we must live in an anointing, in a power, in a transformation, and in a divine attainment where we cease to be, where God becomes enthroned so richly.

> INTERPRETATION OF A MESSAGE IN TONGUES: "It is He! He came forth and emptied Himself of all, but Love brought to us the grace and then offered up Himself to purge us so that we might be entire and free from all things. We would then 'see Him who was invisible' and be changed by the power that is divine and be lost to everything but the immensity of the mightiness of a Godlikeness, for we must be sons of God with promise in the world."

We must be—we must be! We must not say, "It is not for me." Oh, no; we must say, "It is for us."

And God cast Satan out. Oh, I do thank God for that. Yes, beloved, but God could not have cast him out if he had even been equal of power. I tell you, beloved, we can never *"bind the strong man"* (Matt. 12:29 KJV) until we are in the place of binding. I thank God that Satan had to come out. Yes, and how did he come out? By the Word of God's power. And, beloved, if we get to know and understand the principles of our inheritance by faith, we will find out Satan will always be cast out by the same power that cast him out in the beginning. He will be cast out to the end because Satan has not become more holy but more vile.

If you think about the last day upon earth, you will find out that the greatest war—not Armageddon, but the war beyond that—will be between the hosts of Satan and the hosts of God. And how will it take place? With swords, dynamite, or any human power? No! It will take place by the brightness of His presence (2 Thess. 2:8), the holiness of His holiness, the purity of His purity; where darkness cannot remain, where sin cannot stand, where only holiness and purity will remain. All else will flee from the presence of God into the Abyss forever.

And God has saved us with this Word of power over the powers of sin. I know there is a teaching and a need of teaching of the fidelity of the Word of God with power. And we need to eat and drink of this Word. We need to feed upon it in our hearts. We need that holy revelation that ought always to take away the mists from our eyes and reveal Him.

ALWAYS ADVANCING

Beloved, don't forget that every day must be a day of advancement. If you have not made any advancement since yesterday, in a measure you are a backslider. There is only one way for you between Calvary and the glory, and it is forward. It is every day forward. It is no day back. It is advancement with God. It is cooperation with Him in the Spirit.

Beloved, we must see these things, because if we live on the same plane day after day, the vision is stale; the principles lose their earnestness. But we must be like those who are catching the vision of the Master day by day. And we must make inroads into every passion that would interfere, and we must bring everything to the slaughter that is not holy. For in these days God wants us to know that He wishes to seat us on high. Don't forget it.

The principles remain with us—if we will only obey—to seat us on high. Hallelujah! And let us still go on building because we must build this morning. We must know our foundation. We must be able to take the Word of God and make it clear to people, because we will be confronted with evil powers.

A DEAF MAN HEARS

I am continually confronted with things that God must clear away. Every day something comes before me that has to be dealt with along these lines. For instance, when I was at Cazadero, California, seven or eight years ago, among the first people that came to me in those meetings was a man who was completely deaf. And every time we had the meeting—suppose I was rising up to say a few words—this man would take his chair from the ordinary row and place it right in front of me. And the Devil used to say, "Now you are done." I said, "No, I am not done. *'It is finished!'* (John 19:30)."

The man was as deaf as possible for those three weeks. And then in the meeting, as we were singing, this man became tremendously disturbed as though he were in a storm. He looked in every direction, and he became like someone who had almost lost his mind. And then he took a leap. He started on the run and went out among the people and right up one of the hills. When he got about sixty yards away, he heard singing. And the Lord said, "Your ears are open." He came back, and we were still singing. That stopped our singing. And then he told us that when his ears were opened, he could not understand what it was. There was such a tremendous noise he could not understand it. He thought something had happened to the world, and so he ran out of the meeting. Then, when he got away, he heard singing. I met this man later in Oakland, and he was still hearing perfectly.

Oh, the Devil said for three weeks, "You cannot do it." I said, "It is done!" As though God would ever forget! As though God could ever forget! As if it were possible for God ever to ignore our prayers!

RECEIVING GOD'S GLORY

The most trying time is the most helpful time. Most preachers say something about Daniel and about the Hebrew children, Shadrach, Meshach, and Abednego, and especially about Moses when he was tried and in a corner. Beloved, if you read the Scriptures, you will never find anything about the easy times. All the glories came out of hard times.

And if you are to be really reconstructed, it will be in a hard time. It won't be in a singing meeting, but at a time when you think all things are dried up, when you think there is no hope for you and you have passed up everything. That is the time that God makes the man. It is when you are tried by fire that God purges you, takes the dross away, and brings forth the pure gold. Only melted gold is minted. Only soft wax receives the seal. Only broken, contrite hearts receive the mark as the Potter turns us on His wheel, shaped and burned to take and keep the heavenly mold, the stamp of God's pure gold.

We must have the stamp of our blessed Lord, who *"was marred more than any man"* (Isa. 52:14). And when He touched human weakness, it was reconstructed. He spoke out of the depths of trial and mockery and became the Initiator of a world's redemption. Man never spoke as He spoke (John 7:46)! He was full of order and made all things move until the people said, *"We never saw anything like this!"* (Mark 2:12). He is truly the *"Son of God with power"* (Rom. 1:4), with blessing, with life, and with maturity, and He can take the weakest and make them into strength.

GOD CAN FILL YOU NOW

God is here now in power, in blessing, in might, and is saying to you, my brother, and to you, my sister, "What is it? What is your request?"

Oh, He is so precious; He never fails; He is so wonderful! He always touches the needy place. He is so gentle; He never breaks the bruised reed (Isa. 42:3). He is so rich in His mighty benevolence that He makes the smoking flax to flame (v. 3).

May God move us now to see that He must have a choice from us. Oh, how precious He is! There is no passage so precious to me as when He said, *"With fervent desire I have desired to eat this Passover with you before I suffer"* (Luke 22:15).

Oh, that lovely, benevolent, wonderful Jesus! Before the Garden experience, knowing about the cross and Gethsemane, there the love of Jesus, that holy Jesus, could say, *"With fervent desire."* It was *"the joy that was set before Him"* (Heb. 12:2). Will it be missed? Is it possible for *"the joy that was set before Him"*—to make us fully matured saints of God, with power over the powers of the Enemy, filled with the might of His Spirit—to be missed?

Surely this is our God, for there is no other god who answers like this. Let me entreat you right now to pay any price. Never mind what it costs; it is worth it all to have His smile, to have His presence—truly, more than that—to have the same desire that He had to win others for Him.

When I see His great desire to win me, I say, "Lord, remold me like that. Make me have the desire of salvation for others at any cost." Thank God He went through. He did not look back. He went right on.

You never need to be afraid of joining yourself to this Nazarene, for He is always a King. When He was dying, He was a King. Yes, if ever there was any man who spoke in tongues, I believe that Jesus spoke in tongues, for there was no interpretation. And if any man ever spoke truth, He spoke the truth when He said, *"It is finished!"* (John 19:30).

Thank God it is finished. And I know, because it is finished, that everything is mine. Thank God everything is mine: things in heaven, things in earth, things under the earth. He is all power over all. He is in all. He is through all (Eph. 4:6). Thank God He is for all.

And I say to you, without contradiction, that Jesus has so much more for you than you have any conception of. Just like the two sons of Zebedee—did they know what they asked? Certainly they had no conception of what they asked.

> *But Jesus...said, "...Are you able to drink the cup that I am about to drink, and be baptized with the baptism that I am baptized with?" They said to Him, "We are able."* (Matt. 20:22)

Were they able? No, but it was their hearts. Have a big heart! Have a big yes! Have a big "I will!" Have a great desire, though you are blind to what is to follow.

And the sons of Zebedee also wanted what He had. I believe that all believers want the same. Did they drink? Yes, He said they would. Did they see His baptism? Yes, He said they would (v. 23). But they had no idea what it meant, what the cup was. But the cup was drunk to the dregs. Yes, His cup was different. But because of His cup, our cup runs over (Ps. 23:5). Oh, *"surely goodness and mercy shall follow* [you]" (v. 6). Your cup runs over. There may be many cups before the cup is full. But oh, hallelujah anyway, only let it be His will and His way, not my way. Oh, for His way only, and His plan, His will only!

Let the mantle fall from Him onto you today. (See 2 Kings 2:9–15.) *"If you see me when I am taken from you, it shall be"* (v. 10), Elijah said. And Elisha kept his eye on Elijah. The mantle is to fall, the mantle of power, the mantle of blessing.

And I ask you now, seeing that you have this spiritual revelation in the body, in the earthly tabernacle, what are you going to do? If the body is yielded sufficiently until it perfectly becomes the temple of the Spirit (1 Cor. 3:16), then the fullness will flow, and the life will be yielded to you and given to you as you have need of it. May God mold us all to believe it is possible now not only for the rivers, but also the mightiness of His boundless ocean, to flow through us.

You should do as you are led to do. No pressure ought to be needed for you as you see your need before God and know He is here to supply your need. Therefore, why should we have to be entreated to seek the best of all when God is waiting to give without measure (John 3:34) to each and every one? Do as the Lord leads you, and let Him direct you in whatever way.

CHAPTER SIX

FAITH'S TREASURES

I believe that there is only one way to all the treasures of God, and it is the way of faith. There is only one principle underlying all the attributes and all the beatitudes of the mighty ascension into the glories of Christ, and it is faith. All the promises are *"Yes"* and *"Amen"* to those who believe (2 Cor. 1:20).

Let's turn to Hebrews 11:1–10:

Now faith is the substance of things hoped for, the evidence of things not seen. For by it the elders obtained a good testimony. By faith we understand that the worlds were framed by the word of God, so that the things which are seen were not made of things which are visible. By faith Abel offered to God a more excellent sacrifice than Cain, through which he obtained witness that he was righteous, God testifying of his gifts; and through it he being dead still speaks. By faith Enoch was taken away so that he did not see death, "and was not found, because God had taken him"; for before he was taken he had this testimony, that he pleased God. But without faith it is impossible to please Him, for he who comes to God must believe that He is, and that He is a rewarder of those who diligently seek Him. By faith Noah, being divinely warned of things not yet seen, moved with godly fear, prepared an ark for the saving of his household, by which he condemned the world and became heir of the righteousness which is according to faith. By faith Abraham obeyed when he was called to go out to the place which he would receive as an inheritance. And he went out, not knowing where he was going. By faith he dwelt in the land of promise as in a foreign country, dwelling in tents with Isaac and Jacob, the heirs with him of the

same promise; for he waited for the city which has founda-
tions, whose builder and maker is God. (Heb. 11:1–10)

God has a way to bring us to faith, and it never comes by any human means. It always comes by divine principles. You cannot know God by nature; you get to know God by an open door of grace. He has made a way. It is a beautiful way so that all His saints can enter in by that way and find rest. The way is the way of faith; there isn't any other way. If you climb up any other way, you cannot work it out.

SAY "AMEN" TO JESUS

There are several things that are coming before me from time to time, and I find that anything is a failure if it does not have its base right on the Rock, Christ Jesus. He is the only Way, the Truth, and the Life (John 14:6). But praise God, He is the Truth; He is the Life; and His Word is spirit and life-giving (John 6:63). And when we understand it in its true order to us, we find that it is not only the Word of Life, but it quickens, opens, fills, moves, changes, and brings us into a place where we dare to say, "Amen!" There is a lot in an amen. I find you can have zeal without faith. And I find you can have any amount of things without faith. The following examples show the difference between the amen of faith and having zeal or other emotions without faith.

As I looked into the twelfth chapter of the Acts of the Apostles, I found that the people who were waiting all night praying for Peter to come out of prison had zeal, but they did not have faith. (See Acts 12:3–17.) They were so zealous that they even allowed themselves to eat only unleavened bread, and they prayed. It seems as if there is much that could be commended to us from this passage, but there is one thing missing. It is faith. You will find that Rhoda had more faith than all the rest of them. When the knock came at the door, she ran to it, and the moment she heard Peter's voice she ran back again with joy, saying that Peter stood before the gate.

And all the people said, "You are mad. It isn't so." And she made mention of what she saw. The people had no faith at all. But they said, "Well, God has perhaps sent an angel."

But Rhoda said, "It is Peter." And Peter continued knocking. They went and found it was so. They had zeal but no faith. And I believe there is quite a difference.

God wants to bring us into an activity where we will take hold of God in a living way. We need to rest and always see the plan of God.

There was such a difference between Zacharias and Mary. Zacharias and Elizabeth definitely wanted a son, but even when the angel came and told Zacharias that he would be the father of a son, he was full of unbelief. And the angel said, *"You will be mute and not able to speak...because you did not believe"* (Luke 1:20). But look at Mary. When the angel came to Mary, she said, *"Let it be to me according to your word"* (v. 38). This was the beginning of the amen, and the presentation of the amen was when she nursed Jesus.

Believe that there can be a real amen in your life that can come to pass. And God wants us to have the amen that never knows anything else other than amen: an inward amen; a mighty, moving amen; a Godlikeness amen. This amen is what says, "It is," because God has spoken. It cannot be otherwise. It is impossible to be otherwise.

CHANGED BY GOD

Beloved, I see all the plan of life where God comes in and vindicates His power and makes His presence felt. It is not by crying or groaning. It is because we believe. And yet, I have nothing to say about it except that sometimes it takes God a long time to bring us through the groaning and crying before we can believe.

I know this as clearly as I know anything, that no man in this place can change God. You cannot change Him. There is a very good passage in Charles Finney's lectures, and it says, "Can a man who is full of sin and all kinds of ruin in his life change God when he comes out to pray?" No, it is impossible. But as this man labors in prayer and groans and travails, because his tremendous sin is weighing him down, he becomes broken in the presence of God. When he is properly melted in perfect harmony with the divine plan of God, then God can work in that clay. God could not do so before.

Prayer changes hearts, but it never changes God. God is the same today and forever (Heb. 13:8); He is always full of love, full of entreaty, and full of helpfulness. If you always come into the presence of God, you can have what you come for. You can take it away and use it at your disposal. And there is nothing you can find in the Scriptures where God ever charges you for what you have done with what He has given you. God scolds no man, but you can come and come again, and God is willing to give if you believe.

INTERPRETATION OF A MESSAGE IN TONGUES: "It is the living God. It is the God of power who changes things, changes us. 'It is He who has formed us, not we ourselves,' and transformed us because it is He who comes in and makes the vessel ready for the immensity of its power working through us, transforming us into His will, His plan, for He delights in us."

God delights in us. *"When a man's ways please the LORD,"* then He makes all things to move accordingly (Prov. 16:7).

TAKEN AWAY BY GOD

Now we come to the Word, this blessed Word, this holy Word. I want to go to the fifth verse of the eleventh chapter of Hebrews:

By faith Enoch was taken away so that he did not see death, "and was not found, because God had taken him"; for before he was taken he had this testimony, that he pleased God.

When I was in Sweden, the Lord worked mightily there in a very blessed way. After one or two addresses, the leaders called me and said, "We have heard very strange things about you, and we would like to know whether they are true because we can see the doors are opening to you. We can see that God is with you, and God is moving, and we know that your work will be a great blessing to Sweden."

"Well," I said, "what is it?"

"Well," they said, "we have heard from good authority that you preach that you have the resurrection body." When I was in France, I had an interpreter that believed this thing, and I found out after I had preached once or twice through the interpreter that she gave her own expressions. And, of course, I did not know that she was doing this. Then I said, "Nevertheless, I will tell you what I really believe. If I had the testimony of Enoch, I would be off. I would like it, and I would like to go. Evidently no one in Sweden has the testimony of Enoch, or they would be off, because the moment Enoch had the testimony that was pleasing to God, off he went."

I pray that God will so quicken our faith, for we have a long way to go maybe before we are ready. Being taken away was in the mind of God. But remember, being taken away by God comes along the lines of holy obedience and walking with pleasure with a perfectness of God and walking together with God in the Spirit. Some others have had touches of it. It is lovely; it is delightful to think about those moments when we have walked with God and had communion with Him; when our words were lifted, and we were not made to make them, but God made them.

Oh, how wonderful is that smile of divine communication that is truly of God, where we speak to Him in the Spirit and where the Spirit lifts and lifts and lifts and takes us in! Oh, there is a place of God where God can bring us in, and I pray that God by His Spirit may move us so we will strive to be where Enoch was as he *"walked with God"* (Gen. 5:24).

As Paul divinely put it by the Spirit, I don't believe that any person does not have an open door into everything that is in the Scriptures. I believe the Scriptures are for us. In order that we may apply our hearts to understand the truth, I say, "Oh, for an inroad of the mighty revolution of the human heart to break it so that God can plan afresh and make all within us say, 'Amen!'" What a blessed experience it truly is.

Supernatural Faith from God

There are two kinds of faith that God wants to let us see. I am not speaking about natural things but divine things. There is a natural faith, and there is a saving faith. The saving faith is the gift of God. All people are born with the natural faith. But this supernatural faith is the gift of God. Yet there are limitations in this faith. Faith that has no limitation in God can be seen in the twenty-sixth chapter of Acts. This is a very wonderful chapter. I want to define, express, or bring into prominence the difference between the natural faith and this faith that I am going to read about, beginning at the sixteenth verse:

> But rise and stand on your feet; for I have appeared to you for
> this purpose, to make you a minister and a witness both of the

things which you have seen and of the things which I will yet reveal to you. I will deliver you from the Jewish people, as well as from the Gentiles, to whom I now send you, to open their eyes, in order to turn them from darkness to light, and from the power of Satan to God, that they may receive forgiveness of sins and an inheritance among those who are sanctified by faith in Me. (Acts 26:16–18)

Is that the faith of Paul? No, it is the faith that the Holy Spirit is giving. We may have much revelation of a divine plan of God through the gifts in the Lord's order, and when He speaks to me, I will begin operating in the gifts.

I see here just a touch of the gifts, where Paul, through the revelation and the open door that was given to him on the way to Damascus, saw he had the faith of salvation. I notice that as Ananias laid his hands upon him, there came a power, the promise of the Holy Spirit, that filled his body. And then I notice in that order of the Spirit, he walked in the comfort of the Holy Spirit, which is a wonderful comfort. (See Acts 9:1–19.) Oh, tell me if you can, is there anything to compare to what Jesus said: "When the Holy Spirit comes, *'He will teach you all things, and bring to your remembrance all things'* (John 14:26)"? Surely this is a Comforter. Surely He is the Comforter who can bring to our memories and minds all the things that Jesus said.

And all the ways He worked is the divine plan of the Spirit to reveal to us until every one of us, without exception, tastes of this angelic, mighty touch of the heavenly as He moves upon us. The baptism of the Holy Spirit is the essential, mighty touch of revelation of the wonders, for God the Holy Spirit has no limitations along these lines. But when the soul is ready to enter into His life, there is a breaking up of fallow ground and a moving of the mists away, bringing us into the perfect day of the light of God.

And I say that Paul was moved upon by this power, and yet Jesus said to him, "As you go, you will be changed, and in the changing I will take you from revelation to revelation, open door to open door, and the accomplishment will be as My faith is committed to you."

Oh, hallelujah, there is saving faith. There is the gift of faith. It is the faith of Jesus that comes to us as we press in and on with God, a place where we can always know it is God.

AN EXAMPLE OF FAITH

I want just to put before you this difference between our faith and the faith of Jesus. Our faith comes to an end. Most people have come to a place where they have said, "Lord, I can go no further. I have gone so far; now I can go no further. I have used all the faith I have, and I just have to stop now and wait."

Well, brother, thank God that we have this faith. But there is another faith. I remember one day being in northern England and going around to see some sick people. I was taken into a house where there was a young woman lying on her bed, a very helpless case. It was a case where her reason had gone, and many things were manifested there that were satanic, and I knew it.

She was only a young woman, a beautiful child. Then the husband, who was quite a young man, came in with a baby, and he leaned over to kiss the wife. The moment he did, she threw herself over on the other side of the bed, just as a lunatic would do, with no consciousness of the presence of the husband. That was very heartbreaking. And then he took the baby and pressed the baby's lips to the mother. Again, another wild kind of thing happened. So he said to a sister who was attending her, "Have you anybody to help?"

"Oh," she said, "we have had everything."

But I said, "Have you no spiritual help?"

And her husband stormed out and said, "Help? You think that we believe in God after we have had seven weeks of no sleep and of maniac conditions? You think that we believe God? You are mistaken. You have come to the wrong house."

And then a young woman about eighteen or so just grinned at me and walked out of the door, and that finished the whole business. That brought me to a place of compassion that something had to be done for this woman; it did not matter what it was.

And then with my faith—thank God for the faith—I began to penetrate the heavens, and I was soon out of that house, I will tell you, for I never saw a man get anything from God who prayed on the earth. If you are to get anything from God, you will have to pray into heaven, for it is all there. If you are living on the earth and expect things from heaven, they will never come. If you want to touch the ideal, you must live in ideal principles.

And as I saw in the presence of God the limitations of my faith, there came another faith, a faith that could not be denied, a faith that took the promise, a faith that believed God's Word. And I came from that presence back again to earth, but I was not the same man under the same condition that confronted me. But in the name of Jesus, I was a man with a faith that could shake hell and move anything else.

I said, "Come out of her in the name of Jesus!" And she rolled over and fell asleep and wakened in fourteen hours, perfectly sane and perfectly whole. Oh, there is faith, the faith that is in me. And Jesus wants to bring us all into a place in line with God where we cease to be, for God must have the right-of-way, of thought, and of purpose. God must have the way.

WALK WITH GOD

There is a process along these lines. *"Enoch walked with God"* (Gen. 5:24). That must have been during hundreds of years as he was penetrating, and going through, and laying hold, and believing, and seeing that he had gotten to such cooperation and touch with God that things moved on earth and were moving toward heaven. And surely God came for the last time.

It was not possible for him to stop any longer. Oh, hallelujah! And I believe that God similarly wants to bring all of us into line with His will so that we may see signs, wonders, and various miracles and gifts of the Holy Spirit. For this is a wonderful day, the day of the Holy Spirit. It is a blessed day. If you would ask me any time, "When would you have liked to come to earth?" I would tell you, "Just now!" Oh, yes, it suits me beautifully to know that the Holy Spirit can fill the body. It is wonderful just to be a temple of the Spirit, just to manifest the glory of God! It is truly an ideal summit, and everyone can reach out his hand and have God take it and lift him up.

For the heart that is longing, God makes the longing cry. Sometimes we have an idea that there is some special thing in us that does it. No, beloved. If you have anything at all worth having, it is because God has love to give you.

I truly say that there is a plan of God for the purpose of this life. Enoch walked with God. God wants to raise the conditions of saints to walk with Him and talk with Him. I don't want to raise myself up, but it is true that if you do not find me in conversation with man, I am in conversation with God.

489

One thing God has given to me from my youth up—and I am so thankful—is no taste or relish for any book but the Bible. And I can say before God that I have never completely read a book except the Bible, so I know nothing about books. As I have glanced into books, I have seen in them a little of what good people call a good book. Oh, but how much better it is to get the Book of books that contains nothing but God. If a book is commended because it has something about God in it, how much more will the Word of God be the food of the soul, the strengthening of the believer, and the building up of the human order of character with God, so that all the time the reader is being changed by the Spirit of the Lord from one state of glory into another (2 Cor. 3:18).

This is the ideal principle of God. I have something to say about those who have gone, because Paul said, "It is better to go than to stop." (See Philippians 1:23–26.) But oh, I am looking forward to and believing the fact that He is coming again. And this hope in me brings me to the same place as the man of faith who looked for a city that human hands have not made. (See Hebrews 11:8–10.) There is a city that human hands have not made, and by faith we have a right to claim our position right along as we go.

THE IDEAL PLAN OF FAITH

I will turn now to Hebrews 11:6: *"But without faith it is impossible to please Him, for he who comes to God must believe that He is, and that He is a rewarder of those who diligently seek Him."*

I often think that we make great failures along these lines because of an imperfect understanding of His Word. I can see it is impossible to please God along any lines but faith, for everything that is not of faith is sin (Rom. 14:23).

God wants us all to see that the plan of faith is the ideal and principle of God. And when I remember and keep in my thoughts the beautiful words from the twelfth chapter of Hebrews, it is wonderful as I read the second verse: *"Looking unto Jesus, the author and finisher of our faith."* He is the Author of faith. Jesus became the Author of faith. God worked the plan through Him by forming the worlds and making everything that there was by the Word of His power (Heb. 1:1–3). Jesus Christ is the Word (John 1:1). God so manifested this power in the world, forming the worlds by the word of Jesus.

I see that on this divine line of principle of God, God has chosen Him, ordained Him, clothed Him, and made Him greater than all because of one principle, and on this principle only. And this principle is the love of God that gave the joy. It was the joy of the Lord to save. Because of this exceeding, abundant joy of saving the whole world, He became the Author of a living faith. And everyone is changed by this faith from grace to grace. We become divine inheritors of the promises, and we become the substance.

There is one ideal only, and that is that God is working in this holy principle of faith. It is divine.

> INTERPRETATION OF A MESSAGE IN TONGUES: "It is God installated through the flesh, quickened by His Spirit, molded by His will, until it is so in order, until God's Son could not come unless we went, for His life is in us."

Thank God for that interpretation. God's Son, this life, this faith, cannot move from glory unless I move from the earth. And we should meet right in heaven. Thank God for this faith, this principle, this life, this inheritance, this truth, this eternal power working in us mightily by His Spirit!

FAITH THROUGH THE WORD

Oh, thank God for His Word! Live it. Be moved by His Word. We will become flat and anemic and helpless without this Word. You are not any good for anything apart from the Word. The Word is everything; the Word has to become everything. When the heavens and the earth are melted away, then we will be as bright as, and brighter than, the day because of the Word of God.

We know it is *"living and powerful, and sharper than any two-edged sword,"* dividing soul and spirit, joints and marrow, and thoughts of the heart (Heb. 4:12)! God's Word is like a sword piercing through. Who could have a stiff knee if he believed in that Word?

The Word is so divinely appointed for us. Think about it. How it severs the soul and the spirit! Take it in; think it out; work it out. It is divine. See it; it is the truth.

The soul, which has all the animal, all the carnal, all the selfishness, all the evil things—thank God for the truth of the Word that the corruption of the soul will never inherit that place. The corruption of the soul must go from where it came. It is earthly and sensual. But the two-edged sword divides it so it will have no power. And the Spirit of the life of Jesus is over it, ruling it, controlling it, and bringing it always to death.

Flesh and blood will not inherit the kingdom of heaven (1 Cor. 15:50). So I see it is necessary for us to have the Word of God piercing even to the dividing of soul and spirit. Then I notice the joints and marrow must have the Word of God to quicken the very marrow.

Many people in Australia came to me with double curvature of the spine, and instantly they were healed and made straight as I put hands upon them. But no man is able except the divine Son of God, and His power moved upon these curvatures of the spine and straightened them. Oh, the mighty power of the Word of God! God must have us in these days so separated on every line as we proceed along the lines of God and see what the Word of God must bring forth. As it destroys, it brings forth. You can never live if you have never been dead. You must die if you want to live (Matt. 10:39). It was the very death of Jesus that raised Him to the highest height of glory.

Every death-likeness is a likeness to the Son of God. And all the time the Word of God must quicken, flow through, and move upon us until these ideals are in us, until we move in them and live in them.

INTERPRETATION OF A MESSAGE IN TONGUES: "The living God is lifting you out of yourself into Himself."

COME TO GOD IN GLORY

We must be taken out of the ordinary and be brought into the extraordinary. We must live in a glorious position over the flesh and the Devil and everything of the world. God has ordained us, clothed us within, and manifested His glory upon us so that we may be the sons with promise, of Son-likeness to Him. What an ideal! What a Savior! What an ideal Savior! And to be like Him! Oh, yes, we can be like Him. The ideal principle is for God to make us like Him.

Then I see another truth. How do you come to God? Where is God? Is He in the ceiling, in the elements, in the air, in the wind? Where is God? He who comes to God—where is He? God is in you (Eph. 4:4–6). Oh, hallelujah! And you will find the Spirit of the living God in you, which is the prayer circle, which is the lifting power, which is the revelation element, which is the divine power that lifts you.

He who comes to God is already in the place where the Holy Spirit takes the prayers and swings them out according to the mind of the Spirit. For who has known the mind of Christ, or who is able to make intercession, except the mind of the Spirit of the living God (1 Cor. 2:11)? He makes intercession. Where is He? He is in us. Oh, this baptism of the Holy Spirit is an inward presence of the personality of God that lifts, prays, takes hold, and lives in us with a tranquillity of peace and power that rests and says, "It is all right."

God answers prayer because the Holy Spirit prays, your advocate is Jesus, and the Father is the Judge of all. There He is. Is it possible for any prayer to be missed on those lines? Let us be sure that we are in this place now.

"He who comes to God must believe that He is, and that He is a rewarder of those who diligently seek Him" (Heb. 11:6). He who comes to God must believe that God is. You cannot help it. You must believe He is already in the temple.

But some people have not yet entered into the experience because they have never come out. But God said to Abraham, "Come out, come out." (See Genesis 12:1.) And if you have never heard the voice of God telling you to come out, you may be in the wilderness a long time before you enter in. Now, look at the ridiculousness of Abraham, that is, from the human viewpoint. Look at it in Hebrews 11:8: *"By faith Abraham obeyed when he was called to go out to the place which he would receive as an inheritance."* What a silly man he was—*"not knowing where he was going"* (v. 8)! Why, that was the very secret of power. Everything was there. If there is anything that I know that is worth knowing, it is what God is always teaching me about Himself.

There is something about wanting to follow God's mind until we will be what He wants us to be all the time. God has ordered it so. God has planned it so. God wills it. God has no other method or plan of saving ruined man except by man. And when man remains in the place where God has called him, so that he can be a perfect man following God's plan for him, then he will surely have reached the attitude where God has said, "Come out, for I have a place for you, and you can never reach the place without Me. But I am willing that you should be for Me so that I may be for you."

Oh, this God of grace! Oh, this willingness for God to let us see His face! Oh, this longing of my soul that cannot be satisfied without more of God! Oh, it is this, more of God, that I want! I feel that I am the youngest man in the world.

Unless God does something, I would be an awful failure. But surely He will do it. He has brought us in so that He might take us out. And God will never leave us in an unfinished place.

It is all divine order. There is nothing wrong in the plan of God. It is all in perfect order. To think that God can make a mistake is the biggest blunder that a man makes in his life. God makes no mistakes. But when we are in the will of God, the plan works out admirably because it is divine and thought-out by the almightiness of God.

Oh, beloved, have you come out yet? You say, "Out of what?" Out of what you know you didn't want to be in. Why should I answer your questions when you can answer them yourselves? It would be a waste of time. No need of going on that line. But God knows where you are and where you ought to be. Many of you heard the voice of God long ago, but still you have not obeyed. Will you come out? God says, "Come out!" But you say, "Where will I go? Where will I come out?" Come out into God, unto God, oh, hallelujah!

I think it is just about time to come out. It is such a mistake to hold on and not obey Him when you hear His voice. But when we obey, it is so sweet! So I will stop at this time because God probably has something better to teach you in the Spirit as you obey His call and obey His "Come out." God has something better for you than I can tell you. Oh, I say to you, "Come out," and I will leave you either to sit still or come out. Amen!

CHAPTER SEVEN

THE INHERITANCE OF FAITH

here are things in Romans 4 that will bring a revelation of what God intends for the man who believes. The great plan of God's salvation is redemption in its fullness. I know that prayer is wonderful, and not only changes things but changes you. I know that the man of prayer can go right in and receive the blessing from God; yet I tell you that if we grasp this truth that we have before us, we will find that faith is the greatest inheritance of all.

May God give us faith that will bring this glorious inheritance into our hearts, for it is true that the just will live by faith (Rom. 1:17), and do not forget that it takes a just man to live by faith. May the Lord reveal to us the fullness of this truth, which God gave to Abraham.

LOOKING TO GOD'S PROMISE

For twenty-five years Abraham had the promise that God would give him a son. For twenty-five years he stood face to face with God on the promise, every year expecting to have a son. There was Sarah becoming weaker, and Abraham's own stamina and body were becoming frailer. Natural conditions were so changing both Sarah and him that, as far as they could see, there was no such thing as seeing their bodies bring forth fruit. And, if they had looked at their bodies as some people do theirs, they would probably have remained as they were forever. But Abraham dared not look either at Sarah or himself in that respect. He had to look at God. You cannot find anywhere that God ever failed. And He wants to bring us into that blessed place of faith, changing us into a real

495

substance of faith, until we are so like-minded that whatever we ask, we believe we receive, and our joy becomes full because we believe (John 16:24). I want you to see how God covered Abraham because he believed.

Hear what God said to Abraham, and then see how Abraham acted. He was among his own people and his own kindred, and God said to him, "Come out, Abraham, come out!" And Abraham obeyed and came out, *"not knowing where he was going"* (Heb. 11:8). You will never go through with God in any area except by believing Him. It is "Thus says the Lord" every time, and you will see the plan of God come right through when you dare to believe. He came right out of his own country, and God was with him. Because he believed God, God overshadowed him.

I am as confident as possible that if we could get to the place of believing God, we would not need to rely on a dog in the yard or a lock on the door. All this is unbelief. God is able to manage the whole business. It doesn't matter how many thieves are about; they cannot break through or steal where God is.

I want, by the help of God, to lead you into the truth, for nothing but the truth can set you free (John 8:32). Truth can always do it. It is impossible, if God covers you with His righteousness, for anything to happen to you that is contrary to the mind of God.

When God sets His seal upon you, the Devil will not dare to break it. He will not dare to break in where you are. You know what a seal is, don't you? Now then, when God puts His seal upon you, the Devil has no power there. He will not dare to break that seal and go through, and God puts His seal upon the man who believes Him.

There are two kinds of righteousness. There is a righteousness that is according to the law, the keeping of the law, but there is a better righteousness than that. You ask, "What could be better than keeping the law?" The righteousness that sees God and obeys Him in everything is better. The righteousness that believes that every prayer uttered is going to bring the answer from God is better. There is a righteousness that is made known only to the heart that knows God. There is a side to the inner man that God can reveal only to the man who believes Him.

We have many scriptural illustrations to show us how God worked with those people who believed Him. I have many definite instances in my life where God came, where God was, where God worked, and where God planned. And here is one of the greatest plans of all, where God works in this man Abraham exactly opposite to human nature. There were many good points about Sarah, but she had not reached the place. She laughed when she heard she would have a son in her old age, and then denied having done so (Gen. 18:12, 15). Before that, when they had waited a time and she had seen that their bodies were growing frailer, she said, "Now, it will be just as good for you to take Hagar for a wife and bring forth a son through her." (See Genesis 16:1–3.) But that was not the seed of Abraham that God had spoken about, and that caused a great deal of trouble in the house of Abraham.

There are times when you dare not take your spouse's advice. The man who walks with God can only afford to follow God's leadings, and when He leads you, it is direct and clear. The evidence is so real that every day you know that God is with you, unfolding His plan to you. It is lovely to be in the will of God.

INTERPRETATION OF A MESSAGE IN TONGUES: "Glory to God! He is the Lord of Hosts who comes forth into the heart of the human life of man and speaks according to His divine plan. And as you live in the Spirit, you live in the process of God's mind and act according to His divine will."

And so there is a higher order than the natural man, and God wants to bring us into this higher order where we will believe Him. In the first place, God promised Abraham a son. Could a child be born into the world, except on the line of the natural law? It was when all natural law was finished and when there was no substance in these two persons, Abraham and Sarah, that the law of the Spirit brought forth a son. It was the law of faith in the God who had promised.

BORN OF GOD

And then we are brought to the time when our blessed Lord was conceived. I hear Mary saying to the angel, *"Let it be to me according to your word"* (Luke 1:38), so that the Man Christ Jesus was brought forth along the same lines. I see before me faces I know, and I can see that these men are born, not of blood, or by the will of the flesh, but of God (John 1:13). We have the same law in our midst now: born of God! And sometimes I see that this power within us is greater when we are weak than when we are strong, and this power was greater in Abraham as days went by than when he was strong.

Looking at him, Sarah would shake her head and say, "I never saw anybody so thin and weak and helpless in my life. No, Abraham, I have been looking at you, and you seem to be going right down." But Abraham refused to look at his own body or Sarah's; he believed that the promise would happen.

Suppose you come for healing. You know as well as possible that, according to the natural life, there is no power in your body to give you that health. You also know that the ailment from which you suffer has so drained your life and energy that there is no help at all in you, but God says that you will be healed if you believe. It makes no difference how your body is. It was exactly the helplessness of Sarah and Abraham that brought the glorious fact that a son was born, and I want you to see what sort of a son he was.

He was the son of Abraham. His seed is the seed of the whole believing church—innumerable as the sands upon the seashore (Gen. 22:17). God wants you to know that there is no limitation with Him, and He wants to bring us to a place where there will be no limitation in us. This state would be brought about by the working of the Omnipotent in the human body, working in us continually—the One who is greater than any science or any power in the world—and bringing us into the place to comprehend God and man.

I want you to see that Romans 4:16 has a great message for us all:

Therefore it is of faith that it might be according to grace, so that the promise might be sure to all the seed, not only to those who are of the law, but also to those who are of the faith of Abraham, who is the father of us all.

Think about those words, *"Therefore it is of faith that it might be according to grace."* Some of you would like a touch in your bodies; some would like a touch in your spirits; some would like to be baptized in the Holy Spirit; some want to be filled with all God's power. It is there for you: *"That the blessing of Abraham might come upon the Gentiles in Christ Jesus, that we might receive the promise of the Spirit through faith"* (Gal. 3:14).

Now, come on the lines of faith again. I want you to see that you can be healed if you will hear the Word. Now, some people want healing; maybe some need salvation; maybe others want sanctification and the baptism of the Spirit. The verse from Romans says it is by faith, that it might be by grace. Grace is omnipotence; it is activity, benevolence, and mercy. It is truth, perfection, and God's inheritance in the soul who can believe. It is by faith. Grace is God. You open the door by faith, and God comes in with all you need and want. It cannot be otherwise, for it is *"of faith that it might be according to grace"* (Rom. 4:16). It cannot be by grace unless you say it will be so.

This is believing, and most people want healing by feeling. It cannot be. Some even want salvation on the same lines, and they say, "Oh, if only I could feel I was saved!" It will never come that way. There are three things that work together. The first is faith. Faith can always bring the second thing—a fact—and a fact can always bring the third thing—joy. So God brings you to hear the Scriptures, which can *"make you wise for salvation"* (2 Tim. 3:15), which can open your understanding and make you so that if you will hear the truth, you will go out with what you want. Then you have power to shut the door and power to open the door.

DARE TO BELIEVE!

Let us now look step by step at another verse that is mightier still, and you will find it is very wonderful: *"As it is written, 'I have made you a father of many nations'"* (Rom. 4:17). Here are Sarah— her body is almost dead—and Abraham—his body is almost dead. "Now," says Abraham, "God has made me a father of many nations, and there is no hope of a son according to the natural law, no hope whatever." Here God says, *"I have made you a father of many nations,"* and yet Abraham has no son. During the past twenty years of waiting, conditions have grown more and more hopeless, and yet the promise has been made.

Now, how long have you believed and still suffered from rheumatism? How long have you been waiting for the promise and it has not come? Did you need to wait? Look here! I want to tell you that all the people who are saved *"are blessed with faithful Abraham"* (Gal. 3:9 KJV). Abraham is the great substance of the whole keynote of Scripture; he is a man who dared for twenty-five years to believe God when everything got worse every day. Oh, it is lovely and perfect. I do not know anything in the Scriptures as marvelous, as far-reaching, and as full of the substance of living reality to change us if we will believe God. He will make us so different. This is a living faith that changes us and makes us know that *"[God] is, and that He is a rewarder of those who diligently seek Him"* (Heb. 11:6). God is a reality. God is true, and in Him there is no lie or *"shadow of turning"* (James 1:17). Oh, it is good! I do love to think about such truths as these.

Oh, beloved, there is not a subject in the whole Bible that makes my body aflame with passion after God and His righteousness as this does. I see that He never fails. He wants the man to believe, and then the man will never fail. Oh, the loveliness of the character of God!

"A father of many nations" (Rom. 4:17). You talk about your infirmities—look at this! I have never felt I have had an infirmity since I understood this chapter. O God, help me; I feel more like weeping than talking tonight. My cup runs over as I see the magnitude of this living God.

> *Therefore it is of faith that it might be according to grace, so that the promise might be sure to all the seed, not only to those who are of the law, but also to those who are of the faith of Abraham, who is the father of us all (as it is written, "I have made you a father of many nations") in the presence of Him whom he believed; God, who gives life to the dead and calls those things which do not exist as though they did; who, contrary to hope, in hope believed, so that he became the father of many nations, according to what was spoken, "So shall your descendants be."* (Rom. 4:16–18)

It is almost as if Abraham had said, "I won't look at my body. I won't look at my infirmities. I believe God will make the whole thing right." Some of us can say, "What does it matter if I have not heard for over twenty years? I believe my ears will be perfect." God is reality and wants us to know that if we will believe, it will be perfect. *"Who gives life to the dead and calls those things which do not exist as though they did."* There is no limitation of possibility.

Then God tested Abraham and Sarah still further than that. Oh, it is blessed to know you are tested. It is the greatest thing in the world to be tested. You never know what you are made of until you are tested. Some people say, "Oh, I don't know why my lot is such a heavy one," and God puts them into the fire again. He knows how to do it. I can tell you, He is a blessed God. There is no such thing as a groan when God gets hold of you. There is no such thing as lack to those who trust the Lord. When we really get in the will of God, He can make our enemies to be at peace with us (Prov. 16:7). It is wonderful.

I wonder if you really believe that God can quicken what is dead. I have seen it many times. The more there was no hope, Abraham *"believed in hope"* (Rom. 4:18 KJV). Sometimes Satan will cloud your minds and interfere with your perception so that the obscure condition is brought right in between you and God, but God is able to change the whole position if you will let Him have a chance. Turn your back on every sense of unbelief, and believe God. There are some who would like to feel the presence of the touch of God; God will bring it to you. Now, I wish people could come to this place.

Abraham had a good time. The more he was squeezed, the more he rejoiced; and being not weak in faith, he did not consider his own body, which was weak when he was about a hundred years old, or the deadness of Sarah's womb. He did not waver through unbelief, but he was strong in faith, giving God the glory (vv. 19–20). God knows. He has a plan; He has a way. Do you dare trust Him? He knows.

I am here, saved by the power of God, because of the promise that God made to Abraham: "As the countless sands upon the sea-shore and as the stars in multitude and glory, the seed of your son will be!" (See Genesis 22:16–18.) It is for us now. The Scripture says to us that the delaying of the promise and the testing of Abraham were the seed of all those in future generations who would believe in God:

> [Abraham was] *fully convinced that what He had promised He was also able to perform. And therefore "it was accounted to him for righteousness." Now it was not written for his sake alone that it was imputed to him, but also for us. It shall be imputed to us who believe in Him who raised up Jesus our Lord from the dead.* (Rom. 4:21–24)

THE PROMISE FULFILLED

We have another place in the Scriptures, and I want to touch upon it now. Isaac was born. And you find that right in that house where Isaac was and where Ishmael was, there were the seed of promise and the seed of flesh. You find there was strife and trouble right there, for Ishmael was teasing Isaac. And you will find as sure as anything that there is nothing that is going to hold you except the Isaac life—the seed of Abraham. You will find that the flesh life will always have to be cast out. And Sarah said, *"Cast out* [Hagar] *and her son"* (Gen. 21:10). It was very hard to do, but it had to be done. You may say, "How hard!" Yes, but how long did it have to be? It had to be until submission came. There will always be jealousy and strife in your hearts and lives until flesh is destroyed, until Isaac controls and rules in authority over the whole body. And when Isaac power reigns over you, you will find that your whole life is full of peace and joy.

Then the time came when this son Isaac grew up to be a fine young man, perhaps twenty years of age—we are not told—but then came another test. God said to Abraham, "Take your son Isaac, and offer him to Me upon the mount that I will show you." (See Genesis 22:2.) Do you think that Abraham told anybody about that? No, I am sure he didn't. Isaac was near to his heart, and God said he had to offer him on the altar. There he was—Isaac, the heart of his heart—and God said he was to be the seed of all living. What did he have to do but believe that, just as miraculously as Isaac came into the world, God could raise him even if he were slain (Heb. 11:17–19)? Did he tell Sarah about the thing? No, I am certain he did not, or else he would not have gotten away with that boy. There would have been such a trial in the home. I believe he kept it to himself. When God tells you a secret, don't tell anyone else. God will possibly tell you to go and lay hands on some sick one. Go, do it, and don't tell anyone.

One thing I know is that Satan does not know my thoughts; he only knows what I let out of my mouth. Sometimes he suggests thoughts in order to get to know my thoughts, but I can see that God can captivate my thoughts in such a way that they may be entirely for Him. When God gets upon your hearts, you will see that every thought is captive, that everything is brought into obedience and is brought into a place where you are in dominion because

Christ is enthroned in your life (2 Cor. 10:4–5). God reveals deep and special things to some people. Keep your counsel before God.

I see this: Abraham could offer Isaac. "Tell me how," you say. I believe that God wants me to tell you how so that you may know something about your trials. Some people think they are tried more than other people. If you knew the value of them, you would praise God for trials more than for anything. It is the trial that is used to purify you; it is the fiery furnace of affliction that God uses to get you in the place where He can use you. The person who has no trials and no difficulties is the person whom God does not dare allow Satan to touch because this person could not stand temptation. But Jesus will not allow any man to be tempted more than he is able to bear (1 Cor. 10:13).

The Scriptures are the strongest evidence of anything you can have. Before Abraham offered Isaac, he was tried, and God knew he could do it. And before God puts you through the furnace of afflictions, He knows you will go through. Not one single temptation comes to any man more than he is able to bear, and with the temptation, God is always there to help you through. Don't you see that was exactly the position in Abraham's case?

If you know you need the baptism of the Holy Spirit, and you know it is in the Scriptures, never rest until God gives it to you. If you know it is scriptural for you to be healed of every weakness, never rest until God makes the healing yours. If you know that the Scriptures teach holiness, purity, and divine-likeness—overcoming under all conditions—never rest until you are an overcomer. If you know that men who have gone in and have seen the face of God, have had the vision revealed and have had all the Scriptures made to be life in their lives, never rest until you come to it. You say, "Do you have a Scripture to prove it?" Yes, the Scripture says, *"That you…may be able to comprehend with all the saints what is the width and length and depth and height; to know the love of Christ"* (Eph. 3:17–19).

INTERPRETATION OF A MESSAGE IN TONGUES: "Oh, hallelujah! This blessed inheritance of the Spirit is come 'to profit withal,' teaching you all things, and making you understand that the will of God comes not by observation, but holy men of old spoke and wrote as the Spirit gave them power and utterance. And so today the Holy Spirit must fill us with this same initiative of God."

We must live in the fire. We must hate sin; we must love righteousness. We must live with God, for He says we have to be *"blameless and harmless"* amid the crooked positions of the world (Phil. 2:15). I look at you now, and I say God is able to confirm all I have been saying about trials and testings, which are the greatest blessings you can have. God wants to make sons everywhere like Jesus. Jesus was a type of the sonship that we have to strive to attain. You don't know how I feel when I am speaking about the loftiness of the character of Jesus, who was a firstfruit to make us pure and holy. And I see Jesus going about clothed with power. I likewise see every child of God clothed with power, and I see every detail. Jesus was just the firstfruit, and I know that is the pattern of God.

God has not given us a pattern that would be impossible to copy. Jesus hated sin, and this hatred is the greatest luxury we can have in our lives. If I have a hatred for sin, I have something that is worth millions. Oh, the blood of Jesus Christ, God's Son, cleanses us from all sin (1 John 1:7). I feel somehow that the hope of the church for the future is to be purified and made like Jesus: pure in heart, pure in thought. Then, when you lay your hands upon the sick, Satan has no power. When you command him to leave, he has to go. What a redemption! What a baptism! What an anointing! It is ecstasies of delight beyond all expression for the soul to live and move in Him who is our being. (See Acts 17:28.)

CHAPTER EIGHT

FULL! FULL! FULL!

Only believe! All things are possible; only believe (Mark 9:23)! Praise God, He has made all things possible. There is liberty for everyone, whatever the trouble. Our Lord Jesus says, *"Only believe"* (Mark 5:36). He has obtained complete victory over every difficulty, over every power of evil, over every depravity. Every sin is covered by Calvary.

Who are of the tribe of Abraham? All who believe in Jesus Christ are the seed of faith, Abraham's seed. If we dare come believing, God will heal; God will restore and will lift the burden and will wake us up to real, overcoming faith. Look up; take courage! Jesus has shaken the foundations of death and darkness. He fights for you, and there is none like Him. He is the great I AM. His name is above every name. As we believe, we are lifted into a place of rest, a place of conformity to Him. He says to us as He did to Abraham, *"I will bless you...and you shall be a blessing"* (Gen. 12:2). He says to us as He did to His people of old, *"With lovingkindness I have drawn you"* (Jer. 31:3). Hallelujah!

> He'll never forget to keep me,
> He'll never forget to keep me;
> My Father has many dear children,
> But He'll never forget to keep me.

Believe it. He will never forget.

LIVE BY THE POWER OF THE SPIRIT

In the sixth chapter of Acts, we read of the appointment of seven deacons. The disciples desired to give themselves wholly to *"prayer and to the ministry of the word"* (Acts 6:4), and they said to the brothers, *"Seek out from among you seven men of good reputation, full of the Holy Spirit and wisdom, whom we may appoint over this business"* (v. 3). And they chose Stephen, *"a man full of faith and the Holy Spirit"* (v. 5), and six others. We read that Stephen, *"full of faith and power, did great wonders and miracles among the people"* (v. 8 KJV), and his opponents *"were not able to resist the wisdom and the Spirit by which he spoke"* (v. 10). When his opponents brought him before the Sanhedrin, all who sat in the council looked steadfastly on him, and they *"saw his face as the face of an angel"* (v. 15).

I see many remarkable things in the life of Stephen. One thing moves me, and that is the truth that I must live by the power of the Spirit at all costs. God wants us to be like Stephen: full of faith and full of the Holy Spirit. You can never be the same again after you have received this wonderful baptism in the Holy Spirit. It is important that we should be full of wisdom and faith day by day and full of the Holy Spirit, acting by the power of the Holy Spirit. God has set us here in the last days, these days of apostasy, and wants us to be burning and shining lights in the midst of an indecent generation (Phil. 2:15). God is longing for us to come into such a fruitful position as the sons of God, with the marks of heaven upon us, and His divinity bursting through our humanity, that He can express Himself through our lips of clay. He can take clay lips and weak humanity and make an oracle for Himself of such things. He can take frail human nature and by His divine power make our bodies suitable to be His holy temple, washing our hearts whiter than snow.

Our Lord Jesus says, *"All authority has been given to Me in heaven and on earth"* (Matt. 28:18). He longs that we would be filled with faith and with the Holy Spirit, and He declares to us, *"He who believes in Me, the works that I do he will do also; and greater works than these he will do, because I go to My Father"* (John 14:12). He has gone to the Father. He is in the place of power, and He exercises His power not only in heaven but also on earth, for He has all power on earth as well as in heaven. Hallelujah! What an open door to us if we will only believe Him!

The disciples were men after our standard as far as the flesh goes. God sent them forth, joined to the Lord and identified with Him. How diverse Peter, John, and Thomas were! Impulsive Peter was always ready to go forth without a stop. John, the beloved, leaned on the Master's breast, and how different that was! (See John 13:21–26.) Thomas had a hard nature and defiant spirit: *"Unless I...put my finger into the print of the nails, and put my hand into His side, I will not believe"* (John 20:25). What strange flesh! How peculiar they were! But the Master could mold them. There was no touch like His.

Under His touch, even stony-hearted Thomas believed. O God, how You have had to manage some of us! Have we not been strange and very peculiar? But, when God's hand comes upon us, He can speak to us in such a way, He can give us a word or a look, and we are broken. Has He spoken to you? I thank God for His speaking. Behind all of His dealings, we see the love of God for us. It is not what we are that counts, but what we can be as He disciplines, chastens, and transforms us by His all-skillful hands. He sees our bitter tears and our weeping night after night. There is none like Him. He knows; He forgives. We cannot forgive ourselves; we oftentimes would give the world to forget, but we cannot. The Devil won't let us forget. But God has forgiven and forgotten. Do you believe self or the Devil or God? Which are you going to believe? Believe God. I know the past is under the blood and that God has forgiven and forgotten, for when He forgives, He forgets. Praise the Lord! Hallelujah! We are baptized to believe and to receive.

FULL OF FAITH AND POWER

In making provision for the serving of tables and the daily distribution, the disciples knew who were baptized with the Holy Spirit (Acts 6:1–3). In the early days of the church, all who did the work had to be men full of the Holy Spirit. I am hungry that I may be more full, that God may choose me for His service. And I know that the greatest qualification is to be filled with the Spirit. The Holy Spirit has the divine commission from heaven to impart revelation to every son of God concerning the Lord Jesus, to unfold to us the gifts and the fruit of the Spirit. He will take of the things of Christ and show them to us (John 16:14).

Stephen was a man full of faith and the Holy Spirit. God declares it. God so manifested Himself in Stephen's body that he became an epistle of truth, *"known and read by all"* (2 Cor. 3:2). He was full of faith! Such men never talk doubtfully. You never hear them say, "I wish it could be so" or "If it is God's will." They have no *ifs*; they know. You never hear them say, "Well, it is not always so." They say, "It is sure to be." They laugh at impossibilities and cry, "It will be done!" A man full of faith hopes against hope (Rom. 4:18). He shouts while the walls are up, and they come down while he shouts. God has this faith for us in Christ. We must be careful that no unbelief and no wavering are found in us.

"Stephen, full of faith and power, did great wonders and signs among the people" (Acts 6:8). The Holy Spirit could do mighty things through him because he believed God, and God is with the man who dares to believe His Word. All things were possible because of the Holy Spirit's position in Stephen's body. He was full of the Holy Spirit, so God could fulfill His purposes through him. When a child of God is filled with the Holy Spirit, the Spirit *"makes intercession for the saints according to the will of God"* (Rom. 8:27). He fills us with longings and desires until we are in a place of fervency like a glowing fire. We do not know what to do. When we are in this place, the Holy Spirit begins to work. When the Holy Spirit has liberty in the body, He conveys all utterance into the presence of God according to the will of God. Such prayers are always heard. Such praying is always answered; it is never bare of result. When we are praying in the Holy Spirit, faith is evident, and as a result the power of God can be manifested in our midst.

When some of the various synagogues arose to dispute with Stephen, *"they were not able to resist the wisdom and the Spirit by which he spoke"* (Acts 6:10). When we are filled with the Holy Spirit, we will have wisdom.

THE POWER OF THE SPIRIT

Praise God! One night I was entrusted with a meeting, and I was guarding my position before God. I wanted approval from the Lord. I saw that God wants men full of the Holy Spirit, with divine ability, filled with life, a flaming fire. In the meeting a young man stood up. He was a pitiful object with a face full of sorrow. I said, "What is it, young man?"

He said he was unable to work, and he could scarcely walk. He said, "I am so helpless. I have consumption and a weak heart, and my body is full of pain."

I said, "I will pray for you." I said to the people, "As I pray for this young man, you look at his face and see it change."

As I prayed, his face changed. I said to him, "Go out, run a mile, and come back to the meeting."

He came back and said, "I can now breathe freely."

The meetings were continuing, and I missed him. After a few days I saw him again in a meeting. I said, "Young man, tell the people what God has done for you."

"Oh," he said, "I have been able to work and make money."

Praise God, this wonderful stream of salvation never runs dry. You can take a drink; it is close to you. It is a river that is running deep, and there is plenty for all.

In a meeting a man rose and said, "Will you touch me? I am in a terrible situation. I have a family of children, and because of an accident in the pit, I have had no work for two years. I cannot open my hands." I was full of sorrow for this poor man, and something happened that had never happened before. We are in the infancy of this wonderful outpouring of the Holy Spirit, and there is so much more for us. I put out my hand, and before my hands reached his, he was loosed and made perfectly free.

I see that *"Stephen, full of faith and power, did great wonders and signs among the people"* (Acts 6:8). This same Holy Spirit filling is for us, and right things will be accomplished if we are filled with His Spirit. God will grant it. He declares that the desires of the righteous will be granted (Prov. 10:24). Stephen was an ordinary man made extraordinary in God. We may be very ordinary, but God wants to make us extraordinary in the Holy Spirit. God is ready to touch and transform you right now.

Once a woman rose in the meeting asking for prayer. I prayed for her, and she was healed. She cried out, "It is a miracle! It is a miracle! It is a miracle!" That is what God wants to do for us all the time. As surely as we get free in the Holy Spirit, something will happen. Let us pursue the best things, and let God have His right-of-way.

All who sat in the council looked steadfastly on Stephen and *"saw his face as the face of an angel"* (Acts 6:15). It was worth being filled with the Holy Spirit for that. The Spirit is breaking through. There is a touch of the Spirit in which the light of God will truly radiate from our faces.

The seventh chapter of Acts is the profound prophetic utterance that the Spirit spoke through this holy man. The Word of God flowed through the lips of Stephen in the form of divine prophecy so that those who heard these things were *"cut to the heart"* (Acts 7:54). But he, being full of the Holy Spirit, looked up steadfastly into heaven and saw the glory of God and Jesus standing on the right hand of God, and he said, *"Look! I see the heavens opened and the Son of Man standing at the right hand of God!"* (v. 56). Stephen was full of the Holy Spirit right to the end. He saw Jesus standing. In another part of Scripture we read of Him seated at the right hand of God (Eph. 1:20). That is His place of authority. But here we see that He arose. He was so keenly interested in that martyr Stephen. May the Lord open our eyes to see Him and to know that He is deeply interested in all that concerns us. He is *"touched with the feeling of our infirmities"* (Heb. 4:15 KJV).

"All things are naked and open to the eyes of Him" with whom we are connected (v. 13). He knows about that asthma. He knows about that rheumatism. He knows about that pain in the back, head, or feet. He wants to loose every captive and to set you free just as He has set me free. I hardly know that I have a body today. I am free from every human ailment, absolutely free. Christ has redeemed us. He has power *"over all the power of the enemy"* (Luke 10:19) and has worked out our great victory. Will you have it? It is yours; it is a perfect redemption.

And they stoned Stephen, who called upon God, *"'Lord Jesus, receive my spirit.' Then he knelt down and cried out with a loud voice, 'Lord, do not charge them with this sin.' And when he had said this, he fell asleep"* (Acts 7:59–60). Stephen was not only filled with faith, but he was also filled with love as he prayed just as his Master had prayed, *"Father, forgive them"* (Luke 23:34).

It is God's thought to make us a new creation, with all the old things passed away and all things within us truly of God (2 Cor. 5:17); to bring in a new, divine order, a perfect love and an unlimited faith. Will you have it? Redemption is free. Arise in the activity of faith, and God will heal you as you rise. Only believe, and receive in faith. Stephen, full of faith and of the Holy Spirit, did great signs and wonders. May God bless to us this passage and fill us full of His Holy Spirit and through the power of the Holy Spirit reveal Christ in us more and more.

The Spirit of God will always reveal the Lord Jesus Christ. Serve Him; love Him; be filled with Him. It is lovely to hear Him as He makes Himself known to us. He is *"the same yesterday, today, and forever"* (Heb. 13:8). He is willing to fill us with the Holy Spirit and faith just as He filled Stephen.

CHAPTER NINE

HAVE FAITH IN GOD

FOR ASSUREDLY, I SAY TO YOU, WHOEVER SAYS TO THIS MOUNTAIN,
"BE REMOVED AND BE CAST INTO THE SEA," AND DOES NOT DOUBT
IN HIS HEART, BUT BELIEVES THAT THOSE THINGS HE SAYS WILL
BE DONE, HE WILL HAVE WHATEVER HE SAYS. THEREFORE I SAY TO
YOU, WHATEVER THINGS YOU ASK
WHEN YOU PRAY, BELIEVE THAT YOU RECEIVE THEM,
AND YOU WILL HAVE THEM.
—MARK 11:23–24

These are days when we need to have our faith strengthened, when we need to know God. God has designed that the just will live by faith (Rom. 1:17), no matter how he may be fettered. I know that God's Word is sufficient. One word from Him can change a nation. His Word is *"from everlasting to everlasting"* (Ps. 90:2). It is through the entrance of this everlasting Word, this incorruptible seed, that we are born again and come into this wonderful salvation (1 Pet. 1:23). *"Man shall not live by bread alone, but by every word that proceeds from the mouth of God"* (Matt. 4:4). This is the food of faith. *"Faith comes by hearing, and hearing by the word of God"* (Rom. 10:17).

GOD'S WORD IS SURE

Everywhere men are trying to discredit the Bible and take from it all that is miraculous in it. One preacher says, "Well, you know, Jesus arranged beforehand to have that colt tied where it was and for the men to say just what they did." (See Mark 11:1–6.) I tell you, God can arrange everything. He can plan for you, and

511

when He plans for you, all is peace. All things are possible if you will believe (Mark 9:23).

Another preacher says, "It was an easy thing for Jesus to feed the people with five loaves. The loaves were so big in those days that it was a simple matter to cut them into a thousand pieces each." (See John 6:5–13.) But he forgets that one little boy brought those five loaves all the way in his lunch basket. There is nothing impossible with God. All the impossibility is with us when we measure God by the limitations of our unbelief.

Reaching Out in Faith

We have a wonderful God, a God whose ways are *"past finding out"* (Rom. 11:33) and whose grace and power are limitless. I was in Belfast one day and saw one of the brothers of the assembly. He said to me, "Wigglesworth, I am troubled. I have had a good deal of sorrow during the past five months. I had a woman in my assembly who could always pray the blessing of heaven down on our meetings. She is an old woman, and her presence is always an inspiration. But five months ago she fell and broke her leg. The doctors put her into a plaster cast, and after five months they broke the cast. But the bones were not properly set, and so she fell and broke the leg again."

He took me to her house, and there was a woman lying in a bed on the right-hand side of the room. I said to her, "Well, what about it now?"

She said, "They have sent me home incurable. The doctors say that I am so old that my bones won't knit. There is no nutriment in my bones. They could not do anything for me, and they say I will have to lie in bed for the rest of my life."

I said to her, "Can you believe God?"

She replied, "Yes, ever since I heard that you had come to Belfast, my faith has been quickened. If you will pray, I will believe. I know there is no power on earth that can make the bones of my leg knit, but I know there is nothing impossible with God."

I said, "Do you believe He will meet you now?"

She answered, "I do."

It is grand to see people believe God. God knew all about this leg and that it was broken in two places. I said to the woman, "When I pray, something will happen."

Her husband was sitting there; he had been in his chair for four years and could not walk a step. He called out, "I don't believe. I won't believe. You will never get me to believe."

I said, "All right," and laid my hands on his wife in the name of the Lord Jesus.

The moment hands were laid upon her, she cried out, "I'm healed."

I said, "I'm not going to assist you to rise. God will do it all." She arose and walked up and down the room, praising God.

The old man was amazed at what had happened to his wife, and he cried out, "Make me walk; make me walk."

I said to him, "You old sinner, repent."

He cried out, "Lord, You know I believe."

I don't think he meant what he said; anyhow the Lord was full of compassion. If He marked our sins, where would any of us be (Ps. 130:3)? If we will meet the conditions, God will always meet us if we believe *"all things are possible"* (Mark 9:23).

I laid my hands on him, and the power went right through the old man's body. For the first time in four years, those legs received power to carry his body. He walked up and down and in and out of the room. He said, "Oh, what great things God has done for us tonight!"

"Whatever things you ask when you pray, believe that you receive them, and you will have them" (Mark 11:24). Desire God, and you will have desires from God. He will meet you on the line of those desires when you reach out in simple faith.

A man came to me in one of my meetings who had seen other people healed and wanted to be healed, too. He explained that his arm had been set in a certain position for many years, and he could not move it. "Got any faith?" I asked.

He said that he had a lot of faith. After prayer he was able to swing his arm round and round. But he was not satisfied and complained, "I feel a little bit of trouble just there," pointing to a certain place.

I said, "Do you know what the trouble is with you?"

He answered, "No."

I said, "Imperfect faith." *"Whatever things you ask when you pray, believe that you receive them, and you will have them."*

Did you believe before you were saved? So many people want to be saved, but they want to feel saved first. There never was a man who felt saved before he believed. God's plan is always the following: if you will believe, you will see the glory of God (John 11:40). I believe God wants to bring us all to a definite place of unswerving faith and confidence in Himself.

In our text from Mark, Jesus uses the illustration of a mountain. Why does He say a mountain? If faith can remove a mountain, it can remove anything. The plan of God is so marvelous that if you will only believe, all things are possible (Mark 9:23).

LOVE HAS NO DOUBTS

There is one special phrase from our text to which I want to call your attention: *"And does not doubt in his heart"* (Mark 11:23). The heart is the mainspring. Imagine a young man and a young woman. They have fallen in love at first sight. In a short while there is a deep affection and a strong heart love, the one toward the other. What is a heart of love? It is a heart of faith. Faith and love are kin. In the measure that the young man and the young woman love one another, they are true. One may go to the north and the other to the south, but because of their love, they will be true to one another.

It is the same when there is a deep love in the heart toward the Lord Jesus Christ. In this new life into which God has brought us, Paul told us that we have *"become dead to the law through the body of Christ, that* [we] *may be married to another; to Him who was raised from the dead"* (Rom. 7:4). God brings us into a place of perfect love and perfect faith. A man who is born of God is brought into an inward affection, a loyalty to the Lord Jesus that shrinks from anything impure. You see the purity of a man and woman when there is a deep natural affection between them; they disdain the very thought of either of them being untrue. In the same way, in the measure that a man has faith in Jesus, he is pure. He who believes that Jesus is the Christ overcomes the world (1 John 5:5). It is a faith that works by love (Gal. 5:6).

When we have heart fellowship with our Lord, our faith cannot be daunted. We cannot doubt in our hearts. As we go on with God, there comes a wonderful association, an impartation of His very life and nature within. As we read His Word and believe the promises that He has so graciously given to us, we are made partakers of His very essence and life. The Lord is made a Bridegroom to us, and we are His bride. His words to us are spirit and life (John 6:63), transforming us and changing us, expelling what is natural and bringing in what is divine.

It is impossible to comprehend the love of God as we think along natural lines. We must have the revelation from the Spirit of God. God gives liberally. He who asks, receives (Matt. 7:8). God is willing to bestow on us *"all things that pertain to life and godliness"* (2 Pet. 1:3). Oh, it was the love of God that brought Jesus, and it is this same love that helps you and me to believe. God will be your strength in every weakness. You who need His touch, remember that He loves you. If you are wretched, helpless, or sick, look to the God of all grace, whose very essence is love, who delights to give liberally all the inheritance of life and strength and power that you are in need of.

BE CLEANSED TODAY

When I was in Switzerland, the Lord was graciously working and healing many of the people. I was staying with Brother Reuss of Goldiwil, and two policemen were sent to arrest me. The charge was that I was healing the people without a license. Mr. Reuss said to them, "I am sorry that he is not here just now; he is holding a meeting about two miles away, but before you arrest him I would like to show you something."

Brother Reuss took these two policemen down to one of the lower parts of that district, to a house with which they were familiar, for they had often gone to that place to arrest a certain woman who was constantly an inmate of the prison because of continually being engaged in drunken brawls. He took them to this woman and said to them, "This is one of the many cases of blessing that have come through the ministry of the man you have come to arrest. This woman came to our meeting in a drunken condition. Her body was broken, for she was ruptured in two places. While she was drunk, the evangelist laid his hands on her and asked God to heal her and deliver her."

The woman joined in, "Yes, and God saved me, and I have not tasted a drop of liquor since."

The policemen had a warrant for my arrest, but they said with disgust, "Let the doctors do this kind of thing." They turned and went away, and that was the last we heard of them.

We have a Jesus who heals the brokenhearted, who lets the captives go free, who saves the very worst (Luke 4:18). Do you dare spurn this glorious Gospel of God for spirit, soul, and body? Do you dare spurn this grace? I realize that this full Gospel has in great measure been hidden, this Gospel that brings liberty, this Gospel that brings souls out of bondage, this Gospel that brings perfect health to the body, this Gospel of entire salvation. Listen again to the words of Him who left the glory to bring us this great salvation: *"Assuredly, I say to you, whoever says to this mountain, 'Be removed,'...he will have whatever he says"* (Mark 11:23). Whatever!

I realize that God can never bless us when we are being hardhearted, critical, or unforgiving. These things will hinder faith quicker than anything. I remember being at a meeting where there were some people waiting for the baptism and seeking for cleansing, for the moment a person is cleansed the Spirit will fall. There was one man with red eyes who was weeping bitterly. He said to me, "I will have to leave. It is no good my staying unless I change things. I have written a letter to my brother-in-law and filled it with hard words, and this thing must first be straightened out." He went home and told his wife, "I'm going to write a letter to your brother and ask him to forgive me for writing to him the way I did."

"You fool!" she said.

"Never mind," he replied, "this thing is between God and me, and it has got to be cleared away." He wrote the letter and came again, and immediately God filled him with the Spirit.

I believe there are a great many people who want to be healed, but they are harboring things in their hearts that are like a blight. Let these things go. Forgive, and the Lord will forgive you. There are many good people, people who mean well, but they have no power to do anything for God. There is just some little thing that came in their hearts years ago, and their faith has been paralyzed ever since. Bring everything to the light. God will sweep it all away if you will let Him. Let the precious blood of Christ cleanse you from all sin (1 John 1:7). If you will only believe, God will meet you and bring into your lives the sunshine of His love.

CHAPTER TEN

THE HOUR IS COME

Yes, I believe! I hope that our hearts and minds might come to that place of understanding where we realize that it is possible for God to take all our human weaknesses and failures and transform us by His mighty power into a new creation if we *"only believe"* (Mark 5:36). What an inspiration it is to give God the supreme place in our lives! When we do, He will so fill us with the Holy Spirit that the government will rest upon His shoulders. (See Isaiah 9:6.) I hope that we will believe and come into the holy realm of the knowledge of what it means to yield our all to God. Just think of what would happen if we only dared to believe God! We need a faith that leaps into the will of God and says, "Amen!"

THE LORD'S SUPPER

There is no service so wonderful to me as the service of partaking in the Lord's Supper, the Holy Communion. The Scriptures say, *"This do, as often as you* [do] *it, in remembrance of Me"* (1 Cor. 11:25)—you do it in remembrance of Him. I am sure that every person in this place has a great desire to do something for Jesus, and what He wants to do for us is to keep us in remembrance of the Cross, the Burial, the Resurrection, and the Ascension, for the memory of these four events will always bring you into a place of great blessing. You do not need, however, to continually live on the cross, or even in remembrance of the cross, but what you need to remember about the cross is, *"It is finished"* (John 19:30). You do not need to live in the grave, but only keep in remembrance that *"He is risen"* (Matt. 28:6) out of the grave and that we are to be seated *"with Him in glory"* (Col. 3:4). The institution of the Holy Communion is one of those settings in Scripture, a time in the history of our Lord Jesus Christ, when the mystery of the glories of Christ was being unveiled. As the Master walked on this earth, the multitudes would gather with eagerness and longing in their hearts to hear the words that dropped from His gracious lips. But there were also those who had missed the vision. They saw the Christ, heard His words, but those wonderful words were like idle tales to them.

When we miss the vision and do not come into the fullness of the ministry of the Spirit, there is a cause. Beloved, there is a deadness in us that must have the resurrection touch. Today we have the unveiled truth, for the dispensation of the Holy Spirit has come to unfold the fullness of redemption, that we might be clothed with power; and what brings us into the state where God can pour upon us His blessing is a broken spirit and a contrite heart (Ps. 51:17). We need to examine ourselves to see what state we are in, whether we are just religious or whether we are truly in Christ.

The human spirit, when perfectly united with the Holy Spirit, has but one place, and that is death, death, and deeper death. In this place, the human spirit will cease to desire to have its own way, and instead of "My will," the cry of the heart will be, "May Your will, O Lord, be done in me."

GOD'S WORD IS TRUE

And He sent Peter and John, saying, "Go and prepare the Passover for us, that we may eat." So they said to Him, "Where do You want us to prepare?" And He said to them, "Behold, when you have entered the city, a man will meet you carrying a pitcher of water; follow him into the house which he enters. Then you shall say to the master of the house, 'The Teacher says to you, "Where is the guest room where I may eat the Passover with My disciples?"' Then he will show you a large, furnished upper room; there make ready."

(Luke 22:8–12)

It is one thing to handle the Word of God, but it is another thing to believe what God says. The great aim of the Spirit's power within us is to so bring us in line with His perfect will that we will unhesitatingly believe the Scriptures, daring to accept them as the authentic, divine principle of God. When we do, we will find our feet so firmly fixed upon the plan of redemption that it will not matter where our trials or other things come from, for our whole nature will be so enlarged that we will no longer focus on ourselves but will say, *"Lord, what do You want me to do?"* (Acts 9:6).

Every believer should be a living epistle of the Word, one who is *"known and read by all men"* (2 Cor. 3:2). Your very presence should bring such a witness of the Spirit that everyone with whom you come in contact will know that you are a sent one, a light in the world (Matt. 5:14), and last of all, a biblical Christian.

Those disciples had to learn that whatever Jesus said must come to pass. Jesus said, very slowly and thoughtfully I believe,

> *Behold, when you have entered the city, a man will meet you carrying a pitcher of water; follow him into the house which he enters. Then you shall say to the master of the house, "The Teacher says to you, 'Where is the guest room where I may eat the Passover with My disciples?'"* (Luke 22:10–11)

That is the way that Jesus taught them. Beloved, let me say this, there was no person in Palestine who had ever seen a man bearing a pitcher of water. It is an unknown thing. Therefore, we find Jesus beginning with a prophecy that brought that inward knowledge to them that what He said must come to pass. This is the secret of the Master's life: prophecy that never failed. There is no power that can change the Word of God. Jesus was working out this great thought in the hearts of His disciples, that they might know that it would come to pass. After Jesus had given that wonderful command to Peter and John, those disciples were walking into the city, no doubt in deep meditation, when suddenly they cried out in amazement, "Look! There he is! Just as the Master has said."

When I was in Jerusalem, I was preaching on Mount Olivet, and as I looked down to my right I saw where the *"two ways met,"* where the donkey was tied (Mark 11:4 KJV). I could see the Dead Sea, and all the time I was preaching I saw at least one hundred and fifty women going down with pitchers and then carrying them back on their heads, full of water. But I did not see one man. However, Jesus said that it had to be a man, and so it was, for no one could change His word.

Some have said to me that He had it all arranged for a man to carry a pitcher of water. I want to tell you that God does not have to arrange with mortals to carry out His plans. God has the power to hear the cry of some poor needy child of His who may be suffering in England, Africa, China, or anywhere else, saying, "O God, You know my need." And in New York, Germany, California, or some other place, there is a disciple of His on his knees, and the Lord will say to him, "Send help to that brother or sister, and do not delay it." And the help comes. He did not need to get a man to help Him out by carrying a pitcher of water. He works according to His Word, and Jesus said a man would carry water.

What did those disciples do as they saw the man? Did they go forward to meet him? No, they waited for the man, and when he came up, they probably walked alongside of him without a word until he was about to enter the house. Then I can hear one saying to him, "Please, sir, the Master wants the guest chamber!" "The guest chamber? Why, I was preparing it all day yesterday but did not know whom it was for." With man things are impossible, but God is the unfolder of the mysteries of life and holds the universe in the hollow of His hand. What we need to know now is that *"the LORD thy God in the midst of thee is mighty"* (Zeph. 3:17 KJV), and He works according to His Word.

THE WORD OF GOD LIVES TODAY

> *When the hour had come, He sat down, and the twelve apostles with Him. Then He said to them, "With fervent desire I have desired to eat this Passover with you before I suffer; for I say to you, I will no longer eat of it until it is fulfilled in the kingdom of God." Then He took the cup, and gave thanks, and said, "Take this and divide it among yourselves; for I say to you, I will not drink of the fruit of the vine until the kingdom of God comes." And He took bread, gave thanks and broke it, and gave it to them, saying, "This is My body which is given for you; do this in remembrance of Me."*
> (Luke 22:14–19)

It takes the Master to bring the Word home to our hearts. His was a ministry that brought a new vision to mankind, for *"no man ever spoke like this Man!"* (John 7:46). How I love to hear Him preach! How He says things! I have watched Him as He trod this earth. Enter into the Scriptures, and watch the Lord. Follow Him; take notice of His counsel, and you will have a story of wonders. The Book speaks today. It is life, and it looms up full of glory. It reflects and unfolds with a new creative power.

The words of Jesus are life (John 6:63)—never think they are less. If you believe them, you will feel quickened. The Word is powerful; it is full of faith. The Word of God is vital. Listen: *"The word...did not profit them, not being mixed with faith in those who heard it"* (Heb. 4:2). There has to be hearing in order to have faith. Faith is established and made manifest as we hear the Word (Rom. 10:17). Beloved, read the Word of God in quietude, and read it out loud so that you can hear it, for *"he who hears My word"* (John 5:24), to him it gives life.

Listen: *"With fervent desire"* (Luke 22:15); *"the hour has come"* (Mark 14:41). He speaks. From the beginning of time, there has never been an hour like this. These words were among the greatest that He ever spoke: *"The hour has come."* What an hour, for the end of time had come. "What?" you ask. Yes, I repeat it, for the redemption of the Cross, the shedding of the blood, brought in a new hour.

Time was finished and eternity had begun for every soul who was covered with the blood. Until that hour all people lived only to die, but the moment the sacrifice was made, it was not the end but only the beginning. Time was finished, and eternity had begun. The soul, covered with the blood, has moved from a natural to an eternal union with the Lord. Then the commandment, "You shall not," which had so worried the people and brought them into such dissatisfaction because they could not keep the Law, was changed into a new commandment. It was no more, "You shall not," but, *"I delight to do Your will, O my God"* (Ps. 40:8). *"In Adam all die"* (1 Cor. 15:22), but now *"the hour has come"* (Mark 14:41). *"In Christ all shall be made alive"* (1 Cor. 15:22). Instead of death will be the fullness of life divine.

"I have a desire to eat this Passover with you before I suffer. I know that within a few moments the judgment hall awaits Me." Do you think that I could be in Jerusalem and not want to pass through the gate that He went through? Do you think that I could be in Jerusalem and not want to pass over the Brook Kidron? Could you imagine my being in Jerusalem and not wanting to go into the Garden or view the tomb where His body was laid? I knelt down at that holy place, for I felt that I must commune with my Lord there.

While I was in Jerusalem, I preached many weeks outside the Damascus Gate, and God mightily blessed my ministry. It is wonderful to be in the place where God can use you. As I was leaving Jerusalem, some Jews who had heard me preach wanted to travel with me, and they wanted to stay at the same hotel where I was staying. When we were sitting around the table eating, they said, "What we cannot understand is that when you preach we feel such power. You move us. There is something about it; we cannot help but feel that you have something different from what we have been used to hearing. Why is it?"

I replied that it was because I preached Jesus in the power of the Holy Spirit, for He was the Messiah, and He causes a child of His to so live in the reality of a clear knowledge of Himself that others know and feel His power. It is this knowledge that the church today is very much in need of.

Do not be satisfied with anything less than the knowledge of a real change in your nature, the knowledge of the indwelling presence and power of the Holy Spirit. Do not be satisfied with a life that is not wholly swallowed up in God.

There are many books written on the Word, and we love clear, definite teaching on it. But go to the Book, and listen to what the Master says. You will lay a sure foundation that cannot be moved, for we are born again by the incorruptible Word of God (1 Pet. 1:23). We need that simplicity, that rest of faith, that brings us to the place where we are steadfast and immovable. How wonderful the living Word of God is!

Can you not see that the Master was so interested in you that He would despise the shame and despise the cross (Heb. 12:2)? The judgment hall was nothing to Him; all the rebukes and scorn could not take from Him the joy of saving you and me (v. 2). It was that joy that caused Him to say, "I count nothing too vile for Wigglesworth; I count nothing too vile for Brown; for My soul is on the wing to save the world!" How beautiful this is! How it should thrill us! He knew that death was represented in that sacred cup, and yet He joyfully said, *"With fervent desire I have desired to eat this Passover with you before I suffer"* (Luke 22:15). Take the bread, drink of the cup, and as often as you take it, remember (1 Cor. 11:24–25). In other words, take the memory of what it means home with you; think on it, and analyze its meaning.

Jesus brought in a new creation by the words of His ministry. *"Among those born of women there has not risen one greater than*

John the Baptist; but he who is least in the kingdom of heaven is greater than he" (Matt. 11:11). Jesus said that *"the kingdom of God is within you"* (Luke 17:21) and that He would *"no longer drink of the fruit of the vine until that day when* [He drank] *it new in the kingdom of God"* (Mark 14:25). He also said that every person who has the new nature, the new birth, has the kingdom of God within him. If you believe God's Word, it will make you so live that the kingdom of God will always be increasing; and the whole creation of the kingdom of God will be crying, "Come, Lord Jesus, come!" (see Revelation 22:20), and He will come.

As we come to the time of the breaking of bread, the thought should be, "How should I partake of it?" If before His death He could take it and say, *"With fervent desire I have desired to eat this Passover with you before I suffer"* (Luke 22:15), we should be able to say, "Lord, I desire to eat it to please You, for I want my whole life to be for You!" What grace there is! As the stream of the new life begins to flow through your being, allow yourself to be immersed and carried on with an ever increasing flow until your life becomes a ceaseless flow of the river of life, and then it will be *"No longer I...but Christ...in me"* (Gal. 2:20).

Get ready for the breaking of bread, and in doing so, remember. Get ready for partaking of the wine, and in doing so, remember Him.

CHAPTER ELEVEN

FILLED WITH GOD'S FULLNESS

TO THOSE WHO HAVE OBTAINED LIKE PRECIOUS FAITH WITH US
BY THE RIGHTEOUSNESS OF OUR GOD AND
SAVIOR JESUS CHRIST.
—2 PETER 1:1

God has always had a person whom He could illuminate and enlarge until there was nothing hindering the power of God flowing out to a world in need. This *"like...faith"* is the gift God is willing to give us, in order, if need be, that we may subdue kingdoms, work righteousness, and stop the mouths of lions (Heb. 11:33). It is the ability to triumph under all circumstances because our helper is Almighty God, and He is always strong and faithful. The faithful—living in the divine order of victory—always have a good report because God has taken His place in them. The divine Author brings to our minds "Thus says the Lord" every time. If any man would speak, *"let him speak as the oracles of God"* (1 Pet. 4:11), having the Word of God as the standard for all need.

This *"like...faith"* is the same faith that Abraham had. It counts the things that are not as though they are (see Romans 4:17), and it believes that what God has is the essence of the substance of the power of eternal life.

Jesus is the Word, and if you have the Word, you have faith: *"like...faith."* There is no way into the power and deep things of God without a broken spirit. We should be erasing from ourselves and allowing God to take the reins and rule. Faith in God and power with God lie in the knowledge of the Word of God. We are no better than our faith. *"For whatever is born of God overcomes the world. And this is the victory that has overcome the world; our faith"* (1 John 5:4). If you believe in Him, you are purified, for He is pure. You are strengthened, for He is strong. You are made whole, because He is whole.

THE LIVING PRINCIPLE

You may receive all His fullness because of the revelation of Him. This *"like...faith"* is imparted in all the principles of the Word of God. Faith is the living principle of the Word of God. If we are led by God's Spirit, we will definitely be led into the deep things of God and His truth. The revelation of Him will be so clear that we will live by His life.

Now, beloved, I cannot understand God except by His Word, not by impressions, feelings, or sentiment. If I am going to know God, I am going to know Him by His Word. There is a divine act for every man who is born of God when God comes in, working in him a personality of Himself—Christ formed in us.

God is almighty; there is no limitation. And His purpose is to bring many souls to glory (Heb. 2:10). He speaks about *"His divine power* [which] *has given to us all things that pertain to life and godliness, through the knowledge of Him"* (2 Pet. 1:3). God's Word is multiplication—yesterday, today, and forever the same.

God wants to give a great multiplication in the knowledge of Himself. Then faith will be used, and we will know the wonderful flow of the peace of God. If we open ourselves to God, God will flow through us.

If we know God hears us when we pray, we know we have the petition we have desired (1 John 5:15).

THE LIVING WORD

One man gave some marvelous descriptions of God's Word:

1. supernatural in origin
2. eternal in duration
3. inexpressible in valor
4. infinite in scope
5. regenerative in power
6. infallible in authority

7. universal in application
8. inspired in totality

He went on to say that we should:

1. read it through
2. write it down
3. pray it in
4. work it out
5. pass it on

The Word of God changes a man until he becomes an epistle of God. The Word transforms the mind, changes the character from grace to grace, and gives us an inheritance in the Spirit, until we are conformed—God coming in, dwelling in us, walking in us, talking through us, and eating with us. There is no God like our God. I believe in the Holy Spirit.

God is love. *"He who abides in love abides in God"* (1 John 4:16). God wants to take ordinary men and bring them out into extraordinary conditions.

God has room for the thirsty man who is crying out for more of Himself.

It is not what we are, but it is what God wants us to be.

Blessed are the poor in spirit, for Christ is the kingdom of heaven. (See Matthew 5:3.) Beloved, let us rededicate ourselves afresh to God! Every new revelation means a new dedication.

Let us seek His face, and let us take away from this meeting the desire of our hearts. For God has promised to fulfill, fill full, the desire of those who fear Him.

> Like, like faith,
> Like fulfillment. Amen.

Chapter Twelve

A Living Faith

P raise God! There is something that brings us all to this meeting. What will it be like when we get rid of this body of flesh and when Jesus is the light of the city of God (Rev. 21:23)? Nevertheless, God means for us to *"put on the whole armor of God"* (Eph. 6:11) while we are here. He wants us to be covered with the covering of His Spirit and to grow in grace and the knowledge of God (2 Pet. 3:18).

Oh, what God has laid up for us, and what we may receive through the name of Jesus! Oh, the value of the name, the power of the name; the very name of Jesus brings help from heaven, and the very name of Jesus can bind evil powers and *"subdue all things to Himself"* (Phil 3:21). Thank God for victory through our Lord Jesus Christ.

The Author of Our Faith

For the sake of saving us, He *"endured the cross, despising the shame"* (Heb. 12:2). How beautiful it is to say with our whole will, "I will be obedient unto God." Oh, He is lovely; He is beautiful. I do not remember Him ever denying me anything when I have come to Him; He has never turned me away empty. He is such a wonderful Savior, such a Friend that we can depend on with assurance and rest and complete confidence. He can roll away every burden.

Think of Him as the exhaustless Savior, the everlasting Friend, One who knows all things, One who is able to help and deliver us. When we have such a Source as this, we can stretch out our hands and take all that we need from Him.

Let's turn to the eleventh chapter of Mark's gospel.

And Jesus went into Jerusalem and into the temple. So when He had looked around at all things, as the hour was already late, He went out to Bethany with the twelve. Now the next day, when they had come out from Bethany, He was hungry. And seeing from afar a fig tree having leaves, He went to see if perhaps He would find something on it. When He came to it, He found nothing but leaves, for it was not the season for figs. In response Jesus said to it, "Let no one eat fruit from you ever again." And His disciples heard it. (Mark 11:11–14)

The fig tree dried up from the roots (v. 20). We may think we have faith in God, but we must not doubt in our hearts. *"Whatever things you ask when you pray, believe that you receive them, and you will have them"* (v. 24). This is a very wonderful verse.

VICTORY THROUGH THE WORD

The great theme of this discussion is the theme of faith, so I will talk about faith. Your inactivity must be brought to a place of victory. Inactivity—what wavers, what hesitates, what fears instead of having faith—closes up everything, because it doubts instead of believing God. What is faith? Faith is the living principle of the Word of God. It is life; it produces life; it changes life. Oh, that God today might give us a real knowledge of the Book! What is in it? There is life in it. God wants us to feed on the Book, the living Word, the precious Word of God.

All the wonderful things that Jesus did were done so that people might be changed and made like Him. Oh, to be like Him in thought, act, and plan! He went about His Father's business (Luke 2:49) and was eaten up with zeal for His house (Ps. 69:9). I am beginning to understand 1 John 3:2: *"Beloved, now we are children of God; and it has not yet been revealed what we shall be, but we know that when He is revealed, we shall be like Him, for we shall see Him as He is."* As I feed on the Word of God, my whole body will be changed by the process of the power of the Son of God.

But if the Spirit of Him who raised Jesus from the dead dwells in you, He who raised Christ from the dead will also give life to your mortal bodies through His Spirit who dwells in you. (Rom. 8:11)

The Lord dwells in a humble and contrite heart and makes His way into the dry places, so if you open up to Him, He will flood you with His life. But be sure to remember that a little bit of sin will spoil a whole life. You can never cleanse sin; you can never purify sin; you can never be strong if in sin; you will never have a vision while in sin. Revelation stops when sin comes in. The human spirit must come to an end, but the Spirit of Christ must be alive and active. You must die to the human spirit, and then God will quicken your mortal body and make it alive. Without holiness no man will see God (Heb. 12:14).

THE DIVINE POWER OF FAITH

We have a wonderful subject. What is it? Faith. Faith is an inward operation of that divine power that dwells in the contrite heart and can lay hold of the things not seen. (See Hebrews 11:1.) Faith is a divine act; faith is God in the soul. God operates by His Son and transforms the natural into the supernatural.

Faith is active, never dormant. Faith lays hold; faith is the hand of God; faith is the power of God. Faith never fears; faith lives amid the greatest conflict; faith is always active; faith moves even things that cannot be moved. God fills us with His divine power, and sin is dethroned. *"The just shall live by faith"* (Rom. 1:17). You cannot live by faith until you are just and righteous. You cannot live by faith if you are unholy or dishonest.

The Lord was looking for fruit on the tree. He found *"nothing but leaves"* (Mark 11:13). There are thousands of people like that. They dress up like Christians, but it is all leaves. *"By this My Father is glorified, that you bear much fruit"* (John 15:8). The Lord has no way in which to get fruit except through us. We cannot be ordinary people. To be saved is to be an extraordinary man, an exposition of God. When Jesus was talking about the new life, He said, *"Unless one is born again* [of God], *he cannot see the kingdom of God....That which is born of the flesh is flesh, and that which is born of the Spirit is spirit"* (John 3:3, 6).

In order to understand His fullness, we must be filled with the Holy Spirit. God has a measure for us that cannot be measured. I am invited into this measure: the measure of the Lord Jesus Christ in me. When you are in this relationship, sin is dethroned, but you cannot purify yourself. It is by the blood of Jesus Christ, God's Son, that you are cleansed from all sin (1 John 1:7).

When Jesus saw nothing but leaves, He said to this tree: *"'Let no one eat fruit from you ever again.' And His disciples heard it"* (Mark 11:14). The next morning as they passed the same place, they saw the fig tree dried up from the roots (v. 20). You never see a tree dry up from the roots. Even a little plant will dry from the top. But God's Son had spoken to the tree, and it could not live. He said to them, *"Have faith in God"* (v. 22).

We are members of His body. The Spirit is in us, and there is no way to abide in the secret place of the Lord except by holiness.

Be filled with the Word of God. *"For the word of God is living and powerful, and sharper than any two-edged sword, piercing even to the division of soul and spirit, and of joints and marrow"* (Heb. 4:12). Listen, those of you who have stiff knees and stiff arms today, you can get a tonic by the Word of God that will loosen your joints and that will divide even your joints and marrow. You cannot move your knee if there is no marrow there, but the Word of God can bring marrow into your bones.

Is there anything else? One of the greatest things in the Word of God is that it discerns the thoughts and intentions of the heart (v. 12). Oh, that you may all allow the Word of God to have perfect victory in your bodies so that they may be tingling through and through with God's divine power! Divine life does not belong to this world but to the kingdom of heaven, and the kingdom of heaven is within you (Luke 17:21).

God wants to purify our minds until we can bear all things, believe all things, hope all things, and endure all things (1 Cor. 13:7). God dwells in you, but you cannot have this divine power until you live and walk in the Holy Spirit, until the power of the new life is greater than the old life.

Jesus said to His disciples, "If you will believe in your hearts, not only will the tree wither, but the mountain will also be removed." (See Matthew 21:21.) God wants us to move mountains. Anything that appears to be like a mountain can be moved: the mountains of difficulty, the mountains of perplexity, the mountains of depression or depravity—things that have bound you for years. Sometimes things appear as though they could not be moved, but you can believe in your heart and stand on the Word of God, and God's Word will never be defeated.

Notice again this Scripture: *"Whatever things you ask when you pray, believe that you receive them, and you will have them"*

(Mark 11:24). First, believe that you get them, and then you will have them. That is the difficulty with people. They say, "Well, if I could feel I had it, I would know I had it." But you must believe it, and then the feeling will come. You must believe it because of the Word of God. God wants to work in you a real heart faith. I want you to know that God has a real remedy for all your ailments. There is power to set everybody free.

CHAPTER THIRTEEN

THE BLESSED REALITY OF GOD

NOW FAITH IS THE SUBSTANCE OF THINGS HOPED FOR, THE
EVIDENCE OF THINGS NOT SEEN. FOR BY IT THE ELDERS
OBTAINED A GOOD TESTIMONY.
—HEBREWS 11:1–2

God has moved me to discuss the marvelous, glorious reality of God's Word. How great our faith should be, for we cannot be saved except by faith. We cannot be kept except by faith. We can only be baptized by faith, and we will be caught up by faith; therefore, what a blessed reality is faith in the living God.

THE NATURE AND THE WORD OF GOD

What is faith? It is the very nature of God. Faith is the Word of God. It is the personal inward flow of divine favor, which moves in every fiber of our being until our whole nature is so quickened that we live by faith, we move by faith; and we are going to be caught up to glory by faith, for faith is the victory! Faith is the glorious knowledge of a personal presence within you, changing you from strength to strength, from *"glory to glory"* (2 Cor. 3:18), until you get to the place where you walk with God, and God thinks and speaks through you by the power of the Holy Spirit. Oh, it is grand; it is glorious!

God wants us to have far more than what we can handle and see, and so He speaks of *"the substance of things hoped for, the evidence of things not seen."* With the eye of faith, we may see the blessing in all its beauty and grandeur. God's Word is from everlasting to everlasting (Isa. 40:8), and *"faith is the substance."*

If I would give some woman a piece of cloth, scissors, needle, and thread, she could produce a garment. Why? Because she had

532

the material. If I would provide some man with wood, a saw, a hammer, and nails, he could produce a box. Why? Because he had the material. But God, without material, spoke the Word and produced this world with all its beauty (Heb. 11:3). There was no material there, but the Word of God called it into being by His creative force. With the knowledge that you are born again by this incorruptible Word, *"which lives and abides forever"* (1 Pet. 1:23), you know that within you is this living, definite hope, greater than yourself, more powerful than any dynamic force in the world, for faith works in you by the power of the new creation of God in Christ Jesus.

Therefore, with the audacity of faith, we should throw ourselves into the omnipotence of God's divine plan, for God has said to us, *"If you can believe, all things are possible to him who believes"* (Mark 9:23). It is possible for the power of God to be so manifest in your human life that you will never be as you were before, for you will be always going forward from victory to victory, for faith knows no defeat.

The Word of God will bring you into a wonderful place of rest in faith. God intends for you to have a clear conception of what faith is, how faith came, and how it remains. Faith is in the divine plan, for it brings you to the open door so that you might enter in. You must have an open door, for you cannot open the door. It is God who does it, but He wants you to be ready to step in and claim His promises of all the divine manifestations of power in the name of Christ Jesus. It is only thus that you will be able to meet and conquer the Enemy, for *"He who is in you is greater than he who is in the world"* (1 John 4:4).

Living faith brings glorious power and personality; it gives divine ability, for it is by faith that Christ is manifested in your mortal flesh by the Word of God. I do not want you to miss the knowledge that you have heard from God, and I want you to realize that God has so changed you that all weakness, fear, inability—everything that has made you a failure—has passed away. Faith has power to make you what God wants you to be; only you must be ready to step into the plan and believe His Word.

A TRIUMPHANT POSITION IN GOD

The first manifestation of God's plan was the cross of Calvary. You may refuse it; you may resist it; but God, who loves you with an everlasting love (Jer. 31:3), has followed you through life and will follow you with His great grace, so that He may bring you to a knowledge of this great salvation.

God, in His own plan for your eternal good, may have brought something into your life that is distasteful, something that is causing you to feel desperate or to feel that your life is worthless. What does it mean? It means that the Spirit of God is showing you your own weakness so that you might cry out to Him, and when you do, He will show you the Cross of redemption. Then God will give you faith to believe, for faith is *"the gift of God"* (Eph. 2:8).

God, who has given us this faith, has a wonderful plan for our lives. Do you remember when God brought you to this place of salvation, how the faith He gave you brought a great desire to do something for Him, and then He showed you that wonderful open door? I was saved over sixty-seven years ago, and I have never lost the witness of the Spirit. If you will not allow your human nature to crush your faith and interfere with God's plan in its wonderful divine setting, you will mount up like the eagles (Isa. 40:31). Oh, the wonderful effectiveness of God's perfect plan working in us with the divine Trinity flowing through humanity, changing our very nature to the extent that we cannot disbelieve but must act faith, talk faith, and in faith sing praises unto the Lord! There is no room for anything that is not faith, for we have passed beyond the natural plane into a new atmosphere: God enclosed and enclosing us.

Faith is an increasing position, always triumphant. It is not a place of poverty but of wealth. If you always live in fruitfulness, you will always have plenty. What does it say in our text? *"The elders obtained a good testimony"*! The man who lives in faith always has a good testimony. The Acts of the Apostles were written because the lives of the apostles bore the fruit of active faith. To them, faith was an everyday fact. If your life is in the divine order, you will not only have living, active faith, but you will also always be building up someone else in faith.

What is the good of preaching without faith? God intends that we should so live in this glorious sphere of the power of God that we will always be in a position to tell people of the act that brought the fact. You must act before you can see the fact. What is the good of praying for the sick without faith? You must believe that God will not deny Himself, for the Word of God cannot be denied. I believe this message is given in divine order so that you may no longer be in a place of doubt but will realize that *"faith is the substance"* (Heb. 11:1)! Beloved, even with all the faith we have, we are not even so much as touching the hem of God's plan for us. It is like going to the seashore and dipping your toe in the water, with the great vast ocean before you. God wants us to rise on the crest of the tide and not keep paddling along the shore. Oh, to be connected with that sublime power, that human nature may know God and the glory of the manifestation of Christ!

The Word of God is eternal and cannot be broken (John 10:35). You cannot improve on the Word of God, for it is life, and it produces life. Listen! God has begotten you to a living hope (1 Pet. 1:3). You are born again of the Word that created worlds. If you dare to believe, such belief is powerful. God wants us to be powerful, a people of faith, a purified people, a people who will launch out in God and dare to trust Him in glorious faith, which always takes you beyond what is commonplace to an abiding place in God.

CHAPTER FOURTEEN

THE SUBSTANCE OF THINGS HOPED FOR

H ebrews chapter eleven is a wonderful passage; in fact, all the Word of God is wonderful. Not only is it wonderful, but it also has power to change conditions. Any natural condition can be changed by the Word of God, which is a supernatural power. In the Word of God is the breath, the nature, and the power of the living God, and His power works in every person who dares to believe His Word. There is life though the power of it, and as we receive the Word of faith, we receive the nature of God Himself.

It is as we lay hold of God's promises in simple faith that we become *"partakers of the divine nature"* (2 Pet. 1:4). As we receive the Word of God, we come right into touch with a living force, a power that changes nature into grace, a power that makes dead things live, and a power that is of God, that will be manifested in our flesh. This power has come forth with its glory to transform us by divine acts into sons of God, to make us like the Son of God, by the Spirit of God who moves us on from grace to grace and from *"glory to glory"* (2 Cor. 3:18) as our faith rests in this living Word.

FAITH IS A FOUNDATION

It is important that we have a foundation truth, something greater than ourselves, on which to rest. In Hebrews 12:2 we read, *"Looking unto Jesus, the author and finisher of our faith."* Jesus is our life (Col. 3:4), and He is the power of our life. We see in the fifth chapter of Acts that as soon as Peter was let out of prison, the Word of God came: *"Go...speak...all the words of this life"* (v. 20).

There is only one Book that has life. In this Word we find Him who came that we might have life and have it more abundantly (John 10:10), and by faith this life is imparted to us. When we come into this life by divine faith—and we must realize that it is by grace we are saved through faith, and that it is not of ourselves but is the gift of God (Eph. 2:8)—we become partakers of this life. This Word is greater than anything else. There is no darkness in it at all. Anyone who dwells in this Word is able under all circumstances to say that he is willing to come to the light so that his deeds may be seen (John 3:21). But outside of the Word is darkness, and the manifestations of darkness will never desire to come to the light because their deeds are evil (vv. 19–20). But the moment we are saved by the power of the Word of God, we love the light and the truth. The inexpressible divine power, force, passion, and fire that we receive are of God. Drink, my beloved, drink deeply of this Source of life.

"Faith is the substance of things hoped for" (Heb. 11:1). Someone said to me one day, "I would not believe in anything I could not handle and see." Everything you can handle and see is temporary and will *"perish with the using"* (Col. 2:22); but the things not seen are eternal and will not fade away (2 Cor. 4:18; 1 Pet. 1:4). Are you dealing with tangible things or with the things that are eternal, that are facts, that are made real to faith? Thank God that through the knowledge of the truth of the Son of God I have within me a greater power, a mightier working, an inward impact of life, of power, of vision, and of truth more real than anyone can know who lives in the realm of the tangible. God manifests Himself to the person who dares to believe.

But there is something more beautiful than that. As we receive divine life in the new birth, we receive a nature that delights to do the will of God. As we believe the Word of God, a well of water springs up within our hearts. A spring is always better than a pump. But I know that a spring is apt to be outclassed when we get to the baptism of the Holy Spirit. It was a spring to the woman at the well, but with the person who has the Holy Spirit, it is flowing rivers. Do you have these flowing rivers? To be filled with the Holy Spirit is to be filled with the third person of the Godhead, who brings to us all that the Father has and all that the Son desires, and we should be so in the Spirit that God can cause us to move with His authority and reign by His divine ability.

I thank God that He baptizes with the Holy Spirit. I know He did it for me because others heard me speak in tongues, and then I heard myself. That was a scriptural work, and I don't want anything else, because I must be the epistle of God. A whole epistle of the life, of the power, and of the resurrection of my Lord Jesus must be emanating through my body. (See 2 Corinthians 3:3.) There are wonderful things happening through this divine union with God Himself.

"[God] *has in these last days spoken to us by His Son, whom He has appointed heir of all things, through whom also He made the worlds*" (Heb. 1:2). By this divine Person, this Word, this Son, God made all things. Notice that it says that He made the worlds by this Person and made them out of the things that were not there (Heb. 11:3). Everything we see was made by this divine Son. I want you to see that as you receive the Son of God, and as Christ dwells in your heart by faith (Eph. 3:17), there is a divine force, the power of limitless possibilities, within you. As a result of this incoming Christ, God wants to do great things through you. By faith, if we receive and accept His Son, God brings us into sonship, and not only into sonship but into joint-heirship, into sharing together with Him all that the Son possesses (Rom. 8:16–17).

WE HAVE DIVINE AUTHORITY

I am more and more convinced every day I live that very few who are saved by the grace of God have a right conception of how great their authority is over darkness, demons, death, and every power of the Enemy. It is a real joy when we realize our inheritance along this line.

I was speaking like this one day, and someone said, "I have never heard anything like this before. How many months did it take you to think up that sermon?"

I said, "My brother, God pressed my wife from time to time to get me to preach, and I promised her I would preach. I used to labor hard for a week to think something up, then give out the text and sit down and say, 'I am done.' Oh, brother, I have given up thinking things up. They all come down. And the sermons that come down stop down, then go back, because the Word of God says His Word will not return to Him void (Isa. 55:11). But if you get anything up, it will not stay up very long, and when it goes down, it takes you down with it."

The sons of God are made manifest in this present earth to destroy the power of the Devil. To be saved by the power of God is to be brought from the realm of the ordinary into the extraordinary, from the natural into the divine.

Do you remember the day when the Lord laid His hands on you? You say, "I could not do anything except praise the Lord." Well, that was only the beginning. Where are you today? The divine plan is that you increase until you receive the measureless fullness of God. You do not have to say, "I tell you it was wonderful when I was baptized with the Holy Spirit." If you have to look back to the past to make me know you are baptized, then you are backslidden.

If the beginning was good, it ought to be better day by day, until everybody is fully convinced that you are filled with the might of God in the Spirit, *"filled with all the fullness of God"* (Eph. 3:19). *"Do not be drunk with wine, in which is dissipation; but be filled with the Spirit"* (Eph. 5:18). I don't want anything other than being full and fuller and fuller, until I am overflowing like a great big vat. Do you realize that if you have been created anew and born again by the Word of God that there is within you the word of power and the same light and life as the Son of God Himself had?

God wants to flow through you with measureless power of divine utterance and grace until your whole body is a flame of fire. God intends each soul in Pentecost to be a live wire—not a monument, but a movement. So many people have been baptized with the Holy Spirit; there was a movement, but they have become monuments, and you cannot move them. God, wake us out of sleep lest we should become indifferent to the glorious truth and the breath of the almighty power of God. We must be the light and salt of the earth (Matt. 5:13–14), with the whole armor of God upon us (Eph. 6:11, 13–18). It would be a serious thing if the enemies were about and we had to go back and get our shoes. It would be a serious thing if we had on no breastplate.

How can we be furnished with the armor? Take it by faith. Jump in, step in, and never come out, for this is a baptism to be lost in, where you only know one thing and that is the desire of God at all times. The baptism in the Spirit should be an ever increasing endowment of power, an ever increasing enlargement of grace. O Father, grant to us a real look into the glorious liberty You have designed for the children of God (Rom. 8:21), who are delivered from this present world, separated, sanctified, and made suitable for

Your use, whom You have designed to be filled with all Your fullness.

JUST BELIEVE!

Nothing has hurt me so much as this, to see so-called believers have so much unbelief in them that it is hard to move them. There is no difficulty in praying for a sinner to be healed. But when you touch the "believer," he comes back and says, "You did not pray for my legs." I say you are healed all over if you believe. Everything is possible to those who believe (Mark 9:23). God will not fail His Word, whatever you are. Suppose that all the people in the world did not believe; that would make no difference to God's Word; it would be the same. You cannot alter God's Word. It is from everlasting to everlasting, and they who believe in it will be *like Mount Zion, which cannot be moved"* (Ps. 125:1).

I was preaching on faith one time, and there was a man in the audience who said three times, "I won't believe." I kept right on preaching because that made no difference to me. I am prepared for a fight any day, the fight of faith. We must keep the faith that has been committed to us. I went on preaching, and the man shouted out, "I won't believe." As he left, he cried out again, "I won't believe."

The next day a message came saying there was a man in the meeting the night before who had said out loud three times, "I won't believe," and as soon as he got outside, the Spirit said to him, "You will be mute because you did not believe." It was the same Spirit who came to Zacharias and said, *"You will be mute and not able to speak until the day these things take place, because you did not believe my words"* (Luke 1:20).

I believe in a hell. Who is in hell? The unbeliever. If you want to go to hell, all you need to do is to disbelieve the Word of God. The unbelievers are there. Thank God they are there, for they are no good for any society. I said to the leader of that meeting, "You go and see this man and find out if these things are so."

He went to the house, and the first to greet him was the man's wife. He said, "Is it true that your husband declared three times in the meeting that he would not believe and now he cannot speak?"

She burst into tears and said, "Go and see." He went into the room and saw the man's mouth in a terrible state. The man got a piece of paper and wrote, "I had an opportunity to believe. I refused to believe, and now I cannot believe and cannot speak." The greatest sin in the world is to disbelieve God's Word. We are not of those who draw back, but we are of those who believe (Heb. 10:39); for God's Word is a living Word, and it always acts.

One day a stylishly dressed lady came to our meeting and stepped on up to the platform. Under her arm, going down underneath her dress, was a concealed crutch that nobody could see. She had been helpless in one leg for twenty years, had heard of what God was doing, and wanted to be prayed for. As soon as we prayed for her, she exclaimed, "What have you done with my leg?" Three times she said it, and then we saw that the crutch was loose and hanging and that she was standing straight up.

The lady who was interpreting for me said to her, "We have done nothing with your leg. If anything has been done, it is God who has done it."

She answered, "I have been lame and have used a crutch for twenty years, but my leg is perfect now." We did not suggest that she get down at the altar and thank God; she fell down among the others and cried for mercy. I find that when God touches us, it is a divine touch—it is life and power—and it thrills and quickens the body so that people know it is God. Then conviction comes, and they cry for mercy. Praise God for anything that brings people to the throne of grace.

God heals by the power of His Word. But the most important thing is, Are you saved? Do you know the Lord? Are you prepared to meet God? You may be an invalid as long as you live, but you may be saved by the power of God. You may have a strong, healthy body but may go straight to hell because you know nothing of the grace of God and salvation. Thank God I was saved in a moment, the moment I believed, and God will do the same for you.

God means by this divine power within you to make you follow after the mind of the Spirit by the Word of God until you are entirely changed by the power of it. You might come on this platform and say, "Wigglesworth, is there anything you can look up to God and ask Him for in regard to your body?" I will say now that I have a body in perfect condition and have nothing to ask for, and I am sixty-five. It was not always so. This body was a frail, helpless body, but God fulfilled His Word to me according to Isaiah and Matthew: He took my infirmities and my diseases, my sicknesses, and by His stripes I am healed (Isa. 53:5; Matt. 8:17).

✦ It is wonderful to go here and there and not even notice that you have a body because it is not a hindrance to you. He took our infirmities; He bore our sicknesses; He came to heal our broken-heartedness (Luke 4:18). Jesus wants us to come forth in divine-likeness, in resurrection force, in the power of the Spirit, to walk in faith and understand His Word. That is what He meant when He said He would give us power *"over all the power of the enemy"* (Luke 10:19). He will subdue all things until everything comes into perfect harmony with His will. Is He reigning over your affections, desires, and will? If so, when He reigns, you will be subject to His reigning power. He will be the authority over the whole situation. When He reigns, everything must be subservient to His divine plan and will for us.

See what the Word of God says: *"No one can say that Jesus is Lord except by the Holy Spirit"* (1 Cor. 12:3). *"Lord"!* Bless God for-ever. Oh, for Him to be Lord and Master! For Him to rule and con-trol! For Him to be filling your whole body with the plan of truth! Because you are in Christ Jesus, all things are subject to Him. It is lovely, and God wants to make it so to you. When you get there, you will find divine power continually working. I absolutely believe that no man comes into the place of revelation and activity of the gifts of the Spirit except by this fulfilled promise of Jesus that He will bap-tize us in the Holy Spirit.

GOD KNOWS AND CAN HEAL

I was taken to see a beautiful nine-year-old boy who was lying on a bed. The mother and father were distraught because he had been lying there for months. They had to lift and feed him; he was like a statue with flashing eyes. As soon as I entered the place, the Lord revealed to me the cause of the trouble, so I said to the mother, "The Lord shows me there is something wrong with his stomach."

She said, "Oh no, we have had two physicians, and they say it is paralysis of the mind."

I said, "God reveals to me it is his stomach."

"Oh no, it isn't. These physicians ought to know, they have X-rayed him."

The gentleman who brought me there said to the mother, "You have sent for this man; you have been the means of his coming; now don't you stand out against him. This man knows what he has got to do."

But Dr. Jesus knows more than that. He knows everything. All you have to do is call on Jesus, and He will come down. Divine things are so much better than human things, and they are just at your call. Who will interfere with the divine mind of the Spirit that has all revelation, that understands the whole condition of life? The Word of God declares He knows all things (1 John 3:20) and is well acquainted with the manifestation of our bodies, for everything is naked and open before Him to whom we must give account (Heb. 4:13). Having the mind of the Spirit, we understand what the will of God is. I prayed over this boy and laid my hands on his stomach. He became sick and vomited a worm thirteen inches long and was perfectly restored. Who knows? God knows. When will we come into the knowledge of God? When we cease from our own mind and allow ourselves to become clothed with the mind and authority of the mighty God.

UNBELIEF HINDERS GOD'S POWER

The Spirit of God wants us to understand there is nothing that can interfere with our coming into perfect blessing except unbelief. Unbelief is a terrible hindrance. As soon as we are willing to allow the Holy Spirit to have His way, we will find that great things will happen all the time. But oh, how much of our own human reason we have to get rid of, how much human planning we have to become divorced from. What would happen right now if everybody believed God? I love the thought that God the Holy Spirit wants to emphasize the truth that if we will only yield ourselves to the divine plan, He is right there to bring forth the mystery of truth.

How many of us believe the Word? It is easy to quote it, but it is more important to have it than to quote it. It is very easy for me to quote, *"Now we are children of God"* (1 John 3:2), but it is more important for me to know whether I am a son of God. When the Son was on the earth, He was recognized by the people who heard Him. *"No man ever spoke like* [Him]" (John 7:46). His word was with power, and that word came to pass. Sometimes you have quoted, *"He who is in you is greater than he who is in the world"* (1 John 4:4), and you could tell just where to find it. But brother, is it so? Can demons remain in your presence? You have to be greater than demons. Can disease lodge in the body that you touch? You have to be greater than the disease. Can anything in the world stand against you and hold its place if it is a fact that He who is in you is greater than he who is in the world? Do we dare stand on the Word of God and face the facts of the difficulties before us?

"Faith is the substance of things hoped for" (Heb. 11:1). Faith is the Word. You were begotten of the Word; the Word is in you; the life of the Son is in you; and God wants you to believe.

CHAPTER FIFTEEN

THE WAY OF FAITH

In Romans 4:16 we read, *"It is of faith that it might be according to grace,"* meaning that we can open the door, and God will come in. What will happen if we really open the door by faith? God is greater than our thoughts. He puts it to us: *"exceedingly abundantly above all that we ask or think"* (Eph. 3:20). When we ask a lot, God says "more." Are we ready for the "more"? And then the "much more"? We must be, or we will miss it.

We may be so clothed with the Spirit of the Lord in the morning that it will be a tonic for the whole day. God can so thrill us with new life that nothing ordinary or small will satisfy us after that. There is a great place for us in God where we won't be satisfied with small things. We won't have any satisfaction unless the fire falls, and whenever we pray we will have the assurance that what we are about to pray for is going to follow the moment we open our mouths. Oh, this praying in the Spirit! This great plan of God for us! In a moment we can go right in. In where? Into His will. Then all things will be well.

We can't get anything while we are asleep these days. The world is always awake, and we should always be awake to what God has for us. Awake to take! Awake to hold it after we get it! How much can you take? We know that God is more willing to give than we are to receive. How will we dare to be asleep when the Spirit commands us to take everything on the table? It is the greatest banquet that ever was and ever will be—the table where all you take only leaves more behind. It is a fullness that cannot be exhausted! How many are prepared for abundance?

THE WORD MUST COME TO PASS

And Jesus went into Jerusalem and into the temple. So when
He had looked around at all things, as the hour was already
late, He went out to Bethany with the twelve. Now the next
day, when they had come out from Bethany, He was hungry.
And seeing from afar a fig tree having leaves, He went to see if
perhaps He would find something on it. When He came to it,
He found nothing but leaves, for it was not the season for figs.
In response Jesus said to it, "Let no one eat fruit from you
ever again." And His disciples heard it.   (Mark 11:11–14)

Jesus was sent from God to meet the world's needs. Jesus lived
to minister life by the words He spoke. He said to Philip, *"He who*
has seen Me has seen the Father....The words that I speak to you I
do not speak on my own authority; but the Father who dwells in Me"
(John 14:9–10). I am persuaded that if we are filled with His words
of life and the Holy Spirit, and Christ is made manifest in our mortal flesh, then the Holy Spirit can really move us with His life and
His words until *"as He is, so are we in this world"* (1 John 4:17).
We are receiving our life from God, and it is always kept in tremendous activity, working in our whole nature as we live in perfect contact with God.

Jesus spoke, and everything He said must come to pass. That
is the great plan. When we are filled only with the Holy Spirit, and
we won't allow the Word of God to be taken away by what we hear
or by what we read, then comes the inspiration, then the life, then
the activity, then the glory! Oh, to live in it! To live in it is to be
moved by it. To live in it is to be moved so that we will have God's
life and God's personality in the human body.

By the grace of God I want to impart the Word and bring you
into a place where you will dare to act upon the plan of the Word,
to so breathe life by the power of the Word that it is impossible for
you to go on under any circumstances without His provision. The
most difficult things that come to us are to our advantage from
God's side. When we come to the place of impossibilities, it is the
grandest place for us to see the possibilities of God. Put this right
in your mind, and never forget it. You will never be of any importance to God until you venture in the impossible. God wants people
to be daring, and I do not mean foolishly daring. *"Be filled with the*

Spirit" (Eph. 5:18). When we are filled with the Spirit, we are not so much concerned about the secondary thing. We are concerned about the first thing, which is God's.

※ Everything evil, everything unclean, everything satanic in any way, is an objectionable thing to God, and we are to live above it, destroy it, and not allow it to have any place. Jesus didn't let the Devil answer back. We must reach the place where we will not allow anything to interfere with the plan of God.

Jesus and His disciples came to the tree. It looked beautiful. It had the appearance of fruit, but when He came to it, He found nothing but leaves. He was very disappointed. Looking at the tree, He spoke to it. His destructive power is shown forth here: *"Let no one eat fruit from you ever again"* (Mark 11:14). The next day they were passing by the same way, and the disciples saw the tree *"dried up from the roots"* (v. 20). They said to Jesus, *"Look! The fig tree which You cursed has withered away"* (v. 21). And Jesus said, *"Have faith in God"* (v. 22).

As I said previously, there isn't a person who has ever seen a tree dried from the roots. Trees always show the first signs of death right at the top. But the Master had spoken. The Master dealt with a natural thing to reveal to these disciples a supernatural plan. If He spoke, it would have to obey. And God, the Holy Spirit, wants us to understand clearly that we are the mouthpieces of God and are here for His divine plan. We may allow the natural mind to dethrone that, but in the measure we do, we won't come into the treasure that God has for us.

The Word of God must have first place. It must not have a second place. In any measure that we doubt the Word of God, from that moment we have ceased to thrive spiritually and actively. The Word of God is to be not only looked at and read, but also received as the Word of God to become life right within our life. *"Your word I have hidden in my heart, that I might not sin against You"* (Ps. 119:11).

"I give you the authority...over all the power of the enemy" (Luke 10:19). There it is. We can accept or reject it. I accept and believe it. It is a word beyond all human calculation. *"Have faith in God"* (Mark 11:22). These disciples were in the Master's school. They were the men who were to turn the world upside down. (See Acts 17:1–6.) As we receive the Word, we will never be the same; if we dare to act as the Word goes forth and are not afraid, then God will honor us.

547

"The LORD of hosts is with us; the God of Jacob is our refuge" (Ps. 46:7). Jacob was the weakest of all, in any way you like to take it. But God is the God of Jacob, and He is our God. So we may likewise have our names changed to Israel.

As the Lord Jesus injected this wonderful word, *"Have faith in God"* (Mark 11:22), into the disciples, He began to show how it was to be. Looking around Him, He saw the mountains, and He began to give a practical application. A truth means nothing unless it moves us. We can have our minds filled a thousand times, but it must get into our hearts if there are to be any results. All inspiration is in the heart. All compassion is in the heart.

Looking at the mountains, Jesus said,

> *Whoever says to this mountain, "Be removed and be cast into the sea," and does not doubt in his heart, but believes that those things he says will be done, he will have whatever he says.* (Mark 11:23)

That is the barometer. You know exactly where you are. The man knows when he prays. If his heart is right, how it leaps! Any man who does not hate sin is no good for God and never makes progress in God. You are never safe. But there is a place in God where you can love righteousness and where you can hate iniquity until the Word of God is a light in your being, quickening every fiber of your body, thrilling your whole nature. The pure in heart see God (Matt. 5:8). Believe in the heart! What a word! If I believe in my heart, God says I can begin to speak, and whatever I say will come to pass (Mark 11:23).

THERE IS NO DEFEAT WITH GOD

Here is an act of believing in the heart. I was called to Halifax, England, to pray for a lady missionary. I found that it was an urgent call. I could see there was an absence of faith, and I could see there was death.

I said to the woman, "How are you?"

She said, "I have faith," in a very weak tone of voice.

"Faith? Why are you dying? Brother Walshaw, is she dying?"

"Yes."

To a friend standing by, I said, "Is she dying?"

"Yes."

Now, I believe there is something in a heart that is against defeat, and this is the faith that God has given to us. I said to her, "In the name of Jesus, now believe, and you'll live." She said, "I believe," and God sent life from her head to her feet. Her friends dressed her, and she lived.

"Have faith" (Mark 11:22). It isn't saying you have faith. It is he who believes in his heart. It is a grasping of the eternal God. Faith is God in the human vessel. *"This is the victory that has overcome the world; our faith"* (1 John 5:4). He who believes overcomes the world (v. 5). *"Faith comes by hearing, and hearing by the word of God"* (Rom. 10:17). He who believes in his heart—can you imagine anything easier than that? He who believes in his heart! What is the process? Death! No one who believes in his heart can live according to the world. He dies to everything worldly. He who loves the world is not of God (1 John 2:15). You can measure the whole thing up and examine yourself to see if you have faith. Faith is a life. Faith enables you to lay hold of what is and get it out of the way for God to bring in something that is not (Rom. 4:17).

Just before I left home I was in Norway. A woman wrote to me from England saying she had been operated on for cancer three years before but that it was now coming back. She was living in constant dread of the whole thing, since the operation was so painful. She asked if it would be possible to see me when I returned to England. I wrote that I would be passing through London on the twentieth of June. If she would like to meet me at the hotel, I would pray for her. She replied that she would go to London to be there to meet me.

When I met this woman, I saw she was in great pain, and I have great sympathy for people who have tried to get relief and have failed. If you preachers lose your compassion, you can stop preaching, for it won't be any good. You will only be successful as a preacher if you let your heart become filled with the compassion of Jesus. As soon as I saw her, I entered into the state of her mind. I saw how distressed she was. She came to me in a mournful spirit, and her whole face was downcast. I said to her, "There are two things that are going to happen today. One is that you are to know that you are saved."

"Oh, if I could only know I was saved," she said.

"There is another thing. You have to go out of this hotel without a pain, without a trace of the cancer."

Then I began with the Word—oh, this wonderful Word! We do not have to go up to bring Him down; nor do we have to go down to bring Him up (Rom. 10:6–7). *"The word is near you, in your mouth and in your heart' (that is, the word of faith which we preach)"* (v. 8). I said, "Believe that He took your sins when He died on the cross. Believe that when He was buried, it was for you. Believe that when He arose, it was for you. And now He is sitting at God's right hand for you. If you can believe in your heart and confess with your mouth, you will be saved." (See verse 9.)

She looked at me saying, "Oh, it is going all through my body. I know I am saved now. If He comes today, I'll go. How I have dreaded the thought of His coming all my life! But if He comes today, I know I will be ready."

The first thing was finished. Now for the second. I laid my hands upon her in the name of Jesus, believing in my heart that I could say what I wanted and it would be done. I said, "In the name of Jesus, I cast this out."

She jumped up. "Two things have happened," she said. "I am saved, and now the cancer is gone."

> Faith will stand amid the wrecks of time,
> Faith unto eternal glories climb;
> Only count the promise true,
> And the Lord will stand by you.
> Faith will win the victory every time!

So many people have nervous trouble. I will tell you how to get rid of your nervous trouble. I have something in my bag, one good dose of which will cure you: *"I am the LORD who heals you"* (Exod. 15:26). How this wonderful Word of God changes the situation!

"Perfect love casts out fear" (1 John 4:18). *"There is no fear in love"* (v. 18). I have tested that so often, casting out the whole condition of fear, and the whole situation has been changed. We have a big God, only He has to be absolutely and exclusively trusted. The people who really do believe God are strong, and the righteous *"will be stronger and stronger"* (Job 17:9).

At the close of a certain meeting, a man said to me, "You have helped everybody but me. I wish you would help me."

"What's the trouble with you?"

"I cannot sleep because of nervous trouble. My wife says she has not known me to have a full night's sleep for three years. I am just shattered."

Anyone could tell he was. I put my hands upon him and said, "Brother, I believe in my heart. Go home and sleep in the name of Jesus."

"I can't sleep."

"Go home and sleep in the name of Jesus."

"I can't sleep."

The lights were being put out, and I took the man by the coat collar and said, "Don't talk to me anymore." That was sufficient.

He went after that. When he got home, his mother and wife both said to him, "What has happened?"

"Nothing. He helped everybody but me."

"Surely he said something to you."

"He told me to come home and sleep in the name of Jesus, but you know I can't sleep."

His wife urged him to do what I had said, and he had scarcely gotten his head on the pillow before the Lord put him to sleep. The next morning he was still asleep. She began to make a noise in the bedroom to awaken him, but he did not waken. Sunday morning he was still asleep. She did what every good wife would do. She decided to make a good Sunday dinner and then awaken him.

After the dinner was prepared, she went up to him and put her hand on his shoulder and shook him, saying, "It is time for you to wake up." From that night that man never had any more nervousness.

A man came to me for whom I prayed. Then I asked, "Are you sure you are perfectly healed?"

"Well," he said, "there is just a little pain in my shoulder."

"Do you know what that is?" I asked him. "That is unbelief. Were you saved before you believed or after?"

"After."

"You will be healed after."

"It is all right now," he said. It was all right before, but he hadn't believed.

The Word of God is for us. It is by faith, so that it might be by grace (Rom. 4:16).

unbelief

faith →
works by love

CHAPTER SIXTEEN

THE WAY TO OVERCOME

Now let's take a look at 1 John 5. The greatest weakness in the world is unbelief. The greatest power is the faith that works by love (Gal. 5:6). Love, mercy, and grace are bound eternally to faith. Fear is the opposite of faith, but *"there is no fear in love"* (1 John 4:18). Those whose hearts are filled with a divine faith and love have no question in their hearts as to being caught up when Jesus comes.

The world is filled with fear, torment, remorse, and brokenness, but faith and love are sure to overcome. *"Who is he who overcomes the world, but he who believes that Jesus is the Son of God?"* (1 John 5:5). God has established the earth and humanity on the lines of faith. As you come into line, fear is cast out, the Word of God comes into operation, and you find bedrock. All the promises are *"Yes"* and *"Amen"* to those who believe (2 Cor. 1:20).

When you have faith in Christ, the love of God is so real that you feel you could do anything for Jesus. Whoever believes, loves. *"We love Him because He first loved us"* (1 John 4:19). When did He love us? When we were in the mire. What did He say? *"Your sins are forgiven you"* (Luke 5:20). Why did He say it? Because He loved us. What for? That He might bring many sons into glory (Heb. 2:10). What was His purpose? That we might be with Him forever.

The whole pathway is an education for this high vocation and calling. How glorious this hidden mystery of love is! For our sins there is the double blessing. *"Whatever is born of God overcomes the world. And this is the victory...our faith"* (1 John 5:4). To believe is to overcome.

I am heir to all the promises because I believe. It is a great heritage. I overcome because I believe the truth, and the truth makes me free (John 8:32). Christ is the root and source of our faith, and because He is in our faith, what we believe for will come to pass. There is no wavering. This is the principle: he who believes is definite. A definite faith brings a definite experience and a definite utterance.

There is no limit to the power God will cause to come upon those who cry to Him in faith, for God is rich to all who will call upon Him (Rom. 10:12). Stake your claim for your children, your families, your coworkers, that many sons may be brought to glory. As your prayer rests upon the simple principle of faith, *"nothing will be impossible for you"* (Matt. 17:20).

The root principle of all this divine overcoming faith in the human heart is Christ, and when you are grafted deeply into Him, you may win millions of lives to the faith. Jesus is the Way, the Truth, and the Life (John 14:6), the secret to every hard problem in your heart.

"Love has been perfected among us in this: that we may have boldness in the day of judgment; because as He is, so are we in this world" (1 John 4:17). *"Everyone who has this hope in Him purifies himself"* (1 John 3:3). God confirms this faith in us so that we may be refined in the world, *"not having spot or wrinkle or any such thing"* (Eph. 5:27).

It is the Lord who purifies and brings us to the place where the fire burns up the dross, and there He anoints us with fresh oil, so that at all times we may be ready for His appearing. God is separating us for Himself, just as He separated Enoch for a walk with Himself. Because of a divinely implanted faith, he had the testimony before his translation that he pleased God (Heb. 11:5). As the Day of the Lord hastens on, we, too, need to walk by faith until we overcome all things. By our simple belief in Jesus Christ, we walk right into glory.

Chapter Seventeen

Only Believe

I want you to be full of joy, enough joy to fill a deep well. If you have to make it happen, there is something wrong. If God makes it happen, there is always something right. We must be careful to see that God means something greater for us than we have ever touched.

Go Forward

I have thought a great deal about momentum. I find there is such a thing as trusting in the past. When a train has gotten to a certain place, some people get out, but some go on to the end of the journey. Let us go far enough. There is only one thing to do: stay fully aware and always be pressing on. It will not do to trust in the past. Let us go forward. When it comes to the power of momentum, the past will not do. We must have an inflow of the life of God manifested, because we are in that place of manifestation.

I want you to sing now what I sing in all my meetings: "Only Believe."

> Only believe, only believe,
> All things are possible, only believe.
> Only believe, only believe,
> All things are possible, only believe.

The importance of that chorus is that right there in the middle of it is that word *only*. If I can get you to see that when you can get rid of yourself and your human help and everything else and have only God behind you, then you have reached a place of great reinforcement. You have reached a place of continual success. If you help yourself—in the measure you help yourself—you will find that the life of God and the power of God are diminished.

I find so many people trying to help themselves. What God wants is for us to cling to Him absolutely and entirely. There is only one grand plan that God has for us: *"Only believe"* (Mark 5:36). If we believe, we will have absolute rest and perfect submission. When God has entirely taken charge of the situation, you are absolutely brought into everything that God has, because you dare to *"only believe"* what He says.

Conditions on God's side are always beyond your asking or thinking. The conditions on your side cannot reach the other side unless you come into a place where you can rest on the omnipotent plan of God; then His plan cannot fail to be successful. God wants me to press into your heart a living truth: only believe and have absolute rest and perfect tranquillity and allow God to absolutely take charge of the whole situation. You can then say, "God has said it, and it cannot fail." All His promises are *"Yes"* and *"Amen"* to those who believe (2 Cor. 1:20). Are you ready to sing it now? "Only believe, only believe. / All things are possible, only believe."

THERE IS NO CONDEMNATION

Look at Romans 8:1–17. We have a tremendously big subject before us, but it will be one that will be helpful. It is in the realm of spiritual vitality. I want to speak to you on life because I find that there is nothing that is going to help you reach, press into, or live this higher life, except this divine life, which will always help us if we yield ourselves absolutely to it. Not only do we get exercised by this divine light, but we are kept in perfect rest, because God is giving us rest. And it is needed in this day, for this is a day when people everywhere are becoming self-contented in natural things, and when everywhere there is no definite cry or prayer within the soul that is making people cease from everything and cry out for God and the coming of the Son.

So I am intensely eager and full of desire that I may by some means quicken or move you on to a place where you will see what the Spirit has for you. Life in Christ is absolutely different from death. Life is what people long for because of everything it has in it. Death is what people draw back from because of what it has in it.

This light of the life of the Spirit, which God wants me to bring before you, is where God has designed for us to live, in freedom from *"the law of sin and death"* (Rom. 8:2).

So you can see I have a great subject, which is from the divine mind of the Master. You remember what the Master said. He said that He who lives for himself will die. He who seeks to live will die, but he who is willing to die to himself will live (Luke 17:33). God wants us to see that there is a life that is contrary to this life.

The Spirit of the Lord reveals the following to us in the Word of God: *"He who believes in the Son has everlasting life; and he who does not believe the Son shall not see life"* (John 3:36). The unbelieving person is living and walking about but not seeing life. There is a life that is always brought into condemnation, which is living in death. There is a life that is free from condemnation—living in the Life.

> **INTERPRETATION OF A MESSAGE IN TONGUES:** "God the Author, the Finisher, the bringing into, the expression in the human life, changing it from that downward grade and lifting it and bringing it into a place of revelation to see that God has designed me to be greater than anything in the world."

I want you all to understand today that the design of God's Son for us is to be so much greater in this world than we have ever comprehended. God's design is not for me to stay where I was when I came into this room. God's plan is that the spiritual revelation will bring me into touch with a divine harmony. God wants me to touch ideals today; He wants me to reach something more. My eyes are looking up; my heart is looking up. My heart is big and enlarged in the presence of God, for I want to hear one word from God: "Come up higher." God will give us that—the privilege of going higher into a holy association.

There is a word of helpfulness in the first verse of Romans 8: *"There is therefore now no condemnation."* This is the most important thing in all the world; there is nothing to be compared to it. It is beyond all you can think. The person who is under no condemnation has the heavens opened above him. This person has the smile of God upon him. This person has come into the realm of faith and joy and knows that his prayers are answered. I know that He hears me when I pray—I know I have the petition (1 John 5:15).

So God the Holy Spirit would have us to understand that there is a place in the Holy Spirit where there is no condemnation. This place is holiness, purity, righteousness, higher ground, and being more perfected in the presence of God. This "higher ground" state is holy desire. It is perfection where God is bringing us to live in such a way that He may smile through us and act upon us until our bodies become a flame of light ignited by Omnipotence. This is God's plan for us in the inheritance. It is an inheritance in the race that God wants us in today. This race, this divine race, this crowned race, this divine place, is for us today.

There is no condemnation. The great secret of the plan of God for those who are in it is to see our covering. Oh, the covering; oh, the enfolding; oh, those eyes, those lovely eyes, that lovely Jesus, that blessed assurance of being strengthened, that knowledge of the "Rock of Ages, cleft for me," that place where I know I am! And that joy unbounding where I know there are neither devils nor angels nor principalities nor powers to interfere with that life in Christ (Rom. 8:38–39)! It is wonderful!

"No weapon formed against you shall prosper" (Isa. 54:17). God makes us devil-proof, whether evil reports or good reports (2 Cor. 6:8) are spread about us. The power of the Most High God has put us in Christ. If we had put ourselves in, it would have been different. We were in the world, but God took us out of the world and put us into Christ, so God today by His Spirit wants us to see how this regenerative power, this glorious principle of God's high thoughtfulness, is for us. God wants me to leave myself in His sweetness. Oh, there is a sweetness about the Lord; oh, there is a glorious power behind us when God is behind us; there is a wonderful going before when He goes before us. He said, "I will go before you, and I will be your rear guard." (See Isaiah 52:12.) Glory to God!

> It reaches me, it reaches me,
>   Wondrous grace it reaches me;
> Pure, exhaustless, ever flowing,
>   Wondrous grace it reaches me.

THE WORD MAKES US FREE

I can see this order of life that God has for us now: it is to make me free from the law of sin and the law of death (Rom. 8:2).

Praise the Lord! And I find that all sin leads down; it is like gravity. But I find that all faith lifts up into a place of admiration of God. So God wants to spread forth His wings and show that He is able, He is Almightiness, and He is able to preserve what we have committed to Him (2 Tim. 1:12), because He is our Lord. He is not only our Creator, but also the One who preserves us. Not only has He redeemed me, but He is also preserving me. I see I cannot do any of these things by myself, but He has made it possible that if I believe, He will do it.

I absolutely believe that the Word I am preaching to you is sent forth by the power of the Spirit. I find that God has strengthened your hands and is preparing you for the race, the race that is set before you (Heb. 12:1). It is the divine plan I want to ask for in my life so that I may be absolutely in the place where I am preserved from all evil. These are days when Satan seeks to be very great. Oh, yes, he is tremendously busy seeking those whom he may devour (1 Pet. 5:8), but I am finding out that God has blessed me and has blessed us so that we will be in a place where we are more than overcomers (Rom. 8:37).

Being more than overcomers is to have a shout at the end of the fight. It not only means overcoming, but it also means being able to stand when we have overcome, and not fall down. I count it a great privilege that God has opened my eyes to see that His great plan has been arranged for us before the foundation of the world (Eph. 1:4–6), and we may all just come into line with God to believe that these things that He has promised must come to pass to whoever believes.

Turn back once more to the thought that no man, whoever he is, will ever make progress unless he learns that he is greater than the Adversary. If you don't learn, if you don't understand, if you don't come into line today with the thought that you are greater than the Adversary, you will find out that you have a struggle in your life. I want to breathe through you today a passage that is in Scripture, which is, *"He who is in you"* (1 John 4:4). I don't want to take anybody out of his bearings; I want to be so simple that everyone who hears this truth will know that he has a fortification, that he has the oracles of God behind him. In truth he has the power of God with him to overcome Satan through the blood of the Lamb (Rev. 12:11). *"Who is he who overcomes...but he who believes that Jesus is the* [Christ]?" (1 John 5:5); for it is he who overcomes the world, even through his faith (v. 4).

Now, faith is the supreme, divine position where God is entrenched, not only in the life, but also through the life, the mind, and the body. You will never find that you are at all equal against the power of the Enemy except on the authority that you have an authority laid down within you. He who believes in his heart is able to move the mountain (Mark 11:23), but you do not believe in your heart until your heart is made perfect in the presence of God. As you think in your heart, so you are (Prov. 23:7). *"Blessed are the pure in heart, for they shall see God"* (Matt. 5:8). These are the people who see this truth that I am presenting to you today, and it is in them, and that makes them *"more than conquerors"* (Rom. 8:37). They have life over sin, life over death, life over diseases, life over the Devil. Praise the Lord!

INTERPRETATION OF A MESSAGE IN TONGUES: "'God is not the author of confusion' but the Author of peace, and brings to life and focuses the eye until it sees God only, and when you come there you will stand."

Oh, the thought, the standing, the pure hands, the clean hearts—God the Holy Spirit has designed this for us within the plan of this realm of grace. God's plan is hidden, lost, completely lost to the Devil, who is not able to come near. God covers; He hides; we are sealed; bless the Lord! We are sealed until the day of redemption (Eph. 4:30). We so believe in the authority of the Almighty that we triumph in this glorious realm. Oh, this divine touch of God to the human soul brings us all to say *"all things are possible"* (Matt. 19:26).

> Praise the Lord 'tis so, praise the Lord 'tis so,
> Once I was blind but now I see,
> Once I was bound but now I am free,
> Through faith I have the victory,
> Praise the Lord 'tis so.

And so the Lord has a great plan for us to see today, or rather to bring us to our wealth in Christ. Our wealth is so rich, beyond all comparison. *"Deep calls unto deep"* (Ps. 42:7). The Lord has prepared for us not only a sonship, but also an heirship, not only an heirship, but also a joint-heirship (Rom. 8:17). We are not only feeling the breath of God, but the breath of God is also moving us.

We are not only touching fire, but fire is also burning everything that cannot stand fire. And so in this holy sea of life, this divine inheritance for us, I see the truth so full of *"joy unspeakable"* (1 Pet. 1:8 KJV) today, and I see it and I read it to you. *"There is therefore now no condemnation to those who are in Christ Jesus"* (Rom. 8:1). Oh, hallelujah!

THE LAW OF LIFE

Then I notice clearly that we must see and we must always get the facts of these truths. It is a law. Well, there is a law of gravity, and there is a law of life, and we must see the difference and live in life that ceases to die. On the other hand, we must live a life that continues to die and to die daily, because when we die, we receive life. In that life, the baptism of the Holy Spirit is a baptism into a death, into a likeness unto death, into the Son of Man in His likeness. The baptism of the Holy Spirit is purifying, energizing, and it brings the soul to where it touches ideal immensity. God wants us to have no other plan in our minds but this.

Now come along with me, for the Lord has many things to say to us. I see that the Devil wants to destroy. Now listen, you will find that John 10:10 is more real than ever. It says that the Devil comes to steal because he is a thief, and then if he can steal, he will destroy: he will kill, and then he will destroy. I also find that Jesus comes along with a flood tide of refreshment and says, "I have come with life, with life and abundance of life." (See verse 10.) Abundance of life means that you live in an activity of divine inspiration, that you never touch the other thing. You are above it. You are only in association with it to pray it through or to cause the salt to be saltier or the light to be brighter until others can see the way. It is a foundation of God's principle, and everyone who knows it says that is God.

I will go a little further to help you. I find out that whatever you learn from me—I say it without fear of any contradiction—God has given you another chance of seeing light and life. If you fail to seize the opportunity, you will find you will be worse tomorrow. God speaks through me to tens of thousands all over. God is sending me forth to stir the people to diligence. Mine is not an ordinary message. You will never find I have an ordinary message. The past tense is an ordinary message. I must be on fire. The day is too late for me to stop; I must be catching fire; I must be in the wing. I am intensely in earnest and mean all I say now.

Within are the thoughts to impregnate you today with a desire from heaven, to let you see that you do not have to give place to the Devil, neither in thought nor in word. And I pray to God the Holy Spirit that you will be so stirred that you will have a conviction come over your soul that you dare not disbelieve any of the truth, but rather your whole body will be aflame with the epistle of truth. *"He who has seen Me has seen the Father"* (John 14:9). Is that so? Oh, He said, "I and my Father will come and dwell in you." (See verse 23.) Yes, and when He comes to dwell in us, it is to be the epistle; it is to be the manifestation, the power; it is to be the Son of God working miracles, destroying the power of the devils, casting out evil spirits, and laying hands on the people so they who were dying under the power of the Devil will live.

This is life divine, and this is God's thought for you now, if you will not fail to recognize the good hand of God coming to us, God speaking to us of these deep things of Himself that mean so much for us. Oh, bless God that I am entrusted with such a Gospel, with such a message, but first it burns in me. (See Jeremiah 20:9.)

You cannot bring anything to anybody else before you have reached it first yourself. You cannot talk beyond your wisdom. God brings you to test these things; then, because you desire to handle and because you chance to eat these things, out of the eating and digesting of these things will come the refining fire and the flood tide upon the dry ground. This is so because we will be a flame of fire for God: divine inspiration, catching the vision all the time and walking in the Holy Spirit. Oh, bless the Lord!

> I know the Lord, I know the Lord,
> I know the Lord has laid His hands on me.

Glory to Jesus! Is that good hand of God on me only? No! No! No! God has come to more than me, but the important thing is that we recognize the hand of God and the voice of God and that we recognize the power of God. We need to recognize how to be careful and gentle and how to have wisdom to abide in the anointing and to keep in the place where God is not only consuming fire, but also purifying fire. Glory to God! Oh, for this holy, intense zeal. Oh, that God would give us today this zealous position, which will absolutely put us in a place where we know this day that God has spoken to us. We know that once more this day God has brought before us another opportunity. This day—thank God that in His grace and kindness He has opened the way, beloved. The Lord speaks once, even more so, twice. God unfolds the kingdom to you, but He expects you to jump in and go through.

SWEPT UP IN FAITH

"There is therefore now no condemnation" (Rom. 8:1). I would not trade this truth for the money in a million banks. What does it mean? There is condemnation that comes to us if we know that we ought to be further on in the race than we are. Something has stopped us.

Freedom from condemnation means so much to me. I know I was baptized with the Holy Spirit. Jesus is the life, but the Holy Spirit came to reveal the life. Jesus is the truth, but the Holy Spirit is the Spirit of that truth. So I must see that God has so much for me today. I notice that to be without condemnation I must be in the just place with God.

It is a wonderful thing to be justified by faith, but I find there is a greater place of justification than this. I find this: because Abraham believed God, He accounted it to him as righteousness (Rom. 4:3). That was more than the other. God accounted it to him as righteousness because Abraham believed God. He imputed no sin, and therefore He gave him wings. When He imputed no sin, He lifted Abraham into the righteousness of God, lifted him out of himself into a place of rest, and God covered him there. Abraham has not received anything from the Lord that He is not willing to give to anyone now. I am seeing today that whatever I have reached, I am only on the rippling of the wave of the surface of God's intense zeal of love and compassion. He is always saying nothing less than this: "Come on." So I am going forward.

I am here with a whole heart to say, "Come with me," for the Lord has spoken good concerning His people, and He will give them the land of promise. *"No good thing will He withhold"* (Ps. 84:11). So I know that God is in the place to bless today, but I want you to catch the fire. I want you to come out of all your natural propensities, for I tell you nothing is as detrimental to your spiritual rising as your natural mind and your body. Nothing will destroy your spiritual life but your own self. Paul knew that, and therefore he said, "I count myself as rubbish." (See Philippians 3:8.)

Is there anything else? Yes! Paul said, *"I did not immediately confer with flesh and blood"* (Gal. 1:16). He was getting very near this truth. I tell you there are a good many natural associations. As a Jew he came over to the plan of redemption, where everything was absolute foolishness and rank hypocrisy in Jewish estimation.

Is there anything else? Certainly! "If I can only win Him." (See Philippians 3:8.) Oh, what understanding there was in Paul, what beautiful character! What God had revealed to him about this Nazarene King was worthy to make him come into line to see. I can understand today that God breathed upon Paul absolutely. It is the breath of divine order; it is the breath of desire. God breathes on, and as He breathed on him I see this.

Oh, to know! To know that so many years ago, God baptized me, and I can say without a shadow of a doubt that God has swept me on. You know it! How I have always longed to go. I tell you, if you come to that place, you will have to say no to a thousand things in your natural order, for your own heart will deceive you. Be careful of your friends and relatives; they are often a damp rag or a wet blanket. God wants us to lean on Him and go on with Him and dare to believe Him. There is no condemnation (Rom. 8:1). Oh, how sweet the thought! Never mind, I am not here to crush or to bruise anyone. I am here in the Holy Spirit order I know: to make you long to come on, long to obey, long to say to everything that is not the high order of holiness, "Regardless of who misses the right path, I will go through."

> I'm going through, Jesus, I'm going through;
> I'll pay the price whatever others do;
> I'll take the way of the Lord's despised few;
> I'm going through, Jesus, I'm going through.

It is worth it all, praise the Lord, worth it all. Thank God, quickened by the Spirit, I have covered over forty-four thousand miles. You cannot comprehend it with your mind; it is too vast. At all places God in His Spirit has been moving me. I have seen the glory of God moving. I have had the pleasure of seeing two thousand people in the morning and over five thousand in the evening to hear me preach. What opportunities! What times of refreshment! What wonderful things one sees, and I realize that nothing from the past would do. You cannot rely upon anything in the past, and so I am realizing the truth now. It is this: I see it is a whole burnt offering; I see it is an offering in righteousness; I see it is an offering that is accepted; and I see it is a daily offering.

No past sanctification is good enough for today, and I find that this life leads you on to see that it is sanctification with an inward desire of being more perfected every day. While I know I was wonderfully saved, I find that it is being saved that moves me toward perfection. While I see salvation has designs within it for the coming of the King, I see it enriches me with a ceaseless warmth so that I cannot get out of it. Nothing will do unless I am absolutely heated up with this life, because I must see the King.

Since it came, Pentecost has been spoken against, and if there is not someone rising up against you, if there is not a war on, you are doing a bad job. I tell you this in sincerity: if you are not making the people mad or glad, there is something amiss with your ministry. If you leave people as you found them, God is not speaking through you. So, there must be an intensity of enlargement of this divine personality, of God in the soul, so absolutely bringing you to a place where you know it would be awful to remain two days in the same place. I do not know how it sounds, but I tell you, it is intense zeal.

Come on a little nearer now. There are opportunities. God has the right-of-way to the heart and life to bring them to a place where opportunities are made for the possibility of being accomplished. I am realizing that God must impress upon your heart, around you, wherever you are, that He has an opportunity for you today. It will stand right in front of you, and by that means you will be brought into a place where you will convince the people because God is there. Without the shadow of a doubt, the Word of God is effective and destroying, and it brings about perfect life.

CLOTHED IN FAITH

I am going to close with one Scripture passage, because of the importance of it. I want to give you one more word of life. Turn with me to the fifth chapter of 2 Corinthians—it will have something to do with this important treasure. I see that if I preach anything less than these things, I find I miss the whole opportunity of my life. I must have a ministry of faith; I must have clothing for this ministry of faith; I must have the Spirit of Life to manifest this ministry of faith; and then I must have the convincing evidence through the power of the Spirit of imparting that to the lives of the people. I pray that you will lay hold of this truth.

We have here in this fifth chapter of 2 Corinthians one of the best things that God has given me now for some time, this ministry of life. *"For we who are in this tent groan, being burdened, not because we want to be unclothed, but further clothed, that mortality may be swallowed up by life"* (v. 4). Here is one of the greatest truths that was in this Pentecostal evidence, or life in evidence, or the evidence in the life. I find that Jesus is not coming to fetch the body—that is perfectly in order; we cannot get away from the fact—but Jesus is coming for the life in the body. The body may die, but that body will not be in the glory. God will give us a body, and the only thing He is going to give is life. The life is not your life, but it is His life in you. He who dwells in God has God dwelling in him (1 John 4:16). Jesus came to give us His life. Paul said, "Now I live, yet not I, but He lives His life in me." (See Galatians 2:20.) In Colossians we read that when He who is our life appears, then we will appear (Col. 3:4).

You will find that you do not have a desire outside the desire of pleasing Him. There is a joy, or fullness of expression of all the joy, where you see His life being manifested in your mortal body, and that makes you so free from the natural life. Then you are joined up to the supernatural. Paul said he wanted to go, not to be unclothed but clothed upon (Phil. 1:21–23; 2 Cor. 5:4). There is a thought. Do we want to go? No! No! That is not the order of the body; that is not the order of the natural man; that is not the order of the human. What does he want? He wants to be so clothed upon; that is the first thing, clothed upon. When? Now!

Is there anything else? Yes! It is the life clothed upon and the life within the body eating up every mortality, every sense, every human desire, everything that has caused grief, sorrow, brokenness of heart, and has interfered with our rest, stopping the shining of our faces, making us feel how sorry we are. God wants to have His way with us, to live in us to eat up everything, until the body will only be a body filled with the Spirit life. Then the body will only be an existence as the temple for the Spirit. But the body will be preserved blameless. The body, the soul, and the spirit will be blameless in the world(1 Thess. 5:23), and the coming of the King will take the life and change it to present it with Him. God will bring us there.

As surely as I have had this fellowship with you in the Spirit, as surely as your heart has been warmed, I say to you: never mind the past. You may have a thousand things that spoil you; forget them. Know that God has overcome for you so that you will overcome and will be presented faultless, even more so, spotless in the presence of the King. This life will eat up mortality—hallelujah!

The law of the life of the Spirit of Christ will make you *"free from the law of sin and death"* (Rom. 8:2). Can I attain this today? This is a problem; "I have failed a thousand times," you say. Never mind. Is your heart warmed? Do you want to be conquered, or do you love to come into line with Him? Will you pay the price for it? What is the desire of your heart? You may be sorry for the past, but let God have you for the future. You would not like to remain as you were before you came here. I know you would not; you exactly feel the position. You say, "Lord, forgive everything of the past, but help me, Lord, today to offer an offering in righteousness before You. Today I give myself afresh."

CHAPTER EIGHTEEN

BY FAITH

We read in the Word that *"by faith Abel offered to God a more excellent sacrifice than Cain"* (Heb. 11:4). We also read that *"by faith Enoch was taken away so that he* [would] *not see death"* (v. 5); *"by faith Noah...prepared an ark for the saving of his household"* (v. 7); *"by faith Abraham obeyed when he was called to go out to the place which he would receive as an inheritance"* (v. 8).

There is only one way to all the treasures of God, and that is the way of faith. All things are possible, even the fulfilling of all promises is possible, to him who believes (Mark 9:23). And it is all by grace; *"by grace you have been saved through faith, and that not of yourselves; it is the gift of God"* (Eph. 2:8).

There will be failure in our lives if we do not build on the base, the Rock Christ Jesus. He is the only Way. He is the Truth. He is the Life (John 14:6). And the Word He gives us is life-giving. As we receive the Word of Life, it quickens, it opens, it fills us, it moves us, it changes us, and it brings us into a place where we dare to say amen to all that God has said. Beloved, there is a lot in an amen. You never get any place until you have the amen inside of you. That was the difference between Zacharias and Mary. When the Word came to Zacharias, he was filled with unbelief until the angel said, *"You will be mute...because you did not believe my words"* (Luke 1:20). Mary said, *"Let it be to me according to your word"* (v. 38). And the Lord was pleased that she believed that there would be a performance of what He had spoken. When we believe what God has said, there will be a performance.

BELIEF BECOMES FACT

Let's look at the twelfth chapter of Acts, and we will find that there were people waiting all night and praying that Peter might come out of prison. But there seemed to be one thing missing despite all their praying, and that was faith. Rhoda had more faith than all the rest of them. When the knock came at the door, she ran to it, for she was expecting an answer to her prayers. The moment she heard Peter's voice, she ran back and announced to them that Peter was standing at the door. And all the people said, "You are mad. It isn't so." That was not faith. When she insisted that he was there, they said, "Well, perhaps God has sent his angel." But Rhoda insisted, "It is Peter." And Peter continued knocking. They went out and found it so. What Rhoda had believed had become a glorious fact. (See verses 5–16.)

Beloved, we may do much praying and groaning, but we do not receive from God because of that; we receive because we believe. And yet sometimes it takes God a long time to bring us through the groaning and the crying before we can believe.

I know that no man by his praying can change God, for you cannot change Him. Charles Finney said, "Can a man who is full of sin and all kinds of ruin in his life change God when he starts to pray?" No, it is impossible. But when a man labors in prayer, he groans and travails because his tremendous sin is weighing him down, and he becomes broken in the presence of God. When properly melted, he comes into perfect harmony with the divine plan of God, and then God can work in that clay. He could not before. Prayer changes hearts, but it never changes God. He is *the same yesterday, today, and forever"* (Heb. 13:8): full of love, full of compassion, full of mercy, full of grace, and ready to bestow this and communicate that to us as we come to Him in faith.

Believe that when you come into the presence of God you can have all you came for. You can take it away, and you can use it, for all the power of God is at your disposal in response to your faith. The price for all was paid by the blood of Jesus Christ at Calvary. Oh, He is the living God, the One who has power to change us! *"It is He who has made us, and not we ourselves"* (Ps. 100:3). And it is He who purposes to transform us so that the greatness of His power may work through us. Oh, beloved, God delights in us, and when a man's ways please the Lord, then He makes all things move according to His own blessed purpose.

Communion with God

We read in Hebrews 11:5, *"By faith Enoch was taken away so that he did not see death;...before he was taken he had this testimony, that he pleased God."* I believe it is in the mind of God to prepare us for being taken away. But remember this, being taken away comes only on the line of holy obedience and a walk according to the good pleasure of God.

We are called to walk together with God through the Spirit. It is delightful to know that we can talk with God and hold communion with Him. Through this wonderful baptism in the Spirit that the Lord gives us, He enables us to talk to Him in a language that the Spirit has given, a language that no man understands but that He understands, a language of love. Oh, how wonderful it is to speak to Him in the Spirit, to let the Spirit lift and lift and lift us until He takes us into the very presence of God! I pray that God by His Spirit may move all of us so that we walk with God as Enoch walked with Him. But beloved, it is a walk by faith and not by sight (2 Cor. 5:7), a walk of believing the Word of God.

I believe there are two kinds of faith. All people are born with a natural faith, but God calls us to a supernatural faith that is a gift from Himself. In the twenty-sixth chapter of Acts, Paul told us of his call, how God spoke to him and told him to go to the Gentiles:

> *To open their eyes, and to turn them from darkness to light, and from the power of Satan unto God, that they may receive forgiveness of sins, and inheritance among them which are sanctified by faith that is in me.* (Acts 26:18 KJV)

The faith that was in Christ was to be given by the Holy Spirit to those who believed. From this point on, as Paul yielded his life to God, he could say,

> *I am crucified with Christ: nevertheless I live; yet not I, but Christ liveth in me: and the life which I now live in the flesh I live by the faith of the Son of God, who loved me, and gave himself for me.* (Gal. 2:20 KJV)

The faith of the Son of God is communicated by the Spirit to the one who puts his trust in God and in His Son.

UNDERSTAND GOD'S WORD

I believe that all our failures come because of an imperfect understanding of God's Word. I see that it is impossible to please God on any other line except by faith (Heb. 11:6), and everything that is not of faith is sin (Rom. 14:23). You say, "How can I obtain this faith?" You see the secret in Hebrews 12:2: *"Looking unto Jesus, the author and finisher of our faith."* He is the Author of faith. Oh, the might of our Christ, who created the universe and upholds it all by the might of His power (Heb. 1:3)! God has chosen Him and ordained Him and clothed Him, and He who made this vast universe will make us a new creation. He spoke the Word, and the stars came into being; can He not speak the Word that will produce a mighty faith in us? This One who is the Author and Finisher of our faith comes and dwells within us, quickens us by His Spirit, and molds us by His will. He comes to live His life of faith within us and to be to us all that we need. And He who has begun a good work within us will complete it and perfect it (Phil. 1:6), for He is not only the Author but also the Finisher and Perfecter of our faith.

For the word of God is living and powerful, and sharper than any two-edged sword, piercing even to the division of soul and spirit, and of joints and marrow, and is a discerner of the thoughts and intents of the heart. (Heb. 4:12)

How the Word of God severs the soul and the spirit—the soul that has a lot of carnality, a lot of selfishness in it, a lot of evil in it! Thank God, the Lord can sever from us all that is earthly and sensual and make us a spiritual people. He can bring all our selfishness to the place of death and bring the life of Jesus into our being to take the place of that earthly and sensual thing that is destroyed by the living Word.

The Word of God comes in to separate us from everything that is not of God. It destroys. It also gives life. He must bring to death all that is carnal in us. It was after the death of Christ that God raised Him up on high, and as we are dead with Him, we are raised up and made to sit in heavenly places in the new life that the Spirit gives (Eph. 2:6).

God has come to lead us out of ourselves into Himself and to take us from the ordinary into the extraordinary, from the human into the divine, and to make us after the image of His Son. Oh, what a Savior! What an ideal Savior! It is written,

> *Beloved, now we are children of God; and it has not yet been revealed what we shall be, but we know that when He is revealed, we shall be like Him, for we shall see Him as He is.*
>
> (1 John 3:2)

But even now, the Lord wants to transform us *"from glory to glory,"* by the Spirit of the living God (2 Cor. 3:18). Have faith in God, have faith in the Son, have faith in the Holy Spirit; and the triune God will work in you to will and to do all the good pleasure of His will (Phil. 2:13).

CHAPTER NINETEEN

LIKE PRECIOUS FAITH

W e are so dull of comprehension because we so often let the cares of this world blind our eyes, but if we can be open to God, we will see that He has a greater plan for us in the future than we have ever seen or dreamed of in the past. It is God's delight to make possible to us what seems impossible, and when we reach a place where He alone has the right-of-way, then all the things that have been misty and misunderstood are cleared up.

GOD'S GIFT TO US

Let's look at 2 Peter 1:1–8:

To those who have obtained like precious faith with us by the righteousness of our God and Savior Jesus Christ: Grace and peace be multiplied to you in the knowledge of God and of Jesus our Lord, as His divine power has given to us all things that pertain to life and godliness, through the knowledge of Him who called us by glory and virtue, by which have been given to us exceedingly great and precious promises, that through these you may be partakers of the divine nature, having escaped the corruption that is in the world through lust. But also for this very reason, giving all diligence, add to your faith virtue, to virtue knowledge, to knowledge self-control, to self-control perseverance, to perseverance godliness, to godliness brotherly kindness, and to brotherly kindness love. For if these things are yours and abound, you will be neither barren nor unfruitful in the knowledge of our Lord Jesus Christ.

This *"like precious faith"* (2 Pet. 1:1) that Peter was writing about is a gift that God is willing to give to all of us, and I believe God wants us to receive it so that we may subdue kingdoms, work righteousness, and, if the time has come, stop the mouths of lions (Heb. 11:33). Under all circumstances we should be able to triumph, not because we have confidence in ourselves, but because our confidence is only in God. It is always those people who are full of faith who have a good report, who never murmur, who are in the place of victory, who are not in the place of human order but of divine order, since God has come to dwell in them.

The Lord Jesus is the Divine Author and brings into our minds the "Thus says the Lord" every time. We cannot have anything in our lives except when we have a "Thus says the Lord" for it. We must see to it that the Word of God is always the standard of everything.

This *"like precious faith"* is for us all. But there may be some hindrance in your life that God will have to deal with. At one point in my life, it seemed as if I had had so much pressure come over my life to break me up like a potter's vessel. There is no other way into the deep things of God except by a broken spirit. There is no other way into the power of God. God will do for us *"exceedingly abundantly above all that we ask or think"* (Eph. 3:20) when He can bring us to the place where we can say with Paul, "I live no longer" (see Galatians 2:20), and Another, even Christ, has taken the reins and the rule.

We are no better than our faith. Whatever your estimation is of your ability, or your righteousness, you are no better than your faith. No one is ever any better than his faith. He who believes that Jesus is the Son of God overcomes the world (1 John 5:5). How? This Jesus, upon whom your faith is placed—the power of His name, His personality, His life, His righteousness—are all made yours through faith. As you believe in Him and set your hope only on Him, you are purified even as He is pure (1 John 3:3). You are strengthened because He in whom you trust is strong. You are made whole because He who is all your confidence is whole. You may receive of His fullness, all the untold fullness of Christ, as your faith rests wholly in Him.

I understand God by His Word. I cannot understand God by impressions or feelings. I cannot get to know God by sentiments. If I am going to know God, I am going to know Him by His Word. I know I will be in heaven, but I cannot determine from my feelings that I am going to heaven. I am going to heaven because God's Word says it, and I believe God's Word. And *"faith comes by hearing, and hearing by the word of God"* (Rom. 10:17).

GOD'S REAL WORKING

There is one thing that can hinder our faith: a conscience that is seared. Paul sought to have *"a conscience void of offence"* (Acts 24:16 KJV). There is a conscience that is seared, and there is a conscience that is so opened to the presence of God that the smallest thing in the world will drive it to God. What we need is a conscience that is so opened to God that not one thing can come into and stay in our lives to break up our fellowship with God and shatter our faith in Him. And when we can come into the presence of God with clear consciences and genuine faith, our hearts not condemning us, then we have confidence toward God (1 John 3:21), *"and whatever we ask we receive from Him"* (v. 22).

In Mark 11:24 we read, *"Therefore I say to you, whatever things you ask when you pray, believe that you receive them, and you will have them."* Verse twenty-three speaks of mountains removed and difficulties cleared away. Sugarcoating won't do. We must have reality, the real working of our God. We must know God. We must be able to go in and converse with God. We must also know the mind of God toward us, so that all our petitions are always on the line of His will.

As this *"like precious faith"* (2 Pet. 1:1) becomes a part of you, it will make you so that you will dare to do anything. And remember, God wants daring men: men who will dare all, men who will be strong in Him and dare to do exploits (Dan. 11:32). How will we reach this place of faith? Give up your own mind. Let go of your own thoughts, and take the thoughts of God, the Word of God. If you build yourself on imaginations, you will go wrong. You have the Word of God, and it is enough.

A man gave this remarkable testimony concerning the Word: "Never compare this Book with other books. Comparisons are dangerous. Never think or say that this Book contains the Word of God. It is the Word of God. It is supernatural in origin, eternal in duration, inexpressible in value, infinite in scope, regenerative in power, infallible in authority, universal in interest, personal in application, inspired in totality. Read it through. Write it down. Pray it in. Work it out. And then pass it on."

And truly the Word of God changes a man until he becomes an epistle of God. It transforms his mind, changes his character, moves him on from grace to grace, makes him an inheritor of the very nature of God. God comes in, dwells in, walks in, talks through, and dines with him who opens his being to the Word of God and receives the Spirit who inspired it.

When I was going over to New Zealand and Australia, there were many there to see me off. An Indian doctor rode in the same car with me to the docks and boarded the same ship. He was very quiet and took in all the things that were said on the ship. I began to preach, of course, and the Lord began to work among the people. In the second class of the ship, there was a young man and his wife who were attendants for a lady and gentleman in the first class. And as these two young people heard me talking to the people privately and otherwise, they were very much impressed. Then the lady they were attending got very sick. In her sickness and her loneliness, she could find no relief. They called in the doctor, and the doctor gave her no hope.

And then, when in this strange dilemma—she was a great Christian Scientist, a preacher of it, and had gone many places preaching it—they thought of me. Knowing the conditions, and what she lived for, knowing that it was late in the day, that in the condition of her mind she could only receive the simplest word, I said to her, "Now, you are very sick, and I won't talk to you about anything except this: I will pray for you in the name of Jesus, and the moment I pray you will be healed."

And the moment I prayed she was healed. That was this *"like precious faith"* in operation. Then she was disturbed. I showed her the terrible state she was in and pointed out to her all her folly and the fallacy of her position. I showed her that there was nothing in Christian Science, that it is a lie from the beginning and one of the last agencies of hell. At best it is a lie: preaching a lie and producing a lie.

Then she came to her senses. She became so penitent and brokenhearted. But the thing that stirred her first was that she had to go preach the simple Gospel of Christ where she had preached Christian Science. She asked me if she had to give up certain things. I won't mention the things; they are too vile. I said, "No, what you have to do is to see Jesus and take Jesus." When she saw the Lord in His purity, the other things had to go. At the presence of Jesus, all else goes.

This opened the door. I had to preach to all on the boat. This gave me a great chance. As I preached, the power of God fell, conviction came, and sinners were saved. They followed me into my cabin one after another. God was working there.

Then this Indian doctor came. He said, "What will I do? Your preaching has changed me, but I must have a foundation. Will you spend some time with me?"

"Of course I will."

Then we went alone, and God broke the fallow ground. This Indian doctor was going right back to his Indian conditions under a new order. He had left a practice there. He told me of the great practice he had. He was going back to his practice to preach Jesus.

If you have lost your hunger for God, if you do not have a cry for more of God, you are missing the plan. A cry must come up from us that cannot be satisfied with anything but God. He wants to give us the vision of the prize ahead that is something higher than we have ever attained. If you ever stop at any point, pick up at the place where you have left off, and begin again under the refining light and power of heaven. God will meet you. And while He will bring you to a consciousness of your own frailty and to a brokenness of spirit, your faith will lay hold of Him and all the divine resources. His light and compassion will be manifested through you, and He will send the rain.

Should we not dedicate ourselves afresh to God? Some say, "I dedicated myself last night to God." Every new revelation brings a new decision. Let us seek Him.